P9-EDV-518

Books and Beyond

Books and Beyond
The Greenwood Encyclopedia
of New American Reading

VOLUME 3: N–S

Edited by
KENNETH WOMACK

GREENWOOD PRESS
Westport, Connecticut • London

Library of Congress Cataloging-in-Publication Data

Books and beyond : the Greenwood encyclopedia of new American reading / edited by Kenneth Womack.
   p. cm.
   Includes bibliographical references and index.
   ISBN: 978-0-313-33738-3 (set : alk. paper) — ISBN: 978-0-313-33737-6 (v. 1 : alk. paper) — ISBN: 978-0-313-33740-6 (v. 2 : alk. paper) — ISBN: 978-0-313-33741-3 (v. 3 : alk. paper) — ISBN: 978-0-313-33742-0 (v. 4 : alk. paper)
   1. Books and reading—United States—Encyclopedias. 2. Reading interests—United States—Encyclopedias. 3. Popular literature—United States—Encyclopedias. 4. Fiction genres—Encyclopedias. 5. American literature—History and criticism. 6. English literature—History and criticism. I. Womack, Kenneth.
Z1003.2B64   2008
028'.9097303—dc22   2008018703

British Library Cataloguing in Publication Data is available.

Library of Congress Catalog Card Number: 2008018703
ISBN: 978–0–313–33738–3 (set)
      978–0–313–33737–6 (vol. 1)
      978–0–313–33740–6 (vol. 2)
      978–0–313–33741–3 (vol. 3)
      978–0–313–33742–0 (vol. 4)

First published in 2008

Greenwood Press, 88 Post Road West, Westport, CT 06881
An imprint of Greenwood Publishing Group, Inc.
www.greenwood.com

Printed in the United States of America

The paper used in this book complies with the
Permanent Paper Standard issued by the National
Information Standards Organization (Z39.48–1984).

10 9 8 7 6 5 4 3 2 1

Contents

N

NATIVE AMERICAN LITERATURE

Prior to 1968—the dawn of an era known as the "renaissance" of American Indian literature—most literary scholars would have struggled to name a single Native American literary work. However, with the 1960s came profound social transformation; Civil Rights activism, including a new phase of feminism, prevailed throughout the rest of the century. Both movements galvanized advancements on multiple fronts by Native Americans and other disfranchised groups. Nowadays, by contrast, nearly all Americanists, and even some undergraduate literature majors, can name at least a few Native writers.

Definition. Still, no concise definition of "Native American literature" exists. Debates revolve around definitions of "literature," as well as conceptions of "Native" identity. Such debates do not resolve with the passage of time; on the contrary, they continue to broaden and deepen.

Significant philosophical and literary critical developments, along with the steadily increasing body of works written by American Indians, have facilitated our understanding of Native American literary art in recent years. Ironically, these same developments make defining the field more difficult. In general, a crisis in terminology has transformed intellectual (and to an extent, popular) discourse throughout the late twentieth and early twenty-first centuries. During the twentieth century, political, social, and intellectual revolutions continually focused on the powers of language, which in the aftermath of structuralism and deconstruction, are no longer presumed to access "truth" about objective "reality." Intellectual inquiry proceeds in a state of heightened awareness of how language shapes experience and ideas according to perceptual and conceptual screens, which are themselves sustained by discourse. Scholars across diverse disciplines, including even the physical sciences, ponder the verbally constructed frames of reference that define their fields of study. The West has witnessed a widespread shift of intellectual attention onto the nature of representation.

Questions about the meaning of the terms "American" and "literature" arise from this intensely self-conscious frame of mind. After the 1960s, critics concerned with ethnic and gender politics began, for instance, to ask why the word "America" has implicitly meant "United States," and to object to the definition of "American" literature primarily as an Anglocentric, masculine enterprise. Beginning in the 1980s, New Historical critics, confronting traditional disciplinary boundaries, asked whose writings, and what kinds of writing qualify as "literature," as opposed to "popular," historical, or anthropological material. Indeed, the last half of the twentieth century saw a substantial erosion of conventional, Eurocentric conceptions of who, and what, counts as "American" and "literary." Therefore, defining "Native American literature"—with its many nonwestern features eluding Eurocentric generic classification—presents a noteworthy challenge.

Since 1968, and N. Scott Momaday's publication of *House Made of Dawn*, which expressed multicultural themes from Navajo, Pueblo, Kiowa, and Eurocentric cultures, an expanded critical vocabulary and more suitable frames of reference have become available for scholarly discussion of Native literature. The pre-1968 material—a variety of traditional stories, songs, chants, oratory, ceremonial works, nonfiction and autobiographical works—is no longer exclusively the province of historians, folklorists and anthropologists with non-literary and non-tribal (Eurocentric) perspectives; it has become newly "visible" for critical reassessment by both Native and non-Native literary scholars. Such a reclamation project is daunting, for inclusion of these early works leads to more, rather than fewer questions about the intellectually constructed boundaries defining fields of academic inquiry.

Before the European colonization of North America, over 300 indigenous tribes existed; they spoke more than 200 different languages. Though none of these languages were orthographic, petroglyphs and pictographic varieties of expression nevertheless amounted to a kind of "writing" that belies descriptions of tribal cultures as purely "oral." Tribal "literature" thus includes these iconographic forms of representation among a variety of other modes that, until recently, fell outside the print-oriented, Eurocentric vision of the "literary." Today, we understand Native American literature to include such material as both content and contextual background.

Pre-twentieth century written texts frequently reveal the heavy-handed editorial interference of non-Indians. Before 1968, there were few unmediated Native literary voices, and even today, finding "pure" cultural and literary artifacts is impossible.

ESTABLISHING DATES FOR CONTEMPORARY AMERICAN INDIAN LITERATURE

Using the year 1968, and the publication by N. Scott Momaday (Kiowa/Cherokee, 1934–) of his Pulitzer Prize-winning *House Made of Dawn*, to mark the beginning of an Indian literary "renaissance" compares to using the year 1798, and the publication of *The Lyrical Ballads* by Wordsworth and Coleridge, to mark the beginning of the British Romantic Period. To do so is clarifying, but also somewhat arbitrary and misleading. Native American literary forms existed long before 1968, just as romanticism existed long before 1798. However, the pinpointed year is heuristically useful; it focuses our thoughts around key questions.

Contemporary written works are cross-cultural forms, and even some of the oldest tribal stories sometimes hint of cross-cultural connections with ancient European lore. "Deer Woman" (1991), by Paula Gunn Allen (Laguna/Metîs, 1939–), and the old Dakota tale that inspired it, suggest this kind of connection. A story from *Dakota Texts* (1932), collected by Ella Deloria (Yankton-Dakota, 1889–1971), and Allen's narrative both feature magical beings who lure ignorant, innocent characters and hold them captive; both stories are vaguely allusive of Washington Irving's "Rip Van Winkle." Irving's romance, in turn, is informed by German folklore. Along with Jungian archetypal critics and New Historicists, one may speculate from sophisticated perspectives about the circulation of such apparently transcultural elements; however, neither traditional nor contemporary Native American literature is comprehensible from within exclusively Eurocentric critical frames of reference. Today's Native writers emphasize this fact in works requiring the reader's knowledge of indigenous cultural contexts and interpretive practices.

Twentieth-century efforts to preserve indigenous cultural material have included recordings and films; moreover, Native people now write, record, film, and publish their own works. Still, even in the hands of Native artists, both writing and audio-visual technology are western modalities. Electronic media freeze narration and performance in time, thus failing to render important experiential dimensions of tribal dramatic arts that are usually based on different spatial, temporal, and other cosmological paradigms. Translation of older works into English, as well as the creation of newer works in English rather than tribal languages, present additional, formidable barriers to unmediated preservation. In fact, many contemporary Native writers deal overtly in their art with questions about how to render tribal worlds and ways in the English language, and in Eurocentric genres.

Finally, definitions of "Native American literature" sometimes turn on identity politics, on questions contesting not only which modes of expression, but also which writers may be counted as Native American. Some insist that DNA alone determines "Indian" identity, but arguments develop over "blood quantum"— whether one is full-blood, half-blood, mixed-blood, or partly white, black, Mexican, and so on. Others contend that being "Indian" is a result of cultural experience, such as growing up "on the rez." N. Scott Momaday and Gerald Vizenor (White Earth Anishinaabeg, 1934–) probably represent the polar extremes in this controversy. On the one hand, Momaday claims that being an Indian is mostly a matter of having a certain self-conception, a way of knowing oneself and the world that stems from super-consciousness or collective memory. On the other hand, Vizenor declares that there is no such thing as an "Indian"; an "Indian" is a verbal, historical, cultural construction. He believes that the term misleadingly defines individuals and homogenizes hundreds of North and South American indigenous groups. Like Vizenor, Sherman Alexie (Spokane/Coeur d'Alene, 1966–) argues, controversially, that Native identity today is less a matter of bloodline or culture than of politics. Thus, attempting to define Native American literature and identity, we may concur with David Murray—nowadays, "every term seems contested" (2005, 81).

History. In an arena of legitimately contested terms, the best strategy for discussing Native American literature may be to invoke as few such terms as possible. Useful in an historical overview of Native American literature, however, are the conventional distinctions between pre- and post-1968 works, and between works (usually pre-1968) originally composed in tribal languages and those originally composed in English.

Native American Literature Before 1968. Consisting of oral and, to a lesser extent, iconographic forms of expression (rock art, sandpainting, pictographic narrative, and performative gesture, for instance), the pre-colonial, indigenous repertoire included foundational stories, ceremonial and ritual performances, songs, chants, prayers, and merely entertaining or instructive tales. With the eradication of hundreds of tribes following colonization, much of this traditional material was lost. Nevertheless, much has survived through successive generations in tribal memory; it informs the contextual background of contemporary Native literature that must be engaged if a reader hopes to comprehend these works.

Indigenous cosmologies, a key part of this context, are communicated through foundational stories, which range from the tribally specific, such as the *Diné bahane'* (Navajo), *Hactin* and *Black Hactin* stories (Apache), and the *Basket Dice Game* (Pawnee), to the relatively pan-tribal, such as the Earth Diver narratives common among North American groups. Foundational works address questions about the origins of life, both material and spiritual, and the interconnections among beings and places on the earth. These works often center around the deeds of culture heroes and trickster characters, usually the world's first inhabitants following its creation by spiritual entities—not entirely separate "gods," but individual manifestations of the all-pervasive Creator. Heroes and tricksters are responsible for the preservation or destruction of the worlds the creators have made. Culture heroes include, for instance, Monster Slayer and Child of Water (twin figures known by various names among southwestern tribes and clans), Pine Root and Beaded Head (Cree), Hisagita misa (Seminole), I'itoi (Pima), and Beaver Man (Yukon), among many others. Some best known pan-tribal tricksters are Coyote, Raven, Glooscap, and Winabojo, who sometimes resemble or even double as culture heroes. Tricksters and heroes might be shape-shifters, have animal relatives or helpers, and move between dimensions of reality in ways that ordinary beings cannot.

Indigenous ceremonial and ritual works are integrally connected to foundational narratives. The Hero Twins play important roles, for example, in Navajo healing ceremonies such as *Blessingway*, *Nightway*, and others. Though ceremonies are frequently kept secret by tribes and groups within tribes, parts of some are preserved in writing. In the late nineteenth and early twentieth centuries, for instance, Washington Matthews, Elsie Clews Parsons, Ruth Benedict, Franz Boas and others undertook such projects, usually with the assistance of tribal people. Recording ceremonials is often controversial because of their sacred status and power, and because Native Americans justifiably resent Eurocentric appropriation of their spirituality, whether intellectually or commercially motivated. After all, not until 1978, with U.S. congressional passage of the American Indian Religious Freedom Act, were Native people allowed the free and legal practice of their religions. Today, cultural preservation continues, but with tribal members taking the lead and sometimes engaging in cooperative efforts with such organizations as the Smithsonian Institution (the National Museum of the American Indian) in Washington, D.C., and the Heard Museum in Phoenix, Arizona. Some museums, such as the Hatathli Museum at Diné College in Tsaile, Arizona, are located on tribal college campuses and thus entirely under tribal management.

Ceremony and ritual are also conducted through the songs, chants, and prayers that make up another category of traditional Native literature. According to the Navajo *Blessingway*, the world was created through song. Songs heal, tell stories, give power to individuals undergoing initiations into clans and societies, open psychic channels to higher knowledge, and preserve memories and information. Songs are sometimes gifts to humans from plants or animals. Songs may be dreamed or inherited. Some songs are also prayers.

Finally, traditional literature also includes a vast array of entertaining and instructive works. Coyote's foolishness, Crow's tendency to gossip, and other characters' general misbehavior in humorous tales make people reflect on the worst of human traits. Making us laugh at the human predicament, they remind us of our imperfections and responsibilities to ourselves, to others, to all creation. Instructive stories also include historical accounts of heroic deeds and significant events; parables that teach morality, ethics, and values; and tales that provide models for behavior, or explain natural phenomena.

During the late eighteenth century and, increasingly, during the nineteenth, a variety of written autobiographies and other accounts of Native life began to appear as more and more Indians "learned paper." Many of these, such as *Black Hawk, An Autobiography* (1833), fall into the "as-told-to" category—works dictated by Indian authors to non-Indian editors who, intentionally and unintentionally, shaped the stories they were told. Examples include Frank Linderman's collaborations with Plenty-Coups (Crow) in 1928 and Pretty-Shield (Crow) in 1930, and Ruth Underhill's partnership with Maria Chona (Tohono O'odham) in 1936.

Culturally assimilated Indians writing in English also produced their own texts. One well-known and frequently anthologized work by Samson Occum (Mohegan, 1723–92), *A Sermon Preached at the Execution of Moses Paul, an Indian* (1772), warns a mixed audience of Indians and whites concerning alcohol. Occum's sermon and *A Choice Collection of Hymns and Spiritual Songs* (1774) are the first works published in English by an Indian writer.

The first autobiography written in English by a Native American is *Son of the Forest* (1829), by William Apess (Pequot, 1798–1839). Apess's well-developed political awareness shows in this text, and in *An Indian's Looking Glass for the White Man* (1833), where he chastises whites for their widescale destruction of Native communities. Nevertheless, like Occum, Apess was Christianized and deeply assimilated into Eurocentric culture. Such early Native American autobiographers worked within the strictures of Eurocentric generic forms (Christian redemption narrative, for example) that shape the narrator's self-representation. Thus, as scholar H. David Brumble III contends, Native "lifewriting" must be distinguished from Eurocentric "autobiography" owing to different underlying conceptions of "self." Brumble identifies six types of "life-story" antecedent to European contact: coup tales (tales of daring encounters with enemies), informal accounts of experiences or achievements, self-examinations, self-vindications, educational narratives, and stories of vision and power quests.

Well-known pre-1968 written autobiographies include *Life, History, and Travels of Kah-ge-ga-gah-bowh* (1847), by George Copway (Ojibwe, 1818–1869); the autobiographical *Life Among the Piutes* (1883) by Sarah Winnemucca (Paiute, 1844–1891); *Indian Boyhood* (1902), and *From the Deep Woods to Civilization* (1916), by Charles A. Eastman (Santee Sioux, 1858–1939), who also wrote *The Soul of the Indian* (1911), a work addressing indigenous spirituality and the Ghost Dance phenomenon of the 1890s; and *Talking to the Moon* (1945), by John Joseph Mathews (Osage, 1894–1979). Reprinted in 1972 and after, *Black Elk Speaks*, Nicholas Black Elk's spiritual autobiography as told to John Nichardt, has been admired since its first appearance in 1932. As-told-to autobiographies continue to appear well into the late twentieth century: John (Fire) Lame Deer (Lakota), in *Lame Deer, Seeker of Visions* (1972), and Mary Brave Bird in *Lakota Woman* (1990), both collaborated with Richard Erdoes to produce popular texts of this type.

Native nonfiction and lifewriting have a longer continuous history than written fiction. In fact, Native Americans published no written works of fiction before the 1820s, when Jane Johnson Schoolcraft (Ojibwe, 1800–1841) wrote poems and stories for her own magazine, *The Literary Voyager, or Muzzeniegun* (1826–27). In 1833, Elias Boudinot (Cherokee, 1804–1839), published the first novel by a Native American, *Poor Sarah; or The Indian Woman* (1833); Boudinot was also the editor of the first tribal newspaper, the *Cherokee Phoenix*, printed in both Cherokee and English. However, better known is *The Life and Adventures of Joaquin Murieta, the Celebrated California Bandit*, by John Rollin Ridge (Cherokee, 1827–1867), which appeared in 1854. Some years later, S. Alice Calahan (Muscogee-Creek, 1868–1894) published *Wynema* (1891).

Other notable early Native American authors include poet and short story writer Emily Pauline Johnson (Canadian Mohawk, 1861–1913); poet and journalist Alexander Posey (Muscogee, 1873–1908); Mourning Dove (Okanogan/Colville 1882–88?–1936), whose autobiographical novel, *Cogewea, the Half-Blood* (1927), highlights Indian women's issues; John Joseph Mathews, whose works include a history, *Wah'Kon-Tah* (1932), and a novel, *Sundown* (1934), as well as the previously cited autobiography; John Milton Oskison (Cherokee, 1874–1947), who wrote both nonfiction and fiction, including *Wild Harvest* (1925) and *Black Jack Davey* (1926); Zitkala-Så (Gertrude Simmons Bonnin, Yankton Dakota, 1876–1938), who recorded traditional stories in *Old Indian Legends* (1901), and *American Indian Stories* (1921); [George] Todd Downing (Choctaw, 1902–1974) a writer of mystery and detective fiction; and D'Arcy McNickle (Metîs Cree/Salish, 1904–1977), best known for three novels, *The Surrounded* (1936), *Runner in the Sun* (1954), and *Wind from an Enemy Sky* (1978). McNickle's *The Surrounded* was admired as the most complex work of fiction by a Native writer before N. Scott Momaday's *House Made of Dawn*, with which it shares thematic concerns.

Also enjoying a measure of fame in the early twentieth century were Lynn Riggs (Cherokee, 1899–1954), whose play, *Green Grow the Lilacs* (1931) was staged as *Oklahoma*, and William Penn Adair "Will" Rogers (Cherokee, 1879–1935), who during the 1920s wrote columns for the *New York Times* and the *Saturday Evening Post* that occasionally addressed Indian concerns. Since 2000, several American literary scholars have begun to note the influence of such pre-1968 non-narrative material—journalism, speeches, treaties, and popular nonfiction genres—on contemporary Native American writing, most obviously, perhaps, in the speeches and writings of Sherman Alexie.

Native American Literature Since 1968. American Indian writers emerging since 1968 include novelists, short story writers, poets, nonfiction writers, and dramatists, most of whom publish in more than one genre. They are included in anthologies of American literature as well as in a proliferating number of anthologies of Native American literature. Among the best known are Kenneth Rosen's *The Man to Send Rain Clouds: Contemporary Stories by American Indians* (1974); Duane Niatum, *Carriers of the Dream Wheel* (1977) and *Harper's Anthology of Twentieth-Century Native American Poetry* (1988); Simon Ortiz's *Earth Power Coming: Short Fiction in Native American Literature* (1983); Clifford E. Trafzer's *Blue Dawn, Red Earth: New Native American Storytellers* (1996); Joy Harjo and Gloria Bird's *Reinventing the Enemy's Language: Contemporary Native Women's Writings of North America* (1997); Mimi D'Aponte's *Seventh Generation: An Anthology of Native American Plays* (1999); Jaye T. Darby and Hanay Geiogamah's *Stories of Our Way: An Anthology of American Indian Plays* (1999); and John L. Purdy and James Ruppert's *Nothing But the Truth: An Anthology of Native American Literature* (2001).

Browsing through these anthologies affords insight into both stable and evolving patterns in post-1968 Indian writing. We may observe, for instance, the integral relationship between contemporary works and their tribal, traditional predecessors. Momaday's *House Made of Dawn* and *The Way to Rainy Mountain* (1969), together with *Ceremony* (1977) and *Storyteller* (1981) by Leslie Marmon Silko (Laguna, 1948–), clearly articulate important topical and structural paradigms informing indigenous oral and written storytelling; these texts present fictive worlds complexly interlaced with foundational stories and tribal cosmologies. In Momaday's *House*, the protagonist, Abel, is physically, emotionally, and spiritually ill, partly because of his experiences as a soldier in World War II, and partly because he is ignorant of his Puebloan identity. Returning home to Walatoa (Jemez Pueblo) and recognizing his identity as a Dawn Runner lead to his gradual healing. Momaday's narrative unfolds as Abel recovers, and the reader discovers, an Indian "reality" alternative to that of mainstream U.S. society. The author spins an intricate web of Navajo, Pueblo, Kiowa, and Eurocentric tropes and allusions that readers must negotiate accurately if they wish to assume the participatory reader's role in this demanding text.

Like *House*, Momaday's autobiographical *The Way to Rainy Mountain* undertakes a cross-culturally informative task. Three kinds of prose—United States history, tribal stories, and the author's personal experiences—choreograph the reader's role. In the top halves of recto pages, the reader finds the "official" view of the dominant society, while the bottom halves contain italicized, autobiographical matter. Verso pages bear Kiowa stories and tales that pertain to U.S. history, as well as to Momaday's own self-definition. The three bodies of information, and their respective discursive modes, cast significant light upon one another, inviting readers to reassess dominant society perspectives.

In *Ceremony*, Silko develops a plot similar to Momaday's in *House*. Like Momaday's Abel, Silko's protagonist, Tayo, is a spiritually ailing, World War II veteran on a healing vision quest. With the help of a powerful mixed-blood Navajo healer, he finds his way back home to Laguna Pueblo to become a storyteller with world-sustaining responsibilities. As Tayo's story unfolds, it incorporates into itself Navajo and Pueblo foundational stories that are at first presented separately, as lyrical, italicized passages within the text. This textual orchestration implies that for Tayo, to heal is to meld with Native culture, to comprehend and wield the creative-destructive potentiality of words.

Like Momaday and Silko's works, most writing by Native Americans emphasizes this power of language. Moreover, these works collectively articulate a fundamental structural pattern of American Indian written narrative. Indeed, William Bevis has argued that a separation-illness-return-recovery pattern informs Native American narrative, comparable to the way the *bildüngsroman* pattern informs the western novel. Well-known Indian writers whose novels, poetry, short stories, plays, and other works variously reiterate these topical and structural features include James Welch (Blackfeet/Gros Ventre, 1940–2003), Louise Erdrich (Turtle Mountain Ojibwe, 1954–), Anna Lee Walters (Pawnee-Otoe-Missouria, 1946–), Robert Conley (Cherokee, 1940–), Linda Hogan (Chickasaw, 1947–), and others.

For Native writers, the use of western literary forms to convey tribal worldviews poses monumental challenges. Post-1968 writers develop strategies for transforming these genres to their own purposes. Momaday and Silko's technique of interweaving foundational material into their works is an intertextual strategy that also negotiates basic differences between western and indigenous conceptions of time. Western forms are constructed around Eurocentric notions about space and time; representation of nonwestern realities within such western forms thus requires much ingenuity. To dramatize the role that traditional and foundational stories play in the lives of characters is to dramatize for the audience the indigenous experience of the presence of the past. Unlike the western temporal paradigm of "clock" time (linear time, the measured, industrial time of "progress"), the indigenous temporal paradigm is cyclic (natural, seasonal), emphasizing an eternal present that enfolds not only past and future, but also other dimensional worlds (such as the world of spirits). American Indian writing depicts worlds based on such alternative spatio-temporal models, despite significant formal resistance presented by western, written genres. Momaday and Silko's works, again, provide definitive examples. Both Abel in *House* and Tayo in *Ceremony* must align their present-time lives with the lives of other-dimensional characters in foundational stories; their lives are, in essence, coterminous with the lives of foundational characters in the "one story," the never-ending story of Creation. To be out of sync with the "story" is to lose one's identity, one's connections to family, society, humanity, and the earth.

To meet such aesthetic challenges, post-1968 Native writers exploit a variety of postmodern textual strategies. Much literary critical discussion explains how postmodern developments have facilitated communication of indigenous messages. Using multiple narrators, engaging readers in self-reflexive reader roles, developing nonlinear organizational tactics, and focusing attention on the nature of language, discursive forms, and representation are only a few of the postmodern techniques that Native artists have adapted to serve their purposes. Like Momaday in *The Way to Rainy Mountain*, Silko in *Storyteller*, and Anita Endrezze (Yaqui/mixed European, 1952–) in *Throwing Fire at the Sun, Water at the Moon* (2000), they have also introduced fascinating multi-generic forms. Native American writing is frequently also metatextual, instructing the audience about the interpretive practices necessary for reading the text even as they are reading it. Silko's *Ceremony* and *Almanac of the Dead* (1991) are replete with metatextual cues, as are *Ghost Singer* (1988), by Anna Lee Walters, and *Eye Killers* (1995) by A.A. Carr (Navajo/Laguna, 1960–).

In American Indian literary works since 1968, we may also observe that content and themes have shifted gradually away from preoccupation with the past and the near impossibility of living in the dominant society, to a revisionary emphasis on the future—to the subversive transformation of the dominant society. Gerald Vizenor's works, in particular, exemplify this trend. Insisting on the powers of language to construct reality, he also deploys the destructive and deconstructive powers of language to undermine cultural stereotypes. In his fiction and nonfiction, we observe these dynamic, transformative forces in the hands of Native narrators and characters who are determined, according to Vizenor as literary critic in *Earthdivers: Tribal Narratives on Mixed Descent* (1981), to create a "new urban turtle island" (xi). One such creator himself, Vizenor employs an array of transformative tactics, ranging from revisions of tribal lore, to the invention of new terms such as "imagic," "survivance," and "postindian," to the use of "fictional characters with real names" (*Darkness in Saint Louis Bearheart*, 1978, xxi). Novels and short stories by Canadian Native Thomas King (Cherokee/European, 1943–) also fit into this postmodern revisionary category. *Green Grass, Running Water* (1993), *Truth and Bright Water* (1999), and many of King's short stories disrupt both Eurocentric and Native stereotypes. In *Green Grass*, Native Americans rent John Wayne movies, "edit" them to include significant changes, and then return them to video stores where they become transformational instruments within popular culture.

Equally revisionary agendas but less overtly postmodern tactics characterize the works of other contemporary Native authors. Linda Hogan's novels, stories, poems, and essays outline a future inhabited by powerful, rather than victimized indigenous people. In *Solar Storms* (1995) and *Power* (1998), young female protagonists resist pressure from both tribal and U.S. society to control their destinies. Such characters embody hope for a new generation of Native people to heal the past through efficacious participation in the present. Though Hogan's and other future-oriented works such as *Almanac of the Dead* by Silko, *Eye Killers* by Carr, and *Indian Killer* (1996), by Sherman Alexie, honestly confront serious problems without easy resolutions, their emphasis on the renewed presence of empowered Native Americans reminds readers of ancient Native prophecies foretelling the end of colonial domination.

Trends and Themes. These observable trends in post-1968 Native writing corroborate Paula Gunn Allen's claim in her critical study, *Song of the Turtle: American Indian Literature, 1974–1994* (1996). She identifies two phases in the development of Native American literature since the 1970s. In works from the early 1970s through the early 1990s, she sees a healthy expression of anger about history, combined with a pronounced sense of "renewal and hope," particularly in the tendency of these works to convey information about Native identity and cosmology to a diverse, receptive audience. Beginning in the early 1990s, Allen observes a shift toward concern with contemporary Native life, with urban Indian experience, and with designs for the future.

Post-1968 writers best known as novelists are Momaday, Vizenor, Silko, Welch, Hogan, Erdrich, Walters, Alexie, Conley, King, Louis Owens (Cherokee/Choctaw, 1948–2003), Michael Dorris (Modoc, 1945–1997), and Greg Sarris (Miwok/Pomo, 1952–). Also notable are Carr, Susan Power (Standing Rock Sioux, 1961–), Gordon Henry (White Earth Chippewa, 1955–), LeAnne Howe (Choctaw, 1951–), and Debra Magpie Earling (Bitterroot Salish, 1957–). Short story writers include most of these novelists, along with Allen, Endrezze, Ralph Salisbury (Cherokee, 1924–), Beth Brant (Mohawk, 1941–), Carter Revard (Osage, 1931–), Peter Blue Cloud (Mohawk, 1933–), and Duane Niatum (S'Klallam, 1938–), among many others.

Though novels and short stories (during and after the twentieth century) feature more prominently in popular culture than other genres, a discussion of Native American literature must include a few words about poetry and drama. Momaday's "Earth and I Give You Turquoise" (1958), patterned on oral chant and articulating the foundational theme of indigenous connection with the land, inspired his generation of Native poets including Simon Ortiz (Acoma, 1941–), Silko, Hogan, Welch, Joy Harjo (Muscogee Creek, 1951–), Vizenor, Lance Henson (Cheyenne/Oglala, 1944–), Revard, and others. Native American poets address many of the same issues as novelists, and often even more directly borrow from traditional oral genres such as song, prayer, and chant. A major contemporary writer, Joy Harjo transforms many of her poems into lyrics, which she and her bands, *Poetic Justice*, and later, *Arrow Dynamics*, in turn have set to a multicultural pastiche of musical styles. Her most recent works include *A Map to the Next World* (2000), and *How We Became Human: New and Selected Poems* (2002). Louise Erdrich is also well known for her poetry. Like her novels, many of her poems deal with cultural and spiritual experiences of people attempting to preserve indigenous lifeways and values within an unreceptive, sometimes hostile, dominant society. One of her most frequently anthologized poems, "Jacklight" (1984) and several of her recent ones in *Original Fire: Selected and New Poems* (2003), deal directly with bicultural individuals and situations in the lyrical style typical of her narrative works. "Captivity" (1984) is a fascinating poem in which the speaker assumes the voice of Mary Rowlandson, author of the famous colonial narrative of Indian captivity, but tells a somewhat different story.

Other widely published, post-1968 poets (many of whom also write novels, short stories, and nonfiction) are Hogan, Ortîz, Blue Cloud, Mary Tall Mountain (Athabascan, 1918–1994), Jim Barnes (Choctaw, 1933–), Lance Henson (Cheyenne, 1944–), Geary Hobson (Cherokee-Quapaw-Chickasaw, 1941–), Maurice Kenny (Mohawk, 1929–), Roberta Hill Whiteman (Oneida, 1947–), Allison Hedge Coke (Cherokee, 1958–), Wendy Rose (Hopi/ Miwok, 1948–), Diane Glancy (Cherokee, 1941–), Ray Young Bear (Mesquakie, 1950–), Luci Tapahonso (Navajo, 1953–), Armand Garnet Ruffo (Ojibway, 1955–), and Gloria Bird (Spokane, 1951–).

Like poetry, Native American theatre does not enjoy as high a profile as fiction. Nevertheless, it has developed steadily alongside other genres since the 1970s. Hanay Geiogamah (Kiowa/Delaware, 1945–) is well known for *Body Indian* (1972) and two other plays published together in *New Native American Drama: Three Plays* (1980). Diane Glancy is the most prolific of today's Native playwrights, and her works include *War Cries* (1997) and *American Gypsy: Six Native American Plays* (2002). Tomson Highway (Cree, 1951–) is a recognized Canadian Native playwright best known for his comedy, *The Rez Sisters* (1988). Many of these playwrights earned reputations in theatre companies such as the Native American Theater Ensemble (NATE), Spiderwoman Theater, Red Earth Performing Arts Company, and Echo Hawk, all founded in the 1970s. Throughout the 1980s, other companies appeared, including Indian Time Theater and Washington's First American Theater/Free Spirit Players. Unfortunately, American Indian theatre productions in the United States are still rare; the situation is somewhat better in Canada, but even there, the relatively small number of venues, in general, inhibits the development of indigenous theatre.

Literary nonfiction, including autobiographical and "life" writing, is an increasingly visible genre in both American and Native American letters. Most of the writers previously mentioned, including Momaday, Silko, Vizenor, Hogan, Allen, Elizabeth Cook-Lynn (Dakota, 1930–), and many others have written nonfiction and autobiographical essays concerned with indigenous experience. Particularly popular when it appeared was Michael Dorris's *The Broken Cord* (1989), which recounts the short, tragic life of his (and Louise Erdrich's) adopted son who suffered from fetal alcohol syndrome. Other significant contributions to nonfiction are Silko's *Sacred Water* (1993), and *Yellow Woman and a Beauty of the Spirit: Essays* on *Native American Life Today* (1996), Louise Erdrich's *The Bluejay's Dance: A Birthyear* (1995), and Hogan's *The Woman Who Watches Over the World: A Native Memoir* (2001). Collective "life writing" includes *Life Lived Like a Story: Life Stories of Three Yukon Native Elders* (1990) by Julie Cruikshank with Angela Sidney (Tagish/Tlingit, 1902–), Kitty Smith (S. Tuchone/Tlingit, c. 1890–), and Annie Ned (S. Tuchone/Tlingit, c. 1890s–), a clan history melded with commentary on the land; the three female elders offer the book as a message to the younger generation.

Selected Authors. Novelists, poets, playwrights, short story and nonfiction writers from the post-1968 "renaissance" have established enduring trends and themes in American Indian literature. Grounded in Native cosmologies and shaped by unique historical forces, the following basic thematic emphases will undoubtedly prevail throughout the foreseeable future: concern with collective and individual identity, including matters of gender; focus on preservation of ancient knowledge, traditions, and practices; attention to marginalization of Native people within the dominant society; concern with the natural environment; attention to the continuing effects of history on the present time and thus, insistence on repatriation of tribal artifacts; preoccupation with the power of language and human responsibility for its use; and interest in cross-cultural educational initiatives.

In the twenty-first century, a list of major Native American authors still includes most members of the "renaissance" generation such as Momaday, Silko, Welch, Erdrich, and others we have noted, plus a number of younger writers such as Sherman Alexie, whose works have received a disproportionate amount of attention, doubtless owing to his high public profile as a speaker and filmmaker.

To some extent, all contemporary Native writers concerned with identity must engage with patterns set by Momaday, Silko, and Welch. Momaday's Abel in *House Made of Dawn*, Silko's Tayo in *Ceremony*, Welch's Jim in *The Death of Jim Loney* (1979), and his nameless narrator in *Winter in the Blood* (1974) make very clear the equation of a Native individual's tribal connections with his or her physical, spiritual, emotional, and psychological well-being. Abel, Tayo, and Jim must not only learn their tribal heritage and reestablish contact with their relatives, living and dead, but also literally return home to the geographical spaces inhabited by their tribes. The scholar William Bevis thoroughly addresses this Native foundational theme of returning home in the works of these writers, and Ron McFarland and others have argued that Welch's Jim dies primarily because he is unable to reconnect in these ways; thus, he joins his people in spirit by deliberately arranging his own warrior's death.

Welch's later works, however, particularly *The Indian Lawyer* (1990) and *The Heartsong of Charging Elk* (2000), branch out into a new direction regarding such matters of identity. They entertain controversial questions about assimilation into the dominant society; in so doing, they underscore the message inherent within all of his works—the fact that Native individuals are entitled to freedom from pressure to live up to the ideas of other people (including Native Americans) about Native Americans. Sylvester Yellow Calf, in *The Indian Lawyer*, stops short of complete identification with Native people; though he works on their behalf, he refuses to define himself exclusively in terms of a single cultural frame of reference. In *Heartsong*, Welch's protagonist, Charging Elk, is a nineteenth-century Lakota who joins Buffalo Bill's Wild West Show and goes to France, where he remains by choice even when given a chance to return home. Critics of Welch's later works focus on the author's implied departure from the Native-identity models that he himself helped establish.

Related to the subject of identity, Welch sets precedent questions about gender roles, as well, a subject often explored in Native American literature. Jim Loney's masculine identity is compromised because no place for a traditional Indian warrior or hunter exists in the modern world. Welch suggests that without constructive outlets for their energy, and without desirable roles in either tribal or mainstream society, men like Jim, and like Silko's destructive male characters in *Ceremony* and *Almanac of the Dead*, become prone to alcohol abuse and violence. Welch and his contemporaries explore the consequences of this dilemma for women as well as for men; the female characters in Jim Loney's life, his sister and girlfriend, are forced into compensatory, caretaking roles that distort their own identities. Likewise, though Silko's *Ceremony* features a male protagonist, the novel addresses the key issue of social and cosmological disorder resulting from men's loss of respect for themselves and for women. When Silko's Tayo insults female deities and curses the rain, he intensifies his own plight as well as the suffering of his own people.

Similarly, Louise Erdrich's novels variously address the subject of masculine and feminine roles and power; the interconnected worlds of her novels that are first introduced in *Love Medicine* (1989) feature multi-generational families who must continually renegotiate self-definitions arising from conflicts between tribal and Eurocentric traditions. The conflicts destroy potentially powerful women and men, such as Lulu Lamartine and Gerry Nanapush, and profoundly confuse others, such as Lipsha Morrissey. Even more directly focused on the lives of women, Linda Hogan's *Solar Storms* and *Power* examine the experiences of multiple generations of women as they attempt to survive in the dominant society without sacrificing their Native identities. Hogan portrays the god-like, collective female power of mothers and caretakers in many poems included in *Book of Medicines* (1993), and develops variants of this message in all of her novels.

Not only in fiction but in nonfiction works, Erdrich, Hogan, and Allen also deal with matters of gender. Picking up the thread established in the nineteenth century, when Jane Johnson Schoolcraft, Sarah Winnemucca, Mourning Dove, and others first attempted to correct Eurocentric notions about Indian women and their roles within tribal societies, Allen since the early 1980s has educated her readers through nonfiction works emphasizing past and present roles of Native women, particularly within Puebloan, matrilineal societies. Probably Allen's most famous, groundbreaking work is *The Sacred Hoop: Recovering the Feminine in American Indian Traditions* (1986), a nonfiction discussion of Native literature delineating features that distinguish it from Eurocentric genres. Embodying these features, her novel, *The Woman Who Owned the Shadows* (1983), develops a female protagonist who must recover, and to an extent, reinvent a woman's spiritual tradition lost owing to the European destruction of tribal worlds.

Also speaking on behalf of Native women is the poet, musician, and screenwriter, Joy Harjo, whose art celebrates female strength and endurance in ways that shatter stereotypes not only of Native women, but women in general. Her poetry, frequently recorded as lyrics by her and her bands, reflects her powerfully visual imagination. With co-editor Gloria Bird, in *Reinventing the Enemy's Language: Contemporary Native Women's Writing of North America*, Harjo offers a collection of writings by Native authors exploring the "beautiful survival" of Indian women.

Interwoven with the theme of individual and collective identity is concern with the preservation of ancestral knowledge and lifeways. Momaday, Welch, Silko, Erdrich, Hogan, Walters, and Harjo, among numerous others, connect such preservation with survival itself. Hogan's *Power* equates the near-extinction of the Florida panther with the demise of the Taiga tribe, whose cosmology is founded upon their relationship with this animal. The young girl protagonist, Omishto, bears profound responsibility as the youngest member of the Taiga to figure out how to adapt to twenty-first century life without breaking the hearts of the elders, who adhere to the old ways. However, Hogan's novel—like Silko's *Ceremony*, Walters' *Ghost Singer*, Erdrich's *Tracks*, and A.A. Carr's *Eye Killers*—suggests that even the most powerful traditional knowledge, ceremonies, and rituals are sometimes inadequate to the crises of the present day. Key characters in these books—Betonie in *Ceremony* and Michael Horse in *Mean Spirit* (1990), for instance—frequently display visionary capacities for imagining a future in which tribal lifeways survive in rejuvenated forms. Native humorists Vizenor, King, and Alexie also contribute to this conversation through the development of characters good at disruption and disorganization of the dominant society in ways that open spaces for Native inhabitation on their own terms.

Appearing in several of his works, Vizenor's Almost Brown is an adept transformer of Eurocentric language and technology to Native purposes. In the comical short story, "Feral Lasers" (1991), for example, Almost creates enormous holograms of animals, Native Americans, and American folk and historical figures, then sends them out to wreak havoc among drivers on crowded urban highways. These figures symbolically suggest the ways in which technologically knowledgeable Native people may begin to manage representation and thus attain a larger share of the social and political power that such control entails. In a similar comic vein, Thomas King confronts Eurocentric society with the absurdity of their own thoughts about Indians in his story, "A Seat in the Garden" (1990, 1993), where two white characters are unable to recognize actual Indians, but quite good at conjuring up illusory ones from their own imaginations. Like Vizenor, King implies that Eurocentric ways of seeing and controlling reality can be used by disfranchised outsiders who learn to wield representational power in creatively disruptive ways.

Sherman Alexie joins comic writers Vizenor and King in his own denouncement of Indian stereotypes. Alexie is in some ways like a real-life embodiment of Vizenor's character, Almost. Indeed, in the dialogue among Native writers about who may call him- or herself a "real" Indian, Alexie shares Vizenor's notion that Native identity is more clearly defined by self-creative, individual expression and personal politics than it is by cultural heritage. Well known for his novels *Reservation Blues* (1995) and *Indian Killer*, and for collections of short stories including *The Lone Ranger and Tonto Fistfight in Heaven* (1993), Alexie's ideas are developed in five different genres, including two films, *Smoke Signals* (1998) and *The Business of Fancydancing* (2001). Critic David L. Moore aptly describes Alexie's iconoclastic, comic irony as a style conjoining aesthetics and ethics in a revisionary project for retelling history. Stories in *The Toughest Indian in the World* (2001) suggest that the best way for Native people to break free of stereotypical representation—including their own ideas about themselves—is by adopting a kind of postmodern self-consciousness content with uncertainty and marked by perpetual self-reinvention.

Common to contemporary Native literature is also a concern with alienation, marginalization, and geographical displacement of Native people within the dominant society. Concerned with both past and present—indeed, the present effects of the past—Walters's *Ghost Singer* treats the ongoing consequences of the Long Walk for the Navajo; she instructs the audience not only about the forced removal of the Navajo from Dinétah to Bosque Redondo in eastern New Mexico from 1864 to 1868, but also the ways in which the Long Walk continues to this day to affect the Navajo and many other people. Robert Conley's *Mountain Windsong: A Novel of the Trail of Tears* (1992) asks the reader to ponder the consequences of the forced removal of the Cherokee from their southeastern homeland to Oklahoma Indian Territory during the 1830s.

Forced removal of Native people did not end with the nineteenth century, but continued in various ways well into the twentieth century with consequences extending into the present. Hanay Geiogamah's *Body Indian* and Bruce King's *Evening at the Warbonnet* (1990) are plays that expose the suffering of spiritually and physically damaged Indians living in cities. Subjects of various twentieth-century "relocation" policies of the U.S. government, displaced urban Indians also appear in Momaday's *House Made of Dawn*, Vizenor's *Darkness in Saint Louis Bearheart*, and Silko's *Almanac of the Dead*, Alexie's works, including *Indian Killer*, and in the poems of Hogan, Harjo, Henson, Welch, and Ortíz. Political concerns are reflected in James Welch's poems in *Riding the Earthboy 40* (1971) and in Simon Ortíz's poetry in *Going for the Rain* (1976). Both collections offer Native perspectives on America around the time of the nation's bicentennial year. Combining prose and poetry, Ortiz's *Fight Back: For the Sake of the People, For the Sake of the Land* (1980) and *Sand Creek* (1990) deal with the ongoing historical effects of the 1680s Pueblo Revolt upon contemporary life, and with the implications for American politics of the Sand Creek massacre of 1864.

A third thematic thread connecting major works and authors addresses the western appropriation and industrial destruction of the earth. Environmental damage is not only a material but a spiritual problem from tribal perspectives, for most Native people conceive of the earth not as an inert, commodifiable "resource," but as a living being. Traditional American Indian literature reveals a spiritual relationship among humans, animals, spirit entities, and the North American land, a relationship that continues to inform literary works of the present day. The geographical space one inhabits is not just a physical location but a spiritual home as well. Thus the Long Walk and the Trail of Tears are more tragic for Native people than might be obvious to non-Natives. For the Navajo, to leave or destroy the place inhabited by the Holy People, who shape and sustain the tribe, who include Nilchi, the Holy Wind that is the breath of life, is to wither and die. *Diné bahane',* for instance, teaches that the life patterns of the Holy People and other spirit entities are replicated in the lives of human beings within a cosmos where spiritual and material dimensions are inseparable. Thus, for a person to lose the land where he or she draws breath is to become profoundly displaced, to risk illness, death, and nonbeing. Likewise, for the Cherokee, removal meant leaving behind the place chosen for them by Great Buzzard—the Tsalagi country full of mountains (North Carolina)—for a land they did not know and that did not know them. A fundamental claim of Native literature is that specific places were made for specific people, animals, and spirits, and that centuries of exile cannot alter this fact of creation. In the early years of the twenty-first century, the White River Band of Utes have been returning to Meeker, in Colorado's White River Valley, from a reservation in Utah where they were banished over 100 years ago; this is one of many real-life events underscoring the authenticity of views expressed in literary works.

Even more devastating than appropriation of tribal homelands is the utter destruction of such places by logging, mining, oil-drilling, urban development, and other western forms of encroachment. Mary Tall Mountain's poem, "The Last Wolf" (1981, 1995), is a melancholy testimony to such loss. The speaker addresses the wolf, who seems to search for her throughout the "ruined city" to seek her help. Similar lamentations occur in Silko's *Ceremony*, in its concern with atomic warfare, and *Almanac of the Dead*, which addresses global environmental issues, and Carr's *Eye Killers*, in its focus on the widespread pollution of the Southwest by nuclear testing and uranium strip-mining. Hogan's *Mean Spirit* deals with the U.S. government's repeated exploitation of inhabitants of Indian Territory, particularly the Osage, owing to the discovery of oil on tribal lands. Her more recent novel, *Power*, deals with the destruction of Florida's natural environment, home to the nearly extinct Florida panther. Louise Erdrich's *Tracks* (1998) and *Four Souls* (2004) address logging practices that have laid waste to tribal lands and to the hearts of tribal people in the region of the Dakotas and Wisconsin.

Yet another thematic strand of Native literature concerns tribal demands for the repatriation of property, particularly ceremonial items and human remains. Like Native people who belong in the places the Creator designed for them, tribal artifacts must return to their home lest the world continue to be disrupted by their restless spiritual energy. "Old Students of the New Physics" (1993), a poem by Marilou Awiatka (Cherokee, 1936–), develops this theme. She asks us to ponder the Butterfly Effect, a metaphor used by physicists to illustrate small-scale physical events that can have very large-scale effects: figuratively, a butterfly flapping its wings in one place on the earth may cause a hurricane in another. In Awiatka's poem, when earthmoving equipment in an urban development project scatters bones from an Indian gravesite, the speaker predicts consequences felt far and near. Other literary works dealing with stolen, abused, or misplaced Native artifacts include, as previously mentioned, Carr's *Eye Killers* and Walters's *Ghost Singer*. In *Eye Killers*, prayer sticks brought home by Navajos to Dinétah from Bosque Redondo, and kept safe by Puebloan families, are powerful enough to vanquish modern-day monsters—vampiric creatures representing the European presence in North America. In *Ghost Singer*, part of the plot revolves around stolen objects and human remains wreaking havoc among employees of the Smithsonian Museum of Natural History who come in contact with them. Indeed, Walters's novel, a profound explanation of tribal views on the subject, may have played a significant role in the passing of the Native American Graves Protection and Repatriation Act of 1990. Hogan's *Mean Spirit* (1990) likewise addresses the fate of Indian bones scattered about the land with the arrival of more and more white settlers. Two novels by Louis Owens, *The Sharpest Sight* (1992) and *Bone Game* (1994), deal with a man's repatriation of his veteran brother's bones, and with the threat of their ending up in a museum, the ultimate desecration for Native people. In Erdrich's *The Painted Drum* (1995), a real estate agent sells to a museum some Indian bones that she finds on property she has purchased, but she steals a ceremonial painted drum that should have been, along with the bones, returned to the Ojibwe. Like poet Joy Harjo, who stresses the ways in which social and political problems of the present day are related to imperialist atrocities of the past, Erdrich and others insist that the past cannot be simply forgotten, stored away in archives, or appropriated for present-day use in a Eurocentric agenda.

Still another theme that distinguishes most contemporary American Indian literature concerns the creative and destructive powers of language. Louise Erdrich's Nanapush, an important character in several novels and a narrator in *Tracks*, remarks on the power of language to "cure or kill," a power that Silko's *Ceremony* similarly highlights in a plot driven by the destructive magic of beings showing off their storytelling abilities in a contest of "dark things"; the story of atomic energy escapes its author's control and cannot be called back. The bombings of Hiroshima and Nagasaki and the Cold War nuclear arms race are the result. Such narratives emphasize how potential realities originate in thought, find expression in words, and then take actual shape in material forms and practices. Because of this monumental power of words to create, sustain, and destroy worlds and their inhabitants, Native storytellers believe profound responsibility accompanies language use, and storytelling in particular.

In Hogan's *Power*, Omishto and Ama are caught up in real events that unfold according to an ancient tribal story. The humorous works of writers such as Vizenor and King are rife with tricksters, including Coyote, who manipulate stories and other modes of representation for revolutionary, revisionary purposes. Though King's Coyote in *Green Grass, Running Water* usually claims to have been out of town when bad things happen, the reader entertains no doubts about the material consequences of trickster discourse. A comic element in Momaday's *House Made of Dawn* involves a member of the Native American Church, a "priest of the sun," who observes that part of what is wrong with creation is that after St. John the Divine said in the Bible that, "in the beginning was the Word," he should have been quiet; he should have trimmed the "fat." Instead, he talked too much. Too much talk wreaks havoc. Indeed, a common complaint of Native people about whites is that they talk too much. In Walters's *Ghost Singer*, Indian characters advise whites to "be quiet" so that they might "learn something" about indigenous views of the world.

Finally, we may observe among major American Indian authors an educational initiative comprising another thematic pattern uniting their work. An enduring educational trend in nonfiction writing began, perhaps, with Eastman's *The Soul of the Indian* and continues today in works by Hogan, Silko, Allen, Momaday, and many other major Native writers who have written not only poems, novels, and short stories, but also nonfiction essays and autobiographical pieces serving educational purposes. Ongoing efforts have ranged from Luther Standing Bear's *Land of the Spotted Eagle* (1933), to many works by Vine Deloria, Jr. (Yankton/Standing Rock Sioux, 1933–2005), most recently *The World We Used to Live In: Remembering the Powers of the Medicine Men* (2006). Current works focusing on the distinctiveness of Native worldviews, and suggesting that Native values and practices are needed for the preservation of the world, include *Defending Mother Earth* (1996), by Jace Weaver (Cherokee); *The Tewa World* (1967), by Alfonso Ortîz (San Juan Pueblo, 1939–1997); *Talking Indian* (1992), by Walters; and *Tribal Secrets: Recovering American Indian Intellectual Traditions* (1995), by Robert Warrior (Osage). Not to be overlooked is the powerful instructive message regarding education itself that emerges from Alexie's novel, *Indian Killer*. Insisting that any kind of non-Native intervention in Native cultures, sometimes especially well-intended intervention, is a violation, Alexie attacks cross-cultural adoption, anthropological preservation efforts, and non-Native teachers of Native material.

Contrary to Alexie's radical rejection of non-Indian enthusiasts, many Native authors offer metatextual instruction to their projected readers, who are given important information about history, cultural context, and Native interpretive practices that significantly enhance their understanding of the texts in the process of reading them. *Ghost Singer* offers the reader historical information, as well as information about Navajo and Puebloan cosmology, through characters' dialogue. Silko's *Ceremony*, Conley's *Mountain Windsong*, and Hogan's *Mean Spirit*, among others, do the same. These authors are variously skillful at integrating the necessary "educational" content into plot and character development without artificial digressions.

Critical Views of Native American Literature. Native American literature has enjoyed voluminous critical attention since the 1980s by both Native and non-Native scholars, and the pace of scholarly activity shows no signs of slowing. Moreover, literary critical response to Native literature of all genres has become increasingly sophisticated with each passing decade.

Studies of particular interest, and related to broader social and cultural concerns of the twenty-first century, include Joni Adamson's *American Indian Literature, Environmental Justice, and Ecocriticism* (2001), and Eric Gary Anderson's *American Indian Literature and the Southwest* (1999). Adamson highlights Native American literary and philosophical contributions to global discussions of environmental crisis. Anderson's book is a thought-provoking study of the complex, cultural composition of the American Southwest, and the interconnections between Native and non-Native American literature that this land has inspired.

Also concerned with cultural negotiations between Native and non-Native groups are Gretchen M. Bataille, editor of *Native American Representations: First Encounters, Distorted Images and Literary Appropriations* (2001), and Devon Abbott Mehesuah, *Indigenous American Women: Decolonization, Empowerment, Activism* (2003). These critical studies deal with questions of Native identity, both individual and collective, and its preservation despite adversities of dominant cultural pressure, past and present.

Significant introductory studies of Native literature published within the current decade are Eric Cheyfitz's *The Columbia History of Native American Literature Since 1945* (2005), Joy Porter and Kenneth M. Roemer's *The Cambridge Companion to Native American Literature* (2005), Suzanne Eversten Lundquist's *Native American Literatures: An Introduction* (2004), and Roemer's *Native American Writers of the United States, Dictionary of Literary Biography* (1997).

More specialized studies treating particular literary critical issues include Arnold Krupat's *Red Matters: Native American Studies* (2002), Robert Dale Parker's *The Invention of Native American Literature* (2003), Elvira Pulitano's *Toward a Native American Critical Theory* (2003), Theodore Rios and Kathleen Mullen Sands's *Telling a Good One: The Process of a Native American Collaborative Biography* (2000), Catherine Rainwater's *Dreams of Fiery Stars: The Transformations of Native American Fiction* (1999), and Craig S. Womack's *Red on Red* (1999).

Dealing with Native American poetry are Norma C. Wilson's *The Nature of Native American Poetry* (2001), Kenneth Lincoln's *Sing with the Heart of a Bear: Fusions of Native and American Poetry, 1890–1999* (2000), and Robin Riley Fast's *The Heart as a Drum: Continuance and Resistance in American Indian Poetry* (1999). Fast focuses on the concern with negotiation of physical space in Native poetry, while Lincoln traces intercultural developments, and Wilson develops readings of specific poets' works.

Critical views of Native American theatre are found mostly in reviews and newsletters; a few book-length critical studies have appeared since Per Brask and William Morgan's collaborative study of Native Canadian theatre, *Aboriginal Voices: Amerindian, Inuit, and Sami Theater* (1992), a work pertinent to the study of Native theatre in the United States. Also useful is Hanay Geiogamah and Jaye T. Darby's *American Indian Theater in Performance: A Reader* (2000).

On nonfiction and "life writing," David H. Brumble III remains an authoritative voice. His *American Indian Autobiography* (1988) is an indispensable work, as are Arnold Krupat's *Who Came After: A Study of Native American Autobiography* (1985), and *The Voice in the Margin: Native American Literature and the Canon* (1989), and Gerald Vizenor and A. Robert Lee's *Postindian Conversations* (1999), among others.

Reception

The Many Audiences for Native American Literature. Though Momaday's *House Made of Dawn* received critical attention when it appeared, this novel and most other writing by Native Americans presents difficulties for the average reader, and even for literary scholars who are unversed in Native cultural contexts. Work by Native writers that appeared throughout the 1970s drew a mostly literary and academic audience. Novels by Louise Erdrich that began to appear in the late 1980s probably helped create whatever popular audience exists today for Native writing, for even though her works are steeped in Native culture, their plots and characters are relatively more accessible to the general reader than are most of the writings of her predecessors. By the turn of the twentieth century, the readership for Native works was further expanded owing to multicultural educational agendas in schools and universities where students are introduced to works by minority writers. The growing number of literary critical books and articles on Native works is helpful to those who wish to teach them. Consequently, whereas in 1970, a bookstore patron looking for Native American writing would have come out empty-handed, the same visitor in the 1990s and after could easily fill a cart to include a broad selection of literary critical studies to enhance his or her understanding of the material. Moreover, most current anthologies of American literature contain both traditional and contemporary Native works.

Today's Native American writers share a keen sense of the diversity of their potential audience, which may include other members of their tribe, members of other tribes, Eurocentric people of many ethnicities, and non-Eurocentric, non-tribal people; in other words, there is a global audience for their work, often translated into a variety of languages. With this fact in mind, many Native writers have become impressively inventive of ways to reach their audience. Some of these techniques are developed based on oral storytelling practices, for oral storytellers are traditionally adept at audience accommodation—altering the way a story is told depending on who is listening.

The popular audience for Native American writing, however, as opposed to the scholarly one, remains relatively small, to an extent owing to difficulties the material presents. Though Hollywood films such as *Dances with Wolves* (1990), and film adaptations of popular novels set in Navajo country by Tony Hillerman (not Native

American) are box-office hits, most Native people and scholars of Native literature entertain, at the very least, mixed feelings about this phenomenon. Despite the fact that such works by non-Native people are often composed in good faith and contain accurate information, they nevertheless amount in various degrees to appropriation of Native cultures. Unfortunately, many more people have seen *Dances with Wolves* and the Disney cartoon *Pocahontas* (1995) than are familiar with Sherman Alexie's *Smoke Signals* (1998), or Valerie Red Horse's *Naturally Native* (1999); few have heard of films such as Spitz and Klain's *The Return of Navajo Boy* (2000). Native filmmakers and screenwriters legitimately fear the inevitable co-optation and trivialization that accompany mainstream productions. For instance, when A.A. Carr negotiated with film companies for rights to *Eye Killers*, he withdrew from projects when he was told that the Navajo material would have to be cut. Had he agreed, a film version of his novel would have been little more than another vampire tale set among stereotypical Indians in the Southwest. N. Scott Momaday did collaborate with Richardson Morse and an independent film company to produce a video of *House Made of Dawn* in 1972; starring the Laguna/Santo Domingo actor and poet Larry Littlebird, the film was re-released in 1996, but never drew popular or critical attention.

Like Carr and Momaday, most Native artists prefer not to lose control of their materials to the dominant culture; consequently, movie adaptations of their works are rare to nonexistent. This challenge seems, so far, difficult to overcome.

Bibliography

Alexie, Sherman. *Smoke Signals*. New York: Hyperion, 1998.

Allen, Paula Gunn. *Song of the Turtle: American Indian Literature, 1974–1994*. New York: Ballantine, 1996.

Awiatka, Marilou. *Selu: Seeking the Corn-Mother's Wisdom*. Golden, CO: Fulcrum, 1993.

Bevis, William. Native American Novels: Homing In. In *Recovering the Word: Essays on Native American Literature*. Brian Swann and Arnold Krupat, eds. Berkeley: University of California Press, 1987; 580–620.

Brumble, H. David, III. *American Indian Autobiography*. Berkeley: University of California Press, 1988.

Carr, A.A. *Eye Killers*. Norman: University of Oklahoma Press, 1995.

Erdrich, Louise. "Jacklight." In *Jacklight*. New York: Holt, Rinehart and Winston, 1984.

———. "Captivity," In *Jacklight*. New York: Holt, Rinehart and Winston, 1984.

———. *Love Medicine*. New York: Holt, Rinehart, and Winston, 1984.

———. *The Painted Drum*. New York: HarperCollins, 2005.

Geiogamah, Hanay. *New Native American Drama: Three Plays*. Norman: University of Oklahoma Press, 1980.

Hogan, Linda. *Power*. New York: W.W. Norton, 1998.

———. *Mean Spirit*. New York: Atheneum, 1990.

———. *Solar Storms*. New York: Scribner, 1995.

King, Thomas. "A Seat in the Garden." In *One Good Story, That One*. New York: Harper-Collins, 1993.

———. *Green Grass, Running Water*. Boston: Houghton Mifflin, 1993.

McFarland, Ron, ed. *James Welch*. Lewiston, NY: Confluence, 1986.

Momaday, N. Scott. *House Made of Dawn*. New York: Harper and Row, 1968.

———. *The Way to Rainy Mountain*. Albuquerque: University of New Mexico Press, 1969.

Moore, David L. "Sherman Alexie." In *The Cambridge Companion to Native American Literature*. Joy Porter and Kenneth M. Roemer, eds. New York: Cambridge, 2005; 397–410.

Murray, David. "Translation and Mediation." In *The Cambridge Companion to Native American Literature*. Joy Porter and Kenneth M. Roemer, eds. New York: Cambridge, 2005; 69–83.

Porter, Joy, and Kenneth M. Roemer. *The Cambridge Companion to Native American Literature*. New York: Cambridge, 2005.

Silko, Leslie Marmon. *Ceremony*. New York: Penguin, 1977.

———. *Storyteller*. Boston: Little, Brown, 1981.

Tall Mountain, Mary. "The Last Wolf." In *Listen to the Night: Poems to the Animal Spirits of Mother Earth*. Ben Clarke, ed. San Francisco: Freedom Voices, 1995.

Vizenor, Gerald. *Darkness in Saint Louis Bearheart*. Saint Paul, MN: Truck Press, 1978.

———. *Earthdivers: Tribal Narratives on Mixed Descent*. Minneapolis: University of Minnesota Press, 1981.

———. "Feral Lasers." *Landfill Meditation: Crossblood Stories*. Hanover: University Press of New England, 1991.

Walters, Anna Lee. *Ghost Singer*. Albuquerque: University of New Mexico Press, 1988.

Welch, James. *Heartsong*. Edinburgh: Canongate, 2001.

Further Reading

Allen, Paula Gunn. *The Sacred Hoop: Recovering the Feminine in American Indian Traditions*. Boston: Beacon, 1986; Lundquest, Suzanne Eversten. *Native American Literatures: An Introduction*. New York: Continuum, 2004; Native American Authors Project (Internet Public Library), www.ipl.org/div/natam/; Owens, Louis. *Other Destinies: Understanding the Native American Novel*. Norman: University of Oklahoma Press, 1992; Rainwater, Catherine. *Dreams of Fiery Stars: The Transformations of Native American Fiction*. Philadelphia: University of Pennsylvania Press, 1999; Storytellers: Native American Authors Online, www.hanksville.org/storytellers/index.html; Vizenor, Gerald, ed. *Narrative Chance: Postmodern Discourse on Native American Indian Literatures*. Albuquerque: University of New Mexico Press, 1989; Wong, Hertha D. Sweet. *Sending My Heart Back Across the Years: Tradition and Innovation in Native American Autobiography*. New York: Oxford, 1992.

CATHERINE RAINWATER

NEW AGE LITERATURE

Definition. "Faith is universal. Our specific methods for understanding it are arbitrary. Some of us pray to Jesus, some of us go to Mecca, some of us study sub-atomic particles. In the end, we are all just searching for truth, that which is greater than ourselves," says Vittoria Vetra in Dan Brown's *Angels and Demons* (Brown, 2000, 110). In this quote, Brown encapsulates New Age ideology.

In order to discuss New Age literature, it is first necessary to understand key concepts of the movement that sparked the literature. The predominating concern is the healing of the self, others, and the planet through the raising or expanding of spiritual consciousness. The holistic healing and personal transformation movements were some of the very earliest manifestations of the present-day New Age. Late in the twentieth century, alternative healers began incorporating Eastern healing traditions. Along with Eastern healing traditions come Eastern spiritual beliefs, including chakras (the seven key energy centers in the body), karma, reincarnation, meditation, and yoga. In addition to incorporating Eastern spirituality, the New Age draws upon and often blends ancient forms of knowledge from many paths. It's not at all unusual to find an author illustrating a principle by blending Christian, shamanic, and other metaphysical traditions.

Creating your own reality is another major component: the theory that human beings are co-creators with a Higher Power or the Universe, and, therefore divine, that what we focus on, we bring into being. Certain interpretations of quantum physics seem to support this idea of mind manipulating matter.

Another path to spiritual consciousness is in the channeling of either deceased loved ones or evolved entities who wish to bring knowledge of spiritual truth to the human race. This technique has been utilized from Edgar Cayce to Sylvia Browne.

Two main complications arise when trying to define New Age literature. The first is that two epochs have been assigned the term "New Age." The term was originally coined by Alice Bailey, a channeler, in the 1920s. A later incarnation grew in strength in the 1980s but had its roots in the revolutionary atmosphere of the late 1960s. In *Not Necessarily the New Age*, J. Gordon Melton, author of several authoritative works on the New Age, and on religion, writes a fascinating essay linking the modern-day New Age Movement back to Frank Anton Mesmer's principles, Transcendentalism, Spiritualism, The New Thought Movement, the Theosophical Society, and more (Basil, 1998, 35). For the purposes of this entry, we will concentrate on the latter period, mentioning the older wave inasmuch as it pertains to its influence on the present-day New Age literature.

History. Though the genre is purported to have sprung up in the 1980s with the cultural upheaval of the 1960s having played a significant role, most of the basics were established in the eighteenth-century religious/spiritual search. In fact, in a recent article, Doreen Virtue, author of several books about angels, and a holder of a PhD in Counseling Psychology, attributes many of the ideas in her new book, *DIVINE MAGIC: Seven Sacred Secrets of Manifestation* (2006) to a 1908 book, *Kybalion* (Evolve, 6.1, 4). However, to reach that far back into history is beyond the scope of this entry.

We'll begin in the 1960s, when much of the population was ripe for exploration into a redefinition of values in the wake of the Vietnam War, the draft, and mistrust of the government, and was questioning the validity of the then-current social norms in the midst of civil rights, women's, and other movements. Society was ready for a broader definition of truth. Almost synchronistically,

> [Asian immigration] barriers were lowered in 1965. In the late sixties and early seventies, a new wave of Indian gurus found a receptive audience among young Americans seeking religious inspiration from nontraditional sources . . . This spiritual subculture, which was in many ways the successor movement to the counterculture of the sixties, led directly to the New Age Movement of the eighties. (Diem, 1992, 48)

In addition, information was easily disseminated. Susan Love Brown reminds us that the Baby Boomers were the "first generation to be affected by television" and were "also a highly educated generation—nine out of every ten graduated from high school and half have attended college . . . more than twice as educated as their parents" (Brown, 1992, 91).

Some credit the countercultures' experimentation with drugs as one avenue to expand consciousness. While that was certainly true in the 1960s, Basil, in his introduction to *Not Necessarily the New Age,* detects a shift. "Today, however, the key to enlightenment isn't dope—according to many New Age magazines, such a key is more likely to be raw vegetables." About attending the 1987 Harmonic Convergence celebration at Niagara Falls, he states, "Although there were more than a thousand people [there] for instance, I smelled no pot, only incense" (Basil, 1998, 27).

Three of the most visible authors from the 1970s to 1980s era are Richard Bach, Jane Roberts, and Shirley MacLaine, and Bach's *Jonathan Livingston Seagull* is one of the most well-known stories. The classic 1970 allegory is told much like a parable. Instead of being interested in flying only as it facilitates the getting of food (read: the pursuit of material success), our seagull is determined to reach beyond the ordinary, to fly for the joy of flying and for the joy of perfecting his flight. He yearns to show all gulls that "Instead of slogging forth and back to the fishing boats, there is a reason to live! We can find ourselves as creatures of excellence and intelligence and skill. We can be free! We can learn to fly!" (Bach, 1970, 27).

Because of his disregard for tradition, the Elders banish him. Alone, he increases his flying skills until he encounters two shining seagulls who take him to a new land that he thinks is heaven, but soon he finds out is another level of existence on his climb to perfection. Here, the idea of reincarnation enters. He finds very few other gulls there because, he is told, most gulls have to live "thousands or even tens of thousands of ordinary lives" before they achieve the level he has (Bach, 1970, 55).

He essentially becomes an ascended master and returns to earth to teach others that "We are free. When we are our true selves, there are no limitations" (Bach, 1970, 82). This is the message of so much of New Age literature, that there are no limitations.

When Jonathan Seagull ascends to the next level, he leaves Fletcher, his apprentice, to teach the students. Near the end of the tale, Fletcher tells them, "To begin, . . . you've got to understand that a seagull is an unlimited idea, an image of the Great Gull, and your whole body, from wingtip to wingtip, is nothing more than a thought itself."

From here we launch into another major phenomenon of New Age literature—the series of Seth books. Seth, an entity channeled by Jane Roberts, teaches much of what will later abound in New Age literature. Creating one's own reality by manipulating matter through thought is his most prominent theme in both The *Seth Material* (1970) and *Seth Speaks* (1972). Seth says, "We form the physical world as unselfconsciously as we breathe. . . . Our bodies are the materialization of what we think we are. We are all creators, then, and this world is our joint creation" (Roberts, 1970, 112).

Also, he talks about reincarnation:

> I write this book though the auspices of a women of whom I have become quite fond. To others it seems strange that I address her as "Ruburt," and "him," but the fact is I have known her in other times and places, by other names. She has been both man and woman, and the entire identity who has lived these separate lives can be designated by the name of Ruburt. (Roberts, 1972, 3)

These three things, then—being creators of reality, reincarnation, and having a Being larger than the one manifested in the current incarnation—along with channeling, form the core of New Age ideology.

Someone who brought these ideas to the public in a highly visible way was the already-famous actress and dancer, Shirley MacLaine, when the mini-series based on her book *Out on a Limb* was televised. In her series of autobiographical books in the 1980s, including *Out on a Limb* (1983) and *Dancing in the Light* (1986),

TRENDS AND THEMES

As James R. Lewis states, "When studying an amorphous movement like the new age, one almost always has difficulties deciding where the phenomenon begins and ends . . ." (Lewis and Melton, 1992, 1). The same problem applies to the literature of the movement, since many of the works that can be categorized as New Age fit equally well under other headings. Do self-help manuals that tell us that in order to change our luck we will have to change our way of thinking belong to the realm of the New Age or to the field of psychology? If they say instead we have to change our way of believing, do they then fall under metaphysics?

MacLaine recounts her own spiritual search, including her friend Kevin Ryerson the channeler, out-of-body experiences, past lives, even traveling to a South American city to spot UFOs. Her new work, *The Camino: A Journey of Spirit*, is described as her pilgrimage "called the Santiago de Compostela Camino across northern Spain." It is "a nearly 500 mile-trek across highways, mountains, cities and fields."

"Through a range of astonishing and liberating visions and revelations, Shirley saw into the meaning of the cosmos, including the secrets of the ancient civilizations of Atlantis and Lemuria, insights into human genesis, the essence of gender as sexuality, and the true path to higher love" (shirleymaclaine.com).

Whenever we read that a person can change his/her health or quality of life by changing the focus of his/her thoughts—that thoughts are simply a form of energy from which matter (or reality) is formed—we can be confident that, at least loosely, what we are reading will qualify as New Age.

Often instructional manuals for anything from increasing creativity to developing psychic powers, the genre covers anything from variations on traditional Christianity to Buddhist and Hindu beliefs. Native American spirituality and healing methods are often linked to New Age, as are elements of Wicca. Jungian psychology is drawn from in books on synchronicity, and the literature also takes the form of autobiographies of psychics. Therefore the majority of New Age literature falls under the non-fiction category. However, novelists like Dan Brown, James Redfield, and Richard Bach take these non-fiction concepts and transform them into some engrossing fiction.

Some would even include twelve-step literature. The New Age Encyclopedia points out that its religious affirmations are the type that tends to appeal to New Agers. For example, there is an AA custom of referring to one's "Higher Power" rather than to "God" and of insisting that members are free to define their "Higher Power" in any way that they choose (Melton, 1990, 469).

A common thread that flows through the literature can be found as early as the 1970 book *The Seth Material*. Seth, a disembodied entity channeled by Jane Roberts, states, "In reality you project your own energy out to form the physical world" (Roberts, 1970, 3). This concept is reiterated in the most recent popular books and movies *What the Bleep Do We Know* and *The Secret*. These ideas have become so mainstream that the movies can be found on the shelves of rural video stores and on Internet movie clubs such as Netflix. A host of messages from channeled entities can now be accessed as easily as doing a simple Google search. Major networks carry shows featuring psychics, such as Montel Williams with Sylvia Browne. Other psychics, including James Van Praagh, appear regularly on major television shows, and Echo Bodine has her own radio show.

Context and Issues. The need for spirituality has always existed. Many people find this new form more inclusive and less discriminatory. Like Wicca, New Age addresses, includes, and empowers women, where the church and other male-dominated traditions often had not. Ehud Sperling, president of Inner Traditions/Bear and Company publishing, says:

> What makes the Da Vinci Code exciting . . . isn't the character development or even the setting, it's the whole mystery and magic around a reinterpretation of the Christian mythos. There's a real thirst and a hunger in our society today for a different story around Christianity. (Kalye, 2004, 36)

Judith Rosen's *Publishers Weekly* article, "Casting a Wider Spell," quotes Katie McMillan, publicity manager for Inner Ocean Publishing: "Let's face it, between the war, terrorism, and the economy, people are dealing with issues they may not have ever had to deal with before, and they are looking for the tools that will help them" (Rosen, 2003).

The upside of all of this is that New Age spirituality and the literature that accompanies it do fill a need for spirituality for some who can not find it in traditional establishments, and can enhance the spirituality of others who do fit within mainstream religion. The downside is that, like anything, there *are* charlatans. Frauds existed in the Spiritualism era and still do. This is not to debunk all New Age practitioners. People willing to take advantage of the gullible abound in all walks of life, from used car sales to politics. "There's no arguing the fact that for every legitimate, gifted, honest psychic who's ever existed, there have been thousands and thousands of frauds," says Sylvia Browne (Browne, 2006, 11).

Reception. How is all this received by the "mainstream" public? Many people are comforted by this more inclusive spirituality. That fact is proven by the mere sales numbers of such books and movies. On the other hand, though, there's sentiment by some on the Native American side that whites are ripping off their spiritual practices just like they did their land. Their ways are sacred and not to be "sold." Many Wiccans and Neo-Pagans look down on some of the New Age gurus, viewing them as more concerned with money-making than spirituality. Also, there of course will always be those who insist that others not following the tenets of the religion they themselves follow are worshipping Satan.

As far as the desire for this knowledge by the general public, sales speak for themselves. Judith Rosen again quotes Katie McMillan: "New Age is no longer becoming mainstream; it is mainstream . . ." (Rosen, 2003).

"'New Age titles are still the cash cow,' says Hay House publicity director Jacqui Clark. 'The main difference these days is that New Age has moved into the mainstream market with sales to Target, Walmart and Costco as the norm . . .'" (Rosen, 2003).

Others have found it less popular. The New Age Encyclopedia has found that "Neo-Pagan Witches [. . .] operate with an ethic that forbids them to accept money for initiating or training anyone in the essential practices of the Craft as a religion. [. . .] As a result of this ethic, Neo-Pagans look upon the psychic fairs and New Age expos with open contempt, and consider most New Age gurus to be money-hungry frauds who are exploiting the public by charging exorbitant fees for spiritual practices that can be learned for free within a Neo-Pagan coven." (There are, nevertheless, a few Neo-Pagan Witches who consider themselves to be part of the New Age Movement as well.) (Melton, 314)

Lisa Aldred explains the stance taken by many Native Americans: "By far, the biggest business in New Age appropriation of indigenous spirituality transpires in the publishing industry where plastic medicine men authors are big sellers." About titles by Mary Summer Rain and Lynn V. Andrews, she says, "Native American activists have greatly castigated these works for their trivialization of Native American spirituality" (*American Indian Quarterly* 24.3, 2000).

Within the Catholic community, articles can be found either denouncing the movement as a whole, or somewhat accepting it, and making an effort to understand. "The Devil has much to gain from a witch hunt," says Stratford Caldecott in *Catholic Culture* (June 26, 2002). In this article, the author takes a somewhat amiable stance in attempting to quell the fears Catholics and others may have about New Age beliefs. Instead of demonizing these New Age beliefs, the writer urges the reader to look upon them as an honest quest to connect to the divine. Caldecott calls upon Catholics and the church to rather examine the church from within to discover what it is that needs to be addressed as far as why so many people are looking for something more or different.

The April 2007 issue of *The Sun* features an interview by Diane Covington with John O'Donohue, a poet, philosopher, and former priest. In answer to Covington's questions, he states:

> There is a fierce hunger for spirit at the heart of an American culture that has lost all belief in the old language about God.
>
> New Age spirituality is rising up to try to fill the gap. I do not wish to criticize any system which can nourish people's spirits, but I find that a lot of New Age writing cherry picks the attractive bits from the ancient traditions and makes collages of them; it usually excises the ascetic dimension. In general it is not rigorously thought out, but is what I would call 'soft' thinking. (Covington, 2007, 5–6)

Others denounce New Age thought as a trick of Satan. On the Web site *BibleProbe*, Steve Keohane reviews Texe Marrs's *Ravaged by the New Age*, calling it "a shocking expose of the New Age occultism . . . snatching up our innocent children in its rotten net. It also reveals the hidden plan of New Age leaders to bring our teenagers into hideous bondage through Satan worship and witchcraft" (Keohane).

All in all, this surging interest in redefining spirituality might be best summed up in the words of a *The Da Vinci Code* character:

> It is the beauty and wonderment that serve our souls, not the Grail itself. The beauty of the grail lies in her ethereal nature . . . For some, the Grail is a chalice that will bring them everlasting life. For others, it is the quest for lost documents and secret history. And for most, I suspect, the Holy Grail is simply a grand idea . . . A glorious unattainable treasure that somehow, even in today's chaos, inspires us. (Brown, 2003, 444)

Selected Authors

Mind/Body/Spirit Connection. The mind/body/spirit connection is based on the idea that physical illness is only a symptom of some underlying emotional or spiritual "dis-ease." Practitioners work on the entire being to heal, hence the term "holistic." Furthermore, curing and healing are not the same thing. Curing only eliminates symptoms, and not permanently, since the underlying spiritual cause has not been addressed. Deepak Chopra is one of the leading proponents of this idea.

Chopra, winner of the Einstein award through Albert Einstein college of Medicine, "is one of the best known and widely respected leaders in the field of mind/body medicine in the world today," hailed by *Time Magazine* as "one of the top one hundred heroes and icons of the twentieth century" (enlightenment). Chopra, author of approximately 40 books, most having to do with the connection between healing and spirituality, explains much of his thinking from a Hindu or Buddhist perception, though other spiritual traditions are also employed to make his points. Being a medical doctor, he approaches his information from a scientific standpoint. Early in *The Book of Secrets* (2004), he introduces us to a concept called "cell wisdom." He declares that cells of the body possess a form of intelligence:

> Ten years ago it would have been absurd to speak of intestines being intelligent . . . Now it turns out that the intestines are not so lowly after all. The scattered nerve cells form a finely tuned system for reacting to outside events—an upsetting remark at work, the threat of danger, a death in the family. The stomach's reactions are just as reliable as the brain's thoughts, and just as intricate. Your colon, your liver and your stomach cells also *think*, only not in the brain's verbal language. What people had been calling a "gut reaction" turned out to be a mere hint of the complex intelligence at work in a hundred thousand billion cells. (Chopra, 2004, 7)

In a nutshell, thoughts affect the physical body, causing illness or health.

Sylvia Browne, world-renown psychic and author of 115 volumes on psychic phenomenon, explains in *The Other Side and Back* (2000), the power of the mind to manifest things in the physical body:

> Under hypnosis—when the subconscious mind is in charge—if you're told that the hypnotist's finger is a white-hot poker, and the hypnotist touches you with that finger, a blister will form where you were touched. The body doesn't intervene and say, 'Hold it, you can't fool me, I can't be burned with a finger.' It hears 'white-hot poker' and responds appropriately. (Browne, 2000, 94)

Create Your Own Reality. In an essay titled "The Magical Staff: Quantum Healing in the New Age," Catherine L. Albanese explains the principles of quantum physics as they relate to healing and the formation of reality, referring to Einstein's discoveries:

> At the subatomic level, matter—as it turned out—was not nearly so solid as it first appeared. If light could act like waves in some ways and like particles in others, electrons had become microchameleons. Matter dissolved into energy and then reconfigured itself as matter. (Albanese, 1992, 72)

The curiosity about quantum physics has become so widespread that a film entitled *What the Bleep do We Know?* (2005) is popular enough to be an item on video store shelves. The visually stunning film has Marlee Matlin as Amanda, a recently divorced woman betrayed by her husband, walk through ideas of quantum physics. Interspersed with the action are interview-type sequences with prominent scientists, theologians, psychologist, and the entity Ramtha channeled through J.Z. Knight. In addition, animation aids in illustrating concepts. Some interesting things about cell wisdom and thoughts affecting health are demonstrated in a scene where the main character, a photographer, is assigned to photograph a wedding, a distasteful job to her because of her previous experience with marriage. Animated cell-creatures appear on the screen to demonstrate what happens inside the body when various person's addictions to feeling are aroused: sex, anger, and overeating. Dr. Joe Dispenza, who holds post-graduate degrees in physiology, neurochemistry, and neuro-physiology, states:

> Nerve cells that fire together wire together. If you practice something over and over, those nerve cells have a long-term relationship. If you get angry on a daily basis, if you get frustrated on a daily basis, if you suffer on a daily basis, if you give reasons for victimization in your life, you're rewiring and integrating that neuro-net on a daily basis and that neuro-net has a long-term relationship with all those other nerve cells called an identity.

Hope is offered, though. Dispenza goes on to say, " . . . nerve cells that don't fire together no longer wire together." Therefore, it again comes down to the power of thought and what the individual focuses on—or in this case, refuses to focus on.

In a subway scene, Amanda comes upon a demonstration complete with tour guide on Emoto Masaru's photographs of water molecules. The first molecule is untouched and quite shapeless. The second has been blessed by a Zen Buddhist Monk, and the third was kept in a bottle onto which Masaru had simply taped a label saying "Thank you." These display a strikingly lovely, symmetrical quality. However, the last water molecule, labeled "You make me sick. I want to kill you", is hideous. The point of this sequence arrives when a stranger turns to her and says, "It makes you think, doesn't it? If our thoughts can do that to water, what do you think our thoughts can do to us?" This is the lesson Amanda learns by the end of the movie. Drips of water from the bathroom faucet cause her to remember his words at a time when she is looking in a mirror and saying "I hate you," to herself. Realizing what her thoughts have done to her, she consciously changes her focus and is happy and self-accepting as the film closes.

One reviewer commented that the movie "has the corny, ham-handed feel of an old 16 mm educational film" (Monaghan). Jean Lowerison, however, in her review for *San Diego Metropolitan Magazine* praises it as "a great discussion starter, and it's a pleasure to find a film that actually requires gray matter participation" (Lowerison).

Australian filmmaker Rhonda Byrne talked to *Evolve!* magazine about the process of creating the film and book *The Secret*. She "stumbled upon The Secret in a hundred year old book her daughter gave her" and in an excerpt from chapter four, Byrne cites gratitude as the single most powerful tool to bring about abundance. She quotes Dr. Joe Vitale, a metaphysician:

> It is impossible to bring more into your life if you are feeling ungrateful about what you have. Why? Because these thoughts and feelings you emit as you feel ungrateful are all negative emotions. . . . Those feelings cannot bring you what you want. They can only return what you do not want. Those negative emotions are blocking your own good coming to you. (Evolve!, 6.1, 10)

Vitale states this in the film, as well. This work is an unusual case in which the movie came out before the book. At first the DVD was available only through the Internet, then it became possible to purchase it through book clubs. In 2006, *The Secret* was released in CD and book form (Evolve, 6.1, 10).

The Secret (2006), we find out, is the Law of Attraction. The film puts forth the idea that the Universe is like a giant genie, saying "Your wish is my command." That genie doesn't make any distinction between negative or positive, it just grants whatever a person is focusing on, whether it's poverty or wealth. This film also states that what we focus our thoughts on we bring into being. However, *The Secret* takes it a step farther and says it's what we focus our *feelings* on as well. While we might think positive thoughts on the surface, if feelings of fear or negativity are stronger underneath the surface, *thoughts* will not be enough.

This film depends on such notables as Dr. John Hagelin and Fred Alan Wolf, the Reverend Michael Beckwith, Esther Hicks (*Ask and It is Given*), John Proctor, philosopher, Dr. Denis Waitley, psychologist, and others (most played by actors) to illustrate how the Law of Attraction works. Like *What the Bleep Do We Know?*, dramatizations are used. However, unlike the former film, this film does not depend on animation. The book and film received another boost when *The Secret* and Byrne were featured on Oprah Winfrey's television program in 2007.

The movie answers the question about why people who think they are focusing on positive thoughts sometimes get no results. Affirmations have to be done correctly. If you say "I will get out of debt," the word and idea of "debt" exist in the sentence thereby causing you to focus on debt. Instead, the film tells you, you must visualize yourself having things you want. There is a sequence in which a man in pajamas and robe is sitting in his easy chair pretending to drive the new sports car he is wishing for, making corresponding motions of shifting gears and producing sounds of the car revving up. He is so thorough in his visualization that he even remembers to turn around and lock the car with his imaginary remote locking device when he leaves his chair. This is because passion is a force that brings things into existence even faster.

Criticisms of this film rise both from other New Age practitioners and from the medical community. Health care providers are concerned that seriously ill persons may try to use positive thinking instead of seeking medical treatment.

The overall reception of the book, however, tends to be on the positive side. Rachel Deahl notes in her March 1, 2007 *Publishers Weekly* article that "Simon and Schuster has placed the biggest reorder in its history . . . Going back to press for two million more copies."

In another *Publishers Weekly* article, "The Secret Bashing Begins," Lynn Garrett quips, "you're nobody in spiritual publishing until other authors start lining up to debunk you," and lists *There is More to "The Secret"* by Ed Gungor, *The Secret Revealed: Exposing the Truth About the Law of Attraction* by Jim Garlow and Rick Marschall, and *The Secret of the Secret* by Karen Kelly as publications in the works in opposition to *The Secret* (Garrett, 2007).

Variations on Traditional Christianity. Dorren Virtue holds advanced degrees in counseling therapy. Having authored some 22 books on mind, body, and spirit issues, she serves as founding director of Nashville's WomanKind Psychiatric Hospital. During her career, Virtue has also directed three outpatient psychiatric centers, including, most notably, a center devoted to treating drug and alcohol abuse.

Virtue's *Angels 101* offers a comforting message to those who have grown up with what they consider a punishing God. She says that angels, even Archangels, are available to us always and that they love us unconditionally. "The angels will help you with anything and everything . . . there's nothing too big or too small for them to handle. You needn't worry about bothering the angels, as they're unlimited beings who can help everyone simultaneously . . . Angels have unlimited time, energy and resources" (Virtue, 2006, x).

She goes on to assure readers they don't have to follow any certain religious path to have access to angels (Virtue, 2006, x–xi). She responds to such inquiries as "Why can't I hear my angels?" "I've asked my angels for help, but nothing seems to happen," and "Why don't the angels save everyone, especially innocent children?" Angels and God can't or won't violate free will, she explains. This is an important explanation not only in New Age thinking, but in a lot of traditional religious belief as well: If we refuse to follow our guidance, or if we are stuck in having our prayers answered in a certain way, we won't recognize blessings if they arrive in another form. Also, it seems that we all have a "time" to return home to Heaven, which our souls determine prior to our incarnation (Virtue, 2006, 114–117). This theme, that we create a "blueprint" for our lives before we incarnate on earth, runs through most of the New Age thought, from Seth to Sylvia Browne.

Another uplifting thing Virtue asserts is that God and angels know " . . . while we can grow through suffering, we can grow even faster through peace. And our peacefulness inspires others in a way that suffering cannot" (Virtue, 2006, 121).

The Sacred Feminine. The sacred feminine is not a new concept; it is probably one of the oldest concepts existing. The female life-giving force has been honored since the earliest civilizations. It enjoyed a resurgence in the early women's movement when many women were searching for a spirituality that was personal to them.

This quest for the lost feminine is sometimes called the quest for the Holy Grail and is at the center of Dan Brown's novel *The Da Vinci Code*. Like any good mystery, it starts with a murder. Also, like any good mystery, it is jammed with plot twists, danger, and chases. The central mystery, however, is a metaphysical one: It invites the reader to ponder on the idea of the sacred feminine being lost or suppressed by mainstream Christianity. It goes so far as to conjecture that Mary Magdalene was more than a follower of Jesus—she was his wife. The Grail in this case becomes not a vessel from which to drink, but the vessel of Mary's womb that was carrying the bloodline of Jesus at his crucifixion.

The plot: Robert Langdon, a symbologist and art historian, is called in to interpret symbols on the body of murdered Louvre curator Jacques Sauniere and soon finds himself the prime suspect. He connects the symbols to early Goddess-worshiping imagery, which would be in keeping with the curator's research and publications. He is aided in escaping the French police by Sophie Neveu, a cryptologist on the French force, and, it will later be discovered, the estranged granddaughter of Sauniere.

The two embark on a quest to find the Holy Grail—the one way to prove Langdon's innocence—aided by symbols Leonardo da Vinci encoded within his paintings, particularly of *The Last Supper*. Circumstances cause them to hide in the home of Langdon's friend, Leigh Teabing, where the idea of the Grail being not a cup but a womb is revealed to Sophie, Teabing claiming the figure seated next to Jesus in *The Last Supper* was not John, but Mary Magdalene.

Langdon and Neveu follow the clues in these paintings in search of documents tracing the genealogy of this bloodline, allegedly protected and kept hidden by the Priory of Sion and the Knights Templar.

Meanwhile, another group is just as desperate to find this evidence. In a complicated relationship, a bishop who is the head of Opus Dei, a man he'd saved, and an anonymous mastermind called "The Teacher" are in deadly pursuit of our heroes.

In the end, the pair find information that confirms the Grail, but not the Grail itself. Though the novel does question the church and religion, and the suppression of female divinity within the church, like every well-structured argument, Brown's characters concede in many places within the text that religion has done much good in the world. In fact, a main dilemma in the novel is the fear that exposing the document will go farther toward destroying that good than it will in setting other things right. That conflict is not resolved by the end of the novel.

Controversy over *The Da Vinci Code* has spawned at least a dozen books and a few movies. The first film, of course, is the one based on the novel. While filmmakers must necessarily condense a 454-page novel in order to fit it into a one-and-one-half to two-hour viewing time, some of the shortcomings are glaring. For instance, the red-eyed albino has the most beautiful bright blue eyes. Opus Dei and the Vatican are grossly misrepresented in the film. In the book, Bishop Aringarosa, head of Opus Dei, is a man with something to lose acting on his own for personal gain—the Vatican has threatened to remove its support from Opus Dei, and he's going to blackmail the Vatican with the information he hopes to find. The movie makes it appear that the whole of Opus Dei and the whole of the Vatican are behind the four plus murders and a conspiracy. Brown is much kinder to these two entities, making it clear that the villains are acting separately from these two bodies.

Of documentaries exploring the ideas in this novel, we'll confine ourselves to two: *Breaking the Da Vinci Code* (Grizzly Adams Productions, 2005) and *Beyond the Da Vinci Code* (History Channel, 2005).

The History Channel's production comes off as the more believable of the two, delving into both sides of the issue and featuring experts that propound various views. *Breaking the Da Vinci Code* attempts to debunk *all* of the ideas of Mary Magdalene and the sacred feminine by—basically—nitpicking. This side of the story claims there was no Priory of Sion in 1099; that it wasn't formed until 1956. However, the History Channel does find evidence for this organization as early as 1099. About Gnosticism, *Breaking* claims that the Gnostic texts that include Mary Magdalene as an equal to Jesus weren't written until approximately 300 years after the rest of the Gospels, therefore weren't important. *Beyond the Da Vinci Code* disagrees, saying the Gnostic Gospels were contemporary with the Gospels found in the modern-day Bible—they just weren't found until years later. The reason for this is that Gnosticism was proclaimed a heresy and followers felt compelled to hide any evidence of their beliefs. Also, *Breaking* tries to defend its side of the controversy by saying that books weren't eliminated from the New Testament at the Council of Nicea. A moot point—Brown got his dates wrong, but that does not disprove the sacred feminine a part of early Christianity. The fact remains that gospels **were** eliminated from the New Testament about half a century later and the Gnostic texts were indeed among those. Art historians, though, back up one aspect of debunking the da Vinci conspiracy of couching pagan symbolism in his art, as well as painting Mary instead of John at the right hand of Jesus. In journals of Leonardo da Vinci, they say, can be found notes on his strict adherence to compositional techniques. Also, that he painted many of his younger male subjects looking feminine to emphasize their extreme youth. For instance, the fact that some of these figures do not have beards is because they are as yet too young to grow them. A point well taken. The paintings of *The Last Supper* shown in any of these three movies show Jesus himself with a face as feminine-looking as John's (or Mary's).

A major theme in the New Age thriller, *Angels and Demons* (2000), Dan Brown's "prequel" to his *Da Vinci Code,* is science versus religion. Father Vetra, a Catholic priest and quantum physicist, attempts to reconcile God (religion) and science. He's used a particle accelerator in order to isolate the smallest particle into light/photons, recreates the Big Bang and creates matter (actually, antimatter) with this energy. He believes that he's proved the existence of God with his experiments—connecting to two New Age themes: that we are co-creators with God, and the theory that matter is energy.

Unfortunately, he's found dead at the opening of the novel. Branded into his chest is the word *Illuminati,* the name of a secret society of scientists formed around the time of Galileo to safely discuss scientific matters labeled as heresy by the church. An assassin, who believes he's a descendant of one of the Illuminati's number, steals this canister of antimatter for purposes of destroying the Catholic Church. (If the antimatter comes into contact with matter, there will be an explosion that will destroy nine city blocks.) This time the artist whose clues Langdon follows is Bernini, the sculptor's statues pointing the way across Rome to the ancient Illuminati lair that Langdon and his lovely young acquaintance—again the daughter of the murder victim—must find to capture the mastermind of the plot and retrieve the antimatter before a timer goes off. Ancient arcane symbols of the Illuminati and its offspring—the Masons—are what Langdon and Vittoria Vetra must decode before they even discover that they need to follow the statues.

Channeling. Echo Bodine and Sylvia Browne are psychics who extend very similar messages. Both write books not only to explain psychic phenomena, but also to teach readers how to develop their own psychic talents, often called channeling. They have so much in common, in fact, that Browne is one of the persons Bodine lists in her dedication in *The Gift.*

At the age of 17, Echo Bodine learned that she had psychic powers, as well as innate gift for healing. "Echo Bodine discovered at age 17 that she has psychic powers and the gift of healing" (New World Library). She's appeared on *Sally Jesse Raphael*, *Sightings*, *Encounters*, and other national TV shows and even as the cover story for an April 1992 issue of *Corporate Report* (New World Library). Bodine, author of eight books on psychic phenomenon, was recently featured along with other psychics in Minneapolis' New Age newspaper *Edge Life*, giving predictions for 2007. Here is part of what she had to say:

> It seems to be a year of resolution in many areas, and it has to do with finding a whole new way of approaching things. We've heard a lot about the feminine energy these last few years and I see it being more noticeable than ever before in the new year. Women and men both will be using their intuition. We've come to see that our intellect alone can't bring about the changes we need.
>
> I've seen an obvious movement in the last five years to get people to pay more attention to the still small voice within and we're going to be reaping rewards from that in this new year. It's the new order of things. (Edge Life, Jan. 2007, 14)

Bodine tells us in *The Key* (2002) that there are four types of psychic awareness: clairvoyance, the ability to see the future or spirits; clairaudience, the ability to hear the unseen; clairsentience, being able to feel presences or people's auras; and clairgustance, the ability to smell such things (10). Bodine makes a distinction between ghosts and spirits, claiming that ghosts prefer to hold on to their former lives and identity. Many are filled with self-pity, anger, resentments, fear, or self-loathing. Often they are afraid to go into the light after death for fear of punishment for what they've done in this life, or because they are attached to certain people or locations they don't wish to leave. Also she states possession is possible, especially by ghosts of people that were alcohol or drug addicted in life. They like to take over the bodies of living alcoholics or addicts to feel the high. Spirits, however, are evolved beings that come to earth to guide us. They may be departed family members, or they may be other entities whose work on the other side is to help those on the earth-plane (Bodine, 2002). Sylvia Browne agrees with the spirit guide concept, and she has much the same to say about ghosts. Possession, however, she denies vehemently as "a physical and spiritual impossibility" (Browne, 2006, 92).

Like most New Age adherents, both Bodine and Browne believe that we've all lived before and that those past lives can affect us in this life. As in many traditional religions, the belief is that the individual returns to earth again and again to learn, and to perfect spiritually. Browne, however, discusses reincarnation in every one of her books. She asserts that we incarnate on earth in order to experience and overcome negativity. The subject is treated in depth in the 2001 title *Past Lives, Future Healing*. She recounts case histories in which events in past lives have affected persons in the present incarnation. For instance, in one such chapter, she tells the story of Camille, who came to Browne for help with chronic lower back and hip pain. Sylvia regressed Camille to a past life in 1851 in which she was traveling by covered wagon and the train was attacked by a hostile tribe. "Arrows pierced Camille's lower back and 'left hip.'" In another life, the same woman was thrown from a horse and "her hip and lower spine were shattered . . ." (Browne, 2001, 160).

Her 2006 book *Insight: Case Files from the Psychic World* is a summation of her 50 years working as a psychic. Born on October 19, 1936, in Kansas City, Missouri, she had her first psychic vision when she was three, and met her spirit guide, Francine, when she was eight. This was terrifying to Browne, but her grandmother, Ada Coil, was also psychic and guided Sylvia to make use of her gift. During her college years she feared that these voices she heard from Francine and other spirits proved she was schizophrenic. She says that a psychiatrist diagnosed her as not schizophrenic but psychic. She started a teaching career at the age of 19, but later became a full-time psychic reader (Browne, 2006, 17–24).

Browne describes heaven in *The Other Side and Back* (2000) as "A breathtaking infinity of mountains, and oceans, and vast gardens and forests . . . The landscape with brilliant design and variety . . . temples, concert halls, courtyards, sports arenas . . . and homes to meet every presence's personal preference" (Browne, 2000, 5).

Criticisms arise from many quarters, especially from James Randi, a stage magician, and Robert Lancaster, whose Web sites *James Randi Educational Foundation* www.randi.org/ and *StopSylviaBrowne.com* (respectively) are devoted to disproving Sylvia Browne's psychic claims.

Browne has 115 titles to her credit, including audio books and translations of her works. She also advances the cause of the female principle, devoting a book apiece to Mother God and Father God.

Expanding Consciousness—Maximizing Human Potential. Another author who successfully employed fiction to convey spiritual messages is James Redfield, whose contributions to environmental and humanitarian causes is extensive, and has resulted in Humanitarian of the Year awards from Habitat for Humanity and the

International New Thought Alliance, and in Wisdom Media Group's Worldview Award (enlightenment).

His *Celestine Prophecy* (1993) is a fictional search in South America for some scrolls that are legended to hold nine important spiritual insights. Similar to the later *Da Vinci Code,* these insights are so valued that many will kill for them. The lead character hears about these manuscripts and travels to Peru to search for them in a story in which spiritual insights are constantly revealed. Synchronicity continually pops up—beginning with affordable airline tickets. Throughout his journey, revelations abound and he begins to see through the fabric of existence. Redfield's gone on to write other such tales, including *The Tenth Insight* (1996) and *The Secret of Shambala* (1999).

Then, in 2002 he teamed up with Michael Murphy, a founder of the Esalen New Age community in California and author of *Golf in the Kingdom*, and documentary filmmaker Sylvia Timbers to pen *God and the Evolving Universe*. Their purpose can be best summed up thus:

> For millennia, poets have envisioned times and places in which people lived with joyous accord. Philosophers have long dreamt of good societies. And activists in many fields have embodied such dreams in programs for creative cultural change. We believe that the aspiration for social transformation implicit in such visions and activities is essential to the greater life pressing to be born in us. Our ego-transcendent nature, our larger self, has a fundamental urge to help further the world's advance. This drive, this call, has long been expressed in the dreams of humankind. (Redfield, Murphy, and Timbers, 2002, 157)

One message of this book, along with Deepak Chopra's *The Book of Secrets* and Eckhart Tolle's *A New Earth*, is that in order to experience creation to the fullest, and to actualize a heaven on earth, we must transcend the ego and operate from the pure Being that is behind the ego. Here, ego is not equal to conceit. Ego is a false but very necessary self the soul must don in order to maneuver on the physical plane. However, separation generates the feelings of envy, anger, and fear that lead to war and atrocities when individuals conceive of the ego as being the true and only self. In fact, they all warn us that the planet is in such dire straits that humankind must evolve or die.

Evolution is recounted in *God and the Evolving Universe* from the Big Bang, through animal and human evolution, to the evolutions of art, philosophy, religions, and societies, and the authors say it all culminates in evolution of spirit. Similar concerns are voiced in Eckhart Tolle's *A New Earth* (2005). Tolle espouses being present in the moment.

Tolle, in *A New Earth*, explains how the ego comes into being. The ego attaches itself to and therefore identifies with "things."

> When a young child learns that a sequence of sounds produced by the parents' vocal cords is his or her name, the child begins to equate a word, which in the mind becomes a thought, with who he or she is. At that stage, some children refer to themselves in the third person. 'Johnny is hungry.' Soon after, they learn the magic word 'I' and equate it with their name, which they have already equated with who they are. Then other thoughts come and merge with the original I-thought. The next step are thoughts of me and mine to designate things that are somehow a part of 'I.' This identification with objects, which means investing *things*, but ultimately thoughts that represent things, with a sense of self, thereby deriving an identity from them.

When 'my' toy breaks or is taken away, intense suffering arises. Not because of any intrinsic value the toy has . . . but because of the thought of 'mine.' The toy becomes part of the child's developing sense of self of 'I.'

. . . My toy later becomes my car, my house, my clothes and so on. I try to find myself in things but never quite make it and end up losing myself in them. This is the fate of ego. (Tolle, 2005, 35)

He explains the pain-body, the painful emotions carried since childhood, and demonstrates that it is not the emotions alone that are carried and block pure Presence in each moment, but the thoughts that accompany and shape the emotion. The pain-body, he says, becomes addicted to the chemicals that emotion and thought produce, and, usually totally unaware, persons draw negative situations to themselves to feed the pain-body's addiction. He blames identification with "things" (which include thought patterns) for all the wars, atrocities, and damage to the environment that has been perpetrated. Not only do we identify with objects, but we can also identify with a group, religion, nation, or cause. That in itself is not a bad thing, but the idea of making "me" right and "you" wrong is an identity the ego can attach to and feel the need to strengthen.

His ideas about ego have much in common with Chopra's; it is a false self, one necessary for survival in a physical existence. Chopra tells us:

The ego, we are told, blinds us with its constant demands, its greed, selfishness and insecurity. That is a common theme but a mistaken one, because throwing the ego into the dark, making it an enemy, only creates more division and fragmentation. If there is one reality, it must be all-inclusive. The ego can't be thrown out any more than desire can be thrown out. (Chopra, 2004, 25)

Bibliography

Albanese, Catherine L. The Magical Staff: Quantum Healing in the New Age. In *Perspectives on the New Age*. James A. Lewis and J. Gordon Melton, eds. Albany, NY: State University of New York Press, 1992.

Aldred, Lisa. "Plastic Shamans and Astroturf Sun Dances: New Age Commercialization of Native American Spirituality." *American Indian Quarterly* 24.3 http://www.demo/ american_indian_quarterly (2000).

Bach, Richard. *Jonathan Livingston Seagull*. New York: Macmillan, 1970.

Basil, Robert. Introduction. In *Not Necessarily the New Age*. Robert Basil, ed. New York: Prometheus, 1988.

Beyond the Da Vinci Code, DVD. History Channel. A&E Entertainment. 2005.

Breaking the Da Vinci Code, DVD, directed by David Priest. Grizzly Adams Productions. 2005.

Brown, Dan. *Angels and Demons*. New York: Pocket Books, 2000.

_____. *The Da Vinci Code*. New York: Doubleday, 2003.

Brown, Susan Love. Baby Boomers, American Character and the New Age: A Synthesis. In *Perspectives on the New Age*. James A. Lewis and J. Gordon Melton, eds. Albany, NY: State University of New York Press, 1992.

Browne, Sylvia, and Lindsay Harrison. *Insight: Case Files From the Psychic World*. New York: Dutton, 2006.

———. *The Other Side and Back*. New York: Signet, 2000.

———. *Past Lives, Future Healing*. New York: New American Library, 2001.

Browne, Sylvia, and Antoinette May. *Adventures of a Psychic*. Carlsbad: Hay House, 1990.

Byrne, Rhonda. *The Secret*. New York: Atria Books, 2006.

Caldecott, Stratford. "An Approach to the New Age." *Catholic Culture*. Crux Publications Ltd. 26 June 2002. Ebscohost http://www.search.ebscohost.com.

Chopra, Deepak. *The Book of Secrets*. New York: Harmony Books, 2004.

Clark, Jerome, and Aidan Kelly. *New Age Encyclopedia*. Detroit, MI: Gale Research, Inc., 1990.

_____. "New Thought and the New Age." In *Perspectives on the New Age*. James A. Lewis and J. Gordon Melton, eds. Albany, NY: State University of New York Press, 1992.

Covington, Diane. "The Unseen Life That Dreams Us." *The Sun*. Chapel Hill, NC: The Sun Publishing Company, 2007.

Da Vinci Code, The. DVD, directed by Ron Howard. Columbia Pictures and Image Entertainment, 2006.

Diem, Andrea Grace. "Imagining India: the Influence of Hinduism on the New Age Movement." In *Perspectives on the New Age*. James A. Lewis and J. Gordon Melton, eds. Albany, NY: State University of New York Press, 1992.

Echo Bodine's Bio Page. New World Library. www.newworldlibrary.com/client/client_pages/authorbios/bios/bodine.cfm.

Enlightenment. "James Redfield Biography and Resources." http://www.wie.org.bios.

_____. "Deepak Chopra Biography and Resources." http://www.wie.org.bios.

Evolve! "Divine Magic." Minneapolis, MN: Magus Books, 2007.

_____. "The Powerful Process of Gratitude." Minneapolis, MN: Magus Books, 2007.

Freke, Timothy, and Gandy, Peter. *Jesus and the Lost Goddess*. New York: Three Rivers Press, 2001.

Garrett, Lynn. "The Secret Bashing Begins." *Publishers Weekly* 28 March 2007. http://www.publishersweekly.com.

Kayle, Hillary S. "Inner Traditions/Bear and Company Da Vinci Code Redux." *Publishers Weekly* 6 September 2004. Ebscohost http://www.search.ebscohost.com.

Keohane, Steve. "The Age-Old New Age Movement." *BibleProbe*. http://bibleprobe.com/new_age.htm.

Lowerison, Jean. "The Reel Story." *San Diego Metropolitan Magazine* April 2007. http://www.sandiegometro.com.

Melton, J. Gordon. "A History of the New Age Movement." In *Not Necessarily the New Age*. Robert Basil, ed. New York: Prometheus, 1988.

Miejan, Tim, ed. *Edge Life*. Minneapolis, MN: Leap Publications, January 2007.

Monaghan, John. Detroit Free Press, in *Rotten Tomatoes*, 04/10/07.

Redfield, James, Michael Murphy, and Silvia Timbers. *God and the Evolving Universe*. New York: Tarcher/Putnam, 2001.

Redfield, James. *The Celestine Prophecy*. New York: Warner Books, 1993.

Roberts, Jane. *The Seth Material*. Englewood Cliffs: Prentice Hall, 1970.

Roberts, Jane. *Seth Speaks*. Englewood Cliffs: Prentice Hall, 1972.

Rosen, Judith. "Casting a Wider Spell." *Publishers Weekly* 1 September 2003. http://www.publishersweekly.com

The Secret. DVD. Directed by Drew Heriot. Prime Time Productions, 2006.

Shirley MacLaine's official Web site, "The Book the Camino by Shirley," http://www.shirleymaclaine.com

Tolle, Eckhart. *The Power of Now*. Novato: New World Library, 1999.

_____. *A New Earth*. New York: Dutton, 2005.

What the Bleep do We Know? DVD, directed by William Arntz, Betsy Chasse, and Mark Vincente. Captured Light Industries and Lord of the Wind Films LLC, 2005.

Further Reading

Barrett, Jayme. *Feng Shui Your Life*. New York: Sterling, 2003; Braden, Gregg. *The Isaiah Effect*. New York: Harmony Books, 2000; Bradley, Marion Zimmer. *The Mists of Avalon*. New York: Ballantine, 1984; Browne, Sylvia. *Mother God*. Carlsbad: Hay House, 2004;

Chopra, Deepak. *Creating Affluence: Wealth Consciousness in the Field of Possibilities*. San Rafael: New World Library, 1993; Eisler, Riane. *The Chalice and the Blade*. New York: HarperCollins, 1987; Freke, Timothy, and Gandy, Peter. *The Jesus Mysteries*. New York: Three Rivers Press, 2000; Gawain, Shakti. *Living in the Light*. Novato: New World Library, 1998; Myss, Caroline. *Anatomy of the Spirit*. New York: Harmony Books, 1996; Starhawk and Hillary Valentine. *The Twelve Wild Swans*. New York: HarperSanFrancisco, 2001; Walsch, Neale Donald. *Communion with God*. New York: G.P. Putnam's Sons, 2000; West, Kate. *The Real Witches Craft*. London: HarperElement, 2005; Wilson, Colin. *From Atlantis to the Sphinx*. New York: Fromm International, 1997.

DEBBIE K. TRANTOW

OCCULT/SUPERNATURAL LITERATURE

Definition. Supernatural fiction is a generic term that encompasses a wide range of fields, almost all of which deal with matters that defy science and can be classified as "the unknown." The phrase "supernatural fiction" has fallen out of common usage in recent years, subsumed within the marketing categories of horror or **fantasy,** but the categories that make up the field remain popular and easily definable. These include such basic icons as ghosts, vampires, werewolves, and zombies plus those that fall under the more specific term of occult fiction.

Since some occult knowledge may have a scientific rationale, the occult may be seen as covering a borderland between the natural and supernatural. It can include those subjects that to the majority of us seem strange, such as fortune-telling or divination, but which to practitioners are completely natural. What distinguishes the natural from the supernatural is often a matter of faith and perception and consequently the borders of the supernatural realm are vague and, to the influential mind, believable. It highlights the facts that those things that may be perceived as supernatural—such as hauntings, visions, curses, or dreams-come-true—may be psychological manifestations and reflections of a tortured, drugged, or demented imagination. All too often in fiction the supernatural and madness form an unholy bond.

While supernatural fiction is broad enough to encompass fantasy fiction, by convention the two tend to be kept apart. Supernatural fiction is set in the world we know upon which occult or strange events intrude. Fantasy allows for another world in which stories may be set entirely or in part and which may be governed by rules totally alien to our world.

History. The supernatural features in all of the world's ancient legends, but as the world of ghosts, gods, and demons was a central part of cultural beliefs these tales were simply reflecting an interpretation of the world and were not intended as fiction. These ancient fears of the unknown are deeply inbred and are the basis for the popularity of supernatural fiction. Supernatural manifestations appear in many

---

WHAT DOES *OCCULT* MEAN?

The world "occult" comes from the Latin *occultus*, meaning hidden or concealed, a secret not to be divulged. So while matters occult may still be unknown to many, they are known to a select few. Central to the occult, therefore, is secret knowledge, which may take the form of magic or demonology or witchcraft or other religious beliefs, such as theosophy or obeah.

---

early works of fiction, such as "The Nun's Priest's Tale" (*c*1392) by Geoffrey Chaucer (*c*1343–1400) or Caesar's Ghost in *Julius Caesar* (*c*1599) by William Shakespeare (*c*1564–1616), but these were plot devices used as portents and were not central to the plot. We have to wait for the Age of Enlightenment to allow minds to view the supernatural logically and objectively before it can be reintegrated into fiction. During this transition the progenitor of the true ghost story appeared, "A True Relation of the Apparition of Mrs. Veal" (1706) by Daniel Defoe (*c*1660–1731), an account of an apparent haunting in Canterbury, Kent, in 1705. Defoe's approach was to render the event in story form and in so doing he set the prototype for many basic ghost stories. Defoe had a fascination for the supernatural and his open-mindedness allowed for a more healthy skepticism of the supernatural, distancing the imagination from belief and allowing more objective research. Investigations of apparent hauntings have remained fundamental to supernatural fiction, most notably in one of the most influential of all Victorian ghost stories, "The Haunted and the Haunters" (1859) by Edward Bulwer-Lytton (1803–1873), which brought together the threads of ghost and occult fiction in a detailed exploration of a haunting in both rational and imaginative terms.

Gothic Fiction. That ambivalence between logical skepticism and emotional doubt is what fuels the supernatural tale and led to the eruption of gothic fiction in the late eighteenth century, starting with the success of *The Castle of Otranto* (1765) by Horace Walpole (1717–1797). His attempt at mock medievalism brought with it all the supernatural trappings of rattling chains, ghostly groans, and spiritual manifestations that remain symbolic of the genre, along with the ghosts being both portents of doom and a substitute for guilt. The gothic mood prevailed for over 40 years and its shadow continued to be cast over the Victorian period, influencing the so-called "penny dreadful" cheap fiction of which *Varney the Vampire* (1847), attributed to James Malcolm Rymer (1814–1881), is perhaps the most extreme.

The gothic atmosphere was ideal for the rise in novels of the occult, where those who dabble in demonology or necromancy suffer the inevitable fate. There was a rash of deal-with-the-devil stories including *Vathek*, originally *An Arabian Tale* (1786), by William Beckford (1760–1844) and *The Monk* (1796) by Matthew Gregory Lewis (1775–1818). While *Faust* (Part 1, 1808; Part 2, 1832) by Johann Wolfgang von Goethe (1749–1832) may be the best known deal-with-the-devil story, *Melmoth the Wanderer* (1820) by Charles Robert Maturin (1780–1824), is the epitome, regarded by Everett Bleiler as "one of the most remarkable novels in English and certainly one of the great classics of supernatural fiction" (Bleiler, 1983, 351). It symbolized the figure of the accursed wanderer, which became adopted into vampire fiction, starting with "The Vampyre" (1819) by John Polidori (1795–1821). This drew upon Polidori's mentor, Lord Byron, who became the living embodiment of the accursed wanderer, infusing the vampire with the romantic and tragic image that has remained ever since.

Bulwer Lytton figured strongly in the development of the occult novel, most notably with *Zanoni* (1842) and *A Strange Story* (1861). Their significance lies in the degree of detail that Lytton provides, drawn from his own researches into kabalistic and eastern religions. Although both suffer from Lytton's notoriously excessive prose, they are the prototype of the romantic occult novel which uses genuine knowledge, rather than speculative, as a source for realistic fantasy.

Psychological Explorations of the Supernatural. The desire for more realism saw a significant shift in the supernatural tale during the Victorian period from the gothic extravaganza towards subtler psychological explorations. Key to this was the Irish writer Joseph Sheridan Le Fanu (1814–1873). His early works, such as "The Fortunes of Sir Robert Ardagh" (1838) and "Schalken the Painter" (1839), followed the gothic tradition, but with "The Watcher" in *Ghost Stories and Tales of Mystery* (1851) and especially "Green Tea" (1869), Le Fanu raised the question of whether the ghosts, visible only to the victim, are real or imagined and, if the latter, whether they are drug-induced or a prelude to insanity. Le Fanu rightly does not answer these questions, leaving the reader to decide, and as a consequence he created a whole new school of ghost story. Sullivan has called it "a thoroughly modern tale" and in its modernity "unexpectedly daring" (Sullivan, 1978, 12). Charles Dickens (1812–1870) had recognized that ghosts may as likely be a product of the brain than of the spirit world; Scrooge remarks that there is "more of gravy than of grave" about Marley's ghost in *A Christmas Carol* (1843), but it was Le Fanu who gave voice to the dilemma. The concept was developed by others, none better than Henry James (1843–1916) in "The Turn of the Screw" (1898).

The Golden Age of the Ghost Story. The Victorian age is generally regarded as the Golden Age of the ghost story, encouraged by the growing interest in spiritualism, and though it advanced in the capable hands of Le Fanu and others, the basic story became formulaic. Although there were many talented writers whose stories, individually, are of merit, the overall effect began to pall. Nevertheless the field was notable for the number of women writers who brought characterization and motive to the stories. In Britain these included Margaret Oliphant (1828–1897), Mary Molesworth (1839–1921), Charlotte [Mrs J.H.] Riddell (1832–1906) and, arguably the best of them, Vernon Lee (real name Violet Paget, 1856–1935); plus in America, where the New England ghost story flourished, Sarah Orne Jewett (1849–1909), Elizabeth Stuart Phelps (1844–1911), Mary Wilkins Freeman (1852–1930) and, the mistress of the ghostly tale, Edith Wharton (1862–1937). In their hands the ghost story moved away, generally, from a tale of warning to tales of helplessness where people are trapped by the past. Memories can evoke a potent haunting, especially of a lost loved one, making the story both poignant and effective.

By the end of the Victorian age the old-style ghost story had fallen out of fashion, replaced by a demand for more complex stories displaying a deeper understanding of arcane matters. This took several related forms. The most popular in their day were the spiritualist fantasies of Marie Corelli (1855–1923), starting with *A Romance of Two Worlds* (1886), which propounded a confusing concept of psychic vision and religious theory but which at the heart dealt with past lives and reincarnation. Along similar lines were the theosophical works of Helena Blavatsky (1831–1891), including her stories in *Nightmare Tales* (1892), which point to hidden masters and secret doctrines.

Linked to this pursuit of arcane knowledge is the antiquarian ghost story. Montague Rhodes James (1862–1936), Dean of King's College, Cambridge (and later Provost of

Eton), is generally regarded as the dean of the ghost story, many of which he first recounted to his students and only later collected in *Ghost-Stories of an Antiquary* (1904) and subsequent volumes. James takes the adage that "a little knowledge is a dangerous thing" to frightening extremes in tales that are seldom traditional ghost stories but more often related to ancient evils, once trapped but now released by unwary meddlers. James's horrors are usually very physical, with plenty of teeth and hair. His approach of a learned or amateur investigator delving into matters best left alone and suffering the consequences proved irresistible to others. Not only was he imitated by fellow antiquarians such as Edmund Gill Swain (1861–1938) and R.H. Malden (1879–1951) but also by his contemporaries, such as the brothers A.C. Benson (1862–1925) and E.F. Benson (1867–1940), and his influence continues today.

The Occult Detective. The antiquarian interest also ushered in the dawn of the occult detective, including Van Helsing in *Dracula* (1897) by Bram Stoker (1847–1912), and others in the works of Arthur Machen (1863–1947), Algernon Blackwood (1869–1951), and William Hope Hodgson (1877–1918) with *Carnacki the Ghost Finder* (1913). Both Machen and Blackwood were students of the occult, and members of the kaballistic Order of the Golden Dawn, along with W.B. Yeats and Aleister Crowley, and they used their knowledge in a remarkable range of fiction. Blackwood, who was a nature mystic, took this further. Stories such as "The Willows" (in *The Listener,* 1907) and those collected in *Pan's Garden* (1912) explore man's place in the cosmos and his general insignificance against the vast powers of Nature and beyond.

Both Blackwood and Machen influenced the American writer Howard Phillips Lovecraft (1890–1937). Over time, Lovecraft developed what has since been called the Cthulhu Mythos, built around the idea that alien god-like entities had once been either banished from Earth or imprisoned here, from where meddling humans or some catastrophe may release them. Lovecraft's vision is a blending of science fiction concepts with supernaturalism; the latter meaning, as Blackwood also perceived it, that everything is natural, but that humans are limited in their comprehension so that inexplicable events appear to be supernatural. Like M.R. James, Lovecraft's work was immensely influential. He encouraged fellow writers to contribute to his concept of the Elder Gods, among them Frank Belknap Long (1901–1994), August Derleth (1909–1971), and a young Robert Bloch (1917–1994). It has continued to remain popular throughout the last five decades and even attracted contributions by such literary figures as Colin Wilson (1931–) with *The Mind Parasites* (1967) as well as influencing such writers as Ramsey Campbell (1946–) and Brian Lumley (1937–).

The supernatural story remained popular until the 1930s, especially following the rise of interest in spiritualism after the First World War, with stories by Herbert Russell Wakefield (1888–1964), Leslie Poles Hartley (1895–1972), Walter de la Mare (1873–1956), and Oliver Onions (1873–1961). In "The Beckoning Fair One" (in *Widdershins,* 1911), Onions created what some regard as "the best classical ghost story" (Bleiler, 1983, 391). Although on the surface a haunted-house story, it deftly portrays how the residuum of an evil personality gradually drains that of the new resident and a new personality emerges. The only spectral manifestations are sounds, so slight as to be imagined, and with commendable restraint Onions creates an atmosphere charged with the supernatural.

Supernatural Literature after World War II. The horrors of the Second World War and the rise of commercialism in the 1940s and 1950s led to a waning of interest in the supernatural. Only a few writers persevered in Britain, primarily Dennis Wheatley

> ## MOVIES AND SUPERNATURAL HORROR FICTION
>
> The boom in supernatural horror fiction in the 1970s was encouraged by the cinema, mostly because of the success of *Rosemary's Baby* (1967) by Ira Levin (1929–2007), filmed in 1968, and *The Exorcist* (1971) by William Peter Blatty (1928–), filmed in 1973. These introduced a more violent, physical horror, which made the supernatural more convincing and frightening. It tapped into a mood that had also regenerated interest in fantasy fiction in the late sixties, partly because of the hippie fascination with drugs and alternate religions, but also because of the question of faith at a time when the "God is Dead" movement had taken hold.

(1897–1977) and Robert Aickman (1914–1981). Wheatley's occult thrillers had started before the war with *The Devil Rides Out* (1935) and continued through to *The Irish Witch* (1973). In America authors like H.P. Lovecraft, Frank Belknap Long, Manly Wade Wellman (1903–1986), Robert Bloch, and Ray Bradbury (1920–) had been published in the pulp magazines, notably *Weird Tales*, but this also ceased in the fifties. Although Wellman continued to write weird fiction during the fifties, along with Joseph Payne Brennan (1918–1990), Charles Beaumont (1929–1967), and Ray Russell (1924–1999), many writers, including Bloch and Bradbury, shifted from supernatural fiction to crime and mystery. The spirit of the supernatural was kept alive chiefly by August Derleth. In partnership with Donald Wandrei (1908–1997), he established a specialty publishing business, Arkham House, which reprinted the best of the classic material and encouraged new work. Stephen King called Derleth "an editor of pure genius" (King, 1981, 284) and the books he produced during the horror drought of the mid-twentieth century were a major source of inspiration for the new generation of writers who emerged in the sixties and seventies.

You could not believe solely in evil without also looking for its counterpart, and when, in the 1960s and 1970s, the horrors of the Vietnam War were a daily reminder of the evil that men do, there was some consolation in reading novels of supernatural horror where the evil might be vanquished. There was not only a rash of horror films in the seventies, most notably the sequence starting with *The Omen* (1976), but there was also a resurgence in supernatural fiction. Blatty believed that "*The Exorcist* brought a new legitimacy to the field of horror; in publishing and film-making parlance, horror was now profitable" (Winter, 1990, 62). Several authors emerging at that time were ideally placed and equipped to take advantage of this revival, among them Stephen King (1947–), Peter Straub (1943–), Dean Koontz (1945–), and Anne Rice (1941–) and their work, and those of their imitators and colleagues, not only dominated the horror boom of the next 20 years, but remains preeminent among works since 2000.

Trends and Themes. During the seventies the category "horror" emerged as a publishing niche, subsuming supernatural fiction. The film versions of *The Exorcist* and Stephen King's first novel *Carrie* (1974; film 1976) had emphasized the graphic nature of horror over the supernatural, while non-supernatural films like *The Texas Chainsaw Massacre* (1974) went for all-out gross and became idiomatic of horror, which took on terms like splatterpunk or slash-horror.

One of the trends during the seventies and eighties was to blur the boundaries between themes, creating more doubt and uncertainty about the nature of the inexplicable. There is a case to make, for instance, that *Carrie* is science fiction rather than supernatural, if one interprets the girl's psychic power as emanating from within rather than as the result of a poltergeist.

Three major themes emerged, all with considerable overlap.

1. Magic or strange religion in all its forms, either ancient or black magic, involving demonic (or angelic) entities and ancient gods. This includes secret cults or hidden worlds.

2. Apocalyptic fiction. This is closely related to (1) as it usually involves secret knowledge or the discovery of a lost secret that might give clues to a forthcoming apocalypse.

3. The undead, principally vampires, but including ghosts, possession by spirits, and reincarnation.

It is worth looking at these themes in some detail as it highlights the key writers and trends that developed during the seventies.

Contexts and Issues

(1) Black Magic and the Occult. The rise in interest in satanic and witchcraft fiction was primarily due to the popularity of the book and film versions of *Rosemary's Baby* and *The Exorcist*, though it had been gathering pace during the late sixties with the emergence of the drug culture and the exploration of pagan and other "New Age" religions. Newfound sexual, moral, and social freedoms in the western world had caused many to abandon old values, and to those who remained faithful the social order in the late sixties and early seventies must have seemed like the devil had taken over. The most notorious example was the murders committed by Charles Manson's "Family" in August 1969, which were linked to satanic and apocalyptic beliefs, with Manson being referred to variously as "God" or "Satan" by his followers. The films in turn had their influence. A 17-year-old youth found guilty of murdering a 9-year-old girl in October 1975, in York, England, claimed he was "possessed" after seeing *The Exorcist*. A survey conducted by Birmingham University, England, in 1971 concluded:

> The decline of institutional religion seems to have been offset by the growth of 'super-stitions' or non-Christian beliefs about the supernatural or the meaning of life, and by the rise of a large number of cults such as spiritualism, theosophy, scientology and the flying saucer movement. (*The Times*, 10 April 1971, 2)

The fascination for works of the occult increased. Some were relatively mild, usually set in a remote town where innocents unwittingly stumble upon devil worshippers or other religious cults. New England proved a popular locale for such stories. *Harvest Home* (1973) by Thomas Tryon (1926–1991), became the prototype novel of this approach in the seventies. It was a form parodied, to some degree, by John Updike (1932–) in *The Witches of Eastwick* (1984). Charles L. Grant (1942–2006) developed a series of novels set in the fictional New England town of Oxrun Station (connected series also became a trend during the seventies), starting with *The Hour of the Oxrun Dead* (1977), which involved a covert group of Satanists. John Saul (1942–) worked a variant on the theme in *Cry for the Strangers* (1979) in which a jealously guarded town proves a haven to an emotionally disturbed boy, though all other "strangers" start to disappear. Places of learning also seem ripe for satanic activities, and this dates back long before the popularity of J.K. Rowling's Harry

Potter books. In *Conjure Wife* (1943; expanded, 1952), Fritz Leiber has a college professor discover that his wife is a witch who has been protecting him with her magic. More recently Edward Lee (1957–), one of the writers of more extreme horror, has a college as the focus for a supernatural force in *Coven* (1991), while in *University* (1994; aka *Night School*) Bentley Little (1960–) has an entire college campus gradually meld into a tangible supernatural evil.

Cults, usually satanic, became a stock item, especially after the success of the British cult film, *The Wicker Man* (1973) from the script by Anthony Shaffer (1926–2001). That film involved no supernatural events, but followed the investigations of a policeman into the disappearance of a girl on a remote island, where he falls foul of a pagan group. In *The Night Church* (1982), Whitley Strieber (1945–) depicted a cult that used selective breeding to produce Satanists. In *Servants of the Twilight* (1984), Dean Koontz depicts a cult that has helped deliver a son of Satan, while in *Hell's Creation* (1995) by John Russo (1939–), a mother is so convinced her newborn child is the son of Satan that she gives him to Satanists. Another Satanist cult appears in *Once Upon a Halloween* (2000) by Richard Laymon (1947–2001). In both *Ceremonies* (1984) by T.E.D. Klein (1947–) and *The Song of Kali* (1985) by Dan Simmons (1948–) people stumble across plans by cults to resurrect ancient gods. Ray Garton (1962–), renowned for the extreme physical and sexual imagery in his books, depicts a violently evil Manson-like cult leader called Mace in *Crucifax* (1988), a novel that proved so explicit that it was heavily edited with the uncut version appearing from a small press as *Crucifax Autumn* (1988). Mace is not entirely human, but Garton created him as the embodiment of all the misery and disaffection experienced by youngsters when they are abused or abandoned by their parents. Mace becomes a revenge figure against inhumanity.

Running alongside works of satanic interest have been those exploring both old and new gods. Some of this has arisen because of the New Age movement and an interest in Celtic and other religions. Witchcraft is central to *Dark Sister* (1992) by Graham Joyce (1954–). John Farris (1936–) produced what many regard as one of the best novels to explore voodoo, its African origins, and its impact in the United States, in the southern gothic novel *All Heads Turn When the Hunt Goes By* (1977; aka *Bad Blood*). In *Darkness Comes* (1984; aka *Darkfall*), Dean R. Koontz has the police confront a Haitian priest who uses voodoo to summon creatures to do his killings. The venerable pulp writer Hugh B. Cave (1910–2004), who lived in the West Indies and had direct experience of voodoo ceremonies, incorporated much authentic detail in several of his novels including *Legion of the Dead* (1979), *The Evil* (1981), and *Disciples of Dread* (1989). Inevitably these novels also feature zombies, favorites of the cinema ever since the 1968 film *Night of the Living Dead*, from a script by John Russo and George Romero. Russo returned to the zombie theme on several occasions, including *Inhuman* (1986) and *Living Things* (1988). A more thought-provoking use of voodoo occurs in *Darker Angels* (1997) by Somtow Sucharitkul (1952–) under his alias S.P. Somtow. Set during the American Civil War it develops a deep understanding of the voodoo religion and the role it might play in resurrecting the dead.

Other ancient gods feature increasingly in new fiction. The spirits of the sea are worshipped in *The Devil's Churn* (1996) by Kristine Kathryn Rusch (1960–) while in *Forests of the Heart* (2000) Charles de Lint (1951–) explores the conflict between Celtic spirits that have migrated to America and come into conflict with ancient American powers. A similar idea was explored in *American Gods* (2001) by Neil

Gaiman (1960–) in which various ethnic deities have accompanied their emigrants to America. Other forms of mythical spirits, alien though not necessarily harmful and usually in forests, are revealed in *Wildwood* (1986) by John Farris, *Campbell Wood* (1986) by Al Sarrantonio (1952–), and *The Midnight Sun* (1990) by Ramsey Campbell.

All of these works explore our primitive desire for gods or spirits to help us cope with life. Michael Jordan observed that the world is a frightening place and that if we create gods, the "responsibility for our actions is taken from us and given into the hands of an all-powerful if unseen being" (Jordan, 1992, viii). In a series of stories collected in *Deathbird Stories* (1975), Harlan Ellison (1934–) considered how we have abandoned the old gods and created new ones, spirits borne of greed and violence. In "The Whimper of Whipped Dogs" a woman about to be murdered calls upon the spirit of violence to save her. In "Basilisk" the gods of war manipulate humans for their own ends, while in "The Deathbird" we discover that God has been lying all along and it is time to atone. These stories explore humanity's spiritual reconciliation with the world.

Among conspiracy theorists there has long been a belief that it is not gods but Secret Orders that control history. These date back at least as far as the Rosicrucians and also occur as the Secret Masters in Theosophy. Such secret organizations need not be supernatural. Notable recent examples may be found in *The Illuminatus Trilogy* (1975) by Robert Shea (1933–1994) and Robert Anton Wilson (1932–) and *The Da Vinci Code* (2003) by Dan Brown (1964–). Mark Frost (1953–) combined the conspiracy theories with the supernatural in *The List of 7* (1993) where Arthur Conan Doyle becomes involved in a quest to unearth a secret society that is using supernatural means to take over the world. John Crowley (1942–) questioned the very nature of history in *Aegypt* (1987) and, in its sequels *Love and Sleep* (1994) and *Daemonomania* (2000), charted the rise of cults and the possible end of the world. The sequence may be described as fantasy, but its use of alchemical imagery and metaphysical rationalization places the books firmly in the world of the occult.

The supernatural versions of these works posit some form of secret race or elder gods within our world, the idea most notably explored by H.P. Lovecraft and perpetuated by many of his disciples, including Robert Bloch, whose *Strange Eons* (1979) charts a coming apocalypse as the Elder Gods prepare to return. Lovecraft's fiction aside, there are other forms of hidden worlds. T.M. Wright developed a sequence of books exploring the lost Earth Children, an ancient race surviving hidden in America, which form the basis of mysterious events in *Strange Seed* (1978; revised, 2006), *Nursery Tale* (1982), *The Children of the Island* (1983), *The People of the Dark* (1985), and most recently *Laughing Man* (2003). Vampires may also exist as secret societies as explored further below.

Dean Koontz introduced his own ancient race in *Twilight Eyes* (1987) in which the protagonist has the ability to see "goblins," evil creatures who masquerade as humans. Goblins were created, genetically, by a very ancient advanced civilization, but while that race was wiped out in a nuclear war, the goblins have survived and cause most of the woes on Earth.

Koontz sets this story for the most part in a travelling carnival, which is another form of secret world much beloved by writers. It was perhaps most wonderfully evoked in Ray Bradbury's *Something Wicked This Way Comes* (1962) though its prototype was *The Circus of Dr. Lao* (1935) by Charles G. Finney (1905–1985). The carnival is the lure for the unwary who, once they have arrived, are trapped by their desires or failings. Others who have found evil lurking in the sideshow include Al Sarrantonio in *Totentanz* (1985) and Thomas Monteleone (1946–) in *The Magnificent Gallery* (1987). All of these tap into our dreams for wish-fulfillment. Indeed, all occult novels, especially those involving black magic, explore the mortal desire to reach out for forbidden fruit. If occult fiction teaches us anything, it is to know our place in the world.

(2) Apocalyptic Fiction. The coming end of the millennium brought forth considerably more apocalyptic fiction than usual, and this time a high proportion looked to Armageddon and a religious apocalypse. Most significant in this respect was *The Omen* (1976) by David Seltzer (1940–), the book based on his own film script, and the seminal work on the Antichrist.

The interest in apocalyptic fiction had been rekindled a few years earlier by James Blish (1921–1975) in *Black Easter* (1967) and its sequel *The Day After Judgement* (1971). This developed from the "God-is-dead" belief prevalent in the sixties. In this novel a black magician is commissioned to let demons loose on the world for one night to cause as much chaos as possible. The demons refuse to return to Hell and a satanic city is created on Earth. With God dead, Satan finds he has to fill that role.

Stephen King brought a modern idiom to the idea in *The Stand* (1978), where a plague wipes out much of humankind and Satan, manifested as the Walking Dude, recruits an army for the last battle. George R.R. Martin (1948–) took the idea further by linking Satanism and rock music in *Armageddon Rag* (1983), while in *Swan Song* (1987) by Robert McCammon (1952–) a nuclear war not only virtually wipes out humankind but unleashes an ancient demon determined to take control. Charles L. Grant used the approaching Millennium as the basis for a sequence of four books—*Symphony* (1997), *In the Mood* (1998), *Chariot* (1998), and *Riders in the Sky* (1999)—each volume following the impact of one of the Four Horsemen of the Apocalypse. In quieter mode in *The Last Coin* (1988), James Blaylock (1950—) looks to the coming Armageddon triggered once an obsessive collector has amassed all the silver coins Judas received in payment for betraying Jesus.

The Millennium was also the catalyst for two books by Thomas Monteleone, which blend science and the supernatural. In *Blood of the Lamb* (1993) those seeking to engineer the Second Coming clone a human from the blood on the Turin Shroud. He becomes a Roman Catholic priest with the power of healing and the ability to raise the dead. In the sequel, *The Reckoning* (1999), the priest has been elected Pope and subverts Catholicism to his own ends.

John Shirley (1953–) has always been an author to push the limits. In *Demons* (2000; expanded, 2002), he lets an army of demons loose on the world in the near future. This is no ordinary apocalyptic novel. Shirley looks deep into our souls and at the consequences of our actions or inactions in bringing the Earth to its current state. It is as much a mystical novel as supernatural, exploring consciences and motivations in a world of destruction.

British writer Garry Kilworth (1941–) saw the approaching Millennium as a moment when the war between Heaven and Hell broke loose on Earth. In *Angel* (1993), angels have been sent to Earth to destroy escaped demons, though they do not discriminate between demons and humans. In its sequel, *Archangel* (1994), a Heavenly force tries to protect a convocation of religious leaders seeking to obtain world peace, while Hell does its best to destroy it.

Perhaps the ultimate apocalypse is when Hell breaks loose. The idea of Hell as a real place to visit dates back at least as far as the Greek legend of Orpheus in the

Underworld and Dante's *Inferno* (written *c*1307). In *The Sentinel* (1974) by Jeffrey Konvitz (1944—), a Roman Catholic priest is the guardian of the doorway to Hell and the time has come for the Church to seek a replacement. Dante's version of Hell was revisited in *Inferno* (1976) by Larry Niven (1938—) and Jerry Pournelle (1933—), but an even more disturbing Hell was created by Edward Lee in *City Infernal* (2001) and *Infernal Angel* (2003). Here a young girl discovers she has the power to enter Hell where she goes in search of her dead sister. Lee creates a gothic, Bosch-like Hellscape, but also infuses the book with sharp satire and humor, unusual among his works.

The increase in apocalyptic fiction has been responding partly to a market need encouraged by the Millennium, but the number and content of the novels suggest a deeper need, one related to the growing interest in occult novels, namely that the world has become a more violent and dangerous place and that retribution is nigh.

(3) Vampires and the Undead. The fascination with the undead, especially vampires, has grown significantly since the seventies to the extent that it might be considered a genre in its own right. **Vampire fiction** has always been popular but it received a double boost with the success of both Stephen King's *Salem's Lot* in 1975 and Anne Rice's *Interview With the Vampire* in 1976. *Salem's Lot* successfully transferred the horrors of Dracula's Transylvania to small-town Maine, but it is Rice's novel, the first in her Lestat series, that has had the most impact. In this and the many sequels, especially *The Vampire Lestat* (1984) and *Queen of the Damned* (1988), Rice created an entire culture of vampires living, like a secret society, hidden within our own. The use of New Orleans as a decadent setting is also evocative of an ancient world. Rice portrays the vampires as a race with their own form of honor, building upon the accursed wanderer of Polidori's original image, but now far more multi-layered, and with overt eroticism.

While Rice portrayed vampires sympathetically, they remained otherworldly. In *The Dracula Tape* (1975), Fred Saberhagen (1930–) sought to humanize them. He revealed the true story of Dracula as recounted by the Count himself. Saberhagen showed that Stoker's account of him, via Jonathan Harker, was misrepresentative and that vampires are misunderstood, being as equally forces for good as for evil. On its own, Saberhagen's novel is an ingenious and, at times, credible account. However, Saberhagen continued the series, starting with *The Holmes Dracula File* (1976), with Dracula an adventurer combating various villains, which demoted the Count to a pulp hero.

The idea of seeing humanity through a vampire's perception, however, caught on. Two further series appeared, simultaneously, which traced a romanticized image of the vampire through history. In *The Black Castle* (1978), Les Daniels (1943–) introduced Don Sebastian de Dellanueva, a vampire living in Spain in 1496, at the time of the Inquisition. Sebastian is appalled at the horrors committed by mortals against their own kind. This becomes the central theme to the series with Sebastian witnessing various atrocities committed by humankind over the centuries. In *The Silver Skull* (1979) it's the conquistadores decimating the natives in the New World; in *Citizen Vampire* (1981) it's the horrors of the French Revolution, while in *No Blood Spilled* (1991) it's the violence of British colonial India. In all of these books, Don Sebastian is in search of arcane knowledge and a quest for Truth and discovers that humanity has its own thirst for blood.

The Saint-Germain Chronicles by Chelsea Quinn Yarbro (1942–) follows a similar outline. Yarbro has adapted an historical character, Le Comte de Saint-Germain, who lived in the eighteenth century and who claimed to have discovered the elixir of life and to have lived for centuries. Yarbro treated the Count's elixir of life as blood itself. He was an ideal choice for an honorable vampire, not least because one claim concerning his origin was that he was a Prince of Transylvania. She introduced the Count in *Hotel Transylvania* (1978), which developed as much historical information as we have about him with a storyline featuring Satanists at the court of King Louis XV. Thereafter the 20 books at present in the series range from ancient Rome (*Blood Games*, 1979) to the First World War (*Tempting Fate*, 1982) and many points in between.

The novels by Rice, Daniels, and Yarbro cover a vast timescale. By contrast, despite the title, *The Vampire Tapestry* (1980) by Suzy McKee Charnas (1939–) is a series of snapshots in the life of a vampire, currently masquerading as a professor of anthropology, Dr. Weyland, who has no memory of his previous existences prior to various hibernations. Weyland knows of no others of his kind and tries to keep his true nature a secret, but when it is discovered he has to go on the run.

In *They Thirst* (1981) by Robert McCammon a vampire lord, Count Vulkan, descends on Los Angeles with his evil cohorts, intent on attacking and converting all of the city's inhabitants to vampires, passing the vampire virus on like a plague. In *The Hunger* (1981), Whitley Strieber reverses the situation. His solitary, predatory female must hunt for her mate for it is only the female vampire that is ageless. Although the males do not die they wither, surviving as mere shadows. This novel was a one-off until Strieber returned to his female vampire in *The Last Vampire* (2001), while in *Lilith's Dream* (2002), he developed the series by resurrecting the world's oldest vampire, Lilith. Throughout these books the vampire is shown as superior but persecuted. Indeed, the vampire has become a symbol for many persecuted minorities and Streiber's books struck a chord with the feminist movement. J. Gordon Melton noted: "In contrast with the powerful male vampire, the female vampire of the 1980s emerged with the many new roles assumed by women in the larger culture and as important models (however fanciful) of female power" (Melton, 1994, 698).

In *Fevre Dream* (1982), George R.R. Martin (1948–) produced an overlooked classic of vampire fiction. It is set in 1857 on a Mississippi steamboat that has been chartered by a vampire who has created a potion that inhibits the vampire's lust for human blood. He is in conflict with a leader of other vampires who still yearn for the old days. The conflict portrayed is thus between vampire factions striving for a new world or trying to safeguard the old. Set at the time of increasing unrest about slavery and advancing technology the novel parallels American life.

Many of the vampire novels and series that appeared in the eighties and nineties were by women and their work is often categorized as "**dark fantasy**" rather than occult. In addition to those by Anne Rice and Chelsea Quinn Yarbro are works by Elaine Bergstrom (1946–), Nancy Collins (1959–), Patricia ["P.N."] Elrod (1951–), Poppy Z. Brite (1967–), Storm Constantine (1956–), Laurell Hamilton (1963–), and Karen Koehler (1973–). Their work has emphasized the erotic and generally portrays vampires as benevolent and misunderstood. Most recently the vampire has become a subject for "paranormal romances." Premier among these is the Dark series by Christine Feehan, which began with *Dark Prince* (1999) and has currently reached 14 volumes. Feehan has created the dying race of the Carpathians, supernatural creatures who can shapeshift but who, if they do not find their soul mate, will eventually devolve into soulless vampires.

Vampires created by male writers tend to be more violent and the stories feature more original twists. Perhaps the most extreme work is Ray Garton's *Live Girls* (1987) where a nightclub allows female vampires to prey upon their male victims. In the series that began with *Necroscope* (1986), Brian Lumley's powerful *vamphyri* invade Earth from an alternate reality. John Farris relates vampires to the fallen angels in *Fiends* (1990). Bentley Little's vampire in *The Summoning* (1993) is Chinese rather than Transylvanian, with a fear of jade and willow. Lucius Shepard (1947–) depicts a rich and fascinating vampire culture in *The Golden* (1993), which he also turns into an unusual detective story when the vampires have to solve a murder in their midst.

Dan Simmons looked for a scientific rationale for vampires in *Carrion Comfort* (1989), seeing them as a genetic mutation, though in *Children of the Night* (1992) he resorted to a more traditional view when a child with a unique immune system turns out to be a son of Dracula. Brian Stableford (1948–) also explored a scientific rationale in *Young Blood* (1992), where vampirism is a viral infection. He had used the vampire theme earlier in *The Empire of Fear* (1988), set in an alternate history where the ruling aristocracy in Europe, including Charlemagne and Richard the Lionheart, are all vampires. An adventurer goes into darkest Africa to find the source of the vampire bloodstock and the secret of immortality. Both Brian Stableford and Kim Newman (1959–) have a fascination with the late Victorian period and have used it as a setting to rework the vampire theme against other fictional and historical settings, Stableford in *The Hunger and Ecstacy of Vampires* (1996) and Newman in a sequence starting with *Anno Dracula* (1992), which incorporates Jack the Ripper.

The vampire theme continues to fascinate writers, though in the last decade it has been somewhat diverted by the paranormal romance movement and the popularity of the TV series *Buffy the Vampire Slayer* (1997–2003), which has led to many spin-off and imitative novels. Romance and young adult markets come together in the series by Stephanie Meyer that began with the best-selling *Twilight* (2005), which follows the love between a young girl and a vampire.

The theme has remained more enduring than that of werewolves, which lacked a basic template like *Dracula*, and does not have the romantic or erotic connotations. Such early novels as did explore the theme, such as *The Werewolf of Paris* (1933) by Guy Endore (1900–1970), which equates lycanthropy to cannibalism, never attained cult status, and it has always remained of secondary interest. The most successful of recent books was *The Howling* (1977) by Gary Brandner, made into an influential movie in 1980. Brandner treated werewolves rather like vampires, as creatures who looked for safety among their own kind and existed as a secret community until unearthed and destroyed. Whitley Strieber likewise depicted werewolves, or as he perceived them wolves of superior intelligence, as an ancient race who try to remain secretive. In *Wolfen* (1978) he shows how they choose their prey among the outcasts of society who would not normally be missed. Perhaps the most ambitious werewolf work of recent years is the trilogy by Brian Stableford, *The Werewolves of London* (1990), *The Angel of Pain* (1991), and *The Carnival of Destruction* (1994), which combined various occult and apocalyptic imagery in a late Victorian setting to portray a secret war being conducted throughout London by werewolves combating a reawakening of fallen angels, bent on regaining the Earth.

In *Wolf Moon* (1988), Charles de Lint portrays a werewolf who is a victim and searches for a means to stop his affliction, which is eventually cured by love. It is a story reminiscent of the fairy-tale motif of the beauty and the beast. Although the werewolf theme has less appeal for the paranormal romantics, it does appeal to the feminist movement as it can depict powerful individuals seeking to assert themselves in the world. Of recent works in this vein the most striking is the Women of the Otherworld series by Kelley Armstrong (1968–) that began with *Bitten* (2001). Once again there are werewolves existing as a secretive pack society. A unique female werewolf tries to survive in the human world but finds the call of the wild drawing her back. As the series developed Armstrong incorporated witches and other creatures within her supernatural menagerie.

Unlike vampires and werewolves, which have a powerful physical presence, ghosts are usually intangible. The interest in traditional ghosts faded in the fifties and sixties and took a while to recover in the seventies, although *The Haunting of Hill House* (1959) by Shirley Jackson (1919–1965) and the similar *Hell House* (1971) by Richard Matheson (1926–), both about investigations into haunted houses and both effectively filmed, helped keep the theme alive. From the late seventies onwards there was a shift to making ghosts more violent. It was the double whammy in 1979 of *Ghost Story* by Peter Straub and the film *The Amityville Horror* (1979) based on the 1977 book by Jay Anson (1921–1980) that galvanized this change. Straub had already written two novels featuring malevolent ghosts, *Julia* (1975) and *If You Could See Me Now* (1977), both of which sold well, but it was *Ghost Story*, filmed in 1981, that caught the imagination and became a best seller. Here the ghost of a woman accidentally killed and concealed by a group of men many years before returns in a violent way, able to interact with the world and take her revenge. The events described in *The Amityville Horror* were purportedly true though subsequent challenges have suggested that much of it may have been fabricated. Nevertheless the book, which recounted a violent haunting and psychic infestation of a house where a family had been murdered two years before, became a best seller and catapulted interest in hauntings and possession back into the public conscience. At the same time Stephen King had published his novel of possession in a haunted hotel, *The Shining* (1977), while the first of Clare McNally's popular books, *Ghost House* (1979) appeared, itself very reminiscent of the Amityville story.

A new generation of ghost stories soon established itself, dealing with houses haunted by an evil presence that frequently tried to take possession of or in some way harm the occupant. The film *Poltergeist* (1982) successfully whetted the public appetite further. Such stories include *Cold Moon Over Babylon* (1980) by Michael McDowell, *The Brownstone* (1980) by Ken Eulo (1939–), *A Cold Blue Light* (1983) by Marvin Kaye (1938–) and Parke Godwin (1929–), *A Manhattan Ghost Story* (1984) and *The Waiting Room* (1986) by T.M. Wright, *Familiar Spirit* (1983) by Lisa Tuttle (1952–), *The Night Stone* (1986), *Winter Wake* (1989), and *Dark Silence* (1992) all by Rick Hautala, *Soulstorm* (1986) by Chet Williamson, and *Night Relics* (1994) by James Blaylock. John Saul delighted in stories of ghostly children, which featured in several of his early novels: *Suffer the Children* (1978), *Comes the Blind Fury* (1980), and *When the Wind Blows* (1981). T.M. Wright explored a haunted school in *The School* (1990) while Douglas Clegg (1958–), one of the best of the new generation of writers, developed a sequence of novels about a haunted house that had become a school starting with *Mischief* (2000) and continuing through *Infinite* (2001), *Nightmare House* (2002), and *The Abandoned* (2005).

Reception. Although critics will argue that the bottom fell out of the slash-horror market in the 1990s, since 2000 ghost stories have continued to thrive. Most follow fairly traditional lines, though good writers continue to apply that novel twist. Richard Laymon (1947–2001) brought together vampires and a carnival in *The*

Traveling Vampire Show (2000) in what proved to be one of his last books and which won the Stoker Award as that year's best novel. Diana Barron blended the circus with a far from traditional ghost story in her first novel, *Phantom Feast* (2001). There are plenty of ghostly evils in *The Deceased* (2000) by Tom Piccirilli, *The Darkest Part of the Woods* (2002) by Ramsey Campbell, *The Lovely Bones* (2002) by Alice Sebold, *The Hour Before Dark* (2003) by Douglas Clegg, *Perfect Circle* (2004) by Sean Stewart, and *The Night Country* (2004) by Stewart O'Nan (1961–), plus some rather bizarre haunted (or evil) houses in *House of Leaves* (2000) by Mark Z. Danielewski (1966–), *A Winter Haunting* (2002) by Dan Simmons, *House of Bones* (2003) by Dale Bailey, and *Riverwatch* (2003) by Joseph Nassise. In all of these books, whether by new or accomplished writers, old themes have been given original twists. Although much emphasis remains on gross horror and the macabre, the supernatural is center stage, and not just in the wings. The continued appearance of these books and the popularity of the film *The Sixth Sense* (1999) shows that there is still considerable life in the ghost story.

Selected Authors. Devotees of supernatural fiction tend to remain loyal to their favorite writers so that such longtime authors as Ramsey Campbell, Stephen King, Richard Matheson, and Ray Bradbury, who have been producing material for 40, 50, even 60 years, find much of their work still in print. Readers are as likely to pursue an old book by H.P. Lovecraft or Arthur Machen as they are a new one by Douglas Clegg or Tom Piccirilli. Moreover the popularity of sequels and series means that authors like Anne Rice and Laurell K. Hamilton have a ready-made readership for their next volume.

Currently most popular writers of supernatural fiction tend to be classified either under horror fiction (Tom Piccirilli, Douglas Clegg, Rick Hautala) or fantasy (Charles de Lint, Jonathan Carroll, John Crowley). Occasionally an author will throw everything into the pot, challenging genre definitions. *Serenity Falls* (2003; reprinted in three volumes as *Writ in Blood*, *The Pack*, and *Dark Carnival*) by James A. Moore is a panjandrum of a book that combines just about every archetypal image in supernatural fiction. It starts out as the story of a town cursed by a dying witch 300 years before, but her curse takes many forms, which inflict the town until the apocalyptic final battle. Moore's novel is a kaleidoscope of horrors but within a modern context showing how even tired old images can be sharpened and refocused.

This is evident in the work of Tananarive Due (1966–), one of the strongest new talents of the last decade, who has created several variations on old themes. *My Soul to Keep* (1997) and its sequel *Living Blood* (2001) revisit the deal-with-the-devil theme with a dash of vampirism as a woman discovers that her Ethiopian husband is a 400-year-old immortal. In the sequel she too becomes possessed of the living blood and discovers the powers it grants her. In *The Good House* (2003) Due breathed life into the voodoo novel while in *Joplin's Ghost* (2005) she provides a novel twist on the traditional ghost story. The Afro American culture is potently recreated in all of these books, which are as firmly rooted in the past as in the future.

Cross-genre fertilization has continued to develop, particularly since the early days of Dean Koontz, Stephen King, and Peter Straub, some of whose works were thrillers and mysteries first—and certainly marketed that way for maximum sales— but with the supernatural as seasoning. In recent years, however, these authors, notably Koontz, King, and Straub, have returned to the roots of supernatural fiction to explore new directions.

Dean Koontz, whose books continue to hit the best-seller lists, has also returned more deeply to the supernatural. With *Odd Thomas* (2003), *Forever Odd* (2005), and *Brother Odd* (2006), Koontz has completed a trilogy about Odd Thomas, who can see spirits of the recent dead who remain in limbo. Sometimes Thomas can help them move on and sometimes the spirits, such as that of Elvis Presley, hang about him for reasons he does not know. Thomas can also see *bodachs*, strange wolflike shadows which, like vultures, seem to know of impending, violent deaths. Thomas sometimes tries to stop these deaths before they happen. Other times he helps the police solve murders. Thomas cannot avoid being drawn into these events any more than he can avoid his special talent and, as a result, he can be manipulated as happens in the second book where an evil woman lays a trap for him. As a consequence by the third book Thomas has sought refuge in a monastery hoping to escape his ghosts, but death follows him. These books mark a change for Koontz, not only because for once he has developed a sequence featuring the same character, but also because the book focuses on the supernatural as a form of salvation rather than horror. It is an indication of one growing trend in recent years where the supernatural is not necessarily the focus of the horror, but a means to fight it. This is most evident in the recent work of the two major writers of the last 30 years, Stephen King and Peter Straub.

King's ability to sustain a varied and popular output of considerable proportion is remarkable, though in recent years the significance of his work has been challenged. While there are those who believe that Stephen King *is* American horror fiction, he has plenty of critics. When King received the National Book Foundation Medal in 2003 for services to literature, Harold Bloom remarked that he only wrote what used to be called "penny dreadfuls" (*New York Times,* 15 September 2003). King's most vociferous critic is probably S.T. Joshi who commented:

> King's domination of the bestseller lists over the last two decades has been an unmitigated disaster for the weird tale. By being the chief exemplar of the 'banalization' of horror, he has caused an inferior strain of weird fiction (commonplace, flabby, sentimental work full of 'human interest' but entirely lacking in originality of conception) to gain popular esteem. (Joshi, 2001, 95)

Yet it is almost certain that had it not been for King causing horror fiction (at least, as per the marketing label) to be among the best sellers, publishers would not have been so open to other writers during the seventies and eighties, and the next generation of writers would not have found it so easy to enter the market. King hoped that his success did encourage others. When interviewed in 1990 he commented:

> I'm not sure how much we raised the awareness of horror or gave it any kind of cultural cachet. I'm sure that we allowed a lot of contracts to be signed by a lot of writers, put a lot of money in a lot of pockets that otherwise wouldn't have gone there. And I think that's a wonderful thing . . . because most of the people who are doing it aren't in it for a free ride. They're serious about it. I think now—and I didn't use to think this way—but I think now that we might actually have a serious place in American literature in a hundred years or so. (Wiater, 1990, 100)

The main impact King has had on the content of supernatural fiction is to emphasize the horrific so that the supernatural, if present, has become a means to an end rather than the main feature of the book. Although King has continued to place an emphasis on horror in his non-supernatural books, like *Cell* (2006), several of his more recent books have explored a quieter, more reflective form of the macabre with a stronger emphasis on the therapeutic significance of the supernatural. *Bag of Bones* (1998) is, unusually for King, written in the first person by a best-selling novelist, giving the book a stronger personal feel. The novelist, Mike Noonan, is recently widowed and is suffering writer's block. He is haunted by dreams of his dead wife who seems to be luring him to their lakeside summer home but once there he finds the dreams stronger and the supernatural becomes a driving force to discovering past sins. Here the supernatural makes memories tangible, and King is able to show how the past lives on around us and within us.

King has provided a counterpoint to *Bag of Bones* in *Lisey's Story* (2006), this time the story of a widow coming to terms with the death of her husband, Scott, who had been a writer, after 25 years of marriage. Scott comes alive in the story within her memories as she sorts out his papers, and their close relationship takes her into a private world that Scott had escaped to in his childhood when abused by his father. This world is both a source of imagination and inspiration. King shows how you can draw strength from the past and how hauntings can be as positive as they can be frightening. In these novels King uses the supernatural to stir the emotions through the heart rather than the gut.

Recently King has collaborated again with his friend Peter Straub on *Black House* (2001) a sequel to their 1984 dark fantasy novel, *The Talisman*. Straub has himself been very active in recent years producing a number of novels, three of which won the Bram Stoker Award for the Best Horror novel in their respective years. *Mr. X* (1999) is an extremely complex novel of a man, Ned Dunstan, coming to terms with his bizarre family from which he had been cut off for his own safety when his mother fostered him out as a baby. In particular Dunstan has to confront his real father, the eponymous Mr. X., whom Dunstan had never known, and through whose evil mind part of the story is revealed. There is also the mystery of Dunstan's possible twin brother, a *doppelganger* presence that seems to follow Dunstan like a shadow. Straub draws upon much Lovecraftian lore in depicting the bizarre ancestry of this family, which provides most of the occult element, and though the supernatural is intrinsic to the plot, the novel also works as a mystery, driven by its strong but enigmatic characters.

Straub's other recent award-winning books *Lost Boy Lost Girl* (2003) and *In the Night Room* (2004) also explore family relationships but in a more multi-layered and multi-perspective way. They are complex metafictions which question the basis of reality and perception and in so doing blur the boundaries between the natural and the supernatural and between the real and the fictional. The central character of both novels is the author Tim Underhill who had previously appeared in Straub's dark mystery novels, *Koko* (1988) and *The Throat* (1993). In *Lost Boy Lost Girl* Underhill returns to his hometown of Millhaven where his brother's wife has killed herself. Their son, Mark, is missing, perhaps the victim of a serial killer who seems to be copying a killer from 20 years before. Underhill's quest to find his nephew centers on the house once occupied by this former killer which may or may not be haunted by a young girl, perhaps the killer's daughter. However, in *In the Night Room* we discover that *Lost Boy Lost Girl* is only Underhill's version of events, written to assuage the fate of his nephew, which had remained unsolved. *In the Night Room* seeks to step back and re-explore the real events. Straub is entering the territory of the mystics, discovering that beyond our own belief in events is a further understanding, a truer interpretation, uncorrupted by memory or guilt or pain. But how much can we face that reality?

As with King's recent books, Straub is exploring how memory and reality haunt us and how ghosts may be psychological manifestations of alternate existences. It is this lack of a firm connection to reality that evokes horror and uncertainty, and yet our natural reaction is to retreat into ourselves to escape the horror. Straub has constantly challenged the boundaries between genres recognizing that "it's all about a point of view" (*Locus* #507, April 2003, 66). His novels may thus be seen as fantasies of perception in which the supernatural is but one method of understanding.

Straub's recent work marks one of the high points of supernatural fiction, utilizing basic, age-old themes such as a haunted house, but refashioning it with images not solely from fantasy and horror but from within our own psyche to produce a book that deliberately defies categorization. It is perhaps one of the best examples of a key direction that supernatural fiction may take in the new century, to make us aware that it is us who fashion the world about us, including all things of Heaven, Earth, and Hell.

Bibliography

Bleiler, Everett F. *The Guide to Supernatural Fiction*. Kent, OH: Kent State University Press, 1983.

Jordan, Michael. *The Encyclopedia of Gods*. London: Kyle Cathie, 1992.

Joshi, S.T. *The Modern Weird Tale*. Jefferson, NC: McFarland, 2001.

King, Stephen. *Bag of Bones*. New York: Scribner, 1998.

_____. *Danse Macabre*. London: Macdonald, 1981.

_____. *Lisey's Story*. New York: Scribner, 2006.

Koontz, Dean. *Odd Thomas*. New York: Bantam, 2003.

Melton, J. Gordon. *The Vampire Book*. Detroit, MI: Visible Ink Press, 1994.

Straub, Peter. "Horror's House," *Locus* #507, April 2003.

_____. *In the Night Room*. New York: Random House, 2004.

_____. *Lost Boy Lost Girl*. New York: Random House, 2003.

_____. *Mr. X*. New York: Random House, 1999.

Sullivan, Jack. *Elegant Nightmares*. Athens, OH: Ohio University Press, 1978.

Wiater, Stanley. *Dark Dreamers*. New York: Avon Books, 1990.

Winter, Douglas E. *Faces of Fear*. London: Pan Books, 1990.

Further Reading

Auerbach, Nina. *Our Vampires, Ourselves*. Chicago, IL: University of Chicago Press, 1997; Bleiler, Richard. *Supernatural Fiction Writers: Contemporary Fantasy and Horror*. 2nd ed. New York: Scribner's, 2002; Briggs, Julia. *Night Visitors*. London: Faber, 1977; Campbell, Ramsey. "A Life in Horror," *Locus* #507, April 2003; Cavaliero, Glen. *The Supernatural & English Fiction*. Oxford: Oxford University Press, 1995; D'Ammassa, Don. *Encyclopedia of Fantasy and Horror Fiction*. New York: Checkmark Books, 2006; Datlow, Ellen, and Windling, Terri (& others), eds. *The Year's Best Fantasy and Horror* series. New York: St. Martin's Press, 1988–present; Fonseca, Anthony J. and Pulliam, June Michelle. *Hooked on Horror: A Guide to Reading Interests in Horror Fiction, New Edition*. Westport, CT: Libraries Unlimited, 2003; Frost, Brian J. *The Monster With a Thousand Faces*. Bowling Green, OH: Bowling Green State University Popular Press, 1989; Frost, Brian J. *The Essential Guide to Werewolf Literature*. Madison, WI: University of Wisconsin Press, 2003; Gelder, Ken, ed. *The Horror Reader*. London: Routledge, 2000; Gordon, Joan, and Hollinger, Veronica. *Blood Read: The Vampire as Metaphor in Contemporary Culture*. Philadelphia,

PA: University of Pennsylvania Press, 1997; Heldreth, Leonard G., and Pharr, Mary. *The Blood is the Life: Vampires in Literature*. Bowling Green, OH: Bowling Green State University Popular Press, 1997; Joshi, S.T. *The Weird Tale*. Austin, TX: University of Texas Press, 1990; Joshi, S.T. *The Evolution of the Weird Tale*. New York: Hippocampus Press, 2004; Joshi, S.T., and Dziemianowicz, Stefan. *Supernatural Literature of the World*. Westport, CT: Greenwood Press, 2005; Magistrale, Tone, and Morrison, Michael A. eds. *A Dark Night's Dreaming: Contemporary American Horror Fiction*. Columbia, SC: University of South Carolina Press, 1996; Ramsland, Katherine. *Dean Koontz, A Writer's Biography*. New York: HarperPrism, 1997; Schweitzer, Darrell. *Discovering Modern Horror Fiction – I*. Mercer Island, WA: Starmont House, 1985; Schweitzer, Darrell. *Discovering Modern Horror Fiction – II*. Mercer Island, WA: Starmont House, 1988; Sheehan, Bill. *At the Foot of the Story Tree*. Burton, MI: Subterranean Press, 2000.

MIKE ASHLEY

P

PARAPSYCHOLOGY

Definition. *Parapsychology* is the term introduced in the 1930s by J.B. Rhine, one of the field's pioneers, for the scientific study of scientifically paranormal claims, but belief in the phenomena that parapsychologists attempt to study appears to be as old as humanity itself. The set of phenomena of interest to the parapsychologists is referred to by many names, including *psi powers*, *psychic phenomena*, *paranormal abilities*, and the most popular of all, *extrasensory perception (ESP)*. This last name is of special interest to psychologists, as perception is typically defined as the brain's cognitive processing of information received from the senses. Perception is therefore sensory *by definition*—ordinarily the only circumstances under which it occurs in the absence of sensory input would involve either hallucination or direct stimulation of the brain. This is one of the things that makes psychic research both fascinating and frustrating: If parapsychologists are able to establish convincingly that these phenomena occur, then much of what we know about how the human brain functions (to say nothing of the rest of the physical world, including the basic laws of physics) must be, at best, incomplete and obsolete, and at worst, just plain wrong.

Trends and Themes. The alleged phenomena include the following:

- *Telepathy*—The ability to send or receive information without using the usual sensory apparatus (speaking, hearing, seeing, etc.). Also colloquially referred to as mind reading. Anecdotal evidence abounds for telepathy, as when one "knows" who is calling when the telephone rings, or two close friends or relatives say the same thing at the exact same time (there are of course more parsimonious, but far less exciting, explanations for these situations). A demonstration used by self-proclaimed psychics (and which has been repeatedly tested by parapsychologists) involves *remote viewing*, in which the "sender" travels to a remote (and unknown to the receiver) location and proceeds to concentrate on a landmark, picture, or other stimulus. The "receiver" attempts to form a mental impression of what the sender is seeing, and then draws or describes it. Under very loose testing conditions, remote viewing demonstrations are often successful; under conditions that have been set up to exclude various other ways of accomplishing the feat (several are well known among stage magicians), successes are quite rare.

- *Clairvoyance*—Knowing information without resort to ordinary perception, memory, or inference. Again, anecdotes abound about this sort of thing, and it is what *dowsers* claim to be able to do—they can allegedly detect water or minerals underground (often guided by a gently-held stick or other device). Many laboratory experiments have attempted to demonstrate clairvoyance, usually requiring the subjects to detect the identity of a hidden target object (frequently a card).

- *Psychokinesis (previously known as telekinesis)*—Sometimes referred to as "mind over matter," this is the ability to use the mind to cause physical movement or changes in other objects without resort to normal means of doing so. The term *telekinesis* fell into such disrepute in the early days of psychic research, thanks to the many fraudulent manifestations produced by spirit mediums, that *psychokinesis* is now the preferred term.

- *Precognition*—Knowing of events in advance of their occurrence, again without resort to the usual means of acquiring knowledge. Stories of prophecy abound in religion, mythology, and folklore, and so many people are certainly prepared to believe that such a phenomenon exists. As with other psychic gifts, this one has not been reliably manifested by anyone under controlled conditions.

- *Spirit mediumship*—Some practitioners, known as *mediums*, claim to obtain their extrasensory knowledge from the spirits of the deceased. In the early days of the practice (late-nineteenth century), this information (often spoken by the medium in an eerie voice) was often accompanied by physical manifestations (odd sounds, mysteriously floating objects, ectoplasm, etc.—more information about this follows below), but most current mediums have completely abandoned this approach in favor of a fully vocal approach.

History. The initial burst of interest in scientific study of the paranormal was a direct result of the explosion in popularity of spiritualism (also called *spiritism*) in mid-nineteenth century America and Europe. In spiritualism, which eventually became an organized church based in New England, people interested in communicating with the spirits of the dead would hold *séances*, in which they would gather about a table in a darkened room, holding hands, and ask the spirits to communicate with them. The response would usually come in the form of mysterious rapping noises. Over time, the phenomena involved in séances grew to include such things as trumpets floating in the air and being mysteriously blown, the table rising briefly into the air, and the production of *ectoplasm*, or ghost substance, a mysterious shimmering product that the medium would pull from thin air, or sometimes from various body parts, and wave about.

The birth of the Spiritualist movement can be dated quite precisely: The first séances were held in 1848, in the Hydesville, New York, home of the teenage Fox sisters (Margaret and Kate), who decided to have a bit of fun at their parents' expense. Margaret had developed the ability to produce loud rapping sounds with her toes, which seemed to be mysterious communications from beyond when performed in a dark room with everyone holding hands on the tabletop. Very soon the Fox sisters were performing séances with a wide range of people, and others followed their lead until people all over Europe and America were communicating with the dead, and performing ever more elaborate variations on their initial deception.

Within a few years, some eminent men of science, believing the phenomena to be real, began to investigate the conditions under which they occurred. The first attempt to describe a method of investigating these phenomena (and to provide a theory of sorts to explain them) was produced by the French author Léon-Dénizarth-Hippolyte Rivail, writing under the pseudonym Allan Kardec, primarily in two books: *Le Livre des Esprits* (1856) and *Le Livre des Mediums* (1861).

Kardec's interest in the subject seems to have begun when he met two young mediums, whose father was known to him, and they told him (or rather, the spirits whose words were coming through them told him) that he had an important spiritual mission to carry out. The resulting "spiritist theory" which he detailed in his books was the result of responses produced by these mediums via rapping and planchette movement (the trick best known today as the Ouija™ board). Indeed, the pseudonym was provided by the spirits as well: both *Allan* and *Kardec* were alleged to have been his names in prior lives. The spirits even told him what to call the book.

Le Livre des Esprits become an instant sensation, making converts to his brand of spiritualism all over Europe. Kardec founded the Parisian Society of Psychologic Studies, which met in his home on Fridays in order to receive, via automatic writing (another standard medium technique), further instructions from the spirits. One outgrowth of this organization was his editorship of *La Revue Spirite*, which he continued to produce until his death (though not thereafter; it is still published today by the World Spiritist Congress).

Kardec's impact on his world was remarkably far-reaching: Napoleon III even sent for him several times to discuss the teachings in *Le Livre des Esprits*. In the wake of the founding of Kardec's organization, other such groups were rapidly formed throughout Europe and America. As with most spiritual movements, schisms were evident early on, however, as the French version of Spiritualism differed markedly from the American in Kardec's endorsement of the idea of compulsory reincarnation—in Kardec's books, it is made clear that all are required to live multiple lifetimes. This is an odd feature of Kardec's teachings, given that he followed up his early successes with books such as *The Gospel as Explained by Spirits* (1864), *Heaven and Hell* (1865), and *Genesis* (1867), whose target audience couldn't be expected to be particularly receptive to the doctrine of reincarnation.

Context and Issues

"Psychical Research"Takes Hold. As the phenomena produced by mediums began to attract the attention of more scientifically minded observers as well, these men also became interested in investigating the claims of mind readers, hypnotists, and fortune-tellers. Soon they had formed formal organizations, and their "psychical research" was a respectable and rapidly growing enterprise. The Society for Psychical Research formed in London in 1882; the American Society for Psychical Research, today the Parapsychological Association, followed in 1885. Early in their investigations, they began to document a few things about the conditions under which such phenomena seemed more likely to occur. A successful séance, for example, required darkness—the materializations would not occur in a well-lit room, and the spirits would often not communicate at all. The presence of very skeptical people, who might watch very closely, also seemed to make the spirits less likely to turn up. Despite these inconvenient facts, several skillful "superstar" mediums emerged (D.D. Home and Eusapia Palladino are probably

the best known) over several decades following the Fox sisters' initial break-through, and they were instrumental in attracting the interest of serious scientists. Sir William Crookes, the great chemist (known for, among other accomplishments, the discovery of thallium, as well as early developments in the field of chemical fertilizer), for example, became interested in spiritist phenomena following the death of his brother. After attending a séance with the Fox sisters, Crookes was instrumental in getting other scientists to take more seriously the phenomena they produced, along with validating the levitation and table-tilting of D.D. Home. Following his example, the Society for Psychical Research counted several members of the British Royal Society among its early constituency. Alfred Russel Wallace, best known as Charles Darwin's chief competitor for the discoverer's role in the saga of evolutionary theory, also dabbled in psychical research, attending séances and speculating on the sources of the phenomena witnessed therein.

Despite the legitimizing influence of Crookes, Wallace, and other prominent scientists (in America, William James was also an early enthusiast), Home and Palladino were also frequently caught cheating. This was readily overlooked by clients as well as by some of the prominent scientists, who were quick to accept the idea that too-close scrutiny prevented the rather shy spirits from showing up. People who *openly* deceived others for a living (especially such magicians as Houdini), however, began to take notice of these competitors who claimed their miracles were real. Houdini, still the best known of all conjurers, made a second career of attending séances and exposing fraud therein.

Harry Houdini's (born Erich Weiss; 1874–1926) A Magician among the Spirits. Unlike most who arrived in a medium's parlor, Houdini was uniquely qualified to detect the trickery involved in spirit manifestations. Early in his career, he and his wife hosted regular séances for a Midwestern medicine show, during which he would cause tables to tip and float, while he also played musical instruments, all while tied to his chair! After his career as an escape artist took off circa 1899, Houdini left the stage medium business behind and largely forgot about it.

His interest was revived in the early 1920s when he befriended Sir Arthur Conan Doyle, author of the Sherlock Holmes mysteries. Theirs was an odd friendship, balancing Houdini's professional skepticism with Doyle's extreme credulousness (among other things, he wrote a book endorsing the clearly faked photos three young girls took of fairies at Cottingley). Having become a Spiritualist leader, Doyle introduced Houdini to several prominent mediums in hopes of convincing him of the reality of the manifestations they produced. Far from being converted to Spiritualism, Houdini immediately recognized the fairly obvious tricks he had given up earlier in his career, and was offended at their deception of grieving people hoping only to reunite with their loved ones. He was especially sympathetic toward the victims, as he was still tormented by the unexpected death of his own mother a decade earlier.

He set out to show that the business of psychic readings, far from being helpful to those left behind, was in fact built on their exploitation. An early book on the subject, *Miracle Mongers and their Methods* (1920), set the template for the far more influential *A Magician among the Spirits* (1924). Houdini made big changes in his stage act, in order to demonstrate far and wide that as a mere magician, he could not only reproduce all the effects associated with the mediums, but could actually perform them more convincingly. He went beyond reproducing their effects, however, going so far as to attend séances and expose the trickery while it was occurring. This had the added benefit, of course, of keeping his name before the public at a time when he was becoming too old to continue performing the very physically demanding stunts on which he built his career.

According to his book, Houdini frequently attended séances in disguise, with both a reporter and police officer in tow, so that he could simultaneously have the medium arrested for fraud and have a story about the incident (prominently featuring Houdini's own role, naturally) published in the local newspaper. He would also sometimes forego the disguise, instead challenging local mediums in the cities where he performed to demonstrate their powers on stage. The most noteworthy of these challenges involved a medium who went by the name of Margery (real name: Mina Crandon), billed as "The Boston Medium." Margery had already convinced some prominent scientific investigators, a committee put together by *Scientific American*, that she was the real deal. When the committee sent Houdini to investigate, however, he found that she was just like all the other mediums he had seen, using the same fraudulent techniques (he published a separate pamphlet concerning this case, entitled *"Margery" The Medium Exposed*, expanded to book length as *Houdini Exposes the Tricks Used by Boston Medium "Margery"*). Among other things, he reported catching her ringing an electric bell with her foot and levitating a table by leaning over and lifting its edge with her head. So confident was he of her methods that he offered her $10,000 to demonstrate her abilities on stage at Boston's Symphony Hall. The only condition attached to the prize was that she produce a manifestation he could not duplicate. When she refused, Houdini recreated her entire act for the audience, and subsequently went on to do so as a permanent part of his stage act.

Following his success with Margery, he went on to expose the methods used by many other famous mediums, including the Fox sisters, as well as the single most famous medium of the time, Eusapia Palladino. These exposés, and the stories behind them, make up the bulk of *A Magician among the Spirits*.

The impact of earlier exposures of fraud on the popularity of the mediums had been quite minimal (a common reaction: The spirits don't always respond, so of course they have to cheat sometimes—that doesn't mean it isn't real on the other occasions! This justification continues as a major part of the arsenal of certain psychic performers today), even when the originator of the movement admitted her fraud: In 1888 (40 years after getting it all started, but 36 years *before* Houdini's book), Margaret Fox, by this time a widow, told her story and gave public demonstrations of how the effects were achieved.

Because of his high media profile and name recognition, Houdini was far more effective. The book was quite influential in starting the decline of the large-scale popularity of spirit mediums, as it became much harder for them to justify the need for darkness in order for their effects to occur (ectoplasm, for example, was far less convincing to readers who knew it was usually cheesecloth coated with luminous paint). They have never completely gone away, however—the National Spiritualist Association of Churches still boasts 3000 members, and they still hold séances. Furthermore, spiritualist resorts are still in business: Just as children go to summer camps to learn outdoor skills or improve their athletic abilities, thousands of (mostly elderly) spiritualists attend such places as Camp Chesterfield in Indiana to communicate with the departed. Camp Chesterfield (still in operation) became well known outside spiritualist church circles in 1976, with the publication of M. Lamar

Keene's *The Psychic Mafia*. Keene spent years as one of the camp's top mediums, and his book lays out in great detail the extent to which not much had changed from the previous century. It was ultimately conscience that led Keene to abandon the camp and publish its secrets: Among other things, he expresses some regret over the large amounts of money his congregations would donate to the church "building fund," all of which was destined not for construction but rather for Keene's own wallet. The book reveals numerous tricks of the trade that had not previously been exposed, such as the technique used to "apparate" items that the attendees had lost. Often, the items had in fact been surreptitiously stolen from their homes by church accomplices. The book also goes into great detail regarding the use of common, simple magician's tricks to convince the audience that the medium is actually in touch with the spirits.

Keene's book had the usual impact of such exposés on the fraud being exposed: Almost none. Not only are spiritualist churches still in business, the last quarter of the twentieth century and the turn of the millennium saw several waves of new spiritualist practitioners boasting new approaches to the same old thing.

In the mid-1980s, a new wave of mediums emerged, with a new name: channelers. Gone were the physical manifestations, and thus gone also was the need for the cover of darkness. Furthermore, to make their statements even harder to pin down, the new mediums did not claim to be in touch with spirits of dead friends or relatives of their audience, but rather with ancient wise beings removed from the present (and thus from specific details known to the audience) by thousands of years.

Rather than answering questions, these mediums would enter a trance, after which their body language and voice would change, indicating that their bodies had been taken over by entities who wished to speak to the modern world. The most successful of these was certainly JZ (the initials stand for Judy Zebra) Knight. A pretty, small blonde woman, she believes she has been taken over by a 35,000-year old, 8-foot-tall male warrior named Ramtha, from the lost continent of Atlantis. In addition to performing for years to capacity crowds, she published several best-selling books about her experiences, the best known of which is *A State of Mind: My Story*. From the back cover of the 1988 paperback edition:

> . . . he spoke to her with vital spiritual messages for our time. This visionary event changed her life and was to change the lives of countless others all over the world as they flocked to see and hear JZ Knight "channel" the teachings of Ramtha on the eternal paths of unconditional love. . . .the thrilling quest of the spirit that has led to a UFO encounter, miraculous healing, visits from the ever-watchful dead, and—most of all—an eternal wisdom that points to a future of radiant, limitless hope for us all.

The vague positivity of this description is typical of the content of her channelled communications as well, although Knight also frequently appears to espouse a sort of feminist-apocalyptic vision, in which men are brutal creatures who eroticize violence and who must be removed from power and replaced by women—an odd philosophy for a great male warrior from the past. Knight was part of a wave of channelers that crested and broke in the late 1980s, and most have faded back into obscurity. Knight is still making an impact on the entertainment world, however. Some of her followers, members of the Ramtha Foundation, were behind two pop-culture phenomena in the new millennium. The first, the 2005 semi-documentary film *What the Bleep Do We Know?*, explores a variety of esoteric subjects with the help of various on-screen experts (physicists, neuroscientists, etc.), among which Knight appears (with the on-screen credit *Ramtha*). The movie caused a bit of a sensation at film festivals and had a popular run at the box office.

Some of the same production team was behind a 2006 publishing success, the book and accompanying movie entitled *The Secret*. The book is credited to Rhonda Byrne, and the film incorporates the same blend of slick production values and alternative interpretation of science (some would say misrepresentation) that made *What the Bleep . . .* such a success. The producers have taken full advantage of modern technology, spreading the book and movie through a Web site that describes the book/film as follows:

> The Secret reveals the most powerful law in the universe. The knowledge of this law has run like a golden thread through the lives and the teachings of all the prophets, seers, sages and saviors in the world's history, and through the lives of all truly great men and women. All that they have ever accomplished or attained has been done in full accordance with this most powerful law. . . .The Secret explains with simplicity the law that is governing all lives, and offers the knowledge of how to create—intentionally and effortlessly—a joyful life. This is the secret to everything—the secret to unlimited happiness, love, health and prosperity. This is the secret to life. (www.thesecret.tv)

As it turns out, the secret is fairly straightforward: Byrne proposes that in order to attain whatever we wish, we simply have to believe fervently that we shall attain it, and it will come to pass. The universe wants us to be happy, and we just need to make clear what we desire.

The channelers were not the only ones to begin a new mediumistic ascendancy in the last several decades—there are currently several popular entertainers (such as Sylvia Browne, John Edward, and James Van Praagh) who have become successful by claiming to communicate with the dead in yet another, somewhat old-fashioned, manner. Like the channelers, they've eliminated the need for darkness, but are still using a very old technique known among magicians as *cold reading*. In cold reading, the medium asks many questions and zeros in on specific information based on the answers that are given. The person receiving the reading will often only remember the questions to which the answer was "yes" (hits), while forgetting about the much larger number of misses.

These mediums have mostly had little impact in publishing, with the exception of Sylvia Browne, who has many books to her credit. Some concern the expected messages of comfort from the "other side"—both in the books and in her public readings with the bereaved, she claims that her information is provided by a "spirit guide" named Francine. These works include, among others, *Temples on the Other Side: How Wisdom from "Beyond the Veil" Can Help You Right Now* (2008), *Sylvia Browne's Lessons for Life* (2004), *Sylvia Browne's Book of Angels* (2004), *Conversations from the Other Side* (2002), and the forthcoming *End of Days: What You Need to Know Now about the End of the World* (2008). Uniquely among current mediums, however, Browne has also positioned herself as a spiritual leader, founding a church called the *Society of Novus Spiritus*, which she presents as a Gnostic form of Christianity. Her books therefore also include such explicitly religious titles as *The Two Marys: The Hidden History of the Mother and Wife of Jesus* (2007), *Sylvia Browne's Book of Angels* (2004), and *If You Could See What I See: The Tenets of Novus Spiritus* (2006).

The Emergence of Scientific Parapsychology. Given the continuing current popularity of mediums who claim to communicate with the dead, it is important to note that the *scientific* study of psychic phenomena abandoned the notion that psychics were actually communicating with the dead over a century ago. In the late nineteenth century, the Society for Psychical Research had already begun to turn its attention toward paranormal phenomena beyond those manifested by the spirit mediums. In an 1886 two-volume collection of reports of ghosts and contact with the dead, entitled *Phantasms of the Living*, Society members Edmund Gurney and Frederic W.H. Myers speculated that some of the apparitions they studied were actually due to *thought-transference* (a theory, incidentally, about which Alfred Russel Wallace then wrote a highly critical paper), for which they coined a new word: *Telepathy*.

By the early twentieth century, psychical researchers had become less interested in the spirit mediums, and were concentrating their attention more fully on telepaths and clairvoyants. As their methods became more rigorous and quantitative, and psychologists began to take over a field previously dominated by physical scientists, the new science began to find a home at major universities. Pride of place for publishing the first report of an experiment on clairvoyance (card guessing, in this case) goes to John Coover, the first holder of a Fellowship in Psychical Research at Stanford University. In the monograph *Experiments in Psychical Research*, he published the results of four large studies, involving 100 research participants. Somewhat prophetically for the field of study as a whole, he concluded that he had found nothing supportive of belief in ESP. Perhaps in part because of his willingness to publicize his negative results, Coover is largely forgotten even among those who know the parapsychological literature well.

Selected Authors. James Banks Rhine (1895–1980) is known to nearly everyone with even a passing interest in parapsychology. In 1934, he cofounded and became director of the Parapsychology Laboratory at Duke University, located in North Carolina. Rhine and his wife, Louisa, first went to Duke to join the psychology department and work with William McDougall, who shared their interest in paranormal phenomena, and soon this shared interest took psychical research in a new and altogether more scientific direction.

Although he agreed with Houdini after a session with Margery, the Boston medium, that she was guilty of fraud and trickery, Rhine was nonetheless fascinated by telepathy and similar phenomena, and he wanted to establish the study of this more scientifically observable subject matter as a subject distinct from the study of those who claimed communion with the dead. It was Rhine who shook off the phrase "psychical research" with its attendant baggage and popularized the more scientific-sounding *parapsychology* (a term used as far back as 1889 by the psychologist Max Dessoir) to replace it. He also introduced the terms *extrasensory perception* and *psychokinesis*, and was easily the most influential of all parapsychologists, both in his methods and in his ability to popularize the field in his books, articles, and lectures.

More than through books, Rhine's influence came via the publication of a research journal. He founded the *Journal of Parapsychology* in 1937, thus providing American parapsychologists with a respectable peer-reviewed journal in which to publish their findings. The *Journal* is still published today, appearing semiannually. Twenty years after founding the journal, Rhine was also instrumental in founding the Parapsychological Association. In the lab at Duke he developed, with his colleague Karl Zener, the most popular piece of equipment in parapsychology, the Zener cards. The Zener cards are a deck made up of five simple symbols, one on each card: star, circle, square, cross, and wavy lines. The Zener cards were widely used in ESP experiments, in which the participant was required to identify a hidden target card from a set of five known possible targets. In a telepathy experiment, the cards were viewed by a remote person (the sender) who attempted to "transmit" the information to the participant. In a clairvoyance experiment, the participant would simply attempt to identify the order of the cards, without anyone looking at them first.

Rhine's first book, *Extra-Sensory Perception* (1934), may well be the most important book in the history of parapsychology, if only because it gave the world (via its title) a new term for the phenomena of telepathy and clairvoyance. The book's publication was also a watershed event in that it started a new era of publishing on parapsychology and on paranormal phenomena in general. *Extra-Sensory Perception* established the pattern that would be followed thereafter, in which experimental work is largely ignored (and when not ignored, largely ridiculed) by the scientific community but becomes massively popular when sold directly to the public in book form. In this book, Rhine reached exactly the opposite conclusion from that reached by Coover: That "it is independently established on the basis of this work alone that Extra-Sensory Perception is an actual and demonstrable occurrence" (162).

This seminal work was followed in rapid succession by a popular treatment of the research, *New Frontiers of the Mind: The Story of the Duke Experiments* (1937), which sold quite well and was rapturously received by reviewers outside the scientific community, who compared Rhine to Copernicus and to Darwin, among others. Extra-sensory perception had entered the popular lexicon, as had the idea that it was scientifically testable using the Zener cards, and both have endured in the popular imagination ever since. *New Frontiers* was followed over the next several decades by many more books, some co-authored by his wife, Louisa Rhine, a prolific psychic researcher in her own right. The Rhines' entire body of work continued to champion the view that Rhine's lab results consistently demonstrate the reality of extra-sensory perception, in the face of the equally consistent failure of other laboratories to replicate his results when adequate precautions against cheating were taken. Significant titles include the following: *The Reach of the Mind* (1947), *New World of the Mind* (1953), *Parapsychology, Frontier Science of the Mind: A Survey of the Field, the Methods, and the Facts of ESP and PK Research* (1957), *Extra-Sensory Perception after Sixty Years: A Critical Appraisal of the Research on Extra-Sensory Perception* (1967—co-authored with J.G. Pratt).

It should be noted that two years after Rhine began his studies of ESP at Duke (in 1927, working with William McDougall), Pulitzer Prize-winner Upton Sinclair published *Mental Radio* (1929) detailing a series of clairvoyance experiments he conducted with his wife. The book was a popular seller, and the extent to which the idea of clairvoyance was seen as a legitimate topic for study at the time is perhaps best illustrated by the fact that Albert Einstein wrote a preface to the book. In the preface, Einstein stresses Sinclair's honesty and integrity, as well as the dubious nature of the phenomenon itself:

> . . . it is out of the question in the case of so conscientious an observer and writer as Upton Sinclair that he is carrying on a conscious deception of the reading world; his good faith and dependability are not to be doubted. So if somehow the facts here set

forth rest not upon telepathy, but upon some unconscious hypnotic influence from person to person, this also would be of high psychological interest. (in Sinclair 1929)

This passage is sometimes presented as indicating an endorsement of paranormal abilities on Einstein's part. It does not indicate any such thing, but he was clearly open to further study of the phenomena, especially the idea that something psychological rather than paranormal is at work. The additional introduction by Rhine's collaborator, William McDougall, is less guarded:

> The experiments in telepathy, as reported in the pages of this book, were so remarkably successful as to rank among the very best hitherto reported. The degree of success and the conditions of experiment were such that we can reject them as conclusive evidence . . . only by assuming that Mr. and Mrs. Sinclair either are grossly stupid, incompetent and careless persons or have deliberately entered upon a conspiracy to deceive the public in a most heartless and reprehensible fashion. (from Sinclair 1929)

Then came the (temporary) decline of academic parapsychology. Despite Rhine's continuing conviction that the body of research supported the reality of ESP, however, the ongoing lack of replicable evidence had lost his quest most of the little remaining support it enjoyed in the academic scientific community by the end of the 1950s. In 1962, with several decades of research having failed to conclusively demonstrate the existence of any paranormal phenomena, Duke University followed the lead of most other major institutions and quietly distanced itself from parapsychological research. Without the university's continuing support, Rhine moved off campus and founded the Parapsychological Laboratory's successor, the Foundation for Research on the Nature of Man (now the Rhine Research Center), up the street from Duke.

As the 1970s dawned, and brought with them a new wave of "occult" fads (including such things as astrology, Kirlian photography, UFOlogy, pyramid power, the Bermuda Triangle, transcendental meditation practitioners claiming to be able to levitate, etc.), Rhine became quite concerned for the future of parapsychology, as well as its popular image as an experimental science. Many parapsychologists took a positive and uncritical approach to such ideas as the ability of pyramids to focus undefined "energies" to keep blades sharp and prevent food from spoiling when kept under them. Rhine recognized, correctly, that this was eroding the credibility of their continuing research on ESP.

Despite Rhine's concerns, parapsychological research has continued unabated, though it has remained marginalized, with very few degree programs in parapsychology still in existence. Despite the large number of universities in the United States, for example, only two still maintain active parapsychology programs.

This has not halted innovation, however—parapsychology has come a long way from card-guessing experiments. In the early 1970s, even as the number of parapsychology labs dropped dramatically, the productivity of those remaining researchers remained high, and a number of new, more sophisticated paradigms arose to replace the old Zener cards with high technology.

Work in scientific parapsychology continued in the 1970s. Helmut Schmidt, a German-born parapsychologist who worked at the Rhine Research Center, began in the late 1960s to conduct experiments on micro-psychokinesis, or micro-PK, in which subjects attempt to influence the generation of random numbers by computers. He continued this research in the 1970s, and has written many scholarly articles in which he claims to have demonstrated a slight human mental influence on the operation of machines, an influence he explained in terms of quantum mechanics. This has become a common explanatory mechanism for parapsychologists in the ensuing years, although few people outside of physics actually *understand* quantum mechanics. Other researchers have conducted hundreds of experiments attempting to replicate his findings, frequently claiming to have found further support for micro-PK.

Meanwhile, Stanley Krippner, Montague Ullman, and Charles Honorton were using the sleep lab at Maimonides Medical Center in Brooklyn to conduct experiments in dream telepathy, collected in the volume *Dream Telepathy* (1973), edited by Ullman and Krippner. In these experiments, which involved over 100 participants, one person would attempt to "send" thoughts to a second person, while the second person was sleeping. The second person was then awakened and asked to describe his/her dreams, and the dreams were examined for evidence of the sent content. The authors claim to have found, in many instances, a significant relationship between what was sent and what was dreamt. The volume also contains two papers by Honorton that purport to present strong scientific evidence for precognitive dreams. Throughout recorded history, people have of course believed to varying degrees in the ability of dreams to sometimes predict the future—Honorton was the first to claim scientific proof of the phenomenon.

Honorton's dream research is noteworthy mostly for inspiring the next stage of his research, which introduced a highly touted recent parapsychological paradigm: The *ganzfeld* experiment, widely regarded by parapsychologists as the best evidence for paranormal ability so far. The word *ganzfeld* means "total field" in German and is used to refer to a technique of sensory deprivation that creates an absolutely uniform visual field. The usual procedure involves taping halves of ping-pong balls over the experimental subject's eyes. A bright light is then pointed at the eyes, creating a visual field without discontinuities. In addition to the bright light, the subject usually wears headphones playing pleasant noise, such as the sound of surf. Parapsychologists believe the pleasant, relaxed state thus produced is highly conducive to the reception of psychic signals. After the subject (receiver) has spent about 15 minutes in this state, a sender is given a target image, randomly selected from four possible pictures, which were in turn randomly selected from a larger pool of possibilities.

The sender concentrates on the picture for a prearranged interval, while the receiver, in a soundproof room, freely describes all mental impressions that occur during this period. At the end of the session the receiver selects from the four the picture that best matches his impressions. Over a large number of trials, the receiver could expect to get 25 percent correct by chance. An actual rate of correct responses significantly above this level is assumed to be evidence of ESP. Honorton and others have claimed success rates in some experiments as high as 55 percent, but various psychologists (most notably Ray Hyman) have written extensive critiques faulting both the methodology and the statistical techniques involved.

Both the random-number and ganzfeld techniques found new life in the hands of Robert Jahn, a Princeton University physics professor and dean who established the Princeton Engineering Anomalies Research (PEAR) laboratory to conduct parapsychological research in 1979. Though his background is in physics and engineering, he became convinced that the human mind directly influences the world around it, an idea described fully in *Margins of Reality: The Role of Consciousness in the Physical World* (1987, co-authored by Brenda J. Dunne). In the book, they claim to have replicated Schmidt's random number generator findings, and thus to have demonstrated the reality of micro-PK. In 2007, the PEAR lab at Princeton University shut down, but its work continues at a new nonprofit organization, International Consciousness Research Laboratories.

Carrying on Jahn's ideas, however, is fellow physicist Dean Radin, author of the popular (in its fifteenth printing as of late 2006) *The Conscious Universe: The Scientific Truth of Psychic Phenomena* (1997).In the book, Radin introduces a now fairly popular interpretation of psychic phenomena in terms of quantum mechanics (which often makes little sense to most of the physics community Recognizing the extent to which other scientists reject his ideas, he treats this rejection as temporary setback on the road to a forthcoming validation. From the introduction:

> In science, the acceptance of new ideas follows a predictable, four-stage sequence. In Stage 1, skeptics confidently proclaim that the idea is impossible because it violates the Laws of Science. This stage can last from years to centuries, depending on how much the idea challenges conventional wisdom. In Stage 2, skeptics reluctantly concede that the idea is possible, but it is not very interesting and the claimed effects are extremely weak. Stage 3 begins when the mainstream realizes that the idea is not only important, but its effects are much stronger and more pervasive than previously imagined. Stage 4 is achieved when the same critics who used to disavow any interest in the idea begin to proclaim that they thought of it first. Eventually, no one remembers that the idea was once considered a dangerous heresy. . . .
>
> The idea discussed in this book is in the midst of the most important and the most difficult of the four transitions—from Stage 1 into Stage 2. While the idea itself is ancient, it has taken more than a century to conclusively demonstrate it in accordance with rigorous, scientific standards.

After the long dry spell in the world of celebrity (non-medium) psychics prompted by the decline of the spiritualists, popular parapsychology came back in a big way in the 1970s, and at the center of this revival was a tall, handsome, Israeli-born psychic named Uri Geller (1946–). Geller burst onto the international stage with an original, if underwhelming, claim to psychokinetic ability: He appeared to bend silverware, keys, and other small metal objects with his mind. In addition, he claimed to be able to reproduce drawings made by people at some distance from him—sometimes in the next room, sometimes in another part of the world. Uri Geller's genius was in convincing apparently reputable scientists (with no experience of magicians' methods) of his skills, and then parlaying the publicity attendant on their published articles and books into further television appearances and books of his own.

In 1972, for example, Russell Targ and Harold Puthoff conducted a series of tests of Geller and another young psychic, Ingo Swann, focusing on the drawing-reproduction trick described above, to which Targ and Puthoff gave a new name: remote viewing (Honorton's *ganzfeld* experiments simply represent a refinement of this technique, which attempts to more thoroughly control for the possibility of cheating). After numerous revisions to remove some of the odder material, the highly respected British science journal *Nature* published Targ and Puthoff's "Information Transmission under Conditions of Sensory Shielding" in October 1974. This publication led to a substantial amount of respectful, positive publicity both for the psychics and the authors, with even the *New York Times* treating it as a serious scientific paper. What none of the publicity mentioned was that *Nature* had decided to publish the article to let the rest of the scientific community evaluate the quality of current paranormal research. The article was accompanied by an editorial that explained this, and which used such words as "weak," "naïve," and "flawed" to describe the research.

Despite the collective yawn of the scientific community, Targ and Puthoff went straight to the public with a summary of their experiments, entitled *Mind Reach: Scientists Look at Psychic Ability*. The book featured a foreword by *Jonathan Livingston Seagull* author Richard Bach, and an introductory essay by respected anthropologist Margaret Mead, in which she indicates that the research described in the book uses solid laboratory science to confirm the existence of remote viewing. Elsewhere in the book, Targ and Puthoff create a new term to refer to Geller's apparent ability to weaken metal with his mind: *The Geller Effect*, which also became the title of Geller's successful autobiography. The book was co-authored by Guy Lyon Playfair, who has written many other books on paranormal topics, with a special focus on hauntings and reincarnation.

Geller has ridden the wave of publicity ever since, with frequent television appearances and a continuing stream of books and products, most now available via his Web site. His repertoire has varied little since the early 1970s: A typical TV appearance includes the bending of silverware and the guessing of drawings made by other guests. One venture presented him as a health practitioner of sorts; the book *Mind Medicine*, a 1999 publication, barely mentions his putative powers and instead offers a wide range of fairly ordinary health-related advice on the power of such things as relaxation and meditation.

James Randi (1928–), Canadian-born magician and escape artist, had a highly successful career as a stage performer from the 1950s into the 1970s, but since the early 1960s he has been primarily known for picking up where Houdini left off, as the world's leading skeptical investigator of paranormal, occult, and supernatural claims. In the beginning of this phase of his career, he carried around a blank check for $10,000, which he promised to anyone who could show, under proper observing conditions, evidence of any paranormal, supernatural, or occult power or event. With inflation and the participation of some generous donors, the prize is up to over $1 million today, and has never been given away.

THE AMAZING RANDI VERSUS THE AMAZING GELLER

James Randi achieved his greatest fame with his ongoing battle with Uri Geller, whose frequent television appearances (and his insistence that his powers were real and that he never used tricks) offended Randi, who saw not a psychic but a magician, with a very limited repertoire, when he looked at Geller. They also bothered *The Tonight Show's* then-host, Johnny Carson (a skeptical ex-magician himself), who called Randi in as a consultant on ways to prevent Geller from cheating. The result was an embarrassing 22-minute appearance in 1973 during which he was unable to perform any of his usual feats. (Videos of the Geller *Tonight Show* appearance are available on You Tube, www.youtube.com.) Following this experience, Randi went on to write an entire book detailing ways to duplicate many of Geller's *psychic* feats without resort to any paranormal gifts. *The Magic of Uri Geller* was first published in 1975, and was retitled, more directly, *The Truth about Uri Geller* in 1982. It remains in print under that title, despite numerous lawsuits Geller has directed Randi's way. Contrary to the content of Geller's legal complaints, Randi does not state that Geller is definitely a fraud— he simply points out that Geller does nothing that cannot be done better using simple magician's tricks. Despite Randi's investigations, Uri Geller continues to perform around the world and has an extensive Web site.

James Randi has investigated psychic Uri Geller a number of times, and in addition to publishing *The Magic of Uri Geller* in 1975 (retitled *The Truth about Uri Geller* in 1982) he provided further information on Geller's history, including an entire chapter devoted to what he considers the poor methodology of Targ and Puthoff (Randi titles the chapter "The Laurel and Hardy of Psi"), in *Flim-Flam* (1980). Among many other problems, Randi believes that in one of the more famous tests of Geller (the one that was written up in *Nature*), the room in which Geller was placed to isolate him from the "senders" actually had a hole in the wall through which Geller could hear the experimenters discussing the stimulus item. The book also includes chapters on many other odd beliefs of the 1970s, including the presence of space aliens in ancient Egypt (and the resulting pyramid power), the Bermuda Triangle, and the Houdini-Doyle conflict over the Cottingley fairies, as well as an excellent history of the Fox sisters and the early days of psychical research.

Randi's mantra is a simple one: Extraordinary claims require extraordinary evidence. If a person is claiming something that is not possible given our current understanding of the world, then it is unlikely to be true, and substantial scientific evidence should be required of that person before his claim is believed. His devotion to the pursuit of truth against a rising tide of nonsense and pseudoscience earned him a MacArthur Foundation "genius" grant (a prize usually given to people pursuing groundbreaking academic research) in the 1980s, which he put toward his efforts to expose the tricks of phony faith-healers. In 1976 he was a founding fellow of the Committee for the Scientific Investigation of Claims of the Paranormal (CSICOP, made up of leading scientists and thinkers in a variety of disciplines), and he has more recently left CSICOP behind (in part as a result of their being named as co-defendants in lawsuits filed against Randi by Geller and others) to form his own organization, the James Randi Educational Foundation. The JREF serves as a clearinghouse of information on pseudoscience, skepticism, and the paranormal, and also hosts an annual conference ("The Amazing Meeting") devoted to those topics.

Given parapsychology's ongoing failure to produce replicable psychic events involving humans, it is somewhat unsurprising that some authors have turned to the animal world instead. Most prominent in this field is Rupert Sheldrake. He has a PhD in biochemistry, but has chosen to focus his attention on a wide range of paranormal topics, frequently jumping on current paranormal bandwagons. He has joined the ranks of Jahn and Radin, for example, with *The Presence of the Past: Morphic Resonance and the Habits of Nature* (1995), and *Chaos, Creativity, and Cosmic Consciousness* (co-authored by Terence McKenna, Ralph Abraham, and Jean Houston, 2001), in which he and his colleagues attempt to use complex systems theory to explain how psychic powers work. In books such as these, he has added an explanatory piece of jargon to the parapsychological lexicon: *morphic resonance*, a term for the process he believes underlies telepathy. The basic idea is that all living things generate a morphic field (which cannot be measured), and that these fields interact in ways that we cannot currently detect.

Sheldrake has in the last decade or so moved toward a rather unusual career path focused on studies of two phenomena: The sense of being stared at and psychic pets. He has attempted to give a scientific foundation to the fairly ancient folk belief that people can sense when they are the object of staring, claiming to have experimentally demonstrated that people really can tell when somebody out of their line of sight is staring. His primary work on this is the book *The Sense of Being Stared At: And Other Aspects of the Extended Mind* (2003), in which he argues that, thanks to morphic resonance, the mind is able to sense this phenomenon without resort to the usual senses. Other scientists and reviewers have been fairly merciless in their criticism of his methods, but Sheldrake has accepted this criticism with a wry sense of humor, collecting and responding to his critics' objections in an issue of the *Journal of Consciousness Studies*, with a piece called "Sheldrake and his Critics: The Sense of Being Glared At" (2005).

Sheldrake has also become convinced that our pets, especially dogs, have far more sensitive psychic gifts than their owners, an idea he explored thoroughly in *Dogs that Know When Their Owners are Coming Home: And Other Unexplained Powers of Animals* (2000). In the book he claims that experiments show that even when owners come home at unusual times, and dogs are prevented from in any way seeing or hearing any signs that they are coming, the dogs nonetheless begin to become restless or excited shortly before the owner's arrival. Like the staring research, this has been largely ignored or dismissed by the scientific community, including other parapsychologists, but the book has been quite successful.

Reception. Despite over a century of research into psychic phenomena, the field of parapsychology remains a publishing success but a scientific failure. The essential problem is that a large portion of the scientific community, including most research psychologists, regards parapsychology as a pseudoscience, due largely to its failure to move on beyond null results in the way science usually does. Ordinarily, when experimental evidence fails repeatedly to support a hypothesis, that hypothesis is abandoned. Within parapsychology, however, more than a century of experimentation has failed even to conclusively demonstrate the mere existence of paranormal phenomena, yet parapsychologists continue to pursue that elusive goal, and readers continue to accompany them.

Bibliography

Browne, Sylvia. *Sylvia Browne's Book of Angels*. Carlsbad, CA: Hay House, 1993.
———. *Sylvia Browne's Lessons for Life*. Carlsbad, CA: Hay House, 2004.
———. *If You Could See What I See: The Tenets of Novus Spiritus*. Carlsbad, CA: Hay House, 2006.
———. *The Two Marys: The Hidden History of the Mother and Wife of Jesus*. New York: Dutton, 2007.
Byrne, Rhonda. *The Secret*. New York: Atria Books, 2006.
Geller, Uri. *Mind Medicine*. Boston: Element Books, 1999.
———. *Uri Geller's Mindpower Kit*. New York: Penguin Studio, 1996.
Geller, Uri, and G.L. Playfair. *The Geller Effect*. New York: H. Holt, 1987.
Gurney, Edmund, F.W. Myers, and F. Podmore. *Phantasms of the Living*. London: Trubner and Co., 1886.
Houdini, Harry. *A Magician among the Spirits*. New York: Arno Press, 1972 (1924).
———. *Houdini exposes the tricks used by the Boston medium "Margery" to win the $2500 prize offered by the Scientific American. Also a complete exposure of Argamasilla, the famous Spaniard who baffled noted scientists of Europe and America, with his claim to X-ray vision . . .* New York: Adams Press, 1924.
———. *Miracle Mongers and their Methods: A Complete Exposé*. Buffalo, NY: Prometheus, 1981 (1920).
Hyman, Ray. *The Elusive Quarry: A Scientific Appraisal of Psychical Research*. Buffalo, NY: Prometheus, 1989.

Jahn, Robert, and Brenda Dunne. *Margins of Reality: The Role of Consciousness in the Physical World.* San Diego, CA: Harcourt Brace Jovanovich, 1987.

Kardec, Allan. *The Spirits' Book (Le Livre des Esprits).* Albuquerque, NM: Brotherhood of Life, 1993.

————. *Book on Mediums (Le Livre des Mediums).* Boston: Colby and Rich, 1874.

Keene, M. Lamar, and Allan Spraggett. *The Psychic Mafia.* Buffalo, NY: Prometheus, 1997, 1976.

Knight, J.Z. *A State of Mind: My Story.* New York: Warner, 1987.

McMoneagle, J. *The Stargate Chronicles: Memoirs of a Psychic Spy.* Charlottesville, VA: Hampton Roads, 2002.

Morehouse, D. *Psychic Warrior: Inside the CIA's Stargate Program: The True Story of a Soldier's Espionage and Awakening.* New York: St. Martin's, 1996.

Radin, D. *The Conscious Universe: The Scientific Reality of Psychic Phenomena.* New York: HarpersEdge, 1997.

Randi, James. *Flim-Flam!* Buffalo, NY: Prometheus, 1982.

————. *The Truth about Uri Geller.* Buffalo, NY: Prometheus, 1982.

Rhine, J.B. *ExtraSensory Perception.* Boston: B. Humphries, 1964.

————. *New Frontiers of the Mind: The Story of the Duke Experiments.* New York: Farrar & Rinehart, 1937.

Sheldrake, Rupert. *Dogs that Know When Their Owners Are Coming Home.* New York: Crown, 1999.

————. "Sheldrake and his Critics: The Sense of Being Glared At." *Journal of Consciousness Studies* 12.6 (2005).

————. *The Sense of Being Stared At.* New York: Crown, 2003.

————. *The Presence of the Past: Morphic Resonance and the Habits of Nature.* New York: Times Books, 1995 (1988).

Sheldrake, Rupert, T. McKenna, and R. Abraham. *Chaos, Creativity, and Cosmic Consciousness.* Rochester, VT: Park Street Press, 2001.

Sinclair, Upton. *Mental Radio.* Springfield, IL: C.C. Thomas, 1962 (1929).

Targ, R., and H. Puthoff. *Mind Reach: Scientists Look at Psychic Ability.* New York: Delacorte, 1977.

Ullman, M., S. Krippner, and A. Vaughan. *Dream Telepathy.* New York: Macmillan, 1973.

What the Bleep Do We Know? Dir. by Mark Vicente, Betsy Chasse, and William Arntz. Twentieth Century Fox. 2005. 108 mins.

Wolman, B.B., ed. *Handbook of Parapsychology.* New York: Van Nostrand Reinhold, 1977.

Further Reading

James Randi Educational Foundation. www.randi.org; Rupert Sheldrake, Biologist and Author. www.sheldrake.org; Uri Geller's Web site. www.urigeller.com.

LUIS A. CORDÓN

PHILOLOGICAL THRILLERS

Definition. Philological thrillers base their suspense effect on mysteries soluble by scholarship or learning. Plots are pivoted on matters requiring the attention and skill of a protagonist well versed in history and literature, often requiring in-depth linguistic command of classical Greek and Latin, and with broad cultural knowledge. Specialization on the part of the investigator in some arcane subject or sign system/language is mandatory. Usually following the structure of the action thriller with its leading up to a final showdown the learned hero must also possess a modicum of physical prowess, and all in all turn out to command mental and physical resources more than matching those of his vile opponent. In a

TYPES OF PHILOLOGICAL THRILLERS

Like all generic fiction somewhat blurred at the genre edges, the philological thriller seems to subdivide into mysteries to do with antiquity, notably ancient Egypt, mysteries to do with the origins and circumstances of the Christian faith, mysteries about the Knights Templar (the latter two categories often, by force of their shared concerns, fused into one), and a group with no distinct shared thematic emphasis but sharing the central issue of a mystery, the solution of which depends on successful philological enquiry, exhibiting the element of ancient and/or coded texts in need of interpretation.

perspective of time setting the philological thriller typically usually works in terms of a tension between a past containing mysteries in need of interpretation and a present inviting or necessitating such interpretation and, which is essential, making such interpretation possible (e.g., Dan Brown's *The Da Vinci Code*). In cases where such tension is not activated because of events taking place completely in the past, the approach of the investigator is markedly modern (e.g., Umberto Eco, *The Name of the Rose*). As the mystery of the philological thriller involves specialist knowledge for its unravelling, an important characteristic of this kind of thriller is its strong efforts to ensure the reader's appreciation of what is at stake, hence its prominent didactic elements, which may often amount to what is known from popular-science writing.

History. Dan Brown's *The Da Vinci Code* (2003) was, in market figures, the culmination of a literary trend with increasing mass appeal since Umberto Eco's very learned but nonetheless best-selling *The Name of the Rose* (1980). There is a history of philological-thriller elements before Eco, but to talk of a (sub-) genre as such would hardly make any sense. Indeed, it is even only to a superficial reading that Eco's novel may be said to be the first instance of the modern *bona fide* philological thriller. *The Name of the Rose*, as it appears with all desirable clarity from Eco's separately published *Postscript to The Name of the Rose* (1983), the novel was meant to argue against the Newtonian rationalism that pervades most thrillers. Based on semiotics, Eco's specialty as a scholar, the novel is a practical but always subtle demonstration of how meaning is constructed and works by systems of signs. Nonetheless, it makes sense, despite authorial intention, to read the work as a rather straight story of uncovering a secret of immense importance to certain clerics of the medieval church, a secret of a nature only immediately appreciable by philologists and literary historians familiar with Antiquity.

No doubt the good quest-cum-mystery yarn of Eco's novel secured an audience beyond the literary and semiotic connoisseurs, who recognize it, in accordance with Eco's intention, as a work in an anti-rationalist tradition embracing writers before him, like Jorge Luis Borges and Vladimir Nabokov, and after, like Thomas Pynchon and Paul Auster. We may take it that it is exactly this quest-cum-mystery quality that two decades later appealed to the perhaps even larger audience of Dan Brown's *The Da Vinci Code*. Dan Brown's best seller from 2003 is the work that gathered up narrative and thematic elements in a particularly successful combination in terms of reader appeal. It may consequently be considered the common reference work in the genre, a status given irrespective of criteria to do with evaluative criticism.

Central to the philological thriller is a quest for some knowledge deemed of crucial importance, of such an importance indeed that the generally accepted historically based self-understanding of modern (Western) society is in for radical adjustment. In the case of Eco it was the lost—and eventually lost again!—manuscript of Aristotle's treatise on comedy, considered unsound for proper religious observance. In the case of Brown it was the dogma-thwarting notion of a feminine lineage from Christ. Such involvement of searching for tradition-disturbing basics resembles the famous quests for the Holy Grail catalogued by European mythology and literature. We find the myth material to do with the Holy Grail in medieval romance cycles in the Romance languages as well as in English. It found expression in the operas of Richard Wagner, here merging with elements from Nordic mythology, and later also in, for instance, the fiction of such different writers as Lawrence Durrell (*The Avignon Quincunx*), J.R.R. Tolkien (*Lord of the Rings*), and J.K. Rowling (Harry Potter). Victorian adventure fiction (e.g., H. Rider Haggard) often involves the solution of riddles needing a scholarly approach combined with muscular activities.

Trends and Themes. Philology, from classical Greek meaning the love of words, and a concept and term introduced as late as the early nineteenth century in the context of modern university enquiry, presupposes a common culture constituted by written language—texts—accessible by methods relying on the philologist's textual instruments such as what we today would call linguistics, historiography, and literary study, often extending its practices to draw on related domains within anthropology, psychology, and so on.

Central to the philological thriller is the common attribution of extraordinary power to language and other cultural constructs. The phenomenon is well known in the observing of religious and quasi-religious practices. For the transformation—transubstantiation—of the bread and wine of the Eucharist into the body of Christ the Roman Catholic liturgy requires a verbal formula including the Latin words *Hoc est corpus meum*. Although inherently nothing mysterious in the Latin words they have come to be associated with the metaphysical transubstantiation depending on faith, an association all the more apparent in the layman's lack of understanding of the Latin that has resulted in the expression *hocus pocus*, designating that which cannot be immediately understood. To Plato the poets posed a danger to the polity, since their words were capable of arousing feelings contrary to the common sense needed for everyday transactions. To the Nordic Vikings the runes had power of fate. And in most civilizations the written word has carried more importance, in, say, business matters, than oral understandings, although oaths, affidavits, and so on, by having been uttered, do carry legal consequences. In other words, language has traditionally served a double purpose as both means of communication and—more or less powerful—object of communication. Arguably, also the pervasive postmodernist climate of recent decades with its predilection for a "textual" or "verbal" approach to existence has made philological enquiry of topical interest.

Eco radicalized philological enquiry by way of semiotics, a theory of signs developed from the Swiss philologist Ferdinand de Saussure's posthumous publication *Cours de linguistique generale* (1916) consisting of students' lecture notes taken 1906–11, with notable contributions from linguistic scholars such as the Dane Louis Hjelmslev and the American Charles Peirce. In his notes for his novel, *Postscript to The Name of the Rose* (1983), Eco himself draws attention to the way he treats language and text conventions to challenge and redirect interest in cultural-, text-, and language-dependent constructs. The philological enquiry at the heart of the story, the discovery of the lost treatise by Aristotle on comedy, a companion piece to the Greek philosopher's famous and philologically fully processed treatise on tragedy, is the kind of work requiring the philological expertise represented by the "investigating officer," the English monk William of Baskerville, whose procedures parallel and complement the present-day philological work of the author of the novel.

Whereas Eco undertakes to question and put at risk cultural conventions taken for granted in Western culture and thereby joins forces with contemporary philosophical work deconstructing seemingly cultural givens pioneered by the French philosopher Jacques Derrida, Dan Brown's center of interest in his best seller is in the ancient "conspiracy theory" regarding the possible issue of Christ and the existence of a female Christian tradition. The way to the (re-)discovery of this alternative to established Christian dogma is a chain of riddles left by the guardians of the heresy. Unlike Eco's mystery that leaves the investigator and the reader enmeshed in the net of language, Brown's protagonist, the symbologist professor Robert Langdon, and the reader with him, is able to break the code insofar as it is constituted by a series of enigmatic ciphers, but will have to negotiate himself the theological implications of Langdon's quest into apocryphal Christianity.

Contexts and Issues. Structurally, philological thrillers generally follow the broad outlines of the action thriller, the learned labor in the study accompanied by the physical exertions that the pursuit of the implications of the paperwork entail, with or without the heightened danger presented by rivals invariably less given to intellectual sorting out than the protagonist and his/her entourage. A shared trait of most philological thrillers is their two-epoch setting. The mystery or riddle belongs to the past, whereas its solution is a matter of present-day effort calling for all the state-of-the-art tools of the modern scholar.

As the modern philologist—historian, linguist, Egyptologist, and so on—relies very much on technological resources, and as the mystery handled by the philological scholar may very well be in the area of text-dependent science, the philological thriller shares some ground with its cousin the scientific thriller. Also the historical novel, to the extent it is characterized by preoccupation with some problem requiring the scrutiny of texts, and the historical whodunit, may be said to be cousins. The parallel-world explorations of regular science fiction may share elements with the reconstructions of the past in terms of either counter-factual or complementary-factual events.

The philological thriller is characterized by the quest for origins, factual or fictional. As such the application of philological instruments and procedures are made to work in relation to a set of elements existing prior to or outside of the fiction, so to speak. A variety of the philological thriller could be said to exist in the strong tradition in the English academic whodunit (e.g., Michael Innes, pseudonym of the literary historian J.I.M. Stewart), for letting the plot revolve around matters to do with literature, to the point of hinging the plot on some literary element, a tradition playfully honored in the more recent crime novels of Colin Dexter (featuring Inspector Morse) and Reginald Hill (featuring the investigating duo of Dalziel and Pascoe).

In generic perspective the philological thriller is a hybrid. It combines features from the straight mystery whodunit with its sleuth combining hard evidence and intuition for the investigation of crime, the action thriller with its dependence on crude suspense construction, the political thriller with its potential for consideration of matters of (geo)political importance, the regular realist novel with its invitation to empathy, and the historical novel with its reconstructions of plausible pasts. Sam Bourne's *The Last Testament* from 2007, to choose a novel in the wake of *The Da Vinci Code*, is a good illustration of the way that these elements are joined to create a successful philological thriller.

The central event in Bourne's novel is the appearance of old Babylonian clay tablets after the pillage of the Iraqi National Museum in Baghdad in April 2003. Among the clay tablets is one that turns out to be the will of Old Testament Abraham, assigning ownership of Mount Moria, the present-day sacred site in central Jerusalem, facing claims from his two sons Isaac and Ishmael, celebrated by Jews and Muslims respectively. If it can be proved that either one received the land from Abraham, it would give the successful side a legitimate claim rooted in history. The political thriller is in evidence in the importance of the old tablet for current political and military efforts. The mystery element is in the efforts on the part of the two protagonists to get to the root of the matter. The action is in the chases following upon the competition for control of the tablet, with Israeli, Palestinian, and American agents chasing one another. The historical aspect is in the building up of the whole background of Old Testament historiography and archaeology. The empathy is secured by a realist portrayal of Maggie Costello, professional negotiator suffering from past trauma and being first presented as Washington housewife and very much living in a recognizable everyday world. The philological element is a code-breaking involving first the specialist appraisal of the tablet's cuneiform language. In this case it is not the domain of the protagonist(s), but of the character that furnishes the inciting event of the plot, and who is immediately killed. But by the flashback narrative technique the reader is allowed to follow his investigation and interpretation of the tablet, except for the circumstance that information as to the exact nature of Abraham's decision is protracted for structural suspense reasons until the very end. The philological aspect here also applies to the mastery of the Internet resource of Second Life, without which the endeavors of the protagonists would have come to nothing.

Reception. Usually relegated to the popular-fiction dump of the adventure novel or mystery story by its very topic, setting, and thematic issue—murder in the medieval monastery—Umberto Eco's *The Name of the Rose* created quite a critical stir at the same time as the general reading public took warmly to it. It was published at a time when deconstruction, metafictional concerns, and attention to intertextuality were sweeping the literary-critical landscape worldwide. It could be read as an ingenious murder mystery, modelling itself deliberately on the Sherlock Holmes stories, or as a slyly devised practicing of linguistic and literary-critical theories centring on the epistemological implications of language and culturally conditioned verbal constructions such as (non)fictional texts, or it could be read as a warning against the tendency by the powers that be to exercise censorship, or, and surely by most readers, as just a gripping yarn. Eco in one fell swoop set a new and critically acclaimed standard for the historical suspense story turning it into a trend-setting philological thriller.

Eco's novel rekindled interest in the Middle Ages generally, reflected in both academe and entertainment. No doubt his approach to language and other cultural constructs as systems of signs propelled interest in language and language-derived issues. Since language is a kind of cipher agreed upon for its meaning in a given culture, the urge to look into cipher proper is a natural consequence. Literary criticism contemporary with Eco's novel welcomed instances of language games, such as we find in the fiction of British Julian Barnes (*Flaubert's Parrot* (1984)), Lawrence Norfolk (*Lemprière's Dictionary* (1991)), and Iain Pears (*An Instance of the Fingerpost* (1997)) or by American Allan Kurzweil (*A Case of Curiosities* (1992)), or Susan Sontag (*The Volcano Lover* (1992)). Whereas the success of Eco's book resulted first and foremost indirectly as an encouragement in this upsurge of narrative integrating themes of self-reflection in the text, the success of Dan Brown's *The Da Vinci Code* lacked the academic acclaim bestowed on Eco's book with its invitation to sheer enjoyment at the same time as critical scrutiny according to taste and training. The reason is not far to seek. The mystery in Brown's novel may be hard for the fictional characters involved to solve and it may, as it has certainly done, give rise to lively theological debate, but only to the extent that its solution is a matter of reading on and thus dealing in a very basic way with the sign nature of language—understanding the words on the page—does it offer a challenge. Arguably, the work of Eco and Brown between them, however different their intentions and literary executions, opened the field for seeking out the lacunae or mysteries of the past—a lost Aristotelian manuscript in the case of Eco, generation in Christ's family in the case of Brown—and offering a bid for fictional redress. Ancient Egypt, Ancient Greece and Rome, the Crusades and the Knights Templar, and a host of other historical figures, events, or complexes ripe for conjecture opened themselves up to writers' and readers' interest alike. Since Eco's *The Name of the Rose* there has been an increasing production of philological thrillers. Accelerating conspicuously since Dan Brown's best seller, most of them go unheeded by academic literary criticism, but they obviously satisfy a hungry craving on the part of the reading public.

Selected Authors

Mysteries Related to Antiquity, Notably Ancient Egypt. The ancient Egypt of the pharaohs constitutes a particularly inviting site for the genre of the philological thriller. Although many of the riddles to do with social, religious, and political life were more or less solved after the interpretation of the Rosetta stone made hieroglyphs readily accessible as a language, there still remains considerable material for thrilling stories, both in the old civilization itself and in the history of its discovery. Preeminent among those who have written suspenseful tales about ancient Egypt, based on his own expertise as a world-renowned Egyptologist, is Christian Jacq. His novels, most of them gathered together in series (*Ramses*, *Stone of Light*, *Queen of Freedom*, *Judge of Egypt*, *Mysteries of Osiris*, and *Vengeance of the Gods*) lean toward the historical novel, but have distinct traits of the philological thriller.

Among those who have tried their hands on the Kingdom of the Nile are Tom Holland with *The Sleeper in the Sands* (1998), Arthur Phillips with *The Egyptologist* (2004), Matthew Reilly with *Seven Ancient Wonders* (2005), Paul Sussman with *The Last Secret of the Temple* (2005), and Nick Drake with *Nefertiti—the Book of the Dead* (2006), all of them relying on philological means to explain and explore phenomena sparking off danger and drama.

Regarding ancient Greece and Rome philological work has been carried out in bulk since the Renaissance; indeed, it was the rediscovery of Greece through Rome—and through the medieval heritage of Rome—that triggered philology as a line of academic enquiry.

Homeric echoes and Greek mythology are the subject of modern-Greek-and-Byzantine-history specialist Roderick Beaton's *Ariadne's Children* (1995), making the archaeological work on the Minoan civilization in Crete the basis of an exciting plot, and A.J. Hartley making Mycaenean Greece the background of American Museum drama in *The Mask of Atreus* (2006). Novels about ancient Rome have been staple fare in the genre of the historical novel, with Edward Bulwer-Lytton's *The Last Days of Pompeii* (1834) as the perhaps best known, and best loved, of its kind. The British writer Robert Harris offers his angle on the volcanic eruption of the Vesuvius in 79 AD in *Pompeii* (2003) with the variation of having a state-employed water engineer "read" the signs of the imminent catastrophe. The philological interest habitually associated with generations of Latin-school pupils reading the speeches and letters of Cicero is the background of the same writer's portrayal, through sources accessible by philological effort, in his novel *Imperium* from 2006.

Disputed Origins of the Christian Faith. In this category Dan Brown's *The Da Vinci Code* (2003) has pride of place. The murderous lengths to which orthodox Christianity, here in the shape of the Opus Dei organization within the Roman Catholic Church, will go in order to protect dogmatic vested interests found a ready public, ever craving and welcoming conspiracy theories. The popular response to the novel showed that fiction's claims on reality were readily accepted for reality itself. No doubt the offering of a female link to Christ chimed in with a readership since the 1970s raised on gender consciousness. With a bearing on Dan Brown we find also Kathleen McGowan's *The Expected One—Book One of the Magdalene Line* (2006). The author depicts her heroine Maureen Paschal pursuing signs of Mary Magdalene having been seen by people from various cultures throughout the centuries. It goes without saying that this is a venture that, as soon as dogmatic apologists become aware of her, promises serious threats to Maureen. Michael Cordy offers his approach to the question of numinous genealogy in *The Miracle Strain* (1997), a story bridging across to the science thriller in that it has its protagonist, a gene scientist, start work on divine genes.

Knights Templar and the Crusades. The Knights Templar and the Crusades of the Middle Ages saw their justification as the protectors of the Christian faith against Islam, the great imperialist of the time in the lands of the Bible. In concrete terms the Knights Templar were a partly religious, partly mundane order of knights supervising the control with the holy places in the present-day Middle East. As soldiers and warriors they, so to speak, kept open access from the European West to the various holy places and shrines. Associated with the knights was a rich mythology about their passing on from generation to generation the guarding of relics and powerful documents, the most important of them all being the Holy Grail, Christ's drinking cup from the Last Supper. Also in this area the historical novel has long held its own, with Sir Walter Scott's *Ivanhoe* (1820) and various nineteenth-century workings of the Robin Hood stories referring to the crusading Richard Lionheart, as central in this tradition. In Raymond Khoury's *The Last Templar* (2005) we are offered a story that moves between 1291 and present-day New York. The decrypting of an old document plays the central role and justifies the designation of philological thriller. The identical structure of narration, switching between the Middle Ages and the now we have in Kate Mosse's *Labyrinth* (2005). The whereabouts of the Holy Grail will only be revealed to the person in possession of the Trilogy of the Labyrinth, a book preserving in its entirety the truth about the grail. The Knights Templar having something of considerable importance is likewise the subject of Steve Berry's *The Templar Legacy* (2006), a story that throws long glances back into the Middle Ages at the same time as it unfolds its plot by counter-pointing events in contemporary Copenhagen and the south of France.

Whatever the nature of any secret held by the medieval order of knights and its relation to Christian dogma, there seems to be boundless opportunities in this line of fiction.

Assorted Philological Thrillers. Ancient civilizations and Christianity are favorite haunts of the philological thriller, but a good many works of exciting fiction have made use of a need for, or at any rate a sympathizing with, philological competence as the motor of a story, and with an everything but conventionally heroic philologist in a central role. Mention has been made of Umberto Eco and his *The Name of the Rose,* followed by other Eco works deserving the designation of philological thriller, such as *Foucault's Pendulum* (1988; with a bearing on the Knights Templar) and *The Mysterious Flame of Queen Loana* (2004).

In Eco's genuinely learned tradition we find Dame Antonia Byatt's *Possession: A Romance* (1990), about two literary researchers gradually uncovering great secrets in their efforts, which to begin with seem like so much lit crit-career-sustaining drudgery. Also in the kind of literature distinctly not designed for the best-seller lists we have Lawrence Norfolk's *Lemprière's Dictionary* (1991), a story of a young English scholar setting out to write a mythological dictionary. In his research and as a result of his dictionary work he discovers startling things about his father, things that seem to have a very dramatic and deadly bearing on his surroundings while at the same time reflecting his literary endeavors. In this book Eco's and other semiologists' notion of the world in terms of sign systems is made of central importance. In Matthew Pearl's *The Dante Club* (2003) the authentic work by New England philologists and literary critics on a new American translation of Dante form both the background, and, as it turns out, the foreground of deadly events in picturesque campus surroundings. There is no need to be able to read *The Divine Comedy* in the original medieval Italian, but a certain familiarity with the work makes for a more satisfactory response. Ian Caldwell and Dustin Thomason soon after published *The Rule of Four* (2004). Here we have to do with a story in which the progression of the plot keeps pace with the gradual translation of a medieval document in Latin and six other languages, *The Hypnerotomachia Poliphili*. It turns out that working on the old texts previously cost the on-the-point-of-graduating Tom Sullivan's philologist father his life. And more violence is in store, as Tom and his Princeton roommates concentrate beyond the call of curriculum duty on the secrets of the document. In *The Romanov Prophecy* (2004), Steve Berry anticipated his Crusades story by a story set in present-day Russia. When the American lawyer Miles Lord is sent to the Russian archives in Moscow to find documents justifying the claim of the Romanovs on the Russian throne, the dreary work in the vaults has dramatic repercussions. Leaning to the side of conspiracy theory—what actually happened when the Bolsheviks executed the Czar family and did they all die?— Berry makes archive enquiry into a very dangerous discipline. Also to do with recent history, but necessitating the mind of the trained philologist we have Elizabeth Kostova's *The Historian* (2005). This is a Dracula story that closes in on that monster by a combination of careful work on old texts and muscular action in brisk interaction. Old texts and strange artifacts form the key to an old secret in John Fasman's *The Geographer's Library* (2005), a story that centers on medieval alchemy. Switching between 1145 and present-day provincial New England a journalist is asked to write the obituary of an Estonian professor of history, who has died while in the United States. The story proceeds along with the collection and interpretation of 15 artifacts. But the interests of others are ignited as the journalist makes his enquiries.

It seems as if philology is a rich vein for fiction with a wide audience appeal. Certainly since the end of the twentieth century it has been mined with increasing interest and imagination by contemporary writers. Unfortunately there is no critical literature to cover the whole field as presented above. This is partly due to the fact that "philological thriller" has yet to be recognized as a useful designation for a kind of literature enjoying popular appeal but to a superficial glance of immense variety. Partly it is due to the fact that this kind of fiction has suddenly, almost tsunami-like, flooded the book market, with the consequence of virtually stunning those attempting to compare and categorize. As for critical curiosity it is recommended to search for sources under specific author names or in treatises on suspense fiction generally.

Bibliography

Barnes, Julian. *Flaubert's Parrot*. New York: Knopf, 1985.
Beaton, Roderick. *Ariadne's Children*. New York: St. Martin's, 1996.
Berry, Steve. *The Romanov Prophecy*. New York: Ballantine, 2004.
———. *The Templar Legacy*. New York: Ballantine, 2006.
Brown, Dan. *The Da Vinci Code*. New York: Doubleday, 2003.
Bourne, Sam. *The Last Testament*. London: Harper, 2007.
Caldwell, Ian, and Dustin Thompson. *The Rule of Four*. New York: Dial, 2004.
Eco, Umberto. *The Name of the Rose*. San Diego: Harcourt Brace Jovanovich, 1983.
Fasman, John. *The Geographer's Library*. New York: Penguin, 2005.
Harris, Robert. *Pompeii*. New York: Random House, 2003.
Holland, Tom. *The Sleeper in the Sands*. Boston: Little, Brown, 1998.
Khoury, Raymond. *The Last Templar*. New York: Dutton, 2005.
Kostova, Elizabeth. *The Historian*. Boston: Little, Brown, 2005.
Kurzweil, Alan. *A Case of Curiosities*. San Diego: Harcourt Brace Jovanovich, 1992.
McGowan, Kathleen. *The Expected One*. New York: Simon & Schuster, 2006.
Mosse, Kate. *The Labyrinth*. New York: G.P. Putnam, 2005.
Norfolk, Lawrence. *Lemprière's Dictionary*. New York: Harmony, 1991.
Pearl, Matthew. *The Dante Club*. New York: Random House, 2003.
Pears, Iain. *An Instance of the Fingerpost*. New York: Riverhead, 1998.
Phillips, Arthur. *The Egyptologist*. New York: Random House, 2004.
Sontag, Susan. *The Volcano Lover*. New York: Farrar, Straus, Giroux, 1992.

Further Reading

de Saussure, Ferdinand. *Cours de linguistique generale*. Paris: Payot, 1972; Eco, Umberto. *Postscript to The Name of the Rose*. San Diego: Harcourt Brace Jovanovich, 1984.

LARS OLE SAUERBERG

POETRY

Definition. "Poetry, the art of articulation, renders us inarticulate when it comes to defining it." So proclaims David Lehman, series editor of the wildly successful *Best American Poetry*, in his forward to the 2002 edition. One of the most popular texts used in college poetry classrooms, *Sound and Sense*, acknowledges that "people have always been more successful at appreciating poetry than defining it" (2002, 3). If people whose livelihoods depend upon their cogent definitions of poetry fumble and hesitate, the average reader can be forgiven her or his tentative stabs at a definition. Most of us know a poem when we see one but when pressed to define one, retract almost every definition or characteristic as we articulate it. Young children associate poetry with its rhyme, and while it is true that poetry often contains

---

WHAT IS POETRY?

In his famous explorations of the differences between poetry and prose, William Carlos Williams (1883–1963) elliptically announced that "prose has to do with the fact of an emotion; poetry has to do with the dynamization of emotion into a separate form. . . . poetry: new form dealt with as a reality in itself. . . . [T]he form of poetry is related to the movements of the imagination revealed in words—or whatever it may be" (1970, 133). And Wallace Stevens's definition announces that a poem is "the cry of its occasion." "A poem should not mean / But be," says Archibald MacLeish.

---

rhyme, we cannot define poetry by its presence. Much poetry does not rhyme. We may point out that poetry is created from the basic unit of a line, so we may identify poetry as writing that is preoccupied with that unit; however, the line, too, becomes a blurry characteristic, particularly when one examines the genre of prose poems or Language poetry, both of which confound our understanding of what constitutes a line. Rhythm or regular meter frequently marks poetry, but even that characteristic cannot be offered as part of an unwavering definition.

Poets themselves often present ambiguous definitions of poetry, couched around what it *contains* and what it *does* rather than what it *is*, definitions that suggest that each poem creates its own parameters.

In her introduction to the *Best American Poetry 2004*, poet Lyn Hejinian writes "What is, or isn't, a poem? What makes something poetic? These questions remain open. And the fact that there are no formal answers is one source of the vitality of the art form" (2004, 9). Influential poetry critic Helen Vendler remarks that "[w]e have been conscious, too, that a poem can be any one of a number of things, from a whimsical couplet to a sublime sequence" (1987, x). The definition of poetry, like some of its most intriguing examples, resists closure.

When Vendler does define poetry, she offers a list of features: intensity, a point, concentration of the form, and melody (1987, xxx), and this listing technique for defining poetry is common. Most handbooks of literary terms and poetry textbooks will define poetry according to its content and purpose along with one or two of its most salient features. Some will call poetry a rhythmic, imaginative expression intended to supply pleasure, offer an idea of significance, or engage in some manner with meaning, frequently marked by its concentrated and organized use of language. And that's where the definition will begin: a poem is an attempt to communicate some idea of importance through language that is frequently concerned with itself as an artistic medium. For in treating language as art, the definition allows but does not require attention to sound and rhyme, rhythm, image and metaphor, compression and intensity in the definition of the genre.

Identifying poetry's basic material as language rather (as is often the case) than the line allows poetry to exist on the page or on the stage, to offer complete sentences or merely sounds, even symbols. In the broad swath of printed, recorded, and audio-visually taped materials that constitutes current American poetry, more appears to fall under the rubric of poetry than ever before. In James Longenbach's discussion of this expansion of the genre in 2004, he intones that "[i]t's difficult to complain about poetry's expanding audience, but it's more difficult to ask what a culture that wants poetry to be popular wants poetry to be" (2004, 6). Poetry is still the "emotion recollected in tranquility" that it was when Wordsworth said so. And it is still marked by attention to image and metaphor, line breaks and rhythm, sound, compression. But it is also now gesture and voice inflection, meaning divorced from words, ideas divorced from sentimentality. The profusion of genres, schools, and even events that identify themselves as poetry or poetic have pushed the already broadly outlined definitions of poetry even further. Poet Marvin Bell announced in 2003 that "Poetry is a great big Yes: Yes to formalists, yes to free verse writers, yes to surrealists, yes to political poets, yes to the poets of wordplay and slippery self-consciousness" (131). His description responds to the expansion of poetry's definition, which has always been the most slippery of definitions.

The Tendency toward Dichotomies. As welcoming and all-inclusive as contemporary poetry seems to be, any discussion of poetry must navigate the bifurcation that constantly dominates the world of poetry and the interpretations and assessments of it. Longtime editor of the *Cambridge History of American Literature* Sacvan Bercovitch acknowledged that poetry was one of the two most problematic areas covered under the rubric of "American Literature" during the past 20 years, in part because of the multiple simultaneous concepts that render the split. Critics disagree not only on what schools or movements may be included under the rubric of poetry, but also on what specific parameters should be used to differentiate between those schools. Most critics prefer to speak in terms of dichotomies, for example, yet Robert Hass's review of American poetry published in 2001 convinced him of three traditions, and the triad of traditions he notes does not contain mention of any oral traditions. Granted, he speaks in an introduction to the best poetry published and therefore restricted to the printed medium, but he offers no qualifiers to his list of poetic traditions.

As is the case in almost all histories of various art forms, each burgeoning new trend or radical challenge to the prevailing artistic practices rejects the philosophies and the features that hold sway. As the new trend accumulates adherents and those adherents gain popular acceptance, important awards, or critical acclaim, its experimental, radical slant against or relationship to the mainstream eventually shifts from the position of radical outsider to prevailing insider.

We could identify the acceptable, mainstream poetry as traditional, if we keep in mind that what falls into this category is ever-shifting. Traditional does not mean for all time, but rather, for some *recent* period of time. And we also must remember that what is traditional at any given moment very likely occupied the position of challenger or avant-garde prior to its ascent (some would call it descent) to the category of traditional.

DO YOU PREFER YOUR POETRY RAW OR COOKED?

One of the rather static rifts has divided the poetic world between the realm of acceptable or mainstream, and that which challenges the status quo, or the avant-garde. Robert Lowell (1917–77) rather famously divided the two into the "raw" and the "cooked" in his acceptance speech for the National Book Award for poetry in 1960, with *cooked* referring to that "marvelously expert and remote" poetry of the accepted mainstream academic poetry and *raw*, to that which challenged it.

Despite the near-constant stream of poetic schools and movements from avant-garde to status quo, then back out again, one line over which the two realms divide has remained rather consistent for approximately the past half-century. Most twentieth-century schools of poetry have organized themselves in relationship to the position of the self in the poem and the poem's fashioning—or not—of its speaker. Alternately described by critics as the absence or presence of the speakerly self in the poetry, as impersonal versus personal or objective or subjective content, as cooked compared to raw, as poetry keening toward the universal arrayed against that of the local, this essential line over which the poets and critics split the discussion has remained fixed pretty much since the midpoint of the twentieth century.

Another way the world of American poetry is presented as bifurcated focuses on the division between academic and popular judgment, between the worlds of high and low culture, of elitists and commoners. Poetry and criticism emanating from the academy—what university writers' workshop faculty members and students study and write, what journals housed in those universities publish, what published critics deem worthy of their attention, what movements in and schools of poetry constitute the syllabi in college poetry classes—often deviates severely from the poetry that popular audiences demand and applaud, that which average Americans will purchase or that which members of the public will attend. However, in the same way that experimental challenges to the status quo eventually become part of the world of mainstream poetry, so is there constant traffic between the poetic worlds of low and high culture. What is at one point eschewed by the realm of academic presses and classrooms because of its origins among the masses or from the streets rather than from within the walls of institutions of higher education eventually enters academia. Today's academic poets were often yesterday's popular, radical, marginal, even street poets and enjoy a symbiotic or at least connected relationship. The two categories feed each other.

The connectedness of these two worlds must remain in view whenever one assesses the current state of poetry. While at the same time that many have lamented the deplorable decline of national reading practices, and anyone particularly interested in poetry could specifically lament the infrequency with which poets' books are read (let alone purchased), the numbers of Americans—particularly young Americans—who consider themselves poets, participate in local poetry events, apply to Master of Fine Arts (MFA) programs in poetry, and submit poetry to journals and presses that publish it have surged. Public interest in and community activism to promote poetry are also very high. A recent summation of the state of American poetry noted that reading "is in chronic decline" particularly among the 18–24-year-olds at the same time that the President of the Poetry Foundation, John Barr, predicts of "a new Golden Age for poetry" (Walker, 2004, 93–94). A best-selling book of poetry is purchased by only 500 Americans, but the National Poetry Slam competition can fill a major stadium in a large city, with the price of admission roughly equivalent to the cost of that best-selling book of poetry.

History

The American Tradition of Poetry. A complete understanding of the current state of American poetry requires familiarity with the development of the American tradition in poetry, a tradition of mavericks inaugurated in Walt Whitman (1819–1892) and Emily Dickinson (1830–1886) in the nineteenth century, whereby "American" poetry became associated with or defined by the challenge it proffered to whatever tradition was currently in vogue. Within the context of this association of "American" with challenge of the status quo, we can look at the specific movements of the previous century whose reactions to the status quo continue to exert defining forces on the current trends in the genre.

Most surveys of American poetry root the national tradition in Whitman, who offers the first successful American challenge to the status quo. Dickinson also figures predominantly in the establishment of a distinctly American tradition; however, only a few of her poems were published in her lifetime, and some additional publications followed shortly after her death, but a scholarly collection of her work did not appear until midway through the twentieth century. Her challenge to the status quo entered critical consciousness a full century after Whitman's. Stemming from European epic traditions, particularly British poetry, American poetry of the mid-nineteenth century centered itself on the impersonal, universal, objective, cooked side of the poetic divide. The dominance of the epic, particularly Virgil's Latin epic *The Aeneid*, in scholarly traditions handed to the United States from England, allowed little room for poetic exploration of either the local or of the autobiographical. There was no room for the poet to craft a speakerly "I" within his work. Rigid structures with regular, prescribed meter and rhyme also dominated the world of published poetry.

Into this poetic world Whitman avowed something "transcendent and new" in his poetry, challenging the deeply entrenched epic tradition that dominated intellectual strains of poetry, while at the same time he avoided the unfaltering metrics and rhyme scheme of the poetry so widely read during the American nineteenth century. His "Song of Myself," always central to the various iterations of *Leaves of Grass*, brashly revises Virgil's epic promise to sing of arms and of a man whose fate had made him fugitive; Whitman boldly sings, "I celebrate myself, / And what I assume you shall assume, / For every atom belonging to me as good belongs to you." His democratizing assertion of equal possession ("every atom belonging to me as good belongs to you") was a direct challenge to the poetic traditions that celebrated mythic, long-dead but singular national heroes such as Aeneas and Odysseus. In her summary of Whitman's project, Helen Vendler points out that America itself "was to be democratic, not monarchic; free, not feudal; revolutionary, not traditional; America, new in spirit, was to be new in art" (1987, xiv–xv). If the European epic traditions celebrated the epic journey of their nations' founding fathers, often part-divine offspring of the gods, Whitman's celebrates the meandering of his own poetic self, which he also identifies as "Divine . . . inside and out."

Compared to the carefully planned and rigidly executed epic structure, which demands divisions into books or cantos, Whitman's epic (a term his preface disavows) presents 52 sections of such variant length and focus that critics continue to wrangle over the exact dividing lines of those sections, to say nothing of the debate over the topic and meaning of the sections. His individual lines defy all attempts at scansion in hopes of discovering a regular meter, an attempt obliterated already in the first section, where the short line "I celebrate myself" coexists with the run-on lines that catalog what about himself he celebrates: "My respiration and inspiration. . . . the beating of my heart. . . . the passing of blood and air through my lungs, / The sniff of green leaves and dry leaves, and of the shore and darkcolored sea-rocks, and of hay in the barn[. . . .]" More than comfortable with ambiguity of meaning, Whitman's poem revels in its contrary nature, famously catechizing, "Do I contradict myself? / Very well then . . . I contradict myself[.]" Rather than impose an external structure that dictates meter, line length, rhyme scheme, and division of content, Whitman's poetry employs organic form, the notion that the idea or concept of the literary work dictates its structure or allows the work to grow into its form.

Initially derided and dismissed by many influential critics, Whitman has since come to occupy the seminal place in American poetry. In Whitman, American poetry also obtains its first, tradition-forming icon of resistance: in the tradition of Whitman, the poets deemed most central to the American tradition of poetry continue to be those whose work resists classification. Numerous conflicting current schools of poetry claim Whitman as an antecedent. A perfect illustration of his confounding of categorization is that despite his claim that his poem is *not* epic, most studies of the modernist epics begin with Whitman. At the same time, beat and confessional poets also cite him and *Leaves of Grass* as precursor and influence. In his poetic challenge to the mid-nineteenth-century American status quo, Whitman crafted poetry that embraced both sides of the apparent dichotomies that have come to describe poetry, most notably the partition set between the roles of the self in the poetry. This dual embrace also marks some of the most exciting poets publishing today and those poets most definitively linked to an American tradition.

Twentieth-Century Poetic History

High Moderns and New Critics. Whitman serves as an iconic example of the quintessential American poet's trajectory from upstart to paradigm, a trajectory that specific movements have followed as well as individual poets. Of particular concern to anyone who wishes to study contemporary poetry are the upstart movements that reacted to what was, at the midpoint of the twentieth century, the overwhelming mainstream and academic acceptance of the high modern poets and power of the new critics to interpret that poetry. For those movements—the confessional school, the Black Arts movement, and Language poetry—both hearkened back to strong elements of previous poetic traditions and advanced or broadened the definition of what was acceptable within poetry. Each of these three movements became a powerful force in and of itself, asserting in time its own indelible mark on the shape of American poetry and becoming that against which future movements reacted.

The early poetry of Theodore Roethke (1908–1963) and Robert Lowell (1917–1977) and the many historically based, culturally allusive, intellectually driven poems of Ezra Pound (1885–1972), T.S. Eliot (1888–1965), Wallace Stevens (1879–1955), HD (Hilda Doolittle, 1886–1961), and William Carlos Williams, including the devotion of many of them to the epic form, suggested that the high modern poet's role was to serve as a voice for his or her time without necessarily crafting a speakerly self in the poem that narrates that voice. In the dichotomy noted above, much of the high moderns' poetry would fall on the absent, impersonal, objective, universal side of the line. Following an earlier, self-described imagist devotion to no idea but in things, these poets focused on epic poems like Pound's *Cantos*, H.D.'s *Helen in Egypt* and *Trilogy*, T.S. Eliot's *The Wasteland*, William Carlos Williams's *Paterson*, and Hart Crane's (1899–1933) *The Bridge*. An indication of the importance that these poets presumed accompanied them and their work is evidenced in the rather humorous fact that Pound gave a copy of his *Cantos* to Mussolini (who misunderstood them if he read them at all) and defined his project, an epic poem, as a poem "that contains history." In a focus from things to history, the speakerly self was easily obscured.

Of course, reducing all these poets to simplified summaries that outline the similarities among them fails to value the complexity or subtlety of the individual poets and some of their most enduring poems. Even the quintessentially impersonal poem *The Wasteland*, written by the poet who coined the term *objective correlative*, can be persuasively argued as a personal grouse, as the poet's facsimile edition asserts. And William Carlos Williams supplies an equally confounding body of work that much more closely mirrors Whitman's embrasure of competing traditions.

Interpretations of high modern poetry were dominated by a group of critics and then an intellectual movement known as New Criticism, which firmly established itself in the academies of the United States. These critics evaluated poetry according to its ability to craft complex yet unified explorations centered on some theme of universal significance, furthering the presumption that good poetry was objective poetry. The best poems were those that employed the most formal poetic elements in this unified statement, crafting "well-wrought urns" whose aesthetically pleasing surface rested upon a structurally complex yet perfect interior. The best readings were those that accounted for as many of these elemental features as possible. The text itself supplied all the reader needed in order to ascertain this statement. In fact, autobiographical details and authorial intention were not to enter into the discussion of the work unless the work itself invited the reader to do so. The poem's effect on the reader also could not be included in the evaluation of the piece. At its most basic, New Criticism focused on text over act: *how* a poem conveyed its meaning was far more central to its value than why the poet said it, what occasioned the writing of the poem in the first place, or how readers responded to it.

Mid-century Challenges to the New Critics

Confessional Poetry. Confessional poetry presented the first significant challenge to the readings of the new critics and the writings of the high moderns. Confessional poetry brings private, personal details and issues into the public arena of poetry, often through direct addresses of the audience and the use of the first-person pronoun. As Whitman proffered his radical departure from the rhyme and rhythmically rigid poetic forms of his era, the confessional poets of the late 1950s and 1960s reacted against rigidly confined content matter established in the mainstream, academic poetry of their day. In direct violation of poetic trends and principles, confessional poets crafted poetry in which the speakerly self was very much present, very much personal and often autobiographical, focusing not on universal but extremely personal issues.

The confessional poets—often most deeply associated with Sylvia Plath (1932–1963), Anne Sexton (1928–1974), Robert Lowell, W.D. Snodgrass (1926–), Theodore Roethke, and Diane Wakoski (1937–)—popularized the practice of writing from the first person in poetry that was distinctly autobiographical, without the intervention of a poetic persona. It was not narrated upon a world stage, as many of the High Modernist epics were, but rather, it tended to focus on the poet's own life, particularly among those moments limited to the poet's immediate family or times of crisis. If under the scrutiny of the new Critics elements of "good" poems revealed issues of universal significance (itself a much contested entity), in the hands of confessional poets, national or mythic materials often revealed the poet's own emotional or mental breakdown.

This is not to say that the sole subject of confessional poetry is the self. On the contrary, poets in this movement presented poems that revealed how the personal is political. Many participants in this movement used their poetry to issue scathing critiques of American culture at the mid-century, especially those portions of culture deemed inappropriate for polite conversation or public discussion. Many critics suggest that Allen Ginsberg (1926–1997) wrote what could be identified as one of the earliest confessional poems in 1956, with "Howl," a poem that hearkens back to the rhythms of Whitman's self-described barbaric yawp and reclaims the poet's right to employ the first-person pronoun and write about personal experience, but this first-person poem reveals personal disillusionment and disaffection with empty American consumerism in the postwar era. Anne Sexton's bitter fairy-tale revisions in *Transformations* (1971) exposes the false promise of happiness in marriage, where parents are "never bothered by diapers or dust, / never getting a middle-aged spread." As described by Diane Wood Middlebrook, the work of confessional poets "investigates the pressure on the family as an institution regulating middle-class private life" (1993, 636) at a time when the nuclear family was depicted in all forms of popular culture as a source of sustenance and support.

In the poetry of the women in particular, the picture of middle-class family life contradicted the images television sitcoms and mass advertisement campaigns promoted, of the happy homemaker bedecked in a cashmere twin set and pearls and a scrubbed, cheerful family whose biggest concern was Junior's B on Friday's spelling test. The family life revealed in confessional poetry included domestic and substance abuse, mental instability, sexual promiscuity, and rage at many forms of victimization, among other topics considered taboo in polite and popular society. In fact, many young readers of confessional poetry still gravitate toward the depiction of a young woman's rage simply because it is so rare to see women's rage acknowledged at all, in Sylvia Plath's "Daddy."

The legacy of the confessional poets is enormous. Initially lambasted by the critical establishment, confessional poets soon earned the nation's most prestigious awards (W.D. Snodgrass won the Pulitzer Prize and Lowell won the National Book Award in 1960), entered the most austere anthologies, and secured a place in the canon of American poetry. Their success gave permission to all future poets to plumb their own experiences for poetic inspiration, and to complain, if need be, about those experiences. And to a large extent, much of the poetry popular with Americans since 2000 is just that: one person offering public confession of certain experiences and thoughts, sometimes without much attention to the artistry of the language. At least one critic has complained that "[t]o a large swath of the general public now, that's what poetry is" (Walker 2004, 97): confessional prose without metaphor, compression, rhythm, use of sound, or attention to language. The "autobiographical encounter," to use poet Gregory Orr's term, has become not just acceptable, but mainstream in contemporary American literature, so much so that critics still identify the demarcations in American poetry as those between confessional and avant-garde.

The other deep legacy of the confessional poets is the emphasis on voice that still predominates most discussions of poetry, both written and performed. Most poetry workshops are designed to help emergent poets discover their own voice, poets of renown are discussed according to the uniqueness of their voice, and some of the most well-respected treatises on poetry start with or emphasize the role of voice in poetry. Among the most influential of poetry critics, Helen Vendler introduced *Part of Nature, Part of Us*, her collection of essays published in 1980, with the admission that her "own preference is to focus on poets one by one, to find in each the idiosyncratic voice wonderfully different from any other," noting that what lingers in her memory of the poets are "the voices of genius" (1980, x). A later Vendler publication was titled, tellingly, *Voices & Visions*. And a 2004 review of three contemporary poets opened with "We think of ourselves as *having* voices, but these days our poets *are* voices. That is to say, the word 'voice' has come to be synonymous with the word 'poet' in all of those venues in which we discuss poetry" (Martin 2004, 34). The confessional poets ensured this continued focus on voice as something the poet develops rather than just imparts onto the poem, and its implication, then, that the voice in poetry is always also the poet's own.

Black Arts. Another important challenge both to high modernism and to the affiliation of "good" poetry with that coming from American universities surfaces in the Black Arts or Black Aesthetic movement of the 1960s. Inspired by both the successes of the civil rights movement and the radical militant stance of Black Nationalism, Black Arts emerged as a way for African American artists to pursue distinctly African American art forms. Chief among its tenets were the beliefs that one couldn't separate the artist from his or her community and that in order for African American art to flourish, it needed to develop its own aesthetic values separate and distinct from those that descended from or were rooted in European or white American art forms. It sought to provide support and space for African American artists to develop and present their art to an audience comprised of African Americans.

Poetry written by those of African descent in America, when it was discussed or published at all in mainstream presses and journals, was always presented as peripheral to the primary activities of poetic development. The chronicles of American poetic history have always ghettoized or separated out poetic schools or movements populated by significant numbers of non-white poets, and many continue to do so today. Granted, many such movements deserved discussion in their own right; however, consistently addressing African American poets under the rubric of the Harlem Renaissance, the Black Arts movement, or even under a currently popular category of black poets, serves to foster a misunderstanding about the centrality of non-white, particularly black, poets to the development and significance of the genre as a whole.

Many reference sources will devote a chapter or section to one of the two movements mentioned above but not address a single non-white poet in its pantheon of poets of import and significance. The effect of such treatment may be a false popular consensus that the poets who participated in those movements—or the black poets not specifically part of those movements—are insignificant. This exclusion of black voices and black experiences was even more pronounced in the 1960s than it is today.

An instrumental participant in and shaper of this movement, Amiri Baraka (1934–) describes in his autobiography about the moment he realized that he could never write poetry like that which the *New Yorker* published unless he were to become someone alien to himself. The language he uses focuses on how "out" he feels from this world—from the poetic world that in this country, at that time, published almost exclusively white writers. The black writers who did publish, most famously Gwendolyn Brooks, who had by that time already won a Pulitzer Prize for her poetry in 1950, were not calling attention to their art as distinctly African American art. Not yet.

Born LeRoi Jones, Baraka attended Rutgers and Howard, following which he joined the United States Air Force. He moved to Harlem shortly after the assassination of Malcolm X, where he founded the Black Arts Repertory Theatre/School and was a major force in the Black Arts' search for a distinctly Black Aesthetic. Remaining true to the notion that an artist must remain rooted in his community and create art for his people's sake, Baraka lived, worked, and performed in Harlem. The dedication to and awareness of the audience's role crucial to the development of one's art prefigures the current spoken word movement's attention to its audience. Furthermore, the Black Arts movement in general and Baraka's commitment to Harlem in particular reinforced the vibrant primary role of the urban setting in poetry. Eastern coastal cities had long been identified as meccas for poets, as centers of poetic life, but more so for the publishing houses and major universities located within than because of the distinctly urban lifestyle that fostered poetic communities, communities nourished in coffee houses and apartment meetings, in street life and in neighborhoods.

Concomitant with forging a new system of aesthetic valuations, the Black Arts movement also charted the history of art created by artists of African descent and, in so doing, established historical artistic timelines and traditions that hearkened back to African sources. Paradoxically, in examining African and African American art *in isolation* from other traditions, namely other American ones, Baraka and others reminded critics and historians of elements from Africa and African American art that are *central* to our understanding and development of American art. The spoken word has been identified (and is so here) as a revolution, yet the Black Arts movement reminds us that orality remains a cultural fixture both in the various griot traditions of oral African communities and throughout the history of African American literature.

The African griot traditions and specifically the Gicaandi competitions, as well as the tradition of the dozens among some African Americans, should be acknowledged as some of the foreparents of current slam poetry and poetry bouts. In the Gicaandi competitions, a seed-filled gourd rattled an accompaniment for the contestants, who competed against each other with songs, riddles and conundrums, wise sayings and wisecrackings, often performed by moonlight in the town square. So the audience was asked to participate in this ritual competition of verbal sparring performed rhythmically. The gicaandi, or gourd, rooted the performer to his community, as it was grown locally in special plantings. Its traditions were inherited, with a griot father teaching his son the history lessons and details of cultural importance along with all of the improvisional, performative techniques with which to craft his poetry. The griot subtly crafted each performance to match the particulars of his audience. Similarly, in the ritualized insults of the dozens, the audience is crucial as the insults are intended more for their entertainment than for the opponent's shame.

Even our current avant-garde movement, with explicit origins in the Language poetry movement (see below) must acknowledge the conceptual contribution of African American poetry, especially that which was fostered by the Black Arts movement. In its frequent employment of blues- and jazz-inspired elements in poetry, the Black Arts movement occasionally celebrated artistic elements merely for their own sake. Within jazz the celebration of sound for its own sake, in the use of scat, predates the Language poetry movement that calls heightened attention to the material of poetry—the words and even letters themselves. So the new Black Arts poets' use of and references to jazz already celebrated the material apart from its referent or its references to anything other than itself. Scat is celebration of sound as sound, not of sound as representative of something else.

Furthermore, in directing our critical gaze at the history of African American poetry, where orality reigns as *a* if not *the* dominant feature, the Black Arts artists reminded the United States of a long-established tradition of orally performed poetry that predates the current performance poetry craze. Numerous African American poets crafted poems—many of them sermons—with the intended medium of oral performance, not the silent page. James Weldon Johnson's "Creation" from *God's Trombones: Seven Negro Sermons in Verse* (1927) is one such poem that begs, even demands, to be performed. Gwendolyn Brooks coined a term, *preachment*, with which to address and discuss it; so prevalent is the sermonic mode in African American poetry. One could argue, in fact, that African American preachers are the new world equivalents of the African griots, as their community-saving roles and public language performance methods are nearly identical.

Language Poetry. Though many Americans are likely less aware of the Language poetry movement than they are of the confessional poets or Black Arts, this movement, too, has profound influence on the current trends in both academic and popular poetry, particularly in the way its approach to language in poetry has remained synonymous with the definition of avant-garde or experimental poetry. Often written out as L=A=N=G=U=A=G=E, in homage to one of the two prominent early Language poetry journals, the movement, which began in the 1970s, was enabled in part by structural theorists and linguists, who insist that and reveal how language shapes and dictates humans' perceptions of their own experiences. Like virtually all significant movements in the genre, this one challenged mainstream poetry and organized itself around a radical political stance, as its practitioners believed that traditional verse form, conventional syntax, and linear narrative—those aspects of mainstream poetry and other writing they disavowed—"transmit[ted] conservative ideologies" (Gilbert 2001, 567).

The work of such linguists as Ferdinand de Saussure, who explored the arbitrary connection between the signifier and the signified, the utterance and the referent, laid the groundwork for the philosophical underpinnings of this movement. Translated into English and made widely available in the United States in the 1950s, Saussure's work called attention to the deep structure of language (or *langue*)—the relationships and differences that govern our language rules—rather than the surface phenomena of the individual utterances (or *parole*). Since utterances (or words, signifiers) refer to the concepts they represent only by dint of social convention ("tree" represents a large organic growth composed of trunk, limbs, and foliage only because all speakers of English have agreed to relating the word "tree" to our concept of tree, not because of any inherent features of a tree in the utterance itself), we must acknowledge the arbitrary nature of the words we use to represent concepts.

From these ideas arose the theory of structuralism, a mode of interpreting meaning that searches for the underlying patterns that structure our language (and, by extension, our literature). Given the arbitrary relationship between words and concepts, structuralists posit that all patterns are those perceived by the human mind and imposed onto our language. As we learn language, we learn to privilege or recognize some differences but not others. So, a young child in early stages of vocabulary development learns to recognize the difference between dogs and cats as significant because those are the early words he learns, but those differences between a poodle and a German shepherd are coded in the language and offered to him as insignificant differences, ones not worthy of note just yet. The language, therefore, doesn't *reveal* the world to him but it *shapes* the way he perceives the world. In governing our perceptions of the world, language controls our experiences of the world.

This assertion that language structures meaning and not the other way around was crucial to the Language poets' project. The movement placed complete emphasis on the language of the poem, calling self-conscious attention to the words and letters themselves, often breaking up words to reveal smaller words subsumed within the larger ones, creating non-words, or grouping letters or symbols according to their size or shape. For example, skinny letters might form a line of poetry, like ilklih, or a poem or a line may be composed entirely of symbols, as in Armand Schwerner's (1927–99) "Tablet III," which includes the lines "+ + + + + + + + + / + + + + + + + + + + + / + + + +. . . . . tremble" (1983, 66). The poetry rarely offered what in prose would be considered complete sentences (in fact, Ron Silliman 1946–, one of Language's practitioners claimed to be part of the creation of the "new sentence") in part to remind us that poetry offers readers not someone's "voice," but someone's voice as mediated and conveyed by language. Therefore language itself is always the subject of poetry, and the word or letter alone serves as the material. Language poets could have used as their motto one of William Carlos Williams's assertions, made much earlier in *Spring and All:* "[T]he word must be put down for itself" (1923, 102). To Language poets, their strategy was simply more honest than others. They didn't pretend that there was some external idea the language was trying to convey: the language dictated the idea; the language IS the idea.

Central to the Language poetry movement was the notion of an active reader, whose action was inspired rather than hampered by what may appear as obscure poetic text. The initial barriers to understanding arising from the text's difficulty, so the practitioners argued, invited repeated returns to the text. Furthermore, in calling attention to the role of language itself in controlling and shaping meaning, poets of this movement hoped to train readers to question the agenda of their other encounters with language. Aware that language usage in popular culture directs consumer attention to just that—consumption—and away from issues that might inspire radical political action (or any political action), Language poets posited that language as used in popular culture served as a means of social control.

As scat within jazz reminded listeners that the basic material, the stuff of jazz, is sound—not music—Language poets reminded readers of poetry that the stuff of poetry is language, not meaning.

Many Language poets emphasized the human role within language development (the human process of perceiving and imposing patterns) by devising and imposing outrageous structural requirements onto their poetry. A particular success example of this is Lyn Hejinian's (1942–) *My Life*, written when she was 37 years old and comprised of 37 sections of 37 sentences each. When she revised it eight years later, she added eight sentences to each pre-existing section and an additional eight sections to represent the additional years of her life since the original publication date.

In the same way that the autobiographical, speakerly self of the confessional poet, who reports internal observations in a consistent voice, continues to be affiliated with acceptable mainstream poetry, the experimental approach espoused by Language poets that privileges attention to the medium of language itself over the relationships between language and its referents remains identified as the avant-garde. Yusef Komunyakaa (1947–) even calls such poets the "*new* avant garde, those exploratory poets . . . [who] introduce tonal and linguistic flux as the center of the poem" (1993, 15, italics mine). Komunyakaa criticizes them for what "seems" like their "attempt to undermine the importance of recent history . . . anything goes because the poet or the poem's speaker doesn't exist. It's death in language" (1993, 15).

Komunyakaa's comment embodies the dichotomy that still dominates poetic discussions. He eschews the avant-garde in favor of poetry "that embodies content"

(1993, 17). Self-referential poetry—that which uses language to call attention to its linguistic creation without offering someone's (presumably the poet's) thoughts about an event that exists beyond the poem's parameters—was not worthy of the designation best, in his opinion. His comment testifies to the power the mid-century poetic movements still wield over contemporary poetry.

Trends and Themes. As alluded to in Marvin Bell's "Yes!" above, poetry in the United States currently is enjoying a wave of popularity, as the spoken word revolution and technically savvy poets and community-builders create spaces for virtually any voice to be heard. The widespread availability of Internet access has democratized poetry as well, with ordinary Americans (some without any or much formal training in reading poetry) making public comments about some of the nation's most well-educated and well-paid critics. James Longenbach's recent book *The Resistance to Poetry* points out that there are over 300,000 Web sites devoted to poetry, and that in rankings of terms most frequently inserted into Internet search engines, the term *poetry* ranks eighth, above both *football* and the *Bible* (2004, 6). Americans can buy books of poetry online, read the collection, then return to the online bookseller to write a review of that book; and many do just that, so University of Chicago critic Harold Bloom can be identified as "grumpy" by an anonymous Amazon.com reader because of his emotionally expressive introduction to *The Best of the Best American Poetry 1988–1997*. In the same way that any consumer can describe how a certain shoe runs narrow in an online description at Zappos.com or assess a professor's grading difficulty on ratemyprofessor.com, so can ordinary readers of poetry "publish" their review of poetry and evaluate other published reviews.

Occasional Poetry and the Post-9/11 Response. The many hands that craft poetry also reinforce the many purposes of poetry, and the trend of poetry as more than aesthetic object has also marked American poetic activity since 2000. Among its supra-aesthetic roles include "its function in times of war and peace, its role in subverting dominant ideologies, its purpose in communicating the concept of American identity" (Gwiazda, 2004, 462). Perhaps no war has dominated the American imagination (not to mention electoral politics, national budget decisions, even changes to our concepts of personal liberties and acceptable intrusions in or erosions of them) as the War on Terror that emerged in the aftermath of the September 11, 2001, attacks on the World Trade Center and the Pentagon. Virginia Woolf noted during World War I that war always moves people to poetry, and the twenty-first century so-called War on Terrorism is no exception. Immediately after 9/11 our nation witnessed a renewed outpouring of poetry and a renewed faith in poetry to express our collective emotions and make the first move toward healing our sense of national or collective grief. Internet-enabled forwarding of poetry that seemed to speak to the shock of 9/11 made instant household names of poets such as W.H. Auden, whose "September 1939" shot over countless wireless connections. Numerous newspapers printed poems to the editor rather than or in addition to letters to the editor, poems which were written not for their aesthetic value but simply to convey the writer's strong emotion. So numerous are such letters that Internet Web sites devoted to bad 9/11 poems published in local newspapers emerged. Trained poets responded to 9/11 as well, with poems contributed to anthologies devoted expressly to the subject of 9/11 and with shifting poetic techniques that the poets attribute in interviews explicitly to either 9/11 or a post-9/11 world, attitude, or mentality.

Most notorious of the 9/11 poems was Amiri Baraka's. Baraka was heretofore best known for his seminal work with the Black Arts movement of the 1960s. His poem in response to the attacks, "Somebody Blew Up America," caused an uproar after he read it at the Geraldine Dodge Poetry Festival in September 2002. Several lines from this 200+-line poem were extracted as examples of Baraka's allegedly anti-Semitic stance. When the Anti-Defamation League charged Baraka with hate speech, New Jersey Governor McGreevey asked Baraka to resign his post as the state poet laureate, but Baraka refused on the grounds that his accusers were misreading his poem.

The lines purported to be anti-Semitic—"Who knew the World Trade Center was gonna get bombed/Who told 4000 Israeli workers at the Twin Towers/To stay home that day/Why did Sharon stay away?"—Baraka claims are actually an "attack" on anti-Semitism (see amiribaraka.com). His questions are rhetorical, designed to encourage the reader to question who truly knew and why those who knew did nothing.

The answer to that question, who knew?, as all of Baraka's answers, is complicated. The totality of the poem is an invective against imperialism, a litany of abuses against minorities Baraka sees as systemic in the United States, an encouragement to question how the current presidential administration has used the 9/11 attacks to pursue an agenda and pass acts such as the Patriot Act otherwise unacceptable to the American people and identified by Lyn Hejinian as "nefarious policies"; and as such, this poem is no different from the kinds of poems Baraka has written throughout his career, particularly since 1974 when he renounced his former black nationalist stance and embraced world socialism/Leninism-Marxism.

The unprecedented reliance on poetry and poets to speak for a national moment reinforces an affirmative answer to the question posed by Dana Gioia: Can Poetry Matter? American popular use of the Internet, willing attendance at spontaneous readings, the profusion of sincere if untrained poetic responses sent out for local but public view seems to repeat Marvin Bell's emphatic "Yes!"

If we are in a new Golden Age for poetry as the president of the Poetry Foundation claims, some of the supporting evidence would include the selection of various levels of poets laureate. Our nation names a national poet laureate, and 37 states name one as well. In recent years, many cities, including some mid-sized ones, have begun to name their own poet laureates. One might expect San Francisco and New York City to boast its own laureate, so married are the cities of the nation's coastal poles to our poetic traditions, but some might be surprised to learn that midwestern cities such as Kansas City, the Quad Cities, and even Grand Rapids, Michigan, have named their own poet laureate.

During their tenure as poet laureate, titleholders are charged with promoting the reading, writing, and appreciation of poetry among the public. How they do so remains up to the individual laureates. Our national poets laureate since 2000 include Stanley Kunitz (2000), Billy Collins (2001–2003), Louise Glück (2003–2004), Ted Kooser (2004–06), Donald Hall (2006–2007), and Charles Simic (2007–present).

Certainly the broadening of poetry's outreach net nourished by the various laureates is partially responsible for sustaining the country's 250 MFA (Master of Fine Arts) programs, its 500 presses and its 2000 journals that publish poetry, 1100 of them nationally circulated. Poetry has truly been wrested from the exclusive hands of the universities with successful programs like Billy Collins's (1941–) program Poetry 180. This program supplies a poem a day for high schools to share with their students on each of the 180 days of the school year. Another program designed to bring poetry to the masses is the People's Poetry Project, which brings together folk, ethnic, inner city, and literary poets as it turns Lower Manhattan into a poetry village for three days. Such programs guarantee that the future of America's poetry lies in many people's hands, if not in many elite hands.

Spoken Word Revolution. What in the late 1980s may have been identified as a trend in American poetry must by now, in 2007, be acknowledged as at least one of, if not *the* most reinvigorating forces in the genre: spoken word poetry. Spoken word is an umbrella term for poetry *performed.* It reaches its audience via oral (often also theatrical) transmission, thereby diminishing the centrality or importance of the printed word. As a performance, the poetry frequently attempts to engage its audience in ways not available through the printed medium. For example, in many poetry slams, judges of the poetry are randomly selected from the audience, or the audience's applause becomes the scoring system, with the loudest and most enthusiastic audience responses marking the winning poems. So central is the spoken word revolution to current American poetry that Roger Gilbert deemed the performance culture "the most significant development in American culture" (2001, 568) of the final two decades of the twentieth century.

Slam Poetry. The birth and growth of poetry slams, coupled with their cousins, poetry bouts, and the numerous urban venues that sprung up in support of both have welcomed those for whom academic poetry was either stale or inaccessible. Winners of and participants in the National Poetry Slam and of the now-defunct World Heavyweight Poetry Bout were and continue to be predominantly young and urban, often with working-class roots and frequently people of color. Their energy, passion, and humor make the spoken word revolution attractive to producers of visual media, and part of its swift rise to prominence must be attributed to its media coverage and savvy incorporation of and connections to other forms of media. MTV, for instance, played and plays a large role in promoting the works of particular poets, most notably perhaps of Maggie Estep (1962–), so-called poet laureate of MTV. With this coverage, winning one of these competitions could launch a poet's career, and so frequently have careers been thereby launched that now, after more than 20 years, slam poets and academic poets are, in some cases, synonymous, as the winners accept positions at prestigious universities, earn book contracts with mainstream or academic presses, and continue to win some of poetry's most coveted national (often academic) awards. Slam poets have been known to win the Yale Younger Poets Award, for instance, and Pulitzer Prize winning poets have been known to compete in slam contests.

In a local slam the rules may be determined by the organizers of the event, but in a National Slam pre-set rules govern the competition in the organizers' attempt to be fair to all contestants. All poems must be work written by the poets themselves and be read aloud in three minutes or less, with point deductions incurring incrementally for every 10 seconds the poet exceeds this time limit. No props or costumes are allowed, though some interesting debates about what constitutes either have ensued. (Apparently if a poet's bare chest can be considered a prop has yet to be definitively determined.) The five judges score each poem on a point system to reflect both the writing of the poem and its performance, with zero representing the lowest possible score and 10, the highest. The high and low scores for each poem are discarded and the rest, added together, resulting in 30 points as the highest possible score for any single poem. Judges hold their scores up on large cards, Olympic style.

All of the rules and protocols are designed to enliven the event and draw the audience into an active relationship with the poet. It is precisely this keen audience awareness that both rejuvenates the current popular perception of poetry and recalls some of the oldest forms of poetry.

Poetry slams, which celebrate spoken word poetry, descend from numerous predecessors, some of which are as old as the genre of poetry itself. The primary epics of the world (primary epic refers to an epic which exists first in oral form, as opposed to secondary epics, which exist first in written form) were originally delivered to their audiences via public, spoken performances, and these poems form the bedrock of many an academic department, course, or lecture. Within the epic tradition, bards or griots would perform the epic over numerous nights, often to his audience's participatory beat. The best bards always paid careful attention to audience, shaping the story to praise, ridicule, or otherwise add material unique to each particular performance's audience members. The rhythmic participation of the audience facilitated the community learning that was to occur during these performances, as primary epics often were used to teach the audience members their national history, instill a sense of national pride, teach them about proper modes of citizenship, and celebrate the achievements of their culture. So integral to the genre of epic poetry is its oral history that many theorists proclaimed the genre dead once it transitioned to a primarily print or literary one.

In delineating slam's predecessors, one could and ought to look to numerous sources both within and without the United States. The bardic traditions of oral societies, including Greek and African, should be noted, with both epic and lyric histories taken into account. Specific moments in American poetic history, such as Allen Ginsberg's "Howl" and Amiri Baraka's "Nation Time" come to mind, with Ginsberg's subsequent trial for obscenity foreshadowing Sarah Jones's recent run-in with the FCC over the alleged indecency of one of her performance poems/songs. The poetry happenings and open mike nights that flourished in the late 1950s and through the 1960s certainly contributed to the current atmosphere, offering the notion of spontaneous readings perhaps moderated by a skilled or entertaining emcee, welcoming anyone with courage to proclaim themselves poets and perform on-the-spot for an audience. Numerous West Indian dub poets such as Linton Kwesi Johnson (1952–) and Jean "Binta" Breeze (1956–) have been performing spontaneous, improvised, musically centered poetry that would be difficult to distinguish in some cases from performance poetry; and the Four Horsemen, a Canadian group of poets, added to an American appetite for vigorously read poetry.

What is of special interest regarding these non-Western, non-European origins of spoken word performances is that it reflects the relatively contemporary emphasis on globalization and democratization in both poetry and the world at large. As modern technologies make instant communication with virtually any part of the world a possibility for the average American, the parameters of what subject matter can enter American poetry, what constitutes a predecessor to an American poetic trend, and, indeed, who is considered an American poet constantly expand.

Despite the numerous claims of ancestry, slam poetry as its own event holds a rather specific history. Poetry slams began in 1984 with public poetry readings at the Get Me High lounge, then the Déjà vu Bar in Chicago, organized by Marc Smith. The year 1985 marked the first Uptown Poetry Slam as well as coverage by the *Chicago Tribune*, and the formation of the Chicago Poetry Ensemble, which began holding its slams in 1986 at the Green Mill, a Chicago jazz landmark. These early readings coincided with increasing national—if controversial—attention on performance art, perhaps most notable for Marc Smith when Chicago performance artist Karen Finlay lost an NEA (National Endowment for the Arts) grant for a piece in which she smeared chocolate pudding over and into her body. By 1987, Ann Arbor, Michigan, began holding its own slams, quickly followed by slams in New York City, San Francisco, and Fairbanks, Alaska. The urban movement embracing young poets was born.

Cities began sending teams to compete at what by 1991 was dubbed the National Poetry Slam. In 1992, 17 cities sent teams to the competition, including the first Native American team. Another first followed in 1993 with the first Canadian team, paving the way for additional international teams in future years. Much as winning the competition is connected to a potential future as a professional poet, the real purpose of the slams is to promote the writing, enjoyment of, and learning from poetry. The rallying cry of the competitions since 1994 has been "the points are not the point; the point is the poetry," a dictum found on the Web site and often repeated.

The energetic performances of the poets combined with the competitive atmosphere translated well into visual mediums, evidenced in 1996, when the documentary *Slam Nation* was filmed and released at the Sundance Film Festival two years later, featuring a stand-out performer from Team Nuyorican, Saul Williams (1972–). The documentary series *The United States of Poetry* and *Have You Heard the Word* aired on PBS featured slam and other competitions and helped to spread the popularity of slams even more quickly.

Nuyorican Poets Café. Founded by poet and professor Miguel Algarin in 1973, the Nuyorican Poets Café established as its mission to create a multicultural venue that both nurtures artists and exhibits a variety of artistic works. Founded close on the heels of the Black Arts movement, the Café reacted to some of the same feelings of alienation and disconnection Baraka and other black poets experienced when they assessed the contemporary American poetry scene. With prizes awarded and publications selected primarily by white men, poets whose experiences and sensibilities— as well as whose voices—were forged in multicultural settings did not view the traditional path to poetic fame as a conduit to an audience that would value their work: enter an MFA program, learn under a famous white poet, submit poetry to a contest judged by white poets, and publish your prize-winning poetry in a journal edited by a white poet and read by hundreds more of the nation's white poets.

Even more than 20 years after the Café's founding, the guest editor of one of the most successful annual poetry publications announced her strategy to correct for this "literary apartheid" (Rich, 1996, 19), and Web sites devoted to exposing the nepotism of major poetry prizes—contests which award the prize money or publication contract to the judges' students, friends, or lovers even before all the entries are read—continue to suggest an inbreeding or good old boys' (or woman's) club cultivated among the nation's elite and predominantly white MFA instructors and press editors (see Foetry.com).

The quick success of the Café is testament to the validity of its poets' perceptions. There was an audience hungry for their work, but that audience wasn't necessarily in the universities. Its constant attempt to "put the poem into action," as Algarin promised, enlivened the world of American poetry with its reminder of poetry's long relationship with the world of theatre.

This venue has become of the most recognized poetry venues of the nation, and its high profile alumni have demonstrated significant success crossing over into other artistically defined cultural arenas. Its team won the National Poetry Slam in 1996, the year *Slam Nation* was filmed. Although he was not the individual winner of that year, Saul Williams of Team Nuyorican, who is featured in the film, saw his poetic career launched. He later performed the role of an ex-con poet in the film *Slam* and has seen four of his books to print, two of them with MTV Books. The PBS series on African American art in the twentieth century, *I'll Make Me A World*, closed its six-part series with Williams reciting one of his poems, and his musical album, *Amethyst Rock Star*, has met with critical praise.

Concurrent with Marc Smith's attention to poetry slams, Terry Jacobus, a student of poets Ed Dorn (1929–1999), Robert Creeley (1926–), and Anne Waldman (1945–), began Poetry Bouts, slightly different in nature from slams. In a poetry bout, two poets clash one-on-one with each other, with one round of spontaneous composition on a topic selected at that moment. As such, the poetry bouts claim to be the origin of competitive poetics. The first bout, with Terry Jacobus pitted against Gregory Corso (1930–2001), occurred in 1981. This event, like the slam, saw phenomenally swift growth, particularly in the reputation of the poets it attracted. Made part of the Taos Poetry Circus in 1982 and continued until its demise in 2003, the World Heavyweight Poetry Bout winners have included Jimmy Santiago Baca (1952–), Saul Williams, Wanda Coleman (1946–), Simon Ortiz (1941–), Gregory Corso, Ed Dorn, Sekou Sundiata, Quincy Troupe, Jr. (1939–), Patricia Smith, Anne Waldman, and four-time winner Sherman Alexie (1966–). Many of these poets have earned crossover success in other genres, with CDs, film credits, and radio commentaries on their resumes.

Contexts and Issues

Use of Multi-Media. Sherman Alexie, Saul Williams, and Sarah Jones (1973–) are accurate representatives of the new directions poetry has taken into the worlds of performance and media other than print, as all three are successful in multiple artistic genres. Alexie continues the tradition of poetry and poets in performance, as his own tours seem more akin to stand-up comedy than they do to traditional poetry. His successful film *Smoke Signals*, a collaboration between Alexie and Cheyenne/Arapaho Indian Chris Eyre based on one of the short stories from Alexie's collection *The Lone Ranger and Tonto Fistfight in Heaven*, probably did more to bring him to the awareness of a poetry-reading public than his first two books of poetry, *The Business of Fancydancing* and *I Would Steal Horses*. Alexie also demonstrates the ability of the radical avant-garde challenger to move into positions of power and influence, with his numerous prestigious awards and academic posts. His short stories have earned selection in *The Best American Short Stories of 2004*, *Pushcart Prize XXIX of the Small Presses*, *The O'Henry Prize Stories 2005*, and he was named Artist in Residence to the University of Washington for both 2004 and 2006.

Poetry's successful marriage with the world of musical production also marks the years since 2000. Nuyorican Poetry slam winner Reg E Gaines wrote the libretto for the Broadway musical *Bring in da Noise, Bring in da Funk*. When Def Poetry Jam appeared on Broadway in the fall of 2002, it did so under the production of Russell Simmons, Def Jam recording label founder. In fact, much has been written about the black poetry to be found in rap and hip-hop, and some may suggest that to simply remove the instrumental backdrop from rap or hip-hop would result in spoken word. Despite that oversimplification, the poetic movement did and does benefit from the money and fame of the musical world. A Broadway stage alive with dancers can, indeed, put a poem into action.

Like fellow Nuyorican Poets Café poet Saul Williams, Sarah Jones enjoys success in the world of performance, even garnering a 2006 Tony Award for her one-woman show *Bridge & Tunnel*. Jones represents as well some of the connections between poetry and music. She also achieved notoriety when she successfully sued the FCC for its censorship of her song "Your Revolution," for indecency, itself a playful response to Gil Scot Herron's "The Revolution Will Not Be Televised" (Jones's chorus repeats "your revolution will not be between these thighs"). Like many of the slam poets, Jones involves herself in political and civic activism, taking up such projects as protesting discriminatory laws against women and disparities in health care practices that follow racial and ethnic lines. Her 2003 tour of *Surface Transit*, another one-woman show, frequently scheduled talkbacks and Question & Answer sessions after the performance, allowing Jones further arenas to advance her activist projects.

Protest Poetry. Sarah Jones's use of her poetic stage for a soapbox is part of a larger awareness that poetry can be and currently is an appropriate vehicle for protest. Just as each war produces its flurry of poetry that in its graphic or realistic content serves to denounce the war that produced it (one thinks of Wilfrid Owen, Siegfried Sasson, even Homer's *The Iliad*, as icons of detailed violence that laments the situations that produced them), so does war inspire protest at home.

The nations turning to poetry in the immediate aftermath of 9/11 emboldened poets to use this bright spotlight to their advantage. As the U.S. administration pushed for war, poets pushed for peace. On the eve of war in Iraq, on February 17, 2003, the Lincoln Center presented Poems Not Fit for the White House, a poetic response to the possibility of war: a resounding no.

Another vibrant protest movement is spearheaded by the People's Poetry Project, this one protesting the disappearance of the world's languages—and with it, the poetry composed in those languages—as the very technologies that increase the speed of worldwide communication also reduce the number of languages in which that communication occurs. Its Declaration of Poetic Rights and Values clearly establishes its reasons for preserving the world's oral, written, and ceremonial poetry in the language in which it was composed as part of its efforts to retain humanity's creative genius, invested in its poetry.

Culture Wars. This constellation of activities associated with the spoken word has not been without its well-heeled critics. Most famous, perhaps, is critic Harold Bloom's pronouncement that the spoken word marks the "death of art" in the *Paris Review*. However, Bloom's summation may be better understood in the context of American poetry and the culture wars.

Bloom operates from a critical position that was schooled during the New Critics' heyday, and he places a rather narrow definition onto what he would deem "good" poetry. To him, aesthetics is all, and in his determination of aesthetics, a poet's or a poem's purpose—if it is anything other than to impress the well-educated reader with its tightly controlled use of meter, rhyme, ambiguity—cannot be considered in that aesthetic evaluation. His infamous introduction to the *The Best of the Best American Poetry* reveals his belief that the United States is overrun with a culture of resentment, with angry professors leading the charge against those who would value craft. In that introduction, he hurls an angry invective against his editorial predecessor, Adrienne Rich (1929–), who, in his words, created in her edition of the series "a monumental representation of the enemies of the aesthetic who are in the act of overwhelming us. It is of a badness not to be believed, because it follows the criteria now operative: what matters most are the race, gender, sexual orientation, ethnic origin, and political purpose of the would-be poet" (1998, 16). He remarks that he could not find a single poem included in Rich's edition that was worthy of inclusion in the *Best of the Best*.

By her own admission, Rich was not seeking primarily the most aesthetically complex or pleasing poems. Her project was to include those poems that are "especially urgent, lively, haunting, resonant, demanding to be reread" (1996, 15). As Rich points out in her introduction to the *Best American Poetry* of 1996, most literary magazines in this country are edited by white men. And the list she supplies of major U.S. poetry prizes "administered largely by white judges and bestowed largely on white men" includes the Ruth Lilly Prize, Kingsley Tufts Prize, Academy of American Poets fellowship, Pulitzer Prize, and National Book Critics Circle Award (1996, 18). It is this "literary apartheid" (Rich 1996, 19) that the commitment to a multicultural venue fights.

The antagonism between Bloom and Rich should be understood in the larger context of the culture wars marking American society. The 2004 elections and the media focus on blue vs. red states reminded us that the brief moments of national unity heralded in our collective response to 9/11 were over. The culture wars suggest that what polarizes Americans are hot-button issues, with ideology rather than any factor such as religion, race, or social class acting as the divisive factor. Those who are pro-Affirmative Action are likely also pro-choice, anti-gun, environmentalists who believe global warming is a real threat and that Americans have the right to die with dignity and with medical intervention if need be. They tend to reject Intelligent Design, favor the separation of church and state, and support same-sex marriage.

Fox News commentator Bill O'Reilly calls such people Secular-Progressives and those on the other side of the ideological divide, Traditionalists. The Traditionalists are the ones engineering the backlash against such race-, gender-, class- , and sexual orientation-sensitive social movements that demanded civil rights and affirmative action. California, Washington, and, as of 2006, Michigan's so-called "Civil Rights Initiatives" ban affirmative action that given preferential treatment to groups based on race, gender, color, ethnicity, or national origin for public employment, education, or contracting purposes. Each state or city court that recognizes same-sex unions galvanizes the Traditionalists to mount a campaign for a Defense of Marriage Acts, with 40 states as of January 2007 with a DOMA on the books and resulting Web sites to keep lawyers updated on the interpretation of those acts.

Identity Politics. Bloom, Rich, and spoken word poetry fit into the culture wars with Bloom representing the Traditionalists; Rich, the Secular-Progressives; and spoken word, the ground in which the Secular-Progressives work out their identity politics. Identity politics is the practice whereby members of minority groups identify themselves according to shared discrimination they have endured as members of that group and agitate for social change based on what that discrimination has denied them. Ironically, to determine both whether or not some benefit has been systematically denied to members of that particular group and to chart progress in re- or instating those benefits requires that all members identify themselves as such. If the goal of identity politics is to level some heretofore uneven playing field (as is often the case) and erase the results of the difference that caused the unevenness in the first place, that very difference must first be marked and thereby made visible again. For example, were a university to redress the claims of lesbian faculty members that they were unfairly passed over for promotion and pay increases, that university would first need to ask all members to identify themselves according to their gender and sexual orientation, specifically marking lesbians as such. If their complaint was that their gender compounded by their sexual orientation was the difference that accounts for the pay discrepancy, that very difference would first have to be invoked in order for the effects of the institutional discrimination *because* of that difference to be reduced or erased.

As various groups organized around identity politics and agitated for inclusion in university curriculum as well as national publications, American poetry publications—both primary and secondary sources—enjoyed surges in anthologies and critical collections devoted to each minority group. This trend began with the Black Arts movement of the 1960s and the feminist movement of the 1970s, both of which sought to recover past writers either forgotten or ignored, thereby revealing or establishing a tradition of black or woman's art. Both movements also supported emergent writers, support that continues today. Each movement that organized around an aspect of identity—the American Indian Movement, the post-Stonewall gay rights groups like Act Up, for example—worked to recover and promote writers and poets who represented them and contributed to an artistic tradition that foregrounds issues of particular concern to members of that group. Their success can be measured in both the changing parameters of the national debates and, often more hopefully, in the burgeoning publications that include or focus on those issues of concern. Though civil rights and specific, legal protection for gay and lesbian Americans have been slow in coming, the ever-increasing critical attention given to poets who identify themselves (or who have been identified) as gay or lesbian testifies to the success of identity politics to bring gay and lesbian issues to the attention of our nation's scholars and students.

The annual *American Literary Scholarship* section devoted to poetry from the 1940s to the present, for example, notes that from 2001–2003, scholarship on closet lesbian Elizabeth Bishop "far exceeds that on any other poet of the period" (2003, 425). A first-rate poet of major import, Bishop's command of critical attention nonetheless is boosted by college courses devoted specifically to lesbian issues. Ask Google to find poetry anthologies with *lesbians* as a keyword and 768 hits appear. Harold Bloom and new critics would cringe at the thought of a poet's sexual orientation or a poem's subject matter serving as selection criteria for inclusion in an anthology, but they work with a limited view of poetry's purpose, particularly in the context of current American culture. Traditional views of poetry hold that its purpose, to borrow Piotr Gwiazda's descriptions, is to serve "as an object of aesthetic contemplation," whereas the secular-progressive view is that poetry may also serve as "a vehicle for social change" (2004, 462). In the years since 2000, poetry publications suggest that poetry *is* being used—frequently—by those who hope to effect change.

Reception. The questions that a student of poetry would ask now are the same questions they would ask since poetry was first spoken, or written. Is poetry primarily an oral or a written art? What is its primary purpose? Does it serve to entertain, or is its purpose to inform, educate, enrage? Should its subject remain rooted in the personal, the local, or must it move toward the oft-ridiculed "universal," or national? Is poetry now wildly popular or caught in a dismal state of affairs?

These questions are not rhetorical, nor are they simple to answer. To examine popular American poetry since 2000 is to track developments in several media that embrace and excite the young of our country and to bemoan; to roam the latest applications of the most recent technologies and to be thrown into a study of classical and pre-literate histories. The most exciting and important trends in American popular poetry continue to be the multiple manifestations of the same movement: to get poetry out of the exclusive hands of the elite and the academic and into the hands of the masses, particularly the young. The spoken word revolution dominates this trend and illustrates how poetry has reinvigorated itself by simultaneously returning to some of poetry's origins, reminding its contemporary audience that the written form is a late-comer to poetry, and capitalizing on new technologies and other forms of popular cultural media. Performance, specifically dramatic performance, as well as the celebration of sound and music that marks the world's earliest poetic forms, have been the vehicles through which countless new, young Americans have been introduced to poetry, often in flashy, slickly produced events.

Selected Authors. Any discussion of poets in a venue such as this would be ridiculously limited and revelatory of the author's own biases. This discussion will not prove an exception to that rule. However, three will be presented for their command of the critical attention and their relationship to the largest prize the world offers poets, the Nobel Prize for Literature. One, Derek Walcott, has already earned that prize; yet he remains an active poet and, according to some criteria, remains an "American" poet. The other two poets are perhaps most likely of all the American poets writing today to win the prize in the future, if critical attention is any indication.

A discussion of popular American poetry would not be complete without addressing one of the most astounding best-selling books of poetry, Derek Walcott's *Omeros*. Though one can question including Walcott in a list of "American" poets because of his birthplace, the Caribbean island of St. Lucia, by virtue of his long tenure at universities in the United States and with a broad definition of America that includes the various Americas, compounded with the amazing sales of his poetry within our country, he is an American poet to be reckoned with, publishing two books of poetry since 2000: *Tiepolo's Hound* in 2000 and *The Prodigal* in 2004.

Winner of the 1992 Nobel Prize for Literature, Walcott was born in 1930 in Castries, St. Lucia, to a schoolteacher mother and civil servant father (who died before Derek and his twin brother, Roderick, reached their second birthday). His 325-page poem, *Omeros*, published by Farrar Straus Giroux in 1990, cemented his reputation not only as the premier Caribbean poet, but also as the "very man by whom the English language lives," according to his friend and fellow Nobel-prize winning poet Joseph Brodsky. Its publication and subsequent widespread appeal are widely accepted as the catalyst for Walcott's Nobel Prize.

What astounds about Walcott's success with *Omeros* is that the brisk sales of his long and culturally dense but masterful poem testified as early as 1990 that a poetry resurgence was on its way to the United States. Perhaps only one other recent American book, Toni Morrison's *Beloved*, has so quickly entrenched itself in the canon of U.S. literature classrooms. That Walcott did so with poetry, and an epic poem no less, almost baffles the mind.

Perhaps, we can read in Walcott several trends converging to contribute to that success. Just as identity politics seems to offer a boost to some poets whose member group is currently active in the academy, demanding courses and attendant anthologies and critical scholarship to support those courses, Walcott's poem appeared two years shy of the five-hundredth anniversary of Christopher Columbus's so-called discovery of the New World. Many thinkers and cultural critics were interested in assessing the legacy of Columbus, and in the pantheon of New World voices whose very existence was forged in the often violent histories that converged on the New World between 1492 and 1992, Walcott presented an example of artistic near-perfection that even the New Critics would agree was worthy of the designation "best" poetry.

Titled with the Greek word for Homer and divided into seven books of multiple chapters each, with the first and final two books set in St. Lucia and the middle three in Africa, the United States, and Europe, the poem, like Walcott himself, contributes to a new American definition that is globally inclusive. Walcott has made much of the fact that his last name along with his brown skin and green eyes testify to his varied ancestry—Dutch, African, and British. Rather famously, one of his poems declares "either I'm nobody or I'm a nation." As his very body carries the strains of several world cultures converging upon him, so, too, does his poetry retain the several literary heritages he claims. The characters with whom Walcott populates this narrative poem further suggest the deliberate relationship between this poem and *The Iliad* and *The Odyssey* alluded to in the poem's title.

Walcott also embraced several genres, notably poetry and drama, at a time when poetry reinvigorated itself by reminding its audience of its dramatic roots. Walcott began his career as a playwright, with his earliest writing successes in drama. He spent many years nourishing the Trinidad Theatre Workshop, which he founded and for which he wrote his early plays; and his first post-Nobel publication was a stage version of *The Odyssey*, his Caribbean-infused reworking of Homer's text, composed primarily in verse. The Stratford Festival of Ontario, Canada, is staged this play for its 2007 season. And like some of his younger poetic contemporaries, he has also made forays into musical theatre, though with rather disastrous results: his longtime collaboration with Paul Simon on *Capeman* resulted in a financial flop. He has even included his own watercolor paintings as cover art and within his books of poetry.

The contemporary avant-garde, the exploratory poets for whom language itself is both barrier to understanding and stuff of meaning, can find much in Walcott's poetry to admire. For Walcott the poet, among the maladies cured by the convergence of cultures in the Caribbean is no less than the problem of language. Often questioned for his apparent bifurcated devotion to the Caribbean as a place on the one hand and the language and literary traditions of Western Europe on the other, Walcott asserts in *Omeros* his right to all of the beauties of the English language, described in his earlier poem "A Far Cry from Africa" as "the English tongue I love." In *Omeros* Walcott writes that "this language carries its cure" (1990, 323).

Most notable may be that near the millennium's end, with one decade remaining, Walcott offered up what he has described as a love poem to St. Lucia, his home island, that simultaneously serves as an epic reassessment of Caribbean culture. The astoundingly beautiful and technically perfect poetry contained in this assessment celebrates the achievements of those in the Caribbean who, in the words of the poem, "walked. / They survived. There is the epical splendour." When Walcott uses his poetry to "give those feet a voice," his vision transforms a history built on pain and forced migration, marked by poverty, into a testament of beauty.

The poets since 2000 who continue to garner the most critical attention and praise—those most likely identified as The Major Poets compared to the merely influential poets or A Major Poet—remain those in the inclusive, paratactic tradition of Whitman and Williams. Our current poets who practice a both/and form of poetics, who, in Vernon Shetley's words, "find some kind of middle way between the alternatives of a poetry descended from Eliot . . . [and] oppositional politics of a figure like Ginsberg" (1993, 16–17) are those who remain our most interesting, our most significant.

Jorie Graham. One of the most exciting and prolific of those poets is Jorie Graham (1951–), longtime faculty member of the Iowa Writers' Workshop now at Harvard. Like the most profound American poets, Graham deftly and masterfully dances the line that so often has divided poetry, redefining the dichotomy often aligned over the absence or presence of the poem's speakerly self, the impersonal poem against the personal, the confessional mode in which the poet-as-I reveals the self arrayed against the avant-garde mode in which issues of the poet's voice become obsolete as language itself is presented as the only material of poetry. Kirstin Hotelling Zona describes this as Graham's "dance between autonomy and contingency" (2005, 669)—the poetic self that shapes its destiny only as it realizes its dependence upon and existence only within the contexts of relationships. Graham crafts a poetic persona hungry for meaning, and presents that persona in the act of creating that meaning, simultaneously embracing and abjuring the power and responsibility involved in the act of making that meaning. Like Whitman, she fuses features from both sides of the poetic divide, "locat[ing] writerly authority not in the ruptured referent, nor in the lyric 'I' who appears to choose one action over another, but in the play *between* these positions—between presence and absence, desire and dislocation—from which the 'I' emerges" (Zona 2005, 670).

Graham's nine books of poetry, three since 2000, and her resume of achievements have secured her position as Major Poet. Following a trilingual childhood abroad, Graham earned a BA from New York University (1973) and an MFA from Iowa (1978). She has earned an Academy of American Poets Prize, a Whiting Award, and a Pulitzer (for *Dream of a Unified Field*), and been awarded both a Guggenheim fellowship and an NEA grant. Even when critics pen mixed reviews of her books, they are forced to admit the intellectual rigor and the beautiful poetics that mark her writing, as well as the uncanny way she locates her work at the nexus of the debate about poetry, embodying the oppositions and making out of them poetry that unites previously separated worlds. James Longenbach identifies her "acts of inclusion" as the defining feature of her distinct voice and formidable achievements, referring to various, often opposing, poetic traditions infused into her poetry.

From Graham's debut book of poetry, *Hybrids of Plants and Ghosts* (1980) to *Never* (2002), what many critics have noted is the range of Graham's poetry. Each book takes a new direction, sometimes to the bafflement or consternation of critics who enjoyed the poetics of the previous one. Especially laudatory readings have been published in two of the most prestigious literary journals since 2000, one in *PMLA* and another in *Contemporary Literature*, and one of the nations most formidable poetry critics, Helen Vendler, makes Graham one of three poets who are the subject of a recent book.

Graham has said that she writes for the "harried" reader and much has been said about her "breathless" lines, both of which might yield an impression of a poetic world crowded with images or hurried in its presentation. But Graham is also an unceasing advocate for poetry—revealed both by the unflagging interest in and encouragement to the younger poets she teaches, and in her undogged defense of the art. She appears to bristle in interviews only when poetry is identified as marginal and when questions about the proliferation of bad poetry are posed. Her emphasis on the ways poetry can put us in contact with sets of values not affiliated with other forms of learning—how it can inspire curiosity, teach ambiguity—makes her a champion of all forms of poetry. Only in the economic sense, she insists, is poetry marginal, and she suggests that economic value holds little real value to that associated with the heart's knowledge.

Another prolific poet whose command of critical attention derives from her mastery of both sides of a poetic divide is Louise Glück (1943–). Former poet laureate and winner of most prizes awarded to poets, including a Pulitzer in 1993, the Academy of American Poets Prize, the Sara Teasdale Memorial Prize, Glück's poetic hallmarks include archetypal symbolism, mythic subject matter, formal experimentation, and the use of epic material in poetry that foregrounds "the personal, the occasional, the interior" (Murnaghan and Roberts, 1992 4). As is the case with Jorie Graham, however, Glück's poetry evades all categories set to it. Her "need to resist [the closed self's] seduction is her great theme," writes James Longenbach in 2004. Like Plath, who employs myth to embody a personal or speakerly self in the poetry, Glück eschews both confessional and intellectual traditions at the same time that her poetry toys with them. Her poetry is simultaneously personal and distant from the persona, with classical figures such as Penelope and Odysseus representing a contemporary couple caught in the process of a dissolving marriage, as is the case in her 1996 collection *Meadowlands*.

Her most recent poetry collection, *Averno* (2006) may indeed be her "masterpiece," as the *New York Times Book Review* announces, a collection that announces Glück's self-positioning with the world's most notable poets (the title refers to the Italian lake that ancient Romans believed ran to the underworld, immortalized in Virgil's *Aeneid*). The poems in this collection promise to reveal "a theory that explains everything," yet that theory comes from the persona of the poet who takes "it upon myself / to become an artist, / to give voice to these impressions."

The frequency with which these three poets publish and, even more so, command critical attention suggest that they are the future of American academic poetry. The future of American popular poetry lies with us all.

Bibliography

Algarin, Miguel, and Bob Holman, eds. *Aloud: Voices from the Nuyorican Poets Café*. New York: Henry Holt, 1994.

Baraka, Amiri. "Somebody Blew Up America." http://www.counterpunch.org/poem1003.html.

Bell, Marvin. "The Poetry Scene: No One Way." In *The Spoken Word Revolution: Slam, Hip-hop, & the Poetry of a New Generation*. Mark Eleveld, ed. Naperville, IL: Sourcebooks, 2003.

Bloom, Harold. "Introduction." *The Best of the Best American Poetry 1988–1997*. New York: Scribners, 1998.

Gilbert, Roger. "Contemporary American Poetry." In *A Companion to 20th Century Poetry*. Neil Roberts, ed. Oxford: Blackwell, 2001.

Gioia, Dana. *Can Poetry Matter?: Essays on Poetry and American Culture*. St Paul, MN: Graywolf, 2002.

Glück, Louise. *Averno*. New York: Farrar, Strauss, Giroux, 2006.

Graham, Jorie. "The Glorious Thing: Jorie Graham and Mark Wunderlich in Conversation." Interview with Mark Wunderlich. *American Poet*. (Fall 1996): 20–23.

———. *Hybrids of Plants and Ghosts*. Princeton, NJ: Princeton University Press, 1980.

———. *Never*. New York: Ecco, 2002.

Gwiazda, Piotr. "The Aesthetics of Politics/The Politics of Aesthetics: Amiri Baraka's 'Somebody Blew Up America.'" *Contemporary Literature* 45.3 (2004): 460–485.

Hass, Robert. "Introduction." *Best American Poetry 2001*. New York: Scribners, 2001.

Have You Heard the Word? TV Ontario, 1994.

Hejinian, Lyn. "Introduction." *Best American Poetry 2004*. New York: Scribners, 2004.

Kearful, Frank. "Poetry: The 1940s to the Present." *American Literary Scholarship*. Durham, NC: Duke University Press, 2003, 425–474.

Komunyakaa, Yusef. "Introduction." *Best American Poetry 2003*. New York: Scribners, 2003.

Lehman, David. "Forward." *Best American Poetry 2002*. New York: Scribners, 2002.

Longenbach, James. *Modern Poetry After Modernism*. New York and Oxford: Oxford University Press, 1997.

———. *The Resistance to Poetry*. Chicago and London: University of Chicago Press, 2004.

Martin, Charles. "The Three Voices of Contemporary Poetry." *The New Criterion* 22.8 (April 2004): 34–37.

Middlebrook, Diane Wood. "What Was Confessional Poetry?" In *The Columbia History of American Poetry*. Jay Parini, ed. New York: Columbia University Press, 1993.

Murnaghan, Sheila and Deborah H. Roberts. "Penelope's Song: The Lyric Odysseys of Linda Pastan and Louise Glück." *Classical and Modern* Literature 22.1 (1992): 1–33.

"The People's Poetry Language Initiative: A Declaration of Poetic Rights and Values." People's Poetry Project. http://peoplespoetry.org.

Rich, Adrienne. "Introduction." *Best American Poetry 1996*. New York: Scribners, 1996.

Schwerner, Armand. *Sounds of the River Naranjana & THE TABLETS I–XXIV*. Barrytown, NY: Station Hill, 1983.

Shetley, Vernon. *After the Death of Poetry: Poet and Audience in Contemporary America*. Durham, NC: Duke University Press, 1993.

The United States of Poetry. Washington Square Films, 1996.

Vendler, Helen. *The Breaking of Style: Hopkins, Heaney, Graham*. Cambridge, MA: Harvard University Press, 1995.

———. *Part of Nature, Part of Us*. Cambridge, MA: Harvard University Press, 1980.

———. *Voices & Visions*. New York: Random House, 1987.

Walcott, Derek. *Omeros*. New York: Farrar, Straus, Giroux, 1990.

———. *The Prodigal*. New York: Farrar, Straus, Giroux, 2004.

———. *Tiepolo's Hound*. New York: Farrar, Straus, Giroux, 2000.

Walker, Jeanne Murray. "A Comment on the State of the Art: Poetry in 2004." *Christianity and Literature* 54.1 (Autumn 2004): 93–110.

Williams, William Carlos. *Spring and All. 1923. Imaginations*. New York: New Directions, 1970.

Zona, Kirstin Hotelling. "Jorie Graham and American Poetry." *Contemporary Literature* 46.4 (Winter 2005): 667–687.

Further Reading

African-American Review 37.2–3 (Special Issue on Amiri Baraka); Arp, Thomas, and Greg Johnson, eds. *Perrine's Sound and Sense: An Introduction to Poetry*. Tenth edition. Boston, MA: Heinle & Heinle, 2002; Brown, Fahamisha Patricia. *Performing the Word: African American Poetry as Vernacular Culture*. New Brunswick, New Jersey, and London: Rutgers University Press, 1999; Glazner, Gary Mex, editor. *Poetry Slam: The Competitive Art of Performance Poetry*. San Francisco: Manic D P, 2000; Otten, Thomas. "Jorie Graham's ___s." PMLA 118 (2003): 239–253; Perloff, Marjorie. "William Carlos Williams." *Voices and Visions*. 157–203; poets.org.

MICHELLE DEROSE

R

REGIONAL FICTION

Definition. In his essay, "The Regional Motive," novelist, essayist, poet, and environmentalist Wendell Berry confesses that he knows "no word that is more sloppily defined . . . or more casually understood" than "regionalist" (Berry 1972, 63). Because it lacks intellectual dimensions, the "regional" label leaves a writer feeling branded and embarrassed. The label is more embarrassing than other modifiers of contemporary American fiction writers because it implies that the writer is either a mouthpiece for over-storied regions (such as New England, the South, Appalachia, or the Midwest) or a fetishizer of the remains of rurality in America. Forced to negotiate received notions of places and vernacular expression, regionalists confront a dialectic clash between preservation and renewal. The most innovative regional fiction defies the traditional iconography of standard regions, disturbs reader expectations about vernacular expression, and dismantles encyclopedic ownership of place.

With this progressive agenda, it would seem that regional fiction is beginning to merge with "literary fiction," with its focus on the larger cultural and human problems often eclipsed by excessive interest in local detail. However, the entire genre of regional fiction, from the most traditional to the most innovative texts, retains an adverse relationship to official literary culture for a couple of reasons. First, as Marilynne Robinson indicates, the very existence of a "regional" category reveals "a cultural bias that supposes books won't be written in towns you haven't heard of before" (qtd. in Kowalewski 2003, 7). Secondly, regional fiction has internalized the distinction between regional and non-regional writing insofar as it elevates the importance of place over its mere necessity as a background upon which to stage a character's psychological development or "soul search." In this sense, regional fiction has the potential to destabilize the distinction between setting and narrative voice. On the other hand, there remains a nostalgic model of regional fiction, which preserves vernacular relics for no other reason than that they are scarce. In this sense, regional fiction is either dismissed or revered as a genre purporting to contain "authentic" representations of rural places and folk wisdom. To a large degree, regional fiction is persistently popular because, in America, the question of authenticity is asked on so many fronts.

For instance, in November 1998, the State Department issued a publication entitled *Outline of American Literature*, the final section of which was entitled "The New Regionalism." This section of the publication claims that regionalism is making "a triumphant return in American literature, enabling readers to get a sense of place as well as a sense of time and humanity" (*Outline*, 1998). Similarly, but on a more literary front, Joyce Carol Oates has recently called the regional voice the universal voice. Her prose poem "My Faith as a Writer," printed in the front matter of her collection of craft essays, *The Faith of a Writer* (2003) and reprinted on her lecture tour pamphlets, reads as follows:

> Through the local or regional, through our individual voices, we work to create art that will speak to others who know nothing of us. In our very obliqueness to one another, an unexpected intimacy is born.
>   The individual voice is the communal voice.
>   The regional voice is the universal voice. (Oates 2003, 2)

Even in her introduction to the *Oxford Book of American Short Stories*, Oates answers the question "Is American literature at its core a literature of regions?" in the affirmative, asserting that contemporary writers resemble one another "along lines that have less to do with traditional American themes than with . . . highly specific, brilliantly realized American places" (Oates 1992, 15).

This curious endorsement from both the federal government and the literati indicates that the question of region is important to both the political and cultural engines of American public opinion. As the State Department publication indicates, regional fiction is popular because it "enables" curious readers to assume a "sense of place." It thus facilitates a manner of thinking territorially, which helps explain why the State Department has a stake in its comeback. Regional fiction is also, as Oates indicates, a fiction that builds cosmopolitan and humanist connections from the raw materials of the unique timbres of our own voices. It is uniquely "American," these claims suggest, to think territorially and to think that specificity is a pathway to universal, trans-territorial, humanity. Like Whitman, whose careful inventory of body parts "sings the body electric," the regional fiction writer uses the specificity of place to generate tangible patterns of commonality.

Regional fiction became popular in American literature in the late nineteenth century, primarily as a category of realism devoted to representing local specificity. The genre, usually understood as "quaint" representations of places outside the beltway of industrial progress, satisfies reader fantasies about a preindustrial past. Originally solicited elite periodicals, such as *The Atlantic Monthly*, regionalism entered literary history as a genre whose subject (people and places untouched by national standardization) serves a social need (to pacify anxiety about rapid standardization). As Stephanie Foote argues, this category of realism gained popularity because it "represented various sections of the consolidating nation to an audience that was conscious of itself as a national elite" (Foote 2001, 4). In other words, regional fiction allowed middle-class urban readers to think that the disappearance of locally diverse rural communities was part of a natural progression, not a revisable byproduct of industrial progress. Late-nineteenth century regional fiction was remarkably anti-modern. Its stories were set outside the patterns of industrial progress, in what Brodhead calls "zone[s] of backwardness where locally variant folkways prevail" (Brodhead 1994, 150). In this sense, regionalism can be defined as a form of cultural incubation, wherein literary representation preserves the cultures and landscapes threatened by the ongoing procession of modern progress. In the late twentieth century, regional fiction has achieved a renaissance of popularity. The reason is similar; contemporary globalization has introduced another concentric circle by comparison to which the value of the smaller, tangible spheres to which people actually feel the bond of affiliation appear to be in jeopardy.

A definitional obligation to address early in explaining regional fiction is the distinction between "regionalism" and "local color." Where literary regionalism refers to literature that is specific to a particular set of geographical coordinates, local color is a feature of realism that facilitates the production of regional fidelity. Local color differs from realist representation in that it "subordinated plot to the revelation of personality . . . capture[d] the speech patterns of unlettered Americans . . . [and] distinctly rejected any sense of capturing Truth" (Nagel 1997, xxii). Local color, then, is a representational tool that facilitates regional fiction. Though it is possible to *do* local color without writing a regional text, it is impossible to read a regional text that is devoid of local color. Local color is basically a mode of realism that captures the peculiarities local to places outside the literary mainstream, a mode of representation that highlights the specificity of places not yet on literary maps. As Hamlin Garland explains, "Local color in a novel means that it has such quality of texture and back-ground that it could not have been written in any other place or by any one else than a native" (Garland 1894, 53–54).

The formal properties of regional fiction are (1) a setting that is outside the world of modern development but whose existence is in some discernible way being threat-ened by modern development, (2) the inclusion of characters and cultural features that personify some form of humanity that has been sacrificed in the name of progress, and (3) a concerted effort to employ local knowledge and to textualize the peculiarities local to the region in which the piece is set. For instance, vernacular dialect and "foreign" cultural traditions are often a focus of regional fiction.

Considering these defining properties, many see regional fiction as engaging in conservative cultural work. Looking at the same characteristics, others argue that regional fiction resists unchecked modernization. Recently scholars have argued that what looks like nostalgia is in fact the type of anti-modern ambivalence that drives literary modernism. The difference between modernism and regionalism, though one sees few differences after reading Sherwood Anderson's *Winesburg, Ohio* (1919), is the obvious preference in the latter for realist representation. In addition, regional fiction differs from modernist anti-modernism in that its moral urge is similar to that of nature writing. Regional fiction is now studied as a genre that synthesizes the clashes of opposing concepts such as "city" and "country," "center" and "margin," "tradition" and "modernity," even "masculinity" and "femininity." Instead of favoring one or another side (i.e., leaning too conspicu-ously in the direction of conserving rural values), regional fiction oscillates between sides, producing a symphony of voices and positions whose source of resolution is the reader-writer agreement to survey the whole scene. Regionalism thus treats the delicate textures of its subject gently, sharpening them by emphasizing the contrasting hues needed to represent "the local." This means that the narrator's process of encountering a specific region becomes a process of balancing different perspectives on culture, of accommodating the concentric circles of human affiliation.

Finally, then, regional fiction, regardless of the historical period it is produced in, is an arm of realism that captures the spirit of place. Its practitioners assume that there is enough aesthetic value in specific soil to sustain the art of fiction. Sometimes excessively limited in focus, regional fiction seems conspicuously interested in reinforcing the special existence or value of what is off the beaten path. More specifically, literary works that stay within the lines of region seem to neglect or eclipse the greater social and human issues to which literature is supposed to respond. However, the proponents of regional fiction argue that it represents the confluence between who and where human beings are in the world. Its limited focus, like that of pastoral poetry, induces "universal" themes and resemblance from the grainy details of the local.

History. There is some debate regarding which is the earliest work of regional fiction; the regional coordinates and literary form of each disputed work indicate much about the bifurcated history and development of the genre. Some critics cite the first Southwest humorist work, Augustus Longstreet's *Georgia Scenes* (1835), as the first book-length regional work. Other critics agree that Harriet Beecher Stowe's first novel, set in Maine, *Pearl of Orr's Island* (1862), was the first regional offering. It is generally agreed, however, that the publication of Mark Twain's humorous sketch, "The Celebrated Jumping Frog of Calaveras County" (1865) in New York's *Saturday Press*, and Brett Harte's frontier sketches published in the *Overland Monthly* (1868–1870) inaugurate the "heyday" of regional fiction in America. It would appear, then, that the masculine-inflected, frontier humor sketches were the agenda-setting texts of regional form, and that the serene sketches of the New England countryside represent a second tier of regional form.

However, this master narrative has been revised in recent years, as the early works of Twain and Harte have become attached to the histories of **adventure fiction** and **Western literature** more so than to regional fiction. This is true especially in the wake of feminist revision of regional history. In the 1970s and 1980s, feminist literary critics claimed regional fiction as a "woman's genre," beginning the history of the genre in New England, concentrating mostly on the work of Sarah Orne Jewett. In fact, the first publications of prominent feminist literary critics such as Elizabeth Ammons, Josephine Donovan, Ann Douglas, Judith Fetterley, Marjorie Pryse, and Alice Hall Petry were on the subject of Jewett's New England fiction. This feminist reclamation seems counterintuitive, since the genre's "miniaturism, descriptiveness, and domesticity bears the hallmarks of the dominant nineteenth-century gender ideology, specifically the notion of separate spheres and the dismissal of most women's writing as merely ornamental" (Ammons and Rohy, 1998, xviii). Even after considering the impact of feminist criticism on the history of the genre, any history of regional fiction must begin not by choosing to link the genre to either New England domestic realism or Southwest humorism, but by acknowledging the institutional origins of this bifurcation and gauging the development of regional fiction from within these competing historical narratives.

In *Reading for Realism*, Nancy Glazener argues that regional fiction gained popularity through the efforts of a conglomeration of literary institutions. The "*Atlantic* group," as Glazener calls it, "shared contributors . . . endorsed each other's authority, and based that authority in similar understandings of class-inflected cultural trusteeship" (Glazener 1997, 257). Glazener reveals the meta-editorial chatter among these periodicals, which sought to define fiction written in America as uniquely "American." *Atlantic*-group editors (not the least of which is William Dean Howells) have faith in the ability of regional fiction to, as Foote characterizes it, "construct versions of local culture that can coexist peacefully in a single political entity" (Foote 2001, 9). Yet, as Foote further argues, this faith "conceals, as regionalism itself will, the absence of certain kinds of local cultures, identities, and accents" (9). The primary cultures, identities, and accents that these editors concealed are obviously those which cannot "coexist peacefully," those that do not ultimately bend regional fiction around a nationalist project.

A byproduct of this exclusionary literary nationalism, argues Donna Campbell, is what an 1897 *Atlantic Monthly* editorial terms the "Feminine Principle" and "Masculine Principle" of American fiction. This division is similar to the traditional understanding of the split between domestic local color and untamed naturalist fiction. As Campbell explains, a gendered logic is built into regional fiction. The *Atlantic* editorial, written by novelist James Lane Allen, explains that naturalist writers rebel against the popularity of preservation-centered realism. They dislike, among other things, the assumption that preserving local variance is inherently a good idea. Campbell provides an insightful reading of Stephen Crane's story, "The Monster," as naturalist fiction that deliberately subverts regional conventions in order to expose the conservative logic of regionalism's popularity. Crane's setting, a small town that has lost its economic reason for being, features a self-destructive man on the verge of disaster, for whom small-town rituals are a source of anger and oppression. Presenting local color this way, Crane dramatizes the impulse toward violent self-destruction that has long loomed under the surface of even the most innocuous regional fiction.

New England Regionalism. More important than Crane's critique of regional fiction is Edith Wharton's more popular and fully realized critique in *Ethan Frome* (1911), in which Wharton portrays local knowledge as the raw material of self-destruction. In the famous penultimate scene, Ethan and his star-crossed lover steer their sleigh down a hillside in bucolic Starkfield, Massachusetts, straight into an elm tree. This suicide collision marks the beginning of an ongoing critique of nostalgic representation of rural America. It is Wharton's effort, in her words, to "contradict the 'rose and lavender' pages of native writers . . . Mary Wilkins [Freeman] and Sarah Orne Jewett" (qtd. in Hamblen 1965, 239). *Ethan Frome* is thus a "blackly comic joke, a vision of the genre so extreme as to border on private parody" (Campbell 1997, 172). By using the standard trappings of New England local color (the sleigh, the snowy hill, the innocent lovers) as the instruments of violence, Wharton "confronts local color fiction on its own terms . . . disrupt[ing] and transform[ing] its narrative conventions," ultimately revealing that regions can be crippled by their own quaintness (162). Wharton hopes her anti-local color will catch on as the New England fiction writer's "siren-subject"; she hopes regional writers will answer her prefatory call to crash their "cockle-shell to the rocks," meaning to abandon the "woman's work" of representing the delicate, irrelevant hues of New England (*Ethan Frome*, vii). Wharton's Fromes are deliberately colorless, characters she describes as "scarcely more articulate" than "granite outcroppings" (Wharton 1911, vii). They are recounted through the detached sobriety of an outsider narrator, or "looker-on with scope enough to see it all, to resolve it back into simplicity" (viii–ix). Wharton thus replaces interest in the delicate, exotic, and endangered details of regional difference with a crude formal essentialism wherein difference is reduced to proto-elemental categories like soil and rock. Fetterley and Pryse criticize Wharton for having "treat[ed] regionalism with extreme hostility" (Fetterley and Pryse 2003, 58). But Wharton was hostile not toward regional fiction in general, only toward the fact that popular regional fiction was "[s]uffocatingly claustrophobic; utterly regressive; filled with meaningless whining drone voices of women incapable of development" (58).

In short, Wharton was no fan of the "Feminine Principle." This isn't a surprise, especially considering that her strong suit is the urban social fiction. As Fetterley and Pryse imply, Wharton's New England novellas (which include *Frome* and *Summer* [1917]) read as cautionary tales that warn women writers against market expectations that require them to write nostalgic portrayals of rural America. But they are produced with a fairly standard representational objective. In Wharton's words, her novellas "draw life as it really was in the derelict mountain regions of New England," a life "utterly unlike that seen through the rose-coloured spectacles of my predecessors" (qtd in Fetterley and Pryse 2003, 58). Wharton's critique of rose-colored regionalism is a critique of the kind of reader interest in representations of New England that find roses and lavender where there is only stark granite. The effect of contradicting the "'rose and lavender' pages" of Jewett and Freeman reveals a key moral tension of regional fiction.

Wharton's heartbreaking hues have inadvertently inspired writers to turn to New England for tragic plotlines and even horror. Even the recent State Department publication has taken note of this phenomenon in new regionalism, citing Joyce Carol Oates's "haunting works" of the northeast United States whose "obsessed characters' attempts to achieve fulfillment within their grotesque environments lead them into destruction" (*Outline*, 1998). The publication also notes the fact that Stephen King "generally sets his suspenseful page-turners in Maine—within the same region." Also in Maine, recent novelist G.K. Wuori has started to receive recognition for his short story collection, *Nude in the Tub* (1999), and novel, *An American Outrage* (2000), about the north woods of Quillifarkeag, Maine. According to Kent Ryden, the New England of recent regional fiction is a place "where moral corruption and violence hide behind a static surface" (Ryden 2003, 206). Wharton likely did not intend to replace nostalgic representations with horrifying representations of the New England region. Instead, she seems to have wanted to point out that the basic presuppositions of regional fiction are problematic. The fact that an entire (mostly female) faction of writers somehow depend upon the survival of backwards folkways is troubling to Wharton for obvious reasons. A less obvious problem that writers like Wharton have with the nostalgia tradition is that it makes inventories of provinciality mean as much as, if not more than, the larger cultural or human problems that take root in rural regions.

Since Wharton, much has happened to literary New England. It has become, through Robert Frost's poetry, the site of "the social and emotional costs of living in a poor and declining part of the country"; it has been allegorized by Thornton Wilder's *Our Town* (1938) as "the imaginative property of the entire nation" (Ryden 2003, 206–208). But anyone who has read Stephen King's Castle Rock novels knows that the unseemly side of rural New England is the most enduring in popular fiction. King's horror parallels that of H.P. Lovecraft, as both draw their horror from their native knowledge of place. Both fuse and reuse real historical locations and fictional New England locations. Lovecraft explains his interest in New England by claiming the "night-black Massachusetts . . . is material for a really profound study in group neuroticism; for certainly, none can deny the existence of a profoundly morbid streak in the Puritan imagination" (qtd. in Joshi and Cannon 1999, 2). King, along with Russell Banks, Richard Russo, and lesser-known contemporaries like Ernest Hebert and Wuori, flock to New England settings for similar reasons. This "group neuroticism" has become absorbed into a fiction of isolated, self-destructive blue-collar males. Whether probing the psychic contours of such men or writing plainly of the topology of the region, contemporary New England writers always demonstrate a self-evident correspondence between the region and its wrecked lives. Tragic antiheros are matters of fact, lives that, like the Puritan culture that once ruled the region, have already ended and are told just to get the record straight, to continue Wharton's revision of regional fiction to include the violent impulses indigenous to the American landscape.

Trends and Themes. Though the legacy of New England regionalism is evident in many recent works of fiction, most contemporary regional fiction has more in common with the other side of the original bifurcation in regional fiction, that of the Southwest humorist tradition. New England fiction, and perhaps more importantly scholarship about New England regionalists, has helped the genre mature and develop beyond the nostalgia model. However, New England regionalism tends to focus too heavily on the life and death of a single endangered culture. This mono-cultural thematic center has lost resonance in a literary marketplace eager to absorb the multicultural complexities dramatized in the fiction of Julia Alvarez, Sandra Cisneros, Oscar Hijuelos, Maxine Hong Kingston, Chang-Rae Lee, Leslie Marmon Silko, and Amy Tan. As Dwight MacDonald forecasts in his polemic "Masscult and Midcult" (1961), New England has been "pushed aside by history" and has since the mid-twentieth century been slowly "dwindling to provincial gentility" (MacDonald, 1961, 34–35). In the wake of losing New England as a cultural center of American thought and letters, America's "pluralistic culture" finally becomes realized in the 1960s (35). This pluralism makes the organizing tension of New England fiction, namely that between rurality and urbanity, seem outmoded and of no concern to the larger polity. The obsolescence of New England is contested in the fiction of Anne Tyler, Russell Banks, Richard Russo, and others, but only to the extent that the economic problems facing New England are the problems of America at large. As opposed to the New England strand of regional history, the Southern and Western strand produced some of the earliest examples of cross-cultural contact in regional fiction. From Joel Chandler Harris's racially problematic "Uncle Remus" sketches to George Washington Cable's epic portrait of Creole culture, *The Grandissimes* (1880), fiction of the American South has simultaneously highlighted regional fidelity and dramatized cross-cultural tensions. This fiction is thus thematically more in touch with multicultural America and therefore is a more viable progenitor of fiction in today's era of globalization.

Southern Regionalism. The fiction of the American South is the ideal case study of parallel development of regional fiction and multiculturalism. Indeed, as Andrew Hoberek indicates, literary critics are starting to ask whether "southern literature might be understood as the origin of American multiculturalism and identity politics" (Hoberek, 2000). However, in his survey of contemporary Southern and Western fiction, Robert Brinkmeyer asks the crucial question: "Should we, in these days of the global village of cyberspace, do away with the designation 'Southern' and stop worrying about literary classifications grounded in place and region?" (Brinkmeyer 2000, 3). Though the reasonable answer seems to be yes, scholars of

Southern fiction still focus their inquiries on motifs of place. Such scholarship is problematic when it refuses to acknowledge modern realities, such as the fact that agricultural references to the South as the "Cotton Belt" are less accurate than the corporate reference "Sun Belt." Motivated by nostalgia for a monocultural Southern community, some Southern literary scholarship often clings to the idea that the South is immune to the standardizing effects of corporate capital. On the other hand, some contemporary Southern writers rely too heavily on historical designations such as "Old South" and "New South" to exorcise the troubling ancestors from their regional lineage.

Eudora Welty, Flannery O'Connor, Walker Percy, and Wendell Berry have contributed the most substantial battery of essays on the trend of viewing regional fiction, multiculturalism, and identity politics as parallel phenomena. Welty and Percy represent opposite extremes of the argument, expressing conflicting ideas about the virtues of place-based multiculturalism. Welty sees the regionalist framework of her fiction as an intuitive site for interracial encounter. Her late fiction, most notably *The Optimist's Daughter* (1972), uses this specificity of place not to defend against postmodern spatial amnesia, but to put local-level knowledge and power in the service of larger-scale forms of intimacy. Percy, on the other hand, is reluctant to embrace place and local-level racial tensions. Being more interested in existential and psychological themes, Percy sees place as an accident of birth. His essay "Why I Live Where I Live" explains that the importance of geographical location will diminish as the age of postmodern consumerism takes root, especially considering that most Americans find themselves living in the "nonplaces" of American suburbs. Indeed, Percy's confession that Dixie beer is the only outlet for "authentic" local knowledge of New Orleans for those who live in the satellite suburb of Covington, LA, indicates that, if uninterested in wrestling with enduring historical and racial tensions, there's little reason to write about the South anymore.

Obviously, not all contemporary Southern writers share Percy's pessimism about the bankruptcy of Southern soil. Many think that the Southern writer has an obligation to the legacy of Southern history. Berry, for instance, sees the debate over Southern regionalism as having both political and aesthetic repercussions, as regional protocols have typically been used in Southern literature to monumentalize a particular version of the place and its history. Berry notices that regional thinking promotes "exploitive" marketing strategies that put the "picturesque" and "old charm" qualities of the region in the service of producing a collectible version of the South (qtd. in Wilson 1997, 145). Whether writers use parody, the grotesque, or less refurbished literary conventions to counter this type of appropriation, the important writers of the contemporary South contribute at some level to the type of place-based thinking that overlooks the contemporary similarities among American places.

One needs only to realize how near in chronological time Southern writers are to the "Southern Renaissance" of the 1920s and 1930s, to see why writers *from* the South want to be perceived as also being *of* the South. Unlike New England, whose "Brahmins" of the "American Renaissance" lost currency after the Civil War, the South is still enjoying literary dominance. Proud Southerners today assert that their ground is still rich in divisive, almost prurient, distinction. The history of the South has thus afforded the rest of the United States some measure of awareness of the virtues and limitations of multiculturalism. In fact, as Brinkmeyer notes, the

SOUTHERN FELLOWSHIP

The truth is that local affiliation is still very important to Southern writers. In fact, a "Fellowship of Southern Writers" was founded in 1987. The "fellowship" counts nearly every noteworthy contemporary writer of Southern persuasion as a member. With the anachronistic-sounding name "fellowship," the FSW appears to be as conspicuously interested in imposing its trusteeship on Southern literature as was the *Atlantic* group. The fellowship meets biennially to award numerous prizes to fiction writers who continue to contribute works to the canon of Southern fiction. The fellowship's charter members include such pivotal arbiters of Southern literature as A.R. Ammons, Cleanth Brooks, James Dickey, Ralph Ellison, Shelby Foote, John Hope Franklin, Ernest Gaines, Walker Percy, Reynolds Price, Mary Lee Settle, Elizabeth Spencer, William Styron, Peter Taylor, Robert Penn Warren, Eudora Welty, and C. Vann Woodward. Elected members include contemporary dynamos such as Wendell Berry, Lee Smith, Richard Bausch, William Hoffman, Allan Gurganus, Josephine Humphreys, Bobbie Ann Mason, Kaye Gibbons, Barry Hannah, and Larry Brown. Through their allegiances, these writers advance the argument that where one hails from is an indispensable consideration when evaluating the production of fiction.

culturally conservative Agrarians are important forerunners of recent literary concerns. In addition to being the first to articulate the New Criticism (with John Crowe Ransom's 1938 *The World's Body*), the Agrarians enumerated the virtues of non-acquisitive cultures in ways that anticipate contemporary non-Southern environmentalist writers, such as Edward Abbey, Annie Dillard, John McPhee, and Terry Tempest Williams. Despite their goal of producing a Southern monocultural South, Agrarian documents like Ransom's "Aesthetics of Regionalism" (1934) were the first to interrogate the ideological and literary implications of regional form, exemplifying the warrant that region is socially, rather than geographically, constructed.

This Agrarian sociology still influences alternative taxonomies of recent Southern literature. For instance, Matthew Guinn groups contemporary Southern writers such as Dorothy Allison, Larry Brown, and Harry Crews together as "mythoclasts," or blue-collar writers who reject the dominant cultural legacies of Agrarianism, namely nostalgia for capital "S" Southern aristocracy. These writers delineate the virtues of "poor white trash," an endeavor that has arguably been on the Southern intellectual agenda since W.J. Cash's popular and controversial history of the South, *The Mind of the South* (1941). Contemporary Southern women writers, specifically Bobbie Ann Mason, articulate what Patricia Yeager calls the "crises of whiteness" that have resulted from the success of multicultural models of contemporary fiction (Yeager 2000, 11).

Contexts and Issues. Literary critic Mark McGurl claims that these supposed crises of whiteness are not limited to Southern women writers, but are a concern also of male writers. McGurl lists a slate of successful contemporary male writers—including Wallace Stegner, William Kennedy, and Cormac McCarthy—who "have staged their careers . . . in the continuing tradition of literary regionalism" (McGurl 2005, 119). Using regional writing as a way of breaking into the literary market is not a new tactic. As Brodhead reminds us, all major late-nineteenth century American writers, with the exception of Henry James and Howells, succeeded through regional form (viz., Cable, Jewett, Twain, Charles Chesnutt, Mary Wilkins Freeman, and Abraham Cahan). According to Brodhead, "authors in this [regional] mode typically had their first efforts published" (Brodhead 1994, 165). Wallace Stegner has not only sustained a long career via regional protocols, he has also produced a generation of American writers who capitalize on their regional inflections. Having founded and run the Stanford University writing workshop, Stegner shaped the careers of many influential writers, the list of which includes Edward Abbey, Wendell Berry, Ken Kesey, and Larry McMurtry. Teaching a genre that, according to McGurl, "has always been cultural pluralist . . . a form of appreciation of diversity," Stegner helped young white, male writers attain an "alignment by analogy" to the market requisite of diversity (McGurl 2005, 119).

Unlike McGurl, who encourages readers to view regional fiction as a cheap trick used to break into the literary market, Sally Robinson categorizes such writerly positions as gestures toward "marked" embodiment. This is the writer's earnest impulse to register his distinct presence in an era of "identity politics," which Robinson and colleague Peggy Phelan call "visibility politics" (Robinson 2000, 2). No longer the "historical malady of underrepresented populations" alone, invisibility has become a legitimate problem for white men at the end of the twentieth century (2). As Susan Faludi explains, the 1990s male resembles the 1950s housewife archetype in that "the empty compensations of the 'feminine mystique' are transforming into the empty compensations of the masculine mystique" (Faludi 2000, 40). Faludi's historical explanation for this phenomenon is basically that in the late 1960s, in the wake of the civil rights movement and with the rise of women's and homosexual liberation, white men began to take the role of victim of historical processes. Robinson agrees with Faludi, adding that

> from the late sixties to the present, dominant masculinity appears to have suffered one crisis after another, from the urgent complaints of the "silent majority" following the 1968 presidential election, to the men's liberationists call for rethinking masculinity in the wake of the women's movement in the 1970s, to the battles over the cultural authority of "dead white males" in academia, to the rise of a new men's movement in the late 1980s. (Robinson 2000, 5)

McGurl wants to categorize male-authored regional fiction as the most recent "men's movement." Indeed, even Robinson explains each men's movement in literary terms, noticing how all assertions of white masculinity employ a "language of crisis, . . . vocabulary of pain and urgency to dwell on, manage or heal the threats to a normativity continuously under siege" (5). Through this process of reacting to the changing tide, white men have become *marked men.* In fact, white men are becoming so specialized a group, Robinson claims, that the "enduring image of the disenfranchised white man has become a symbol for the decline of the American way of life" (2). By acquiring "markings," in this case place-based determinants, the masculine reclamation of regionalism, as both McGurl and Robinson conceive of it, perpetuates the prominence of identity politics by making the survival of difference a key objective of literary production. Branding the otherwise bland experience of white men with a retroactive ethnic mark is supposed to equalize the playing field among diverse authors, as it makes white masculinity into another kind of diversity.

In this sense, male writers have appropriated what Mary Louise Pratt calls the "rhetorics of diversity and multiculturalism" that have emerged in contemporary

America. The "import" of these rhetorics, Pratt warns, is "up for grabs across the ideological spectrum" (Pratt 1999, 617). Jonathan Franzen, a leading contemporary fiction writer and occasional arbiter of literary culture, has recently (begrudgingly) acknowledged this misuse of diversity. Regionalism, Franzen claims, "is still thriving" in both American literature and on American campuses (Franzen, 2003, 68). Indeed, some forms of **academic fiction** seem also to be forms of regional fiction, namely Jane Smiley's novel about a fictional midwestern state university *Moo* (1995). Naysayers such as Franzen see regional fiction as a genre hungrily "feed[ing] on specificity" and finding "the manners of a particular region . . . fertile ground" for exploitive literary enterprises (68). Franzen complains that "it's fashionable on college campuses nowadays to say that there is no America anymore, there are only Americas; that the only things a black lesbian New Yorker and a Southern Baptist Georgian have in common are the English language and the federal income tax" (68–69). In short, regionalism has facilitated an almost curricular pathway toward the emergence of a post-national imagination; or, to employ Franzen's pessimism, regional fiction writers and identity politicians alike have become so skilled at delineating the differences among Americans that the United States is beginning to look like a small-scale version of an inassimilable world rather than like a unified national body. The question is whether or not these skills should be used to dismantle commonality, whether or not America's national identity should be debated to the point of being irrevocably splintered. The regional writer ostensibly has no preference, save to represent the living ground local to her experience.

Reception. The most telling barometer of both the reception and gender inflection of regional fiction at large is Oprah Winfrey's agenda-setting book club. Since its inception in the fall of 1996, Oprah's Book Club has frequently selected regional fiction by contemporary women authors. In a sense, the book club is the popular manifestation of the female-centered regional fiction championed in the scholarship of Judith Fetterley, Marjorie Pryse, and others. Oprah's Book Club does some of the same cultural work as this scholarly endeavor. As Foote argues, the "feminist retrievals" of the 1970s and 1980s construct an "alternative literary tradition" that values community over alienation, nature over urban zones, and the values of "cooperation, communication, and a tradition of feminine knowing" (Foote 2001, 33). Oprah's Book Club is a similar and more popularly effective engine of public opinion that values feminine community over masculine alienation. By elevating regional settings and identities as discrete from society at large, however, Oprah's Book Club also threatens to re-inscribe counterproductive cultural divisions.

From its first selection, Jacquelyn Mitchard's *The Deep End of the Ocean* (1996), Oprah's Book Club has favored regional inflections in its women authors. In *The Deep End of the Ocean*, a Wisconsin photographer and housewife loses her son in a Chicago hotel lobby and is reunited with him nine years later. The novel highlights a core binary of regional fiction, the tension between dangerous urban centers and the more innocuous "homeland" of middle-class suburbia. Through the selection of Jane Hamilton's *Book of Ruth* (1989), also in the charter season, Oprah's Book Club recovers and republishes the first novel of a writer whose biographical note highlights the author's quaint regional credentials by stating that she "lives, works, and writes in an orchard farmhouse in Wisconsin." Since then, the book club has popularized subsequent novels by Hamilton. Other female regional novels selected for the book club include: Kaye Gibbons's *A Virtuous Woman* (1989), Marry McGarry Morris's *Songs in Ordinary Time* (1995), Edwidge Danticat's *Breath,*

Eyes, Memory (1995), Billie Letts's *Where the Heart Is* (1995), Joyce Carol Oates's *We Were the Mulvaneys* (1996), Gwyn Hyman Rubio's *Icy Sparks* (1998), Melinda Haynes's *Mother of Pearl* (1999), Tawni O'Dell's *Back Roads* (2000), Christina Schwarz's *Drowning Ruth* (2000), and Lalita Tademy's *Cane River* (2002). In recent years, book-club selections have shifted away from feminine regionalism, favoring instead novels by traditionally canonical "literary" figures (such as Tolstoy, Faulkner, Steinbeck) and contemporary memoirs. This shift appears to be the result of criticism that Oprah might be devoting disproportionate attention to themes of feminine travails. Most apparent, however, is the fact that the shift followed a scandal involving Franzen's being invited, then disinvited, to the list.

Franzen's discomfort, more specifically his claim that the book club includes "enough schmaltzy, one dimensional" novels to give any serious fiction writer pause, sparked a public debate about the virtues and limitations of popularizing "literary fiction." It should have investigated the question of why Oprah found Franzen's *The Corrections* (2001) a novel to shelve alongside feminine regionalism. Stylistically, Franzen differs much from the novelists named above; he is much less invested in realist narration or sentimental tones. On a thematic level, however, *The Corrections* resembles the very novels Franzen considers "schmaltzy." Like the work of Mitchard, Hamilton, Letts, and others on Oprah's list, Franzen's novels question the heartland values and bourgeois complacencies of red-state America. His first novel, *The Twenty-Seventh City* (1988), dramatizes municipal corruption in St. Louis, representing a heartland whose households act as incubators against the multicultural revolution. Continuing this theme in *The Corrections*, Franzen delineates the political, cultural, and psychological decline of the Midwest. The difference between *The Corrections* and the regionally inflected late-twentieth century novels that precede him on Oprah's list is that it does not approach the representation of place as what W.J. Keith calls "a welcome limitation of possibility" (Keith 1988, 10). Rather than uncover the "numinous landscape beneath a desacralized, irradiated, and overdeveloped one," which Michael Kowalewski takes to be the goal of contemporary regional writers, Franzen acknowledges the transformations that globalized capital brings to the Midwest (Kowalewski 2003, 18).

This acknowledgment of the effects of progress on regional landscapes might be the cultural work of twenty-first-century regional fiction. For more than a century, the genre has exploited its difference from the mainstream, entertaining audiences whom Foote describes as "preoccupied with national problems regarding the proper constitution of the citizen" (Foote 2001, 36). Regionalism, according to Foote, has helped those audiences "negotiate their fear of foreigners alongside a romantic longing for rural countrymen" (36). The recent re-appropriation of local knowledge by male writers, though it might be reducible to a marketing ploy, indicates that the regional fiction of tomorrow will be inclusive, not separated into gendered camps, with women regionalists protecting the quaintness and sanctity of place and men regionalists exploring the "territories."

Selected Authors. In fact, gender roles in regional fiction seem to have reversed. For instance, Bobbie Ann Mason exemplifies the exploitive tendencies of the Southwest humorist tradition. Her fiction, according to Fred Pfeil, "allows upscale readers to savor the narrative as a virtual transcription of likeable, down-home stupidity" (Pfeil 1990, 76). Mason's very career mimics the economy of late-nineteenth century regional writers. After leaving the academy in 1979 to become a full-time writer, Mason has published short stories about the "New South" in

The New Yorker and *The Atlantic Monthly.* These stories, later collected in *Shiloh and Other Stories* (1982), feature a "white trash" culture (with strip malls, fast-food, and bad TV) that the reader is positioned to encounter with condescending amusement.

Similarly reminiscent of traditionally masculine modes of regional fiction, is the work of Annie Proulx. In fact, Proulx's career trajectory moves geographically in the direction of male-centered regionalism. Her early novels, *Postcards* (1992) and *The Shipping News* (1993), are set in the typically feminine rural New England. Next, her innovatively structured novel, *Accordion Crimes* (1996), defies locational fidelity by following a Sicilian accordion from the "Old World" to a diverse set of American regions, such as New Orleans, rural Iowa, Maine, and the Mexican border. Finally, Proulx's most recent work has been two short story collections set in rural Wyoming—*Close Range* (1999) and *Bad Dirt* (2004). These collections evoke the spirit of Bret Harte to the extent that they feature "ne'er-do-well antiheroes unlikely to appear" in the promotional literature for the Wyoming region she documents (Kowalewski 2003, 11). Furthermore, these collections ignore the over-storied zones of Wyoming, such as Jackson Hole and Yellowstone, echoing Harte's "pioneering" accounts of the seedy side of the frontier landscape while also highlighting the homoeroticism of the all-male frontier (*Close Range* includes "Brokeback Mountain," the story that Larry McMurtry and Diana Ossana adapted into an Academy Award winning screenplay).

On the other side of both the country and the gender line, New England has recently become the favorite setting for small-town realists such as Ernest Hebert, Russell Banks, and Richard Russo. In *Dogs of March* (1979), Hebert produces the prototypical self-destructive New England everyman in the character of Howard Elman, after whom Banks models Wade Whitehouse, antihero of his novel *Affliction* (1989). Elman is a former foreman of a textile mill who loses his job when the mill is sold to a company from the New South. According to Kent Ryden, Elman is the realistic counterpart to the romanticized "Yankee"; he is "profane and given to drinking, a factory worker who deliberately refuses to farm the fields that he owns, an imperfect father and husband" (Ryden 2003, 209). He has no interest in the physical beauty championed by a previous generation of New England regionalists. Hebert implies that this lack of appreciation is an essential feature of postindustrial New England. This argument is evident in the novel's culminating scene, wherein Elman's ugly trailer home (a symbol of economic decline) obscures the view of the idyllic countryside for which the novel's other main character, an idealistic midwesterner, had left his life in the Midwest.

Similarly, Banks's early works confront the allegorical resonance of blue-collar New England. His story collection, *Trailerpark* (1981) is a storehouse of America's fears about its orphans. In the tradition of Sherwood Anderson's *Winesburg, Ohio*, each story couples a culture in decline with the fears that such decline inspires in the general reader. For instance, the lead story introduces the park through the eyes of its lenient resident manager. Her passive acceptance of her tenants' infractions is challenged when she learns that a tenant is breeding rodents. The guinea pig trailer becomes a metaphor for overpopulation, an image that corresponds with the fear of being outnumbered by undesirable others. As the early 1980s popular imagination is subdued by *pathos*-driven images of the large-scale poverty and overpopulation on remote continents, Banks's small-scale parable reminds the reader of homegrown orphans. The eccentric guinea pig lady, her illogical allegiance to her rodents' natural impulse to reproduce, brings global "epidemics" uncannily close to the reader.

Banks extends this relationship between the shrinking world and the small town in his most recent novel, *The Darling* (2004). The narrator, a middle-aged former 1960s political radical who has made a life out of abandoning anything that takes on even the slightest resemblance of home, moves from rural New England to war-torn Monrovia to reunite with a chimpanzee sanctuary she had abandoned during the Liberian civil war. Banks's international turn is not anti-regional, but a reinvention of regional storytelling that elevates the resemblance of socially disparaged regions throughout the world. The resemblance between old New England and the Third World allows readers to assess the enduring value of local color. Ultimately, Banks, like his predecessor Wharton, champions the destruction of sentimental attachment to local color, but not without dramatizing the complexities of mobilizing the local knowledge of unfamiliar places, such as Monrovia, into fictional narratives that build a version of world citizenship from the common ground of local affiliation with postindustrial economic and cultural realities.

Recent popular novels set in the Midwest also evoke postindustrial moods and landscapes. For example, Whitney Terrell's *The Huntsman* (2001) and Michael Collins's *The Keepers of Truth* (2001) cast a kind of third-world shade on the Midwest. In Terrell's novel, a Kansas City judge claims that there is "no difference between [Kansas City] and the most obscure village on the Congo River that Conrad once went past. . . . And that, then, is the dream, isn't it? . . . that we are not, in fact, so obscure as savages, eh? That we have some reason not to kill and rape?" (Terrell 2001, 341). In short, Terrell represents the "heartland" as a place to "go native," a place so inconsequential as to be a no man's land, or what Tom Lutz calls the "bloody crossroads" between cultures (Lutz 2004, 12). Collins is an Irish citizen who has himself recently gone native in the Midwest, writing a series of murder-plot novels set in the rustbelt detritus of Illinois. Collins strikes a similar logic of resemblance between the Midwest and the Third World. His narrator names the obvious opponent to Midwest economic stability—outsourcing—but for unobvious reasons. His midwestern men have the typical paradox of guilt and contempt regarding sweatshop labor, which simultaneously shuts down factories in the Midwest and makes consumer habits less prohibitive. But more importantly, Collins's male characters "long for . . . immigrant exhaustion" (Collins 2001, 173). Therefore, where Terrell exploits the lawless remoteness of the Midwest, Collins romanticizes the botched camaraderie between its unemployed men and the "women and children . . . of places without names" (173). These narratives of postindustrial resemblance respond to Amitava Kumar's call for fiction that does not simply showcase the diverse cultures that are now available as a result of economic globalization, but that "forge[s] new connections and elaborate[s] on . . . new coalitions and emergent subjectivities" (Kumar 2003, xxiii). Such narratives are setting the agenda for future generations of writers who think territorially.

Bibliography

Ammons, Elizabeth, and Valerie Rohy. "Introduction." *American Local Color Writing, 1880–1920*. New York: Penguin, 1998, vii–xxx.

Banks, Russell. *Trailerpark*. 1981. New York: Perennial, 1996.

———. *The Darling*. New York: HarperCollins, 2004.

Berry, Wendell. "The Regional Motive." *A Continuous Harmony: Essays Cultural and Agricultural*. New York: Harcourt, 1972, 61–68.

Brinkmeyer Jr., Robert H. *Remapping Southern Literature: Contemporary Southern Writers and the West*. Athens: University of Georgia Press, 2000.

Brodhead, Richard. "Regionalism and the Upper Class." In *Rethinking Class: Literary Studies and Social Formations*. Wai Chee Dimock and Michael T. Gilmore, eds. New York: Columbia University Press, 1994, 150–174.

Campbell, Donna. *Resisting Regionalism: Gender and Naturalism in American Fiction, 1885–1915*. Athens: Ohio University Press, 1997.

Collins, Michael. *The Keepers of Truth*. New York: Scribner, 2001.

Faludi, Susan. *Stiffed: The Betrayal of the American Man*. New York: Perennial, 2000.

Fetterley, Judith, and Marjory Pryse. *Writing Out of Place: Regionalism, Women, and American Literary Culture*. Urbana: University of Illinois Press, 2003.

Foote, Stephanie. *Regional Fictions: Culture and Identity in Nineteenth-Century American Literature*. Madison: University of Wisconsin Press, 2001.

Franzen, Jonathan. *The Corrections*. New York: Farrar Straus & Giroux, 2001.

———. *How to Be Alone*. 2002. New York: Picador, 2003.

Garland, Hamlin. "Local Color in Art." In *Crumbling Idols: Twelve Essays on Art Dealing Chiefly with Literature, Painting, and the Drama*. 1894. Jane Johnson, ed. Cambridge, MA: Harvard University Press, 1960, 49–55.

Glazener, Nancy. *Reading for Realism: The History of a U.S. Literary Institution, 1850–1910*. Durham, NC: Duke University Press, 1997.

Gray, Richard. *Writing the South: Ideas of an American Region*. New York: Cambridge University Press, 1989.

Guinn, Matthew. *After Southern Modernism: Fiction of the Contemporary South*. Jackson, MI: University Press of Mississippi, 2000.

Hamblen, Abigail Ann. "Edith Wharton in New England." *New England Quarterly* 38.2 (1965): 239–244.

Hoberek, Andrew. "Reconstructing Southern Literature." *Postmodern Culture*. 11.1 (2000). http://www3.iath.virginia.edu/pmc/text-only/issue.900/11.1.r_hoberek.txt.

Joshi, S.T., and Peter Cannon, eds. *More Annotated H.P. Lovecraft*. New York: Dell Publications, 1999.

Keith, W.J. *Regions of the Imagination: The Development of British Rural Fiction*. Toronto: University of Toronto Press, 1988.

Kowalewski, Michael. "Contemporary Regionalism." In *A Companion to the Regional Literatures of America*. Charles L. Crow, ed. Malden: Blackwell Press, 2003.

Kreyling, Michael. *Inventing Southern Literature*. Jackson, MI: University Press of Mississippi, 1998.

Kumar, Amitava. "Introduction." *World Bank Literature*. Minneapolis, MN: University of Minnesota Press, 2003, xvii–xxxiii.

Lutz, Tom. *Cosmopolitan Vistas: American Regionalism and Literary Value*. Ithaca: Cornell University Press, 2004.

MacDonald, Dwight. *Against the American Grain*. 1962. New York: De Capo Press, 1983.

McGurl, Mark. "The Program Era: Pluralisms of Postwar American Fiction." *Critical Inquiry* 32 (2005): 102–129.

Nagel, James. "Introduction: The Literary Context." In *The Portable American Realism Reader*. James Nagel and Tom Quirk, eds. New York: Penguin, 1997, 20–32.

"The New Regionalism." In *Outline of American Literature*. Kathryn VanSpanckeren, ed. 1998. U.S. Department of State, Washington. 12 June 2005. http://usinfo.state.gov/products/pubs/oal/lit8.htm#regionalism.

Oates, Joyce Carol. "Introduction." *Oxford Book of American Short Stories*. Oxford: Oxford University Press, 1992, 3–16.

———. *The Faith of a Writer: Life, Craft, Art*. New York: HarperCollins, 2003.

Percy, Walker. "Why I Live Where I Live." *Esquire* 93 (April 1980): 35–36.

Pfeil, Fred. *Another Tale to Tell: Politics and Narrative in Postmodern Culture*. New York: Verso, 1990.

Pratt, Mary Louise. "Arts of the Contact Zone." In *Ways of Reading*. David Bartholomae and Anthony Petroksky, eds. New York: St. Martin's Press, 1999, 605–619.

Proulx, Annie. *Close Range*. New York: Scribner, 1999.

Robinson, Sally. *Marked Men: White Masculinity in Crisis*. New York: Columbia University Press, 2000.

Ryden, Kent C. "New England Literature and Regional Identity." In *A Companion to the Regional Literatures of America*. Charles L. Crow, ed. Malden: Blackwell Press, 2003, 195–213.

Terrell, Whitney. *The Huntsman*. New York: Penguin, 2001.

Wharton, Edith. *Ethan Frome*. 1911. New York: Charles Scribner's Sons, 1987.

Wilson, Charles Reagan. "American Regionalism in the Postmodern World." *Amerikanstudien* 42.2 (1997): 145–158.

Yeager, Patricia. *Dirt and Desire: Reconstructing Southern Women's Writing 1930–1990*. Chicago, IL: University of Chicago Press, 2000.

JASON ARTHUR

ROAD FICTION

Definition. The literal road is a structured path that enables someone to transport or relocate people, vehicles, animals, and other objects to another area. The metaphorical road enables someone to travel down a structured way in order to find a personal path, for example, a place in society. The road is also a learning device, incorporating life experience as education, involving learning about different cultures and traditions of dissimilar people in other places. "Simply put, a road story shows that experiences away from home—perspectives gained on the road—reveal and even transform identity. The road dares us to dream of a better life" (Mills 2006, 22).

History. Road fiction began as a genre in the late 1950s and through the 1960s, starting with the emergence of Jack Kerouac and his highly praised novel *On the Road* (1957). Upon publication, *On the Road* was heralded as an inspirational work and its creator as the voice of a new generation: the Beat generation. Taking their name from the pulsating style of jazz and scat, the Beat generation authors composed prose and poetry that had a distinctive rhythmic pattern. Beat also reflected the feelings of many people in postwar America: tired, poor, and abused.

After World War II, travel became more accessible because of automobiles and newly constructed highways. Most automobile production had been suspended for the duration of the war, which had left many people without an affordable means of transportation. With a new sense of mobility, the Beats were able to use this automotive freedom as a source of rebellion—a way to reject the traditional life of a house, steady job, and family that was labeled the American Dream in 1930s and 1940s. "Through their pursuit of mysteries, Kerouac and Ginsberg supplanted the road stories they knew from childhood—the tragedies and screwball comedies of the Depression in which the road story signified hard times and chastity" (Mills 2006, 39). Starving for adventure and excitement, Jack Kerouac, William S. Burroughs, Allen Ginsberg, and friends Lucien Carr and Neal Cassady set out on the road to put the university life behind them and to learn what real life could teach them.

Literature of rebellion often includes thoughts on how to represent new ideas—the presentation of conscious changes in literary style, word use, sentence structure, and even point of view and narration. Jack Kerouac purposefully wrote to change the conservative way of thinking in postwar America. Kerouac was not alone in his new vision. His friend, and sometimes coauthor, Allen Ginsberg wrote poetry in accordance with the spontaneous beat developed by Kerouac. Criticized for being indecent and, more often, vulgar, the Beats wrote about America as they saw it in their travels and from the stories they would share with one another. "Beginning with Kerouac's *On the Road,* however, the Beats initiated an ambitious remapping that went far beyond the theme of the road, becoming a radical experiment in the style and syntax of literary expression" (Mills 2006, 40). The Beats loved the vernacular of other cultures and their changing signifiers, meaning that their slang terms were constantly being reformatted over the years. They drew from the subculture in America; they loved the raw sound of jazz and admired the constant changing of slang words, which fueled their desire to have language become more feeling than meaning. "The writers' experiments with language and with the mobility of meaning have distilled over time into set themes—bebop jazz, sexual freedom, male bonding and rivalry—or have been reduced to their bare predictable narrative patterns—escape, rebellion, renewal" (Mills 2006, 36). The Beat authors craved the slang language being spoken by minorities and the American youth. This new language was being used in music, in new literature and poems, and most importantly, on the street. Kerouac utilized the new "talk" in his first versions of *On the Road* and *Visions of Cody.* Kerouac wrote in *On the Road,* "What's your road, man?—holyboy road, madman road, rainbow road, guppy road, any road. It's an anywhere road for anybody anyhow. Where body how?" (1976, 251). Like the nonsensical lyrics of scat, Kerouac developed the new language of the Beatniks. The new generation now had a new language with which to rebel against conventional American society.

Minority authors had a natural, yet not always appreciated, place in literature. LeRoi Jones found inspiration in Kerouac's *On the Road* and decided to write his own version from a black man's point of view. Ralph Ellison's novel *Invisible Man* was published in 1952, just five years before Kerouac's *On the Road.* Both Ellison and Jones's novels represent the African American man in postwar America. Woman writers, such as Joyce Glassman and Hettie Jones, also took it upon themselves to write from the female point of view, trying to break the stereotypical mold of women on the road and at home.

The Beat generation also sought to expose the subculture or counterculture of American society by openly discussing the growing popularity of drug use. Jack Kerouac, William S. Burroughs, Ken Kesey, and Allen Ginsberg often cited drug use in their works, intending for their readers to help break the taboo of such controversial subjects. They also wanted to break the taboo concerning minorities, not just for women and African Americans, but also for Mexicans and Native Americans, for gays, lesbians, and transgenders, and for the working lower class of Middle America. "The Beats' emulation of minority subcultures also helped to reassert some of the social changes begun by the war, including the demand by minority cultures for representation and the refusal of non-conformists to be labeled 'deviant'" (Mills 2006, 38). These Caucasian men of middle-class families discovered a world that was secret and taboo; they encountered racial and sexual diversity, made friends with drug addicts and the homeless, immersed themselves in the working class, and deliberately learned what poverty was like. Irony, however, can be found in Kerouac's narrative in *On the Road,* when his main character Sal Paradise, a representation of himself, becomes excited to leave his familiar and safe world behind for the excitement of the open road but at several times during his trip becomes frightened of his surroundings and retreats back to familiar ground. African American writer LeRoi Jones, on the other hand, "finds racial salvation on Louisiana's segregated roads" (Mills 53). Kerouac tried to capture life from all angles but could not truthfully report on all of the aspects of a culture that society refused to let him experience; in other words, only a black man can tell you what it is like being a black man.

Landmarks of Road Fiction. One of the aspects of the road, or Beat, authors is their interconnection with each other. They often gave credit to their friends for the style, content, and even titles of their own novels and poems. Without this connection, the Beat counterculture would not have held together for almost two decades, until Kerouac's death in 1969, and continued through the Beats as individual artists into the 1970s through the 1990s. The connection between Jack Kerouac, Allen Ginsberg, William S. Burroughs, Hunter S. Thompson, Tom Wolfe, Ken Kesey, LeRoi Jones, Hettie Jones, and Joyce Johnson can be seen through each other's stories and novels. All of these writers were somehow connected in life, inspiring one another and helping each other transform new literary ideas into a new literary genre.

Jack Kerouac, On The Road *(1957) and "Essentials of Spontaneous Prose" (1958).* Kerouac is regarded as the forefront master of road fiction, a movement he set out to create, though he felt uncomfortable with the title of creator.

Like a traditional quest story, *On the Road* concludes in the same place it started, in New York City. Alter Ego to Kerouac is Salvatore (Sal) Paradise. Ironically, his last name is a paradox to what Sal actually finds on the road. He is interested in humanity and everything that has to do with humanity, including jazz, women, and his friends and other people who are connected to him. He has a fascination with his friends Dean Moriarty and Carlo Marx, the landscape, traveling, and writing about the landscape. Sal, like Kerouac, believes that the narrator is the writer as the creator; he is the man experiencing the experience. He tries his best to write everything that happens down in his notebooks, just as Kerouac himself had done during his own travels that inspired the writing of the novel. He tries to be a truthful witness, finding words for every sight he sees, including those around him, who are just as important to the story as the road itself.

The character Dean Moriarty, inspired by good friend Neal Cassady, is the perfect travel companion: "With the coming of Dean Moriarty began the part of my life you could call my life on the road . . . Dean is the perfect guy for the road because he actually was born on the road, when his parents were passing through Salt Lake City in 1926, in a jalopy, on their way to Los Angeles" (Kerouac 1976, 1). Dean, a free spirit, is imprisoned; "only a guy who's spent five years in jail can go to such maniacal helpless extremes . . . Prison is where you promise yourself the right to live" (236). In marriage, too, Dean finds himself trapped. He is three times married, twice divorced. Prison is representative of any situation in which one feels trapped, whether school, family, or marriage. The restrictions of the war left many Americans needing freedom—personal freedom, educational freedom, freedom of movement, and the right to be themselves in an unconfined society. Kerouac believed that one of the ways to learn about the world, which affected his writing and his life in general, was to travel the roads of the American countryside, learning as he went, exploring the landscapes, and experiencing a life different from that to which he had been accustomed.

Sal finds the difference between the education one can receive at school and the education that one can receive on the road, living the experience of what life has to offer him. He also finds disappointment on the road, not the glamour or glory of traveling. He befriends people of the lower classes and the subcultures, and he is intrigued by them and fears them and their society. Coming from a middle-class family, Sal feels uncomfortable being poor and often retreats back into the world to which he is accustomed, a place that is familiar and safe. Kerouac knew that the road did not have all of the answers. He discovered on his own travels that not every trip was going to be magical or perfect; "the road is life" (Mills 2006, 22). Kerouac experienced, firsthand, the "starving Sidewalks and sickbeds" (1976, 8).

Kerouac set out to change the style of writing and to create a movement in terms of identity. He believed that writing should not be altered or edited once initially written. He thought writing was visceral and natural, which was similar to the position of the surrealist poets of France in the 1940s. They too believed in a constant, undisturbed line of thought called the stream of Consciousness. This concept entitled the writer to continuously write without stopping, creating a unified and blended narrative. Kerouac writes in his essay "Essentials of Spontaneous Prose" (1958), "Time being of the essence in the purity of speech, sketching language is undisturbed flow from the mind of personal secret idea words, blowing on subject of image" (72). This type of writing is considered a kind of literary liberation and challenges the writer to keep focused on the one thought instead of changing from one idea to another.

Kerouac's first draft of *On the Road* was written in three weeks in 1951 on a continuous scroll of Teletype paper. Publishers, however, would not publish his novel because of the controversial content and the unusual experimental writing style. Kerouac edited his manuscript several times before it was finally published six years later in 1957. An unedited version of *On the Road* was published as *Visions of Cody* which was part of one pre-publication version of *On the Road*, in 1972. Kerouac's infatuation with jazz can be seen in the narrative of *Visions of Cody* more than in *On the Road*.

> The Mad Road, lonely, leading around the bend into the openings of space towards the horizon Wasatch snows promised is in the vision of the west, spine heights at the world's end, coast of blue Pacific starry night—nobone half-banana moons sloping in the tangled night sky, the torments of great formations in the mist, the huddled invisible insect in the car racing onward, illuminate.—The raw cut, the drag, the butte, the star, the draw, the sunflower in the grass—orangeubuttered west lands of Arcadia, forlorn sands of the isolate earth, dewy exposures to infinity in black space, home of the rattlesnake and the gopher—the level of the world, low and flat. (1972, 391)

Kerouac used his spontaneous prose to try to capture the landscape in words, rather than focusing on story plot and character traits. He wanted to paint a picture of the landscape by using words. After publication of *On the Road*, Kerouac had the credibility of a successful writer and had the freedom to return to his spontaneous prose style and nonconformist attitude, as can be seen in moderation in *The Dharma Bums* (1958) and *The Subterraneans* (1958).

Allen Ginsberg, "Howl" (1954) and Selected Poems: 1947–1995 *(1996).* Ginsberg met Jack Kerouac during his first year at Columbia University, along with other writers such as William S. Burroughs and John Clellon Holmes. Ginsberg and Kerouac became good friends, and Ginsberg even makes an appearance in Kerouac's novel *On the Road,* as the character Carlo Marx. Being a poet, Ginsberg did not write about his road experiences in the same way as Kerouac, though he admired his spontaneous prose style and spent years applying it to his composition of poetry. He also drew inspiration from French surrealist poet André Breton. Ginsberg was also a part of Ken Kesey's Merry Pranksters and often would perform his poetry on the road with them, "keeping apace with their psychedelic experiments" (Mills 2006, 92).

Ginsberg became good friends with William S. Burroughs after their introduction by mutual friends Lucien Carr and David Kammerer. After Burroughs was arrested for conspiracy to deliver marijuana on the basis of letters found by police that he had written to Ginsberg, he moved his family to Mexico. Ginsberg still kept in touch with Burroughs and encouraged him to continue his writing even after the death of his common-law wife, Joan. Ginsberg traveled with Jack Kerouac to Tangiers, where Burroughs had gone in order to write. Burroughs compiled several manuscripts and sought his friends' advice on how to edit them. Their trip resulted in Burroughs's masterpiece *Naked Lunch.*

Kerouac collaborated with Ginsberg on a film version of the poem "Pull My Daisy," written by Ginsberg, Kerouac, and friend Neal Cassady. The poem had been written in the Beat style scat that Kerouac had employed in his earlier versions of *On the Road.* The film was also titled *Pull My Daisy* and was to be made into an art film version of *On the Road.* Photographer Robert Frank was chosen to direct the movie. "Frank's cinematography in this film—grainy black and white imaged, titled horizons, atmospheric and spontaneous shots—helped lay the aesthetic groundwork for the New American film" (Mills 2006, 61).

Ginsberg became famous for his insight into the American culture and his desire not only to change it but to make it more aware of its subcultures and emerging counterculture. He also attacks the mass-media images such as movies, radio, and television in his poem "I Am a Victim of Telephone" (*Selected Poems* 1996, 141). His dream about changing American society with the innocence of youth as a vehicle became his life passion, and most critics would say that he achieved it.

One of his best-known poems is "Howl," a biographical look at the Beat poets' destructive lifestyle. The Beats' fascination with the subculture of America brought them to less-than-desirable sections of strange cities where they learned the lives of drug addicts and prostitutes. Accused of being immoral and obscene, Ginsberg's poem came under attack from the public, and it was therefore banned in many bookstores across the country. An obscenity trial boosted its popularity, and the Beat generation became famous as champions against censorship, fighting for First Amendment rights. Ginsberg also claimed he wanted to talk about taboo subjects in order to start a conversation, bringing the taboo to light in the public eye and therefore helping to bring about change.

William S. Burroughs, Naked Lunch *(1959).* Burroughs started writing in 1945, resulting in a collaboration with Jack Kerouac about the murder of David Kammerer by a mutual friend, Lucien Carr, called *And the Hippos Were Boiled in Their Tanks.* Allen Ginsberg encouraged Burroughs to continue writing, but it was not until the shooting death of his common-law wife, Joan Vollmer Adams, in Mexico in 1951—for which Burroughs was arrested and convicted absentia of homicide—that he claims he began to really write. In the introduction to *Queer* (1985), he wrote, "The death of Joan brought me in contact with the invader, the Ugly Spirit, and maneuvered me in to a life long struggle, in which I have had no choice except to write my way out" (xxiii). Before Joan died, while in Mexico with Joan and their three children, he had written two novels: *Queer* and *Junkie*. (*Queer* would not published until 1985, and *Junkie* would be published in 1953.) Burroughs and Ginsberg's collection *The Yage Letters,* which was published in 1963, includes correspondence letters between Burroughs and Ginsberg from when Burroughs was in South America. In 1953, because there was no restriction on the use or sale of drugs, Burroughs traveled to Morocco and stayed in a small apartment in Tangiers. Over the next four years, with the help of readily available drugs, he composed a first draft of what would become his most influential novel, *Naked Lunch*. In 1957 Ginsberg and Kerouac traveled to Tangiers to help Burroughs edit his manuscript and shape it into the version that was finally published in 1959. Parts of the *Naked Lunch* manuscript also resulted in three other novels: *The Soft Machine* (1961), *The Ticket That Exploded* (1962), and *Nova Express* (1964). All have the same style of writing as *Naked Lunch,* meaning that while composing the manuscripts, Burroughs used creative techniques such as a nonlinear style, cutting sentences apart and splicing them with other phrases to create an altered sense of reality like the real reality he experienced during his drug-induced writing sessions: "fumbling through faded tape at the pick up frontier, a languid grey area of hiatus miasmic yawns and gaping goof holes" (1959, 63). Burroughs would confuse readers further by editing the pre-published proofs and sending them to the publisher, ironically, in no particular order, resulting in the final unintentional chapter splicing that can be found in the final publication of the novel.

Like Kerouac, Ginsberg, Tom Wolfe, and Hunter S. Thompson, Burroughs enjoyed the ambiguity of his writings, most often created by accident, but his work is still considered as natural writing. The creativity of the nonlinear form was a direct representation of Burroughs and how he lived his life. "The Beats flocked to subcultures that manipulated the precarious nature of language to create new and unexpected meanings" (Mills 2006, 37). Also like Ginsberg, Burroughs's masterpiece went on trial for obscenity soon after its publication. California was the first state to accuse the novel of being obscene, but in 1965 all charges were dropped. In 1966, the Supreme Court of Massachusetts declared that it was not obscene and considered the novel an important contribution to American literature. Several excerpts from the Boston trial are included in the 1991 edition of *Naked Lunch,* published by Grove Press.

> The freeing of the artist in literary presentation is as much a precondition of the desirable creating of adequate opinion on public matters as is the freeing of social inquiry. Artists have always been the real purveyors of news, for it is not the outward happening in itself is news, but the kindling by it of emotion, perception, and appreciation. (xxxiv)

Allen Ginsberg was one of many people to testify for the novel, having experienced the same accusation in 1956 for his poem "Howl."

Burroughs remained friends with Ginsberg throughout his life, supporting him especially during the late 1970s when Burroughs's son William S. Burroughs Jr.

(Billy) became ill from liver cirrhosis. In 1974 Ginsberg found Burroughs a job teaching creative writing at the City College of New York. Burroughs lasted a semester, claiming that he was uninspired by his students "The teaching gig was a lesson in never again. You were giving out all this energy and nothing was coming back" (Morgan 1988, 477).

Burroughs became a cult figure in American popular culture in the 1980s and 1990s. He had cameos in many films, notably a small role as a junkie priest in Gus Van Sant's film *Drugstore Cowboy* (1989). In 1997 he made appearances in the video for U2's song "Last Night on Earth." He also contributed a spoken word performance on a track by Nirvana called "The Priest They Called Him." Burroughs recorded the song "Just One Fix" with the 1990s alternative band Ministry and made an appearance in the video version of the song. He also made an appearance on the television show *Saturday Night Live* in 1981 (Internet Movie Database).

Context and Issues. Since the 1960s, other authors have written about the road and thematically the experiences of the traveler, the adventure and the culture that they encounter, and the culture that they create. Following are some of those books: Erika Lopez's *Flaming Iguanas: An Illustrated All-Girl Road Novel Thing* (1997), Joyce Johnson's *Come and Join the Dance* (1961), LeRoi Jones's *The System of Dante's Hell* (1965), Toni Morrison's *Song of Solomon* (1977), Vladimir Nabokov's *The Annotated Lolita* (1970), Robert M. Pirsig's *Zen and the Art of Motorcycle Maintenance: An Inquiry into Values* (1974), Thomas Pynchon's *The Crying of Lot 49* (1965), Tom Robbins's *Another Roadside Attraction* (1971) and *Even Cowgirls Get the Blues* (1976), Mona Simpson's *Anywhere But Here* (1986), Cormac McCarthy's *The Road* (2006), Don DeLillo's *America* (1971), Barbara Kingsolver's *The Bean Trees* (1988) and *Pigs in Heaven* (1993), Bobbie Ann Mason's *In Country* (1985), Sherman Alexie's *The Lone Ranger and Tonto Fistfight in Heaven* (1993), and Bryan Lee O'Malley's graphic novel *Lost at Sea* (2005). Music and film have also drawn upon the road experience. Bands of the 1960s included the Grateful Dead and Jim Morrison and The Doors, and musicians of the 1970s included Bruce Springsteen and Bob Seager. Road movies have included *Easy Rider* (1969), *Two-Lane Blacktop* (1971), *Alice Doesn't Live Here Anymore* (1974), *Mad Max* (1979), *Mad Max 2: The Road Warrior* (1982), *Thelma and Louise* (1991), *My Own Private Idaho* (1991), *Dumb and Dumber* (1994), *Road Trip* (2000), and *Sideways* (2004), and there have been television shows such as *Route 66* in the 1960s and the commodification of the road in the reality show *Road Rules* in the 1990s.

Hunter S. Thompson (1937–2005). Thompson is best known for his gonzo style of journalism. *Gonzo* is a term he invented to describe this free-flowing, naturalistic writing style, similar to that of Kerouac's spontaneous prose: "one of the basic tenets of gonzo: no revision. Gonzo was to be first-draft, written-at-the-moment . . . a genuinely spontaneous feel" (McKeen 1991, 49). Thompson started his style when deadlines began to expire; instead of sending his editors polished and reworked articles, he would send them his notes, often written by hand from his point of view as representative of the finished article. The style became widely popular. Thompson had always believed that writing should be natural and spontaneous, putting the author himself into the middle of the action. He wrote many of his articles and novels in first person, using his own experiences and encounters as his storylines.

His first full-length published book, *Hell's Angels: A Strange and Terrible Saga* (1967), introduced Thompson as a risk-taker. Like many of the road authors, Thompson became immersed with the subculture of America. The one thing that made his writing different, however, was that Thompson felt that the deeper one submerges oneself into the culture, the better one can write about it, as he demonstrates with his nonfiction piece *Hell's Angels,* based on his travels with the infamous biker gang in late 1965. Because the group was known to dislike outsiders, Thompson presented his assignment for *The Nation,* open and honestly, to the then-leader of the gang, Ralph "Sonny" Barger, with the help of Birney Jarvis, a former Hell's Angels member and police-beat reporter for the *San Francisco Chronicle.* Thompson built a reputation with the gang, ultimately earning their trust. Thompson shared the life of a Hell's Angel for over a year, but then several of the members with whom Thompson was not familiar, who suspected him of profiting from his writings about the gang, demanded a part of Thompson's compensation. Thompson tried to explain to them that although he would be paid for the articles, it was not more than his regular pay. Unconvinced, they gave Thompson a "stomping," as they termed it, meaning that the bikers gave Thompson a severe and brutal beating. His involvement with the gang dwindled, but in letters to friends later in his life, Thompson always held Ralph "Sonny" Barger in high regard and felt no ill will toward him, despite the incident involving his gang members.

Much of American society feared the Hell's Angels because of their disregard for others. Their attitude toward outsiders, the law, and society in general earned them the reputation of being a part of a degenerate society. The outlaw gang gained a quick reputation when they were hired to act as security for a concert for the Rolling Stones in California, which ended in the beating death of one of the spectators by several of the bikers-turned-guards. The opening page of *Hell's Angels* presents the reader with Thompson's witnessed description of the elusive gang:

> The Menace is loose again, the Hell's Angels, the hundred-carat headline, running fast and loud on the early morning freeway, low in the saddle, nobody smiles, jamming crazy through traffic and ninety miles an hour down the center stripe, missing by inches . . . tense for the action, long hair in the wind, beards and bandanas flapping, earrings, armpits, chain whips, swastikas and stripped-down Harleys flashing chrome as traffic on 101 moves over, nervous, to let the formation pass like a burst of dirty thunder. (1996, 3).

Eliot Fremont-Smith (1967), a book reviewer for the *New York Times,* called *Hell's Angel*s an "angry, knowledgeable, fascinating and excitedly written book" that details the gang "not so much as dropouts from society but as total misfits, or unfits—emotionally, intellectually and educationally unfit to achieve the rewards, such as they are, that the contemporary social order offers." These "misfits," such as they were regarded by American culture as a whole, were a part of the subculture that only being on the road could uncover. They existed because of the road, the inspiration of mobility on the road, rebelling against the social norm and doing so in an extreme, but effective manner.

Thompson's best-known novel, *Fear and Loathing in Las Vegas* (1971), originated from a road trip he took with Oscar Zeta Acosta, a popular Mexican American attorney and activist for human rights in Los Angeles. Thompson and Acosta traveled to Las Vegas using Thompson's assignment for *Sports Illustrated* as a reason. Throughout the novel, Acosta is referred to as "my attorney," whereas Thompson appears as his alter ego, Raoul Duke. "'I want you to know that we're on our way to Las Vegas to find the American Dream.' I smiled. 'That's why we rented this car. It was the only way to do it. Can you grasp that?'" (Thompson 1996, 6). Their search for "the American Dream" becomes futile as their penchant for drugs deters them from their path. "The trunk of the car looked like a mobile police narcotics lab" (4). The book, considered a cult classic, became even more popular after the release of the film version in 1998, starring Johnny Depp and Benicio del Toro.

Thompson was always looking for the American dream in his writings, but somehow it always eluded him in his writings and his personal life. The American dream that Thompson was looking for did not exist. Thompson died in 2005 from a self-inflicted gunshot wound to the head in his home in Colorado.

Tom Wolfe (1931–). His journalistic-style novel *The Electric Kool-Aid Acid Test* detailed the adventures of Ken Kesey's Merry Pranksters in the late 1960s. Wolfe's novel became an anthem for the emerging hippie culture of Southern California, with its promotion of drug use, music, and rebellion against conventional American society and the ensuing Vietnam War.

Wolfe, like Kerouac, experimented with new literary techniques such as free association (spontaneous prose), repetition, and overuse of punctuation in order to express the drug-induced hysteria of Ken Kesey and his Merry Pranksters, accounted in *The Electric Kool-Aid Acid Test*. This style of writing, Wolfe called "New Journalism." "[New Journalism] has revolutionized several genres of writing. Thanks to Wolfe, not Kesey, strangers understand that to be 'on the bus' means to have awareness" (Mills 2006, 88–89). Along with E.W. Johnson, Wolfe edited an anthology of journalism titled *The New Journalism*. Unlike Hunter S. Thompson's gonzo journalism, *The New Journalism* claims that the reader will get a better understanding of the narrative if the text is written in third person but recounted from firsthand author experience.

> What really characterizes the New Journalism, at least as it is represented in this book, is first, a certain elusiveness on the part of the writer. The more he puts himself forward, hopping about inside his own story, nattily dressed, bearded, drunk, eccentric, acting up, the less we seem to know about where he stands, because he has made it his job to hide his opinions, or to hint at them only indirectly, or perhaps even to have none. (Wood 1973)

Wolfe itemized the happenings aboard Kesey's "Furthur" bus, keeping detailed accounts of the stories developed by the larger-than-life characters.

Ken Kesey (1935–2001). Kesey is best known for his novel *One Flew Over the Cuckoo's Nest* (1962). The novel was an instant success. The film version was released in 1975 and won five Academy Awards. To coincide with the counterculture of the late 1960s, Kesey hosted a series of parties called "Acid Tests" that included psychedelic themes such as the music of the Grateful Dead, visits from members of the Hell's Angels motorcycle gang, black lights and florescent paint, and hallucinogenic drugs such as LSD. The 1960s icon Timothy Leary, who popularized the term *psychedelic,* was among the guests at Kesey's parties. Out of these parties came the group Kesey put together known as the Merry Pranksters, who traveled across the county in a repainted school bus named Furthur. These journeys are described in detail in Tom Wolfe's novel *The Electric Kool-Aid Acid Test* (1968), utilizing Kerouac's spontaneous prose method. Other members of the Merry Pranksters included Neal Cassady, Allen Ginsberg, and Timothy Leary. The Merry Pranksters are also mentioned briefly in Hunter S. Thompson's book *Hell's Angels: A Strange and Terrible Saga* (1967).

Kesey replaced Kerouac as the voice of the new generation.

> *On the Road* was . . . stance-changing. We all tried to imitate it. Yet, even then, no one considered it the work of a Truly Great Writer. I recall my initial interpretation of the phenomenon, that, yeah, it was a pretty groovy book, but not because this guy Ker-oh-wak was such hot potatoes; that what it was actually was one of those little serendipitous accidents of fate, that's all. (Kesey 1983, 60)

After the release of his second novel, *Sometimes a Great Notion,* in 1964, Kesey decided to stop writing and focus on the film that he was making about his friends: *The Merry Pranksters Search for the Kool Place.* "For Kesey and his collaborators, the road story needed retelling, not because the road had lost its meaning but because the road *novel* had. The Pranksters wanted to enlighten others, not only through LSD and their 'acid tests' but also through America's primary mechanism of altered consciousness—the movies" (Mills 2006, 93). Kesey believed that his movie would be the ultimate road trip, looking for "something wilder and weirder out on the road" (Wolfe 1981, 90), but Kesey failed to finish it. The unfinished acid road trip movie, however, was upstaged by the failure of another acid road trip movie that was released: *Magical Mystery Tour,* produced by the Beatles in 1967.

Kesey continued to write essays, short stories, and plays throughout his life. He and the Merry Pranksters also made appearances well into the 1990s, especially at Phish concerts, a band that is said to resemble the Grateful Dead. Kesey died on November 10, 2001, at his home in Pleasant Hill, Oregon.

LeRoi Jones (aka Amiri Baraka) (1934–). The Beat icons Jack Kerouac and Allen Ginsberg were Jones's early influences, especially with their love for jazz in common. Jones's wife, Hettie Cohen, became a successful Beat author with her memoir about her life with Jones titled *How I Became Hettie Jones* (1996). His decision to marry a white woman shocked some of the literary community, but it was the first step in Jones's rebellion against the racism raging in the country at the time. The publication of his novel *The System of Dante's Hell,* in 1965, propelled him to Beat fame. Mostly inspired by Kerouac's novel *On the Road,* Jones decided to write his own road novel from an African American point of view. Jones was raised in a middle-class family; however, he was also raised in the middle of America's turmoil with racism.

> Selby's hoodlums, Rechy's homosexuals, Burroughs' addicts, Kerouac's mobile young voyeurs, my own Negroes, are literally not included in the mainstream of American life . . . They are Americans no character in a John Updike novel would be happy to meet, but they nonetheless Americans, formed out of the conspicuously tragic evolution of modern American life. (Jones 1963, xiv)

Jones dedicated much of his writing to trying to break the stereotype of black writing; he wrote from his perspective but kept it culturally neutral, not to hide the fact that he was African American, but to blend into literature the black writer's point of view, without making it racially biased. "His belief at the time [was] that a writer's creative individuality—the writer's 'voice'—becomes his only voice" (Mills 2006, 52). Jones admired Kerouac's use of style and language. He felt that Kerouac was able to capture creativity in his writing voice with the use of his spontaneous prose. Similar to Kerouac's character Sal in *On the Road,* Jones's character Roi, in *The System of Dante's Hell,* sets off on the road to discover the real America and to shun the society in which he was raised. Unlike Sal, Roi does not feel displaced in the African American communities. Whereas Sal feels "scared" (Kerouac 1976, 157), Roi rediscovers his lost past and comes to terms with his ethnicity. "If we can bring back on ourselves, the absolute pain our people must have felt when they came onto this shore, we are more ourselves again, and can begin to put history back on our menu" (Jones 1965, 153). Like his character and alter ego Roi, Jones left his wife Hettie to return to the black community. "Hettie, 'the white wife,' was a liability for a young Afro-American male who felt ethnically illegitimate and who wanted now to be black, which tragically for Jones meant being seen as black by both blacks and whites . . . [He became] distanced from his bohemian life and closer to a 'deeper black' identity" (Watts 2001, 141). Later in his life, Jones wrote many critical essays about jazz, blues, and other black-influenced music. He became a professor of African American studies in 1984. In 1989 he won an American Book Award and a Langston Hughes Award for his collection of works. He was named poet laureate of New Jersey in 2002 but was forced to relinquish the title because of the controversy surrounding his poem about 9/11, "Somebody Blew Up America," in 2003.

Women in Writing Road Fiction. Unlike many African American male writers, women authors were often overlooked in the 1950s and 1960s, overshadowed by their male counterparts and dismissed as not having original thoughts among the Beat generation authors. The male authors, such as Jack Kerouac, tried to give women a voice of their own in their works but failed to do so; instead they stereotyped women into roles of caretakers, prostitutes, and wives who were partly responsible for their husbands' misery in marriage. Hélène Cixous states in her 1975 essay "Sorties" that women authors need to develop a separation from male writers, opposing themselves from their points of view. Janet Wolff wrote in her 1993 essay "On the Road Again: Metaphors of Travel in Cultural Criticism" that she believes women are following in the footsteps of their male counterparts, utilizing the same language in their own writings, causing the female authors to become marginalized. "Just as women accede to theory, [male] theorists take to the road . . . [and] the already-gendered language of mobility marginalizes women who want to participate in cultural criticism" (234). She feels that it is necessary for women to develop their own metaphors so that they can be recognized as women writers, instead of following in the same linguistic footsteps of male authors, such as Kerouac, who had popularized the "road" as a male-dominated domain in literature.

Joyce Johnson wrote her own version of *On the Road,* titled *Come and Join the Dance,* in 1961. It was not until the end of the 1990s that she gained fame with the play version of her memoir *Minor Characters,* detailing her life as a woman writer in the 1960s and as Jack Kerouac's girlfriend and representing every other female character that had become a supporting role in the novels written by the popular male authors of that time. As noted previously, Hettie Jones, wife of LeRoi Jones, also made a name for herself later in life with her memoir about her life with Jones and the racism they experienced being a mixed-race couple in the 1960s. Other female writers include Diana di Prima and Carolyn Cassady.

Hélène Cixous expressed belief that "another thinking as yet not thinkable will transform the functioning of all society" (1988, 289). Erika Lopez explores new ways of thinking, living, and traveling, finding her own freedom and adventure in her novel *Flaming Iguanas: An All Girl Road Novel Thing* (1997), in which she not only explores the life of the woman on the road but also explores the lesbian perspective of life on the road. "When you're on the road, you just let your head go. You start thinking about your life, and it's just kind of inevitable. You also lighten up on yourself, because you're not next to other people, so you don't really have anyone to gauge yourself by. You feel quite normal and very much OK about your thinking and who you are . . . You're just there, thinking" (qtd. in May 1997).

Erika Lopez grew up on the road, on welfare and in the middle of the impoverished society Kerouac set out to find. Lopez was raised to speak her mind, and because her mother practiced Quakerism, Lopez was also raised to not be subservient to anyone, a lesson the women of the 1950s and 1960s did not have the luxury to practice.

Joyce Johnson (nee Glassman) (1935–). Joyce Johnson claims that she was "determined . . . to write about sex frankly, unusual for a young women at the time" (qtd. in Tallmer 2003). Sexual freedom—women's freedom—was another theme of road fiction. Johnson's memoir *Minor Characters* won her a National Book Critics Circle Award. The memoir was also turned into a play, titled *Door Wide Open,* in 2003. Based on her life with Jack Kerouac and the rest of the Beat authors and poets,

> *Minor Characters* is first and foremost Joyce's own story, showing us what it was like to be a young woman coming of age in the tumultuous and transitional fifties, as the youth of postwar America chafed against the constraints of a buttoned-up conservative society. (Knight 1998, 167)

Her novel *Come and Join the Dance* (1961) tells the story of a young woman, Susan, who yearns to be free of the confines of university life. She wants to become a rebel. Susan daydreams during her exams and excitedly waits for her time to leave her life of comfort and constraint and travel to Paris. She feels that once she is on her own, things will happen for her. Similar to other Beat authors and poets, Glassman believed that a university education is good, but life experience is better. Susan is given the voice of a strong woman, ready for the road and the experiences that come with it, but she stays true to herself, realizing that no man is able to give her what she cannot give to herself. "She remembered she had a train to catch, suitcases to pick up four blocks away, and a door to close for the last time. She was slipping away from Peter, just as he was slipping away from her. This was the end of something that had been completed" (171). She had no regrets about leaving him to pursue her travels in Paris. Female characters are often given a minor role in novels authored by men, with stereotypical personalities, but written from a woman's perspective, Susan is given an independent personality, a radical change for female characters in the 1950s and 1960s.

As Kerouac's lover from 1957 to 1958, Glassman witnessed his shot to stardom after the publication of *On the Road.* The Beats became famous in American literature, but Glassman still struggled to have her voice heard over the many talented men who were finally getting recognized for their visions. Like Hettie Jones,

Glassman found it difficult to conform to society's preconceived notions of the role of the woman in 1950s and 1960s America. Some of Glassman's fame came from her connections, rather than her talent as a writer. This made Glassman even more determined to make a name for herself based on her own merit.

Hettie Jones (nee Cohen) (1934–). Hettie Jones had to overcome not only the fact that she was a white Jewish woman but also that she was married to a black man and was raising two daughters of mixed race during the 1960s. Being the wife of author and poet LeRoi Jones, Hettie had to fight to make a name for herself in a predominantly male-oriented literary world. "She discusses the manner in which her life as a woman and particularly as a bohemian wife and mother restricted her opportunities to edit, write, and otherwise engage her mind in ways available to her husband, LeRoi" (Watts 2001, 44). Brenda Knight wrote about Hettie in her collection *Women of the Beat Generation* (1998) as being a woman who, from childhood, knew she did not belong in conventional society, in the traditional role of a Jewish woman on Long Island during the 1950s. "Hettie Cohen made a choice to leave behind comfortable Long Island and the fifties' ideal of a cookie-cutter marriage when she went to a women's college in Virginia to study dramas. There she explored the creative arts, discovered jazz, and realized there was no turning back" (360). Thus, Hettie Jones entered into the nonconformist lifestyle of the Beat generation.

Bibliography

Baudrillard, Jean. *America*. Trans. Chris Turner. New York: Verso, 1988.

Beauvoir, Simone de. *America Day by Day*. New York: Grove, 1953.

Belasco, Warren. *America on the Road: From Autocamp to Motel, 1910–1945*. Cambridge: MIT Press, 1979.

Breton, André. *Manifestoes of Surrealism*. Ann Arbor: University of Michigan, 1972.

Burroughs, William S. *Naked Lunch*. New York: Grove Press, 1991. Originally published 1959.

———. *Queer*. New York: Penguin, 1985.

Cain, Chelsea. *Dharma Girl: A Road Trip across the American Generations*. Seattle, WA: Seal, 1996.

Cervantes, Miguel Saavedra de. *The Ingenious Gentleman Don Quixote of La Mancha*. Ed. Joseph R. Jones and Kenneth Douglas. New York: Norton, 1981.

Charters, Ann, ed. *The Beats: Literary Bohemians in Postwar America, Part 2*.

Dictionary of Literary Biography. Volume 16. Detroit, MI: Gale Publishing Group, 1983.

———, ed. *The Portable Beat Reader*. New York: Penguin, 1992.

———, ed. *The Portable Jack Kerouac*. New York: Viking, 1995.

Cixous, Hélène. "Sorties." In *Modern Criticism and Theory*. David Lodge, ed. New York: Longman, 1988, 287–293. Originally published 1975.

Coupland, Douglas. *Generation X: Tales for an Accelerated Culture*. New York: St. Martin's, 1991.

Debord, Guy. *The Society of the Spectacle*. Trans. Donald Nicholson-Smith. New York: Zone, 1995. Originally published 1967.

DeLillo, Don. *America*. New York: Penguin, 1971.

Dettelbach, Cynthia Golomb. *In the Driver's Seat: The Automobile in American Literature and Popular Culture*. Westport, CT: Greenwood, 1976.

Devitt, Amy J. *Writing Genres*. Carbondale: Southern Illinois University Press, 2004.

Ellison, Ralph. *Invisible Man*. New York: Vintage, 1990. Originally published 1947.

Feldman, Paula R. "Joan Didion." In *American Novelists Since World War II*. Jeffrey Helterman and Richard Layman, eds. *Dictionary of Literary Biography*. Detroit, MI: Gale, 1978, 121–127.

Fremont-Smith, Eliot. "Books of the Times; Motorcycle Misfits—Fiction and Fact." *New York Times* 23 February 1967: 33.

Ginsberg, Allen. *Howl and Other Poems.* San Francisco: City Lights Books, 2006.

———. *Selected Poems: 1947–1995.* New York: Harper, 1996.

Helterman and Richard Layman. *Dictionary of Literary Biography.* Volume 2. Detroit, MI: Gale, 1978, 121–127.

Holmes, John Clellon. "The Name of the Game." In *The Beats: Literary Bohemians in Postwar America, Part 2.* Ann Charters, ed. 627–629.

———. "The Philosophy of the Beat Generation." In *The Beats: Literary Bohemians in Postwar America, Part 2.* Ann Charters, ed. 631–636. DLB volume 16. Originally published 1958.

———. "This Is the Beat Generation." In *The Beats: Literary Bohemians in Postwar America, Part 2.* Ann Charters, ed. 629–631. Originally published 1952.

Hunt, Tim. *Kerouac's Crooked Road: The Development of a Fiction.* Berkeley: University of California Press, 1996.

Internet Movie Database. "William S. Burroughs." Retrieved June 6, 2007, from http://imdb.com/name/nm0123221.

Johnson, Joyce [Joyce Glassman]. *Come and Join the Dance.* New York: H. Wolff, 1961.

———. *Minor Characters.* New York: Penguin, 1999.

Jones, LeRoi. *The System of Dante's Hell.* New York: Grove, 1965.

———. *The Moderns: An Anthology of New Writing in America.* New York: Corinth, 1963.

Kael, Pauline. "Woman on the Road." Rev. of *Alice Doesn't Live Here Anymore,* dir. Martin Scorsese. *New Yorker* 13 January 1975: 74–78+.

Kerouac, Jack. "Beatific: The Origins of the Beat Generation." *The Portable Jack Kerouac.* Ann Charters, ed. 565–573. Originally published 1958.

———. "Essentials of Spontaneous Prose." *Evergreen Review* 2.5 (1958): 72–73.

———. *On the Road.* New York: Penguin, 1976. Originally published 1957.

———. "The Vanishing American Hobo." *Holiday* (March 1960): 60–63.

———. *Visions of Cody.* New York: Penguin, 1972.

Kesey, Ken. "Is There Any End to Kerouac Highway?" *Esquire* December 1983: 60–63.

Knight, Brenda. *Women of the Beat Generation: The Writers, Artists and Muses at the Heart of a Revolution.* Berkeley, CA: Conari, 1998.

Lackey, Kris. *Road Frames: The American Highway Narrative.* Lincoln: University of Nebraska Press, 1997.

Least Heat Moon, William. *Blue Highways: A Journey into America.* New York: Fawcett, 1982.

Lopez, Erika. *Flaming Iguanas: An Illustrated All-Girl Road Novel Thing.* New York: Simon, 1997.

May, Sandra. "20 Questions: Interview with Erika Lopez." City Paper.net 1997 July 17. Retrieved March 17, 2007, from http://www.citypaper.net/articles/071797/article001.shtml.

McCarthy, Cormac. *The Road.* New York: Knopf, 2006.

McKeen, William. *Hunter S. Thompson.* Boston: Twayne, 1991.

Mills, Katie. *The Road Story and the Rebel: Moving Through Film, Fiction, and Television.* Carbondale: Southern Illinois University Press, 2006.

Morgan, Ted. *Literary Outlaw.* New York: Avon Books, 1988.

Morrison, Toni. *Song of Solomon.* New York: Plume, 1987. Originally published 1977.

Nabokov, Vladimir. *The Annotated Lolita.* Ed. Alfred Appel Jr. New York: McGraw, 1970.

Pirsig, Robert M. *Zen and the Art of Motorcycle Maintenance: An Inquiry into Values.* New York: Quill, 1979.

Primeau, Ronald. *Romance of the Road: The Literature of the American Highway.* Bowling Green, OH: BGSU Popular Press, 1996.

Robbins, Tom. *Even Cowgirls Get the Blues.* Boston: Houghton Mifflin, 1976.

Simpson, Mona. *Anywhere But Here.* New York: Vintage, 1986.

Tallmer, Jerry. "The Beat of New York in the Fifties." *The Villager*. 2003. http://www.
thevillager.com/villager_4/thebeatofnew.html.

Thompson, Hunter S. *Fear and Loathing in Las Vegas and Other American Stories*. New
York: Random House Modern Library, 1996. Originally published 1971.

———. *Hell's Angels: A Strange and Terrible Saga*. New York: Ballantine, 1996. Originally
published 1967.

Watts, Jerry Gafio. *Amiri Baraka: The Politics and Art of a Black Intellectual*. New York:
New York University Press, 2001.

Wolfe, Tom. "The Chief and His Merry Pranksters Take a Trip with Electric Kool Aid."
World Journal Tribune: New York 29 January 1967:4–7.

———. *The Electric Kool-Aid Acid Test*. New York: Bantam, 1981. Originally published
1968.

———. *The Kandy-Kolored Tangerine-Flake Streamline Baby*. New York: Farrar, 1968.

Wolff, Janet. "On the Road Again: Metaphors of Travel in Cultural Criticism." *Cultural
Studies* 7.2 (1993): 224–240.

Wood, Michael. "The New Journalism." *New York Times* 22 June 1973. Retrieved
March 15, 2007, from http://www.nytimes.com/books/98/11/08/specials/wolfe-jour-
nalism.html.

ANNE BAHRINGER

ROMANCE NOVELS

Definition. The term *romance novel* is used to categorize a type of fiction focused
on stories of successful love. In academic discussions, the word *romance* may be
used to characterize a story of a triumphant or tragic relationship, but in the retail
book industry, it is specifically understood that a book marketed as a romance novel
will conclude on a happy or hopeful note. Naturally, there are numerous novels
classified in other genres (including **erotic literature, historical fiction**, and **chick lit**)
in which romantic relationships play a prominent role in the plot. Whether a book
is regarded specifically as a romance novel or as mainstream fiction depends in part
on authorial intent and publisher specialty: the genre attracts legions of devoted
readers because it promises reliable entertainment in the form of likable protagonists and accessible plots. Many readers become attached to specific authors, series,
or imprints, while others become connoisseurs of a particular subgenre. In recent
years, there has been an upswing in the promotion titles across multiple genres, such
that publications such as *Romantic Times* regularly feature reviews of writers whose
books are primarily marketed, shelved, and nominated for awards in other genres
such as **mystery novels, science fiction**, and **fantasy literature**. These writers
include Janet Evanovich (b. 1943), Lois McMaster Bujold (b. 1949), Elizabeth Bear
(b. 1971), and Naomi Novik (b. 1973).

Be they manuals for writers, promotional brochures aimed at library and bookstore patrons, or Web sites and blogs with reviews and forums for multiple types
of participants, many guides to romantic fiction emphasize the diversity of the field
by outlining its major subgenres. One primary form of distinction is temporal—
that is, the grouping of novels into "historical," "contemporary," and "futuristic."
The Romance Writers of America (RWA), a professional network for both
published and aspiring authors, currently lists the end of World War II (1945) as
the dividing point between "historical" and "contemporary," but Estrada and
Gallagher (1999) set the cutoff year as 1899, "a time distant enough to be considered 'historical' by the masses" (16), whereas the "Browse by Time Period" feature
on the Historical Romance Writers Web site includes listings for the Korean War
(1950–1953) and the Vietnam War (1954–1975). There is general agreement,

however, that the most popular setting for historicals is Regency-era Great Britain. While the future George IV's reign as Prince Regent ran specifically from 1811 to 1820, narratives set in the decades immediately preceding or following that span of time may also be perceived as Regency style if their characterizations or plots originate from events such as the Napoleonic Wars (for instance, veterans of Waterloo reentering society, contending with profiteers, or awakening the interest of bereaved, would-be spinsters). A further distinction is often drawn between traditional Regency romances, which are often characterized as light comedies, and Regency-era historicals, which are generally viewed as longer and more sexualized in content (Beau Monde 2005).

Another primary form of classification within the genre is that of format. There are two major formats: category romances, relatively short novels (approximately 50,000–70,000 words) that are packaged as part of a routinely issued series by their publishers (often 2–6 volumes per month), and single-issue or stand-alone titles (generally between 70,000 and 120,000 words), which are promoted similarly to general fiction titles (and indeed sometimes referred to as mainstream books by some romance industry professionals).

It is important to note that "series" has two separate definitions in this context. In relation to category romances, the term refers to a group of books published under a specific publisher's imprint. The books are written by different authors and are not directly related to each other except in overall theme and tone (for instance, books in Harlequin's American Romance line are promoted as "fast-paced, heart-warming stories about the pursuit of love, marriage and family in America today," while those in the Steeple Hill Love Inspired line depict "Christian characters facing the many challenges of life and love in today's world," and those for Kimanu TRU offer younger African American readers stories about "real-life situations they encounter without being preachy or naive" (eHarlequin.com). In relation to single-issue romances, the term "series" refers to a group of books created by a single author with shared characters (such as protagonists who belong to the same family) and a storyline that is extended from one book to the next. The stories of a particularly engaging clan (such as Nora Roberts's MacGregors) may build into a saga that spans multiple volumes and generations.

A common career trajectory among romance writers is to debut as a category writer and then progress to single-issue work as one gains experience and confidence. In both formats, the majority of authors see their work printed as mass-market paperbacks; hardcover publication is generally reserved for new volumes of especially popular storylines (as well as reissues or omnibus editions of those series' older volumes). For example, Stephanie Laurens's Bar Cynster series commenced with six stand-alone novels about a group of brothers and cousins; these were issued between 1998 and 2001, all as mass-market titles. As the series' fan base solidified, the series expanded into additional stories about characters who had appeared in secondary roles in the earlier novels; three of these were also issued only in mass-market format (2001–2002), but all the others (more than a half dozen to date) have first appeared as hardcover volumes, the series' devotees having proved themselves eager enough for each new installment to pay the additional expense (often listed at three times the mass-market price) rather than wait for the mass-market edition (in Laurens's case, customarily issued 10 months after the hardcover). At the same time, Laurens's Bastion Club storyline formally debuted in 2003 as a mass-market series and has remained in that format.

The Bastion Club series by Laurens demonstrates another narrative strategy that established authors sometimes employ—that of "borrowing" characters or events from their other titles or series for cameos in their newer novels. Laurens's *Captain Jack's Woman* (1997), originally published as a true stand-alone story, is now listed on her Web site (stephanielaurens.com) as a prequel to the Bastion Club series, and characters from the Cynster clan sometimes show up in the ballrooms of Bastion Club narratives. When crafted properly, such scenes reward an author's longtime fans with the pleasure of an in-joke without requiring newer readers to be familiar with books outside of the series.

A third type of subgenre label signals the story's style to would-be readers. Examples of such labels include classic, ethnic, inspirational, paranormal, romantic comedy, sensual, suspense, and time travel. Both the specific labels and their scope vary among publishers, reviewers, and writing instructors, but it is common practice to adopt or develop a system of such labels when discussing the genre as a whole. Coding books by subgenre enables prospective consumers to sift efficiently through the dozens (and sometimes hundreds) of blurbs in a typical review publication or marketing campaign, allowing them to ascertain and assess the titles most likely to match their tastes more quickly.

Authors who specialize in one subgenre and then choose to write in a radically different style sometimes adopt separate names for each type of story in order to manage reader expectations. As Jayne Ann Krentz puts it, "This way readers always know which of my three worlds they will be entering when they pick up one of my books"; as a specialist in suspense novels, Krentz uses her married name for contemporary stories, the name Amanda Quick for historicals, and Jayne Castle for futuristic and paranormal tales (Krentz "Biography"). On the "Frequently Asked Questions" page of her Web site, Sabrina Jeffries cites similar reasons for writing as Deborah Martin and Deborah Nicholas. Authors also may elect to publish their novels under pseudonyms because of other marketing considerations (such as the fear of prolific output being equated with poor quality), contractual obligations (some names are restricted to specific publishers), or personal concerns (Gorlinsky); if an author's name becomes a powerhouse brand, where readers habitually seek out that author's work regardless of subgenre, multiple pseudonyms may become an open secret among booksellers and fans (Little and Hayden 2003, 376) and later formally publicized (292–93).

Selected Authors. The most influential classic in the history of romance novels is *Pride and Prejudice* (1813) by Jane Austen (1775–1817). In addition to remaining popular in its own right (placing third in All About Romance's "Top 100 Romances" poll in 2007 and consistently ranked among the top 25 titles in earlier incarnations of the list), it has inspired more than 60 sequels and adaptations in various media (www.pemberley.com). Austen is credited as the main literary model for Georgette Heyer (1902–1974), who in turn is considered the pioneer of Regency stories as a subgenre of historical romance (Regis 2003, 125–126). Allusions to *Pride and Prejudice* also permeate chick-lit bestseller *Bridget Jones's Diary* (1996) by Helen Fielding (b. 1958), and it has been dubbed "the original chick-lit masterpiece" (Swendson 2005). (Some writers view chick lit as a subgenre of romance, while others treat it as a distinctly separate niche.)

Among nineteenth-century novels, Charlotte Bronte's *Jane Eyre* (1847) also has demonstrated enduring appeal and influence (All About Romance 2007; Falk 1999, 217), as has her sister Emily Bronte's classic *Wuthering Heights* (1847), with its iconic brooding hero, Heathcliff. Among twentieth-century authors, Barbara Cartland (1901–2000) and Kathleen E. Woodiwiss (1939–2007) were two of the romance genre's giants. Cartland composed over 700 novels between the 1920s and her death; habitually dressed in pink and prone to voicing conservative opinions, she catered to the traditional perception of romance novels as chaste, ultra-feminine fare. Woodiwiss was far less prolific, producing just 15 novels across 35 years, but she is revered by many modern writers for revolutionizing the genre; when it first appeared in 1972, *The Flame and the Flower* electrified readers with the scope of its plot (significantly broader than category romances, which had dominated romance publishing up to that point), the feistiness of its heroine, and the explicit details incorporated into its love scenes. The success of Woodiwiss's novels and other stand-alone titles such as Rosemary Rogers's *Sweet Savage Love* (1974) and Bertrice Small's *The Kadin* (1978) encouraged publishers to view long historical romances as commercially viable (Radway 1991, 33–34).

By the advent of the twenty-first century, steamy novels had become very much the norm—enough to invite considerable criticism from both within and outside the field. For example, in one discussion of trends, author Dorothy Garlock (b. 1942) complained that classic storytelling was "being replaced by raunchy erotica published as romance," a lament actively echoed and debated in All About Romance (AAR) forums between 1997 and 2000 (AAR; Authors on the Web 2003; Gracen 1999). When asked about changes in the genre since *The Flame and the Flower,* Woodiwiss suggested that explicit sex had become "overdone" (Wehr and Weiss 2000).

At the same time, interest never wholly waned in milder novels. The Christian romances of Grace Livingston Hill (1865–1947), popular during her lifetime, were regularly reissued during the last quarter of the twentieth century. Janette Oke (b. 1935) has been lauded as the author whose Love Comes Softly series (1979–1989) proved the viability of Christian fiction to modern publishers. In 1999 AAR began "One Foot on the Floor," a periodically updated recommendations list of romances featuring "kisses only" or "subtle sensuality" (www.likesbooks. com/onefoot.html). In 2007 the president of the RWA, Sherry Lewis, observed that both inspirational romance and erotic romance were "two of the hottest subgenres" in the field (Robbins 2007).

Trends and Themes. Writing mavens frequently advise would-be novelists to eschew chasing trends, in part because regular romance readers tend to be very well-versed in their subgenres (and thus quick to detect and dismiss phonies) and in part because books created merely to capitalize on fads may fail to reach retail buyers before the market becomes saturated and interest fades. Moreover, because the perception of trends is often based on local, anecdotal observation rather than global statistical analysis, experts may disagree on whether a pattern is truly in effect: for example, interest in historical romances is commonly thought to have peaked during the 1990s, but some industry professionals contend that the audience for that subgenre never materially decreased. Rather, it may have become less prominent as the markets for other subgenres grew. Nonetheless, some analysts believe historicals fell out of fashion during the early 2000s, returning to favor in 2007 (MacGillivray 2008; Robbins 2007; St. Claire 2007). Other possible trends that have attracted notice in recent years include significant turnover among romance editors (resulting in younger staff and shifting perspectives), the popularity of strong, athletic heroines in other media (such as Buffy the Vampire Slayer), and the success of hero archetypes beyond the "alpha male" of stereotypical bodice-rippers, such as in Vicki Lewis Thompson's Nerd series (Wheless 2007; Vinyard 2004, 93–98).

Some observers believe that the conventional boundaries between romance and other genres have become increasingly flexible, allowing for subgenres such as paranormal romances, romantic mysteries, and time-travel fantasies to flourish. Publishers have become more aware of the sophisticated and diverse tastes of present-day romance readers and have refined their submission and purchasing standards accordingly. For instance, the writing guidelines for the Harlequin Romance imprint stress that "stories must have a global outlook that is mindful of the different lifestyle choices of our readers worldwide" (eHarlequin.com). Another editorial department offers tips on what to avoid among its subgenre specifications—for example, writers of time-travel romances should "beware of philosophizing about the meaning of time, and how the past affects the present. No time machines, please" (Dorchester Publishing 2004).

With Internet access becoming commonplace, both author- and fan-based Web sites and blogs have proliferated. In addition to serving as marketing tools, many sites host forums or encourage extended comment threads that permit authors and readers of romance novels to champion underappreciated texts, commiserate with each other on misconceptions about romance fans, debate appropriate responses to plagiarism scandals, kibbitz about experiences such as attending conventions or chapter meetings, and partake of other interactive opportunities. There is a wide range of tone among these sites, ranging from the demure *Romance Reader* (www.theromancereader.com) to the raucous and blunt *Smart Bitches Who Love Trashy Books* (www.smartbitchestrashybooks.com).

In addition to online communities and local book clubs, romance readers also congregate at regional and national gatherings. These have included the yearly Booklovers extravaganza organized by *Romantic Times* since 1982 and Celebrate Romance! (also known as "CR"), an annual conference founded by romance fans in 1998. For writers, agents, and publishers, the RWA's national and chapter-based conferences provide opportunities to network, attend workshops, and promote their manuscripts or books.

Throughout the 1990s and most of the 2000s, the viability of electronic books (frequently referred to as "e-books") was repeatedly explored by both entrepreneurial and established publishers. The format has not displaced print editions of books to any appreciable degree, but as the devices and interfaces for downloading and perusing e-texts became more affordable and user-friendly, the distribution of romance novels through Web-based vendors received more attention from reviewers and consumers, and the RWA established a special-interest chapter to support authors of electronic and small press titles. The e-book industry has been praised for making available romance novels deemed too non-commercial or risky for print publishers, particularly those by authors who push depictions of erotic adventures, homosexual or polysexual relationships, or paranormal phenomena beyond the perceived limits of conventional taste. Some authors have also earned royalties via the e-publication of older books that had lapsed out of print.

Although romance novels have often been disparaged as "trashy" throwaway stories with short shelf lives, a number of titles in the genre have demonstrated substantial staying power, remaining in print and appearing on top 100 lists (AAR 2007) more than a decade after their first appearance in publishers' catalogs.

Modern classics include *Lord of Scoundrels* (1995) by Loretta Chase (b. 1949), *Outlander* (1991) by Diana Gabaldon (b. 1952), *The Bride* (1989) by Julie Garwood (b. 1946), *MacKenzie's Mountain* (1989) by Linda Howard (b. 1950), *Dreaming of You* (1994) by Lisa Kleypas (b. 1964), and *Paradise* (1991) by Judith McNaught (b. 1950).

Context, Issues, and Reception. The lack of respect accorded to romance fiction by both professional critics and the general public has long been a source of frustration to its fans. Although romance fiction now accounts for over 25 percent of all books sold each year (RWA 2008), its books are frequently condemned as formulaic, trite, and unrealistic and its authors accused of perpetrating fairy-tale myths or soft-core pornography. As with works of science fiction, fantasy, and mystery, the genre classification frequently applied to romance novels is simultaneously an asset and a liability: while the designation helps publicists, booksellers, and librarians identify and promote new titles to readers likely to enjoy them, it can also result in the "ghettoization" of such books, where their separation from mainstream literary fiction encourages academic and "serious" readers to dismiss them as irrelevant fluff. Women seen perusing romances in public still run the risk of being automatically judged as intellectually lightweight or unfulfilled in their relationships; in response to charges that the genre celebrates passive protagonists and patriarchal values, defenders of romantic fiction have repeatedly pointed out the strength, independence, and resourcefulness of its heroines (Allen 2007; Bly 2005; Michaels 2007, 6; Regis 2003, 9–16). Another criticism leveled at romance authors has been that they graft overly modern characterizations or concerns onto historical scenarios, rendering their stories inherently anachronistic; the degree to which works of fiction should be expected to conform to real-life history and culture (as well as the exact nature of said history and culture) is a perennial source of contention among romance readers. The expectations among readers regarding historical verisimilitude vary wildly, and a detail that strikes one reader as an insignificant error may cause another to abandon the story in disgust (and, in the opposite direction, a reader who expresses concern about an item she considers inaccurate may be viewed either as helpfully informative or as unnecessarily nitpicky, depending on the author in question).

A recurring source of debate and tension within the field has been its treatment of non-Caucasian characters. As in the wider world, there has been much heat and little consensus over questions such as if and how an author's description of a Native American or Middle Eastern hero may reflect or perpetuate racist stereotypes, where best to display African American romance novels (in romance? in African American literature? in general fiction?), why Asian American protagonists are rare, if political correctness and historical accuracy are mutually exclusive, if the casts of contemporary romance novels need to become more multicultural, and other concerns. Issues such as the romance industry's perceived role in propagating ageist and heterosexist beliefs have also prompted discussion and analysis.

That said, positive attention to romantic fiction also has increased in recent years, with libraries investing more thought and resources into building collections that offer their patrons the best of the genre (Bouricius 2000; Wyatt et al. 2008). In 2008 the American Library Association's Reading List Council initiated its annual list of the Best Adult Genre Fiction, and it has become common for major public library systems to include romance recommendations on their Web sites (Atlanta-Fulton, Nashville, New York, and Seattle among those doing so).

ROMANCE AWARDS

The RWA bestows a number of awards each year, including ones that recognize booksellers, librarians, and other professionals whose support of the genre has been exceptional. The top awards for novels are the RITAs (named after the association's first president, Rita Clay Estrada), which are currently awarded in 12 categories. Authors who win three or more RITAs in the same category are inducted into RWA's Hall of Fame. The members of the Hall of Fame include Jo Beverley (b. 1947), Justine Dare, Jennifer Greene, Kathleen Korbel, Susan Elizabeth Phillips, Francine Rivers (b. 1947), Nora Roberts, LaVyrle Spencer (b. 1944), Jodi Thomas, and Cheryl Zach (b. 1947). Winners of the RWA's Lifetime Achievement Award have included Estrada, Howard, Krentz, Phillips, Roberts, and Woodiwiss, as well as Heather Graham, Robin Lee Hatcher, Maggie Osborne, and others. The most recent RITA award winners for the Best Traditional Romance category have been *Claiming His Family* by Barbara Hannay (2007); *Princess of Convenience* by Marion Lennox (2006); *Christmas Eve Marriage* by Jessica Hart (2005); *Her Royal Baby* by Marion Lennox (2004); *The Christmas Basket* by Debbie Macomber (2003); *Quinn's Complete Seduction* by Sandra Steffen (2002); *The Best Man & The Bridesmaid* by Liz Fielding (2001); and *Annie, Get Your Groom* by Kristin Gabriel (2000).

Bibliography

All About Romance. *All About Romance: The Back Fence for Lovers of Romance Novels.* http://www.likesbooks.com

———. "Top 100 Romances, November 2007." 2007. http://www.likesbooks.com/top 1002007results.html

Allen, Louise. "My Heroines Are Independent. This Is Not Patriarchal Propaganda." *Guardian Unlimited* December 12, 2007. http://www.guardian.co.uk/commentis-free/2007/dec/12/comment.books

Authors on the Web. "Romance Author Roundtable." 2003. Retrieved January 2, 2008, from http://www.authorsontheweb.com/features/0302-romance/romance-q11.asp

Beau Monde. "About Us." 2005. Retrieved January 21, 2008, from http://thebeaumonde. com/about

Bly, Mary. "A Fine Romance." *New York Times* 12 February 2005.

Bouricius, Ann. *The Romance Readers' Advisory: The Librarian's Guide to Love in the Stacks.* Chicago: American Library Association, 2000.

Chase, Loretta. *Lord of Scoundrels.* New York: Avon, 1995.

Dorchester Publishing. 2004. "Submission Guidelines." Retrieved January 24, 2008, from http://www.dorchesterpub.com/Dorch/SubmissionGuidlines.cfm

eHARLEQUIN.com. "Writing Guidelines." Retrieved January 23, 2008.

Estrada, Rita Clay, and Rita Gallagher. *You Can Write a Romance.* Cincinnati, Ohio: Writer's Digest, 1999.

Falk, Kathryn. *How to Write a Romance for the New Markets and Get It Published!* Columbus, MS: Genesis, 1999.

Gabaldon, Diana. *Outlander.* New York: Delacorte, 1991.

Garwood, Julie. *The Bride.* New York: Pocket Books, 1989.

Gorlinsky, Rachel. "Sensual Romance—What's in a Name?" Retrieved January 23, 2008, from http://sensualromance.writerspace.com/WIAN_Aliases.html

Gracen, Julia. "Too Darn Hot: Romance Fans Clash Over a New Breed of Explicit, Kinky Love Story." *Salon.com* 5 October 1999.

Historical Romance Writers. http://historicalromancewriters.com. Accessed January 20, 2008.

Howard, Linda. *MacKenzie's Mountain.* New York: Mira, 2000.

"Jane Austen Novels and Adaptations." 2008. http://www.pemberley.com/

Jeffries, Sabrina. "About Sabrina—Frequently Asked Questions." Retrieved January 24, 2008, from http://www.sabrinajeffries.com/faqs.php

Kleypas, Lisa. *Dreaming of You.* New York: Avon, 1994.

Krentz, Jayne Ann. *Dangerous Men and Adventurous Women: Romance Writers on the Appeal of the Romance.* Philadelphia: University of Pennsylvania, 1992.

———. "Biography." Retrieved January 23, 2008, from http://jayneannkrentz.com/biography.html

Little, Denise, and Laura Hayden. *The Official Nora Roberts Companion.* New York: Berkley, 2003.

MacGillivray, Deborah. "Historical Romances? The Phoenix of Romance Novels." *Romance Writers Report,* January 2008.

McNaught, Judith. *Paradise.* New York: Pocket Books, 1991.

Michaels, Leigh. *On Writing Romance: How to Craft a Novel That Sells.* Cincinnati, Ohio: Writer's Digest, 2007.

Nashville Public Library. 2006. "Books, Movies & Music: Romance." Retrieved January 19, 2008, from http://www.library.nashville.org/bmm/bmm_books_romance.asp

Radway, Janice A. *Reading the Romance: Women, Patriarchy, and Popular Literature, With a New Introduction by the Author.* Chapel Hill: University of North Carolina, 1991. Originally published 1984.

Regis, Pamela. *A Natural History of the Romance Novel.* Philadelphia: University of Pennsylvania, 2003.

Robbins, Sarah. "Textually Promiscuous: Romance Readers Definitely Read Around." *Publishers Weekly* 19 November 2007.

Romance Writers of America. http://www.rwanational.org. Accessed January 26, 2008.

Schoenberger, Chana R. "E-Bodice-Ripper." *Forbes* 18 July 2007.

St. Claire, Roxane. *RWA Conference Blog* 12 July 2007. http://www.rwanational.org/cs/rwa_annual_conference/rwa_conference_blog

Swendson, Shanna. "The Original Chick-Lit Masterpiece." In *Flirting with Pride and Prejudice: Fresh Perspectives on the Original Chick-Lit Masterpiece.* Jennifer Crusie with Glenn Yeffreth, eds. Dallas: BenBella, 2005, 63–69.

Vinyard, Rebecca. *The Romance Writer's Handbook: How to Write Romantic Fiction & Get It Published.* Waukesha, WI: Writer Books/Kalmbach, 2004.

Wehr, Isolde, and Angela Weiss. "Interview with Kathleen E. Woodiwiss." 2000. Retrieved January 23, 2008, from http://kwoodiwiss.forumwise.com/archive/o_t/t_39/an_interview_with_kathleen.html

Wheless, Karen. "CR2007 Write Up." *Celebrate Romance Conference Blog.* http://www.crspring.com/cr2004-write-up

Woodiwiss, Kathleen. *The Flame and the Flower.* New York: Avon, 1972.

Wyatt, Neal, Georgine Olson, Kristin Ramsdell, Joyce Saricks, and Lynne Welch. "Core Collections in Genre Studies: Romance Fiction 101." *RUSQ—Reference & User Services Quarterly* (January 2008). Available at http://www.rusq.org

Further Reading

All About Romance: The Back Fence for Lovers of Romance Novels, http://www.likesbooks.com; *Dear Author: Romance Book Reviews, Author Reviews, and Commentary,* http://dearauthor.com; Regis, Pamela. *A Natural History of the Romance Novel.* Philadelphia: University of Pennsylvania, 2003.

PEGGY LIN DUTHIE

S

SCIENCE FICTION

Definition. Despite science fiction's familiarity and prominence in contemporary culture, no definition of it commands universal scholarly assent. Certain formal elements, however, do feature in most definitions. First, science fiction is marked by *novelty*—or what Suvin (1979, ix, 3) calls "the novum"—essentially a violation of, or break with, some aspect of historical experience. At the same time, it displays *rationality,* that is, a degree of deference to the worldview and the established theoretical paradigms of modern science. Finally, it contains *realism,* in the sense of literalness and verisimilitude: the events depicted are to be understood as actually happening, even if they have a further, metaphorical level of meaning. Hence, science fiction's presentation of novel phenomena such as innovations in technology is constrained to some extent by its characteristic rationality and realism.

Many works read and discussed as science fiction fit somewhat uncomfortably in a narrative genre that is characteristically focused on technological innovations or their social impact. These works include (1) alternate (or more correctly, alternative) history stories—such as Philip K. Dick's *The Man in the High Castle* (1962), which describes a world where the Axis powers won World War II; (2) stories that describe contact with alien civilizations, even if set in the present and not involving any

---

SCI-FI CHARACTERISTICS

Science fiction is a genre or mode of narrative characterized by *novelty, rationality,* and *realism.* It typically depicts future developments in social organization, science, or technology, and its main thematic focus is on the effects of technological change, whether on individuals or societies. However, this is a somewhat idealized description. Science fiction is extremely varied, and it has been shaped by historical contingencies and commercial realities that have not favored conformity to any abstract ideal.

technological innovations by human beings; (3) stories that describe certain kinds of natural disasters, such as asteroid impacts; (4) postholocaust narratives about the aftermath of a global war; and (5) prehistoric fiction, which speculates about humanity's distant past, as in Jean M. Auel's *The Clan of the Cave Bear* (1980).

Nonetheless, these kinds of narrative do combine novelty, rationality, and realism. Their composition and intelligibility depend, moreover, on modern scientific knowledge or a general sense of human societies' historical contingency. For example, nuclear holocaust stories would be impossible but for the scientific advances that led to the development of nuclear weapons. Stories about asteroid impacts, alien contact, or mankind's distant past were not readily imaginable until science began to describe the vastness of space and depth of time, and to theorize systematically about human origins. Such stories are made possible by a modern, scientific image of the world and of humanity's limited place within it.

A more troubling set of issues arises when science fiction is compared to the modern fantasy genre. Fantasy is notable for its depiction of gods, demons, and other supernatural beings; rationally inexplicable events; or the effective operation of magic in some form. Its plots and character types tend to draw on those found in myth, legend, fairy tale, and romance. Yet, though initially seemingly paradoxical, science fiction and fantasy share an extensively overlapping audience and often exert a similar appeal. To resolve the paradox, we must acknowledge that the contrast is not absolute, that there are certain similarities, as well as differences, between these genres.

Importantly, the work of modern fantasy writers, such as J.R.R. Tolkien or David Eddings, much resembles science fiction in its detailed portrayal of imaginary societies, and sometimes of entire worlds. Moreover, fantasy narratives can display a kind of rationality: the operation of magical forces and methods may be internally consistent within the narrative, not unlike the body of self-consistent natural laws postulated by science. There is a sense that problems are being solved within a set of "rules." Conversely, science fiction's deference to real science can be quite arbitrary, and the fictional science it describes can appear magical. As a result, much of what is marketed as science fiction could be understood as a kind of fantasy with technological trappings.

Science fiction and modern fantasy are not simply equivalent, and science fiction is not merely a variety of fantasy. However, where the emphasis is on extraordinary adventures in exotic societies, magic and superscience are approximately equivalent. Upon reflection, then, it is understandable that many narratives blend science fiction and fantasy elements, that adventure-oriented science fiction and fantasy are particularly likely to blur into each other, and that the two genres have overlapping audience appeal.

As a further complication, a rich body of literary narrative has responded in one way or another to social, economic, scientific, and technological change. Much of this work bears no resemblance to science fiction, but some of it includes obvious science fiction elements, such as the depiction of future social and technological developments. However, it may also display features—for example, a concern for literary style and relatively subtle characterization—that are atypical of what can be called "genre science fiction," that is, narratives produced for a specific, identifiable science fiction market. Historically, most literary science fiction narratives are anti-utopian (or dystopian) in nature.

Much of Thomas Pynchon's fiction—such as *Gravity's Rainbow* (1973) and *Against The Day* (2006)—resembles science fiction's New Wave and cyberpunk styles. Indeed, *Gravity's Rainbow* was a major influence on the cyberpunk writers of the 1980s, such as William Gibson. Another influence was William S. Burroughs's bizarre oeuvre—notably *The Naked Lunch* (1959), *The Soft Machine* (1961), *The Ticket that Exploded* (1962), and *Nova Express* (1966)—which depicts mind control, dystopian forms of social oppression, alien invasion, and transmutations to and from human form.

Popular fiction that emphasizes danger and adventure may not be marketed as science fiction, even when it displays science fiction elements. This is especially true of techno-thrillers by such authors as Michael Crichton. Crichton's *Jurassic Park* (1990), *Prey* (2002), and *Next* (2006), for example, could easily have been badged as science fiction novels if that had been commercially justified. It is often observed (e.g., by Clute, 1999) that the authors and publishers of works with broad appeal may be reluctant to categorize them as science fiction. The practical reality is that the commercial classification of novels as science fiction or as something else (e.g., as "literary" novels or as thrillers) often depends on marketing considerations as much as formal narrative elements.

History. Human societies have always experienced periods of tumultuous change from such causes as war, famine, and plague. However, as Robert Scholes has argued, the idea of future societies with radically different social and economic organization was probably unthinkable before the seventeenth and eighteenth centuries, while the transformation of societies by irreversible technological change became apparent only in the nineteenth (Scholes, 1975, 14–15). For the first time, it became possible to think of a future greatly different from the present as a result of continuing advances in human knowledge and technology.

This breakthrough in conceptualizing the future offered new opportunities for storytelling. Some works written in the early phases of the Scientific Revolution can be seen as prototypes for science fiction; examples include Francis Bacon's *The New Atlantis* (1629), a utopian fragment that glorifies science and technology. However, the modern genre finds more immediate roots in the fiction of Mary Shelley, Edgar Allan Poe, Jules Verne, Edward Bellamy, H.G. Wells, and other literary giants of the Romantic and Victorian ages. During the nineteenth century, imaginative writers increasingly speculated about technological devices not yet invented. They conceived of diverse possible futures, and used imagined places and times as exotic locations for tales of adventure and heroism.

Brian Aldiss (1986, 18) identifies Shelley's *Frankenstein, or The Modern Prometheus* (1818) as the first true science fiction novel, and it does indeed have a respectable claim to the title. It depicts Victor Frankenstein's use of advanced, scientifically based technology to create something entirely new in the world: a repulsive and powerful artificial man. Some of Poe's stories from the 1830s and 1840s also have science fiction elements. However, a substantial body of work that resembles modern science fiction first emerged around 1860, particularly with the stories and novels of Jules Verne.

Verne is best known for novels in which science and technology provide the means to accomplish fantastic journeys, as in *Five Weeks in a Balloon* (1863), *Journey to the Centre of the Earth* (1863), *From the Earth to the Moon* (1865), and *20,000 Leagues under the Sea* (1870). H.G. Wells's career as a writer of what were then known as "scientific romances" commenced a few decades later, with a group of short stories that led up to his hugely influential novella *The Time Machine* (1895) and his first full-length "scientific romance," *The Island of Dr Moreau* (1896). Wells was more didactic and socially concerned, while Verne was more focused on adventure and had an engineer's sense of realism—the plausible depiction of technological novelties.

Though they are the best remembered proto–science fiction authors today, Verne and Wells were certainly not the only writers of their era producing work with elements similar to those of modern science fiction. During the late nineteenth and early twentieth centuries, such elements appeared in many utopias, lost-race novels, and stories of near-future geopolitical disruption. The latter described wars, invasions, and racial conflict, but not necessarily any new technologies or methods of warfare.

Nineteenth-century adventure novels, such as H. Rider Haggard's *She: A History of Adventure* (1886), frequently took place in remote, exotic, and often mildly erotic locations. The use of interplanetary settings merely took this a step further. The first novel by Edgar Rice Burroughs, *A Princess of Mars* (1917)—actually first published in *All-Story Magazine* in 1912—epitomized this trend. It defined one pole of early science fiction, emphasizing action and adventure in an alien setting. Burroughs revitalized the lost-race motif, and he was the major influence in science fiction until the mid-1930s, with many imitators writing similar stories set in faraway places (Clareson, 1990, 11–12). Elements of this style can be found up to the present day.

However, genre science fiction is a newer phenomenon, dating from the 1920s and 1930s, when the genre's direction was shaped by two great American editors: Luxembourg-born Hugo Gernsback and John W. Campbell. Though Gernsback looked for original stories that emphasized futurism, science, and gadgetry, the immediate context for his contribution was the popular success of exotic adventure stories such as those by Burroughs. He first showed this sort of interest with the magazine *Modern Electrics* (1908) and the novel *Ralph 124C41+* (1911), but he did not devote an entire magazine to genre science fiction until the launch of *Amazing Stories* in April 1926 (Clareson, 1990, 14–15). *Amazing Stories* is usually considered the first specialized science fiction magazine, though Gernsback originally coined the term *scientifiction*. He adopted the usage *science fiction* for the first issue of *Science Wonder Stories* in 1929, and it became the established term in 1938, when it was incorporated into the title of Campbell's *Astounding Science-Fiction* (Clareson, 1990, 16).

During the Gernsback era, Verne and Wells came to be thought of as science fiction writers. Their work was often reprinted in genre magazines, alongside new stories that tended to applaud the advance of science and technology. Also during this first era of modern science fiction, the subgenre now known as space opera became an established form. This type of narrative involves action on a galactic scale, or beyond, rather than mere adventure on the local planets of our solar system. Space opera often includes space voyages that are analogous to Earth-bound naval fleets, and it may involve such elements as contact with alien species, war on a colossal scale, descriptions of immensely destructive weapons, and other kinds of superscience. *The Skylark of Space* (1928), by E.E. "Doc" Smith, was the novel that really established the form, and it has been argued that Gernsback's principal contribution to the new genre was the discovery of Smith's exuberant talent (Clareson, 1990, 17).

Science fiction's so-called golden age began in the late 1930s and lasted until the end of the 1940s. In 1937, John W. Campbell began to assume editorial duties at

---

THE FUTURE HISTORY OF HUMANITY

During the golden age of science fiction, Asimov, Clarke, Heinlein, and others developed the concept of a future history of humanity, first formalized by Heinlein but expanded into a complex narrative framework by Asimov. By the end of the 1940s, science fiction had created an intertextual mythos involving the development and fluctuations of future galactic empires (Clareson, 1990, 31–33). This may be viewed as a generic megatext, providing a network of familiar, easily evoked icons that are well understood by dedicated readers (compare Broderick, 1995, 57–63).

---

the magazine *Astounding Stories of Super-Science* (to use its complete title), and in 1938, he officially became the magazine's editor, changing its name to *Astounding Science-Fiction* (it is now called *Analog Science Fiction and Fact*). By 1939, the magazine and the science fiction genre as a whole were being steered by Campbell's strong personality. During this period, he published the first short stories of celebrated British science fiction writer Arthur C. Clarke and established a group of regular contributors who became the major figures in genre science fiction. These included Isaac Asimov, Robert A. Heinlein, L. Ron Hubbard, and A.E. Van Vogt.

Isaac Asimov's original Foundation trilogy became one of the great canonical texts of twentieth-century science fiction. The three volumes appeared in sequence during the early 1950s, and they were a repackaging of a series of stories about the Seldon Plan that had originally been published from 1942 to 1950. Thousands of years in the future, Hari Seldon, founder of the new science of psychohistory, establishes two foundations at the opposite ends of the galaxy. Their mission is to reduce the 30,000-year interregnum of chaos between the predicted fall of the Galactic Empire and the rise of a new empire. Seldon has predicted that this long interregnum can be reduced to only a thousand years, saving untold chaos and suffering.

The stories that comprise the first volume, *Foundation* (1951), trace the early history of the First Foundation and establish Asimov's narrative strategy for the series. At each crisis point for the Foundation, the key to a successful outcome is an insight into the situation that is reached by the Foundation's leaders (and that was achieved in advance by Seldon). Nevertheless, this insight is withheld from the reader until the end of each respective story. Asimov adopts a similar approach in the stories contained in *Foundation and Empire* (1952) and *Second Foundation* (1953), the trilogy's second and third volumes, respectively. All three volumes display Asimov's frequent technique of setting his characters to outguess each other's understandings. Those who most fully grasp the underlying situation are successful.

Three decades later, Asimov returned to this universe with *Foundation's Edge* (1982), which jumps 120 years into the future from the events depicted at the end of *Second Foundation*. Unlike its predecessors, but like other works in the Foundation mythos that followed it, *Foundation's Edge* was conceived from the beginning as a full-length novel: it contains far more descriptive detail and appears designed to exceed the earlier stories/volumes in the complexity of its puzzles.

Asimov's other great achievement during the golden age was the development of one of science fiction's most celebrated and recurrent icons: the mechanical human being, or robot. He devised his famous three laws of robotics to govern his robots' behavior. These laws required them to preserve human life, obey human commands, and preserve themselves, in that order of priority. The possible loopholes inherent in the three laws enabled Asimov to write many ingenious puzzle stories, including two robot detective novels in the mid-1950s, *The Caves of Steel* (1954) and *The Naked Sun* (1957).

In *Foundation's Edge*, Asimov began to unite his Foundation mythos with his robot stories, and he continued this program in further novels published in the 1980s and 1990s: *The Robots of Dawn* (1983), *Robots and Empire* (1985), *Foundation and Earth* (1986), *Prelude to Foundation* (1988), and *Forward the Foundation* (1993, after Asimov's death the previous year). Of all these, *Foundation and Earth* takes the story furthest into the future. These novels supplement the original trilogy with far more background and breadth, and portray the hero, Hari Seldon, at various stages of his life, whether as a swashbuckling young man or in his later years. After Asimov's death, his estate authorized the publication of three more novels along similar lines—the Second Foundation Trilogy—*Foundation's Fear*, by Gregory Benford (1997), *Foundation and Chaos*, by Greg Bear (1998), and *Foundation's Triumph*, by David Brin (1999).

Robert A. Heinlein turned to writing in his early thirties and soon became one of the key figures of the golden age of science fiction. His first novel to appear in book form, *Rocket Ship Galileo*, was published in 1947. It was followed by a string of highly successful novels—the Heinlein juveniles—aimed at what would now be called the young adult market. Like Asimov, he flourished as a leading American science fiction writer for many years after the golden age.

By the late 1940s, science fiction was changing. The atomic bomb and the abrupt surrender of Japan turned the public's attention to science—and hence to science fiction. And some science fiction narratives began to appear in the slick magazines and in book form. At about the same time, new specialized magazines challenged Campbell's hegemony. In 1949, *The Magazine of Fantasy* appeared, edited by Anthony Boucher and J. Francis McComas, which became *The Magazine of Fantasy and Science Fiction* with the publication of its second issue in 1950 (Clareson, 1990, 49). This magazine introduced greater variety, with stories that stepped outside the technocratic vision favored by Gernsback and Campbell. In 1950, the first issue of *Galaxy Science Fiction* appeared. Book publication became increasingly important, and as described by Clareson (1990, 40–49), 1952 was a pivotal year: Donald A. Wollheim became science fiction editor at Ace Books; Betty and Ian Ballantine founded Ballantine Books; and Clifford Simak's *City* was published. The latter was a key work in shifting away from an adulation of technology to critique of modern urban-industrial society. In the same year, Kurt Vonnegut's first novel, the dystopian *Player Piano*, was published.

Such writers as Clifford D. Simak, Kurt Vonnegut, Damon Knight, James Blish, Alfred Bester, Ray Bradbury (who leaned more to fantasy and horror fiction), Frederick Pohl and Cyril M. Kornbluth, Theodore Sturgeon, and Walter M. Miller experimented with form, style, and tone, some of their work presaging the experiments of the 1960s New Wave. *The Demolished Man* (1953) and *The Stars My Destination* (1957), Bester's most successful works, show "obsessed men driven to, if not beyond the borders of sanity" (Clareson, 1990, 71). Pohl and Kornbluth were published in *Galaxy Science Fiction* during the 1950s. Their satirical *Gravy Train* was serialized in 1952, and in the following year it was revised in book form as

The Space Merchants. Miller's *A Canticle for Leibowitz* (1959) is a high point in science fiction's treatment of the nuclear holocaust theme. After a nuclear war, the remnants of human civilization eventually progress to a new Renaissance and beyond—leading, however, to another nuclear war.

During the 1950s, Vonnegut and Bradbury, in particular, brought science fiction to a wider audience than it had previously enjoyed (Clareson, 1990, 49–50). Ray Bradbury is probably best known for *The Martian Chronicles* (1950) and *Fahrenheit 451* (1953). *The Martian Chronicles* portrays the settlement of Mars by humans, and as in much science fiction of the time, the threat of nuclear war underlies its storyline. The first explorers from Earth wipe out the ancient Martian civilization by accident: humans infect the Martians with chickenpox, which is a deadly disease to the latter. A frontier culture develops on Mars, until the long feared nuclear war takes place on Earth in 2005 and Mars is deserted. *Fahrenheit 451* is a satirical depiction of an anti-intellectual future America, where houses are fireproof and "firemen" burn books.

In many ways, though, as Clareson points out (1990, 115–116), the 1950s belonged to Heinlein with the publication and success of the Heinlein juveniles and the reprinting of much of his work from the magazines. The 1960s saw further experimentation, and Heinlein continued to adapt. In 1961, he published his most famed novel of all, *Stranger in a Strange Land,* which celebrates sex and the body (the characters seem to be nude as often as not), advocates open sexual relationships, and satirizes politics, organized religion, and traditional social mores.

During the 1960s and early 1970s, Heinlein wrote several more books, most notably *The Moon is a Harsh Mistress* (1966), which tells the story of a lunar colony's rebellion against Earth analogous to the American Revolution. However, some of his later work lacks shape and discipline, and there was a seven-year gap in his output from 1973 to 1980, when he was plagued by health crises. In the 1980s—prior to his death in 1988—he wrote several novels, of which *Friday* (1982) and the satirical *Job: A Comedy of Justice* (1984) shows him still near his best form.

Other novels to escape the boundaries of the genre and obtain cult status were Vonnegut's *Cat's Cradle* (1963) and his ambiguously science fictional *Slaughterhouse-Five* (1969), which reacts to the political assassinations of the Kennedys and Martin Luther King, the Vietnam war, and the social conflict that troubled America throughout the turbulent 1960s. Frank Herbert's *Dune* (1965) also obtained a huge audience. Its plot involves complex political and religious struggles on a desert world far in the future. *Dune* was followed by many sequels by the author, and since his death in 1986, by a continuing series of sequels and prequels by his son, Brian Herbert, and Kevin J. Anderson.

In the early 1960s, under the editorship of E.J. Carnell and then of the more aggressive Michael Moorcock, the leading British science fiction magazine *New Worlds* began to promote the New Wave style of science fiction. This style largely rejected the genre's tradition of narrative realism, purporting instead to explore the mind's "inner space," a concept that was associated with J.G. Ballard in particular. Strictly speaking, the New Wave comprised a group of writers closely involved with *New Worlds,* and British authors Ballard, Brian Aldiss, and John Brunner were its major exponents. However, the term *New Wave* is often used somewhat more loosely to cover broader changes in the style of American, as well as British, science fiction during the 1960s.

In the United States, Harlan Ellison published his blockbuster anthologies *Dangerous Visions* (1967) and *Again Dangerous Visions* (1972), for which he commissioned stories that might be seen as controversial and subversive. Major American science fiction writers of the 1960s who participated in the transition to a new style are Norman Spinrad—notably with *Bug Jack Barron* (1969)—Thomas M. Disch, Roger Zelazny, Samuel R. Delany, and James Tiptree Jr. (pen name of Alice Sheldon). The writers of the sixties dealt with such subjects as environmental disaster, and they often depicted Western civilization as doomed. Philip José Farmer and Samuel R. Delany explored sexuality with a newfound freedom. The prolific Philip K. Dick—whose stories and novels have perhaps been the subject of more cinematic adaptations than any other science fiction writer's since Verne and Wells—produced much of his best work during the 1960s, including *The Man in the High Castle* (1962) and *Do Androids Dream of Electric Sheep?* (1968).

After this point, the science fiction genre displayed multiple facets, but only a few can be mentioned here. During the mid-1960s and early 1970s, Robert Silverberg, another immensely prolific writer, produced some of his most studied and insightful works, including the award-winning novella "Nightwings" (1969), as well as the novels *A Time of Changes* (1971) and *Dying Inside* (1972). *A Time of Changes* depicts one man's rebellion against an oppressive culture that rejects individuality as an obscenity. *Dying Inside* is a sensitive depiction of the declining powers of a middle-aged man whose telepathic abilities are failing him. Joe Haldeman appeared as a powerful new talent with *The Forever War* (1974), a grim antiwar novel that draws on Haldeman's experience as a soldier in Vietnam. The values of the golden age of science fiction were kept alive in the work of Larry Niven and Jerry Pournelle, most notably in Niven's *Ringworld* (1970) and in the Niven-Pournelle collaboration *The Mote in God's Eye* (1974).

During the late 1960s and throughout the 1970s, there was also a vigorous interest in feminist and racial themes, sexuality, political theories, and utopian visions (the latter sometimes of complex, ambiguous kinds). Key works of the period were Ursula K. Le Guin's *The Left Hand of Darkness* (1969) and *The Dispossessed: An Ambiguous Utopia* (1974), Joanna Russ's *The Female Man* (1975), Marge Piercy's *Woman on the Edge of Time* (1976), Samuel R. Delany's *Dhalgren* (1975) and *Triton* (1976), and Octavia E. Butler's *Kindred* (1979), which uses time travel as a narrative device to examine the American experience of slavery.

The Dispossessed, possibly Le Guin's best known novel, depicts life on Anarres, a hostile desert world whose society is a resource-poor, would-be utopia run along anarchist lines. Though Anarresti society is presented sympathetically, we are led to see its flaws: in particular, it is hostile to individuality and genius. Anarres is contrasted to another world, Urras, which is home to both a luxurious capitalist society and a communist dictatorship of the worst kind. Though the development of an anarchist society on Anarres has fallen short of its founder's revolutionary ideals, there are indications—as the narrative draws to a close—that revolution can be a permanent process and that renewal is beginning.

Russ's *The Female Man* and her other work of this period constitute the science fiction genre's most forthright attack on sexism and sexual inequality. The novel's four main characters—Joanna, Jeannine, Janet, and Jael—live in different realities: one of them evidently lives in our reality, but the others live in realities that diverge widely from ours. Russ's fierce style and hard-edged characterization influenced the cyberpunk writers of the following decade. In particular, her highly capable female warriors—such as Jael in *The Female Man* and Alyx in *Picnic on Paradise* (1968)—provided models for the no-nonsense razor girls of William Gibson's early fiction.

Butler's *Kindred* has obtained widespread praise for the horrifying realism of its depiction of slavery, with its popularity and message enabling it to transcend the science fiction genre. *Kindred* depicts the dilemma of a modern-day African American novelist who finds herself leading a dual life as she is transported repeatedly to a slave plantation in the nineteenth-century South. Her struggle to survive takes an additional twist because she is descended from a brutal slave owner, Rufus, who somehow has the ability to summon his descendants to help him when he is danger. She must assist him to survive, at least until he has the child whose line will one day lead to her own existence.

Delany's huge, enigmatic, sexually explicit *Dhalgren* (1975) was another book that burst out of the confines of science-fiction marketing and found a cult audience. Delany followed up with *Triton* (later republished under the author's preferred title, *Trouble on Triton*). Like *The Dispossessed,* to which it seems a response, *Triton* depicts a world that is not entirely utopian. Delany's focus is more on the personal than the political: the narrative concerns a character who is unable to fit into a seemingly utopian future society, but purely because of his own shortcomings.

As Harris-Fain points out (2005, 98–100), the science fiction field was fragmenting in the late 1970s and early 1980s. It was possible for a reader to focus on a particular type of science fiction, according to taste, but many writers and publishers were looking for something to reunify the field. At this time, Frederick Pohl published what many consider his best solo novel, *Gateway* (1977), which is a prominent example of a veteran writer's adoption of some of the New Wave techniques (Harris-Fain, 2005, 69).

In the early 1980s, Gene Wolfe revived far-future science fiction in his novel series *The Book of the New Sun* (1980–1987) as well as in subsequent series that continued into the 1990s and beyond. The five volumes of the first series—including its coda, *The Urth of the New Sun* (1987)—four volumes of *The Book of the Long Sun* (1993–1996), and three volumes of *The Book of the Short Sun* (1999–2001) can be read as one huge narrative. *The Book of the New Sun,* which commences with *The Shadow of the Torturer* (1980), tells the story of Severian, a journeyman torturer who is ultimately made Autarch, or ruler of the kingdom . He must find a way to renew the dying Sun—for which he travels to a higher universe, Yesod—and plead with an entity closer to the Increate or creator.

Far-future science fiction relies on the fact that we find ourselves in a universe incomprehensibly old and with a similarly incomprehensible number of years still ahead. This subgenre responds to this fact by telling stories about the Earth in a future separated from us by a vast temporal gulf. There is no precise starting point for the far future, but such stories typically involve a planet that is so completely different from the present day as to be almost unrecognizable. The classic example is Jack Vance's *The Dying Earth* (1950), which had numerous sequels and influenced many other writers. Wolfe takes a similar approach on a gargantuan scale. As discussed by Michael Andre-Driussi (2001), far-future science fictional texts such as those by Vance and Wolfe use linguistic techniques that create a sense of strangeness and ancientness. They employ many archaic words or archaic-seeming coinages, and their prose is lush with exotic, often polysyllabic, names for characters and places.

Other writers maintained a hard–science fiction tradition throughout the second half of the twentieth century and into the twenty-first. Their values reflect those shown by Jules Verne and by the writers of the golden age. The precise boundaries of hard science fiction are disputed. In their introduction to *The Hard SF Renaissance,* David G. Hartwell and Kathryn Cramer suggest that the expression "has always signified SF that has something centrally to do with science" (2002, 13). This "something" is somewhat vague, but hard science fiction generally emphasizes logic, problem solving, scientific accuracy, and plausible detail. It often includes realistic depictions of the lives of working scientists, engineers, astronauts, and similar professionals. The hard–science fiction subgenre is epitomized by such works as Hal Clement's *Mission of Gravity* (1954) and Gregory Benford's *Timescape* (1980), a widely admired story of communication across time.

The **cyberpunk** movement of the 1980s synthesizes elements from the New Wave, hard science fiction, and the politically engaged narratives of Delany and Russ. Cyberpunk writers—such as William Gibson, Bruce Sterling, Pat Cadigan, and (later) Neal Stephenson—produced, in effect, a new (or at least revised) science fiction megatext that presents direct interfacing between human minds and advanced computers, events in computer-constructed virtual realities, and the activities of powerful artificial intelligences. The punk aspect of their work involves portrayals of street life, youth rebellion (often against the power of ubiquitous, transnational corporations), tough-guy attitudes and dress codes, and certain recurring images (e.g., of rust, chrome, concrete, reflective glass, and architectural ruins).

William Gibson was born in South Carolina in 1948, but he has lived in Canada since the late 1960s. His work was a dominant presence within the cyberpunk movement's early output, and it has subsequently exerted an enormous influence on American and international science fiction. The movement was showcased in Gibson's early short stories—collected in *Burning Chrome* (1986)—and in his first novel, *Neuromancer* (1984), which was soon expanded into a trilogy whose volumes are *Count Zero* (1986) and *Mona Lisa Overdrive* (1988). Bruce Sterling's anthology *Mirrorshades* (1986) also helped define the spirit of cyberpunk, as it collects important stories by Gibson and other key writers of the 1980s.

Neuromancer, in particular, had a stunning impact on the American and international science fiction communities. It is a linguistically pyrotechnic and conceptually dense crime thriller set in the polluted, high-tech urban jungle of a near-future world in which a vast sprawl of buildings stretches from Boston to Atlanta; nonhuman nature has receded to make way for patterns of streets, Styrofoam, and neon lights; and the world of sensorial experience has lost ground to an artificial cyberspace (Gibson's celebrated coinage, though the idea had precursors) that is the construct of electronic neuro-stimulation. The novel's language is marked by vivid, risky similes and swift sentences; and images and fragments of dialogue intrude in the flow of the narrative in a disorienting way. Gibson conveys the rush and confusion of the hard, amoral—yet sometimes alluring—world in which the novel's events take place. *Neuromancer* synthesizes the influences of *noir* crime writers such as Raymond Chandler, the prose experiments of Alfred Bester, the elements of 1960s New Wave science fiction, and the challenging fictions of William S. Burroughs and Thomas Pynchon.

Since the 1980s, cyberpunk sensibility has been assimilated into much of the science fiction field and beyond into the nonnarrative arts. This, however, has scarcely been the only development. During cyberpunk's heyday, there was a vigorous debate between its advocates and the so-called humanists—notably John

Kessell and James Patrick Kelly—who took a more critical and selective attitude to technology. Standing outside of any subgenre or movement, James Morrow produced darkly satirical narratives, combining science fiction and fantasy elements, whereas Connie Willis became widely acclaimed and multiply awarded, primarily for work that brought new interest and gave vitality to the tradition of time travel narratives.

During the 1980s and 1990s, **space opera's** tradition was also enriched by such writers as C.J. Cherryh, Orson Scott Card, David Brin, Dan Simmons, Elizabeth Moon, Lois McMaster Bujold, Catherine Asaro, and Vernor Vinge, who took space opera in a dazzling variety of directions. Their stories are set against the wide backdrops of the space opera subgenre but with emphases ranging from intellectual speculation and play to action-adventure to unashamed romance.

Through the 1990s and beyond, there was also a distinctive international resurgence of hard science fiction, showcased in Hartwell and Cramer's *The Hard SF Renaissance* (2002). In the United States, this renaissance was strongly associated with the work of Gregory Benford, Greg Bear, and David Brin as well as with Kim Stanley Robinson's Mars trilogy, but numerous other writers also took part, including newer talents such as Ted Chiang. This renaissance was also evident in other English-speaking countries. It can be seen, for example, in the stories and novels of Australian author Greg Egan and in the work of a prominent group of British writers that includes Ken MacLeod, Iain M. Banks, and Stephen Baxter.

For twenty-first-century science fiction, all the boundaries are blurred. Space opera is influenced by hard science fiction and cyberpunk. Prose space opera generally displays a higher degree of realism—and a greater distance from fantasy—than its cinematic equivalent. Science fiction as a whole has become, to an extent, post-cyberpunk: it is permeated by images of alienation, machine intelligence, and posthuman minds and bodies. The megatext has metamorphosed into something darker, harder, and weirder.

Trends and Themes. Science fiction is a thematically rich genre. The three-volume *Greenwood Encyclopedia of Science Fiction and Fantasy* (2005) contains four hundred entries on specific themes, many of which—such as "Alien Worlds," "Aliens in Space," "Aliens on Earth," "Generation Starships," "Mad Scientists," "Planetary Colonies," " Time travel," and "Virtual Reality"—are of relevance mainly or entirely to science fiction rather than fantasy narratives.

As a genre that developed in the wake of the scientific and industrial revolutions of the past four centuries, science fiction tends to make certain assumptions. These include the idea that human experience takes place within a small part of an unimaginably vast space-time continuum, and that it is open to us to imagine the rest. Thus, the genre's canvas comprises the past, present, and future, as well as the depths of interplanetary and interstellar space. It is natural for science fiction authors to speculate about life on other planets, contact between humans and alien life forms, and the possibility of human expansion beyond the confines of planet Earth. It is equally natural for them to imagine travel in time and space—whether to the historical or prehistoric past or to the near or far future.

Science fiction's canvas spreads even further to include entirely different realities. These may be rationalized in various ways—for example, there may be mathematical spaces beyond our own, as in Rudy Rucker's novel of supermathematics, *Mathematicians in Love* (2006), whose main characters travel through a variety of alternative realities. In other cases, alternative histories or realities may be presented as purely imaginary constructs with no explanation as to how they relate to our own world in a physical or metaphysical—rather than thematic—sense.

In principle, science fiction assumes the contingency and mutability of current technologies, economic arrangements, and social forms. The technological and other novelties that it depicts enable its characters to act within constraints—physical, biological, technological, or cultural—that differ from those applying to human beings in historical and contemporary societies. This alteration of expected constraints can be deployed for a wide range of literary effects. In some cases, it enables the exploration of specific aspects of human behaviour, life, or the universe. It also enables authors to speculate about the future or to comment on the customs and values of existing societies by extrapolating their worst tendencies or by viewing a real society from the perspective of an imaginary one with different assumptions.

Thus, the genre has lent itself to the purposes of utopian or visionary speculation, and to various kinds of satire. Of course, the creation of locales separated in space or time—or otherwise—from the reader's society can often function for less didactic purposes. In much science fiction, these locales are used primarily for entertainment: distant worlds can provide exotic settings for conflict and adventure, as in the planetary romances of Edgar Rice Burroughs and the gaudy narratives that typify space opera.

Science fiction narratives tend to include characters whose abilities differ from those of historical humans, sometimes because of their greater inherent powers, sometimes because of their access to innovative and empowering technology. At one extreme, this encourages the creation of superheroes and supervillains—good and evil characters with superhuman powers—and of the spectacle that ensues when they are drawn into violent conflict. Other forms of conflict in science fiction include wars between rival military forces equipped with superweapons and, often, with superpowers' warriors in their ranks. Such forms of superspectacular combat create an affinity with heroic fantasy, with its magical locales and characters, typically deployed for similar purposes.

Inevitably, science fiction's main thematic concern is the consequences of scientific advance and technological change. The genre has always shown a range of attitudes to science and technology, reflecting—and sometimes opposing—tendencies in the Western culture that has nurtured it. In medieval Europe, there was a long tradition of suspicion toward "impious" inquiries into nature—expressed in hostile depictions of magic and alchemy—and this can be seen continuing through the Renaissance and even the age of the Enlightenment. Jonathan Swift's *Gulliver's Travels* (1726), for example, contains merciless satire of Enlightenment-era scientists.

Hostility to science and technology increased in the Romantic period around the beginning of the nineteenth century, as in Mary Shelley's *Frankenstein*. Shelley warned against scientific hubris, but during the later nineteenth century, technological progress came to be a popular value in industrialized nations. There was far more optimism about technological progress in Verne's tales of imaginary voyages, which postulates such devices as Nemo's submarine in *Twenty Thousand Leagues under the Sea* (though the submarine is also an engine of destruction that preys on shipping). The period's techno-optimism culminated in futuristic utopias—such as Edward Bellamy's *Looking Backward: 2000–1887* (1888) and Wells's *A Modern Utopia* (1905)—and in the magazines of the Gernsback era and the golden age.

The science fiction pulp magazines of the Gernsback era valorized science, scientists, and technology, while golden age science fiction was only slightly more cautious in its optimism about technology and the future. Hard science fiction and various forms of space opera continued this golden age optimism in the following decades. By contrast, more literary forms of twentieth-century science fiction conveyed greater pessimism. Even H.G. Wells was more than a Wellsian techno-utopian, but the utopian component of his output produced a backlash—first seen, perhaps, in E.M. Forster's cautionary tale of a machine-dependent future, "The Machine Stops" (1909). Thereafter, Yevgeny Zamyatin, Aldous Huxley, and George Orwell described dystopias in which technology is used as an instrument for totalitarian enslavement, or as the enforcement of a decadent and repugnant form of social stability.

Widespread intellectual rejection of technology followed the destruction of Hiroshima and Nagasaki, and the atrocities of the Nazi death camps. Even within the professional genre, postwar science fiction gave expression to fears of decay or destruction, produced by overreliance on technology or the use of immensely powerful weaponry. The dominant British and American figures of the New Wave era often expressed the vision of a doomed society. In the late decades of the twentieth century and at the turn of the twenty-first, the technophobic imagination focused increasingly on dangers from computers, artificial intelligence, and biotechnology. However, 1980s cyberpunk handled all this with a degree of ambivalence. Cyberpunk writers produced images of a dark future, but they also portrayed advanced technologies as inevitable, adaptable, and alluring. Though potentially dangerous, the invasive technologies depicted by the cyberpunks have their attractions, and the near-future societies portrayed in such novels as *Neuromancer* are not totally dystopian.

Chris Moriarty's *Spin State* (2003) is an example of how all this plays out when contemporary space opera combines with cyberpunk. In the relatively near future, Earth has become uninhabitable. Climate change has led to ecological disaster, though there are plans to restore the global environment and seed the planet with stored genetic material. Meanwhile, most human beings have been evacuated to an artificial construct, the Ring, where various cultures and nationalities remain as suspicious of each other as ever. Thanks to the invention of faster-than-light travel, new societies have also been established on the planets of other star systems. Some of these are under UN control, but others have broken away in defiance—and the authorities seem to have lost track of still others.

Of course, the ambivalent, complex attitudes to technology found in cyberpunk and post-cyberpunk writing are not entirely new. Indeed, a powerful characteristic of science fiction from the beginning was the moral ambivalence of technology. Even Verne sometimes showed dangers in the powerful new technologies that he described and glorified. Part of science fiction's appeal lies in its ability to show advanced technology as dangerous and potentially destructive, while simultaneously revealing its allure and giving it some accommodation within the megatextual value systems that result.

Most imaginable forms of technology receive a mix of positive and negative portrayals in current science fiction. The predicted technology of molecular engineering (or nanotechnology) is one example: while some works show it as offering a world of plenty, it can also be portrayed as a threat by a techno-thriller writer such as Michael Crichton. In Crichton's *Prey* (2002), escaped "clouds" of tiny nanotech devices commence a bizarre parasitism on human victims. By contrast, a number of current authors—such as Neal Stephenson, Wil McCarthy, and the British crop of space opera and hard science fiction writers—attempt to imagine life in a world of economic plenty.

One example is McCarthy's *The Collapsium* (2000) and its sequels in the Queendom of Sol series. Set about five hundred years in the future, this series describes a society in which people can transport themselves around the Solar System, using nanotechnological devices to analyze their bodies as data patterns. Aging and disease have been eliminated by using a "morbidity filter." Among the other inventions of the future age is "wellstone," or programmable matter: a substance capable of mimicking the properties of many naturally occurring materials as well as physically hypothetical ones. People are coming to terms with what all this plenty means for their lives, work, and relationships.

With its frequent depiction of exotic or greatly altered societies, science fiction is also well placed to depict alternative moral outlooks, family arrangements, political forms, and methods of social organization. This gives the genre its cognitive tools for examining a wide range of social issues, from forms of government and the relationship between the state and the individual to sexuality, relations between men and women, and methods of reproduction. The approaches taken may be utopian, dystopian, or simply heterotopian, with the presentation of arrangements that are *different* from those familiar to the reader, yet not entirely good or bad. Its heterotopian impulse gives science fiction some tendency to imply a kind of moral relativism, because many possible social arrangements and moral attitudes are viewed rather dispassionately. On the other hand, perhaps surprisingly, the genre sometimes adopts conservative or even reactionary conventions, as with the widespread depiction of empires in space ruled along the lines of ancient imperial dynasties.

Despite its obvious potential to reimagine love, courtship, sexuality, and marriage, science fiction is frequently quite conservative also in its implied philosophy of sex and gender. Many science fiction narratives appear to assume that the dating and marital customs of their authors' own times and places will last into the near and even distant future. Feminist utopias, however, typically reject traditional relationships between the sexes, including marriage. Some feminist novels, such as Charlotte Perkins Gilman's *Herland* (1915) and Joanna Russ's *The Female Man* describe societies without men. Marge Piercy's *Woman on the Edge of Time* depicts a utopia in which women have achieved freedom from male domination, and sexuality is free of guilt (though not of all interpersonal conflict). Ectogenesis is used to separate reproduction from "recreational coupling," and there is no marriage bond.

Because science fiction examines social changes that arise from the advance of science and technology, it provides an ongoing literary forum for such issues as preservation of monogamy. It sometimes criticizes monogamy from an alien viewpoint, as in Heinlein's *Stranger in a Strange Land,* or describes alternatives, such as the line marriages of the same author's *The Moon is a Harsh Mistress.* Some science fiction narratives describe unusual familial/sexual arrangements for their alien characters—as in Asimov's *The Gods Themselves* (1972)—without considering anything very radical for future humans. However, Anne McCaffrey, Philip José Farmer, Samuel R. Delany, and others have imagined more startling sexual arrangements involving the interactions of humans and nonhumanoid aliens, or even direct human-alien sex, especially in Delany's *Stars in My Pocket Like Grains of Sand* (1984).

Context and Issues. During the 1990s, the biological and computational sciences became particularly prominent within the more general intellectual culture. This was the result of scientific advances, the explosion in rapid, computerized communications, and some foreboding about where biotech and computers might be leading us. Such concerns and emphases are reflected in the science fiction of the 1990s and the new millennium, sometimes accompanied by the striking idea of a coming technological singularity: a point in time where the rate of technological change will approach infinity, perhaps because it falls under the control of minds more powerful than ours.

From its beginnings, science fiction has postulated advances in biology, and it has also depicted the work of biologists, the biology of alien beings, the structure of alien worlds, and mutational changes on Earth. Its specialized concerns have included artificial organic life (as in *Frankenstein*), medical advances, new diseases, the creation of human clones, life extension and immortality, increased physical and cognitive abilities, genetic engineering, and the terraforming of other planets. Despite this variety, however, monstrosity and alien threats to human life have long been the genre's staples when it addresses the biological sciences. Physical or moral monstrosity, it is often suggested, results from human meddling with the stuff of life.

Some authors have resisted the genre's teratological and cautionary impulses, but more optimistic works have usually been the exception: James Blish projects a vision of human adaptation to the environments of other worlds in his short story "Surface Tension" (1952), and something similar is imagined in Joan Slonczewski's *A Door into Ocean* (1986), among others. Some science fiction authors have imagined entire alien ecologies that often resemble those of fantasy, but others—such as those in Le Guin's *The Left Hand of Darkness,* Asimov's *The Gods Themselves*, and Slonczewski's *A Door Into Ocean*—display more cognitive rigor. Octavia E. Butler's radical Xenogenesis novels, beginning with *Dawn* (1987), depict aliens who change constantly through their history as they encounter new species and mix with them.

The most noteworthy saga of terraforming is perhaps Kim Stanley Robinson's Mars trilogy—*Red Mars* (1992), *Green Mars* (1993), and *Blue Mars* (1996)—which describes how Mars is made habitable through centuries of effort, resulting in beneficial but not entirely expected outcomes. Greg Bear's *Blood Music* (1985) provides another exception to science fiction's distrust of biological experimentation: in this novel, a renegade researcher's experiment on his own body eventually leads to a benign transformation of the Earth and humanity. Bear's *Darwin's Radio* (1999) and *Darwin's Children* (2003) are contemporary versions of the idea that a sudden evolutionary change may occur in the human species.

One successful approach during the 1990s renaissance of hard science fiction was that of Nancy Kress, initially in her novella "Beggars in Spain" (1990). This was subsequently reworked and expanded into a successful series of novels: *Beggars in Spain* (1993), *Beggars and Choosers* (1994), and *Beggars' Ride* (1996). Kress's work contains intelligent observation of what might happen if human abilities could be enhanced by genetic engineering. Her main characters are modified human beings whose superior abilities include the capacity to live without sleep and devote the extra hours to self-improvement. The narrative asks such questions as how society would—or should—react to the presence of individuals who might seem to have an unfair advantage over everyone else, in whatever fields of work they choose. Conversely, what duties would such individuals owe to those less fortunate, without losing the integrity of their own extraordinarily impressive lives?

Observation of the rapid pace of technological change has led to the idea—popularized by Vernor Vinge in particular—that humanity is headed for a point of infinite possibility (the aforementioned singularity); it has also led to speculation about the possibility that human beings may be transformed by technological processes into something posthuman, that is, into humans possessing unprecedented physical or cognitive capacities. Vinge's prolific speculations about such issues—initially in his novella "True Names" (1981) and his novel *Marooned in Realtime* (1987)—have made him something of an icon for pro-technology activists—such as those in the transhumanist movement, which favors the enhancement of human capacities.

Post-cyberpunk space opera and related fictional forms typically imagine scenarios in which technology goes *inwards:* it alters human capacities rather than merely altering our environment or providing us with new tools. Robert Reed's *Marrow* (2000), for example, is a disciplined attempt to portray a truly posthuman civilization whose people have indefinitely long lives and extraordinary personal abilities. Reed's characters are technologically enhanced to a degree that makes them immortal and almost indestructible. Individuals are able to pursue the same roles for many thousands of years, and they seem to possess infinite patience. Much of the plot turns on the difficulty of inflicting certain and permanent death, even with the most extreme methods or with deadly weapons specially designed for the purpose. Characters who die convincingly are as likely as not to return chapters later.

In Moriarty's *Spin State,* the characters possess advanced artificial intelligences that have emerged into self-awareness, and that are now struggling for political emancipation, as well as genetically engineered posthumans, some of them "wired" with extensive nonbiological hardware. Indeed, the book's main character, Major Catherine Li, is a "genetic construct" who has managed to alter the official records on her biological background in order to escape a requirement for registration. She works as a UN Peacekeeper, and she is thoroughly wired with "ceramsteel" augmentations.

But there is a paradox about cyberpunk's legacy. Much of what it once described as the future has actually come to pass, while the more extreme ideas, such as uploading human personalities into a virtual reality, may seem implausible. Partly, perhaps, for this reason some of the most notable cyberpunk writers have recently produced narratives that are scarcely identifiable as science fiction at all. Yet, these writers would have been perceived as painting a radical picture of the near future if they had been published only twenty years ago, when cyberpunk was young.

William Gibson's most recent novels—*Pattern Recognition* (2003) and *Spook Country* (2007)—have a cyberpunk feel but no clearly identifiable science fiction elements. Gibson's current mission, it seems, is to portray the present *as if it were* science fiction. Cayce Pollard, the main character of *Pattern Recognition,* lives in a milieu of fashion and design, consulting on corporate design proposals and identifying cool trends a step in advance. She suffers from a hypersensitivity to images and patterns that sometimes induces panic and nausea, but that enables her to perform her job with extraordinary success. Gibson depicts Cayce's comings and goings across several countries; she encounters numerous cultures, subcultures, and strange individuals as she attempts to uncover the identity of a mysterious *auteur* who is releasing cut-up bits of original movie footage on the Internet in an inexplicable order. Cayce's father, we learn, disappeared on September 11, 2001, in New York

City, a year before the events of the book. *Spook Country* is set in the same world—again, a strange version of our own—with a story of espionage, avant-garde art, drug use and abuse, and fancy corporate marketing.

Gibson seems to suggest that in the early years of the new millennium, after such events as the September 11 attacks in 2001, our own world has become alien to us, and it needs to be looked at with fresh eyes. Perhaps Gibson's drift into a literary place that is not quite the house of science fiction also reflects a greater willingness on the part of some writers from the science fiction tradition to write more directly about the contemporary context and its concerns: about such familiar anxieties as the influence of corporations and markets, the allure of fashion and style, the ubiquity of prohibited drugs, the shadows of racial, cultural, and religious tension, and the realities of environmental degradation and climate change. Twenty-first-century science fiction addresses these issues in many different ways—for example, *Spin State* makes reference to a ruined environment on Earth; several cyberpunk and post-cyberpunk works present a future with many racial, linguistic, and cultural demographics; and Kim Stanley Robinson's writings have recently emphasized global warming and its impact (discussed below under "Authors and Their Works").

Gibson's recent novels also reflect a more general convergence of the literary mainstream and more ambitious forms of prose science fiction. Since the 1960s New Wave, if not before, science fiction writers have developed an increasing stylistic sophistication, embracing such values as deep and particularized characterization, complex narrative design, and less literal kinds of story telling.

Like Gibson, Neal Stephenson comes from the science fiction tradition, and he made his mark during the 1990s with such late-cyberpunk novels as *Snow Crash* (1992) and *The Diamond Age* (1995). With *Cryptonomicon* (1999) and his more recent Baroque Cycle of novels (2003–2004), Stephenson can be seen as another writer who challenges the distinction between science fiction and the mainstream. Like Gibson, he shows a strong influence from the writings of Thomas Pynchon—generally placed on the other side of the science fiction–mainstream literary divide—and he has achieved success beyond the confines of a dedicated science fiction readership. *Cryptonomicon,* mainly set during the Second World War, depicts efforts to crack the military code used by the Axis powers, whereas the Baroque Cycle is set in the same reality about 250 years earlier. Though some historical and geographical details are changed from the world that we know, there is little in these books that is truly science fictional.

Kim Stanley Robinson's *The Years of Rice and Salt* (2002) takes a radically different approach to contemporary anxieties, making use of the alternate history form of narrative. It is, perhaps, the most ambitious work of this kind published to date. The book's premise is that the Black Death of the fourteenth century destroyed almost the entire population of Europe, not only one-third or so, creating a political vacuum to be filled by Islam and the Chinese. Christianity and white-skinned humans are essentially wiped out. This novel also uses a fantasy device to reimagine the course of history since the 1300s: its main characters are repeatedly reincarnated after their deaths, with no scientific or pseudoscientific explanation.

Robinson's characters discuss the nature of history among themselves, and the author appears to suggest that major real events, such as the rise of modern science, would have had equivalents even in the absence of European civilization. Mark Bold describes in detail Robinson's use of a world focused on cultures about which

Westerners are seldom educated, which is a profoundly political and timely act. Bold argues that "ignorance of Islamic cultures forms the basis of the stereotyping that is used to justify slaughter of Afghan civilians, oppression of Palestinians, and genocide sanctions in Iraq" (Bold 2002, 136). However, the relatively sympathetic view of Islam suggested by Robinson may be contrasted with the suspicion implicit in some of Dan Simmons' recent fiction (discussed below under "Authors and Their Works").

Reception. As the pace of social and technological change accelerated during the twentieth century, narratives of technological innovation and futuristic prospects became more culturally prominent. Science fiction expanded into new media such as radio, cinema, comics, television, and computer games.

Science fiction concepts first appeared in radio serials starting in the 1930s; *Buck Rogers in the 25th Century* (1932–1947), a space opera serial aimed at a young audience, was probably the first genuine science fiction radio program. Since the 1960s, science fiction radio drama has been rare in the US, but it was relatively common in the 1930s, 1940s, and 1950s. Broadcasts usually took the form of juvenile serials, including the *Superman* series (1940–1952), in which the superhero from Krypton foiled the schemes of various criminals. However, the most famous radio drama of all is a 1938 broadcast by Orson Welles: an adaptation of H.G. Wells's novel *War of the Worlds*. This broadcast produced widespread panic when many listeners mistook it for a genuine news report about an invasion of planet Earth by Martians.

As Peter Nicholls has observed in a detailed encyclopedia entry on science fiction cinema, science fiction has a natural affinity with the cinema, as the latter's illusory qualities "are ideal for presenting fiction about things that are not real" (Clute and Nicholls 1993, 219) Cinematic science fiction began to develop in the early decades of the twentieth century, often showing a Frankensteinian or dystopian edge, as in *Metropolis* (1926), Fritz Lang's portrayal of a mechanized and dehumanizing future city. During the 1930s, there was something of a boom in American science fiction cinema. This included adaptations of notable early science fiction texts, such as Shelley's *Frankenstein* and works by H.G. Wells, though there were also entirely new stories, such as *King Kong* (1933). Again, the predominant emphasis was Frankensteinian, highlighting the self-destructive schemes of mad scientists.

Some early movies were more optimistic about science and technology, notably *When Worlds Collide* (1951) and *Things to Come* (1936), the latter a British celebration of technocratic Wellsianism. Nonetheless, science fiction cinema has often displayed a bias against science and technology—most markedly in the many American and Japanese portrayals of monsters created by the misuse of science—such as the giant ants of *Them!* (1954), and the huge, city-destroying reptile of *Gojira* (1954) and its many sequels. Other movies that influenced American popular culture in the 1950s were *Destination Moon* (1950), *The Thing* (1951), *The Day the Earth Stood Still* (1951), *Forbidden Planet* (1956), and *The Fly* (1958). In general, monsters, aliens, and space exploration provided the icons of 1950s science fiction cinema.

Nicholls regards 1968 as the most important single year in science fiction cinema's history (Clute and Nicholls 1993, 222). That year's movie releases included *Planet of the Apes*, the likeable spoof *Barbarella*, and above all Stanley Kubrick's visionary, cryptic, numinous *2001: A Space Odyssey* (on which the director collaborated with Arthur C. Clarke). The 1960s and 1970s saw a large number of cautionary antitechnology movies, cinematic dystopias, and post-Holocaust movies.

In more recent decades, besides drawing heavily on the conventions of heroic fantasy, adventure movies such as *Star Wars* (1977) have looked back to older forms of science fiction, such as superhero stories and Gernsback-era space opera. *Star Wars* can also been seen as belonging to the tradition of 1930s cinematic space opera, which yielded movies such as *Flash Gordon* (1936). *Star Wars* and its sequels, prequels, and imitations gave more impetus to media tie-in writing, which has sometimes been controversial in the science fiction writing. The frequent resemblance to modern fantasy works applies to science fiction in all media, but with particular force to action-adventure science fiction movies.

During the late 1970s and the 1980s, a new kind of science fiction cinema emerged, perhaps beginning with *Alien* (1979), *The Terminator* (1984), David Cronenberg's remake of *The Fly* (1986), *Predator* (1987), and the sequels to each of these. This was a darker, grittier, sometimes ickier approach to science fiction. To some extent, this type of science fiction was rooted in the Frankensteinian tradition of technophobic horror, but it also had affinities with contemporaneous developments in prose science fiction, as well as in comics, where a darker style was showcased in the 1980s work of Frank Miller. *Blade Runner* (1982) depicts a police hunt for renegade androids in a near-future Los Angeles. Appearing at the same time as the first clearly cyberpunk short stories by Gibson and others—and anticipating *Neuromancer* by two years—*Blade Runner* is pure cyberpunk, imagined for the big screen; its importance as a masterpiece of cyberpunk film is rivalled only by *The Matrix* (1999), and its more recent sequels (*The Matrix Reloaded* and *The Matrix Revolutions,* both released in 2003) and spin-offs.

The history of science fiction comics begins with the space opera comic strips introduced into newspapers in the 1920s and 1930s, such as the *Flash Gordon* strip created in 1934. These led to reprints in comic-book form and then to original comic-book series, such as *Action Comics,* which introduced the figure of Superman in 1938. Superman obtained his own comic book in the following year, and he has provided the inspiration for a huge number of superheroes ever since. By the early 1950s, science fiction comics were popular, with an emphasis on interplanetary adventure and space opera, though a broad range of science fiction types and themes was covered. There were also frequent adaptations of prose science fiction by well-known authors of the time.

The year that transformed modern comic books was 1961, when Marvel Comics—which had published work in a variety of genres through the 1950s—created a new team of superheroes, the Fantastic Four. These characters obtained their superhuman powers through bodily mutation induced by exposure to cosmic rays during a mission in space. During the 1960s, Marvel and DC (which published comics featuring Superman, Batman, Green Lantern, and others) embarked on a rivalry that led to the creation of countless more superheroes and supervillains. Less commercially successful than the superhero comics were comic-book adaptations of movies, television shows, and prose narratives, though there were long-running adaptations of some major science fiction texts from cinema and television.

Some companies began to experiment with collections of stories—or with long, stand-alone stories of considerable complexity, published in a larger and more durable format. The first of these that could plausibly be termed graphic novels began to appear in the early 1970s, and the expression "graphic novel" was popularized towards the end of that decade. This form of publication became established during the 1980s, with the publication of the Marvel Graphic Comic line, including *God Loves, Man Kills* (1982), by Chris Clairmont, which later influenced the X-Men movies; *Maus: A Survivor's Tale* (1986) by Art Spiegelman; the four-volume *Batman: The Dark Knight Returns* (1986) by Frank Miller; and the twelve-volume *Watchmen* (1987) as well as the ten-volume *V for Vendetta* (1982–88), both by Alan Moore. This format has now become a staple within the comic-book industry.

About the same time that the graphic novel reached its initial heights, George R.R. Martin and a group of collaborators—including Roger Zelazny and leading comics writer Chris Claremont—commenced a complementary venture: the *Wild Cards* series of books (1987–). Some of these volumes contain interrelated stories, while others are novels in their own right, composed by either a group of authors or a single author. This ongoing series tells of events in an alternative reality inhabited by superheroes and supervillains, among others, following the accidental release of an alien virus that transforms human DNA. The *Wild Cards* series has itself spun off comic-book adaptations.

While the world of comic books is complex, the general tendency has been for American comics to be dominated by superhero adventures. These have fed back into television, cinematic, and prose science fiction, with numerous adaptations of superhero comic series. Some cinema adaptations—such as those involving Superman, Batman, and Marvel's Spider-Man and X-Men—have achieved high levels of success, often setting box-office records and establishing places among the top-grossing movies of all time. The movies *X-Men* (2000), *Spider-Man* (2002), and their sequels have led to a major resurgence of comic-book superheroes in cinema during the early years of the twenty-first century. These movies have inspired further novelistic spin-offs, including novelizations in prose form of film scripts and entirely original superhero adventures.

The first science fiction television series to be broadcast in the United States was the postwar *Captain Video* (1949–53, 1955–56), which featured a futuristic hero who battled various alien threats with the help of his Video Rangers. This started the practice of aiming science fiction on TV mainly at a young audience. *Captain Video* was followed by many space adventure and superhero programs. However, *The Twilight Zone* (1959–64) and *The Outer Limits* (1963–65) were varied anthology-style programs with more appeal to adults: the former used a mix of science fiction and fantasy, while the latter was focused on science fiction, often reflecting something of the New Wave sensibility of the time. Some of its most famous scripts, including that for the most celebrated episode of all—"Demon with a Glass Hand" (1964)—were written by Harlan Ellison. The 1960s also saw the production of many science fiction or fantasy comedy shows, such as *My Favorite Martian* (1963–66). Drama series of the 1960s included *Voyage to the Bottom of the Sea* (1964–68), *Lost in Space* (1965–68), and *Time Tunnel* (1966–67)—all aimed at children and teenagers—and *The Invaders* (1967–68), which sought a more mature audience.

However, *Star Trek* (1966–69) was ultimately the most successful of the American science fiction shows of the 1960s. It featured the voyages of a giant starship, sent out to explore for new worlds and civilizations. Once again, the episode widely regarded as the best in the original series was one scripted by Ellison: "The City on the Edge of Forever" (1967). Though it did not attract strong ratings, *Star Trek* not only gained an enthusiastic fan base and eventually had many successors and imitators but also became the basis for both a long succession of movies—beginning with *Star Trek: The Motion Picture* (1979)—and numerous spin-off novels and comic books.

Star Trek and the series that followed it maintained a strand of optimism that was not apparent in the dominant prose science fiction of the 1960s and 1970s. *Star Trek* itself was set in a somewhat utopian version of the twenty-fourth century, when humanity has come together in the benign United Federation of Planets. With this backdrop, the series expressed hopes for mankind's survival, maturity, and eventual flourishing in space. However clumsily, it suggested the possibility of a human society without racism, sexism, poverty, or gross inequality. The show's cult following, together with the success of the *Star Wars* movies, led to the creation of many science fiction series in the 1970s and beyond, with fluctuations in priorities and fashions. One notable success was *The X-Files* (1993–2002)—a TV show that investigated the paranormal—with its catchy slogan "the truth is out there."

In the first decade of the twenty-first century, there is an intricate cross-fertilization of American and foreign cinema, comics, television, media-related prose science fiction, and computer games—a new medium that has gained enormous participation, especially among younger people, and that is now a wealthy industry in its own right. For example, the 1999 movie *The Matrix* has spawned feature-length sequels, short animations, comics, games, and other tie-in material. Along with the related genre of modern fantasy, science fiction has become a dominant presence in popular cultures worldwide.

But despite the visibility of science fiction in popular culture—or perhaps because of it—the kinds of science fiction that are best known to the public do not accurately reflect the state of the art in prose science fiction. Cinematic space opera typically resembles the stories that first appeared in the 1920s as much as it resembles current post-cyberpunk forms of narrative. The relatively peripheral superhero variety of science fiction has had great prominence in the cinema, whereas more thoughtful movies with strong science fiction elements—such as *The Eternal Sunshine of the Spotless Mind* (2004)—are frequently not even marketed or discussed as science fiction.

To an outsider, science fiction may appear to be a form of entertainment—a somewhat lurid one—aimed at the youth market, along with pop music and computer games. Of course, the production of entertaining works for children and teenagers is not a contemptible thing, and the most culturally visible works, such as the *Star Wars* movies, are technically dazzling products that gain additional strength and resonance through their respectful treatment of mythic archetypes. The work of writers and others involved in the multimedia complex of science fiction–based entertainment requires high levels of skill, knowledge, and professionalism. Moreover, popular science fiction in all media displays an admirable knowingness, complexity, and capacity for self-scrutiny that may not be apparent to the uninitiated. All that conceded, the most innovative work in prose science fiction is largely obscured.

An ever-expanding body of scholarly and critical writing has emerged that examines, interprets, and evaluates the science fiction genre. This includes encyclopedic volumes such as *The Encyclopedia of Science Fiction* (1993); specialist journals such as *Science Fiction Studies, Foundation: The International Review of Science Fiction* (published by the Science Fiction Foundation) and *Extrapolation* (published by an official academic body, the Science Fiction Research Association); news magazines such as *Locus;* and many semiprofessional and amateur publications (the latter known as "fanzines") that sometimes achieve high standards of analysis. Nonetheless, science fiction is held in relatively low regard by the elite literary culture. Some novelists (or their publishers) avoid the label, even when incorporating science fiction elements into their narratives. Karen Joy Fowler's *Sarah Canary* (1991), for example, avoided science fiction marketing and thereby obtained a broader audience.

In the process of defending science fiction, John Clute (1999) offers additional reasons why it is often dismissed as trash: much science fiction that is prominently marketed as such *really is* trash, he suggests. American science fiction authors have tended to dramatize ideas about the world and technology, as a consequence of which their work can be simplistic both in dealing with complex matters such as human nature and in depicting American triumphalism. These authors also receive a degree of the defensive disparagement from technology-wary humanists. At the same time, Clute argues, science fiction provides a bracing angle for writers to adopt in looking at the world—and at its potential—in a time of constant innovation and crisis.

In the midst of ongoing controversy about science fiction's literary and cultural value, Peter Brigg's *The Span of Mainstream and Science Fiction* (2002) offers a sustained argument that trends in the last few decades have produced a convergence between science fiction and mainstream forms of fiction—however, exactly, these are understood. As discussed above, genre science fiction writers have developed an increasing literary sophistication. Conversely, the major physical, conceptual, and social transformations wrought by science during the nineteenth century and since have prompted mainstream writers to investigate themes that fall within science fiction's domain.

As Jonathan Lethem (1998) has lamented, there has been no true merger of science fiction and the literary mainstream, which often forces writers to choose a career in either one or the other. However, many literary authors have published stories and novels that are formally science fiction, or close to it. Two recent examples, out of many, are John Updike's *Toward the End of Time* (1997) and Philip Roth's *The Plot Against America* (2004); the former portrays the aftermath of a nuclear war between China and America, whereas the latter postulates that the great aviator and notorious anti-Semite Charles Lindbergh stood successfully for the U.S. presidency in 1940. Like Robinson's *The Years of Rice and Salt* and Jack Dann's *The Rebel: An Imagined Life of James Dean* (2004), Roth's book demonstrates the ongoing vitality of the alternate history novel.

Selected Authors. Since the early years of the new millennium, significant work has been written and published by science fiction authors whose careers commenced in several different eras of the genre's development. This underlines the genre's teeming diversity of movements, styles, and subgenres. Some of the distinguished authors who remain productive—such as Robert Silverberg, Frederick Pohl, and Ray Bradbury—have careers stretching back to the 1950s or even earlier. Major American authors from the New Wave era (such as Ursula Le Guin), from the cyberpunk era (such as William Gibson, Bruce Sterling, Pat Cadigan, and Michael Swanwick), and from the hard science fiction tradition (such as Gregory Benford, Greg Bear, and David Brin) continue to produce fine work, as do practitioners of varied forms of space opera—such as Orson Scott Card, Catherine Asaro, and Elizabeth Moon. Accordingly, any discussion of major authors who have been active in recent years must be highly selective.

The recent novels of William Gibson and Neal Stephenson are discussed above under the heading "Contexts and Issues," where the point is made that their work is merging with the mainstream. Something similar may be said of Bruce Sterling, the most aggressive advocate of cyberpunk during the 1980s: Sterling's *Zeitgeist* (2000) and *The Zenith Angle* (2004) are further examples of novels that have emerged from the science fiction tradition but crossed over into territories that resemble the literary mainstream or the techno-thriller genre. Conversely, Richard Powers is the most prominent contemporary example of an American author whose interest in the implications of science and technology almost carries him into the house of science fiction. His career has explored such issues as genetics, artificial intelligence, and virtual reality—as in *The Gold Bug Variations* (1991), *Galatea 2.2* (1995), and *Plowing the Dark* (2000).

Powers's ninth novel, *The Echo Maker* (2006) won the National Book Award and was a finalist for the Pulitzer Prize. Its focus is on cognitive neurology and, particularly, on the mysteries that surround a young man, Mark Schluter, who suffers severe head injuries when he flips his truck at high speed and is subsequently diagnosed with Capgras syndrome. He is unable to accept that his sister, Karin, is really his sister and accuses her of being a fake. Indeed, he starts to think that his dog, his house, and much else in his Nebraska hometown, are cunning facsimiles, which leads him to concoct bizarre explanations for this. A celebrated neurologist, Dr. Gerald Weber—a kind of Oliver Sacks figure—is brought in to assist, but he finds his own personality undermined by his interactions with Mark and others in the town. Throughout, *The Echo Maker* contains meditations on the vulnerability of our selves and our perceptions of the world, a vulnerability that is acted out at many levels.

By contrast, old-fashioned space opera continues to be strongly represented in contemporary science fiction. Its most prominent exponents include Lois McMaster Bujold and Elizabeth Moon. Bujold's main claim to prominence in the science fiction field is based on a series of space opera adventures reminiscent of C.S. Forester's Horatio Hornblower stories (and their earlier science fiction imitators). She writes about the life, vicissitudes, and successes of Miles Vorkosigan, a somewhat unusual hero for such adventures, because he is born with brittle bones and other medical problems. As a result his growth is stunted, and at one stage he fails the physical requirements to join the Service Academy. Nonetheless, Miles gradually rises in rank: in *Diplomatic Immunity* (2002), he is 32 years old and has attained the high post of Lord Auditor. In this book, the Barrayarran Emperor delegates him to deal with a diplomatic problem that involves murder, intrigue, and a colorful cast of characters.

Elizabeth Moon's greatest single success has been her Nebula Award–winning novel *The Speed of Dark* (2002), which is about a profoundly autistic but highly functioning individual, Lou Arrendale, who holds down a difficult job with a large employer. Lou is confronted by a possible cure for his syndrome. In reviewing this novel, Gwyneth Jones describes Lou's choice as a tragic one: "do you want to be normal if it will cost you everything you know and love?" (Jones, 2003, 20). Apart from *The Speed of Dark*, Moon has produced a large body of writing that typically describes adventures in space, often with an emphasis on military operations and tactics, reflecting her own significant experience in active service with the U.S. Marine Corps.

Joe Haldeman's continued success since the mid-1970s represents the flowering of a traditional kind of science fiction. Despite its title, Haldeman's *Forever Peace*

(1997) is not a sequel to his 1970s award-winning novel, *The Forever War,* but they both deal realistically with the horrors of war and war's possible roots in human nature. *Forever Peace* is set in the year 2043, during the Ngumi War, in which a coalition of Western nations led by the United States is attempting to put down the rebellion of an alliance of poor nations.

The early part of the novel focuses on the methods of mid-twenty-first-century warfare, in which Americans use remote-controlled war machines—notably, the robotlike "soldierboys," constructed through advanced nanotechnological manufacturing. In the second half, intrigue and complexity are added when two scientists discover that the completion and operation of an immense particle collider being built around Jupiter could create a new Big Bang and destroy the existing universe. The two scientists, aided by other people, attempt to stop the project and to advance their own plan to alter human nature—by making us more peaceful and putting an end to the cycle of wars—but they are opposed by a fanatical religious cult, the Hammer of God.

Forever Free (1999), however, is a true sequel to *The Forever War,* set after the interspecies war described in the earlier book has actually ended. Told in the first person by William Mandella, the main character of *The Forever War, Forever Free* involves an attempt to hijack an old space cruiser on the planet Middle Finger, where Mandella has settled down with his wife Marygay. The idea is for a group of war veterans and their families to escape the Galaxy and to use relativistic time dilation to travel forty thousand years into the future, when things might be more interesting. However, something goes wrong early in this journey, and the disgruntled vets are forced to return to Middle Finger, where everything has changed much more quickly than expected. This is a surprisingly whimsical book, sometimes a bit self-indulgent, much in the spirit of Heinlein's late novels.

Haldeman's *Camouflage* (2004) is a classic science fiction narrative that would have been successful in the golden age, except for its sexual frankness. In the near future, an alien spaceship is discovered deep beneath the surface of the ocean, and two dangerous nonhuman beings take an interest in it, though initially being unaware of each other. Both are millions of years old, superhuman in many of their abilities, and possessed of similar (though interestingly *not* identical) capacities to change shape and appearance. They both live within human societies, camouflaged as human beings. One of these creatures, the changeling, has gradually become benevolent towards humans, but the other, the chameleon, is driven by an urge to kill and destroy. This sets up a confrontation between good (of a kind) and evil, enlivened by spectacular combat and interspecies sex, all described with vividness and panache that few of Haldeman's peers could equal.

American-born Toronto resident Robert Charles Wilson became a Canadian citizen in 2007, but he has been a significant player in American science fiction since his first novel, *A Hidden Place,* was published in 1986. Wilson's narratives draw on the full breadth of the genre's traditions, particularly hard science fiction and the New Wave. He describes strange transformations of the world, as in *Darwinia* (1998), which is premised on the mysterious replacement in 1912 of the flora, fauna, as well as geographical and geological identity of Europe. In *The Chronoliths* (2001), huge monuments, seemingly from the future, appear suddenly in the early twenty-first-century world. They commemorate victories by somebody named only as "Kuin" in inscriptions on the monuments. The appearance of each Chronolith causes immense local destruction, and, as each new one appears, there is worldwide fear, confusion, and political destabilization. In both of these novels, Wilson concentrates on the reactions of an ordinary American man to the world-changing events and their social repercussions.

Spin (2005) is in a similar mold. A kind of membrane suddenly appears around the Earth, with no explanation, and blanks out the stars and the moon, while selectively letting through the light of the sun. The alien membrane comes to be known as "the Spin," whereas the beings hypothesized as having created it are called "the Hypotheticals." *Spin* is also a love story, depicting the narrator's devotion to his childhood sweetheart over three decades, and the complications and difficulties that their relationship encounters. His life is confusingly entangled with Diane's and her twin brother's from the night when the stars go out. The first published sequel to *Spin*, entitled *Axis* (2007), describes the human colonization of a new world created by the mysterious Hypotheticals.

Vernor Vinge has long been a prophet of Singularity and posthuman future, though this hardly exhausts his immense contribution to science fiction. His most significant achievement in the new millennium is *Rainbows End* (2006), a near-future novel, set in San Diego in 2025. It impressively portrays a world greatly, yet plausibly, altered from our own, one with ubiquitous cybernetic devices and endless conspiracies within conspiracies. This world is, it seems, fast approaching the Singularity or something like it.

At one level, *Rainbows End* is a redemption narrative: the story of a brilliant—but unscrupulous and emotionally cruel—poet, Robert Gu. Gu is restored to mental clarity and youthfulness after suffering from Alzheimer's disease, and he now has to create a new life for himself. He finds that his poetic genius has gone, though he has new talents and a softened personality. He struggles to fit into society after losing two decades as he is gradually transformed into a wiser and kinder person. At another level, Vinge presents a battle of cyberspace geniuses, one of whom is Alfred Vaz. Vaz is a high-level intelligence operative who wants to develop a mind-control technology to enforce world peace—a similar theme to Haldeman's *Forever Peace*, but presented with a quite different authorial attitude. We sympathize with Vaz's goal, even while being led to believe that his methods are unacceptable. Much of the book's mystery lies in the true identity of Mr. Rabbit, Vaz's opponent, who tries to put a stop to the mind-control scheme.

Though *Rainbows End* has many of the trappings of cyberpunk—and its author has a strong claim to have inspired the cyberpunk movement with his fiction of the early 1980s—Graham Sleight shrewdly observes that Vinge's novel does not have a cyberpunk ethos. Whereas Gibson, for example, depicts a world that is socially polarized between the street-smart and the corporate rich, Vinge presents a sunny and nonthreatening middle-class vision (Sleight 2006, 17). The rush towards a posthuman techno-rapture seems to take place within a comfortable suburban bubble. This may, in fact, be astute extrapolation on Vinge's part, but it does raise questions about what role there will be for the poor people of the world in a massively information-rich future.

In *Ilium* (2003) and its sequel *Olympos* (2005), Dan Simmons takes a radically different approach to posthuman possibilities: the events are set several thousand years in the future, long after our world has been transformed by extraordinary technologies. This is a "far future of posthumanity where the distinction between organic and machine blur[s] into insignificance" (Jeffery 2004, 1220). Simmons gradually reveals a complex backstory that requires considerable effort to piece together. The background includes global religious conflict on an unprecedented scale, with the development of biological weapons for mass extermination by political Islamists; the rise of reengineered superhuman beings; colossal engineering projects (such as habitable rings that orbit the Earth); and a space-faring civilization of surprisingly sympathetic, self-conscious robots called "moravecs" (after Hans Moravec, a celebrated robotics guru). Much of the action in the narrative present takes place on the plains of ancient Troy—but it is an alternative version of ancient Troy created by posthuman beings who emulate the powers and personalities of the Greek gods. Simmons weaves together multiple strands of story into what is really a single, immense novel published in two volumes.

Simmons is one of a growing number of science fiction writers who attempt to imagine a truly posthuman future while still engaging the sympathies of human readers. In part, this is achieved by including more-or-less human characters in all the narrative strands, though, as Jeffery recognizes, (2004, 123) the moravecs have the most human-seeming sensibilities of the lot. The *Ilium-Olympos* project represents only one fraction of Simmons's ambitious and growing body of literary work, which also includes important contributions to modern space opera and the horror genre.

As one leading science fiction scholar has remarked (Freedman, 2005, 125–126), Kim Stanley Robinson may be the most accomplished American science fiction writer to emerge since the 1960s and 1970s. Robinson's first two novels, *Icehenge* and *The Wild Shore,* were published in 1984, and since then he has continued to produce complex, humane works of hard science fiction, interspersed occasionally with more whimsical pieces, such as *Escape from Kathmandu* (1989). He is best known for his epic Mars trilogy—which covers two centuries of colonization, terraforming, and revolution on Mars, beginning with the departure of the First Hundred from Earth in 2027. Since then he has written *Antarctica* (1997), a near-future novel of illicit oil drilling and secret feral settlements, and his huge alternate history novel *The Years of Rice and Salt* (discussed above under Context and Issues).

Most recently, Robinson has published a new trilogy focused on the near-future impact of global warming: *Forty Signs of Rain* (2004), *Fifty Degrees Below* (2005), and *Sixty Days and Counting* (2007). Robinson's characters are involved in politics and high-level science administration in a very-near-future Washington, DC. They face accelerating climate change that produces floods in Washington, huge storms along the California coast, the halting of the Gulf Stream, a ferociously bitter winter in North America, the breaking off of enormous tabular icebergs in Antarctica, and the necessary evacuation of Tuvalu, as sea levels rise. American political leaders are slow to accept the new reality, remaining driven by an increasingly irrelevant imperative for economic growth.

The strength of these novels lies in their synthesis of many types of events as the author conveys the idea of a world undergoing change. There are dramatic depictions of disasters interweaved with political machinations, mysteries, and the characters' ordinary lives. We are shown day-to-day work activities and the detail of juggling these with personal demands (looking after children, finding somewhere to live in a new city, and so on). In his review of *Forty Signs of Rain,* Freedman (2005, 129) observes that, at points, it is one of the best novelistic depictions of the institutional practice of science since Gregory Benford's *Timescape* in 1980. That observation could be extended to the other books of the trilogy, and it is even more impressive that Robinson is able to combine the hard–science fiction elements with a finely observed picture of his characters' personal lives.

Robinson does have rivals for preeminence, and they surely include Connie Willis, who has won many major awards in the broader field of science fiction and fantasy. By any reasonable measure, she is the most professionally honored author ever to work in genre science fiction. Willis began writing professionally in the late 1970s, and she emerged as a major talent during the following decade. Her 1982 story "Fire Watch" won both of the science fiction field's premier awards—a Hugo Award and a Nebula Award—and it remains one of the most admired of all time-travel narratives. She won her most recent of many Hugo Awards for "Inside Job" (2005), a humorous fantasy novella. Other highlights of her distinguished career include her *Fire Watch* collection (1985) as well as the novels *Lincoln's Dreams* (1987), *Doomsday Book* (1992), and *To Say Nothing of the Dog* (1998).

Willis displays a fascination with history, and much of her work uses the plot device of a near future in which historians at Oxford University are trained to use time travel to observe the past—often encountering awkward problems or personal dangers, and becoming deeply involved in events. This enables the author to reveal and interpret past eras. She shows them in vivid detail, whether her focus is on the Nazi Blitz (*Fire Watch*), Europe at the time of the Black Death (*Doomsday Book*), or Victorian England (*To Say Nothing of the Dog*). *Lincoln's Dreams* employs a somewhat different device to reveal the past: it is set in the present, but one character is seemingly dreaming the dreams of Confederate general Robert E. Lee.

In *Passage* (2001), Willis presents the highly realistic narrative of a research psychologist's investigation of near-death experiences. The science fictional twist in the tale is that a brilliant neurologist at the same hospital invents a drug that enables these experiences to be manufactured at will. When she uses the drug, the researcher has an apparent experience of wandering the *Titanic* on its ill-fated voyage, allowing Willis to examine another emotionally resonant corner of history's mansions. We see, too, a fine example of the thematic and stylistic convergence between literary mainstream and some ambitious kinds of science fiction. Phenomena described by the neurological sciences are now proving a common source of fascination for supposedly genre writers, such as Willis, and supposedly mainstream writers, such as Richard Powers.

Once again, there is a considerable affinity between thoughtful, technically ambitious science fiction and scientifically literate work from the literary mainstream. There has, of course, been no true merger; and it should not be forgotten that science fiction has become an increasingly visible component of a popular culture whose values are often remote from those of novelists and short story writers from a high literary tradition. Popular science fiction is of interest and value in its own right, whether or not it displays a conventional literary sensibility. But scientific understanding and technological innovation continue to transform our world and the ways in which we perceive ourselves. As long as that remains so, the implications of science and technology will interest artists and writers from many traditions.

It should not, therefore, be surprising to find resemblances between, say, Delany's *Dhalgren* and Pynchon's *Gravity's Rainbow* (in the 1970s), or between a recent novel by a science fiction author, such as *Passage,* and a novel from across the literary divide, such as *The Echo Maker.* Marketing techniques and authorial reputations aside, there is little that distinguishes the most ambitious science fiction writing and the most scientifically aware narratives currently being produced within the literary mainstream. It is salutary to note this convergence, or at least intersection, of traditions: a lively awareness of it may enrich our experience of both.

SCIENCE FICTION AWARDS

World Science Fiction Society presents the annual Hugo Awards at the annual World Science Fiction Convention (WorldCon). Awards are currently presented in 15 categories. Recent award winners in the "Best Novel" category have included *Rainbows End* by Vernor Vinge (2007); *Spin* by Robert Charles Wilson (2006); *Jonathan Strange and Mr. Norrell* by Susanna Clarke (2005); *Paladin of Souls* by Lois McMaster Bujold (2004); *Hominids* by Robert J. Sawyer (2003); *American Gods* by Neil Gaiman (2002); *Harry Potter and the Goblet of Fire* by J.K. Rowling (2001); and *A Deepness in the Sky* by Vernor Vinge.

The Nebula Awards are presented by the Science Fiction and Fantasy Writers of America. Recent winners for "Best Novel" have included *Seeker* by Jack McDevitt (2006); *Camouflage* by Joe Haldeman (2005); *Paladin of Souls* by Lois McMaster Bujold (2004); *Speed of Dark* by Elizabeth Moon (2003); *American Gods* by Neil Gaiman (2002); *The Quantum Rose* by Catherine Asaro (2001); and *Darwin's Radio* by Greg Bear.

Sources: World Science Fiction Society-World Science Fiction Convention Web site. http://www.worldcon.org/index.html, and Science Fiction Writers of America Web site. http://www.sfwa.org/awards

Bibliography

Aldiss, Brian, and David Wingrove. *Trillion Year Spree: The History of Science Fiction.* London: Gollancz, 1986.

Andre-Driussi, Michael. "Languages of the Dying Sun." In *Earth Is But a Star: Excursions Through Science Fiction to the Far Future.* Damien Broderick, ed. Perth: University of Western Australia Press, 2001, 217–236.

Bould, Mark. "Review of *The Years of Rice and Salt,* by Kim Stanley Robinson." *Foundation* 86 (Autumn 2002): 134–136.

Brigg, Peter. *The Span of Mainstream and Science Fiction: A Critical Study of a New Literary Genre.* Jefferson, NC: McFarland and Co., 2002.

Clareson, Thomas D. *Understanding Contemporary American Science Fiction: The Formative Period (1926–1970).* Columbia, SC: University of South Carolina Press, 1990.

Clute, John, and Peter Nicholls, eds. *The Encyclopedia of Science Fiction.* New York: St. Martin's Press, 1993.

———. "In Defense of Science Fiction" *Salon* November 27, 2007. http://www.salon.com/books/feature/1999/05/25/sfdefense/index.html.

Crichton, Michael. *Prey.* New York: HarperCollins, 2002.

Freedman, Carl. "Review of *Forty Signs of Rain* by Kim Stanley Robinson." *Foundation* 95 (Autumn 2005): 125–130.

Haldeman, Joe. *Camouflage.* New York: Ace, 2004.

———. *Forever Peace.* New York: Ace, 1997.

Harris-Fain, Darren. *Understanding Contemporary American Science Fiction: The Age of Maturity, 1970–2000.* Columbia, SC: University of South Carolina Press, 2005.

Hartwell, David G., and Kathryn Cramer, eds. *The Hard SF Renaissance.* New York: Tor, 2002.

Jeffery, Steve. "Review of *Ilium* by Dan Simmons." *Foundation* 91 (Summer 2004): 122–124.

Jones, Gwyneth. "Review of *The Speed of Dark* by Elizabeth Moon." *New York Review of Science Fiction* 177 (May 2003): 20–21.

Moon, Elizabeth. *The Speed of Dark.* New York: Ballantine, 2003.

Powers, Richard. *The Echo Maker.* New York: Farrar, Straus, and Giroux, 2006.

Robinson, Kim Stanley. *Forty Signs of Rain*. New York: Bantam, 2004.

Scholes, Robert. *Structural Fabulation: An Essay on Fiction of the Future*. Notre Dame, IN: Notre Dame University Press, 1975.

Simmons, Dan. *Ilium*. New York: EOS, 2003.

———. *Olympos*. New York: EOS, 2005.

Sleight, Graham. "Review of *Rainbows End* by Vernor Vinge." *New York Review of Science Fiction* 215 (July 2006): 17–18.

Suvin, Darko. *Metamorphoses of Science Fiction*. New Haven, CT: Yale University Press, 1979.

Vinge, Vernor. *Rainbow's End*. New York: Tor, 2006.

Willis, Connie. *Passage*. New York: Bantam, 2001.

Wilson, Robert Charles. *Spin*. New York: Tor, 2005.

Further Reading

Broderick, Damien. *Reading by Starlight: Postmodern Science Fiction*. New York: Routledge, 1995; Clute, John, and Peter Nicholls, eds. *The Encyclopedia of Science Fiction*. New York: St. Martin's Press, 1993; Freedman, Carl. *Critical Theory and Science Fiction*. Middletown, CT: Wesleyan University Press, 2000; Geraghty, Lincoln. *Living with Star Trek: American Culture and the Star Trek Universe*. New York: I.B. Tauris, 2007; *Locus* Online. http://www.locusmag.com/ (accessed November 27, 2007); James, Edward, and Farah Mendlesohn, eds. *The Cambridge Companion to Science Fiction*. Cambridge: Cambridge University Press, 2003; Lethem, Jonathan. "Why Can't We All Just Live Together? A Vision of Genre Paradise Lost." *New York Review of Science Fiction* 121 (September 1998): 1, 8–9. (Originally published in shorter form in *Village Voice* as "Close Encounters: The Squandered Promise of Science Fiction."); Science Fiction Foundation Web site. http://www.sf-foundation.org/ (accessed November 27, 2007); Science Fiction Research Association Web site. http://www.sfra.org/ (accessed November 27, 2007); *Science Fiction Studies* Web site. http://www.depauw.edu/sfs/ (accessed November 27, 2007); Seed, David, ed. *A Companion to Science Fiction*. Oxford: Blackwell Publishers, 2005; Westfahl, Gary. *The Mechanics of Wonder*. Liverpool: Liverpool University Press, 1998; Westfahl, Gary, ed. *The Greenwood Encyclopedia of Science Fiction and Fantasy: Themes, Works, and Wonders* (three volumes). Westport, CT: Greenwood Press, 2005.

RUSSELL BLACKFORD

SCIENCE WRITING (NONFICTION)

Definition. Science nonfiction—or *popular science,* for the general audience—is an omnibus term referring to science-based literature that is not fiction (*popular science* and *pop science* have a slightly derogatory connotation). It includes essentially all literary nonfiction about science, particularly the natural sciences. It is distinct from the specialized literatures of the arts, sciences, and humanities that appear primarily in scholarly journals and university press monographs, and from the technical references and textbooks that are intended for professionals, practitioners, and students in a given field. Popular science literature includes the biography and autobiography of individual scientists, accounts of scientific discovery and technological invention, as well as explanations of scientific ideas and their implications. It is intimately connected to the professional domain of science journalism, drawing many of its practitioners from the ranks of science news reporters and science writers.

Popular science also overlaps with the interdisciplinary scientific monograph, that is, a book published by a scholarly press that is read by scientists outside the author's particular specialty but whose research will nonetheless be influenced by the author's ideas. Some such books receive broader attention, especially if they are in some degree controversial. E.O. Wilson's *Sociobiology* (1975), for example, is regarded by some critics as an extremist argument for the genetic determination of human behavior and thus as a potential rationalization for social injustice (see Ceccarelli 2001 for a discussion of the reception of Wilson's work). The present chapter *excludes* topics such as astrology, UFOlogy, parapsychology, and New Age occultism (that is, the hidden powers of things such as pyramids and crystals), which are more properly regarded as pseudoscience.

Popular science tends to emphasize the *intellectual content* of science—that is, its findings and speculations—rather than its sociological character, its historical development, or even its policy implications. According to Mellor (2003), when written by a scientist, it tends to be didactic in purpose and tone, and it is primarily interested in an *expository* effect (this does not prevent the occurrence of some lively prose, however; e.g., Sagan 1973). When written by a science journalist or other nonscientist, the focus usually shifts toward storytelling, which creates a *narrative* effect by highlighting the dramatic elements of discovery within a particular field (e.g., Gleick 1987); the tone thus often becomes literary or even poetic (e.g., Ferris 1997). Either scientistic or journalistic popular science authors may alternately focus on argumentation, laying out some kind of science-based critique of society's use, misuse, or abuse of science and technology (e.g., Carson 1962; Kolbert 2006; Rees 2003) or, more rarely, an examination of science itself (Smolin 2006; Horgan 1996) to achieve a *critical* effect.

In other words, popular science as a type of literature generally consists of works written by scientists or science journalists who try to explain current ideas and recent developments in a scientific field, usually either from the perspective of an expert scientific "insider" who seeks to teach the lay reader about those ideas or from that of a knowledgeable outside observer who emphasizes the narrative of discovery and the praiseworthy responsibility of particular individuals for some of those developments. A critical popular science also exists that warns a lay audience of problems associated with ignoring social or other ramifications of scientific findings, or that conversely engages in a critique of the practice of science. The underlying point of commonality among all three types of popular science literature is that they are geared toward "popularization," that is, toward making science, scientific knowledge, or scientific habits of mind accessible to a broader audience.

The derogatory connotation of the term *popular science* stems from its implicit contrast with *real science,* that is, the scientific communications produced by scientists for other scientists, rather than for a more general public. Very few scientists are charged in their job descriptions with communicating with the public (Reichhardt 2005); therefore, popular science is taken to be less serious than real science, a distraction from more worthy efforts—at least in the judgment of the review, tenure, and hiring committees evaluating the professional accomplishments of scientists, who tend not to consider themselves responsible for "outreaching" to the public in any case (Brown, Propst, and Woolley 2004). And despite the existence of a few high-profile popular science best sellers, publishers are coming to recognize the category as an increasingly crowded niche with a comparatively limited readership (Reichhardt 2005).

THE RELATIONSHIP BETWEEN POPULAR SCIENCE AND SCIENCE FICTION

In general, popular science is treated with greater respect than is **science fiction,** because as nonfiction, the former can claim for itself the sober mantle of "real science," in contrast to the speculative and ostensibly puerile character of genre fiction. Science fiction writers, for their part, make extensive use of information from popular science as background and inspiration (Sheffield 1999), and those with scientific expertise sometimes write popular science as well as science fiction, as the oeuvre of noted writer Isaac Asimov (1920-1992), whose PhD was in biochemistry, indicates (e.g., Asimov 1972). Similarly, science luminaries better known for their popularizing work have also written science fiction novels (e.g., Sagan 1985; Forward 1980). Additionally, an entire subcategory exists of titles purporting to examine and explain the "science" underlying science-fictional pop culture, of which *The Physics of Star Trek* is an early example (Krauss 1995) and *The Physics of Superheroes* (Kakalios 2005), a more recent one.

History. The emergence of a robust publishing category called *popular science* can be seen as an expression of a basic human desire to make sense of the world, coupled with the existence of both a diffuse reading public and a class of knowledgeable expert writers, conditions which existed as early as the Renaissance in some Italian cities (Eamon 1985). A functional, sociological impetus for science popularization is linked to the growth of science as a domain with a characteristic and paradoxical central feature—namely, science produces knowledge that is on the one hand *universal* in its scope and applicability, but on the other *esoteric* in its origins and provenance. The working out of this tension was part of the early development of science—for example, in the seventeenth century natural philosophers wrangled over how much confidence to place in experimental demonstration vis-à-vis reason-driven theorizing, and over how much public participation in the counsels of science was warranted (Eiseley 1973; Lynn 2001; Shapin and Schaffer 1985).

The sacerdotal character often ascribed to scientists speaking in the public sphere—speaking, that is, as priestly mediators of the natural world—is a product of their access to this abstruse but essential knowledge (Lessl 1989). In the 19th century, popular science essayists and writers emerged in Europe, Australia and the United States to explicate scientific ideas and make the case, however tendentious, for their larger social or cultural meaningfulness (Fyfe 2005; Repp 2000; Lightman 2000; Lucas, Maroske, and Brown-May 2006; Menand 2001). Besides increasing public knowledge of science, the popularization of science garners and shapes public support for scientific enterprise (Bates 2005; Cassidy 2005, 2006); and some scientist-popularizers eventually turn from presenting scientific concepts per se to promoting the principles and practices of scientific inquiry (e.g., Sagan 1973 vs. Sagan 2006; Gould 1977 vs. Gould 1999; Weinberg 1977 vs. Weinberg 2001) in the face of exaggerated or dystopian science-fictional and mass-media images of science (see Nerlich, Clarke, and Dingwall 1999; Petersen, Anderson, and Allan 2005; Schnabel 2003 for discussions). Popular science also enables disparate scientific communities to monitor each other for useful ideas and innovations (Paul 2004).

There is, therefore, a recognized social value in the mission of popularizing science, despite an unwarranted professional stigmatization of those who engage in it

(Shermer 2002). Opinion surveys show that while support for science and scientific research is broad and strong, public knowledge of specific scientific concepts is sparse (Miller 2004; Brown, Propst, and Woolley 2004; Smith 2003; Bainbridge 2002). Given this fact, legislatures, science policy advocates, and science educators have consistently sought to encourage greater public awareness, knowledge, and appreciation of science, motivated by the sense that "scientific literacy"—that is, familiarity with concepts and ideas emerging from the work of science (see DeBoer 2000; Paisley 1998)—is essential for robust economic competitiveness and (more recently) meaningful democratic decision making (Hodson 2003). For example, during the 1920s a national debate took place in Britain over the "neglect of science" in public education, inspiring many scientists to write and publishers to print books on science for the public (Mayer 1997; Bowler 2006).

However, the incorporation of popular science into formal scientific education occurs only on an ad hoc basis (Lam 2005; Wally, Levinger, Grainger 2005). In the 1940s, American comic books published biographical accounts of medical researchers and innovators—such as Louis Pasteur and Walter Reed—as a commercial effort to capitalize on the general success of comic books by making use of educational (i.e., "true life") material (Hansen 2004). Later, during the Cold War, when the Soviet Union's launch of the Sputnik satellite created perceptions of a "science gap," legislation was enacted to support science education (Clowse 1981), itself part of a broader political discussion over the character and form of a national scientific research alliance of private and public research-sponsoring organizations, institutions, and corporations (Greenhill 2000), most of which are little known to the public (Brown, Propst, and Woolley 2004). Some critics suggest that the pressure upon researchers to justify their funding creates an environment in which they are motivated to seek out media attention, thereby contributing to the "hyping" of science (Caulfield 2004). Popularizers of science, on the other hand, attribute their motivation to a desire to share the romance of science, the sense of wonder that it evokes. "*Not* explaining science seems to me perverse," wrote astronomer Carl Sagan (1996), whose 13-part television documentary *Cosmos* and its accompanying book (Sagan 1980) presents a panoramic breadth of scientific ideas and speculation. "When you're in love, you want to tell the world."

Despite the prior existence of some well-known popularizations such as Sagan's work and physicist Steven Weinberg's account of the Big Bang in *The First Three Minutes* (1977), the recent history of popular science publishing begins in many accounts with the publication of physicist Steven Hawking's *A Brief History of Time* (1988), which despite its intellectual density (some reports call it "unreadability") initiated a pop science boom in publishing that lasted through the 1990s (Reichhardt 2005; Tallack 2004). At about the same time, the publication of James Gleick's *Chaos* (1987), with its intimations of a revolutionary new mathematics, drew considerable popular attention to the implications of studying complex dynamic systems. Chaos theory emerged from such studies, and its popularization took on an enormous weight as a metaphor for the fragmented and chaotic postmodern world. Mathematical insights from chaos theory have been used in various scientific disciplines and still receives some attention from science popularizers (Gribbin 2004). Some suggest that the popular science boom has tightened up subsequently, though the precise dimensions of the contraction are disputed (Levin 2005a).

The success of Hawking's book and of science journalist Dava Sobel's *Longitude* (1995)—an account of the solution of a perplexing navigational problem in the 17th century—is cited as the proximate cause of a glut of popular science books, in which "formulaic and regurgitative writing" are the norm—although even the most critical admit the possibility of gold among the dross (Laszlo 2005). Despite experimentations with novelistic and memoir-form popular science (e.g., Levin 2002), a consensus seems to have arisen that the paramount requirement for good popular science is clarity of writing combined with an understanding of the science, rather than literary flair (Aczel 2004). This may mean only that the content of popular science has spilled out of its traditional boundaries; for example, certain playwrights have found great dramatic potential in scientific ideas such as chaos theory (Stoppard 1993) and Heisenberg's uncertainty principle (Frayn 2000). But the overall imperative toward clarity may account for the recent critical and popular success of Bill Bryson's (2003) *A Short History of Nearly Everything,* an overview of scientific ideas. As a travel writer, Bryson is used to clearly explaining unfamiliar territory to his readers.

Trends and Themes. There are a few topic areas in popular science that consistently receive attention from writers of popular science, their publishers, reviewers, and the public. These include the related areas of physics, cosmology, and astronomy on one hand, and biology, genetics, and evolution (and its discontents) on the other. The public fascination with these domains of scientific inquiry can be attributed to their perceived potential for revealing fundamental information about the nature of the cosmos or the character of humanity. Hawking (1988) after all promised in *A Brief History of Time* to show how physics could let us understand the mind of God; and the emergence of a school of literary criticism that seeks to analyze the behavior of fictional characters in evolutionary terms speaks to the power of genetic explanations of human activities (Shea 2005).

Much recent popular science in the domain of physics and cosmology continues to follow in the tradition of Hawking. The author reviews the development of modern physics, beginning with Einstein's insight about the invariance of the speed of light regardless of the speed of the observer and showing how this led to further insights about the composition of matter at subatomic scales and the large-scale history of the universe. After this review, the author turns to a discussion of more recent, speculative developments that build upon the earlier findings or address their implications, such as alternate universes (Kaku 2005b), hidden or "rolled up" dimensions of space-time (Randall 2005), or variations in the speed of light at different times in the history of the universe (Magueijo 2003). The centennial of the publication of Albert Einstein's groundbreaking papers explaining poorly understood experimental findings relating to the nature of light and the behavior of atoms (one of which earned him a Nobel Prize) in 1905 marked a surge in Einstein-related books (Levin 2005b), some by physicists (Kaku 2005a; Rigden 2005) and others by science writers (Fox and Keck 2004)—with the former focusing on the implications of Einstein's physics and the latter seeking to provide the scientist's human context.

Interestingly, a number of books in recent years have been written by physicists who believe that a mistake is being made by the continued commitment of physicists to string theory, which posits that various subatomic particles can be understood as the three-dimensional "projections" of unobservable string-like objects vibrating in some kind of higher-dimensional space (Smolin 2006; Woit 2006). These critiques vary in their vehemence but hinge upon the idea that string theory is so far from testable that it is not truly scientific. Testability (or falsifiability) means that an empirical demonstration would produce different results if an idea were true than if it were false, and so the possibility of experimental refutation is regarded as the *sine qua non* of scientific status for a theory. The critics believe that the focus on string theory is stifling alternatives, and this debate has reached the popular press (Matthews 2006). For their part, advocates of string theory–based approaches point to the construction of the Large Hadron Collider (LHC) in Switzerland as an exciting opportunity for garnering further empirical data that may provide support for string theory models (e.g., Greene 1999; Randall 2005).

With the passing (at least for now) of the heroic age of space exploration—no giant leaps for humanity seem immediately in the offing—books about astronomy and space science have grown narrower in scope, even if their scale remains interplanetary. Science writer Dava Sobel's *The Planets* (2005) is a set of essays, one per planet, that combines scientific information with literary, historical, and even astrological allusions, in an effort to show how the lore of the planets is very much embedded in Western thought. The effect is one of a literate and meditative musing upon the intersection of science and culture. Such efforts are not limited to astronomical science, however: Jennifer Ouellette's *Black Bodies and Quantum Cats* (2005) attempts to illuminate episodes from the history of physics with references to history and popular culture. Planetologist Steve Squyre's *Roving Mars* (2005), on the other hand, is straight narrative. He tells the story of the design, construction, launch, and success of Spirit and Opportunity, two robotic Mars rovers that he helped build. Similarly, astronomer Fred Watson's *Stargazer* (2005) is a historical and technological appreciation of the telescope and its role in astronomy.

Increasingly, however, popular science is drawing upon the cognitive sciences for its material. This is perhaps to be expected, given the extent to which questions about the workings of the brain and its relationship to consciousness and mind have gained prominence in scientific inquiry over the past ten to fifteen years (Horgan 1999). Recent contributions by cognitive scientists to popular science include Daniel Levitin's *This Is Your Brain On Music* (2006), which discusses Levitin's investigations into the psychology of music as well as his own metamorphosis from musician to music-loving scientist. Intellectual territory somewhat more fraught is covered by Louann Brizendine's *The Female Brain* (2006). This book provides an account of a neuropsychiatrist's conclusions about the differences between male and female brains, drawing upon her twenty years of research and clinical practice. Brizendine argues that hormonal and neurological differences between the sexes do in fact make women more language-, emotion-, and memory-oriented and men more sex- and aggression-oriented.

Recent popular science drawing on biology and genetics has notably included a retrospective summary of James Watson's contribution to molecular biology to medicine, law, and technology (Watson and Berry 2003). His codiscovery of DNA's double-helical structure (Watson 1968) made possible more recent innovations in gene therapy, genetic engineering, and genomics. Explanations of evolutionary theory and the operation of natural and sexual selection continue to occupy the attention of science popularizers. In *The Ancestor's Tale* (Dawkins 2004), Richard Dawkins retraces the evolutionary branchings that resulted in humanity moving backwards in time through a series of rendezvous toward the common ancestor of life on earth. The (specious) currency of intelligent design (ID) has moved some science popularizers to an ardent defense of evolution, as in skeptic Michael Shermer's *Why Darwin Matters* (2006), which refutes the various argumentative threads essayed by ID's proponents, such as the "anthropic principle" (the universe seems to have been made especially well suited to us) and "irreducible complexity" (biological features like eyes and the organelles of cells are just too complicated to have evolved by chance) by showing that they don't hold up to scrutiny.

A broader trend to use science to make sense of human action rather than origin is evident in two quite disparate books: science writer Stephen Hall's *Size Matters* (2006) and geographer Jared Diamond's *Collapse* (2005). Hall, himself a short man, is interested in the effect of height on boys' happiness and future success. He outlines the history of research on height and growth and criticizes the medicalization of shortness by using human growth hormone on children. Diamond, on the other hand, is interested in identifying the causal forces at work in broad swaths of human history. His earlier book *Guns, Germs, and Steel* (Diamond 1997) argues that accidents of geography explain how the West came to geopolitical primacy in modern times. *Collapse* (subtitled "How Societies Choose to Fail or Succeed") is a set of case studies that again seeks to isolate the causal features of a particular historical phenomenon: in this case, how societies can emerge, develop, flower, and then—sometimes even in their moment of flowering—collapse and vanish utterly, like the Norse in Greenland or the priesthood of the temples of Angkor Wat did. His answer includes some combination of self-inflicted environmental damage, climate change, and the presence or absence of hostile or unhelpful neighbors, and it is derived from comparative quantitative analysis of the factors he finds in the cases he examines. Similarly, the economist Steven Levitt's *Freakonomics* (Levitt and Dubner 2005) offers counterintuitive, startling conclusions—such as the possibility that the legalization of abortion may lower the crime rate—drawing upon economic (rather than moral) reasoning and analysis.

Finally, scientists continue to debate over the relationship between science and religion, as implicated in the notion of intelligent design discussed above. The lectures posthumously published as *The Varieties of Scientific Experience* (Sagan 2006) seek to convey the literal awesomeness of science as a way of understanding the universe and as a source through which human purpose may be made rather than received. *The God Delusion* (Dawkins 2006), a more controversial and polemical book, tries to explain religious sentiment as the product of our inability to understand the causal features of inanimate objects and the intentionality of animate beings. Other scientists (Collins 2006; Gingerich 2006) seek to provide reasons for their belief in God. Francis Collins—former director of the National Human Genome Research Institute and once an atheist—argues that science and faith are fundamentally compatible, and that the existence of altruism and other examples of moral law strongly suggests the presence of a God to initiate them. Owen Gingerich, an astronomer, asserts the anthropic principle that finds the earth and the universe suspiciously well suited for the emergence of life and intelligence; from this he infers the hand of a benign creator. Finally, sociobiologist Edward O. Wilson (2006) retreats from demonstration to embrace persuasion: he addresses his slim epistle *The Creation* to a Southern Baptist minister in an effort to enroll people of faith into the project of protecting and preserving the environment and the earth's natural resources, bracketing off disputes about faith and reason in order to save what is precious to both.

Context and Issues. The popularization of science occurs against a backdrop in which science stands in tension with other domains of knowledge and belief. In other words, the writer of popular science is potentially addressing a variety of audiences, all of which have different stakes in and commitments to the science at issue. In order to negotiate that variety, the writer of popular science must implicitly or explicitly take stances on the boundaries of science (how can science be distinguished from nonscience?); the relationship between science and society (is science a separate culture, or an integral part of this one?); and the larger purpose of science (is science merely a tool for instrumental, empirical knowledge, or does it fulfill some more transcendental function?).

The ways in which science is bounded off from nonscience is called the "demarcation of science." However, some scholars of science find it difficult to sustain efforts to mark the science-pseudoscience border, efforts which are based on the assumption that there exists a unified entity called science that can be defined with sufficient precision so as to include all desired cases and exclude all undesired ones (Still and Dryden 2004). Thus, a large subgenre within popular science has grown up around efforts to allow laypeople to distinguish the hallmarks of true science from its pseudoscientific imitators. Michael Shermer (2001), for example, attempts to establish principles for detecting the boundaries of science. Drawing upon science historian Thomas Kuhn's (1962) notion of scientific paradigms that shift as new explanations gain adherents, he posits a scientific borderland in which tentative theories and approaches exist until moved, via further examination, to the precincts of either true science or nonscientific pseudoscience. Carl Sagan (1996) proposes that scientific habits of mind (a concern for evidence, an awareness of fallacious reasoning) and a compassionate skepticism are the proper tools for combating pseudoscience.

The question of the culture of science and its relation to the society that supports it has prompted a number of critiques. The best known is probably C.P. Snow's (1959) discussion of the two cultures of science and the arts, finding the two socially, politically, and ideologically diametrically opposed to each other. While Snow's observations are dated with respect to the particular oppositions he observes, the overall notion of opposition continues to resonate in some quarters. Joseph Schwartz (1992), a physicist by training, argues that by conceiving of mathematics rather than visualization as its heart, science has in fact lost touch with nature and thereby alienated itself from the rest of society. The problem has real consequences for the task of science popularization, which therefore must conceive of itself as *translating* the arcane into the mundane, and thereby, having to balance fidelity to the source, and comprehensibility and engagement to the reader (Littmann 2005). Rhetorical examination of such translations in the popular press by science reporters have found that science reporters tend to adopt a celebratory rather than interrogatory tone, and to value decision and action over evaluation and causation (Fahnestock 1986). Popular science sometimes addresses these issues by considering the aesthetics of science (Hamann, Morse, and Sefusatti 2005) as well as by directly confronting the tension between science and the humanities—in some instances calling for the ultimate reduction of humanistic inquiry to explanations rooted in natural science (Wilson 1998), and in others arguing for some sort of détente (Gould 2003).

The tensions between faith and reason, belief and skepticism, the miraculous sublime and the empirical mundane all contribute to the conflict between religion and science. Since the emergence of science, religion has been forced to retreat from many of its claims to causal or empirical knowledge. Thus, many scientists, as well as others who are dissatisfied with an increasingly unemployed "God of the gaps," reconcile science and religion by ascribing to one the domain of facts and the other that of values—what evolutionary biologist Steven Jay Gould (1998) called the "non-overlapping magisteria" of science and faith. Many others also see the conflict as nugatory (Broad 2006); but this solution is not entirely satisfying, given that it insulates science from its moral obligations and religion from its duty to see things as they are as well as how they ought be. Some scientists, motivated by an atheistic sentiment, attempt to debunk religion as superstition (Dawkins 2006; Dennett 2006). But partisans of religion tend not to make the obvious reverse criticism—that science may require moral guidance not available to it internally—at least not too loudly. Instead, some try to reclaim a space for God by suborning the cognitive authority of science for themselves (Dean 2005; Glanz 2001)—thus, the transformation of pseudoscientific creation science into intelligent design theory. By all but the most tendentious of readings, intelligent design counts as pseudoscience, as its currency is due to ideological rather than scientific reasons. But it merits attention not for its own intellectual merits, but rather for the extent to which biology (particularly evolutionary biology, of course) is informed by its self-conscious contrast with creationist advocacy. This results from the cultural tension between science and religion, which also manifests itself in the credence given by some scientists to a strong anthropic principle that wonders why the universe seems to have been made just right for human beings to exist.

Reception. Popular science is presented in the mass media in a variety of forms. Science journalism by newspaper reporters on the "science beat" (Nelkin 1995) and by writers for science-oriented magazines such as *Seed, Scientific American,* and *Discover* provides a training ground for many writers of popular science books. Another common connection of popular science literature to other media is the television tie-in—that is, a televised documentary series explicating a popular science book—or even books and documentaries conceived as synergetic companions to each other. Examples of televised documentaries of popular science include Carl Sagan's 13-episode *Cosmos* series and its lavishly illustrated accompanying volume (Sagan 1980). Sagan's successor is string theorist Brian Greene, whose description of *The Elegant Universe* (1999) was turned into a three-hour television documentary.

The scholarship of popular science occurs in at least two distinct academic communities: (1) studies of public understanding of science (PUS) and the related field of rhetoric of science (RS) as well as (2) research in science education. PUS is a sociological specialty within the broader domain of science and technology studies (STS), which is concerned with the social and cultural dimensions of science and technology (Locke 2001). PUS investigates science in public discourse in all its forms—including museums, classrooms, newspapers, and community forums—while rhetoric of science is interested in the persuasive character of scientific texts. Science educators concern themselves to some degree with the role of popular science in the classroom (e.g., Parkinson and Adendorff 2005). Additionally, scientific communities pay some attention to popular science as a teaching tool and a means of judging the reputation of their discipline in the public eye (von Baeyer and Bowers 2004).

Selected Authors. This section briefly discusses two physical scientists, two biological scientists, and two science journalists who have popularized and written about popular science. The physical scientists are Carl Sagan, an astronomer, and Briane Greene, a physicist known for his work in string theory; the biological scientists are Stephen Jay Gould, a paleontologist, and Richard Dawkins, a zoologist; and the science journalists are Timothy Ferris and Dava Sobel, both of whom began their careers as reporters.

Carl Sagan (1934–1996). Though Albert Einstein certainly eclipsed Carl Sagan in terms of sheer fame, Sagan was the first celebrity scientist to be fully integrated into the popular culture media industry, a fact which had negative consequences for his academic standing: he was refused tenure at Harvard, and the National Academy of Science rejected his nomination for membership (Poundstone 1999). Sagan continued to be a productive scientist even as his popularizing work expanded over the course of his career (Shermer 2002). Sagan's oeuvre included speculation about extraterrestrial intelligence (Sagan 1973), space exploration and colonization (Sagan 1994), the fates of humanity and the earth (Sagan 1997), as well as discussions of the character and significance of scientific knowledge (Sagan 1996, 2006).

Brian Greene (1963–). Brian Greene is a professor of mathematics and physics at Columbia University. He received his PhD from Oxford University in 1987, where he was a Rhodes Scholar upon graduating from Harvard. His research involves superstring theory, which is an attempt to find an overarching formulation from which the different kinds of interactions of matter and energy can be derived, unifying gravity with the other fundamental forces—in brief, a theory of everything of the sort desired by Einstein, and promised—but ultimately not delivered—by Hawking. *The Elegant Universe* (Greene 1999)—winner of the Royal Society's Aventis Prize for Science Books in 2000—discusses this search. His more recent book, *The Fabric of the Cosmos* (Greene 2004), discusses relativity, cosmology, and the nature of space and time.

Richard Dawkins (1941–). Richard Dawkins received his PhD from Oxford University in 1966, and he was for most of his career a professor of zoology at Oxford (following a brief stint at UC Berkeley). In 1995, he became the Charles Simonyi Professor of Public Understanding of Science at Oxford. His popular science explanations of evolutionary theory focus on the notion expounded in *The Selfish Gene* (1976) that fitness in terms of natural and sexual selection refers less to individual organisms than to the genes they comprise, because it is the differential survival of units of replication that selection pressures act upon. *The Blind Watchmaker* (1986), which marshals arguments against the notion of design, was made into a BBC documentary (Dawkins himself has made numerous appearances as a scientific presenter and panelist on British television). His increasingly antagonistic engagement with religious faith, culminating in *The God Delusion* (2006), engenders harsh criticism of both his ideas and his methods (Dean 2006; Holt 2006).

Stephen Jay Gould (1941–2002). Widely regarded as among the most stylistically sophisticated and erudite popularizers of science, Stephen Jay Gould at intervals collected the essays he wrote for *Natural History* magazine (published by the American Museum of Natural History) and compiled them in book form. The first compilation, *Ever Since Darwin,* appeared in 1977; the last, *I Have Landed,* was published in 2002. He was associated with the notion of punctuated equilibrium (the idea that massive die-offs or extinction events occur in the evolutionary record, at which point newly emptied ecological niches become available to be filled). His evolutionary thought has attracted criticism from those who disagree with his critique of adaptationism (the tendency to regard all features of an organism as functional products of evolution rather than as *possible* adaptations needing to be demonstrated as such), including Richard Dawkins (Shermer 2002). Michael

Shermer's even-handed assessment of Gould's output concludes that the essays by the latter embody a philosophy of science—and of the history of science—that holds the value of the past to lie in its service to the present.

Timothy Ferris (1944–). Timothy Ferris is a journalist and professor of journalism who was a reporter in New York City and a writer for *Rolling Stone*. He then took a job teaching English at CUNY in Brooklyn and published *The Red Limit* (Ferris 1977), an account of the astronomical investigations into the expansion of the universe. On the strength of his musical, technical, and scientific expertise, he produced the recording—made of gold and containing sounds of the Earth and its creatures—that was stowed aboard the Voyager space probe, should any extraterrestrials ever come upon it. He has written, narrated, produced, and directed in various combinations audio and video productions for planetariums, news shows, and television documentaries. He is currently an emeritus professor of journalism at UC Berkeley, a consultant to NASA on its long-term space exploration policy, and an amateur astronomer. His books have received critical acclaim from newspapers as well as awards and recognition from scientific societies and educational institutions. Reviews by scientists find him a clear guide to science for laypeople, albeit one given perhaps overmuch to poetical extravagances (Gingerich 1997).

Dava Sobel (1947–). Dava Sobel is a professional science writer, with a background in science reporting and magazine writing. As of 2006–2007, she was the writer-in-residence at the University of Chicago's creative writing program. Sobel is best known for her popular science histories *Longitude* (1995) and *Galileo's Daughter* (Sobel 1999). *Longitude* won enormous praise for the lucidity of its prose and the fascinating story it tells about how the problem of determining longitude at sea was solved, requiring the construction of a reliable clock as well as accurate celestial observation. *Longitude* was also produced as a BBC documentary, and then a dramatized version was aired by the BBC and American cable television. However, recent scholarship and criticism (Charney 2003; Dizikes 2006) takes issue with Sobel's lone genius approach to understanding the history of science, arguing that it misrepresents the collective and consensual character of science. This approach—the "standing on the shoulders of giants" school of scientific history—is out of step with contemporary models of how science works, in which it is viewed as far more enmeshed in its social context than previously thought.

Bibliography

Aczel, Amir. "When Good Novelists Do Bad Science." *The Globe and Mail* January 3, 2004: sec. D: 10.

Asimov, Isaac. *Asimov's Guide to Science*. 3rd ed. New York: Basic Books, 1972.

Bainbridge, W.S. "Public Attitudes toward Nanotechnology." *Journal of Nanoparticle Research* 4.6 (2002): 561–570.

Bates, B.R. "Public Culture and Public Understanding of Genetics: A Focus Group Study." *Public Understanding of Science* 14.1 (2005): 47–65.

Bowler, P.J. "Experts and Publishers: Writing Popular Science in Early Twentieth-Century Britain, Writing Popular History of Science Now." *British Journal for the History of Science* 39 (141) (2006): 159–187.

Brizendine, Louann. *The Female Brain*. 1st ed. New York: Morgan Road Books, 2006.

Broad, William J. "The Oracle Suggests a Truce between Science and Religion." *New York Times*, February 28, 2006: sec. F: 4.

Brown, C.P., S.M. Propst, and M. Woolley. "Report: Helping Researchers Make the Case for Science." *Science Communication* 25.3 (2004): 294–303.

Bryson, Bill. *A Short History of Nearly Everything.* 1st ed. New York: Broadway Books, 2003.

Carson, Rachel. *Silent Spring.* Boston, MA: Houghton Mifflin, 1962.

Cassidy, A. "Popular Evolutionary Psychology in the UK: An Unusual Case of Science in the Media?" *Public Understanding of Science* 14.2 (2005): 115–141.

———. "Evolutionary Psychology as Public Science and Boundary Work." *Public Understanding of Science* 15.2 (2006): 175–205.

Caulfield, T. "Biotechnology and the Popular Press: Hype and the Selling of Science." *Trends in Biotechnology* 22.7 (2004): 337–339.

Ceccarelli, Leah. *Shaping Science with Rhetoric: The Cases of Dobzhansky, Schrodinger, and Wilson.* Chicago, IL: University of Chicago Press, 2001.

Charney, D. "Lone Geniuses in Popular Science: The Devaluation of Scientific consensus." *Written Communication* 20 (3) (2003): 215–241.

Clowse, Barbara Barksdale. *Brainpower for the Cold War: The Sputnik Crisis and National Defense Education Act of 1958, Contributions to the Study of Education no. 3.* Westport, CT: Greenwood Press, 1981.

Collins, Francis S. *The Language of God: A Scientist Presents Evidence for Belief.* New York: Free Press, 2006.

Dawkins, Richard. *The Selfish Gene.* New York: Oxford University Press, 1976.

———. *The Blind Watchmaker.* 1st American ed. New York: Norton, 1986.

———. *The Ancestor's Tale: A Pilgrimage to the Dawn of Evolution.* Boston: Houghton Mifflin, 2004.

———. *The God Delusion.* Boston: Houghton Mifflin Co., 2006.

Dean, Cornelia. "Opting Out in the Debate on Evolution." *New York Times* June 21, 2005: sec. F: 1.

———. Faith, Reason, God, and Other Imponderables. *New York Times* July 25, 2006, 1.

DeBoer, G.E. "Scientific Literacy: Another Look at Its Historical and Contemporary Meanings and Its Relationship to Science Education Reform." *Journal of Research in Science Teaching* 37.6 (2000): 582–601.

Dennett, Daniel Clement. *Breaking the Spell: Religion as a Natural Phenomenon.* New York: Viking, 2006.

Diamond, Jared M. *Guns, Germs, and Steel: The Fates of Human Societies.* 1st ed. New York: W.W. Norton & Company, 1997.

———. *Collapse: How Societies Choose to Fail or Succeed.* New York: Viking, 2005.

Dizikes, Peter. "Twilight of the Idols." *New York Times Book Review,* November 5, 2006: 31.

Eamon, W. "Science and Popular Culture in 16th-Century Italy, the 'Professors of Secrets' and Their Books." *Sixteenth Century Journal* 16.4 (1985): 471–485.

Eiseley, Loren C. *The Man Who Saw through Time.* Rev. and enl. ed. New York: Scribner, 1973.

Fahnestock, J. "Accommodating Science: The Rhetorical Life of Scientific Facts." *Written Communication* 3.3 (1986): 275–296.

Ferris, Timothy. *The Red Limit: The Search for the Edge of the Universe.* New York: Morrow, 1977.

———. *The Whole Shebang: A State-of-the-Universe(s) Report.* New York: Simon & Schuster, 1997.

Forward, Robert L. *Dragon's Egg.* 1st ed. New York: Ballantine Books, 1980.

Fox, Karen C., and Aries Keck. *Einstein: A to Z.* Hoboken, NJ: J. Wiley, 2004.

Frayn, Michael. *Copenhagen.* Methuen Drama pbk. ed [with revisions]. London: Methuen Drama, 2000.

Fyfe, A. "Conscientious Workmen or Booksellers' Hacks? The Professional Identities of Science Writers in the Mid-Nineteenth Century." *Isis* 96.2 (2005): 192–223.

Gingerich, Owen. "Hello to All That." *New York Times Book Review,* 1997: 9.

————. *God's Universe*. Cambridge, MA: Belknap Press of Harvard University Press, 2006.

Glanz, James. "Darwin vs. Design: Evolutionists' New Battle." *New York Times,* April 8, 2001: sec. 1: 32.

Gleick, James. *Chaos: Making a New Science*. New York: Viking, 1987.

Gould, Stephen Jay. *Ever since Darwin: Reflections in Natural History*. 1st ed. New York: Norton, 1977.

————. *Leonardo's Mountain of Clams and the Diet of Worms: Essays on Natural History*. 1st ed. New York: Harmony Books, 1998.

————. *Rocks of Ages: Science and Religion in the Fullness of Life*. 1st ed. New York: Ballantine Pub. Group, 1999.

————. *I Have Landed: The End of a Beginning in Natural History*. 1st ed. New York: Harmony Books, 2002.

————. *The Hedgehog, the Fox, and the Magister's Pox: Mending the Gap between Science and the Humanities*. 1st ed. New York: Harmony Books, 2003.

Greene, Brian R. *The Elegant Universe: Superstrings, Hidden Dimensions, and the Quest for the Ultimate Theory*. New York: W.W. Norton, 1999.

————. *The Fabric of the Cosmos: Space, Time, and the Texture of Reality*. 1st ed. New York: Knopf, 2004.

Greenhill, K.M. "Skirmishes on the 'Endless Frontier': Reexamining the Role of Vannevar Bush as Progenitor of US Science and Technology Policy." *Polity* 32.4 (2000): 633–641.

Gribbin, John R. *Deep Simplicity: Bringing Order to Chaos and Complexity*. 1st U.S. ed. New York: Random House, 2004.

Hall, Stephen S. *Size Matters: How Height Affects the Health, Happiness, and Success of Boys—And the Men They Become*. Boston: Houghton Mifflin Co., 2006.

Hamann, H.T., John Morse, and Emiliano Sefusatti. *Categories on the Beauty of Physics: Essential Physics Concepts and Their Companions in Art and Literature*. 1st ed. New York: Vernacular Press, 2005.

Hansen, B. "Medical History for the Masses: How American Comic Books Celebrated Heroes of Medicine in the 1940s." *Bulletin of the History of Medicine* 78.1 (2004): 148–191.

Hawking, S.W. *A Brief History of Time: From the Big Bang to Black Holes*. Toronto; New York: Bantam Books, 1988.

Hodson, D. "Time for Action: Science Education for an Alternative Future." *International Journal of Science Education* 25.6 (2003): 645–670.

Holt, Jim. 2006. "Beyond Belief." *New York Times Book Review,* October 22, 2006: 1.

Horgan, John. *The End of Science: Facing the Limits of Knowledge in the Twilight of the Scientific Age*. Reading, MA: Addison-Wesley Pub., 1996.

————. *The Undiscovered Mind: How the Human Brain Defies Replication, Medication, and Explanation*. New York: Free Press, 1999.

Kakalios, James. *The Physics of Superheroes*. New York: Gotham Books, 2005.

Kaku, Michio. *Einstein's Cosmos: How Albert Einstein's Vision Transformed Our Understanding of Space and Time, Great discoveries*. New York: W.W. Norton, 2005a.

————. *Parallel Worlds: A Journey through Creation, Higher Dimensions, and the Future of the Cosmos*. 1st ed. New York: Doubleday, 2005b.

Kolbert, Elizabeth. *Field Notes from a Catastrophe: Man, Nature, and Climate Change*. 1st U.S. ed. New York: Bloomsbury, 2006.

Krauss, Lawrence Maxwell. *The Physics of Star Trek*. New York: Basic Books, 1995.

Kuhn, Thomas S. *The Structure of Scientific Revolutions*. Chicago, IL: University of Chicago Press, 1962.

Lam, Lui. "Integrating Popular Science Books into College Science Teaching." July 2005. http://www.pantaneto.co.uk/issue19/lam.htm.

Laszlo, P. "Unfortunate Trends in the Popularization of Science." *Interdisciplinary Science Reviews* 30.3 (2005): 223–230.

Lessl, T.M. "The Priestly Voice." *Quarterly Journal of Speech* 75.2 (1989): 183–197.

Levin, Janna. *How the Universe Got Its Spots: Diary of a Finite Time in a Finite Space.* Princeton, NJ: Princeton University Press, 2002.

Levin, Martin. "Boom to Bust." *The Globe and Mail,* March 26, 2005a: sec. D: 25.

———. "Einsteiniana." *The Globe and Mail,* April 30, 2005b: sec. D: 21.

Levitin, Daniel J. *This is Your Brain on Music: The Science of a Human Obsession.* New York: Dutton, 2006.

Levitt, Steven D., and Stephen J. Dubner. *Freakonomics: A Rogue Economist Explores the Hidden Side of Everything.* 1st ed. New York: William Morrow, 2005.

Lightman, B. "The Visual Theology of Victorian Popularizers of Science: From Reverent Eye to Chemical Retina." *Isis* 91.4 (2000): 651–680.

Littmann, M. "Courses in Science Writing as Literature." *Public Understanding of Science* 14.1 (2005): 103–112.

Locke, S. "Sociology and the Public Understanding of Science: From Rationalization to Rhetoric." *British Journal of Sociology* 52.1 (2001): 1–18.

Lucas, A.M., S. Maroske, and A. Brown-May. "Bringing Science to the Public: Ferdinand von Mueller and Botanical Education in Victorian Victoria." *Annals of Science* 63.1 (2006): 25–57.

Lynn, M.R. "Divining the Enlightenment: Public Opinion and Popular Science in Old Regime France." *Isis* 92.1 (2001): 34–54.

Magueijo, João. *Faster than the Speed of Light: The Story of a Scientific Speculation.* Cambridge, MA: Perseus Book Group, 2003.

Matthews, Robert. "Nothing Is Gained by Searching for the 'Theory of Everything.'" *Financial Times,* June 3, 2006: 11.

Mayer, A.K. "Moralizing Science: The Uses of Science's Past in National Education in the 1920s." *British Journal for the History of Science* 30.104 (1997): 51–70.

Mellor, F. Between Fact and Fiction: Demarcating Science from Non-Science in Popular Physics Books. *Social Studies of Science* 33.4 (2003): 509–538.

Menand, Louis. *The Metaphysical Club.* 1st ed. New York: Farrar, Straus and Giroux, 2001.

Miller, J.D. "Public Understanding of, and Attitudes toward, Scientific Research: What We Know and What We Need to Know." *Public Understanding of Science* 13 (3) (2004): 273–294.

Nelkin, Dorothy. *Selling Science: How the Press Covers Science and Technology.* Rev. ed. New York: W.H. Freeman and Co., 1995.

Nerlich, B., D.D. Clarke, and R. Dingwall. "The Influence of Popular Cultural Imagery on Public Attitudes towards Cloning." *Sociological Research Online* 4.3 (1999): U237–U250.

Ouellette, Jennifer. *Black Bodies and Quantum Cats: Tales from the Annals of Physics.* New York: Penguin Books, 2005.

Paisley, W.J. "Scientific Literacy and the Competition for Public Attention and Understanding." *Science Communication* 20.1 (1998): 70–80.

Parkinson, J., and R. Adendorff. "Science Books for Children as a Preparation for Textbook Literacy." *Discourse Studies* 7.2 (2005): 213–236.

Paul, D. "Spreading Chaos: The Role of Popularizations in the Diffusion of Scientific Ideas." *Written Communication* 21.1 (2004): 32–68.

Petersen, A., A. Anderson, and S. Allan. "Science Fiction/Science Fact: Medical Genetics in News Stories." *New Genetics and Society* 24.3 (2005): 337–353.

Poundstone, William. *Carl Sagan: A Life in the Cosmos.* New York: Henry Holt, 1999.

Randall, Lisa. *Warped Passages: Unraveling the Mysteries of the Universe's Hidden Dimensions.* 1st ed. New York: Ecco, 2005.

Rees, Martin J. *Our Final Hour: A Scientist's Warning.* New York: Basic Books, 2003.

Reichhardt, Tony. "Pumping up the Volume." *Nature* 436.7049 (2005): 326–327.

Repp, K. "Popular Science in the 19th Century: Middle-Class Culture, Science Education and the German Public, 1848–1914." *Journal of Social History* 33.4 (2000): 970–972.

Rigden, John S. *Einstein 1905: The Standard of Greatness*. Cambridge, MA: Harvard University Press, 2005.

Sagan, Carl. *The Cosmic Connection: An Extraterrestrial Perspective*. 1st ed. Garden City, NY: Anchor Press/Doubleday, 1973.

———. *Cosmos*. New York: Random House, 1980.

———. *Contact: A Novel*. New York: Simon and Schuster, 1985.

———. *Pale Blue Dot: A Vision of the Human Future in Space*. 1st ed. New York: Random House, 1994.

———. *The Demon-Haunted World: Science as a Candle in the Dark*. 1st ed. New York: Random House, 1996.

———. *Billions and Billions: Thoughts on Life and Death at the Brink of the Millennium*. 1st ed. New York: Random House, 1997.

———. *The Varieties of Scientific Experience: A Personal View of the Search for God*. New York: Penguin Books, 2006

Schnabel, U. "God's Formula and Devil's Contribution: Science in the Press." *Public Understanding of Science* 12.3 (2003): 255–259.

Schwartz, Joseph. *The Creative Moment: How Science Made Itself Alien to Modern Culture*. 1st ed. New York: HarperCollins Publishers, 1992.

Shapin, Steven, and Simon Schaffer. *Leviathan and the Air-Pump: Hobbes, Boyle, and the Experimental Life*. Princeton, NJ: Princeton University Press, 1985.

Shea, Christopher. "Survivalist Lit: Does Darwin Have Anything to Say About Beowulf and Madame Bovary?" *Boston Globe*, November 6, 2005: sec. E:4.

Sheffield, Charles. *Borderlands of Science: How to Think like a Scientist and Write Science Fiction*. Riverdale, NY: Baen Books, 1999.

Shermer, M.B. "This View of Science: Stephen Jay Gould as Historian of Science and Scientific Historian, Popular Scientist and Scientific Popularizer." *Social Studies of Science* 32.4 (2002): 489–524.

Shermer, Michael. *The Borderlands of Science: Where Sense Meets Nonsense*. Oxford; New York: Oxford University Press, 2001.

———. *Why Darwin Matters: The Case against Intelligent Design*. 1st ed. New York: Times Books, 2006.

Smith, H.A. "Public Attitudes towards Space Science." *Space Science Reviews* 105.1–2 (2003): 493–505.

Smolin, Lee. *The Trouble with Physics: The Rise of String Theory, the Fall of a Science, and What Comes Next*. Boston: Houghton Mifflin Co., 2006.

Snow, C.P. *The Two Cultures and the Scientific Revolution*. Cambridge: Cambridge University Press, 1959.

Sobel, Dava. *Longitude: The True Story of a Lone Genius Who Solved the Greatest Scientific Problem of His Time*. New York: Walker, 1995.

———. *Galileo's Daughter: A Historical Memoir of Science, Faith, and Love*. New York: Walker & Co., 1999.

———. *The Planets*. New York: Viking, 2005.

Squyres, Steven W. *Roving Mars: Spirit, Opportunity, and the Exploration of the Red Planet*. 1st ed. New York: Hyperion, 2005.

Still, A., and W. Dryden. "The Social Psychology of 'Pseudoscience': A Brief History." *Journal for the Theory of Social Behaviour* 34.3 (2004): 265–290.

Stoppard, Tom. *Arcadia*. London; Boston: Faber and Faber, 1993.

Tallack, P. "Echo of the Big Bang: An End to the Boom in Popular Science Books May Actually Raise Standards." *Nature* 432.7019 (2004): 803–804.

von Baeyer, H.C., and E.V. Bowers. "Resource Letter PBGP-1: Physics Books for the General Public." *American Journal of Physics* 72.2 (2004):135–140.

Wally, L.M., N.E. Levinger, and D.W. Grainger. "Employing Popular Children's Literature to Teach Elementary School Chemistry: An Engaging Outreach Program." *Journal of Chemical Education* 82.10 (2005): 1489–1495.

Watson, Fred. *Stargazer: The Life and Times of the Telescope*. 1st Da Capo Press ed. Cambridge, MA: Da Capo Press, 2005.

Watson, James D. *The Double Helix: A Personal Account of the Discovery of the Structure of DNA*. 1st ed. New York: Atheneum, 1968.

Watson, James D., and Andrew Berry. *DNA: The Secret of Life*. 1st ed. New York: Alfred A. Knopf, 2003.

Weinberg, Steven. *The First Three Minutes: A Modern View of the Origin of the Universe*. New York: Basic Books, 1977.

———. *Facing Up: Science and Its Cultural Adversaries*. Cambridge, MA: Harvard University Press, 2001.

Wilson, Edward O. *Sociobiology: The New Synthesis*. Cambridge, MA: Belknap Press of Harvard University Press, 1975.

———. *Consilience: The Unity of Knowledge*. 1st ed. New York: Knopf, 1998.

———. *The Creation: An Appeal to Save Life on Earth*. 1st ed. New York: Norton, 2006.

Woit, Peter. *Not Even Wrong: The Failure of String Theory and the Search for Unity in Physical Law*. New York: Basic Books, 2006.

Further Reading

Bryson, Bill. *A Short History of Nearly Everything*. New York: Basic Books, 2003; Dawkins, Richard. *The Selfish Gene*. New York: Oxford University Press, 1976; Diamond, Jared. *Guns, Germs, and Steel*. New York: W.W. Norton, 1997; Ferris, Timothy. *The Whole Shebang: A State-of-the-Universe(s) Report*. New York: Simon & Schuster, 1997; Gleick, James. *Chaos: Making a New Science*. New York: Viking, 1987; Gould, Stephen Jay. *Ever since Darwin*. New York: W.W. Norton, 1977; Greene, Brian R. *The Elegant Universe*. New York: W.W. Norton, 1999. Horgan, John. *The End of Science*. Reading, MA: Addison-Wesley, 1996. Sagan, Carl. *The Demon-Haunted World*. New York: Random House, 1996; Smolin, Lee. *The Trouble with Physics*. Boston, MA: Houghton Mifflin, 2006; Watson, James D. *The Double Helix*. New York: Atheneum, 1968.

WILLIAM J. WHITE

SEA LITERATURE

Definition. To explore the lasting influence of the sea on the American imagination and thereby explain the popularity of seafaring themes throughout American literary history is by no means an easy task. The universal human fascination with uncharted oceans and adventurous voyages notwithstanding, the sea has always served the dual purpose of arousing desire, to retool Richard Proirier's famous phrase, for "a world elsewhere" and simultaneously providing a powerful imagery that helped to articulate complex human issues of the here and now. Furthermore, seafaring tales usually comprise different levels of human agency: the natural (i.e. the sea) and the technological (the ship), individual skills (navigation, the art of sailing, physical endurance etc.) as much as collective efforts (the ship as a highly complex, social microcosm or the maritime traditions and achievements of a whole nation), and the known world (the port of departure, the ship, the crew) and the unknown, new spaces of the ship's destination. Taking to the sea also always involves a certain degree of risk taking, the readiness to take chances and immerse oneself in a world one can never entirely control. The sea as a literary topic can thus be understood as epitomizing the greatness and tragedy of human life itself. And yet, their apparently universal appeal to the contrary, seafaring tales have not intruded into the collective memory and unconscious of all nations alike. If regional, cultural, and historical differences are important in shaping a people's literary traditions, they are equally instrumental in instilling a popular taste for the sea and its mysteries. The lingering appeal of sea fiction in America is a good case in point.

History. As cultural critic Robert Lawson-Peebles argued "before America existed on the map, it existed in the imagination" (1988, 7). Given that America was as much a product of the imagination as the result of geographic discovery, the narratives and stories that Europeans have used to recreate their initial encounter with the "New World" are heavily indebted to their seagoing experience, an experience that preceded the actual "landings" or "arrivals" in America. From Christopher Columbus's report of his first voyage to the West Indies (1493) to Sir Walter Raleigh's *The Discovery of Guiana* (1595), Richard Hakluyt's *The Principal Navigations, Voyages, Traffiques and Discoveries of the English Nation* (1598–1600), and John Winthrop's programmatic *A Modell of Christian Charity* (1630), which was drawn up in the midst of the hazardous trans-Atlantic passage, the sea and its perils, promises, and traditional mythical connotations figured prominently in the writings of early explorers of America.

Though later generations appeared to have been preoccupied with conquering and settling the "wilderness" that stretched from the Atlantic to the Pacific Ocean, the imagery of the sea never actually lost its hold on the American mind. The most important mode of transportation during the early national period—the one that actually became the symbol of westward migration—was the so-called "prairie schooner" or Conestoga wagon (a reference to the town in Pennsylvania where they were originally built). Named because their white-covered tops seemed to float like graceful sails through the prairie grass, prairie schooners rhetorically invoked the perilous passage to the New World. In his late, experimental prose poem "John Marr and Other Sailors" (1888) Herman Melville adopts the image of the prairie schooner to articulate the (semi-autobiographical) longing for the sea of an old salt who, putting an end to his rovings, finally married and removed to a log house on the western frontier:

> With some of his former shipmates [. . .] he had contrived, prior to this last and more remote removal, to keep up a little correspondence at odd intervals. But from tidings of anybody or any sort he [. . .] was now cut off; quite cut off, except from such news as might be conveyed over the grassy billows by the last-arrived prairie-schooners—the vernacular term, in those parts and times, for the emigrant-wagon arched high over with sail-cloth, and voyaging across the vast campaign. [. . .] To the long-distance traveler [. . .] recent settlements offered some landmarks; but otherwise he steered by the sun. In early midsummer, even going but from one log-encampment to the next [. . .] travel was much like navigation. (Melville 2000, 265–266)

By rhetorically joining the hazards of westward expansion to the earlier crossing of the Atlantic, nineteenth-century Americans both reinforced and added to the cultural heritage that ties America to the sea.

More significantly, seascapes also provided a foil for literary discussions of various national, political, and philosophical issues in America. Just consider the numerous seafaring stories written during the time of the so-called "American Renaissance," when Americans were struggling to define their own idea of a national literature, thereby slowly weaning themselves from the ongoing cultural dominance of Europe. "Because the sea was central to their identity," as critic John

---

ISHMAEL'S VIEW OF THE COMMON SAILOR

No, when I go to sea, I go as a simple sailor, right before the mast, plumb down into the fore-castle, aloft there to the royal mast-head. [...] I always go to sea as a sailor because of the wholesome exercise and pure air of the forecastle deck. For as in this world, head winds are far more prevalent than winds from astern [...], so for the most part the Commodore on the quarter-deck gets his atmosphere at second hand from the sailors on the forecastle. He thinks he breathes it first; but not so. In much the same way do the commonality lead their leaders in many other things, at the same time that the leaders little suspect it. (Melville 1967, 14–15)

Peck reminds us, "Americans turned to the sea to understand themselves" (2001, 94). Ishmael, the principle narrator of Melville's classic sea novel *Moby-Dick* (or *The Whale* (1851)), thus takes to the sea in order to cope with impending "hypochondria," an ailment particularly reminiscent of the Old World. By the same token, he does not want "ever to go to sea as a passenger," nor does he intend to embark on a career "as a Commodore, or a Captain, or a Cook." A true American, Ishmael deliberately abandons the "distinction of such offices" for the community and solidarity of the common sailor.

In maritime literature such as Richard Dana's *Two Years Before the Mast* (1840), Melville's posthumously published novella *Billy Budd, Sailor* (1891), Jack London's *The Sea-Wolf* (1904), Eugene O'Neill's *The Hairy Ape* (1922), Ernest Hemingway's *To Have and Have Not* (1937), Peter Matthiessen's *Far Tortuga* (1975), or Charles Johnson's *Middle Passage* (1990) ships have repeatedly served to articulate concern about the course of American society. Early on, Melville, the experienced salt-turned-writer, depicted the world-as-ship or, as in *Moby-Dick*, the ship-as-world. The Pequod is a human microcosm of its own, a floating world replete with sailors from all walks of life. The economic nature and physical hardships of the whaling business notwithstanding, theirs is a community of equals that cuts across the boundaries of both class and race. As the doomed journey of the vessel reveals, the communitarian ideal of the simple sailor is eventually threatened. Yet as a powerful democratic myth, Melville's idealized treatment of maritime life nevertheless helped to establish the sea as a utopian counter-space to the increasing rigidity and social divisiveness of modern American society.

If we look at the economic conditions from which seafaring parables such as James Fenimore Cooper's *The Pilot* (1824), Melville's *Moby-Dick,* or Edgar Allan Poe's *Arthur Gordon Pym* (1838) sprang, we find that nineteenth-century America—its rapid industrialization notwithstanding—was still a nation that depended heavily on the sea and its allegedly unlimited resources. This is especially true of those Americans who lived near the Eastern shore and participated in one the first truly global businesses, the bloody harvesting of the sperm whale. In the early nineteenth century, according to maritime historian Nathaniel Philbrick, "people didn't invest in bonds or the stock market, but rather in whale ships" (2000, 20). As we can learn from *Moby-Dick,* sperm oil lubricated the machines of the industrial age. If transforming a gigantic sperm whale into oil entailed a quasi-industrial form of work, the hunting of the whale—especially, as whalers pushed farther and farther into as yet uncharted regions of the Pacific—remained a hazardous, myth-laden enterprise. Whalemen, Philbrick argues, were not merely seagoing hunters and factory workers but also explorers whose wondrous maritime adventures continued to haunt the imagination of Americans well into the twentieth century.

Trends and Themes. Although taking to the sea appeared to be the natural inclination and symbolic focus of New Englanders, the land-bound, aristocratic planter society of the South was no less predicated on seafaring goods and tropes. As poet William Carlos Williams remarked, "poised against the Mayflower is the slave ship" (1925, 208–211). Though the slave trade had been legally banned since 1808, the entire system of plantation slavery could not have thrived without the triangular pattern of the transatlantic trafficking in know-how (such as West African rice planting technology in the Carolinas), human cargo (slaves), and, finally, the products of enforced labor (sugar, molasses, rum, cotton, etc.). As historians of the colonial period point out, images of the sea had a firm grip on people of color in the Americas, even if their understanding of the "New World" was never one of mythical homecoming but rather of rejection, disaster, and catastrophe. With an eye on white America's maritime roots the militant black leader Malcolm X quips in his 1965 autobiography: "We didn't land on Plymouth Rock, my brothers and sisters, Plymouth Rock landed on us" (201).

Compared to the utopian interpretations of the sea in early white American sea fiction, the seafaring experience of enslaved Africans differs considerably from that of their masters. "Whereas Columbus conquered 'new' lands for Europeans, thus increasing their mobility and freedom and providing them with new perspectives, the African diaspora," Werner Sollors and Maria Diedrich argue in *The Black Columbiad,* "stands for the end of freedom, for the loss of perspective; [. . .] whites celebrated the New World as their potential paradise, while the African drifted in a world of evil spirits which threatened them with social and physical annihilation" (1994, 5). However, despite the traumatic experience of the so-called "middle passage" sea images spelled out more than merely disaster for African Americans. "For the slave community," as critic Elizabeth Schultz observed, "for whom the sea-crossing would have been an appalling memory, that some [of their] songs should identify the sea as an uncontrollable element is probably not surprising. What is noteworthy, however, is the existence of spirituals and sermons in which an individual either prevails against the sea or harness it to his use" (1995, 234).

To many slaves on the Atlantic coast, the sea signified a means of escape to freedom. Although in some spirituals the implication that the sea may lead to freedom can hardly be missed ("I set my foot on de Gospel ship / [. . .] it landed me over on Canaan's shore / An' I'll never come back no mo'"), others used sea images in a more figurative manner. Because much of African American folklore is derived from the Bible, references to Noah, Jonah, or Moses at the Red Sea are widespread. These images "have overtones of wish-fulfillment, implying that the sea might lead to liberation. [. . .] spirituals and sermons invoking the sea inspired and encouraged the slave community, strengthening both their collective hopes for a savior in this world and individuals' hopes for saving themselves" (Schultz 1995, 234–235).

If the sea often works as separator, border, or dangerous boundary, it is also, as Haskell Springer points out, "the joiner of human beings and the center of their communities" (1995, Introduction 1). This is particularly true of African Americans that had been abducted from their homeland and brought to a strange "new" world where they found themselves, in Olaudah Equiano's famous phrasing, "deprived of all chance of returning to [their] native country" (1995, 56). To the exiled slave population, Africa was irretrievably lost. The desire to cross the Atlantic again and to return to the land of "origin" has therefore become a prominent feature of the African diaspora. Real or imagined, for people of African descent Africa remained the guarantor of a common identity, a mythic source of inspiration and community. In African American writing the sea, therefore, often emerges as a means to bridge the historical and geographical gap between Africa and the descendants of former slaves. By the same token, Barbadian poet Edward Kamau Braithwaite claims that only the return to Africa enabled him to discover his native Caribbean (quoted in Pedersen 1994, 43). Afrocentrist movements such as "Ethiopianism," "Pan-Africanism" or the francophone "Negritude" lend ample proof to the pervasive consciousness of common roots and a shared transatlantic cultural heritage within the African diaspora. In the wake of these earlier attempts to undo the initial separation and dramatic uprooting associated with the middle passage, the sea, and in particular the Atlantic, is now increasingly being reconsidered as a space where routes cross and cultures merge to form an encompassing network of transatlantic exchange. In his path-breaking study *The Black Atlantic* (1993) the British critic Paul Gilroy describes the "ship" as a major driving force in the cultural system of the African diaspora: "The image of the ship— a living, micro-cultural, micro-political system in motion—is especially important for historical and theoretical reasons [. . .]. [It] immediately focuses attention on the middle passage, on the various projects for redemptive return to an African homeland, on the circulation of ideas and activists as well as the movement of key cultural and political artifacts: tracts, books, gramophone records, and choirs" (4). Gilroy's influential study not only paved the way for a wave of new interrogations into transatlantic patterns of cultural exchange, but it also reflects the overriding importance of sea images in American and, especially, African American fiction.

If many African Americans were drawn to maritime occupations for merely practical reasons, the sea often also figured as a mythical, utopian space that promised freedom, equality, and adventure. When resting from his job as a ship caulker in Baltimore, Frederick Douglass mused about the sight of the "beautiful vessels, robed in white, and so delightful to the eyes of freemen" that he had seen as a boy on the Chesapeake Bay:

> I have often, in the deep stillness of a summer's Sabbath, stood all alone upon the lofty banks of that noble bay, and traced, with saddened heart and tearful eye, the countless number of sails moving off to the mighty ocean. The sight of these always affected me powerfully. My thoughts would compel utterance; and there, with no audience but the Almighty, I would pour out my soul's complaint, in my rude way, with an apostrophe to the moving multitude of ships. (1993, 74)

Having thus contemplated the multitude of ships on the Chesapeake Bay, Douglass decided to follow in their wake and attempt the hazardous escape to the north: "Why am I a slave? I will run away. I will not stand it [. . .] I will take to the water. This very bay shall yet bear me into freedom. The steamboats steered in a north-east course from North point; and when I get to the head of the bay, I will turn my canoe adrift and walk straight through Delaware into Pennsylvania" (1993, 74–75). Douglass finally escaped by dressing up as a black sailor and—with the help of forged "seaman's protection" papers—embarked on a ferry to cross the Susquehanna River.

African American writers have repeatedly added to Douglass's visionary "apostrophe to the moving multitude of ships." In the famous opening chapter of *Their*

Eyes Were Watching God (1978), Zora Neale Hurston adopts the same nautical image, although in this instance it is used to express her dissatisfaction with those male would-be sailors that never manage to actually go "aboard":

> Ships at a distance have every man's wish on board. For some they come in with the tide. For others they sail forever on the horizon, never out of sight, never landing until the Watcher turns his eyes away in resignation, his dreams mocked to death by Time. (9)

If for Douglass and Hurston the liberating prospects of a life at sea remained largely a rhetorical figure, for blues poet Langston Hughes taking to the sea represented a crucial moment in the search of an identity of his own. In his autobiography, *The Big Sea* (1940), Hughes describes how he fled the racist atmosphere at Columbia University that at the time was mostly white and how, as an ordinary sailor, he embarked on a merchant vessel headed for Africa:

> Melodramatic maybe, it seems to me now. But then it was like throwing a million bricks out of my heart when I threw the books into the water. I leaned over the rail of the *S.S. Malone* and threw the books as far as I could out into the sea—all the books I had had at Columbia, and all the books I had lately bought to read. [. . .] Then I straightened up, turned my face to the wind, and took a deep breath. I was a seaman going to sea for the first time—a seaman on a big merchant ship. And I felt that nothing would ever happen to me again that I didn't want to happen. I felt grown, a man, inside and out. [. . .] Inside the hot cabin, George lay stark naked in a lower bunk, talking and laughing and gaily waving his various appendages around. Above him in the upper bunk, two chocolate-colored Puerto Rican feet stuck out from one end of a snow-white sheet, and a dark Puerto Rican head from the other. It was clear that Ramon in the upper bunk didn't understand more than every tenth word of George's Kentucky vernacular. But he kept on laughing every time George laughed—and that was often. (Hughes 1940, 3–4)

The liberating aspects of seafaring are equally prominent in Hughes's poetry. In his poem "The Young Sailor," he foregrounds the self-esteem and personal independence often associated with shipboard life: "This strong young sailor / Of the wide seas" (Hughes 1994, 62). Not unlike earlier generations of African American sailors, Hughes ostensibly cherished the relative absence of racial constraint aboard ship. If this freedom, at times, turned out to be treacherous, it was nevertheless real insofar as it provided a way out of the racist environment on the continent and allowed the skilled black mariner a degree of self-assertion and quasi-autonomy unknown in many other professional areas.

To contemporary African American writers of the sea, the infamous middle passage now often represents an imaginary journey into a common past. In Paule Marshall's 1983 novel *Praisesong for the Widow,* the black female protagonist consciously links her own history to the collective history of all African peoples. As Schultz notes, "in the course of Marshall's novel, Avey Johnson, a black matron from North White Plains, is nudged back through her own history, back through the history of her people, with the sea as the setting for each stage of her own psychic rebirth" (1995, 252–253). In close symbolic parallel to the collective trauma of the middle passage, Avey is made to undergo a similar catastrophic yet for her also cleansing seafaring experience. Aboard a battered schooner on her way to the small Caribbean island of Carriacou, choppy seas cause her to vomit in plain view of a motley crowd of men, women, and children. Although Avey is reminded of similar embarrassing moments in her childhood, the ironic, affirmative stance of the people on board, who recontextualize the event as the disposal of "waste and pretense" from Avey's bourgeois black life, enables her to master the imagined humiliation. Having thus symbolically relived her own history through the history of African people, Avey eventually leaves the sea and returns to life in the community.

In his novel *Middle Passage,* which won the National Book Award in 1990, Charles Johnson returns to the 1830s and the world of slavery; the protagonist of the novel, Rutherford Calhoun who is a newly freed slave, embarks on an adventurous journey across the Atlantic to Africa and, later, back to the New World. To his shock and horror Calhoun learns that the vessel, significantly called *The Republic,* is a slave ship whose secret mission is to transport the last survivors of a legendary African tribe, the Allmuseri, from their devastated homeland to America. His journey turns into a symbolic, perilous voyage into the cruel machinery of the slave trade and, even more important, the netherlands of his own, divided psyche. As a freed slave Calhoun is a product of the black and white worlds, a fact that leads to a form of ontological "inbetweeness" that Johnson, in a mix of historical detail and satire, explores with the help of phenomenological philosophy and Zen Buddhism.

From yet a different angle, West Indian writer Caryl Phillips, who teaches at Amherst College, also revisits the former routes of the slave trade. In what amounts to a constant shifting between an imaginary and factual journey across continents, Phillips metaphorically employs the sights and sounds of the (black) Atlantic to investigate the complex cultural heritage of slavery. In his autobiographical travelogue *The Atlantic Sound* (2000), he encodes the sound of waves that break against the slave ship with the mythic ramifications of the African Diaspora. Long after the abominable traffic has ceased, the throbbing, threatening sound of the waves still holds sway, according to this sensitive traveler into our racial past, over the imagination of Africans, Americans, and Europeans alike.

Contexts and Issues. American sea fiction reflects the history of the larger society (including its racial divisiveness), and yet, at the same time, it also transcends the historical context by continuously bringing into focus a number of universal themes and topics. Even though in some cases neither the voyage nor the sea itself takes center stage, authors drawn to the sea usually invest both with a symbolism and meaning that transform the actual seagoing experience into a kind of spiritual journey. If this is true, as we have seen, of the bulk of maritime literature of the nineteenth century—the so-called great age of sail—it is equally true for a large number of contemporary sea fictions, written against the backdrop of rapid technological and ecological change. If in some cases the prevalent mood is rather somber and nostalgic, in others we find an ongoing effort to wrest from the bare, unchanging facts of maritime life a new meaning, an as yet untold story. Regardless of the form that story eventually takes—autobiographical, documentary, or fictional—it often reverberates with references to earlier attempts by other authors to write about the sea. American sea fiction thus betrays a sense of continuity and tradition that in other literary genres critics have come to find problematic. Cutting across a huge variety of narrative techniques and differing authorial agendas, American writers of the sea appear to be bound together by a shared understanding of the importance of the sea as a joining rather than a separating force and, perhaps more important, as a vital ingredient of American identity.

If for Melville and his generation seascapes were often laden with metaphysical, dark philosophical meaning, turn-of-the-century writers such as Stephen Crane, Jack London, Frank Norris, and later dramatist Eugene O'Neill used the sea to probe contemporary theories of biological evolution (Darwinism) and psychoanalysis (Freud and Jung). In this realist-naturalist tradition of American sea literature the captain and his crew act out in representative ways the eternal laws of nature or, as in Crane's "The Open Boat" (1897) and London's "A Thousand Deaths" (1899), the threat of drowning takes on complicated psychological meaning thereby epitomizing the subliminal structure of human consciousness. Other writers of that era such as William McFee (next to London probably the most famous American author of maritime fiction during his time), Lincoln Colcord, Richard Hallet, or Archi Binns, were either trying to wed the increasingly important role of the engineer to the tradition or register the fact that the kind of life aboard ship eternalized in Dana's *Two Years Before the Mast* (1840), as London once noted, "had passed utterly away" (Bender 1988, 150).

Though often neglected by critics and historians of sea literature, the most popular book about an epic sea voyage in modern times, the one that became a model for generations of sailor-writers interested in the physical and psychic challenges of single-handed circumnavigation, is certainly Joshua Slocum's *Sailing Alone Around the World* (1900). An expert sailor and professional captain, Slocum embarked in 1895 on a voyage around the world in a 37-foot sloop of 9 tons that he himself rebuilt from an abandoned hulk. The fact that he decided to use only the sparsest means of navigational technology and generally championed simplicity as the most adequate form of a sailor's life helped to turn his autobiographical book into a maritime classic often compared to Henry David Thoreau's *Walden* (1854). When he writes "I sailed with a free wind day after day, marking the position of my ship on the chart with considerable precision; but this was done by intuition, I think, more than by slavish calculations" (1996, 145) Slocum's view of the alleged benefits of modern science is utterly skeptical. Yet unlike Thoreau's scathing cultural critique before him, his is a rather soft-spoken and ironic assessment of the future course of the world. If Slocum's life embodies a history of the decline of sailing as a commercial activity in America, his epic voyage and the book it spawned were meant to celebrate the tenacity and perseverance of the simple sailor in the face of natural chaos.

To pit man against nature has always been a favorite topic among writers of sea fiction. In the novels and stories of Ernest Hemingway this classic theme increasingly comes to reflect the author's animalistic view of human life. Hemingway, in Joseph DeFalco's words "the most distinguished writer of prose fiction in the twentieth century fully to explore the sea" (1995, 298), showed a life-long interest in the ocean as a metaphor of human conflict and man's existential condition. Of his three major sea novels—*To Have and Have Not* (1937), *The Old Man and the Sea* (1952), and *Islands in the Stream* (1970, posthumously)—*The Old Man and the Sea* is probably the most radical attempt to capture the sea's symbolic significance. Both *Islands in the Stream* and *The Old Man and the Sea* came out of a project that went through several mutations and that Hemingway originally envisioned as his "sea book": a trilogy entitled *The Sea When Young, The Sea When Absent,* and *The Sea in Being.* Though not all segments of the trilogy were published, these later books betray a heightening concern about the sea as a metaphor of existence. This becomes particularly clear in *The Old Man and the Sea* where the protagonist, a Cuban fisherman called Santiago, challenges the forces of biology and the marine environment. Though he is marvelously in tune with the ocean, its creatures and mysteries, Santiago also represents the dualisms and ambivalence of the human relationship with nature. If his is a life, as one critic called it, of "biological brotherhood" (Bender 1988, 195) Santiago's readiness to accept the voracious struggle for survival in nature turns him into a sea hero of tragic dimensions. The story, which is replete with religious and existentialist meaning, represents Hemingway's attempt to write a parable of the sea that is set—contrary to his other seafaring fictions—in an ahistorical situation. Santiago's struggle with the gigantic Marlin becomes a universal story of man's return to harmony in nature and the treacherous ambivalence of this return exemplified by the sharp contrast between Santiago's timeless world and the tourists who at the end of the novella tactlessly disrupt the sacred unity of the old man and the sea.

In Peter Matthiessen's highly acclaimed novel *Far Tortuga* (1975), the nautical setting is wedded to particular socio-historical circumstances such as the declining turtle fishery of the Cayman Islands during the 1960s. However, the tragic death of Captain Raib Avers, one of the last "turtlers," also resonates with larger cultural and moral implications. By some critics judged the best American novelist of the sea since Herman Melville, Matthiessen exploits a number of classic topics in maritime fiction—the last voyage, nautical hazards, the ambiguous character of the captain, mutiny, and the violence and amorality often associated with life aboard ship. However, the blending of different linguistic registers and the unusual psychological depth of the novel turns the seemingly simple tale into an increasing complex story about human fallibility; more generally, its major theme is man's age-old attempt to overcome the vagaries of fate and to bring order, at least temporarily, to a dark and chaotic universe. Matthiessen's challenging narrative technique, as critics often claim, amalgamates postmodern style and traditional sea writing. What is more, *Far Tortuga* and the later *Men's Lives: The Surfmen and Baymen of the South Fork* (1986), a documentary history of the declining fishing communities on eastern Long Island, foreground issues that have become an ongoing concern of writers about the sea in contemporary America: (1) the vanishing world of individuals heroes, workers, or navigators; (2) the problem of increasing mechanization and commercial exploitation in maritime professions; and (3) the disastrous ecological consequences of modern ways of life that appear to threaten a staggering number of marine species, eventually creating a dangerous imbalance between man and nature.

A prominent topic ever since Rachel Carson's environmentalist classic *The Sea Around Us* (1951), ecological concerns loom large in contemporary American literature of the sea. If Matthiessen stands out because of his interest in and detailed knowledge of marine biology, others treat the sea with a similar kind of reverence born from a consciousness of man's dependence on an intact marine habitat. Given the obvious and often irrevocable destruction of wetlands, rivers, and even oceans many authors articulate human responsibility and occasionally a nostalgic longing for the sea as a sustaining, purifying force. One aspect of this new trend in nautical fiction is an emphasis on marine life and the tendency to adopt the animal's point of view. In Hank Searls's novels *Overboard* (1977) and *Sounding* (1982), for example, much of the action is told from the imagined perspective of a pregnant female shark and an aging bull sperm whale. Set against a complementary story line that involves a stranded Soviet nuclear submarine and sprinkled with allusions to Melville's *Moby-Dick*, *Sounding* attempts to reintroduce interspecies communication as an important aspect of sea fiction.

An interesting philosophical twist on this topic is Edward Albee's play *Seascapes* (1975). Albee, the foremost American representative of the theatre of the absurd, confronts an elderly American couple strolling on a New England beach with two human-sized lizards that speak and act like real people. The lizards apparently no longer feel at home in the sea, but the conversation is so hopeless and depressing that they are nearly driven back to their original environment. Against the symbolically rich backdrop of the seascape, the play, for which Albee won his second Pulitzer Prize for drama, explores the alienated, distorted relations between man, animals, and the natural environment. The play also asks fundamental philosophical questions about whether life is worth living, but it decides, as critics pointed out, that there is no alternative.

In an equally surrealistic fashion, postmodern author Kurt Vonnegut also investigates the relationship between humans and marine environments. His 1985 postapocalyptic novel *Galápagos* proffers an alternate version of human history: in the wake of a sudden war a motley group of survivors manage to escape to the Galápagos Islands where they evolve over the course of a million years into a kind of amphibian species. Because their brains have shrunken considerably, they are now able to live a life more in tune with the sea and their natural surrounds.

Selected Authors. Matthiessen, Vonnegut, Joseph Heller, Ken Kesey, or science fiction author Ursula Le Guin are often grouped as postmodern authors with a keen interest in both the metaphorical and ecological ramifications of the sea. However, the one writer best known for repeatedly probing the symbolic interfaces between seafaring and the act of storytelling is novelist John Barth. In a number of intricately woven postmodern fables, Barth effectively juxtaposes the at times erratic, meandering activity of sailing or floating on the water and the conventions of prose fictions. In his first published novel, *The Floating Opera* (1956), the narrative is repeatedly compared to a showboat idly drifting in the Virginia and Maryland tidewater areas. The boat also emerges as a metaphor or mirror of human life in general. As Todd Andrews, the narrator of the story, explains:

> It always seemed a fine idea to me to build a showboat with just one big flat open deck on it, and to keep a play going continuously. The boat wouldn't be moored, but would drift up and down the river on the tide, and the audience would sit along both banks. They could catch whatever part of the plot happened to unfold as the boated past, and then they'd have to wait until the tide ran back again to catch another snatch of it, if they still happened to be sitting there. To fill in the gaps they'd have to use their imaginations, or ask more attentive neighbors, or hear the word passed along from upriver to downriver. Most times they wouldn't understand what was going on at all, or they'd think they knew, when actually they didn't. [. . .] I needn't explain that that's how much of life works. (Barth 1956, 7)

Like many of his postmodern fellow writers Barth often foregrounds the importance of storytelling as the most appropriate analogy to life itself: life holds meaning because it is a story constantly told and re-told, a multifaceted narrative plot that changes with each introduction of a new character or story line. Yet if the act of narration serves well to illustrate Barth's point that life is as quintessentially fabricated, unpredictable, and shifting as the numerous stories it holds in store, the ubiquitous sea imagery in his work emphasizes that point even further.

In Barth's 1982 novel *Sabbatical: A Romance,* perhaps his most successful meditation on his twin interests—boating and storytelling—the action centers around a nine-month sabbatical cruise on a sailboat named *Pokey, Wye I.* The novel is infused with sailing terminology, and its two principal characters, Fenwick Turner, a former CIA agent, and his wife, Susan Seckler, a professor of American literature, blend sophisticated reflections on their past lives and future with nautical metaphors, literary history, and narratological discourse. With *Sabbatical,* as Dennis Berthold observes, Barth "legitimizes sea fiction as a serious academic subgenre and ensures that the most sophisticated contemporary literary critics will have to know a jib from a stay" (1995, 319). Among contemporary writers of sea fiction Barth is certainly among the most formally varied and intellectually challenging. His fascination with similarities between storytelling and the world of sailors and ships can be traced throughout his extensive prose fiction and essay writing. In novel after novel he returned to either ships or the people who navigate them interweaving the tradition of sea fiction with his special interest in authorial self-reflection and the mechanics of storytelling. If in his more recent novels—*Tidewater Tales: A Novel* (1987), *The Last Voyage of Somebody the Sailor* (1991), *Once Upon a Time: A Floating Opera* (1994), or *Coming Soon* (2001)—sea topics figure to varying degrees, all of these works add, each in its own interesting way, to Barth's ongoing obsession with the sailing world and the estuarine tidewater system of his navigational "home turf," the Chesapeake Bay.

Having so far reviewed selected contemporary novels that either employ sea imagery to explore the conflictual relationship between humans and the environment or share an interest in seafaring as an epitome of man's voyage of self-discovery, I want to conclude this essay by mentioning a number of recent popular sea fictions that do not, or at least not exclusively, fall into one of these categories. Following in the wake of Peter Benchley's enormously successful marine thriller *Jaws* (1973), there are quite a few texts that seek to exploit the sensationalism of shipwrecks or natural disasters. Among the more interesting examples are Beryl Bainbridge's dark and brittle tale of the Titanic's fatal voyage, *Every Man for Himself* (1996), and the superbly written first novel of Sebastian Junger, *The Perfect Storm* (1997). Junger recounts the authentic 1991 October storm off the coast of Nova Scotia when natural forces combined to create the "perfect storm" whose conditions could not possibly have been worse. Also based on authentic events are Katherine Anne Porter's *Ship of Fools* (1962), which centers on international travelers going from Mexico to Germany in 1931 aboard the freighter *Vera,* Robert Stone's fictional account of a failed solo circumnavigation race in 1969, *Outerbridge Reach* (1992), and Peter Landesman's *The Raven* (1995), which tells the story of the disappearance of a ship with thirty-six people who had gone out for a day of deep-sea fishing.

There are also numerous novels that turn on naval history and military events such as Tom Clancy's *The Hunt for Red October* (1984), William Brinkley's *The Last Ship* (1988), and David Poyer's *The Med.* (1988), the first book of a series designed around the protagonist Dan Lenson, a graduate from the Naval Academy. An outstanding representative of this category is David Guterson's *Snow Falling On Cedars,* which won the Pen/Faulkner Award in 1995. The novel is set on San Piedro Island, north of Puget Sound; it tells the story of a local fisherman, who in 1954 is found suspiciously drowned, and a Japanese American, named Kabuo Miyamoto, charged with his murder. The gripping tale evolves around a historical incident during World War II when San Piedro's Japanese residents were sent into exile while their neighbors watched.

Finally, I want to mention a group of texts that is informed—like much of American sea literature—by either autobiographical or regional/geographical experiences. A remarkable representative of this tradition is John Casey's 1989 novel *Spartina*. Set on the Southern Rhode Island shore, the story offers a bleak portrait of a region that is dramatically changing under the impact of increasingly new resorts for inland tourists. Though conscious of his own anachronistic lifestyle, the novel's protagonist, fisherman, and boat-builder Dick Pierce, embarks on a heroic project: to finish a half-built 50-foot boat in his backyard so he can fish for red crabs out in deep water and make some real money to support his family. *Spartina* won the National Book Award in 1989; its description of Pierce's complex, grieving character has been repeatedly compared to the best in sea fiction since Melville and Hemingway. Other examples of regionally inspired maritime fiction include William Martin's *Cape Cod* (1992), which follows the involvement of the people of Cape Cod with the sea from the landing of the Mayflower to the present era of whale-watching; Annie Proulx's internationally successful novel *The Shipping News* (1993); James Michel Pratt's saga of three generations of lighthouse keepers off the coast of Massachusetts, *The Lighthouse Keeper* (2000); Tony Horwitz's *Blue Latitudes* (2002), an autobiographical travelogue by a journalist who embarks on a cruise to retrace the nautical legacies of the British navigator James Cook; and Lewis Robinson's collection of stories set on the Maine coast, *Officer Friendly and Other Stories* (2003).

If the present survey of American maritime literature has not nearly covered the staggering number and huge variety of texts in the field, it should have become clear that today the tradition of sea fiction, though constantly transforming itself to meet new challenges and concerns, is as vital a part of the national literary identity as in the days of Cooper, Dana, and Melville. Far from becoming a fringe activity, sea writing in America continues to investigate the ocean's compelling mysteries and to plow its uncharted depth for symbols to articulate our own modern and postmodern version of man's universal fascination with the sea.

Reception. Today, scholars examining the role of the sea in American literary history are confronted with a wave of critical texts that stand in need to be charted and explored. Though in the broadest sense the topic may well include Native American water myths or contemporary seashore environmentalism, in my own approach here I could only present a small number of American writers and discuss ways in which they recreate, question, and thereby continuously reinforce connections (whether imagined or real) between America and the sea. More encompassing, encyclopedic publications include Haskell Springer's *America and the Sea: A Literary History* (1995), Peter Neill's compilation of primary American sea literature *American Sea Writing: A Literary Anthology* (2000), and Jill B. Gidmark's *Encyclopedia of American Literature of the Sea and Great Lakes* (2001). Equally comprehensive though by now also somewhat dated is Myron J. Smith's and Robert C. Weller's *Sea Fiction Guide,* a partially annotated listing of sea writing and authors up to 1976. Other critics have looked more selectively at the tradition and produced case studies such as Patricia Ann Carlson's *Literature and Lore of the Sea* (1986), Bert Bender's *Sea-Brothers: The Tradition of American Sea Fiction From* Moby-Dick *To the Present* (1988), and lately Robert Foulke's topical study *The Sea Voyage Narrative* (2002) and Klaus Benesch's, Jon-K Adams's, and Kerstin Schmidt's *The Sea and the American Imagination* (2004).

Bibliography

Albee, Edward. *Seascape—A Play.* New York: Atheneum, 1975.

Barth, John. *Coming Soon.* New York: Houghton Mifflin Company, 2001.

———. *Once Upon a Time: A Floating Opera.* Boston: Little, Brown and Company, 1994.

———. *The Last Voyage of Somebody the Sailor.* Boston: Little, Brown and Company, 1991.

———. *The Tidewater Tales: A Novel.* New York: Putnam's, 1987.

———. *Sabbatical: A Romance.* New York: Putnam's, 1982.

———. *Lost in the Funhouse.* New York: Doubleday, 1968.

———. *The Floating Opera.* New York: Appleton, 1956.

Bender, Bert. *Sea-Brothers: The Tradition of American Sea Fiction from* Moby-Dick *to the Present.* Philadelphia: University of Philadelphia Press, 1988.

Benesch, Klaus, Jon-K Adams, and Kerstin Schmidt, eds. *The Sea and the American Imagination.* Tübingen: Stauffenburg, 2004.

Berthold, Dennis. "Prose Since 1960." *America and the Sea: A Literary History.* Haskell Springer, ed. Athens/London: The University of Georgia Press, 1995, 307–326.

Carlson, Patricia N., ed. *Literature and Lore of the Sea.* Amsterdam: Rodopi, 1986.

Carson, Rachel. *The Sea Around Us.* New York: Oxford University Press, 1951.

Crane, Stephen. "The Open Boat." *The Works of Stephen Crane. Vol. 5.* Fredson Bowers, ed. Charlottesville: University Press of Virginia, 1969.

Dana, Richard Henry, Jr. *Two Years Before the Mast.* New York: Harper, 1840.

DeFalco, Joseph. "Modernist Prose and Its Antecedents." *America and the Sea: A Literary History.* Haskell Springer, ed. Athens/London: The University of Georgia Press, 1995, 289–306.

Douglass, Frederick. *Narrative of the Life of Frederick Douglass, An American Slave, Written by Himself.* David Blight, ed. Boston/New York: St. Martin's Press, 1993.

Gidmark, Jill B., ed. *Encyclopedia of American Literature of the Sea and Great Lakes.* Westport, Connecticut: Greenwood Press, 2001.

Equiano, Olaudah. *The Interesting Narrative and Other Writings.* Vincent Carretta, ed. New York: Penguin, 1995.

Fabre, Geneviève, and Klaus Benesch, eds. *African Diasporas in the Old and the New World.* Amsterdam: Rodopi, 2003.

Farr, James. *Black Odyssey: The Seafaring Tradition of Black Americans.* New York: Peter Lang, 1989.

Foulke, Robert. *The Sea Voyage Narrative.* (1997) New York/London: Routledge, 2002.

Gilroy, Paul. *The Black Atlantic: Modernity and Double Consciousness.* Cambridge, Massachusetts: Harvard University Press, 1993.

Hemingway, Ernest. *Islands in the Stream.* New York: Scribner's, 1970.

———. *The Old Man and the Sea.* New York: Scribner's, 1952.

———. *To Have and Have Not.* New York: Scribner's, 1937.

Horwitz, Tony. *Blue Latitudes: Boldly Going Where Captain Cook Has Gone Before.* New York: Picador, 2002.

Hughes, Langston. *The Collected Poems of Langston Hughes.* Arnold Rampersad and David Roessel, eds. New York: Vintage, 1995.

———. *The Big Sea.* New York: Knopf, 1940.

Hurston, Zora Neale. *Their Eyes Were Watching God.* 1937. Urbana/Chicago: University of Illinois Press, 1978.

Johnson, Charles. *Middle Passage.* New York: Atheneum, 1990.

London, Jack. *Great Short Works of Jack London.* Ed. Earle Labor. New York: Harper, 1965.

Lawson-Peebles, Robert. *Landscape and Written Expression in Revolutionary America: The Worlds Turned Upside Down.* Cambridge: Cambridge University Press, 1988.

Malcolm X. *Autobiography of Malcolm X.* New York: Grove Press, 1965, 201.

Marshall, Paule. *Praisesong for the Widow.* New York: Dutton, 1983.

Martin, William. *Cape Cod.* New York: Grand Central, 1992.

Matthiessen, Peter. *Men's Lives: The Surfmen and Baymen of the South Fork*. New York: Random, 1986.

———. *Far Tortuga*. New York: Random, 1975.

Melville, Herman. *Moby-Dick*. New York/London: Norton, 1967.

———. *Billy Budd, Sailor*. Harrison Hayford and Merton M. Sealts, Jr., eds. Chicago: University of Chicago Press, 1962.

Peck, John. *Maritime Fiction: Sailors and the Sea in British and American Novels, 1719–1917*. New York: Palgrave, 2001.

Neill, Peter, ed. *American Sea Writing: A Literary Anthology*. New York: The Library of America, 2000.

Pederson, Carl. "Sea Change: The Middle Passage and the Transatlantic Imagination." *The Black Columbiad*. Werner Sollors and Maria Diedrich, eds. Cambridge, MA: Harvard University Press, 1994, 42–51.

Philbrick, Nathaniel. *In the Heart of the Sea: The Tragedy of the Whaleship Essex*. New York: Viking, 2000.

Phillips, Caryl. *The Atlantic Sound*. London: Faber and Faber, 2000.

Poirier, Richard. *A World Elsewhere. The Place of Style in American Fiction*. New York: Oxford University Press, 1966.

Robillard, Douglas, ed. *The Poems of Herman Melville*. Kent, Ohio: The Kent State University Press, 2000.

Schultz, Elizabeth. "African-American Literature." *America and the Sea: A Literary History*. Haskell Springer, ed. Athens/London: The University of Georgia Press, 1995, 233–259.

Slocum, Joshua. *Sailing Alone Around the World*. (1900). London: Adlard Coles Nautical, 1996.

Smith, Myron J., Jr., and Robert C. Weller, eds. *Sea Fiction Guide*. Metuchen, New Jersey: The Scarecrow Press, 1976.

Sobel, Dava. *Longitude: The Story of a Lone Genius Who Solved the Greatest Scientific Problem of His Time*. London: Fourth Estate Limited, 1996.

Sollors, Werner, and Maria Diedrich, eds. "Introduction." *The Black Columbiad: Defining Moments in African American Literature and Culture*. Cambridge, MA: Harvard University Press, 1994.

Springer, Haskell. "Introduction: The Sea, the Land, the Literature." *America and the Sea: A Literary History*. Haskell Springer, ed. Athens/London: The University of Georgia Press, 1995, 1–31.

———. "Call Them All Ishmael?: Fact and Form in Some Nineteenth-Century Sea Narratives." *Literature and Lore of the Sea*. Patricia Ann Carlson, ed. Amsterdam: Rodopi, 1986, 14–22.

Stein, Roger B. *Seascape and the American Imagination*. New York: Clarkson N. Potter, 1975.

Vonnegut, Kurt. *Galápagos*. New York: Delacorte, 1985.

Williams, Williams Carlos. *In the American Grain*. (1925) New York: New Directions, 1956.

Further Reading

Bender, Bert. *Sea-Brothers: The Tradition of American Sea Fiction from* Moby-Dick *to the Present*. Philadelphia: University of Philadelphia Press, 1988; Benesch, Klaus, Jon-K Adams, and Kerstin Schmidt, eds. *The Sea and the American Imagination*. Tübingen: Stauffenburg, 2004; Berthold, Dennis. "Prose Since 1960." *America and the Sea: A Literary History*. Ed. Haskell Springer. Athens/London: The University of Georgia Press, 1995, 307–326; Foulke, Robert. *The Sea Voyage Narrative*. (1997) New York/London: Routledge, 2002; Neill, Peter, ed. *American Sea Writing: A Literary Anthology*. New York: The Library of America, 2000; Carlson, Patricia N., ed. *Literature and Lore of the Sea*. Amsterdam: Rodopi, 1986; Smith,

Myron J., Jr., and Robert C. Weller, eds. *Sea Fiction Guide*. Metuchen, New Jersey: The Scarecrow Press, 1976.

KLAUS BENESCH

SELF-HELP LITERATURE

Definition. The genre of "self-help" literature is known by several other labels, including "self-improvement," "self-actualization," "life skills," "personal growth," and "recovery." The genre is so popular that it merits its own section on the *New York Times* weekly bestseller list, which is titled "Advice, How-To, and Miscellaneous." Books in this genre often fit several other categories utilized by retailers, librarians, and marketers, including art instruction, alternative medicine, business writing, career coaching, diet, etiquette, health, **humor, inspirational literature**, motivational literature, **new age literature**, personal finances, popular psychology, reference, and spirituality. Whereas this entry will use the term "self-help" throughout, many of the guides and manuals regarded as "self-help" books actively urge their readers to seek assistance rather than relying solely on their own resources. Such texts can be regarded as "self-help" in terms of the books' function as starter kits and handbooks rather than stand-alone, self-contained solutions to the readers' issues.

History. Benjamin Franklin (1706–1790), whose many roles included author and publisher, remains an iconic figure to many modern advocates of task and time management. The advice he dispensed through his series of *Poor Richard's Almanacs* (1732–1758) and the manuscript of his autobiography (edited and published in numerous versions after his death) is still quoted widely and frequently, including on the front page of "Franklin planners" ("Dost thou love life? Then do not squander time, for that's the stuff life is made of"). The planners, a calendar-based tool popular among many white-collar employees, are part of a larger, massively influential system developed and marketed by FranklinCovey, a company formed from the 1997 merger of Franklin Quest (the original manufacturer of the planners) and Covey Leadership Center (a training and consulting corporation). The Covey Leadership Center was founded by Stephen R. Covey (b. 1932), who wrote *The Seven Habits of Highly Successful People* (1989). The book sold over 15 million copies during its first two decades in print, appearing on the *New York Times* Business Best Sellers lists well into the first decade of the twenty-first century. Sequels such as *First Things First* (Covey, Merrill, and Merrill 1994), *The Seven Habits of Highly Effective Families* (Covey 1997), and *The Eighth Habit* (Covey 2004) were also bestsellers. Covey's fame is manifest both in the honors he's received, such as being named one of America's twenty-five most influential people (*Time* 1996), as well as the ongoing success of the FranklinCovey company and its stores, workshops, and conferences. The phrase "seven habits" is so recognizable that it is frequently borrowed for headlines to books and articles largely unrelated to Covey or time management; a quick Internet search turns up titles such as the "Seven Habits of Highly Effective Massgoers" (2004), "Seven Habits of Highly Effective Imperialists" (2004), "Seven Habits of Highly Effective Foundries," "Seven Habits of Highly Effective Physical Educators" (2005), and "Seven Habits of Highly Effective Global Private-Public Health Partnerships" (2007).

Another iconic figure in the genre is Dale Carnegie (1888–1955). As with Franklin's autobiography, Carnegie's *How to Win Friends and Influence People* (1936) and *How to Stop Worrying and Start Living* (1948) have been reprinted and repackaged in multiple editions since their original press runs; as with the FranklinCovey corporation, the Dale Carnegie Training company (founded 1912) conducts numerous courses nationwide that are factored into many business budgets.

A contemporary of Carnegie, Minister Norman Vincent Peale (1898–1993), wrote *The Power of Positive Thinking* (1952) and forty-five other books; as with *How to Win Friends and Influence People, The Power of Positive Thinking* remains in print in multiple formats. Peale's platform was religious rather than corporate; the continuation of his legacy has resided in *Guideposts,* an inspirational magazine Peale co-founded with his wife in 1945.

In the secular realm, one of the most influential figures among self-help enthusiasts is talk-show host Oprah Winfrey (b. 1952), whose endorsements have helped secure the success of other household names such as Deepak Chopra (b. 1946), John Gray (b. 1951), Suze Orman (b. 1951), "Dr. Phil" McGraw (b. 1950), and Marianne Williamson (b. 1952). Winfrey, repeatedly named on *Time 100* lists (Mandela 2007), also promotes a number of self-help books via her lifestyle magazine, *O,* which premiered in May 2000. The inaugural theme, "Live Your Best Life," became the title of an anthology (Randol 2005), as well as several tours of motivational seminars conducted by Winfrey and an online workshop that closed in 2006. Individuals whose profiles have been boosted by Winfrey's support have also included physicians Michael F. Roizen (b. 1946) and Mehmet C. Oz (b. 1960), known for their "RealAge" and "YOU" programs for diet and personal care; fitness expert Bob Greene; professional organizer Peter Walsh (b. 1956); and interior designer Nate Berkus (b. 1971).

Not all of Winfrey's endorsements are greeted with enthusiasm or approval. In particular, her support of *The Secret* (Byrne 2007) was fiercely criticized by commentators who found its "ask, believe, receive" variation of positive thinking to be simplistic, materialistic, and even offensive, particularly in its implication that victims of tragedies somehow attract their misfortunes (cf. Birkenhead 2007; Klein 2007; Salkin 2007). However, the book's promise of life-changing revelations attracted enough readers for it to dominate bestseller lists during the better part of 2007. Another popular author promoting the notion of a desire-responsive universe is Michael J. Losier, who teaches workshops on utilizing the *Law of Attraction* (2004) and who has received repeat airtime with Winfrey. Esther and Jerry Hicks are also well-known advocates of "prosperity consciousness"; their most recent book is also titled *Law of Attraction* (2006). Their dispute with Rhonda Byrne over the documentary version of *The Secret* added to the controversy surrounding Byrne's success (Salkin 2007).

Although the popularity of *The Secret* surged in 2007, the concepts it promoted are not wholly new. In addition to Peale, another classic author mentioned in discussions of prosperity consciousness is Napoleon Hill (1883–1970), who penned *Think and Grow Rich* (1937). The book has appeared in several different versions over the years, with several expanded editions produced during the first decade of the twenty-first century.

Trends and Themes

Topical. A primary concern among contemporary readers is finding, establishing, and maintaining a proper balance between professional and personal priorities. Some of the concepts addressing this issue include time management and clutter

---

HELP FOR DUMMIES AND IDIOTS

Two of the most recognizable brands in self-help are the black-and-yellow "Dummies" guides launched in 1991 and the orange-bordered "Complete Idiot's Guides" launched in 1993. Both series began as hip, humorous introductions to the basics of various computer programs. The format proved to be popular enough to expand into nontechnical areas of interest, with both series going strong into their second decades. Sample titles in recent years have included *Grieving for Dummies* (2007), *Baby and Toddler Sleep Solutions for Dummies* (2007), *Frugal Living for Dummies* (2003), *The Complete Idiot's Guide to Creative Visualization* (2005), *The Complete Idiot's Guide to Organizing Your Life* (4th edition, 2005), and *The Complete Idiot's Guide to Managing Your Time* (3rd edition, 2002). The Dummies brand is so recognizable that the 2007 movie *Evan Almighty* featured a book called *Ark Building for Dummies* both in its plot and in its advertising.

---

management. In an appendix to *First Things First,* the authors analyzed the strengths and weaknesses of eight basic approaches covered in the time management literature they surveyed:

> The "Get Organized" Approach (putting things in order)
>
> The "Warrior" Approach (protecting time to get things done)
>
> The "Goal" Approach (focusing on goals)
>
> The "ABC" Approach (concentrating on top priorities)
>
> The "Magic Tool" Approach (using customized planners and other aids)
>
> The "Time Management 101" Approach (treating time management as a specific, acquirable skill)
>
> The "Go with the Flow" Approach (redefining one's frames of reference)
>
> The "Recovery" Approach (examining one's personal hangups)
>
> (Covey, Merrill, and Merrill 1994, 332–341)

One of the newer systems that caught on in the early 2000s is "Getting Things Done" (GTD), which was developed by trainer and consultant David Allen (b.1945) and is promoted through his book of the same name. Allen's prescription for "stress-free productivity" includes exhortations such as his "do it," "delegate it," and "defer it" rules for handling the contents of one's in-box (Allen 2001, 131) and "use your mind to think *about* things, rather than think *of* them" (233).

Another organizational program that acquired numerous adherents during this period was the humor-laced "Sidetracked Home Executives"™ (SHE) system, established by "The Slob Sisters" in 1977 and aimed primarily at homemakers. As with many self-improvement franchises, the SHE system has been propagated through workshops, Web pages, newsletters, media appearances, and other offerings, including books; a revised and updated version of its basic guide, *Sidetracked Home Executives,* was issued in 2001, twenty years after the first edition (Young and Jones 2001). The SHE system has inspired two peppy spinoffs, FlyLady and Company (founded 1999) and The Brat Factor (founded 2006). The FlyLady program, known for its cheerleading style and for slogans such as "Shine Your Sink," has produced books on routine-building and self-care, including *Sink Reflections* (Cilley 2002) and *Body Clutter* (Cilley and Ely 2006), as well as partnering with the "Dinner Diva" and her "Saving Dinner" series (Ely 2003, 2005, 2005a, 2006, 2007). The Brat

Factor occupies a cartoonesque online Web space called "Bratland," where it addresses the issue of self-sabotage, that is, when a person's "Inner Brat" resists the efforts being made to control or eradicate bad habits; the motto of the Brat Factor is "If it isn't fun, it won't get done." The tools sold in the Brat Factor online store include "Mouth Traps"—decals the user places over her own mouth to create time-outs and deter "complaining, snacking, smoking, drinking, or whining."

The theme of self-sabotage is discussed in Judith Wright's books and workshops as well. Wright's specialty is teaching people how to overcome their "soft addictions," her trademarked term for benign-seeming habits that become liabilities from overindulgence, such as watching television and spending time on the Internet. Wright, who runs an institute in her name, is best-known for a 2003 book called *There Must Be More than This,* which was revised and expanded several years later into *The Soft Addiction Solution* (Wright 2006). Wright has also trademarked the concept of "The One Decision," which urges readers to approach and assess their lives in the context of a single guiding principle. The principle, which is up to each reader to define for himself or herself, is framed in epic terms: not unlike *The Secret* and other prosperity consciousness manuals, *The One Decision* tells its disciples that they too will benefit from the laws of attraction:

> Magic happens once you definitely make your One Decision. The very act of committing sends out a message to the universe, and then, and only then, can full resources come to your aid. When you definitely commit, unforeseen support, inspiration, and encouragement come your way. You begin to find synergies and synchronicities in events and things around you. You begin to attract the support of other people who have made deeper life commitments. It requires a leap of faith to make your One Decision, but once you have, resources will appear that you never would have expected. (Wright 2005, 73)

The One Decision program also employs language evocative of epic and spiritual journeys, using phrases such as "The Way of the Heart," "The Keys to the Kingdom," and "The Good Fight" to describe facets of the user's progress toward self-improvement and alluding to heroic fantasies such as *The Fellowship of the Ring* (32–33) and the quest for the Holy Grail (157). Wright's work has been endorsed by a number of eminent authors, including Covey, novelist James Redfield (b. 1950), mystic Andrew Harvey (b. 1952), and "medical intuitive" Caroline Myss.

The search for meaningful work is a central theme in many advice books published since 2001. In *The Answer to How Is Yes* (Block 2002), readers are urged to ask "What" questions instead of "How"-based ones in order to frame their priorities in the context of their personal values rather than measurable results. In *I Don't Know What I Want, But I Know It's Not This* (Jansen 2003), readers are offered multiple self-assessment exercises to help them ascertain what type of career change would best suit their skills and personalities. In *The Anti 9 to 5 Guide* (2007), Michelle Goodman (b. 1976) details the steps women can take to pursue a variety of non-office-based careers or to adjust their professional commitments to make more time for avocations or side gigs. Goodman's observation that "work in the twenty-first century is dramatically different from the way it was in the 1960s, 1970s, 1980s, and early to mid-1990s" (Goodman 2007, 9) is echoed in *Free to Succeed* (Reinhold 2001), a guide for individuals interested in becoming "free agents" such as entrepreneurs, "intrapreneurs" (employees with ownership of special projects), or seasonal workers. The author, a woman known as "The Career Coach" on the job-hunting Web site monster.com, offers prospective free agents a seven-step program for discerning whether they are suited to nontraditional employment and anecdotal examples to illustrate each step.

The word "authentic" and its variations also appeals to modern workers. Readers of *The Authentic Career* (Craddock 2004) are led through stages of "Awareness," "Emotional Ownership," "Interaction," and "Integration," with exercises such as "Weeding the 'Shoulds'" and "The Mandala of Your Life." *Authenticity* (Cappannelli and Cappannelli 2004) is organized in four stages as well: "Exploring Ten Beliefs that May Be Limiting Your Life," "Penetrating Those Thorny Myths that Limit Authenticity," "Turning Deliberately Toward Greater Meaning and Purpose," and "Practicing A Few Simple Strategies that Can Change Your Life." British personal development coach Neil Crofts (b. 1963) runs a large franchise called "Authentic Transformation"; like many other self-improvement companies, its offerings include an electronically distributed newsletter, a team of consultants (called "Authentic Guides"), a schedule of workshops and gatherings (include a retreat-style event termed an "advance"), and several books, including *Authentic* (Crofts 2003) and *Authentic Business* (Crofts 2005). Other titles geared to address aspects of this yearning include *Authentic Happiness* (Seligman 2003), *Something More: Excavating Your Authentic Self* (Breathnach 1998), *The Authentic Heart* (Amodeo 2001), and *Authentic Relationships* (Jacobsen and Jacobsen 2003).

Another trend has been to invoke the Renaissance period of history and its major figures, including artists Michelangelo Buonarroti (1475–1564) and Leonardo Da Vinci (1452–1519). Such books appeal to users who associate the Renaissance with versatile, multi-talented geniuses. In *The Angel Inside,* Chris Widener uses the life and art of Michelangelo to tell a parable about choosing one's path; the book includes an eleven-page "Discussion Guide and Workbook" with sections such as "Embrace the Stages of Chipping, Sculpting, Sanding, and Polishing" and "No One Starts with the Sistine Chapel" (Widener 2004, 103–105). The authors of *The Michelangelo Method* also employ artistic metaphors in their guide to fostering creativity, with one chapter titled "Plan First, Then Chip Away," and two others featuring the word "vision" (Schuman and Paxton 2007). The concept of viewing oneself as a masterpiece also appears in books such as *The Secret,* which quotes Joe Vitale as saying, "You are the Michelangelo of your own life. The David you are sculpting is you" (Byrne 2006, 23); *Sacred Self, Sacred Relationships,* in which the reader is exhorted, "Come to see yourself as the artistic perfection Michelangelo saw hidden in the block of granite" (Jones and Jones 2002, 59); and *The Play of Your Life,* where the user is guided through the search for a new career by thinking of it in terms of "the script," "the audition," and other elements of a dramatic production (Sabatino 2004). In *How to Think Like Leonardo da Vinci* and its workbook, "high performance learning" expert Michael J. Gelb names seven principles in Italian (*curiosita, dimostrazione, sensazione, sfumato, arte/scienza, corporalita,* and *connessione*) that he presents as reflective of da Vinci's skills (Gelb 1998). In *Da Vinci Decoded* (an allusion to Dan Brown's *The Da Vinci Code,* a blockbuster novel in 2003), Gelb encouraged his readers to apply the seven principles featured in the earlier book to spiritual as well as creative matters (Gelb 2004). In *The Da Vinci Method,* Garret LoPorto speaks of a "DaVinci" personality type that he sees as common to most entrepreneurs, including himself, and one that includes a high percentage of individuals with Attention Deficit (Hyperactive) Disorder (ADD/ADHD)

(LoPorto 2005); one headline for the book on its Web site billed it as "The Most Advanced Adult ADD/ADHD Therapy on the Planet!" Disciples of the method are called "DaVincis" and congregate in an online community called "DaVinci Nation."

The theme of advising users that their weaknesses are actually hidden strengths can also be seen in books such as *The Renaissance Soul,* which addresses individuals who can't seem to focus on just one interest; the author repeatedly cites Franklin and da Vinci as examples of successful Renaissance Souls (cf. Lobenstine 2006, 33). Barbara Sher discusses a similar personality type at length in *Refuse to Choose!,* having coined the term "Scanners" to describe individuals who "instead of diving down into the depths of an interest . . . scanned the horizon for many interests." Sher, too, mentions Franklin as a role model, as well as the philosopher Aristotle (384 B.C.E.–322 B.C.E.) and the poet Johann Wolfgang von Goethe (1749–1832) (Sher 2006, xiv).

Another type of weakness that has received significant attention within the past decade is the compulsion of many individuals to repeat behaviors they already know to be unproductive or even self-destructive. One school of thought posits that individuals subconsciously adhere to internal narratives that tend to prevent them from moving forward with their lives; the role these stories play has been examined in books such as *I Could Do Anything If I Only Knew What It Was* (Sher and Smith 1994), with chapters such as "Fear of Success: Leaving the Ones You Love Behind." In its "Going Deeper" section, *The Renaissance Soul* also devotes space to "Rewriting Old Messages" and coping with "Creative Fear and Anxiety" (Lobenstine 2006, 267–292). This theme is central to books such as *Becoming Real: Defeating the Stories We Tell Ourselves that Hold Us Back* (Saltz 2004) and *Bad Childhood, Good Life* (Schlessinger 2006).

Transcending one's baggage is also emphasized in books on overcoming negativity, such as *The Emotional Toolkit* (Mininni 2005). Based on a course called "LifeSkills" that the author began teaching in 1999, *The Emotional Toolkit* employs lists and charts such as "The Emotion Tree" to guide its users toward analyzing and managing distressing feelings. In *Be Nice (Or Else!),* the first step listed under "Take Control of Your Life" is "Eliminate and Cancel Negative Programming" (Claybaugh 2004, 40–47). In *Receiving Love,* relationship therapists Harville Hendrix and Helen LaKelly Hunt examine why individuals "have trouble accepting compliments and positive feedback from their partners and others" (Hendrix and Hunt 2004, 3), tracing it back to hidden triggers and unconscious defenses developed in childhood. This is an extension of Hendrix's "Imago" theory of couples interaction, so called because of his belief that "partners in an adult intimate relationship are, in important ways, mirrors of their caretakers" (Hendrix and Hunt 2004, 289). This theory was first presented in *Getting the Love You Want* (1988), a bestseller that continued to attract new readers during its second decade in print and generated spin-off products such as workbooks, "home video workshops," and sequels titled *Keeping the Love You Find* (Hendrix and Hunt 1992) and *Giving the Love That Heals* (Hendrix and Hunt 1997). The exercises in *Receiving Love* include keeping a "Gift Diary" and practicing "Positive Flooding" (setting aside time to shower one's partner with compliments).

Although many authors in the genre couch their advice in gentle, sympathetic language, the blunt approach favored by personalities such as "Dr. Phil" McGraw and "Dr. Laura" Schlessinger (b. 1947) has also attained a substantial following.

McGraw developed his fan base as a regular on Oprah Winfrey's television talk show in the late 1990s, and he began hosting his own show (produced by Winfrey's company) on television in 2002. His publications have covered both relationships and diet and include *Relationship Rescue* (2000), *Self Matters* (2001), *The Ultimate Weight Solution* (2003), *Family First* (2005), *Love Smart* (2006), as well as workbooks and a cookbook. Schlessinger became a household name with her first book, *Ten Stupid Things Women Do To Mess Up Their Lives* (1994); her publications since have included *Ten Stupid Things Couples Do to Mess Up Their Relationships* (2001) and *The Proper Care and Feeding of Husbands* (2004). Conservative writer Paul Coughlin attracts readers who share his aggravation with the Christian church's treatment of men, which he discusses in books such as *No More Christian Nice Guy* (2005). Coughlin contends that Christianity has focused too much on comfort at the expense of personal growth and deplores the under-masculine image of Christ that he sees churches promoting: "That sweet, Gumby-like Jesus can't save you from a dark night of the soul" (Meadows n.d.). Coughlin's aggressive stance is also evident in *No More Jellyfish, Chickens, or Wimps* (2007), a guide to rearing "assertive" children.

The perception of anxiety, uncertainty, and dissatisfaction with society's current roles for men can also be witnessed in other "male liberation" titles intended to address these symptoms, such as *No More Mr. Nice Guy!* (Glover 2003), *The Way of the Superior Man* (Deida 2004), and *Being the Strong Man a Woman Wants* (Katz 2005). There are also unisex guides to self-assertiveness and conflict management; these include *Anxious to Please* (Rapson and English 2006), *Too Nice For Your Own Good* (Robinson 1997 [2000]), *Don't Be Nice, Be Real* (Bryson 2004), *The Disease to Please* (Braiker 2001), *The Power of Positive Confrontation* (Patcher and Magee 2000), and *The Coward's Guide to Conflict* (Ursiny 2003).

On the distaff side, a prime example of the unsentimental, anti-self-pity approach is *He's Just Not That into You* (Behrendt and Tuccillo 2004), written by two members of the creative team for the *Sex in the City* television show. The book proved to be so popular that it was later abridged into a version subtitled *Your Daily Wake-Up Call* (2005), reformatted into a "pocket guide" (with a pink-ribboned telephone bookmark, 2005), and expanded into a second edition (2006). Rebuttals include *Be Honest—You're Not That into Him Either* (Kerner 2005). Parodies include *He Just Thinks He's Not That into You* (Whitman 2007). Behrendt, a comedian by profession, has since parlayed his reputation as a relationships expert into a short-lived daytime talk show (2006–2007) and additional books co-authored with his wife, Amiira Ruotola-Behrendt, including *It's Called a Break-Up Because It's Broken* (2005).

With many humor books adopting a pseudo-handbook format, and many handbook writers employing sarcasm and irony to entertain their readers, it can be difficult to assess to what extent a book genuinely intends to offer help and when its advice is tongue-in-cheek. This is particularly the case with books with cynical titles. One reviewer called *The Complete A**hole's Guide to Handling Chicks* "basically a how-to book for the sexually frustrated, offering advice—often in handy chart form—on how to have as much meaningless sex as possible. I think it's supposed to be funny, but I've laughed more at books about genocide" (Schaub 2003). Another book in the "telling it as it is" subgenre is *Why Men Love Bitches* (2002), written by comedian Sherry Argov, which received sufficient interest for a follow-up titled *Why Men Marry Bitches* (2006).

The potent combination of satire and how-to can be seen in the enthusiasm nationwide for Southern-flavored guides to manners. One of the classics of this category, *The Southern Belle Primer, or Why Princess Margaret Will Never Be a Kappa Kappa Gamma* (Schwartz 1991), was reissued in 2006 with a new subtitle, *Why Paris Hilton Will Never Be a Kappa Kappa Gamma*. Ronda Rich followed *What Southern Women Know* (1999) with *What Southern Women Know about Flirting* (2005). Gayden Metcalfe and Charlotte Hays provide both irreverence and recipes in *Being Dead Is No Excuse: The Official Southern Ladies Guide to Hosting the Perfect Funeral* (2005) and *Somebody is Going to Die if Lilly Beth Doesn't Catch That Bouquet*, a sequel on organizing weddings (2007). Deborah Ford's GRITS (Girls Raised in the South), Inc. franchise has inspired the formation of the Official Sisterhood of GRITS as well as a series of books, including *The GRITS Guide to Life* (2003), *Puttin' On the Grits: A Guide to Southern Entertaining* (2005), *GRITS Friends Are Forevah: A Southern-Style Celebration of Women* (2006), and *Bless His Heart: the GRITS Guide to Loving (Or Just Living With) Southern Men* (2006).

Another major Southern sisterhood brand features the Sweet Potato Queens, who hail from a Jackson, Mississippi, parade tradition that began in 1982 and now counts more than five thousand regional chapters with names such as "The Sweet Tea Queens," "The Kudzu Queens," and "The Divine Dixie Divas" (www.sweetpotatoqueens.com). The first book in the series, *The Sweet Potato Queen's Book of Love* (Browne 1999), was followed by *God Save the Sweet Potato Queens* (Browne 2001), a combined cookbook and financial planner (Browne 2003), a "field guide" to men (Browne 2004), and a wedding-and-divorce guide in one volume (Browne 2005).

The appeal of advice from other geographic and ethnic perspectives has also been a significant trend during the first decade of the twenty-first century. The elegant, stylish reputation of French women has helped fuel interest in titles such as *French Women Don't Get Fat* (Guiliano 2005) and its sequel, *French Women for All Seasons* (Guiliano 2006); *Entre Nous* (Ollivier 2003); *Joie de Vivre* (Arbor and Whiteside 2003); *All You Need to Be Impossibly French* (Powell 2006); *The French Diet* (Montignac 2005); and *The French Don't Diet Plan* (Clower 2006). Books highlighting the lifestyle approaches of other cultures include *Mediterranean Women Stay Slim, Too* (Kelly and Adamson 2006) and *Japanese Women Don't Get Old or Fat* (Moriyama and Doyle 2005).

During the 2000s, books listing "things to do you die" also represented a trend. Patricia Schultz's "1,000 Places" travel guides inspired a cable television show as well as appearing on the *New York Times* "Advice, How-To and Miscellaneous" bestseller list multiple years (Schultz 2003 and 2007). Other variations on the theme include *2Do Before I Die* (Ogden and Day 2005), *101 Things to Do Before You Die* (Horne 2004), and *1001 Books You Must Read Before You Die* (Boxall 2006), the last title part of a series that also features volumes devoted to music albums, movies, and paintings.

Design. *What Would You Do If You Had No Fear?* (Conway 2004) follows a common handbook design. Printed in a nonstandard 5 1/2" by 7" format (making it larger than mass-market paperbacks but smaller than typical trade-quality soft covers), the book is structured for multiple readings. It is a collection of anecdotes and meditations, primarily from participants in the author's workshops and from her own life. Each anecdote—usually less than five pages long—is given its own title and an epigraph; Conway sometimes concludes the anecdote with another quotation. Then she lists three "Life Challenges" derived from the anecdote for the reader to pursue.

For instance, in "Be Real," Conway begins with a quotation from the Chinese philosopher Lao-Tzu (approximately sixth century B.C.E.): "When you are content to be simply yourself and don't compare or compete, everyone will respect you." She then discusses issues of authenticity and insecurity, incorporating quotations from some of her students and relating how she coped with being raped when she was thirty-four. After emphasizing the value of learning to say "a strong, nonnegotiable 'no'," Conway bookends the discussion with a second quotation from Anonymous: "If I be you, who'll be me?" She then issues three life challenges:

> Take a self-defense class.
>
> Ask who you need to say "no" to. Say it.
>
> Take a meditation class or listen to a guided meditation CD. (Conway 2004, 104–108)

Authenticity (Cappannelli and Cappannelli 2004) displays an identical structure. For instance, one of its chapters is titled "What Needs to Be Done Is (Only) the Doing" and opens with a quote from journalist I.F. Stone (1907–1989). The authors discuss the issue of "the difference between real and imagined action," propose strategies for overcoming one's tendency to overthink, and end with "Today's Reflection," a section in boldface type that concludes, "Today, I will do the next physical actions. Today I will invite greater authenticity and originality in my life" (Cappannelli and Cappannelli 2004, 163–166).

In similar fashion, *The Happiness Makeover* includes fifty-three short chapters with titles such as "What's So Bad About Getting Your Hopes Up?" and "Accept the Duty of Delight" sandwiched by sections on "You Can Be Happier," "Twenty-two Instant Happiness Boosters," and "Loving Your Life." Every section and chapter begins with a quotation; the sources range from anonymous bumper stickers ("Don't believe everything you think") to Isaac Bashevis Singer (1902–1991) and Lao-Tzu (the latter a favorite of such handbooks; words attributed to him also appear in Cappannelli and Cappannelli 2004 and many others). Many of the chapters end with quotations as well, from luminaries such as poet William Butler Yeats (1865–1939) to guests on *Oprah* (Ryan 2005).

Although it is aimed at a hip-hop demographic, *Make It Happen* also follows this basic scheme. Each chapter corresponds to a rule, such as "Rule 1: Find Your Will" and "Rule 10: Flex Purpose, Not Power," with epigraphs from rap stars such as Eminem (b. 1972), Jay-Z (b. 1968), and Kanye West (b. 1977). At the end of each chapter, the "What," "Why," "How," and "But" of each rule is reiterated in the form of a chart (Liles 2005).

Displaying inspirational quotations in the page margins is also a favored tactic. Some books are designed with extra-wide margins to accommodate this; *The Authentic Career* is an example of this strategy (Craddock 2004). In others, such as Judith Wright's books, the quotations are embedded in the page layout as blocks of text with a gray background and border to set them apart from the main content. Pat Croce's *110%* (2001) features two quotations at the top of each section in oversize type, with the title in even larger type in the middle of the page; the lower half of each page contains an average of 3–5 short paragraphs offering the reader suggestions for perspective and action.

Referencing other self-help works and authors is another common practice in this genre. In *The Renaissance Soul,* Lobenstine's citations include *Free to Succeed* (Reinhold 2001), *Wishcraft* (Sher and Gottlieb 2003), a half-dozen how-to books, and *The Artist's Way* (Cameron 1992) (Lobenstine 2006, 145, 157, 160, 281). In the first set of acknowledgments for *Be Nice or Else* (2004), hair salon mogul and motivational speaker Winn Claybaugh states that his mentors have influenced him so much "that my thoughts in this book will border between plagiarism and personal experience"; he enthusiastically describes Louise Hay, Og Mandino, Oprah Winfrey, Marianne Williamson, John Bradshaw, Gerald Jampolski, George Melton, Will Garcia, and Leo Buscaglia as some of the mentors in question (Claybaugh 2004, 191–94). Schlessinger enlists the assistance of other experts for *drlaura.com* features; for example, a column on enticing children to eat their vegetables was authored by Missy Chase Lapine, who had recently produced a book on the same topic (Lapine 2007 and 2007a). The "Reading Corner" of the Web site lists several dozen titles recommended on Schlessinger's radio show, including manuals on decluttering (cf. Peel 2007), fitness (cf. Druxman and Heaner 2007), money management (cf. Economides and Economides 2007), and child raising (cf. Blyth and Winston 2007).

Contexts and Issues. Self-help literature attracts both passionate devotees and vehement skeptics. The market for self-improvement products grew by 50% between 2000 and 2004, with over three thousand new titles published per year (Salerno 2005, 7–8). Some analysts have attributed the surge of interest in the genre to the economic uncertainty and social instability that many individuals felt during this period, prompting them to consult advice manuals as a means of obtaining or regaining control over their lives (cf. McGee 2005, 12–13).

As noted earlier, some self-help authorities readily encourage their readers to make use of the "mountains of motivational messages available" (Croce 2001, 50), and women's magazines such as *Good Housekeeping* regularly quote from published books in their feature articles. Others position themselves as mavericks or contrarians offering common-sense alternatives to mainstream advice. For instance, in *BeliefWorks,* Ray Dodd discusses "seven secret keys" that he insists "are not really secrets at all . . . there is nothing contained in this book you didn't already know" (Dodd 2006, 140). Although Dodd frequently resorts to mystical and elemental terms to discuss dreams and energy, he also devotes a chapter to disputing "the myth of self-improvement," asserting that it can exacerbate one's problems rather than address them. Mireille Guiliano orders her readers to "Banish the diet book! You don't need an ideology or a technology, you need what French women have: a balanced and time-tested relation to food and life" (Guiliano 2005, 6–7). Consultant Jack M. Zufelt openly opposes traditional methods such as goal-setting and affirmations, asserting that other self-help authorities are "wasting people's time and money" (Anderson 2003). The authors of *Authenticity* take pains to stress that their book is different than what they perceive to be standard fare:

[T]his is not one of those soft and fuzzy books that promise you the moon and suggest you can have it effortlessly and immediately. In our experience, finding greater meaning and purpose requires a good deal more than that. . . . we have done our best to avoid the 'chewing-gum answers' and 'feel-good strategies' that tend to evaporate almost as soon as the page is turned or the speaker has left the podium. We also hold too much respect for you to sugarcoat our message. Frankly, we feel the world already has far too much polite information that does not advance our lives. (Cappannelli and Cappannelli 2004, xiii–xiv).

In *The Last Self-Help Book You'll Ever Need,* Paul Pearsall summarizes what he sees as ten tenets of standard self-help advice (including "Thou shalt never be less than thou can be") and then counters them with his "Ten Contrary Commandments" ("Thou shalt celebrate what thou already art") (Pearsall 2005, 80–81). He also devotes space to why he's "Had My Fill of Dr. Phil," citing an interview in which he'd seen "all the toxic elements of self-helpism: compliant thinking, the primacy of celebrity, the application of 'soft science'" (29). One online consultant, Steve Pavlina, deliberately uses the term "personal development" instead of "self-help" to describe his work because "I really don't want to be associated with marketers who promise quick-fix solutions to very difficult human challenges" (Pavlina 2006).

The industry has been the target of a number of books and articles criticizing its practices, which some observers regard as ineffectual at best and predatory at worst. Charges leveled against self-help gurus include fostering unrealistic expectations, promoting unscientific thinking, and judgmental, disingenuous, or hypocritical behavior (cf. Aviram 2001; Anderson 2003; Miller 2005; Hari 2007). The celebrity worship accorded to charismatic but ethically challenged personalities such as Tony Robbins (b. 1960) has also provoked concern and outrage among nonparticipants (Salerno 2005, 75–87).

Mariva Aviram, a self-professed former "self-help addict," argues that many readers do not have the resources to adhere to the programs presented to them, skewering instructions such as "If you have too much to do, delegate tasks to others" with comments such as "This simplistic piece of advice is only useful to a wealthy neurotic workaholic, who, come to think of it, is the self-help market's best friend" (Aviram 2001). Pearsall likewise notes that "self-help books aren't written for the poor," but for dissatisfied middle class workers with the leisure to indulge in self-centeredness (Pearsall 2005, 12).

The strategies promoted in relationship guides such as *The Rules* (Fein and Schneider 1995) and *He's Just Not That into You* (Behrendt and Tuccillo 2004) continue to inspire controversy over whether they are effective, honest, and healthy practices for modern women to follow. Proponents of such strategies argue that they are realistic about gender-based behavior (rather than pretending the differences do not exist) and that they build and reinforce women's self-esteem by urging them not to accept demeaning treatment from insufficiently interested men. Detractors of such books see them as manuals for manipulative mind games and overly simplistic in their characterizations of how relationships should work (e.g., Traister 2004).

Reception. On a less cynical note, the "Books for a Better Life Awards" are a major fundraiser for the New York City chapter of the National Multiple Sclerosis Society, having raised over a million dollars since the program's inception in 1996. The annual awards recognize "the very best in self-improvement publishing" in nine categories: childcare/parenting, first book, inspirational memoir, motivational, personal finance, psychology, relationships, spiritual, and wellness. There is a "Hall of Fame" associated with the event; its members include Jane Brody, Helen Gurley Brown, Deepak Chopra, Dr. Wayne Dyer, Oscar Dystel, John Gray, Judy Collins, Laurence Kirshbaum, Heidi Murkoff, Suzanne Somers, Andrew Weil, Jack Canfield, Mark Victor Hansen, and Peter Workman. The "first book" award is named after Suze Orman.

AWARD-WINNING SELF-HELP BOOKS

Recent winners of "Books for a Better Life Awards" have included these 2006 self-help titles: *Packaging Girlhood: Rescuing Our Daughters from Marketers' Schemes* by Sharon Lamb, Ed.D. and Lyn Miken Brown, Ed.D.; *Social Intelligence: The New Science of Human Relationships* by Daniel Goleman; *What To Eat* by Marion Nestle (North Point Press); and *Crazy Busy: Overstretched, Overbooked and About to Snap* by Ned Hallowell, M.D.

The titles of some self-help guides have become catchphrases that remain in active circulation long after the books' sales have peaked. For instance, the term "Rules Girl" has become shorthand for women who believe in playing "hard to get," as advised by *The Rules* (Fein and Schneider 1995). The concept of "He's just not that into you," made popular through the book of the same name (Behrendt and Tuccillo 2004), has been riffed upon by sportswriters (Plaschke 2007), bloggers on politics and business (Beasley 2007; Fried 2007), and other pundits in discussing situations where they perceive an imbalance of interest among the parties involved.

As with many other genres, a successful self-help book is likely to spawn sequels, accessories, imitators, counterarguments, and parodies. *The Rules* (Fein and Schneider 1995) was followed by *The Rules II: More Rules to Live and Love By* (1997), *The Rules for Marriage: Time-Tested Secrets for Making Your Marriage Work* (2001), and *Rules for Online Dating: Capturing the Heart of Mr. Right in Cyberspace* (2002). Responses to *The Rules* include Barbara De Angelis's *The Real Rules: How to Find the Right Man for the Real You* (1997). Parodies include Nate Penn and Lawrence LaRose's *The Code: Time-Tested Secrets for Getting What You Want from Women—Without Marrying Them!* (1996). It has been cited in attempts to describe other books, such as *What Southern Women Know (That Every Woman Should): Timeless Secrets To Get Everything You Want in Love, Life, and Work* (Rich 1999), which the publisher continues to promote as "*A Southern Belle Primer* meets *The Rules*" (Penguin Group 2007). The authors of *How to Date Like a Man* begin their book by summarizing the plateau they believe their typical reader has reached: "You've tried the Rules, you've tried listening to your married friends, and you've even tried listening to your mother. But you're still eating Chinese takeout with your good *Friends* Monica, Rachel, Ross and Chandler" (Moore and Gould 2000, 3).

Parodies of *The Seven Habits of Highly Effective People* have included *The 7 Habits of Highly Ineffective People* (Minor 1994), the *7 Habits of Highly Defective People* (Crimmins and Maeder 1996), a *McSweeney*'s list (Lloyd n.d.). Dr. Phil is well-known enough to be cited and spoofed on assorted television shows and movies, and he was the inspiration for a *Sesame Street* character called "Dr. Feel."

Dr. Laura, herself parodied on shows such as *Frasier* and *The West Wing*, cheerfully collaborated with the manufacturers of the "Dr. Laura Talking Action Figure," advertising it on her site with the headline "What's Blonde, VERY Talkative, and comes in a Fabulous Package?" The FlyLady shop includes ostrich feather dusters and timers. The wares of diet-related franchises may include aprons, whereas calendars are a staple of time-management programs. Clothing, coffee mugs, jewelry, key rings, license-plate holders, and other items also serve to promote popular brands or concepts.

Selected Authors. The self-help movement does not lack for prominent authors, many of whom have been mentioned already in this entry. Other individuals whose influence was substantial during the first decade of the twenty-first century follow.

Robert Kiyosaki (b. 1947) promotes his investment theories via the "Rich Dad, Poor Dad" series, which includes titles such as *Rich Dad's Escape from the Rat Race* (2005), *Rich Dad's Guide to Becoming Rich without Cutting up Your Credit Cards* (2003), and *Rich Dad's Before You Quit Your Job* (2005).

Dave Ramsey (b. 1960) is another financial advisor, known for his tough-love crusade against debt, which he communicates primarily through his radio show. Ramsey's no-nonsense demeanor and faith-based lifestyle appeal to listeners who regard him as a type of fiscal pastor. As one reporter summed up, "There are thousands of personal finance experts (or 'experts'). There is even a competitive industry of *Christian* personal finance experts. Yet there is only one guy—one bald, middle-aged Christian money guy—who's a favorite of both *60 Minutes* and *The 700 Club*" (Drury 2007). Ramsey's books include *Total Money Makeover* (2007) and *Financial Peace Revisited* (2003), both of which have been republished in updated editions. As with Dr. Laura, Ramsey's Web site includes a reading recommendations section, organized into topical lists that include "Christian Devotional" and fiction titles as well as business and finance classics by Carnegie and others.

One of the leading names in literature on eating disorders is Geneen Roth. The majority of her books were published in the 1990s, but she remains active as a magazine columnist and workshop leader. Spiritual advisor Iyalna Vanzant likewise remains in demand as an instructor and lecturer, although interest in her books appeared to have peaked by 2001.

In the area of creative expression, Julia Cameron (b. 1948) remains active. The "morning pages" ritual featured in *The Artist's Way* (a writing exercise to be performed upon rising every morning) has become a routine practiced by numerous writers; Cameron's follow-up titles have included *The Sound of Paper* (2004), *How to Avoid Making Art* (2005), *and Finding Water* (2006). Susan Ariel Rainbow Kennedy (b. 1954), better known by her initials (SARK), employs a distinctive, colorful style to letter and illustrate her books, cards, and posters; her exuberance is also very much in evidence on her Web site, "Planet Sark," which includes a tribute to her mother titled "Marvelous Marjorie" and an interactive feature where users can consult with her cat Jupiter as a clickable oracle. Her recent publications include *Eat Mangoes Naked* (2001), *Make Your Creative Dreams Real* (2004) and *Fabulous Friendship Festival* (2007).

Bibliography

Allen, David. *Getting Things Done: The Art of Stress-Free Productivity.* New York: Penguin, 2001.

Amodeo, John. *The Authentic Heart: An Eightfold Path to Midlife Love.* New York: Wiley, 2001.

Anderson, Adrienne. "The Last Word on Self-Help?" *Denver Business Journal* 23 June 2003.

Arbor, Robert, and Katherine Whiteside. *Joie de Vivre: Simple French Style for Everyday Living.* New York: Simon & Schuster, 2003.

Argov, Sherry. *Why Men Love Bitches: From Doormat to Dreamgirl—A Woman's Guide to Holding Her Own in a Relationship.* Avon, MA: Adams, 2002.

———. *Why Men Marry Bitches: A Woman's Guide to Winning Her Man's Heart.* New York: Simon & Schuster, 2006.

Aviram, Mariva H. "The Self-Help Industry: New Year's Day Is the Holiday of Self-improvement Junkies." (1 Jan. 2001) www.mariva.com.

Beasley, Ron. "He's just not that into you." *Middle Earth Journal.* (27 April 2007). http://ronbeas2.blogspot.com/2007/04/hes-just-not-that-into-you.html.

Behrendt, Greg, and Amiira Ruotola-Behrendt. *It's Called a Breakup Because It's Broken: The Smart Girl's Breakup Buddy*. New York: Broadway, 2005.

Behrendt, Greg, and Liz Tuccillo. *He's Just Not That Into You: The No-Excuses Truth to Understanding Guys*. New York: Simon Spotlight Entertainment, 2004.

Birkenhead, Peter. "Oprah's Ugly Secret." *Salon*. (5 March 2007). http://www.salon.com/mwt/feature/2007/03/05/the_secret.

Block, Peter. *The Answer to How Is Yes*. San Francisco: Berrett-Koehler, 2002.

Blyth, Myrna, and Chriss Winston. *How to Raise an American: 1776 Fun and Easy Tools, Tips, and Activities to Help Your Child Love This Country*. New York: Crown Forum, 2007.

Boxall, Peter, ed. *1001 Books You Must Read Before You Die*. New York: Universe, 2006.

Braiker, Harriet B. *The Disease to Please: Curing the People-Pleasing Syndrome*. New York: McGraw-Hill, 2001.

Breathnach, Sarah Ban. *Something More: Excavating Your Authentic Self*. New York: Time Warner, 1998.

Browne, Jill Conner. *The Sweet Potato Queens' Wedding Planner: The Sweet Potato Queens' Divorce Guide*. New York: Crown, 2005.

———. *The Sweet Potato Queens' Field Guide to Men: Every Man I Love is Either Married, Gay, or Dead*. New York: Three Rivers, 2004.

———. *The Sweet Potato Queens' Big-Ass Cookbook (and Financial Planner)*. New York: Three Rivers, 2003.

———. *God Save the Sweet Potato Queens*. New York: Three Rivers, 2001.

———. *The Sweet Potato Queens' Book of Love*. New York: Three Rivers, 1999.

Bryson, Kelly. *Don't Be Nice, Be Real: Balancing Passion for Self with Compassion for Others*. 2nd ed. Santa Rosa, CA: Elite, 2004.

Byrne, Rhonda. *The Secret*. New York: Atria/Beyond Words, 2006.

Cameron, Julia. *Finding Water: The Art of Perseverance*. New York: Tarcher/Penguin, 2006.

———. *How to Avoid Making Art (Or Anything Else You Enjoy)*. New York: Tarcher/-Penguin, 2005.

———. *The Sound of Paper: Starting From Scratch*. New York: Tarcher/Penguin, 2004.

——— *The Artist's Way: A Spiritual Path to Higher Creativity*. 10th Anniversary Edition. New York: Tarcher/Penguin, 2002.

Cappannelli, George, and Sedena Cappannelli. *Authenticity: Simple Strategies for Greater Meaning and Purpose at Work and at Home*. Cincinnati: Emmis, 2004.

Cilley, Marla. *Sink Reflections: Overwhelmed? Disorganized? Living in Chaos? The FlyLady's Simple FLYing Lessons Will Show You How to Get Your Home and Your Life in Order—and It All Starts with Shining Your Sink!* New York: Bantam, 2002.

Cilley, Marla, and Leanne Ely. *Body Clutter: Love Your Body, Love Yourself*. New York: Simon & Schuster, 2006.

Claybaugh, Winn. *Be Nice (Or Else!) And What's In It For You*. Laguna Beach, CA: Von Curtis, 2004. http://www.BeNiceOrElse.com.

Clower, Will. *The French Don't Diet Plan: 10 Simple Steps to Stay Thin for Life*. New York: Crown, 2006.

Conway, Diane. *What Would You Do If You Had No Fear? Living Your Dreams While Quakin' in Your Boots*. Maui: Inner Ocean, 2004.

Coughlin, Paul. *No More Jellyfish, Chickens, or Wimps: Raising Secure, Assertive Kids in a Tough World*. Bloomington, Minnesota: Bethany, 2007.

———. *No More Christian Nice Guy: When Being Nice—Instead of Good—Hurts Men, Women And Children*. Bloomington, Minnesota: Bethany, 2005.

Covey, Stephen R. *The 8th Habit: From Effectiveness to Greatness*. New York: Free Press, 2004.

———. *The Seven Habits of Highly Effective Families*. New York: Golden, 1997.

———. *The Seven Habits of Highly Effective People: Restoring the Character Ethic*. New York: Simon & Schuster, 1989.

Covey, Stephen R., A. Roger Merrill, and Rebecca R. Merrill. *First Things First: To Live, to Love, to Learn, to Leave a Legacy.* New York: Fireside, 1994.

Craddock, Maggie. *The Authentic Career: Following the Path of Self-Discovery to Professional Fulfillment.* Novato, California: New World Library, 2004.

Croce, Pat, with Bill Lyon. *110%: 110 Strategies for Feeling Great.* Philadelphia: Running Press, 2001.

Crofts, Neil. *Authentic Business: How to Create and Run Your Perfect Business.* Chichester, United Kingdom: Capstone/Wiley, 2005.

———. Authentic: *How to Make a Living Being Yourself.* Chichester, UK: Capstone/Wiley, 2003.

Deida, David. *The Way of The Superior Man: A Spiritual Guide to Mastering the Challenges of Woman, Work, and Sexual Desire.* Boulder, Colorado: Sounds True, 2004.

Dodd, Ray. *BeliefWorks: The Art of Living Your Dreams.* Charlottesville, VA: Hampton Roads, 2006.

Drury, Susan. "The Gospel According to Dave." *Nashville Scene* (31 May 2007).

Druxman, Lisa, with Martica Heaner. *Lean Mommy: Bond With Your Baby and Get Fit With the Stroller Strides Program.* New York: Center Street, 2007.

Economides, Steve, and Annette Economides. *America's Cheapest Family Gets You Right On the Money: Your Guide to Living Better, Spending Less, and Cashing In On Your Dreams.* New York: Three Rivers, 2007.

Ely, Leanne. *Saving Dinner the Vegetarian Way: Healthy Menus, Recipes, and Shopping Lists to Keep Everyone Happy at the Table.* New York: Ballantine, 2007.

———. *Saving Dinner Basics: How to Cook Even If You Don't Know How.* New York: Ballantine, 2006.

———. *Saving Dinner for the Holidays: Menus, Recipes, Shopping Lists, and Timelines for Spectacular, Stress-free Holidays and Family Celebrations.* New York: Ballantine, 2005.

———. *Saving Dinner the Low-Carb Way: Healthy Menus, Recipes, and the Shopping Lists That Will Keep the Whole Family at the Dinner Table.* New York: Ballantine, 2005.

———. *Saving Dinner: The Menus, Recipes, and Shopping Lists to Bring Your Family Back To the Table.* New York: Ballantine, 2003.

Fein, Ellen, and Sherrie Schneider. *The Rules: Time-Tested Secrets for Capturing the Heart of Mr. Right.* New York: Warner, 1995.

Fried, Wendy. "He's Just Not That into You." *Proxyland* (26 March 2007). http://proxyland.blogspot.com/2007/03/hes-just-not-that-into-you.html.

Gelb, Michael J. *Da Vinci Decoded: Discovering the Spiritual Secrets of Leonardo's Seven Principles.* New York: Delacorte, 2004.

———. *How to Think Like Leonardo da Vinci: Seven Steps to Genius Every Day.* New York: Delacorte, 1998.

Glover, Robert A. *No More Mr. Nice Guy! A Proven Plan for Getting What You Want in Love, Sex, and Life.* Philadelphia: Running Press, 2003.

Goodman, Michelle. *The Anti 9 to 5 Guide: Practical Career Advice for Women Who Think Outside the Cube.* Emeryville, California: Seal, 2007. http://www.anti9to5guide.com.

Guiliano, Mireille. *French Women for All Seasons: A Year of Secrets, Recipes and Pleasure.* New York: Borzoi/Knopf, 2006.

———. *French Women Don't Get Fat: The Secret of Eating for Pleasure.* New York: Borzoi/Knopf, 2005.

Hari, Johann. "The Selfishness of the Self-Help Industry: The Cult of Positive Thinking Blames All The People Who Falter or Fail in Life for Their Own Misfortune." UK *Independent* (12 April 2007). http://www.commondreams.org/archive/2007/ 04/12/469.

Hendrix, Harville. *Keeping the Love You Find: A Guide for Singles.* New York: Pocket, 1992.

———. Getting *the Love You Want: A Guide for Couples.* New York: Holt, 1988. http://www.gettingtheloveyouwant.com.

Hendrix, Harville, and Helen LaKelly Hunt. 2004. *Receiving Love: Transform Your Relationship by Letting Yourself Be Loved.* New York: Atria, 2004.

———. *Giving the Love That Heals: A Guide for Parents.* New York: Pocket, 1997.

Hicks, Esther, and Jerry Hicks. *The Law of Attraction: The Basics of the Teachings of Abraham.* Carlsbad, CA: Hay House, 2006.

Horne, Richard. *101 Things to Do Before You Die.* New York: Bloomsbury, 2004.

Jacobsen, Wayne, and Clay Jacobsen. *Authentic Relationships: Discover the Lost Art of "One Anothering."* Grand Rapids, Michigan: Baker Books, 2003.

Jansen, Julie. *I Don't Know What I Want, But I Know It's Not This: A Step-by-Step Guide to Finding Gratifying Work.* New York: Penguin, 2003.

Jones, Blackwolf, and Gina Jones. *Sacred Self, Sacred Relationships: Healing the World for Seven Generations.* Center City, Minnesota: Hazelden, 2002.

Katz, Elliot. *Being the Strong Man a Woman Wants: Timeless Wisdom on Being a Man.* Toronto: Award, 2005.

Kelly, Melissa, and Eve Adamson. *Mediterranean Women Stay Slim, Too: Eating to Be Sexy, Fit, and Fabulous!* Text by Amaranth Illuminare. New York: HarperCollins, 2006.

Kerner, Ian. *Be Honest—You're Not That Into Him Either: Raise Your Standards and Reach for the Love You Deserve.* New York: Regan Books, 2005.

Kiyosaki, Robert T., with Sharon L. Lechter. *Rich Dad's Escape From the Rat Race: How to Become a Rich Kid by Following Rich Dad's Advice.* New York: Little, Brown, 2005.

———. *Rich Dad's Before You Quit Your Job: 10 Real-Life Lessons Every Entrepreneur Should Know About Building a Multimillion-dollar Business.* New York: Warner, 2005.

———. *Rich Dad's Guide to Becoming Rich Without Cutting Up Your Credit Cards.* New York: Warner, 2003.

Klein, Karin. "Self-help Gone Nutty." *Los Angeles Times* (13 February 2007).

Lapine, Missy Chase. *The Sneaky Chef: Simple Strategies for Hiding Healthy Foods in Kids' Favorite Meals.* Philadelphia: Running Press, 2007.

———. "No Veggie Left Behind." (16 July 2007) http://www.drlaura.com/sah/budget.html.

Lasser, Jonathan. n.d. Review of Behrendt and Tuccillo about.com. (2004). [Accessed June 25, 2007.]

Liles, Kevin, with Samantha Marshall. *Make It Happen: From Intern to President: The Hip-Hop Generation Guide to Success.* New York: Atria, 2005.

Lloyd, Brendon. "7 Habits of Highly Successful People." McSweeney's Internet Tendency. (n.d.) [Accessed July 15, 2007.]

Lobenstine, Margaret. *The Renaissance Soul: Life Design for People with Too Many Passions to Pick Just One.* New York: Broadway, 2006.

LoPorto, Garret. *The DaVinci Method: Break Out and Express Your Fire.* Concord, MA: Media for Your Mind, 2005.

Losier, Michael. *Law of Attraction: The Science of Attracting More of What You Want and Less of What You Don't.* New York: Wellness Central, 2004.

Mandela, Nelson. "Oprah Winfrey." ["Time 100" listing, "Heroes and Pioneers" category.] *Time* (14 May 2007). http://www.time.com/time/specials/2007/time100.

Martin, Courtney E. "Oprah's 'Secret' Could Be Your Downfall." AlterNet (26 March 2007). http://www.alternet.org/movies/49591.

McGee, Micki. *Self-Help, Inc.: Makeover Culture in American Life.* New York: Oxford, 2005.

McGraw, [Dr.] Phil. *Love Smart: Find the One You Want, Fix the One You Got.* New York: Free Press, 2006.

———. *Family First: Your Step-by-Step Plan for Creating a Phenomenal Family.* New York: Free Press, 2005.

———. *The Ultimate Weight Solution: The 7 Keys to Weight Loss Freedom.* New York: Free Press, 2003.

————. *Self Matters: Creating Your Life from the Inside Out*. New York: Simon & Schuster Source, 2001.

————. *Relationship Rescue: A Seven Step Strategy for Reconnecting With Your Partner*. New York: Hyperion, 2000.

Meadows, Truxton. n.d. "Interview with Paul Coughlin." One Flew Over The Church. http://www.oneflewoverthechurch.com/interviews/PaulCoughlin.html. [Accessed July 29, 2007.]

Metcalfe, Gayden, and Charlotte Hays. *Somebody is Going to Die if Lilly Beth Doesn't Catch That Bouquet: The Official Southern Ladies Guide to Hosting the Perfect Wedding*. New York: Hyperion, 2007.

————. *Being Dead Is No Excuse: The Official Southern Ladies Guide to Hosting the Perfect Funeral*. New York: Hyperion, 2005.

Mininni, Darlene. *The Emotional Toolkit: Seven Power-Skills to Nail Your Bad Feelings*. New York: St. Martin's, 2005.

Miller, Laura. "Self-help Nation." Salon.com (12 August 2005).

Minor IV, Herman. *The Seven Habits of Highly Ineffective People: Low-Effort Lessons In Mismanaging For Success*. New York: Carol, 1994.

Montignac, Michel. *The French Diet: The Secrets of Why French Women Don't Get Fat*. New York: DK, 2005.

Moore, Myreah, and Jodie Gould. *Date Like a Man: What Men Know About Dating and Are Afraid You'll Find Out*. New York: HarperCollins, 2000. [2001 paperback edition cited.]

Moriyama, Naomi, and William Doyle. *Japanese Women Don't Get Old or Fat: Secrets of My Mother's Tokyo Kitchen*. New York: Delacorte, 2005.

Ogden, Michael, and Chris Day. *2Do Before I Die: The Do-It-Yourself Guide to the Rest of Your Life*. New York: Little, Brown, 2005.

Ollivier, Debra. *Entre Nous: A Woman's Guide to Finding Her Inner French Girl*. New York: St. Martin's, 2003.

Patcher, Barbara, with Susan McGee. *The Power of Positive Confrontation: The Skills You Need to Know to Handle Conflicts at Work, at Home and in Life*. New York: Marlowe/Avalon, 2000.

Pavlina, Steve. "Is Self-Help a Scam?" *Personal Development for Smart People* (13 March 2006). http://www.stevepavlina.com/blog/2006/03/is-self-help-a-scam.

Pearsall, Paul. *The Last Self-Help Book You'll Ever Need: Repress Your Anger, Think Negatively, Be a Good Blamer, and Throttle your Inner Child*. New York: Basic, 2005.

Peel, Kathy. *Desperate Households: How to Restore Order and Harmony to Your Life and Home*. Carol Stream, Illinois: Picket Fence, 2007.

Penguin Group. Catalog copy for Rich 1999. 2007. http://us.penguingroup.com/nf/Book/BookDisplay/0,,9780399526275,00.html.

Plaschke, Bill. "He's just not that into you." *Los Angeles Times* (20 June 2007).

Powell, Helena Frith. *All You Need to Be Impossibly French: A Witty Investigation into the Lives, Lusts, and Little Secrets of French Women*. New York: Plume/Penguin, 2006.

Ramsey, Dave. *The Total Money Makeover: A Proven Plan for Financial Fitness*. Revised edition. Nashville: Thomas Nelson, 2007.

————. *Financial Peace Revisited*. New York: Viking, 2003.

Randol, Susan. *Live Your Best Life: A Treasury of Wisdom, Wit, Advice, Interviews, and Inspiration from O, The Oprah Magazine*. Birmingham, AL: Oxmoor, 2005.

Rapson, James, and Craig English. *Anxious to Please: 7 Revolutionary Practices for the Chronically Nice*. Naperville, Illinois: Sourcebooks, 2006.

Reinhold, Barbara B. *Free to Succeed: Designing the Life You Want in the New Free Agent Economy*. New York: Plume, 2001.

Rich, Ronda. *What Southern Women Know About Flirting: The Fine Art of Social, Courtship, and Seductive Flirting to Get the Best Things in Life*. New York: Penguin Perigee, 2005.

———. *What Southern Women Know (That Every Woman Should): Timeless Secrets To Get Everything You Want in Love, Life, and Work*. New York: Penguin Perigee, 1999.

Robinson, Duke. *Too Nice For Your Own Good: How to Stop Making 9 Self-Sabotaging Mistakes*. New York: Warner, 2000.

Ryan, M.J. *The Happiness Makeover: How to Teach Yourself to be Happy and Enjoy Every Day*. New York: Broadway, 2005.

Sabatino, Colleen A. *The Play of Your Life: Your Program for Finding the Career of Your Dreams—and a Step-by-Step Guide to Making It a Reality*. Emmaus, Pennsylvania: Rodale, 2004.

Salerno, Steve. *SHAM: How the Self-Help Movement Made America Helpless*. New York: Crown, 2005.

Salkin, Allen. "Shaking Riches Out of the Cosmos: Rivals Claim Credit for The Secret, a DVD and Book that Promote the Power of Wishful Thinking." *New York Times* (25 February 2007).

Saltz, Gail. *Becoming Real: Defeating the Stories We Tell Ourselves That Hold Us Back*. New York: Riverhead, 2004.

SARK. *Fabulous Friendship Festival: Loving Wildly, Learning Deeply, Living Fully with Our Friends*. New York: Three Rivers.

———. *Make Your Creative Dreams Real: A Plan for Procrastinators, Perfectionists, Busy People, and People Who Would Really Rather Sleep All Day*. New York: Fireside, 2004.

———. *Eat Mangoes Naked: Finding Pleasure Everywhere (and Dancing With the Pits)*. New York: Fireside, 2001.

Schaub, Michael. Review of Indante and Marks 2003. *Bookslut* (October 2003). http://www.bookslut.com/propaganda/2003_10_000777.php.

Schlessinger, [Dr.] Laura. *Bad Childhood, Good Life: How to Blossom and Thrive in Spite of an Unhappy Childhood*. New York: HarperCollins, 2006.

———. *The Proper Care and Feeding of Husbands*. New York: HarperCollins, 2004.

———. *Ten Stupid Things Couples Do to Mess Up Their Relationships*. New York: Cliff Street/HarperCollins, 2001.

———. *Ten Stupid Things Women Do To Mess Up Their Lives*. New York: Villard, 1994.

Schultz, Patricia. *1,000 Places to See in the USA and Canada Before You Die*. New York: Workman, 2007.

———. *1,000 Places to See Before You Die*. New York: Workman.

Schuman, Kenneth, and Ronald Paxton. *The Michelangelo Method: Release Your Inner Masterpiece and Create an Extraordinary Life*. New York: McGraw-Hill, 2007.

Schwartz, Maryln. *The Southern Belle Primer, or Why Princess Margaret Will Never Be a Kappa Kappa Gamma*. New York: Doubleday, 2001.

Seligman, Martin E.P. *Authentic Happiness: Using the New Positive Psychology to Realize Your Potential for Lasting Fulfillment*. New York: Free Press, 2002.

Sher, Barbara. *Refuse to Choose! Use All Your Interests, Passions, and Hobbies to Create the Life and Career of Your Dreams*. Emmaus, Pennsylvania: Rodale, 2006.

Sher, Barbara, with Annie Gottlieb. *Wishcraft: How to Get What You Really Want*. 2nd ed. New York: Ballantine, 2003. http://www.wishcraft.com.

Sher, Barbara, with Barbara Smith. *I Could Do Anything If I Only Knew What It Was: How to Discover What You Really Want and How to Get It*. New York: Dell, 1994.

Time. "Time 25." *Time* (17 June 1996). http://www.time.com/time/magazine/article/0,9171,984696,00.html.

Traister, Rebecca. "He loves me, he loves me not." [Review of Behrendt and Tuccillo 2004.] *Salon.com* (6 December 2004).

Ursiny, Tim. *The Coward's Guide to Conflict: Empowering Solutions for Those Who Would Rather Run Than Fight*. Naperville, Illinois: Sourcebooks, 2003.

Whitman, Danielle, pseud. *He Just Thinks He's Not That Into You: The Insanely Determined Girl's Guide to Getting the Man You Want*. Philadelphia: Running Press, 2007.

Widener, Chris. *The Angel Inside: Michelangelo's Secrets for Following Your Passion and Finding the Work You Love.* New York: Currency/Doubleday, 2004. http://www.TheAngelInside.com.

Wright, Judith. *The Soft Addiction Solution: Break Free of the Seemingly Harmless Habits That Keep You from the Life You Want.* New York: Penguin, 2006.

———. 2005. *The One Decision: Make the Single Choice That Will Lead To a Life of MORE.* NewYork: Tarcher/Penguin, 2005.

Young, Pamela, and Peggy Jones. *Sidetracked Home Executives: From Pigpen to Paradise.* New York: Warner, 2001.

Further Reading

Davey, Steve. *Unforgettable Places to See Before You Die.* New York: Firefly, 2004; Indante, Dan, and Karl Marks, pseud. *The Complete A**hole's Guide to Handling Chicks.* New York: St. Martin's, 2003; http://www.theartistsway.com; Butler-Bowdon, Tom. *50 Self-Help Classics: 50 Inspirational Books to Transform Your Life.* Yarmouth, Maine: Nicholas Brealey, 2003; http://www.butler-bowdon.com; http://www.davidco.com; http://www.flylady.net; http://www.franklincovey.com; http://www.oprah.com; http://www.planetsark.com.

PEGGY LIN DUTHIE

SERIES FICTION

Definition. The difficulty in evaluating series fiction results from the various categories that make up the separate category of installment fiction. The terms trilogy, series, multi-part novels, sequence, sagas, and shared universes can be slippery. For example, Isaac Asimov's *Foundation* series and Richard Adams's *Hitchhiker's Guide to the Galaxy* both began as trilogies and then were later added to so that the scope of the original trilogy expanded to a series.

Books published in installments, such as trilogies or tetralogies, are not technically series according to most publisher designations. A trilogy such as J.R.R. Tolkien's *The Lord of the Rings,* for example, is one story divided by the publisher into publishable chunks. As with most trilogies, the story begins in volume one and is completed in volume three. A series, on the other hand, although featuring the same characters and locations, is made up of individually published books with stand-alone plots that can be read without any familiarity with earlier books in the series.

Context and Issues. According to Shannon Hill, an editor at Christian publisher WaterBrook, readers are drawn to series because they allow them to feel they are part of a larger community. (Winner, S10). There is a sense of familiarity that is comforting. Of course this can be said of all series fiction, not just those series with religious overtones. Readers of series fiction can return to a world over and again and join their favorite characters and wander in their favorite locations. Although the plot may be new, the reader can be certain that the experience will be the same.

Series fiction writers work quickly, often giving way to stereotypes and sloppy editing, which in part contributes to the poor critical reception they receive. Many authors release two or three titles per year in order to keep up with the demands of readers. The quality of series varies dramatically, and the success of an author is often based on the character created. In series fiction, the main character may grow but does not change drastically over time. Careers may change and locations may alter, but the inherent qualities of the character remain and are what draw the reader back to share adventures with him or her over and over.

The best series feature characters are well-rounded and grow as the books progress. Often producing works at least indirectly chronological, respected series writers introduce changes into their characters' lives that echo real life changes: career changes, marriage, family, illness (their own or their friends and families), and even death of loved ones. Often derided are those series that are cranked out quickly and follow a formulaic plot template. Although books in these series follow the same characters through many adventures, the characters do not grow or develop in any perceptible ways and the plots are shallow and often contrived. They are riddled with inconsistencies and rarely relate to any previous novels in the series. Children's fiction series and series romances are most frequently targeted with this criticism.

History. In the nineteenth century the growth of the novel as a form and the marketplace as being able to produce buyers of books spurred the development of series novels. On the British front, Mrs. Oliphant's *Chronicles of Carlingford*, Anthony Trollope's *Barsetshire* series, and Sir Walter Scott's *Waverly Novels* were just a few of the popular series offerings. Storylines tracing the rise and fall of families, the changes in a village or city, and the adventures of individual heroes provided their authors a handsome living. In North America, James Fenimore Cooper's *The Leatherstocking Tales* stories embodied the ideal rugged American heroes, and Hawkeye and Natty Bumpo were vastly popular (*The Pioneers* 1823, *The Last of the Mohicans* 1826, *The Deerslayer* 1840).

Eventually, characters from the dime or adventure papers, which were mostly geared toward the lower economic classes, were developed into full length novels, mostly for children. The earliest series of stories for children were overtly moralistic and didactic. They were meant as teaching tools and a way to instill good values and behavior. Horatio Alger published *Ragged Dick* in 1867. The story followed the rise of a young orphan from poverty to success. A seemingly endless stream of novels and stories by Alger continued to be released even after his death in 1899, examples of the tradition of American inventiveness and hard work.

The forty-volume series of Tom Swift books by the Edward Stratemeyer syndicate house name Victor Appleton debuted in 1910. This boy inventor series was the beginning of many that incorporated the Horatio Alger myth of American success. Stratemeyer went on to contribute such series as *Nancy Drew*, the *Hardy Boys,* and the *Bobbsey Twins,* over twenty series in all. The popularity of series fiction for young readers has been constant since the early 1900s and the Stratemeyer Syndicate, producing dozens of novels under such pseudonyms as Franklin W. Dixon and Carolyn Keene, dominated the market. According to a *Smithsonian* article on the Stratemeyer series, 98% of young readers surveyed in 1926 put Tom Swift at the top of their favorite reading list (Watson 1991, 50–59). Tom Swift would be replaced by Harry Potter today, but the love of series fiction continues.

Reception. One of the many criticisms leveled at young readers series is the media tie-ins. When Disney created the television series *Lizzie McGuire,* a book series followed. Series of books now regularly accompany television shows or films, rather than television and film reproducing shows about series (*The Chronicles of Narnia* and the Harry Potter books being notable exceptions). Critics argue that the books in these media tie-ins are of poor quality, pandering only to the desire of readers for more adventures about their favorite characters.

These early series novels are extremely important to scholars of both literature and popular culture for their insight into both what appealed to a changing

> ## "DON'T KILL SHERLOCK HOLMES!"
>
> The availability of books and the ease and relative inexpensive nature of Internet book buying has introduced readers to series and allowed them to complete series in a manner that was not possible before the late 1990s. The Internet has also changed how series are read and shaped by their audiences. Most major series have publisher-sponsored Web sites. Audiences shaped series even in the days of Arthur Conan Doyle's Sherlock Holmes stories; after killing off the tedious Holmes, the outcry of readers demanding his return prompted Doyle to bring back the character he was heartily sick of. Today's series can create enough furor that readers create their own fan sites or blogs. Reader's contributions to these blogs and Web site discussion forums have an impact on the authors and how they develop the series installments.

audience and how these books reflected a changing society. For example, in the late 1950s, the Stratemeyer Syndicate initiated an overhaul of the first 38 *Hardy Boys* titles. The books were edited to bring them up to date and in some instances to remove the racial stereotypes in earlier titles. These editorial changes, which sometimes resulted in entire rewrites of the novels, angered many fans but give a fascinating insight into a changing world and the value of nostalgia attached to childhood favorites.

Trends and Themes

Children and Young Adults. A recent reference book for librarians, *Popular Series Fiction for K-6 Readers* by Rebecca L. Thomas and Catherine Barr (2004), lists almost 1,200 series for young readers. Older series, such as the original *Nancy Drew, Hardy Boys,* and *Anne of Green Gables* are still extremely popular with young readers, but dozens of new series launched each year cater to every interest a child may have from romance to sports to careers.

Like mystery fiction for adults, mystery series for young readers continue to be popular. The *Hardy Boys,* since their 1927 debut, have been featured in five series, the most recent launched in 2005 and called the *Undercover Brothers* series. The newer *Hardy Boys* series, however, have not been as successful as the original 58, which still sell steadily. Nancy Drew, the female counterpart to the Hardy Boys has seen equal popularity over the years, with two new series begun in 2004, *The Nancy Drew Girl Detective* series and *Nancy Drew and the Clue Crew* series.

Nancy Drew was an important character who shaped fiction for girls in a positive direction. Characters such as Nancy and detective nurse Cherry Ames offered female readers characters who were independent, intelligent, and not afraid of adventure. However, romance was often a casualty of the heroine's intelligence and adventurous can-do nature. Boys who are rescued by girls apparently have little interest in pursuing romance, and romance is a hot selling feature for the contemporary girls series. The boom of girls series hit in the 1980s with Francine Pascal's *Sweet Valley High* series. Pascal's novels made a break with the formula inherent in previous series for girls. Critic Stephanie Foote argued that it is not enough for heroines to be beautiful and kind, they must be hardworking, innovative, and powerful as well (Foote 2006, 521). Characters such as Nancy Drew exemplify this ideal. Pascal and her successors, however, jumped on the bandwagon of beautiful, but left out much of the rest.

Critics find many of the newer series geared to teenaged girls to be disturbing. Their characters and locations often replicate popular television series such as the 1990s hit *Beverly Hills 90210* and the more current *OC*. The protagonists are wealthy and mostly white and spend their time in frenzied shopping, gossiping, partying, and sexual encounters in extravagant California locales. Cecily von Ziegesar's *Gossip Girl* and *It Girl* are two series in this genre. Lisi Harrison's *The Clique* enters the world of the wealthy in a series about privileged thirteen-year-olds and their machinations to get in and stay in the Clique. An unusual twist to the rich and beautiful series is Scott Westerfeld's *Uglies* series. In Westerfeld's world, when people turn sixteen, they undergo surgery that makes them supermodel beautiful. When one young girl refuses surgery and runs away, the world is turned upside down.

Although there are still plenty of mature girls series, some authors are beginning to turn away from such provocative material and are providing girls with series that are more realistic and familiar to readers, such as Annie Bryant's *Beacon Street Girls*. The series, aimed at readers in the 9–13 age group, is set in a middle class neighborhood in Brookline, Massachusetts, and features five girls of varying backgrounds and their adventures. The twelve installments focus on the problems of young girls and introduce characters of multicultural backgrounds. *The Babysitter's Club,* published by Scholastic Books from 1986 to 2000, had a wide range of characters with various traits: various racial and religious identities; health problems, such as diabetes and asthma; interests; and talents. A film based on the series was released in 1995. Several series spin-offs have been produced by the series author, Ann Martin, and other ghostwriters.

Sex and violence in young adult series fiction is also countered by Christian series. Series offerings from such publishers as Zondervan and Tyndale, Melody Carlson's *True Colors,* and Robin Jones Gunn's *Christy Miller* and *Sierra Jenson* tackle serious, and not so serious, teenage problems. *Left Behind: The Kids* by Jerry B. Jenkins and Tim LaHaye is based on the enormously popular *Left Behind* series for adult readers. The 40+ book series follows the adventures of five children searching for truth after the Rapture.

For younger children, adventure has reigned since the days of Gertrude Warner Chandler's *Boxcar Children* (1942). In over 100 books, many contributed to the series by authors after Warner's death, the four Alden children continue to solve mysteries and have adventures. The latest adventure is *The Box That Watch Found* (2007). One of the most popular recent series is Mary Pope Osborne's *The Magic Tree House.* Readers follow Jack and Annie in two series, *The Magic Tree House* and the *Merlin Missions* as they travel to other places and times with the help of a magical tree house and Morgan LeFay. The books are extensively researched and teachers can access the research guides that accompany the titles, making for books that are educational as well as enjoyable.

R.L. Stine has been the undisputed leader of horror novels for young readers with his immensely popular *Fear Street* and *Goosebumps* series. His newest series, *Mostly Ghostly,* continues to spread chills. The popularity of J.K. Rowling's Harry Potter books has created a market for fantasy books of all sorts but particularly those including young magicians and witches. The popular *Pirates of the Caribbean* films, featuring Johnny Depp as the pirate Jack Sparrow, have inspired new pirate adventures, the most successful of which has been Rob Kidd's *Jack Sparrow* series aimed at younger readers. Sparrow is a youngster gathering a crew and having adventures on board the *Barnacle.*

Animal protagonists continue to be popular with young readers as well. British author Brian Jacques's *Redwall* series began in 1986 with *Redwall*. The series now has nineteen titles, and the world Jacques has created is beloved by millions of readers (children and adults alike). Margaret McCallister's *Mistmantle* titles follow Jacques's lead.

Daniel Handler, better known as Lemony Snicket, created a spoof of young adult series themselves called *A Series of Unfortunate Events*. The series began with *The Bad Beginning* (1999) and concluded with *The End* (2006). The first book begins with the words, "If you are interested in stories with happy endings, you would be better off reading some other book. In this book, not only is there no happy ending, there is no happy beginning and very few happy things in the middle. . . . I'm sorry to tell you this, but that's how the story goes." The books follow in the darkly humorous tradition of Edward Gorey and Roald Dahl and are geared toward young readers who don't care for sports books for boys or best friend adventures for girls. The Baudelaire Orphans find themselves battling evil Count Olaf and other horrible relatives with whom they are forced to live using their wits to survive. Snicket launched a new series in 2007 with *Vampire Island*.

Creator of ten series and contributor to many more, Katherine A. Applegate is one of the queens of series fiction for young readers. Her *Animorphs* series (1996–2001) included fifty-four titles. In the books, the characters morph into various animals, often saving their city or even the world from aliens or other villains. The destruction of the Earth due to a huge asteroid sends selected families to another planet in the first book of Applegate's *Remnant* series (*The Mayflower Project,* 2001); in the final installment, *Begin Again,* 2003, the Earth is on the brink of being reborn. In *Everworld,* Applegate's characters find themselves in a parallel universe where mythology and reality blend and nothing is as it seems.

Selected Authors

Mainstream Fiction. Series are popular in genre fiction, such as science fiction, romance, mystery, and men's adventure, but mainstream fiction has seen its share of series contributions as well. Honoré de Balzac completed almost 100 titles for his interconnected *La Comédie Humaine*. The novels examined all aspects of early nineteenth century French life from the rural areas to life in Paris to the military. Another French writer, Émile Zola, produced twenty novels in the *Les Rougon-Macquart* cycle, which followed the lives of an extended family during the French Second Empire. Most of William Faulkner's novels and stories are set in Yoknapatawpha County, Mississippi, with characters showing up in various stories. More contemporarily, John Jakes produced the *Kent Family Chronicles* and the *North and South* series following families through generations of American History.

In 1980, Jean Auel released the first book in her *Earth's Children* series, *The Clan of the Cave Bear,* which became a huge bestseller and was made into a movie starring Daryl Hannah. Auel's final installment in the ice age saga is the 2002 *The Shelters of Stone*.

Armistead Maupin first serialized his *Tales of the City* in the *San Francisco Chronicle*. The series followed the lives of several characters, the most popular being Michael Tolliver, a gay man who develops AIDS late in the series, and Anna Madrigal, the eccentric landlady of 28 Barbary Lane, the central setting of *Tales. Tales of the*

City was published in 1978 with a 2007 release, *Michael Tolliver Lives,* updating fans on the life of their favorite character.

Dean Koontz has four titles in the *Odd Thomas* series. Thomas communicates with the dead, helping them to gain justice or otherwise helping them accomplish what they couldn't in life. Dan Brown has offered two thrillers featuring Harvard symbolist Robert Langdon in the extraordinarily bestselling *The Da Vinci Code* (2003) and *Angels & Demons* (2000).

Science Fiction, Fantasy, and Horror. In the world of science fiction and fantasy, worlds created by authors often draw other authors to contribute to them. The worlds expand into universes peopled with the original characters and many new ones. New plots are developed and back stories for older plots and characters created. A canon grows up, mostly unofficial, governing what does and does not belong to the universe and helping direct new material written. In a 2005 editorial, Gary Hoppenstand, the editor of *The Journal of Popular Culture,* bemoaned the damage done by imitators of Tolkien, *Star Trek,* and *Star Wars.* He believes that original science fiction and fantasy writing is being pushed out by the endless installments in the *Star Trek* and *Star Wars* series and series based on Middle Earth imitations (Hoppenstand 2005, 603–604). Two examples of what have come to be known as shared universes are the *Star Trek* and *Star Wars* franchises.

The 1960s television series *Star Trek* has spawned not only movies and additional series (*Next Generation, Deep Space Nine, Voyager,* and *Enterprise*) but also over 700 book titles as well, beginning with Mack Reynolds's *Mission to Horatius* in 1967. Several series have been created within the past decade. *Star Trek: Strange New Worlds I* (1998) is an anthology of short stories culled from a writing competition and edited by Dean Wesley Smith, himself the author of a dozen *Star Trek* adventures. This collection of fan fiction has led to writing careers for many of its contributors and is still going strong at volume ten. Two new series will be launched in 2008, *Star Trek: Terok Nor* and *Star Trek: Klingon Empire.*

Star Trek: The Next Generation currently includes almost seventy titles by various authors. There have been at least six *Deep Space Nine* series, the longest running with almost thirty titles. James Blish, Dean Wesley Smith, and John Vorholt have been some of the most frequent contributors to the *Star Trek* universe of series. Even the most recent spin-off, *Enterprise,* which aired from 2001 to 2005 has spawned a ten-book series.

George Lucas's phenomenal success, *Star Wars,* has produced dozens of novels as well. Based on the early lives or post canonical *Star Wars* lives of characters such as Han Solo or Princess Leia or even on newly invented characters and adventures, the *Star Wars* franchise continues to widen. Spin-offs such as *Star Wars: Boba Fett, Star Wars: Clone Wars,* and *Star Wars: Dark Nest* offer readers more adventures than the slow release of films can provide.

Another shared world is George R.R. Martin's *Wild Cards,* which has expanded to eighteen volumes since the 1986 debut, *Wild Cards,* involves a gene-altering virus of the same name. Superheroes from the comics are alive and well in the hands of the series' authors. Probably the most popular shared universe of all time is the *Myth* series of Robert Asprin, which extends from the 1978 *Another Fine Myth* to the 2002 *Something M.Y.T.H Inc.* Three more series, *Phule's Company, Time Scout,* and *Myth Adventures* also have post 2000 releases. With his former wife Lynn Abbey, Asprin created the *Thieves World* shared universe. The anthologies of stories set in the city of Sanctuary were published from 1979 to 1989 and set the standard for shared universes. A new *Thieves World* anthology, *Sanctuary,* was released in 2002.

Harry Turtledove is one of the masters of series science fiction. He juggles eleven different series, all of which have had installments since 2000; among them are *World War, Great War, Darkness,* and *Pacific War.* Many of his novels are considered alternative history, which is set in an alternate timeline—often uchronian, which means a utopian sort of time period preceding our own. In more contemporary times, this genre often asks the question, "What if?" and stories are called counter-factual histories. For example, what if Confederate forces had won in the Civil War is the question asked in *The Guns of the South: A Novel of the Civil War* (1992). The success of this stand-alone title spurred Turtledove to develop the *Worldwar* and the *Great War* series in which real battles are altered by alternative timelines.

Even former Speaker of the House Newt Gingrich has contributed to alternative history series with his Civil War trilogy and his Pacific War series, addressing the "what ifs" of some of these momentous battles.

Anne McCaffrey's Dragonrider series is one of the best beloved of science fiction and fantasy readers alike. The *Dragonriders of Pern* series began in 1968 and still continues with a 2007 release *Dragon Harper* written with her son Todd McCaffrey.

Many fantasy writers release their books in series, such as David Eddings, Terry Brooks, and R.A. Salvatore. Eddings's Belgeriad series began with the 1982 *Pawn of Prophecy* and was followed by many more installments. His most recent series, written with wife Leigh Eddings, is the *Dreamers* series begun in 2003. In 1977, Terry Brooks burst on the fantasy scene with his Tolkienesque *Sword of Shannara.* Brooks's world was favorably received and he's been adding more volumes to the Shannara saga ever since. The latest is part of the *Genesis of Shannara* saga, *Armageddon's Children* (2006), which brings the Shannara epic to a futuristic Seattle. Salvatore is the author of seven series, several since 2000.

In 1994, Terry Goodkind released the first title in his Sword of Truth series, *Wizard's First Rule.* The series is more mature and graphically violent than many of Goodkind's fantasy counterparts, but the series has attracted legions of followers from the first title. Goodkind's world is a battlefield where the fight for control is ever-shifting between the world of magic and the world of reality, with the material between them flimsy stuff. The hero, Richard Cypher, develops from a man who is thrust into an adventure that he does not understand to a powerful hero whose magic is great. Book eleven, *The Confessor* (2007), is the culmination of the adventures of Richard and Kahlan as they try to save the world they know from darkness.

The current reigning queen of fantasy series is Mercedes Lackey. Lackey has over twenty series, many with titles added since 2000. Her most popular series is set in the land of Valdemar (*Arrows of the Queen,* 1987; *Exile's Valor,* 2003). Valdemar is a fantastical land peopled with magical creatures in a medieval setting. Although the writer of several series, Piers Anthony is best known for his pun-filled Xanth series. The first release, *A Spell for Chameleon* (1977), has been followed by thirty more titles, the most recent, *Air Apparent,* in 2007.

Diana Gabaldon begins her highly praised *Outlander* series in 1991 with *Outlander.* A 1945 nurse joins her husband in post World War II Scotland to rekindle their marriage. She is transported back to the Scotland of the late 1770s and so the time travel adventures begin. Gabaldon's books are a combination of fantasy, history, and romance, but the author insists that her titles do not fit neatly in any particular genre. In the sixth book of the series, *A Breath of Snow and Ashes* (2005), Gabaldon meticulously follows her characters as they make preparations for the American Revolution.

Horror novels have succumbed to the demands of series readers as well. One of the longest running series in the horror genre is V.C. Andrews's *Flowers in the Attic* series with its many spin-offs, sequels, and prequels. Andrews wrote the first five in the early eighties but died in 1986. The series has been continued by various authors since that time. Seven of the series have been developed since 2000, including the most recent Secrets line.

Vampires seem to be a popular creature around which series are built. Anne Rice's New Orleans *Vampire Chronicles* debuted with *Interview with the Vampire* (1975). The vampire Lestat was played by Tom Cruise in the box office rendition of the movie in 1994. Rice's latest installment in the *Chronicles* is *Blood Canticle* (2003). Laurell K. Hamilton's *Anita Blake, Vampire Hunter* series first appeared in 1993. In a future time when the United States has provided vampires with equal rights, Blake takes on various clients who need her skills in necromancy. *Blood Noir* (2008) is the fourteenth Anita Blake installment. A more lighthearted vampire series is set in the Buffyverse of the television series *Buffy the Vampire Slayer*, played by Sarah Michelle Gellar from 1997 to 2003. Dozens of Buffy novels for both young adults and a more mature audience have been released.

Stephen King, the undisputed master of horror fiction is not known for series fiction. His *Dark Tower* sequence, however, is a seven-title series begun in 1982 with *The Gunslinger*. The final installment, *The Dark Tower*, was released in 2004.

Men's Adventure and Westerns. Nick Carter was a fictional detective popular in the dime novels of the 1880s. His popularity has led to a long-running series of books as his identity continued to morph through the 1990s. The hero's name eventually became the pseudonym for a string of authors who wrote Nick Carter novels, including Martin Cruz Smith. There were 261 *Nick Carter: Killmaster* novels published between 1964 and 1990, in which Carter's character was a spy for the AXE agency.

Even more prolific were the Mack Bolan series, which produced over 570 installments. Don Pendelton created the *Executioner* series and contributed 41 titles to the popular action-adventure genre, which has been described as the equivalent to romance fiction for women. After his death in 1995, the series was continued by house authors. Over the years, Bolan has battled Mexican drug lords, Russian spies, and a host of other enemies. Pendleton discussed his character on his Web site: "Bolan lives large, responding to the challenge of life, remaining alive and remaining human in the process. Success in living means growth, achievement, beating the challenge and maturing toward a meaningful evolutionary plateau" (http://www.don-pendleton.com/executionerseries.html). Men may be attracted to the heroism of Bolan, but according to the Don Pendleton Web site, over forty percent of Bolan fans are female. The formula of the hero still drives sales. Six titles, including *Devil's Playground*, have been released in 2007 alone.

William W. Johnstone is one of the masters of the adventure series for men. He is best known for his westerns, but he also wrote in the science fiction, military, and horror genres. Several of his series, including the western series *Mountain Man* and *Blood Bond*, have been continued after his death in 2004 by J.A. Johnstone.

Johnstone himself was the quintessential adventurer, with stints in the French Foreign Legion and the military. In *Out of the Ashes* (1983), the first book in the *Ashes* series, Ben Raines searches for his missing family in post-apocalyptic America. The 34th entry in the series is *Escape from the Ashes* (2003) and follows Raines's plane crash in Canada. The *Mountain Man* story has followed Smoke Jensen through 34 titles so far. Living for revenge and to wipe out bands of desperados, Jensen is forced to keep moving. Readers follow ex-CIA agent John Barrone in the *Code Name* series and the blood brothers Sam Two Wolves and Matt Bodine in the *Blood Bond* line.

Clive Cussler is another household name in the adventure genre. His character, Dirk Pitt, has appeared in nineteen novels. Cussler, like his character Pitt, is an adventurer. A diver, he has recovered many shipwrecks and has established the nonprofit agency NUMA (National Underwater and Marine Agency), which is the premise for his NUMA series. The Pitt novels feature high tech weapons and tools and many of the same elements that make Indiana Jones and James Bond so popular, beautiful women and nefarious villains among them.

Westerns are the quintessential men's adventure novels. Zane Grey, Max Brand, and Louis L'Amour are the leaders of this genre of gunslingers, cattle rustlers, and Old West shootouts. Although Grey, famous for *Riders of the Purple Sage* (1912), died in 1979; Brand, the prolific author of westerns died in 1944 in World War II; and L'Amour, equally prolific, died in 1988, their bibliographies have continued to be added to by ghost writers. But new writers are creating Western series to cater to a readership that is not ready to let go of the Old West. Bryce Harte writes the Creed series; *Creed: Arkansas Raiders* (2001) is the tenth in the series. Elmer Kelton has been writing westerns since the 1950s, and his Texas Rangers series is going strong with his 2008 release *Hard Trail to Follow*. Hundreds of titles have been published in the long-running Tabor Evans's *Long Arm* series since the series debut, *Longarm*, appeared in 1978.

Mystery and Detective Fiction. Mystery and detective fiction by its nature lends itself to series. The detective, either professional or amateur, is inquisitive, resourceful, and persistent, all traits that make for great mystery solving. Readers of mysteries are very loyal and will buy dozens of novels by the same author. Lillian Jackson Braun is a case in point. Braun debuted retired journalist Jim Qwilleran in the 1966 *The Cat Who Could Read Backwards*. Qwilleran and his Siamese cats Koko and Yum Yum live in a small Northern community, and with the help of Koko, Qwilleran solves mysteries. Braun, in her nineties, continues to produce a new installment of her *The Cat Who* series almost every year. It is difficult to tell who is more popular to readers, the cats or the detective as fans wait anxiously for each of the twenty plus books that Braun has released thus far. Readers enjoy *The Cat Who* series not only for its interesting characters and the exploits of the amazing Koko, but for the feeling of "coming home" they experience each time they return to the Northern Midwest town of Pickax.

One of the most respected writers of any genre is Lawrence Block. Block has created several series characters: Bookstore owner and cat burglar Bernie Rhodenbarr, Cold War spy Evan Tanner, and former police officer and recovering alcoholic Matt Scudder. As Scudder grows, he gives up the booze but not his moral ambiguity. A detective in the hard-boiled tradition, Scudder operates below the radar of traditional law enforcement. The books are gritty and violent, but the New York City location is palpably realistic. What draws readers to the series is its refusal to provide the elements of hard-boiled mystery fiction in conventional or stereotypical ways. The good guys in Scudder's world are not always good, the bad not always so bad.

With Marcia Muller's introduction of detective Sharon McCone in the 1977 *Edwin of the Iron Shoes,* a new day dawned for women's detective fiction. The hard-boiled P.I. is a predominantly male role, and until McCone appeared, women were not part of the private eye scene in any visible numbers. Married to hard-boiled detective author Bill Pronzini, himself the creator of a long running series, Muller was influenced to develop McCone as a softer version of the male archetype. *The Ever Running Man* (2007) is number twenty-four in the series. Although Muller has had success with McCone, the wildly popular Kinsey Millhone and V.I. Warshawski have given writers of female detectives solid role models as well.

Sara Paretsky's first V.I. Warshawski novel *Indemnity Only* was released in 1982 and introduced readers to strong, capable female characters who are not victims but rather the protectors of victims. Thirteen novels later Paretsky still has her detective searching for justice on issues of community and social responsibility.

Kinsey Millhone is one of the best-recognized female sleuths being published today. She was introduced by Sue Grafton in the 1982 *A is for Alibi. T Is for Trespass* (2007) is her twentieth Millhone installment. Like Paretsky, Grafton's novels tackle social themes in an effort to understand the "whys" behind the murders investigated.

Husband-wife teams in mystery fiction have always been popular. J.D. Robb's sleuthing team is anything but the usual in her *In Death* series, which numbers 26 titles and is set in a New York fifty years in the future. In the 1995 debut, *Naked in Death,* police lieutenant Eve Dallas meets her future husband Roarke, a suspect in the first installment. Dallas is praised as a strong, intelligent woman, and the book's fast pace and suspense has earned Robb an even wider audience. She has written dozens of romance titles as Robb and other fiction as Nora Roberts.

Equally popular are series based on the lives of famous people, often novelists themselves. Stephanie Barron's series of mysteries based on the life of Jane Austen debuted with *Jane and the Unpleasantness at Scargrove Manor* in 1996. The most recent release is *Jane and the Barque of Frailty* (2006). Elliott Roosevelt writes mysteries about a fictitious Eleanor Roosevelt who solves mysteries in the White House (*Murder at the President's Door,* 2001). The author of several series, Laurie R. King is best known for her Mary Russell series set in England during World War I. The debut novel in the series is the highly acclaimed *The Beekeeper's Daughter* (1994). Russell solves mysteries with the retired Sherlock Holmes, whom she eventually marries. There have been many Sherlock Holmes pastiches, but King's is different, and applauded, because she adds female interest to Holmes's adventures, giving Russell an identity of her own.

Patricia Cornwell's 1990 *Postmortem* introduced mystery readers to the world of Kay Scarpetta, Chief Medical Examiner for the State of Virginia, and opened the floodgates to a slew of forensic mysteries. Cornwell's novels employ all of the features of forensic science in her Scarpetta mysteries. *Book of the Dead* (2007) is number fifteen. Kathy Reichs is a forensic anthropologist for Quebec, medical examiner for North Carolina, and anthropology professor at the University of North Carolina, Charlotte. Her books about Temperance "Tempe" Brennan are filled with the same forensic expertise as Patricia Cornwell's. Brennan debuted in *Deja Dead* (1997). The television series *Bones* is based on Reichs and her character.

Jeffery Deaver has introduced a new type of forensic scientist. Injured while working a case, Lincoln Rhymes is now a quadriplegic, able to move only a finger. Rhyme is not an easy man to work with, but his wide ranging forensic expertise is a hot commodity. In *The Bone Collector* (1997), Rhyme begins working with Amelia Sachs who becomes indispensable as both his eyes and legs and as his lover. Deaver's Lincoln Rhyme series is praised for the books' dizzyingly fast-paced and twisted plot lines. *The Broken Window* is scheduled for a 2008 release. A new series debuts with the 2007 *The Sleeping Doll* and stars Kathryn Dance, a kinesics analyst who appeared in the Rhyme title *The Cold Moon* (2006).

Along Came a Spider, the first in a series of nursery rhyme titled books, appeared in 1993 and, much to his reader's delight, has been followed by twelve more Alex Cross novels, seven of them bestsellers. Cross is a psychologist who works with the police department to track killers.

Although there have been several popular series featuring gay and lesbian characters (Joseph Hanson's Dave Brandstetter for one), one of the most popular characters has been Laurie King's San Francisco-based Kate Martinelli, a lesbian homicide detective. King's first Matinelli novel, *A Grave Talent* (1993), won the Edgar Award for the best first crime novel of the year. Detective Kate Delafield stars in Lambda Award-winning Katherine V. Forrest's mystery series (*Hancock Park*, 2004). Ellen Hart's lesbian character, Jane Lawless, is a restaurant owner in Minneapolis; *Night Vision* (2006) is the fourteenth in the series.

In 1990 Walter Mosley achieved critical acclaim with his first Easy Rawlins book, *Devil in a Blue Dress*. Rawlins, a war veteran, solves crimes in post World War II Los Angeles. Mosley's novels follow Rawlins through time; the first novel is set in 1948, and the most recent, *Blonde Faith* (2008), takes place in the post Vietnam era. A series featuring Fearless Jones and his sidekick Paris Minton is also set in the Los Angeles of the 1950s. A third series character is Socrates Fortlow (*Walkin' the Dog*, 1999). His novels are seen as providing strong social commentary on the life of African-Americans in a volatile period of American history.

Along with focusing on social issues, African-American authors often infuse their mysteries with family dynamics as well. Former *Essence* magazine editor Valerie Wilson Wesley's Tamara Hayle is a Newark, New Jersey, ex-cop turned private eye. Wesley's novels follow Hayle as she struggles to raise her son. Barbara Neely created Blanche White, a nosy forty-year-old domestic who frequently finds trouble. *Blanche on the Lam* (1992) was her first appearance and won the Agatha, the Macavity, and the Anthony awards.

Unquestionably the most popular author to feature Native American characters is Tony Hillerman. Tony Hillerman created Joe Leaphorn, a member of the Navajo Tribal Police in New Mexico, and his partner Jim Chee. His novels, beginning with *The Blessing Way* (1970), became very popular for their authentic depictions of Navajo life and the Southwest. Although he has written other mysteries and nonfiction titles, the Leaphorn/Chee novels are the most popular. The most recent title is the 2003 *Sinister Pig*.

Set on a fictional South Carolina resort island, Carolyn Hart's "Death on Demand" series features an attractive, wealthy couple, Annie and Max Darling. They own a mystery bookshop and also work together to solve the many real mysteries that come their way. The author reveals in the books a familiarity with esoteric mystery fiction that appeals to devotees of the genre.

One of the most successful mystery series is Elizabeth Peters's Amelia Peabody. Peters has set dozens of books in nineteenth century Egypt, where Peabody and her husband excavate tombs and historical locations. The novels, begun in 1975, are strongly colored by Peters's own background in Egyptian archaeology. Yearly installments in the Amelia Peabody series are eagerly awaited by the millions of fans of the series and have been awarded many mystery fiction kudos. *Tomb of the Golden Bird* (2006) is the eighteenth Peabody novel.

An example of a television series spawning a novel series is the popular *Murder, She Wrote,* a mystery series starring Angela Lansbury that aired from 1984 to 1996. The series, initially set in the small New England town of Cabot Cove, eventually followed Lansbury's character, mystery writer Jessica Fletcher, as she traveled around the country. Donald Bain's first installment in the series is *Gin and Daggers* (1989), and two titles are scheduled to be released in 2008. The series, one of the longest running drama series, is dear to many reader's hearts as well.

Romance. Harlequin romances are the most widely recognized romance publications in the world. The North American division of the British Mills and Boon publishing empire, Harlequin has been distributing romances in various series for over fifty years. Each month, titles are released in over a dozen different series, each series having its own characteristics. For example, the Harlequin Romance line has mildly sensuous titles and the Blaze line contains higher levels of sensuality. Other lines are Historical, Intrigue, Medical Romances, and four series in Spanish (Deseo, Bianco, Jazmin, and Julia). There is also a NASCAR line for racing fans. One of Harlequin's imprints, Kimani Press, releases series geared toward an African American audience.

Notable fantasy writers such as Mercedes Lackey have contributed to the Harlequin Romance's Luna line. The line offers readers fantasy focused on romance and sensuality. The series, launched in 2004, features romance/fantasy novels by several well-known fantasy and science fiction writers. Lackey's contribution, *The Fairy Godmother* (2004), combines humor and romance in its depiction of a world where its inhabitants must live out their lives in fairy tale tradition.

Other than the success of Janet Dailey's American series, in which a romance was set in each of the fifty states, series or category romances generally do not follow the series definition of repeat characters or locations. They do not need to be read in any particular order, although they are numbered. Highly formulaic, a Harlequin romance is short, under 250 pages, and always ends happily ever after. The heroines are dispatched to locations all over the world and they are involved in every type of vocation possible, from high-stakes professional careers to single moms. Because Harlequin was hesitant to publish American authors and titles with a more American sensibility, Simon and Schuster launched its Silhouette imprint in 1980 to put a different spin on formula romances. The line charged authors to create heroines who were stronger and more self-sufficient than their Harlequin counterparts. Other publishers followed suit and category romances began a publishing phenomenon. As the market expanded, however, the books became more formulaic and the quality waned.

The most successful author to begin her career in the world of category romance and cross over to noncategory books is Nora Roberts. Roberts has many series to accompany her stand-alone romance titles. One of the most prolific romance writers working today, Roberts, who also writes under the name J.D. Robb, has produced over twenty romance series. Roberts is a highly respected romance author, having almost 200 books to her credit since 1981. She sold her first manuscript to Silhouette Books in 1981, *Irish Thoroughbred,* as part of the *Irish Hearts* series. Her *Calhoun Women* series is one of the most popular Silhouette series ever.

Roberts has won many romance genre awards, several for her *McGregor* series alone. Part of her success lies in her inclusion of elements from other genres such as mystery and fantasy.

Christian Fiction. A new trend that many Christian publishing houses contribute to, a response to the increasing demands on readers' time and attention, is the release of smaller series. Sales of series installments, excepting more established authors, tend to wane after the third release. To broaden their series offerings, publishers such as Tyndale, a major Christian publisher, have begun to release nonserial series. These series provide readers with the same characters and locations, but the individual titles do not need to be read in chronological order. Readers are not obligated to read earlier titles to feel comfortable with later releases.

Even Harlequin has gotten on the Christian romance bandwagon, offering God-centered romances, sans sex, with its Love Inspired line. Conservative, often fundamentalist, values are highlighted in these works with women frequently giving up the roles of powerful women and finding love and happiness in laundry and raising children.

Beverly Lewis's *Annie's People* series (*The Brethren*, 2006) and Wanda E. Brunstetter's *Brides of Lancaster County* and *Daughters of Lancaster County* are just a few of the series that now feature the simple lives of the Pennsylvania Amish. Jan Karon's Mitford saga is set in a North Carolina mountaintop village and follows the life of Father Tim Kavanaugh. The acclaimed series, begun in the 1994 *At Home in Mitford* culminates in the series conclusion *Light from Heaven* (2005). The series is beloved for its nostalgic look at a small town and the simple religious lives of its inhabitants. Gilbert Morris's *House of Winslow* series debuted in 1986, and the fortieth installment, *The White Night,* concluded the series in 2007.

The Left Behind series is undoubtedly one of the largest publishing phenomena the world of Christian publishing has ever seen. The books, written by Tim LaHaye and Jerry B. Jenkins, are located in the time of the Rapture, a Christian idea that encompasses a time when Jesus Christ returns to the Earth to take select individuals to meet God in Heaven. The first title in the series, *Left Behind: A Novel of the Earth's Last Days* (1995), has been followed by almost a dozen more titles, an extensive series for children (*Left Behind: The Kids*), movie adaptations, and several spin-off series (*Left Behind: End off State, Left Behind: Military*).

Bibliography

Auel, Jean. *The Shelters of Stone.* New York: Crown, 2002.

Cornwell, Patricia. *Book of the Dead.* New York: G.P. Putnam's, 2007.

Deaver, Jeffrey. *The Bone Collector.* New York: Viking, 1997.

Don Pendleton Web Site. http://www.donpendleton.com/executionerseries.html. Accessed on April 30, 2008.

Foote, Stephanie. "Bookish Women: Reading Girls' Fiction: A Response to Julia Mickenberg." *American Literary History* 19.2 (2007): 521–526.

Goodkind, Terry. *The Confessor.* New York: Tor, 2007.

Grafton, Sue. *T Is for Trespass.* New York: G.P. Putnam's, 2007.

Handler, Daniel. *The Bad Beginning.* New York: HarperCollins, 1999.

———. *The End.* New York: HarperCollins, 2006.

Hillerman, Tony. *Sinister Pig.* New York: HarperCollins, 2003.

Hoppenstand, Gary. "Series(ous) SF Concerns." *The Journal of Popular Culture* 38.4 (May 2005).

LaHaye, Tim, and Jerry B. Jenkins. *Left Behind: A Novel of the Earth's Last Days*. Wheaton, IL: Tyndale House, 1995.

Mosley, Walter. *Devil in a Blue Dress*. New York: Norton, 1990.

Peters, Elizabeth. *Tomb of the Golden Bird*. New York: William Morrow, 2006.

Rice, Anne. *Blood Canticle*. New York: Alfred A. Knopf, 2003.

Thomas, Rebecca L., and Catherine Barr. *Popular Series Fiction for K-6 Readers*. Westport, CT: Libraries Unlimited, 2004.

Warner, Gertrude Chandler, and Robert Papp. *The Box That Watch Found*. Morton Grove, IL: Albert Whitman and Co., 2007.

Watson, Bruce. "Tom Swift, Nancy Drew and Pals All Had the Same Dad." *Smithsonian* 22.7 (October 1991): 50–59.

Winner, Lauren F. "The Series Still Rules." *Publishers Weekly* 28 August, 2006. S10–S11.

Further Reading

Agosto, D.E., S. Hughes-Hassell, and C. Gilmore-Clough. "The All-White World of Middle-School Genre Fiction: Surveying the Field for Multicultural Protagonists." *Children's Literature in Education* 34.4 (December 2003): 257–275; Benson, Christopher. "What's Behind the Boon in Black Mystery Writers?" *Ebony* (September 2003); Billman, Carol. *Secret of the Stratemeyer Syndicate: Nancy Drew, the Hardy Boys, and the Million Dollar Fiction Factory*. New York: Ungar, 1986; Charles, John A., and Mosley, Shelley. "Getting Serious about Romance: Adult Series Romance for Teens." *Voice of Youth Advocates* 25.2 (June 2002): 87–93; Darbyshire, Peter. "The Politics of Love: Harlequin Romances and the Christian Right." *Journal of Popular Culture* 35.4 (Spring 2002): 75–87; Erisman, Fred. *Boys' Books, Boys' Dreams, and the Mystique of Flight*. Fort Worth: Texas Christian University Press, 2006; Erisman, Fred. "Stratemeyer Boys' Books and the Gernsback Milieu." *Extrapolation* 41 (Fall 2000): 272–282; Foote, Stephanie. "Deviant Classics: Pulps and the Making of Lesbian Print Culture." *Signs: Journal of Women in Culture and Society* 31 (2005): 169–190; Heising, Willetta L. *Detecting Women Pocket Guide: Checklist for Mystery Series Written by Women*. 3rd ed. Dearborn: Purple Moon Press, 1999; Heising, Willetta L. *Detecting Men: A Readers Guide and Checklist for Mystery Series Written by Men*. Dearborn: Purple Moon Press, 1998; Inness, Sherrie, Ed. *Nancy Drew and Company: Culture, Gender, and Girls' Series*. Bowling Green: Popular Press, 1997; Inness, Sherrie, Ed. *Nancy Drew and Company: Culture, Gender, and Girls' Series*. Bowling Green: Popular Press, 1997; Jones, Patrick. *What's So Scary about R.L. Stine?* Lanham, Maryland: Scarecrow Press, 1998; Kensinger, Faye R. *Children of the Series and How They Grew, or a Century of Heroines and Heroes, Romantic, Comic, Moral*. Bowling Green, Ohio: Bowling Green State University Popular Press, 1987; Lanes, Selma. *Down the Rabbit Hole: Adventures and Misadventures in the Realm of Children's Literature*. New York: Atheneum, 1971; Langbauer, Laurie. *Novels of Everyday Life: The Series in English Fiction, 1850–1930*. Ithaca, New York: Cornell University Press, 1999; Molson, Francis J. "The Boy Inventor in American Series Fiction: 1900–1930." *The Journal of Popular Culture* 28.1 (Summer 1994): 31–48; O'Rourke, Meghan. "Nancy Drew's Father: The Fiction Factory of Edward Stratemeyer." *The New Yorker* 80 (8 November 2004): 120–129; Romalov, Nancy Tillman. "Mobile Heroines: Early Twentieth Century Girls Automobile Series." *The Journal of Popular Culture* 28.4 (Spring 1995): 231–243; Rye, Marilyn. "Changing Gender Conventions and the Detective Formula: J. A. Jance's Beaumont and Brady Series." *The Journal of Popular Culture* 37.1 (2003): 105–119; Sands, Karen, and Marietta Frank. *Back in the Spaceship Again: Juvenile Science Fiction Series Since 1945*. Westport, Connecticut: Greenwood Press, 1999; Simkin, John E., ed. *The Whole Story: 3000 Years of Sequels and Sequences*. Melbourne: Thorpe, 1996; Thomas, Rebecca L., and Catherine Barr. *Popular Series Fiction for Middle School and Teen Readers*. Westport, Connecticut: Libraries Unlimited, 2005; Volz, Bridget D., Cheryl P. Scheer, and Lynda B. Welborn. *Junior Genreflecting: A Guide to Good Reads and Series*

Fiction for Children. Westport, Conn.: Libraries Unlimited, 2000; Watson, Victor. *Reading Series Fiction: From Arthur Ransome to Gene Kemp*. London and New York: Routledge Farmer, 2000; Westfahl, Gary. "Going Where Lots of People Have Gone Before, or, The Novels Science Fiction Readers Don't See." *Interzone* 170 (August 2001): 54–55.

PATRICIA BOSTIAN

SPACE OPERA
Definition

> In these hectic days of phrase coining, we offer one. Westerns are called "horse operas," the morning housewife tear-jerkers are called "soap operas." For the hacky, grinding, outworn spaceship yarn, or world-saving for that matter, we offer "space opera."
>
> —Arthur Wilson "Bob" Tucker, 1941

Tucker's disparaging description still influences perceptions of space opera today. Considered a subgenre of science fiction, space opera is usually seen at best as "for fun," as Brian Aldiss puts it, and at worst, hack writing barely deserving of the infamous sci-fi pulp magazines of the 1930s and 1940s. Up until the late 1970s, space opera was a dismissive term applied to the type of "hacky, grinding, outworn" sci-fi writing Tucker vilifies, which was, in essence, a western or a romance transposed to outer space.

Elements of the early space opera are introduced with willful abandon in an effort to entertain, whereas the plausibility of those elements—virtually instantaneous galactic travel, worlds with impossible aliens, and the ever-so-slightly-bigger-and-better death ray—are blithely ignored. Its pejorative status is highlighted by William Sims Bainbridge, who describes space opera as that which uses "the physical props of hard science without the underlying intellectual themes" (1986, 77), meaning that the physical conditions of the universe in which space opera functions usually run contrary to known science. Bainbridge's description furthers the notion that

---

A RECIPE FOR SPACE OPERA

Brian Aldiss wittily described the subgenre as that which takes "a few light years and a pinch of reality and inflate thoroughly with melodrama, dreams, and a seasoning of screwy ideas" (9). Aldiss then listed a number of defining elements of space opera:

- Earth in peril
- Quest
- Hero
- Aliens and exotic creatures
- Blood running down the palace steps
- Ships launching into the louring dark
- Beautiful women
- Evil villain
- Happy ending (1974, 10)

To which we can also add:

- Cosmic backdrop
- Sweeping, swashbuckling action
- Often stilted dialog (and even narration)
- Enough superlatives to fill a galaxy

space opera is primarily action and flash (deriving from the Sturm und Drang movement of eighteenth-century Germany as well as the romance novels of the eighteenth and nineteenth centuries) and virtually devoid of ideas, a traditional distinction between writing literature and merely writing.

Trends and Themes. Not all of these characteristics are endemic to space opera; certainly most works of traditional or hard science fiction employ many of these same operatic qualities. As Tzvetan Todorov brilliantly points out in *Genres in Discourse,* the borders of any genre remain opaque, nebulous, and subject to constant scrutiny and redefinition. Many early practitioners of hard science fiction—such as Isaac Asimov, Arthur C. Clarke, or Robert Heinlein—would have been horrified to have their works referred to as space opera. Yet many of the qualities denoting space opera run rampant through their works. The entry on **science fiction** in this work offers a much more detailed definition of hard science fiction; but at its essence, hard science fiction is *science* fiction; space opera is science *fiction.*

Early space opera can also be distinguished from planetary romance, its sister subgenre, which, while making use of extraterrestrial settings, comes closer to fantasy than science fiction because the story invariably resembles pre-technology Earth and incorporates qualities like swordplay and magic, to name a few. Planetary romance or early space opera is perhaps best exemplified by Leigh Brackett's *The Sword of Rhiannon* (1949). In space opera, planets—and, similarly, the ubiquitous spaceport bar—serve generally as ports of call; the real action is in space and spaceships. And rather than relying on magic, space opera will rely on what can be called superscience, an instance of which is the sudden development of a regeneration drug that can restore the hero to perfect, symmetrical health just as he has had his eyes plucked out and his limbs amputated—without, of course, even a scar—as is the case in E.E. Smith's Lensman series. Pre–1980 space opera focused on the tale, not the idea, was often tinged with a nostalgic affection, and indulged freely in extravagance. It was also unmistakably masculine.

In 1974, Aldiss famously declared space opera dead. In a sense, he was correct; the old space opera had passed away, but the late 1970s saw the birth of what has become widely known as *the new space opera.* Although the new space opera still bears many of the old earmarks—the epic scale, the exotic setting, the earth in peril—it pays closer attention to real science and realistic characters. It also takes on the literary quality of exploring and expounding ideas, and it pays homage to the space battle royale—so much so, in fact, that some purists argue in favor of a separate military science fiction or even military space opera category. But the scope, size, and qualities of military science fiction, even when grounded on firm science, make moot most attempts to distinguish it from space opera. The new space opera, though better and more literary than its forerunner, still engenders Aldiss's qualities of "great images, excitements, and aspirations" (1974, 10).

History. Although a few critics argue that space opera's roots can be traced to such early writers as Jules Verne and H.G. Wells, most tend to agree on two primary literary figures of the 1920s as being credited with originating the subgenre: E.E. "Doc" Smith and Edmond Hamilton.

E.E. "Doc" Smith (1890–1968). Born in Sheboygan, Wisconsin, Edward Elmer Smith is most noted for his two space opera sagas, the four-volume Skylark series and the more popular six-book Lensman series. Smith earned two degrees in chemical engineering from the University of Idaho, went on for both a Master's and a PhD, and worked for a few years at the National Bureau of Standards in Washington, DC.

A prolific writer, Smith infused much of his fiction with his scientific knowledge, though usually just as a starting point. As his stories progressed, their scientific bases would become increasingly outlandish.

Skylark. The first Skylark novel, *The Skylark of Space,* originally ran serially in the August–October 1928 issues of *Amazing Stories,* the first magazine devoted solely to science fiction and published by the influential Hugo Gernsbeck. Smith had actually begun writing it in 1915 with the aid of a neighbor, Lee Hawkins Garby. It was Garby who allegedly suggested that Smith first try his hand at writing science fiction, to which he agreed, provided she write the love interest portions of the story. Both are listed as authors of the work.

In the novel's very first sentence, young scientist-hero Richard Seaton has just discovered the peculiar qualities of unknown metal X in his laboratory: under the proper conditions it stimulates the conversion of other metals into pure energy, and in turn it can generate a field of energy capable of propelling ships beyond the speed of light. Seaton's discovery piques the interest of a former colleague, the evil Dr. Marc "Blackie" DuQuesne, who steals Seaton's secret. Both men recognize that metal X and its amazing properties hold the secret to space travel, and they simultaneously begin building spaceships—Seaton with the aid of his millionaire inventor friend M. Reynolds Crane, and DuQuesne allied with the nefarious World Steel Corporation. Seaton's ship is the eponymously named *Skylark.* DuQuesne kidnaps Dorothy Vaneman, Seaton's lovely socialite fiancée, and a galactic pursuit ensues that brings both ships and crews into contact with such wonders as dead stars, startling technological leaps, and eventually an alien race on the planet Osnome, populated by the evil Mardonalians and the benevolent Konalians. At first deceived by the Mardonalians, both Seaton and DuQuesne realize they must join forces with the Kondalians to defeat their new mutual nemeses, which they promptly do.

Even while indulging in the hyperbolic "bigger, better, faster" episodic qualities of what has come to be known as the linchpins of early space opera, Smith nonetheless accomplishes a few admirable feats. While much of his technological advances defy known physics (such as faster-than-light travel and time dilation), the energy for his galactic star drive resembles, if only vaguely, the process of cold fusion and obeys the general principles of matter-to-energy conversion; the gravity well surrounding the dead star conforms approximately to the properties of a neutron star's gravity horizon; on Osnome, humans encounter both slavery and the practice of rudimentary eugenics, which in this case involves euthanizing flawed members of society. In this regard, *The Skylark of Space* can be said to follow one of the mandates of hard science fiction by engaging in extrapolative scientific thought, both technologically and socially.

Smith composed the remaining three novels of the series on his own, Mrs. Garby opting not to participate. *Skylark Three* also appeared serially in *Amazing Stories* (1930) with new villains—the Fenachronians, who possess vastly superior technology and who are naturally bent on destroying the Earth—and a new supertechnology developed by Seaton and Crane, an impenetrable energy shield known as the Zone of Force. Osnome, as luck would have it, is part of a fantastic fourteen-sun system rife with planets and intelligent species. Seaton and Crane encounter a number of these species (most importantly the Norlamin, key allies in the next book), acquiring and synthesizing technology as they go, all the while fending off the continuing plottings of DuQuesne. In an apparent extension of the euthanistic eugenics of *The Skylark of Space,* Seaton resolves the threat of Fenachrone by not only destroying the entire planet but also tracking down and eliminating the few Fenachronians who managed to escape planetary annihilation; DuQuesne is also immolated. The story ends with Seaton being named the new Chief of the Galactic Council.

For *Skylark of Valeron,* Smith switched publishing milieus, opting to run the story in *Astounding Stories* from August 1934 through February 1935. Seaton's primary foe this time is the Chlorans, who are attempting to conquer Valeron, and his secondary foes are DuQuesne (who had substituted a dummy and thus avoided immolation), a number of Fenachronians (who had eluded Seaton in the previous work), and also a couple of more metaphysical foes: a colony of beings that are pure intellect, first briefly encountered in *The Skylark of Space,* and inhabitants of the fourth dimension that Seaton and company traverse while fleeing the beings of pure intellect. Skylark of course becomes yet bigger, faster, and more powerful, its main improvement being a centralized artificial brain that, among other amazing feats, can synthesize matter directly from energy as well as both map and travel the entire galaxy. DuQuesne temporarily conquers the Earth, until Seaton "disembodies" his foe's intelligence, locking it in a Niven-like stasis box and sending it drifting off into the ether of eternal space.

Smith did not write the series' final installment, *Skylark DuQuesne,* until 1965, when it ran in *If* magazine, and it marks Smith's later tendencies to explore mental powers over technological ones, in which he indulges more freely in his Lensman series. DuQuesne has once again escaped his fate but run afoul of the latest foe, the Llurdi, a race of Vulcan-like purely logical beings bent on domination. The Chlorans also return in a much more malevolent form, but they are defeated in the novel's climactic battle. Peace is negotiated with the Llurdi, the remaining Fenachrone become allies, and DuQuesne, seemingly reformed, departs for a distant galaxy to set up his own empire, accompanied by his new fiancée, Dr. Stephanie de Marigne.

Lensman. In the third *Skylark* installment, Smith had begun experimenting with technological power versus mentalic power, a relationship he explores much more fully in his Lensman series.

The Lensman series comprises either four, six, or seven novels, which is due to its interesting publication history. Smith had begun conceiving his Lensman universe as early as the late 1920s, envisioning it as a four-volume work. Each appeared in serial form in *Astounding* magazine: *Galactic Patrol* (1937–1938), *Gray Lensman* (1939–1940), *Second-Stage Lensmen* (1941–1942; sometimes *Lensman*), and *Children of the Lens* (1947–1948). Smith had begun with a detailed outline for the entire saga, which helped make Lensman's plot much more complicated and consistent than Skylark's. Following the final installment's publication, Smith contracted with Fantasy Press to issue the works in hardcover. Lloyd Eshbach, Fantasy Press's owner, convinced Smith to rewrite one of the author's earlier works, *Triplanetary,* so that it would not only fit into the Lensman universe but also serve as a prequel. Eshbach then suggested that Smith also write a new work, *First Lensman,* to act as a bridge between the prequel and the series proper. Fantasy Press published the revised *Triplanetary* in 1948 and *First Lensman* in 1950, then released the original four-volume Lensman series between 1950 and 1954. Smith revised the original four-volume series in order to make the two new prequels consistent, and as a result a number of discrepancies between the original and the first publication in book form exist. Further, F. Orlin Tremaine, the *Astounding* editor who had contracted with Smith for Lensman, had left the magazine in 1938 to begin his own rival publication, *Comet.* The new magazine struggled financially, and Tremaine asked Smith for a contribution, hoping the author's fame and popularity would resuscitate his struggling enterprise. In response Smith wrote "The Vortex Baster," his initial foray into what would become *Masters of the Vortex,* an ancillary Lensman story set parallel to but not dependent upon the plots and characters of his Lensman series. Unfortunately, Smith's effort did not help Tremaine; "The Vortex Blaster" appeared in the final issue of *Comet,* though subsequent truncated Vortex tales ran in *Astounding* throughout 1942, until Smith elaborated on the story and published it in novel form in 1960, returning to *The Vortex Blaster* in name. This seventh Lensman novel seems to be set in the series' chronology between *Second-Stage Lensmen* and *Children of the Lens.*

The revised *Triplanetary* introduces two ancient races with highly developed mentalic powers, the benevolent Arisians and the power-hungry, invading Eddorians. Though possessing superior mental powers, the Arisians realize the Eddorians pose a significant threat because the aggressive race's mental powers rival their own; coupled with the Eddorians' technological supremacy, this gives the Eddorians the edge. The Arisians begin eugenics programs on a number of planets, including Earth, hoping over time to breed not only intelligent life but also a superior race to serve as galactic guardians. A couple billion years pass and humans begin to develop, garnering the attention of the Eddorians, who send Gharlane, Second of Eddore, to interfere with human history and ensure that the race never develops. But with the aid of Arisians disguised as humans, inhabitants of Earth (a.k.a. Tellus in the series) survive and begin populating the solar system, though they quickly find themselves plagued by space pirates (the Eddorians disguised). *Triplanetary* introduces Virgil Samms, First Lensman, and Rod Kinnison, whose ancestor, Kimball Kinnison, is the central hero of the four-book original Lensman series.

The bridge novel, *First Lensman,* describes the formation of the Galactic Patrol and introduces the lens itself, a gift to Samms from the Arisians. The lens is a lower-order artificial life form created by the Arisians that is fitted to a unique wearer (no one else can wear it), enabling its possessor a range of advanced mental powers, including the ability to communicate with any other life form and limited mind-reading capabilities. Samms uses the lens to visit various races and recruit from among their numbers to populate the Galactic Patrol, a marked departure by Smith from run-of-the-mill depictions of aliens as *other.* In *First Lensman,* aliens operate as fully functional and equal partners to humans. Earth faces a massive attack by space pirates—the Boskonians—but it is saved by the nascent Galactic Patrol.

The four volumes of the original Lensman series can be viewed as an organic whole. Generations have passed and humanity has established a foothold in the galaxy, but the Boskonians continue to be a formidable foe. Gradually Kimball Kinnison and his fellow Lensmen perceive that the Boskonian pirates are not a loose affiliation of brigands but the organized, purposeful fighting force of an even greater foe operating on an intergalactic scale. The fighting rages for years and is characterized by larger and more fantastic displays of technology, energy, and subterfuge—hyperspatial tubes, superdreadnaughts, planet-destroying energy beams, immense battles between huge space navies, secret councils that rule world-spanning empires, second- and third-stage lensmen, and the culmination of the Arisians' secret, humanity-spanning eugenics program in the form of Kinnison's five offspring, the children of *Children of the Lens.* These children can meld their own minds into what Smith calls The Unit, creating a mental force beyond even the Arisians. Further, The Unit can also channel the mental energies of all the other Lensmen—there are billions by now—which they use to finally penetrate the defensive shield surrounding the Eddorians' planet, vaporizing both the shield and the Eddorians.

Edmond Hamilton (1904–1977). "The Monster God of Mamurth," published in the August 1926 edition of *Weird Tales,* marked Hamilton's entry into the science fiction field. Though Hamilton gained a sizable readership for his numerous novels and short stories written during the 1920s and 1930s, his career is singularly marked by the Captain Future series. Hamilton was born in Pennsylvania and entered college at the age of 14, but he never finished it.

A highly productive writer who early in his sci-fi career earned the nickname "World Wrecker"—because many of his stories involved a galactic menace that could be neutralized only by destroying entire planets—Hamilton wrote hundreds of science fiction novels and short stories, several under a series of pseudonyms. He wrote even more novels and short stories in the horror and detective genres when his science fiction sales lagged. From 1946 on, when he married Leigh Brackett, another sci-fi author of note who also wrote the screenplay for *Star Wars V: The Empire Strikes Back,* his writing is marked by a more pensive and realistic style (a change usually credited to Brackett's influence). In that same year Hamilton was hired by Mort Weisinger, an old collaborator, to work at *DC Comics.* Weisinger had been a science fiction fan ever since reading *The Skylark of Space* as well as the early Buck Rogers series, and he had also collaborated with Hamilton several times, even lending a significant hand in the creation of Captain Future. Hamilton remained affiliated with *DC Comics* until 1966, lending his hand to countless Batman and Superman story lines.

Most of the Captain Future novels were published under their own *Captain Future* label and put out by Pines Publications. The first, *The Space Emperor,* appeared in early 1940 and was later reprinted as *Captain Future and the Space Emperor;* it serves to provide much of the series' exposition. Captain Future himself is Curtis Newton, the son of the brilliant scientist Roger Newton and Elaine, who are slain by the evil scientist Victor Kaslan while working in their moon laboratory. Raised by the giant robot Grag, the android Otho, and Simon Wright, the elderly scientific accomplice of the Wrights who exists now as a disembodied brain in a plastic case, Curtis becomes a Doc Savage-like paragon of virtue, intelligence, and physical prowess who vows to spend his life zipping around the galaxy (and in later adventures, through multiple dimensions and across time) in his ship, *The Comet,* righting wrongs and fighting evil.

Captain Future magazine published seventeen of the Captain Future adventures, with the remaining ten works appearing from 1946–1951 in *Startling Stories,* sometimes under Hamilton's Brett Sterling alias. Pines Publications also published a number of Captain Future comics, featuring a different Captain Future, under its *Nedor Comics* label. A year after Hamilton's death, a Japanese anime company began a series of 52 "Captain Future" episodes. While many qualities, plot lines, and characters diverged considerably from Hamilton's creation, the show was clearly based on Hamilton's work.

Perhaps more readily than in any other genre, science fiction lends itself to the sequel and even the series. Any piece of fiction must invent plot and character, but science fiction often needs to invent also new worlds and new races, and once that extra investment is made, authors are often loath to abandon it all after a single work. Although it can be argued that neither Smith nor Hamilton invested a great deal of creativity in making those worlds and races plausible, their inventive energy is nonetheless impressive. But when a series starts with a dramatic climax that involves destroying an entire marauding race by annihilating their entire planet, writing subsequent installments becomes rather a challenge. It is easy to see why both writers engaged in increasingly hyperbolic elements as their series continued, and that very hyperbole came to define early space opera.

That is not to say that they ignored actual science entirely. Both were highly intelligent and based much of their extrapolative technology on known scientific principles of the time, and they were often dogmatic in explaining how the inventions and technologies supposedly worked. Space opera does not altogether shirk sound science, but neither does it allow mere science to get in the way of a good story. The Smith-Hamilton era also saw the genesis of Buck Rogers (1928) and Flash Gordon (1935), two serialized swashbucklers who helped amplify and aggrandize science fiction in both the pulps and the movie theatres.

From the 1930s through the late 1970s, a number of luminaries made significant contributions to the space opera field, though many of them would cringe at having the label applied to their works—as would many of their fans. The figure who held the most sway during this period—along with Hugo Gernsback, who is often credited with creating science fiction as a genre and whose editorship was characterized by soliciting and encouraging space opera stories—was John W. Campbell, a sometimes space opera writer whose real influence lay in his position as editor of *Astounding Science Fiction*. Campbell ushered in a host of new young writers such as A.E. van Vogt, Robert Heinlein, and Isaac Asimov. Originally credited with moving the genre away from its operatic elements and more toward hard science, Campbell nonetheless began subscribing to baseless scientific notions in the early 1950s, including psionic powers and anti-Newtonian propulsion, which led many writers to believe that Campbell's vision of science was actually commercialized pseudoscience. His overbearing personality and truculence eventually drove many of the leading science fiction authors away from Campbell. But he also presided over what is generally referred to as the golden age of science fiction, a period ranging from the late 1930s to the 1950s.

The most important figure in the chronological progression of space opera after Smith and Hamilton is Jack Williamson. His Legion of Space series, first appearing in 1934, takes place in the thirtieth century and details the efforts of the Legion as it battles the Medusae, a race bent on conquering and inhabiting Earth because their own home planet has begun to spiral into its own star. Williamson, who died in 2006, continued writing well into his nineties and was an early influence on Asimov and others.

In 1946 A.E. van Vogt produced his first novel, *Slan,* which inverts the usual evil-alien paradigm by making ordinary humans villains intent on destroying the Slan. A product of eugenically evolved humans, the Slan are near supermen who possess psychic abilities, vastly superior intelligence, and supranormal strength and stamina. Other notable space opera works by van Vogt include *The Weapon Shops of Isher* (1951) and *Cosmic Encounter* (1980).

Arthur C. Clarke, generally considered one of the "Big Three" of science fiction and recognized as writing a style of science fiction based on extrapolation of sound science, nonetheless wrote a few works that could easily be categorized as space opera. Chief among them is *Childhood's End* (1953), given that Clarke dabbles with notions of the occult, of humanity's ascension into a hive-mind mentality, and of the existence of a race of Overlords and, above them, the Overmind, which uses the Overlords to guide certain races through their stage of transcendence from corporeal to ethereal existence. *Childhood's End* represents an exception in Clarke's oeuvre; he is otherwise widely recognized for the high quality of his science, as in his close adherence to known physics in *2001: A Space Odyssey* (although the existence of the monolith can be seen as problematic) and even in the hyperfilament he speculates about in *The Fountains of Paradise* (1979). He is even credited with being the first to recognize the importance of using geostationary positions for communications satellites.

Probably the best known name in science fiction is Isaac Asimov, who, like Clarke, is usually lauded for writing hard science fiction. An early Campbell disciple, Asimov's contributions to the field both in terms of literature and influence are extensive. "Nightfall" was recognized by the Science Fiction Writers of America as the best science fiction short story of all time, and the Foundation series was awarded a Hugo Award for best science fiction series of all time. But Foundation is pure space opera, comprising the original three volumes published in the early 1950s as well as its later four volumes, appearing from 1982 to 1993. Ostensibly, even his Robot series can be included, since he eventually folded R. Daneel Olivaw (as well as a few of his other stories and favorite themes) into Foundation's galactic empire. Foundation, admittedly influenced by Gibbons's *History of the Decline and Fall of the Roman Empire,* incorporates Hari Selden's theories of psychohistory, vast armadas careening through hyperspace, an empire that spans an entire galaxy, and startling technological and mentalic advances.

No list of space opera authors can be comprehensive, and the likes of Jack Vance, Vernor Vinge (as well as his ex-wife, Joan Vinge), Andre Norton (more noted for her fantasy works), and even Robert Heinlein could be incorporated here, along with dozens of other names. But by the mid-1960s, science fiction had begun to transform under the influence of the New Wave writers. Michael Moorcock is generally credited with originating the movement when he assumed editorship of *New Worlds* magazine in 1964; Harlan Ellison is often touted as the movement's primary initial writer and proponent. Science fictional New Wave advocated bringing the entire genre closer to the mainstream, primarily by sacrificing scientific integrity for literary style while simultaneously encouraging more experimentation—in short, foregrounding space opera's penchant for telling the tale rather than adhering to sound science, even as the New Wave writers eschewed space opera as hack writing. The New Wave writers felt they were distinguishing their brand of science fiction by focusing more intently on psychological and sociological aspects, and their writing trended toward a more pessimistic view of humanity. Leading New Wave writers include such note worthies as Moorcock, Ellison, J.G. Ballard, Philip K. Dick, Ursula K. Le Guin, Samuel Delany, Roger Zelazny, Robert Silverberg, Leigh Brackett, and Brian Aldiss.

Disdain for anything with even a whiff of space opera reached its height during the late 1960s and early 1970s, which prompted Aldiss's declaration that the genre was dead. But, like Twain's obituary, the death knell was premature, and space opera's fortunes experienced a radical reversal in the late 1970s. In the mid-1970s, Lester Del Rey attempted to redefine space opera by returning it to its roots as a nonliterary or even antiliterary art form, rejecting what he called the failed experiment of the New Wave movement and its Modernist roots (Hartwell and Cramer

2006, 15–16). Del Rey's influence was very slight until about 3 p.m. on May 25, 1977, at which time George Lucas and 20th Century Fox released *Star Wars* on the world. An unabashed space opera, *Star Wars* transfixed an entire generation, redefining space opera as the best-selling popular science fiction entertainment. As noted earlier, Brackett even wrote the script for the second Star Wars installment, *The Empire Strikes Back*. *Star Wars* demonstrated to the hard sci-fi writers—to the entire world, actually—that space opera could be an immense commercial success while simultaneously receiving, at the very least, moderately favorable literary and cinematic reviews. Lucas and company also showed that space opera could be rollicking good fun. Its early sense of awe and wonder had returned.

Context and Issues. By the middle of the 1980s, the space opera renaissance was in full swing. Yet the literary inclinations of the New Wave movement influenced the resurgence of what is frequently called the new space opera, with its practitioners bringing new literary savvy to the genre and the lines between space opera and hard science fiction becoming once again blurred. Many of the names listed here also appear in the accompanying entry on science fiction, and with good reason. The new space opera writers were more cognizant of being at least reasonably account-able to science, were capable of infusing their works with philosophical ideas and symbolism, and still managed to tell an engaging tale. The new movement's vanguard was primarily British, led by the likes of Alastair Reynolds, John Clute, and Iain Banks, though by 1990 a new breed of American writers began to estab-lish a foothold, especially because new space opera, though still not fully considered hard science fiction or even fully literary, bore a much more favorable imprimatur. Among publishers, Baen Books was the first noteworthy house to openly advocate for the new space opera and a new core of writers, with Del Rey and Tor soon following suit.

An impressive number of writers published the bulk of their space opera canons in the 1980s and 1990s, though few have produced much since 2000. These writers, in varying degrees, contributed heavily to refiguring and reconstituting space opera by bringing to their craft more complexity of character, a greater attention to science, and the infusion of themes and ideas, whether political, religious, cultural, or philosophical. What follows is a brief discussion of the major works and ideas of three of these authors.

Steven Barnes (1952–) initially came to prominence coauthoring several works with Larry Niven, starting with *Dream Park* (1981), followed by *The Descent of Anansi* (1982), *Achilles' Choice* (1991), and *Saturn's Race* (2000); the two writers also teamed with Jerry Pournelle for the two-volume Heorot series. Barnes also con-tributed one work each to the *Star Trek* and *Star Wars* sagas, the latter appearing in 2004, and he singlehandedly wrote several works as well.

Along with Greg Bear and Gregory Benford, David Brin (1950–) comprise the affectionately named Killer B's of science fiction, so called largely because of their collaborative efforts in writing the "final" trilogy in Asimov's Foundation series, though Brin had long before established himself as a sci-fi writer of note with his award-winning Uplift novels, beginning with *Sundiver* (1980) and concluding with *Heaven's Reach* (1998). While largely a work of military space opera, the Uplift stories serve as a paean to evolutionary theory, and they also incorporate and develop ideas of genetic engineering, democracy, and racial consciousness. In other works, such as *Glory Season* (1993) and *Kiln People* (2002), Brin explores the effects of technology on humanity. Brin also gained some notoriety for writing a few articles criticizing what he felt were the antidemocratic principles and attitudes underlying the immensely popular *Star Wars* and *Lord of the Rings* works. His only space opera work since 2000 is *Forgiveness* (2001), a graphic novel contributing to the Star Trek: The Next Generation series.

Dan Simmons (1948–) gained widespread popularity and acclaim for his four-volume Hyperion Cantos (though he followed the tetralogy with a 1999 short story, "Orphans of the Helix," which continues the same story line). Simmons mines Greek mythology for his most recent space opera undertaking, *Ilium* (2003) and its sequel, *Olympos* (2004), just as he borrows from classic literature for his award-winning Cantos. The titles are drawn from the poetry of John Keats—Keats, in fact, appears as a cybrid character—and the initial format borrows liberally from the pilgrimage motif of Boccaccio's *Decameron* and Chaucer's *The Canterbury Tales*. Simmons's Cantos revolve around the Shrike, a four-armed, armored machine with spikes covering its body. The Shrike has been built by a far-future machine god, and it can manipulate time to torture beings—pilgrims—in an effort to lure a human god from the future. Clearly the antagonist of the first two novels, the Shrike begins to act benevolently in subsequent tales. The Cantos gradually develop into a cautionary tale about militaristic religion, with the heroes battling the Pax, an extension of the Catholic Church that has spread its dominance over most of the galaxy, largely with the aid of the cruciform, a quasi-organic artifact that allows regeneration of the dead.

Reception. Only in the past two decades has space opera began to garner serious critical attention, albeit limited, which is mainly due to the longstanding perception of space opera as hack writing. Prior to 1990 critical examinations of space opera were virtually nonexistent, largely because the term was anathema. But since its rejuvenation in the late 1970s and beyond, space opera has slowly become a fertile object for critical analysis. Kathryn Cramer, William H. Hardesty III, David G. Hartwell, and especially Gary Westfahl reside at the forefront of a small cadre of literary critics who have examined space opera in some detail, tracing its origins and finding in the new space opera no small merit. The bulk of the critical attention has come in the last ten years, and it frequently takes the form of some sort of reconsideration of the genre, though feminist perspectives on space opera are beginning to appear with greater regularity.

In his "Space Opera" chapter in *The Cambridge Companion to Science Fiction,* Westfahl points to space opera's burgeoning commercial appeal as well as its trend of garnering the bulk of the major science fiction awards since around 1990 as primary reasons why the genre is attracting better writers and receiving more critical attention (Westfahl 2003, 205). David Pringle points to space opera's steadily increasing level of sophistication and literary merit in the past decade, though he argues also that the subgenre should be divided even further into planetary romances, which he feels are distinctly different (Pringle 2000, 39, 46). Hartwell and Cramer are perhaps the most vocal and insistent critics calling for a reassessment of space opera's literary merits, finding that the new space opera is a "colorful, dramatic, large-scale science fiction adventure, competently and sometimes beautifully written" (Hartwell and Cramer 2006). *Locus* magazine, a near-annual winner of various science fiction awards for its reportage on science fiction and fantasy, even devoted its August 2003 issue exclusively to articles and interviews on the new space opera.

Further, television and film manifestations of space opera have similarly progressed from the days of Flash Gordon and Buck Rogers. While 1960s and 1970s offerings like *Dr. Who, Star Trek, Star Wars,* and especially the original *Battlestar Galactica* still bore many of the clichés of the old space opera, already the seeds of the new space opera can be seen as several of these undertakings began to concern themselves with ideas and issues underlying the basic entertainment quotient. Even in Ridley Scott's *Alien* (1979) were themes like militarism, xenophobia, masculinity, and abortion being embedded in sophisticated and challenging ways. And although some of the most recent TV and movie issues can still rally around the older notions of space opera—consider *Galaxy Quest* and *Total Recall*—by presenting sheer entertainment on a vast scale that blithely disregards the physical laws of time and space, series like Joss Whedon's *Firefly* (and its subsequent cinematic issue, *Serenity*) and Ronald D. Moore's 2003 reincarnation of *Battlestar Galactica* have garnered wide critical acclaim, with the latter earning Peabody, Hugo, and Saturn awards.

With a cadre of new, talented, and literary writers producing a steadily increasing stream of space opera, Tucker's notion of the genre as filled with hacky, outworn yarns seems to have been fully put to rest.

Selected Authors. Contemporary, or new, space opera authors can be divided into three groups: those whose primary corpora came in the 1980s and 1990s but who are still contributing a handful of works; those who established themselves in the genre in the 1990s but continue to write extensively; and those who are new writers and whose work starts almost exclusively in 2000. Continuing the trend of the new space opera, each of these writers infuses his or her works with better science, more deeply complex characters, and political and philosophical musings and explorations.

Group 1: Human-Alien Interactions. If there is one dominant characteristic of the writers in this group, it is their penchant for exploring human-alien interactions. By and large these writers invest a great deal of thought and complexity in developing their alien species without simply demonizing them, even though plots often center around human-alien conflict. The novels frequently depict the intricacies and difficulties of intercultural interaction, serving as a metaphor for the panoply of contemporary global politics.

Kevin J. Anderson (1962–) wrote a few contributions on his own to the Star Wars galaxy of novels and many more as coauthor with wife Rebecca Moesta before teaming up with Brian Herbert in a series of immensely popular prequels to Frank Herbert's Dune series. Anderson has also recently novelized *The League of Extraordinary Gentlemen* (2003) and *Sky Captain and the World of Tomorrow* (2004) as well as contributed three *X-Files* books and a novel set in the *StarCraft* computer game world.

Orson Scott Card's (1951–) primary contribution to space opera is the highly touted and multiple award-winning Ender's Game series (generally known as the Enderverse), begun in 1977 as a novelette appearing in *Analog.* He expanded the story to book length in 1985 and followed it with seven other installments. A practicing Mormon, Card's religious views permeate not only the Ender's Game series but also most of his other works, including The Homecoming Saga and The Tales of Alvin Maker, though arguably both of these series lean more toward fantasy and alternate history than science fiction despite the former's setting in distant space. But at the heart of each lies what has become Card's principal protagonist— the brilliant young boy, possessing superior talents, whose internal struggles with morality and the burdens of sin and guilt dominate his passage through life, earmarked by seeking ultimate redemption. Both *Ender's Game* and its sequel,

Speaker for the Dead, won both the Hugo and the Nebula Awards, making Card the only author to win both of science fiction's highest awards in consecutive years. Card has recently been adding short stories to the Ender's Game series, stories which have been published mostly on line. In 1999 he began a string of novels paralleling the Ender tales called The Shadow Series, alternately referred to in some circles as the Bean Quartet, because the works center around Julian "Bean" Delphiki, a supporting character from *Ender's Game.* Originally comprising four books, Card has announced a fifth work in the series, as well as another Ender work, but no details have yet been released. Further, plans to make *Ender's Game* into a movie have been in the works since 2003, though screenplay issues have made the film's production dubious, despite an announcement by Fresco Pictures that they intend to release a film version no sooner than 2008.

While C.J. Cherryh's (1942–) voluminous output of fiction spans a number of genres, the bulk of her work is usually classified as space opera and functions within two primary arenas Cherryh has created, the Alliance-Union universe and the Foreigner universe. Comprising twenty-four novels and a handful of short story anthologies to date—including *Downbelow Station* (1981) and *Cyteen* (1988), Cherryh's two Hugo-winning works—the Allied-Union stories begin in the near future and trace humanity's gradual expansion to the stars, eventually including roughly twenty sentient alien species. Her Foreigner universe spans nine novels thus far, most of them published since 2000, and traces the exploits of the crew members of starship *Phoenix* as they find themselves stranded in space with no way to return to Earth. Cherryh has been widely lauded for developing complex and realistic alien species and examining human interactions with the *other,* and for paying close attention to such cultural nuances as language, environment, politics, and racial self identity. The politics in her novels have been described as having a moderate conservative leaning. Cherryh is also one of the few space opera writers who has garnered scholarly attention, primarily in *The Cherryh Odyssey* (2004), a compilation of articles edited by Edward Carmien.

David Drake (1945–) has also written numerous works spanning multiple genres, with his space opera works falling predominantly into the militaristic, right-leaning category. Drake, like Simmons, often draws heavily on mythology. Hammer's Slammers, his first series of space operas begun in 1979 with an eponymously named novel (1987), borrows freely from the tales of Jason and the Argonauts, *The Iliad,* and *The Odyssey.* In 1998 Drake inaugurated his latest space opera series, titled the RCN (Republic of Cinnabar Navy) series, which evokes Horatio Hornblower's exploits. He has written five works thus far, with a sixth issue planned for 2008. The RCN series revolves around Daniel Leary, an RCN officer, and Adele Mundy, a librarian who eventually also takes a commission in the RCN, at the center of an epic battle against the evil, totalitarian Alliance of Free Stars. Unlike Hammer's Slammers, the RCN series focuses more on character development and political intrigues, though space battles still abound. Drake has also contributed to a number of works wherein he is listed as coauthor, though by his own admission his contribution has been plot and character outlines, which the other writer then finishes. In this vein he has teamed primarily with Eric Flint.

Writing extensively in both fantasy and science fiction, including contributions to the Star Wars and Star Trek universes (in the latter, primarily for the animated TV series of the 1970s), Alan Dean Foster (1946–) is best known in space opera circles for his Humanx Commonwealth stories, which commences with *The Tar-Aiym*

Krang (1972), and which has two more volumes forthcoming. Most of these works recount the adventures of Philip Lynx ("Flinx") and his female Alaspinian Miniature Dragon, or minidrag, companion, Pip. Because of his empathic powers and his remarkable spaceship, *Teacher,* Flinx becomes a renegade; Pip is also empathic, though non-sapient. Flinx's adventures detail his search for his unknown biological father, his encounters with mysterious artifacts, his attempts to flee the Commonwealth government, his interactions with numerous alien species, and his discovery of a source of malignancy in the Great Emptiness that threatens the entire galaxy by consuming all life on any planet it encounters. One of Foster's most common motifs is the intricacies between life forms and their environment, often making their symbiotic coexistence one of the key elements of his novels.

Group 2: The Female Writer and Character. If the first group is marked by alien culture, the second group is dominated by the female—both as writer and as character. Three of the four authors below are female, while the fourth, David Weber, is most noted for his Honor Harrington tales, which center around a strong female protagonist. While Doc Smith was given kudos for some of his strong female characters, they enjoyed only minor significance. For the writers in this group, the female, whether writer or character, becomes far more prominent.

Catherine Asaro (1955–) was born in Oakland, California, and has earned multiple science degrees: a BA in chemistry, an MA in physics, and a PhD in chemical physics. She was a physics professor at Kenyon College until 1990, at which time she founded Molecudyne Research in Maryland. In addition, she has taught mathematics and ballet, has served as a NASA consultant and as a visiting scientist at the Max Planck Institute for Astrophysics, and has written a handful of fantasy novels.

Asaro's professional writing career (save for one short story in 1993) began with 1995's *Primary Inversion,* which introduces readers to her Skolian Empire, within which most of her novels are set. In reality, the Skolians are but one of three empires, along with their enemies, the Eubian Traders and the Terrans (also known as Allieds). The Skolians try to balance themselves politically between the other two, and they are ruled by the ancient and somewhat democratic Ruby Dynasty, which is often fraught with internal struggles. They possess limited empathic and telepathic talents, enhanced through pico- and nanotechnology. The Eubian Traders are ruled by the Aristos, products of a genetic engineering program gone awry, and their empire is built entirely upon a slave economy. The Allieds, last to join the interstellar scene (in the year 2122), spend much of the series simply trying to stay out from underfoot.

The Skolian series' publication history does not follow a chronological timeline, nor is it dedicated to continually expanding and developing a linear plot. Instead, Asaro has written a number of stories that, though set within her primary Skolian universe, can often stand alone as individual works. *Spherical Harmonic* (2001), for example, reengages the series' main story lines after several side stories have taken place in previous works. The work starts to unify plot developments from previous Skolian episodes like *The Last Hawk* (1997) and *The Quantum Rose* (2000; Nebula Award winner for Best Novel) while developing the character of Dhyianna (Dehya) Selei, the Ruby Pharaoh, who had been a minor, elusive figure to this point. Further, *Spherical Harmonic* is part of a four-volume subset of the Skolian series that traces the aftermath of one of the series' major events, the Radiant War. Two of her most recent contributions to the series, *Schism* (2004) and *The Final Key* (2005), function best in tandem, following a contiguous character and plot line, though the former actually comprises a triad of three short stories. The most recent Skolian novel is *The Ruby Dice,* which brings back one of the leading protagonists from early story lines, Imperator Kelric, to the forefront. *The Ruby Dice* appeared in 2006 in novella form and is due out in expanded form in late 2007 or early 2008.

Asaro intermixes a great deal of current, advanced, and accurate physics with highly developed romances among her characters into her novels. She will switch off between male and female protagonists, though each is generally a strong, independent, autonomous personality. Reviews, though occasionally mixed (depending on the particular novel), have generally been quite favorable. James Schellenberg finds *Primary Inversion* "a serendipitous find" (challengingdestiny.com), and her most recent Skolian works have received nearly universal praise. SciFi.com's Paul Di Filippo, for example, likens *Schism* and *The Final Key* to Frank Herbert's Dune saga in the way Asaro's characters, politics, and action all mature and achieve high levels of sophistication and interest. And his fellow site critic, Lois H. Gresh, raves that *Schism*—and, indeed, the entire Skolian series—is nothing short of excellent.

Lois McMaster Bujold (1949–) has become one of the most popular and most critically acclaimed writers in new space opera almost exclusively on the strength of her extended Vorkosigan chronicles. Her four Hugo Awards for Best Novel tie her with Robert Heinlein, and she has received two Nebulas as well. After working for a number of years as a pharmacy technician, she turned her hand to writing science fiction—a love she acquired from her father.

Bujold wrote her first three novels before making a single sale. *Twilight Zone Magazine* bought the third volume in late 1984, and about a year later, Baen Books purchased and published all three. Like Asaro, the publication dates of Bujold's Vorkosigan novels do not follow the series' chronology, nor do they all center on her principal protagonist, Miles Vorkosigan.

Even before birth Miles suffers physical impairment due to an assassination attempt against his mother, Cordelia Naismith, and father, Aral Vorkosigan. Constrained by a weakened body and short physical stature, Miles often overcompensates. He confronts the universe with daring and audacity, usually managing to extricate himself from the resulting disastrous circumstances by his brilliance and éclat. By the age of seventeen he tricks a number of colleagues into believing he has recruited them for the infamous Dendarii Mercenaries, and by their very exploits, the mercenary band is formed. Succeeding in a series of secretive campaigns and political subterfuges, Miles continues to ascend the hierarchy of his home world of Barrayar.

Barrayar was initially settled mostly by Russian, Greek, and French pioneers traveling via wormholes, the principal form of interstellar travel in the series. The wormholes themselves all originate in close proximity in an area called the Wormhole Nexus, a region of space inhabited by an array of varying cultures residing on planets and military space stations that guard the entry points. Reintegrated into galactic civilization after generations of isolation, Barrayar is almost immediately invaded by the neighboring Cetagandan Empire, but it manages to fend off the attack. Miles doesn't officially enter the story line until the 1991 novel *Barrayar,* and his exploits assume center stage in the next novel chronologically, *The Warrior's Apprentice* (1986), the second of Bujold's initial three-novel output. Most of the ensuing novels, novellas, and short stories recount Miles's ongoing exploits.

Though her recent work has been primarily fantasy, Bujold has written two Vorkosigan novels since 1999: *A Civil Campaign* (1999) and *Diplomatic Immunity*

(2002), both furthering Miles's adventures. *A Civil Campaign* develops the love interest between Miles and Ekaterin Vorsoisson, whom he had met in the previous novel. Because of his failing health, Miles has abandoned his military career and is now an Imperial Auditor. As is his wont, Miles pursues Ekaterin impetuously, proffering an embarrassing offer of marriage at a party gone terribly awry, which she refuses. Their relationship complicates further when two seats on the vaunted Council of Counts become available. Miles, acting as his father's deputy, controls one of the votes, and as such is courted and even blackmailed by the two Barrayarans vying for one of the open seats. The blackmail serves to implicate Miles in the death of Ekaterin's former husband. Miles's efforts are further muddied by the Emperor's impending marriage and the arrival of Miles's clone-brother, Mark, who is in the midst of an illicit affair of his own. Miles's persistence and honor prevail, and he and Ekaterin wed. *Diplomatic Immunity* commences as Miles and Ekaterin begin their honeymoon, which is interrupted by a diplomatic entanglement in Quaddiespace. Quaddies are four-armed-no-legged, genetically created beings first introduced in *Falling Free* (1988). They are raised as slaves to live and work entirely in the freefall of outer space, but rendered obsolete when artificial gravity is developed. They escaped their servitude and now inhabit a remote planetary system; but early in *Diplomatic Immunity* a situation arises at Graf Station in Quaddiespace, requiring Miles's intervention. Ordered to avoid a major diplomatic fiasco, Miles naturally exacerbates the already tense situation. While evading assassination attempts and uncovering clues that widen the mystery, Miles manages to avert a war between Cetaganda and Barrayar, even as he runs into an old flame. Between these two most recent novels, Bujold also wrote an intervening novella, "Winterfair Gifts" (2002), which retells the Miles-Ekaterin wedding from the perspective of Roic, Miles's armsman.

Bujold's science is not on a par with Asaro's, though her ability to sustain an extended plot line and develop complex characters is more deft. Sfsite.com's Regina Lynn Preciado, in reviewing the entire Vorkosigan saga, calls Bujold "a master writer whose prose continues to impress with every book"; Sfreviews.net's T.M. Wagner also touts the entire series. In July 2006 Baen Books promised a new Vorkosigan novel from Bujold in the near future.

Elizabeth Moon (1945–) earned Bachelor's degrees in both history and biology, and she also served time in the U.S. Marine Corps as a 1st Lieutenant. She won a Nebula Award for best novel for *The Speed of Dark* (2003) and garnered a Hugo nomination for her earlier work, *Remnant Population* (1997). She has worked variously as a sign painter, a draftsman, and as a columnist with a weekly county newspaper; she has also busied herself with a number of community activities.

Moon first established herself as a fantasy writer in the late 1980s with her trilogy entitled The Deed of Paksenarrion, to which she later added two more works; some critics have pointed out the trilogy's strong resemblance to the *Dungeons & Dragons* board game and modules. Her first venture into space opera was the Familias Regnant series, comprising seven volumes published from 1993 to 2000 and met with somewhat mixed but promising reviews. In 2003 Moon launched a new space opera series known collectively as Vatta's War. Four books have come out so far, with a fifth, *Victory Conditions,* slated for a 2008 release. The series chronicles the struggles of Kylara Vatta, a young woman born into the family of an interstellar shipping corporation who bucks her sinecure with the family business to try her hand at military life. In the first novel, *Trading in Danger* (2003), Kylara is forced to resign from the military and instead takes captaincy of an old freighter her family has designated for the scrap yards. When she deviates from her simple mission, she quickly becomes entangled with space pirates and a planetary war, in which she must rely on her military training to turn certain disaster into a profitable victory for herself and her family. In the subsequent novels, political intrigues and military battles intensify as her father's corporate headquarters are attacked, leaving both her parents dead. Though her military training serves her in good stead, Kylara must adapt to political intrigues, shifting alliances, commercially driven interests, and betrayals, as well as become adept at diplomacy.

Moon is noted for her strong female protagonists who must embark upon a *bildungsroman* that entails encountering betrayal and loss to achieve autonomy and recognition, and to learn the value of loyalty. Her series tend to start slowly, to mediocre reviews, until she gains her footing with character and plot, from which point the stories and the critical regard both accelerate. Moon schooled herself in stories of space pirates and planetary adventure at the heels of Anne McCaffrey, with whom she coauthored The Planet Pirates trilogy in the early 1990s.

David Weber (1952–), in addition to collaborating with such space opera notables as John Ringo (see below), has established himself in the genre largely on the strength of his Honor Harrington series, affectionately known as the Honorverse. Weber's space opera is heavily militaristic, coupled with a complex interplay of politics. Generally politicians play the roles of foils to the exploits of the military characters; thus, the politics of his novels, especially in the Honorverse, tend toward libertarianism, emphasizing the importance of individual actions over governmental enterprise. Weber has devoted tremendous energy to fully fleshing out his Honorverse, most especially the various navies, which strongly parallel the navies of Britain and France at the time of the Napoleonic Wars. Harrington herself is an amalgam of Horatio Hornblower (with whom she shares initials) and British Admiral Lord Nelson.

On Basilisk Station (1993) inaugurated the Honorverse, presenting Honor Harrington as a fresh-faced graduate of the Royal Manticorian Navy's Advanced Tactical Course commanding her first ship, the *Fearless*. Banished to Basilisk Station for repeated tactical failures during simulated war games, Harrington catches wind of The People's Republic of Haven's plans to overrun Basilisk Station and conquer its system. Through a desperate and costly military maneuver Harrington exposes the plan, allowing her home world of Manticore time to bolster its defenses. The Honorverse currently spans seventeen novels, including four anthologies, and follows Harrington's continued military and diplomatic career as she repeatedly demonstrates her mettle in a constant stream of space battles and political intrigues. By the time of *At All Costs* (2005), the series' most recent work, Harrington has become a dame, a duchess, a countess, and an admiral of the fleet, even as the balance of power between Manticore and Haven has shifted dramatically in favor of the latter.

In addition to the Honorverse, Weber has developed a number of other space opera series, both individually and in tandem with other writers. His solo efforts include the Heirs of Empire trilogy, whereas his collaborations span the four-volume Empire of Man series with John Ringo and the highly touted 1632 universe, coauthored by Eric Flint. He has also cowritten with Linda Evans and Steve White.

Ad Astra Games has, in the past two years, put out two books detailing aspects of the Honorverse as part of what they are calling their *Jayne's Intelligence Review* series: *The Royal Manticoran Navy* (2006), covering the navy's history, ship classifications, battles, and even uniforms and insignia; and *The Navy of the People's Republic of Haven* (2007), which performs much the same task in detailing Manticore's foe, the planet Haven.

Group 3: New Faces on the Scene. With the immense popularity of space opera over the past two decades, the genre has seen an explosion of works by countless writers. The writers in this group represent newer, promising faces on the American space opera scene. Under its "space opera/space epics/space romance" listing, for example, scifan.com lists over eight hundred titles published since 2000. Although economic and political considerations show signs of becoming earmarks of post–2000 space opera, contemporary fiction in the genre bears the indelible stamp of the military battle. First and foremost among new space opera writers of the third millennium stands John Ringo (1963–). Having traveled widely and pursued careers in marine biology and database management, Ringo began publishing in 2000, and he has already issued, both individually and as coauthor, over thirty-five books. He writes almost exclusively in the military space opera vein (he served in the military as a paratrooper), and his works tend to reflect his outspoken, military-flavored conservative views. His works are almost always part of an extended series.

Ringo's first novel, *A Hymn before Battle* (2000), introduced his Posleen War series (also referred to as The Legacy of Aldenata), currently standing at eight volumes with five more planned. Ringo wrote the first four on his own, and he has been cowriting the volumes since the fifth issue, *Cally's War* (2006). Earth is recruited by the peaceful Galactic Federation in their eons-long war against the aggressive, centauroid Posleen. The Galactic Federation enlists the aid of the Darhel to help humanity train and develop advanced technology, though the Darhel are duplicitous in their aims. Humans, outnumbered and outgunned, retaliate against the Posleen in unorthodox but effective ways, led by the courageous Captain Michael O'Neal. By the third novel—*When the Devil Dances* (2003)—however, Earth's forces have been overwhelmed, leaving only pockets of resistance (including O'Neal) hindered by the blundering interference of inept politicians. Ringo's post–9/11 politics surface clearly in the novel, as it takes the series down a darker path and explores the idea of an all-out militaristic response to an attack on America. In the afterword, in fact, he calls 9/11 a wake-up call for America and urges the United States to fight. As the series develops, the Darhel are discovered to have been controlling and manipulating humanity for thousands of years, greater emphasis is given to the heroic actions of the individual in combat situations, Earth's allies are revealed as hoping that the war ends in mutual destruction, and huge, massively destructive weaponry is developed, which enables humans to begin to prevail. Though the series shifts focus from its characters to the battles and the weaponry as it progresses, the forthcoming works promise to turn their attention back to more thorough and detailed character development.

Ringo's next series, *Empire of Man,* is cowritten with David Drake. It satirizes contemporary environmentalist movements while basing its story line on Xenophon's *Anabasis,* the story of 10,000 Greek troops stranded in hostile Persia in 400 B.C.E. The four-volume series begins with Prince Roger MacClintock marooned on planet Marduk while on a diplomatic mission. Fortunately, he is accompanied by the Bravo Company of the Bronze Battalion of the Empress's Own Regiment, and in the course of their world-girding trek in hopes of commandeering an imperial ship to return home, all the while battling both flora and fauna, the pampered prince grows in true *bildungsroman* tradition, learning responsibility and loyalty while becoming a warrior himself, gaining new respect for and from his battle-hardened marines. As the battalion steadily diminishes, its marines are forced to strike a number of political alliances in the midst of their many battles. The first three novels all detail the Prince's trudge to and conquest of the spaceport, and they tend to become repetitive. Prince Roger begins to assume Henry the Fifth-like proportions, as suggested by the fourth book's title, *We Few* (2005), taken directly from Henry's St. Crispin's Day speech just before the Battle of Agincourt, in Shakespeare's noted work. In the final installment, Prince Roger and his band finally return home, only to find that his mother, the Empress, has been usurped by traitors and that he stands accused of regicide. Roger must once again draw on his new-found leadership skills and his trusty marines to set things aright.

Ringo is also in the midst of three other series. The four-volume Council Wars continues his military space opera bent, but it also presents an intriguing mix of hard science and magic, though the magic is in the Arthur C. Clarke sense that any sufficiently advanced technology is indistinguishable from magic. The series begins with its own Edenic fall from grace and traces the exploits of Herzer Herrick, chiseled from the image of the classic Greek warrior. Paladin of Shadows currently spans four books, with a fifth, *A Deeper Blue,* slated for a mid-2007 release. The series confronts directly a couple of the themes and ideas raised in Council Wars, primarily the troubled hero and deeply rooted male desires; the first book, *Ghost* (2005), also takes square aim at the perceived liberalism of higher education. Council Wars started leaning into the fantasy realm, whereas Paladin of Shadows is more thriller than science fiction, though still with heavy military overtones. In 2006 Ringo also wrote *Into the Looking Glass,* and has teamed with Travis Taylor (see below) for its sequel, the much more space-operatic *Vorpal Blade* (2007). Like Weber, Ringo's novels demonstrate a libertarian inclination with even greater emphasis on the importance of the male military figure.

Tony Daniel (1963–) began his science fiction writing career with a pair of non-fiction essays published 1990, followed by several short stories and a pair of novels in the 1990s. He spent several years involved with the drama group Automatic Vaudeville in New York City, wrote and directed a film entitled *American Bohemian,* served as the Senior Story Editor at Scifi.com's Seeing Ear Theater, and spent a couple of years as a radio dramatist. Daniel currently lives near Dallas with his wife, daughter, and son.

He is often confused with the Tony Daniel of Dark Horse Comics fame, whose work often slides into the science fiction realm. But Tony Daniel, the science fiction author, entered the space opera arena with *Metaplanetary* (2002), an oblique reference to Doc Smith's *Triplanetary* and the first release of a trilogy in progress. Extending Daniel's 1998 novella "Grist" and set a thousand years in the future, the novel's central trope is the Met, a network of cables extending throughout the inner solar system that serves as both communication and transportation. Society within the Met's influence is hegemonic, ruled by the monomaniacal Director Ames. The Met cannot be extended beyond the asteroid belt, and life in the outer system is at best a loose confederacy of rebels and cloudships, which are human personalities downloaded into massive spaceships poised to venture forth to the distant stars. The bulk of *Metaplanetary* is spent building Daniel's technology-infused world and setting the stage for the incipient clash between these two disparate cultures. The war commences in the second book, *Superluminal* (2005), which occupies most of the story line; the second volume also contains extensive appendices to help sort the multitude of characters and concepts.

Daniel's two space opera entries examine the line between human and artificial, the symbiosis between humans and technology, and the nature of existence, the last showing the influence of the author's own existentialist leanings. *Metaplanetary* was well received; David Soyka, writing on Sfsite.com, describes the novel as "Heinlein meets Gibson and Stephenson, with a dash of Tom Robbins," recognizing both Daniel's post-cyberpunk and hard sci-fi influences. Though receiving similar plaudits, *Superluminal* was generally perceived as suffering from "middle book syndrome," which is characterized by plot lines only marginally extended in anticipation of the next novel. And Stuart Jaffe writes that character development in the second installment was thin, though he still found *Superluminal* "an astounding achievement in world-building" (infinityplus.co.uk).

Travis "Doc" Taylor has a series of scientific degrees, culminating in a PhD in optical science and engineering from the University of Alabama in Huntsville, and he has worked on several programs for both the Department of Defense and NASA. His education and background bring a hard-edged science to his works, with their scope and timbre falling clearly within the parameters of new space opera. Taylor holds a black belt in martial arts and a pilot's license. He lives with his wife and daughter in northern Alabama.

Warp Speed (2006), Taylor's inaugural novel, and its sequel, *The Quantum Connection* (2007), are near-future, harder science fiction tales. His space opera works start with *Von Neumann's War* (2006), written with Ringo. The novel, which was met with lukewarm reviews, couples Taylor's hard science with Ringo's militaristic style in describing contemporary Earth's invasion by self-replicating machines (Von Neumann machines). Taylor and Ringo also teamed up for *Vorpal Blade,* due for a fall 2007 release, and the sequel to Ringo's *Into the Looking Glass.* The book's press release describes it as a return to the "good old days" of science fiction with space marines, fantastic weaponry, and BEMs (bug-eyed monsters). Taylor also has undertaken his own largely space-operatic Tau Ceti series. Neither the first installment, *One Day on Mars* (fall 2007), nor its sequel, *The Tau Ceti Agenda* (2007–2008), have been released, and Travis's Web site describes the former as "24 on Mars" and the latter as a "non-stop space navy, Armored Environment Suit Marines, configurable hovertanks and fighting mecha, space fighters, spies, senators, presidents, a mass exodus, and multiple nuclear explosions!"

Scott Westerfield (1963–) is probably better known for his young adult books, but he has also had success writing hard science fiction. He earned a degree in philosophy from Vassar in 1985, and he has worked variously as a factory worker, substitute teacher, software designer, and textbook editor. He splits his time between New York City and Sydney, Australia. His wife is Australian author Justine Larbalestier.

Westerfield's foray into space opera currently spans two novels, *The Risen Empire* and *The Killing of Worlds,* both released in 2003. Originally a single book entitled *Succession,* the work was split into two books due to its length, though the full version with the original name was nonetheless issued later in 2003. In the distant future an 80-world human empire has been ruled by the same man for over 1,600 years, thanks to a parasite that can keep the mind and body active after death. The emperor bestows this gift on a select but growing number of elites, with the result that the living must work ever harder to sustain the growing dead, or Risen, population, which, per force, makes the empire torpid. But in a neighboring empire, another culture has arisen. The Rix, cyborgs who worship artificial intelligence, wish to liberate the worlds of the Risen Empire, and they begin by kidnapping the emperor's sister while trying to seed an emergent artificial mind. The emperor's Imperial Navy intervenes, but not before the sister is killed and her mind seeded. The newly sentient mind, however, has also discovered a secret regarding the emperor and the Risen, and planetary war hangs in the balance as a result. *The Killing of Worlds* escalates the action. While Imperial Navy Captain Laurent Zai is on a desperate mission to destroy a Rix battle cruiser, a lone Rix commando named Herd begins a trek across the planet Legis to seize a polar communications array to essentially free the seeded AI mind, delivering the emperor's closely guarded secret.

Westerfield's two novels speculate on the nature of sentience, the rights of privilege in the face of dwindling resources, and political exigency. While not as highly lauded as his hard sci-fi works, such as like *Evolution's Darling* (2000), the *Succession* novels were still celebrated as a cut above standard space opera fare. Mark L. Olson, writing for Nesfa.org, reviews Westerfield's work enthusiastically. Scifi.com offered two somewhat competing opinions of the two volumes. Paul Witcover found the first book hurried and overly dependent on cliffhangers, but he still recommends the work; Paul Di Filippo, writing about *The Killing of Worlds,* describes Westover's writing as poetic and balletic.

John C. Wright (1961–) began writing science fiction novellas in the mid-1990s, but he did not publish his first book, *The Golden Age,* until 2002, which quickly developed into a trilogy after receiving early critical praise. Wright graduated from William and Mary's College of Law, but he abandoned his law career and turned to journalism for financial reasons. In a 2002 interview with Nick Gevers of Sfsite.com, Wright proclaims, "I am a space opera writer. Perhaps I am the last of my kind. I like large themes, thunder, fury, and wonder. Why blow up a city when you can blow up a world? Why launch a starship one kilometer long, when you can launch a super-starship a thousand kilometers long? Why build space armor out of carbon-steel when you can build it out of adamantium?" Wright, his wife, and three children live in Centreville, Virginia. Another professed libertarian, his novels often explore the tensions between individual and societal rights. Wright has also received acclaim for his fantasy trilogy, Chronicles of Chaos.

Set 10,000 years in the future and infused with a great deal of classical references, Wright's Golden Age trilogy is built upon technology's transformation of humans into virtually immortal, though stagnant, beings (somewhat similar to Westerfield's seeded humans). The central character, for instance, is named Phaethon, and he finds himself suddenly out of favor. Over the course of the novel, he learns that selected bits of memory—his as well as the memories of others—have gone missing. His particular gap extends upwards of 250 years. Drawing on his legal background, Wright's novel culminates in a well-constructed courtroom scene that leaves Phaethon an exile and sets the stage for the subsequent two works. The title of the second book, *The Phoenix Exultant* (2003), refers to Phaeton's ship, the most magnificent ship ever built, and his quest to regain its possession. His journey takes him through a vastly changed yet wondrous solar system as well as layers of murky deception as he seeks to uncover the identity of his enemy. The trilogy's conclusion, *The Golden Transcendence* (2004), takes on more of the trappings of the new space opera as a high-tech war breaks out and the future of humanity hangs in the balance. More than one reviewer has compared Wright's trilogy to the Matrix trilogy: both involve a human battle against world-dominating machine intelligences, both question—à la Plato's "Allegory of the Cave"—the nature of reality, and both seek an ultimate determination of truth, which has been occluded by labyrinthine obscurity.

The entry on space opera is far from finished. Its growing popularity and increasing critical attention continue to lure writers old and young: established writers like Mike Moscoe (writing as Mike Shepard) and his Kris Longknife series or Walter Jon Williams' Dread Empire's Fall both demonstrate the trend of writers swerving from established genres to try their hands at space opera, whereas new writers such as Scott Gamboe and C.J. Merle may prove to leave indelible marks in the field. They, too, merit serious consideration, as do many more authors whose numbers continue to swell the field of space opera writers to the very stars.

Bibliography

Aldiss, Brian. *Space Opera: An Anthology of Way-Back-When Futures.* London: Weidenfeld and Nicolson, 1974.

Anderson, Kevin J. *The League of Extraordinary Gentlemen* (movie novelization). New York: Pocket Books, 2003.

———. *Sky Captain and the World of Tomorrow* (movie novelization). New York: Onyx, 2004.

Asaro, Catherine. *Catch the Lightning.* New York: Tor, 1996.

———. *The Final Key.* New York: Tor, 2005.

———. *The Last Hawk.* New York: Tor, 1997.

———. *Primary Inversion.* New York: Tor, 1995.

———. *The Quantum Rose.* New York: Tor, 2000.

———. *Schism.* New York: Tor, 2004.

———. *Spherical Harmonic.* New York: Tor, 2001.

Asimov, Isaac. *Foundation.* New York: Gnome Press, 1951.

———. "Nightfall." *Astounding* Sept. 1941. 9–34.

Bainbridge, William Sims. *Dimensions of Science Fiction.* Cambridge: Harvard University Press, 1986.

Brackett, Leigh. *The Sword of Rhiannon.* New York: Ace, 1953.

Brin, David. *Forgiveness.* La Jolla, CA: WildStorm Productions, 2001.

———. *Glory Season.* New York: Bantam, 1993.

———. *Heaven's Reach.* New York: Bantam, 1998.

———. *Kiln People.* New York: Tor, 2002.

———. *Sundiver.* New York: Bantam, 1980.

Bujold, Lois McMaster. *Barrayar.* New York: Baen, 1991.

———. *A Civil Campaign.* New York: Baen, 1999.

———. *Diplomatic Immunity.* New York: Baen, 2002.

———. *Falling Free.* New York: Baen, 1988.

———. *The Warrior's Apprentice.* New York: Baen, 1986.

———. "Winterfair Gifts." In *Irresistible Forces.* Catherine Asaro, ed. New York: New American Library, 2004.

Card, Orson Scott. *Ender's Game.* New York: T. Doherty, 1985.

———. *Speaker for the Dead.* New York: Tor, 1986.

Carmien, Edward, ed. *The Cherryh Odyssey.* San Bernardino, CA: Borgo Press, 2004.

Cherryh, C.J. *Cyteen.* New York: Warner Books, 1988.

———. *Downbelow Station.* New York: Daw, 1981.

Clarke, Arthur C. *Childhood's End.* New York: Ballantine, 1953.

————. *The Fountains of Paradise.* New York: Harcourt Brace Jovanovich, 1979.

Drake, David. *Hammer's Slammers.* New York: Baen, 1987.

Drake, David, and John Ringo. *We Few.* New York: Baen, 2005.

Clarke, Arthur C., and Stanley Kubrick. Screenplay, *2001: A Space Odyssey.* Director Stanley Kubrick. 1968.

Daniel, Tony. *Metaplanetary.* New York: EOS, 2001.

————. *Superluminal.* New York: EOS, 2004.

Di Filippo, Paul. Rev. of *The Final Key,* by Catherine Asaro. http://www.scifi.com/sfw/ issue452/books.html (accessed 3 May 2007).

————. Rev. of *The Killing of Worlds,* by John C. Wright. http://www.scifi.com/sfw/issue339/ books.html (accessed 3 May 2007).

Foster, Alan Dean. *The Tar-Aiym Krang.* New York: Ballantine, 1972.

Gevers, Nick. "Ferocious Poet's Heart Commanding: An Interview with John C. Wright." (April 2002). http://www.sfsite.com/05a/jcw127.htm (accessed 3 May 2007).

Gresh, Lois H. Rev. of *Schism,* by Catherine Asaro. http://www.scifi.com/sfw/ issue396/books2.html (accessed 3 May 2007).

Hamilton, Edmond. *Captain Future and the Space Emperor.* New York: Popular Library, 1967.

————. "The Monster God of Mamurth." *Weird Tales* (August 1926).

Hartwell, David G., and Kathryn Cramer, eds. *The Space Opera Renaissance.* New York: Tor, 2006.

Jaffe, Stuart. Rev. of *Superluminal,* by Tony Daniel. (26 February 2005). http://www.infinity-plus.co.uk/nonfiction/superluminal.htm (accessed 27 April 2007).

Jayne's Intelligence Review: The Navy of the People's Republic of Haven. Cedar Falls, IA: Ad Astra Games, 2007.

Jayne's Intelligence Review: The Royal Manticoran Navy. Cedar Falls, IA: Ad Astra Games, 2006.

Moon, Elizabeth. *Remnant Population.* New York: Baen, 1999.

————. *The Speed of Dark.* New York: Ballantine, 2003.

————. *Trading in Danger.* New York: Ballantine, 2003.

Niven, Larry, and Steven Barnes. *Achilles' Choice.* New York: Tor, 1991.

————. *Descent of Anansi, The.* New York: Tor, 1982.

————. *Dream Park.* Huntington Woods, MI: Phantasia Press, 1981.

————. *Saturn's Race.* New York: Tor, 2000.

Olson, Mark L. Rev. of *The Risen Empire,* by Scott Westerfield. http://nesfa.org/reviews/ Olson/RisenEmpire.html (accessed 7 May 2007).

Preciado, Regina Lynn. Rev. of the Vorkosigan series, by Lois McMaster Bujold (2004). http://www.sfsite.com/05a/mv175.htm (accessed 4 April 2007).

Pringle, David. "What is This Thing Called Space Opera?" In *Space and Beyond: The Frontier Theme in Science Fiction.* Gary Westfahl, ed. Westport, CT: Greenwood, 2000, 35–47.

Ringo, John. *Ghost.* New York: Baen, 2005.

————. *A Hymn Before Battle.* New York: Baen, 2000.

————. *Into the Looking Glass.* New York: Baen, 2005.

————. *When the Devil Dances.* New York: Baen, 2002.

Ringo, John, and Julie Cochrane. *Cally's War.* New York: Baen, 2006.

Ringo, John, and Travis S. Taylor. *Von Neumann's War.* New York: Baen, 2006.

————. *Vorpal Blade.* New York: Baen, 2007.

Schellenberger, James. Rev. of *Primary Inversion,* by Catherine Asaro. Challengingdestiny. com (29 October 1997). http://www.challengingdestiny.com/reviews/inversion.htm (accessed 17 April 2007).

Simmons, Dan. *Ilium.* New York: EOS, 2003.

————. *Olympos.* New York: EOS, 2005.

———. "Orphans of the Helix." In *Far Horizons*. Robert Silverberg, ed. New York: Avon Eos, 1999. 207–258.

Smith, Edward Elmer. *Children of the Lens*. Reading, PA: Fantasy Press, 1954.

———. *First Lensman*. Reading, PA: Fantasy Press, 1950.

———. *Galactic Patrol*. Reading, PA: Fantasy Press, 1950.

———. *Gray Lensman*. Reading, PA: Fantasy Press, 1951.

———. *Second Stage Lensmen*. Reading, PA: Fantasy Press, 1953.

———. *Skylark DuQuesne*. New York: Pyramid Books, 1967.

———. *Skylark of Valeron*. Reading, PA: Fantasy Press, 1949.

———. *Skylark Three*. Reading, PA: Fantasy Press, 1948.

———. *The Vortex Blaster*. New York: Gnome Press, 1960.

Smith, Edward Elmer, and Lee Hawkins Garby. *The Skylark of Space*. Cranston, RI: Southgate Press, 1946.

Soyka, David. Review of *Metaplanetary*, by Tony Daniel. 2001. http://www.sfsite.com/08a/mp109.htm (accessed 18 May 2007).

Taylor, Travis S. *The Quantum Connection*. New York: Baen, 2005.

———. *The Tau Ceti Agenda* commentary. http://www.doctravis.com/node/36#comment (accessed 18 May 2007).

———. *Warp Speed*. New York: Baen, 2004.

Todorov, Tzvetan. *Genres in Discourse,* translated by Catherine Porter. Cambridge: Cambridge University Press, 1990.

Van Vogt, A.E. *Cosmic Encounter*. New York: Doubleday, 1980.

———. *Slan*. Sauk City, WI: Arkham House, 1946.

———. *The Weapon Shops of Isher*. New York: Greenberg, 1951.

Wagner, T.M. Review of *The Warrior's Apprentice*, by Lois McMaster Bujold (2004). http://www.sfreviews.net/warriorsapp.html (accessed 4 April 2007).

Weber, David. *At All Costs*. New York: Baen, 2005.

———. *On Basilisk Station*. New York: Baen, 1993.

Westerfield, Scott. *Evolution's Darling*. New York: Four Walls Eight Windows, 2000.

———. *The Killing of Worlds*. New York: Tor, 2003.

———. *The Risen Empire*. New York: Tor, 2003.

Westfahl, Gary. "Space Opera." In *The Cambridge Companion to Science Fiction*. Edward James and Farah Mendlesohn, eds. Cambridge: Cambridge University Press, 2003, 197–208.

Williamson, Jack. *The Legion of Space*. Reading, PA: Fantasy Press, 1947.

Witcover, Paul. Review of *The Risen Empire*, by Scott Westerfield. http://www.scifi.com/sfw/issue307/books2.html (accessed 18 May 2007).

Wright, John C. *The Golden Age*. New York: Tor, 2002.

———. *The Golden Transcendence*. New York: Tor, 2003.

———. *The Phoenix Exultant*. New York: Tor, 2003.

Further Reading

Aldiss, Brian, ed. *Space Opera: An Anthology of Way-Back-When Futures*. London: Westfield and Nicolson, 1974; Eisenhour, Susan. "A Subversive in Hyperspace: C. J. Cherryh's Feminist Transformation of Space Opera." *New York Review of Science Fiction* 1 (October 1996): 4–7; Hardesty III, William H. "Semiotics, Space Opera and *Babl-17*." *Mosaic* 13.304 (1980): 63–69; Hartwell, David G. "Nine Ways of Looking at Space Opera: Part I." *New York Review of Science Fiction* 212 (August 2006): 17–21; Hartwell, David G. "Nine Ways of Looking at Space Opera: Part II." *New York Review of Science Fiction* 213 (September 2006): 19–21; Hartwell, David G. "Nine Ways of Looking at Space Opera: Part III." *New York Review of Science Fiction* 214 (October 2006): 17–19; Hartwell, David G., and Kathryn Cramer. "Space Opera Redefined." In *Speculations on Speculation*. James Gunn and

Matthew Candelaria, eds. Lanham, MD: Scarecrow Press, 2005, 259–265; Lamont, Victoria, and Dianne Newell. "House Opera: Frontier Mythology and Subversion of Domestic Discourse in Mid-Twentieth Century Women's Space Opera." *Foundation: The International Review of Science Fiction* 34.95 (2005): 71–88; Monk, Patricia. "Not Just 'Cosmic Skull-duggery': A Partial Reconsideration of Space Opera." *Extrapolation* 33.4 (1992): 295–316; Sanders, Joe. "Space Opera Reconsidered." *New York Review of Science Fiction* 1 (June 1995): 3–6; Stableford, Brian. "Space Opera." In *Encyclopedia of Science Fiction.* John Clute and Peter Nicholls, eds. London: Orbit, 1999, 1138–1140; and Westfahl, Gary. "Beyond Logic and Literacy: The Strange Case of Space Opera." *Extrapolation* 35. 3 (1994): 176–185.

JOHN CARLBERG

SPECULATIVE FICTION

Definition. "Speculative fiction" has become a term used within the last twenty years by American authors, readers, and literary scholars to refer collectively to writing that is often categorized into generic subsets of popular literature of the fantastic: **science fiction**, gothic fiction, horror, **fantasy, magic realism,** and **utopian fiction.**

Speculative writing is not different from popular genre fiction that includes fantastical or supernatural elements. Rather, speculative fiction is an *idiom,* or phrase, that allows for a broader interpretation of what can be considered literature of the fantastic. The term "speculative" has become more accepted as scholars, readers, publishers, and authors alike recognize that many texts that have fantastical or supernatural elements often combine aspects of several popular genres. As a result, such texts cannot be easily categorized as one particular genre or another. Separating or classifying writers and their works into rigid genre categories does an injustice to the complexity of authors' fiction. As critics Jane Donawerth and Carol Kolmerten point out, "Most theorists admit that notions of utopia, science fiction, and fantasy overlap to some degree" (Donawerth and Kolmerten 1994, 2). Anne Cranny-Francis agrees, stating, "No text is the unequivocal construct of a single genre . . . it is difficult to find a text which does not exhibit some characteristics of other genres" (Cranny-Francis 1990, 20).

For example, Elizabeth Kostova's *The Historian* (2005) could be considered both detective and horror fiction, given that the narrative involves a father and daughter bent on proving the existence of the legendary vampire Dracula and solving the mystery of his resting place. Rather than be constrictively labeled as either detective or horror fiction, *The Historian* can be recognized as a text that integrates various genres of fantastical literature if placed under the *rubric,* or category, of speculative fiction.

Further, speculative fiction encompasses those works that are not generically classifiable because they refuse a distinction between mundane and supernatural occurrences. In this sense, speculative fiction is synonymous with Tzvetan Todorov's definition of the "fantastic." In his seminal *The Fantastic: A Structuralist Approach to a Literary Genre,* Todorov classifies a text as fantastic if its action exists between the real and the imaginary. According to Todorov, "uncanny phenomena [can be explained] in two fashions, by types of natural causes [the real] and supernatural causes [the imaginary]. The possibility of a hesitation between the two creates the fantastic effect" (Todorov 1973, 26). In other words, Todorov understands the fantastic as literature that produces a certain sensation or feeling in the reader, one of uncertainty as to whether the events described are "true."

Often, the rationale for categorizing a text as science fiction or horror is predicated on the fact that the reader understands that the text explores an unreal world or improbable events. For instance, in a novel such as Octavia Butler's *Fledgling* (2006), the vampire creatures are supernatural, and the novel itself is grounded in an alternate version of the world we know. However, in Kathryn Davis's *The Thin Place* (2006), the whole point of the novel is to question our division of existence into what is real and what is imaginary. The novel's title itself refers to a location "where spirits of the dead can reach through the ether to spirits of the living" (Balée 2006, 482), in this case a New England town called Varennes. In Varennes, a young girl, Mees, has the power to bring the dead back to life. Such an ability would seem fantastic, yet Davis presents Mees's power as complementing the magical and unknown qualities of the natural world we inhabit. Davis underscores the fantastical aspects of the everyday by emphasizing the instability of the earth itself: "Aside from the obvious holes and tunnels made by animals and people, rabbit warrens, subway systems, missile silos, rumpus rooms, it [the earth] seems solid enough, though in fact it's a set of interlocking pieces, sometimes bound tightly together and sometimes drifting far apart" (Davis 2006, 34). In this way, the earth becomes a metaphor for reality; like the planet's surface, our sense of reality can shift and alter to include extraordinary occurrences.

Given *The Thin Place*'s intermixing of the mundane and the amazing, it might be tempting to label the novel as magic realism. Magic realism is a genre in which supernatural elements or events are integrated seamlessly into a realistic setting without surprise or commentary from the characters. Important writers of magic realism include Latin American authors Gabriel García Márquez, Luis Jorge Borges, and Isabel Allende. Because of its inclusion of fantastical elements, magic realism can be incorporated within a discussion of speculative fiction. However, works such as *The Thin Place* are more aptly titled speculative fiction than magic realism because they do foreground the supernatural and ponder its meaning, rather than cast the fantastic as unremarkable. For instance, in *The Thin Place,* Mees is acutely aware that her ability is extraordinary, and she contemplates the purpose and consequences of her power. In this way, the term "speculative fiction" can apply to texts that do not fit easily into the category of magic realism or the popular genres that explore alternate worlds and realities.

The term speculative fiction allows one not only to avoid dividing texts into rigid genre categories but also to recognize that the purpose behind various related popular genres is a "shar[ed] . . . emphasis on the imaginative freedom of alternate worlds" (Donawerth and Kolmerten 1994, 3–4). Critic Darko Suvin explains this freedom by characterizing the speculative mode as "literature of cognitive estrangement" (Suvin 1979, 4). Though Suvin applies this definition more specifically to science fiction, his words accurately describe the work that all types of speculative fiction perform. "Cognitive estrangement" is a literary device by which writers "displace the story setting to another time and/or place, immediately denaturalizing the society portrayed in the text" (Cranny-Francis 1990, 193). This estrangement allows the writer to critique social problems and inequities from a distance, enabling both author and reader to contemplate and explore scenarios in which those cultural issues might be ameliorated or improved.

Understood as literature of cognitive estrangement, the term speculative fiction enables one to recognize texts that might not otherwise either fit a certain genre category or authors who have not previously or consistently written literature with fantastical aspects. An example of both points is Cormac McCarthy's *The Road* (2006), a harrowing novel in which the love, tensions, and pain of a father-son relationship play out against the backdrop of a post-apocalyptic America. Though set in a futuristic, nuclear winterized landscape, it would be hard to categorize *The Road* as science fiction, given the novel's focus on an emotional, familial relationship rather than the technological or political conditions that have brought about the decimation of civilization. McCarthy never explains how or why the destruction occurred. The reader is told only that "The clocks stopped at 1:17. A long shear of light and then a series of low concussions" (McCarthy 2006, 45). Instead, conceit of apocalypse becomes a means by which McCarthy cognitively estranges readers from everyday life to bring them a new perspective on parent-child relationships. Writer Michael Chabon notes that McCarthy forces us to acknowledge and confront a parent's unspoken nightmare:

> *The Road* is not a record of fatherly fidelity; it is a testament to the abyss of a parent's greatest fears. The fear of leaving your child alone, of dying before your child has reached adulthood . . . And above all, the fear of knowing—as every parent fears—that you have left your children a world more damaged, more poisoned, more base and violent and cheerless and toxic, more doomed, than the one you inherited. (Chabon 2007)

As a result, readers are forced to rethink their understanding of what being a "good" parent means and of what they are obligated to do for their children.

Further, by terming *The Road* "speculative fiction," one acknowledges that McCarthy's novel includes certain fantastical, speculative "what if" elements that might be found in science or horror fiction, but one also recognizes that McCarthy is not an author of traditional popular genre fiction (such as previous works *Blood Meridian* (1985) and *All the Pretty Horses* (1992) show). In fact, given that genre fiction can be stigmatized as consisting of nonliterary, unimaginative popular literature, many writers would be hesitant to have their work labeled as genre fiction because it might detract from their writing being recognized as complex and innovative work.

As various cultural studies scholars such as Raymond Williams (1983), John Fiske (1989a), and Geoffrey Nowell-Smith (1987) have pointed out, the distinction between what might be considered "high" literary art and "low" popular culture is not only arbitrary but often elitist because it assumes that a book that sells many copies cannot be interesting, creative, and innovative writing. Nevertheless, fairly or not, science fiction, horror, and other popular genre writing are still not considered serious fiction worth studying. As a result, a horror novel such as Scott Smith's *The Ruins* (2006), which was critically lauded as both a complex and frightening narrative of American tourists in Mexico, one in the tradition of recognized American horror masters such as H.P. Lovecraft and Stephen King, can yet be dismissed by some as a nonliterary work that has little purpose beyond entertaining the reader. However, by labeling *The Ruins* as speculative writing rather than horror fiction, one could potentially remove the stigma of "genre fiction" so that the novel could be viewed as innovative, interesting work rather than one that mechanically follows basic genre rules.

It is because of such genre rules that popular genre fiction is often dismissed. Much popular fiction does adhere to clichéd characters and repetitive storylines; indeed, a genre is usually identifiable by a certain set of expected parameters, or rules, which govern it. For example, mysteries often consist of a detective who is able to identify a criminal based on his or her ability to notice details or clues that others cannot see. The popularity of such genre fiction is that the reader can expect similar story arcs, characters, and situations in each book. There are relatively few surprises and, as such, the narrative becomes safe and comforting for the reader. They are almost ritualistic narratives that satisfy a reader's need for constancy and a return to a stable status quo. Such texts are opposed to "literary" fiction, which is seen as striving to avoid set rules by creating challenging narratives that do not reward a reader with stable, desired outcomes.

However, as critics such as Cranny-Francis have argued, so-called literary writing cannot be entirely free from genre conventions. Further, popular fiction writers are often notable because they work within the genre to subvert its rules in order to challenge social conventions, prejudices, and limitations. Thus, the creation of the term "speculative fiction" enables one to eschew a rigid division between the popular and the literary. The phrase acknowledges that a text might at once contain genre conventions, deviations from those conventions, and a purpose beyond entertainment and yet be widely read by the general public. For instance, the aforementioned *The Historian* spent many weeks on the *New York Times* bestseller list as a new take on the traditional vampire narrative. However, it is also a novel that is intricately plotted and well-written, and one that demands a great deal of historical and cultural knowledge on the part of the reader.

Trends and Themes

Gender, Race, and Sexuality in Speculative Fiction. The Historian also provides another example of how speculative fiction subverts the division between the literary and the popular: its ability to challenge the traditional gender roles prevalent in popular genre writing. As a female author, Elizabeth Kostova is writing in a genre (horror/vampire fiction) usually occupied by male writers and readers. By creating a speculative narrative focused on a heroine rather than a hero, Kostova alters the typical genre convention of a male protagonist who drives the action of the story. Such a feminist narrative is literary in its subversion of popular expectations and at the same time appealing to female readers of genre fiction, a readership that is often disregarded. In addressing women writers of genre fiction, Cranny-Francis points out that their feminist take on traditional masculine genre writing "give[s] the traditional male readership, whether of fantasy, utopian fiction, detective fiction . . . a new and stimulating perspective. The important recognition in this statement is that there is an existing readership worth tapping. . . . People of all ages, classes, genders, and races read genre fiction" (Cranny-Francis 1990, 3).

In this way, Natalie M. Rosinsky argues that the term "speculative fiction" becomes necessary because traditional genre definitions are "limited and value-laden" in terms of who writes and reads genre fiction and why (Rosinsky 1984, 115n. 2). When women write genre fiction, they are "continually crossing the boundaries which delimit the operation—formally/aesthetically/ideologically—of the traditional generic text and, in so doing, showing that those boundaries exist" (Cranny-Francis 1990, 19). In other words, when imagining alternative constructions of gender roles—a strong female protagonist versus a helpless heroine, for example—female authors might employ a popular genre to do so, but they undermine the very conventions of that genre that normally relegate female characters to subordinate or derogatory roles.

Given such nontraditional genre texts, the term speculative fiction becomes important in terms of characterizing women authors, as well as writers of color or gay and lesbian writers. The attempt to divide the imaginative writing of women and writers of color into rigid generic categories is problematic because inevitably those texts that do not precisely fit the definitions of "science fiction," "utopian fiction," and so on, risk being excluded from consideration as belonging to a tradition of writing in the speculative mode. As noted previously, popular genre fiction such as science fiction and horror has been viewed as writing by white, heterosexual men for a similarly apportioned audience. However, writers from historically disenfranchised groups, including women, writers of color, and gay and lesbian writers, might choose to write in a popular genre mode in order to imagine alternate realities that explore, question, and reimagine traditional hierarchies of power and that argue for cultures that are free of sexism, racism, and homophobia. Such writers write not with the purpose of conforming to genre conventions but with the intent of participating in what Cranny-Francis describes as the "ideological struggle" (Cranny-Francis 1990, 19) of confronting and challenging white masculine power at the turn into the twenty-first century. The problem that women writers, writers of color, and nonheterosexual writers face when working in popular genre fiction is that their work might not be recognized as such because they are not the traditional writers of this fiction, and their work, which alters genre conventions, is not properly acknowledged as literature of the fantastic.

For example, although African American writers Octavia Butler and Samuel Delaney are today readily appreciated as important authors of the fantastic, other African American writers, such as Jewelle Gomez and Tananarive Due, have received far less notice for publishing interesting and provocative popular genre fiction. Due is gaining notoriety, as evidenced by *The Boston Globe* review of her novel *The Living Blood* (2001): "Due has become . . . a talented storyteller who stands tall among her horror cohorts Anne Rice and Stephen King" (Jones 2001). However, the fact that the reviewer describes Due as a "horror" writer shows how limiting such categories are for writers of color. For instance, Due's novel elides conventional boundaries of horror fiction by including elements of African magic and folklore. By working within the horror genre yet refusing its limitations, Due cannot be categorized accurately as a writer of traditional horror fiction. This point is true for Butler and Delaney as well, whose work cannot be considered correctly as "science fiction," given that their imaginative work does not always involve a discussion of science, technology, or future worlds. Employing the term speculative fiction opens up the definition of what constitutes imaginative literature. As a result, writers who do not fit the typical white, male, heterosexual profile of popular genre authors and who do not write conventional genre fiction can be recognized as contributing to and enriching the tradition of popular imaginative writing.

Because the rubric speculative fiction enables one to recognize a diverse group of writers as creating literature of the fantastic, it further allows one to trace traditions of imaginative writing among women writers, writers of color, and gay and lesbian authors. Usually, such literary lineages are reserved for white, male, heterosexual writers of the fantastic. For example, Stephen King's work is influenced by earlier horror writers such as H.P. Lovecraft and Sheridan LeFanu, and H.G. Wells's and Edgar Rice Burroughs's science fiction thrillers about Mars and invading Martians are the forbears of Kim Stanley Robinson's acclaimed Mars trilogy. However, such lineages among women, writers of color, and gay and lesbian writers of the fantastic

AFRICAN AMERICAN SPECULATIVE FICTION

There exists a rich tradition of African American literature of the fantastic that is rarely critically recognized, with the exception of editor Sheree R. Thomas's collections *Dark Matter: A Century of Speculative Fiction from the African Diaspora* (2000) and *Dark Matter: Reading the Bones* (2004). The truth is that African American writers wrote in the speculative mode from the turn of the century into the twentieth century and on. One such early imaginative popular writer is Pauline E. Hopkins, who has not been recognized as a speculative writer for two primary reasons: first, her novel, *Of One Blood* (1903), cannot be easily generically categorized (it combines African adventure, mystery, science fiction, and gothic narratives); and second, Hopkins casts African American mothers as heroes in her speculative fiction, whereas traditionally most popular genre fiction has viewed racial difference as a social threat or has refused to acknowledge race altogether. By employing the more expansive term speculative fiction, Hopkins can be linked to later African American writers of the fantastic, such as Butler, Delaney, Due, Gomez, Toni Morrison (*Song of Solomon* (1977), *Beloved* (1987)), and Toni Cade Bambara (*The Salt Eaters* (1980)), all of whom use the supernatural to imagine ways of overcoming racism and its legacy in American culture. Were it not for the broader category of speculative fiction, writers such as Morrison (who is often considered a "literary" writer rather than an author of popular fiction) would not be placed alongside Butler or Hopkins, though all three participate in using the fantastic in analogous ways.

remain obscure because these men and women have not been celebrated as important authors of popular imaginative literature.

Using the term speculative fiction can illuminate historical connections among diverse writers and texts that would otherwise not be understood as comprising similar traditions and themes in imaginative writing. On the other hand, many writers of color reject the label "speculative" for their fiction, which imagines events or possibilities beyond what is traditionally considered probable. This rejection is based on the argument that definitions of "real" and "imaginary" have been defined by Western culture and white writers. However, for those writers of color, what white culture might consider fantastic and unreal is in fact possible. In her essay "The Site of Memory," Toni Morrison writes, "The work that I do frequently falls, in the minds of most people, into that realm of fiction called fantastic, or mythic, or magical, or unbelievable. I'm not comfortable with those labels" (Morrison 1987, 2294). For Morrison, relating what she calls the "truth" of life includes the strange and seemingly improbable that is for her nonetheless possible as part of the fabric of existence. Similarly, some of the fantastical occurrences that are woven throughout Ana Castillo's *So Far From God* (1993) serve to distinguish the Chicano/a community of Tome, New Mexico, from the surrounding white culture. For instance, the death and resurrection of a three-year-old girl, nicknamed La Loca, is understood within the community as a miraculous, if somewhat frightening, event; however, the incident is explained away as "epilepsy" by the white doctors in Albuquerque. Therefore, although broadening the definition of imaginative writing, the category of speculative fiction can also work to reinforce the division between the real and the imaginary that much nonwhite literature of the fantastic attempts to undermine.

Current Speculative Fiction. To understand themes and trends in current speculative writing, it is useful to consider briefly how twenty-first century speculative fiction motifs can be distinguished from imaginative writing of the preceding century. Although this article cannot address all such themes fully, it seeks to outline the preeminent concerns of today's speculative writers and the new ways in which the speculative mode is being employed by contemporary authors.

Much speculative writing in the twentieth century, particularly in the first half, employed popular writing to make challenges to the cultural status quo more palatable because, as noted earlier, the fantastic uses cognitive estrangement to displace social critiques to another time or place. In this way, the critique may be tempered by the distance created between the action of the text and real life. An example from the world of popular **comic books** would be *The X-Men*. Created by Stan Lee and Jack Kirby in 1963, the comic followed the exploits of its titular characters, also known as "mutants," who represent the "next step" in human evolution because of their superpowers. The ostracizing (in one storyline to labor camps) of mutants by average humans can be read as a coded critique of racism, anti-Semitism, and homophobia in American culture. This interpretation of the underlying message of *The X-Men* comic is underscored by the motivations of lead villain, Magneto, a Jewish Holocaust survivor. For Magneto, the human prejudice against and fear of the mutants is no different than the desire of the Nazi regime to construct Jews as enemies of the state and so justify their liquidation. In this way, *The X-Men* becomes a speculative means of addressing the horrible consequences of prejudice against a group of people who are labeled as different; however, the comic did so in a way that did not address the subject in a direct manner during a time when an open critique of these subjects might have alienated a mostly white, male readership.

For twenty-first century speculative fiction, there is less need to embed social critique within an imaginative narrative for the sake of making that critique more palatable to readers. Issues of racism, sexism, and homophobia are now more widely discussed and acknowledged in contemporary society, and so the focus of current speculative fiction is not so much to make such critiques acceptable but to use cognitive estrangement to help readers see social inequities or questions about the nature of reality in new and startling ways.

One recurrent theme in contemporary speculative fiction is a focus on social changes wrought by the ability to access information via the Internet and other technologies widely available since the millennium. For example, many twenty-first century speculative texts pessimistically portray as impossible the desire of characters to understand themselves and their identity by gathering data and information about past events. This theme arises from society's twenty-first century craving to accumulate, sort, and have access to information through various media sources, most importantly the Internet. Such data grants its users seemingly more and more insight into what has transpired to bring society to its present point. Concurrently, seminal twenty-first century events such as 9/11 or the Iraq War have encouraged people to explore how such historical moments came to be. Further, an event such as 9/11 produces a longing to return to a time before such a devastating occurrence in an effort to recapture a sense of peace, nostalgia, and innocence through an exploration of earlier aspects of American history.

However, current speculative fiction, by using the imaginary to question our ability to know the past and the truth with accuracy and objectivity, suggests that such desires cannot be fulfilled and are perhaps even dangerous to pursue. Donna Tartt's novel, *The Little Friend* (2002), explores these points. Tartt's speculative novel combines elements of the fantastic and mystery genres with the Southern Gothic style of

American writers William Faulkner and Flannery O'Connor to tell the story of twelve-year-old Harriet Dufresnes and her efforts in 1970s Alexandria, Mississippi, to solve the cold case murder of her older brother, Robin. Harriet was an infant when nine-year-old Robin disappeared from a family Mother's Day gathering, only later to be found strangled and hanging from a tree. Though she never knew Robin, Harriet is acutely aware that her family, particularly her mother, have been psychologically damaged since the tragic and mysterious circumstances of her brother's death. In part what drives Harriet to fixate on her brother's murder is a sense that if his death could be understood and information gathered to show what happened, somehow this knowledge will bring closure and peace to a family that continuously lives with the heartbreaking pain of not knowing how or why Robin died.

In her narrative, Tartt uses elements of the speculative to show that such closure, such knowledge of the past, is not possible. There is a sense of unreality about the past and people's recollection of it and even a questioning of the stability of the present. No one can quite remember the exact circumstances or moments before Robin disappeared, and when Harriet questions her family members, they each give different stories or evade answering altogether. Harriet's sister, Allison, who was four when Robin disappeared and was presumably the last to see him alive, lives in a kind of alternate dream world, to her as real as the everyday reality of the other characters: "Alison yawned. How could you ever be perfectly sure when you were dreaming and when you were awake? . . . Repeatedly during the day, as she drifted around her own house . . . she asked herself: Am I awake or asleep? How did I get here?" (Tartt 2002, 103). As a result, Alison cannot provide Harriet with any clues about what happened to their brother. Further, Harriet's great aunt, Libby, adds to the sense of the fantastic and unknowable by recounting that three days before Robin was murdered, a man's hat appeared in her bedroom mysteriously out of nowhere. Libby uses this incident to illustrate to Harriet that there are some things, like Robin's death, which defy explanation: "All I'm saying is that there are an awful lot of things in the world we don't understand, honey, and hidden connections between things that don't seem related at all" (Tartt 2002, 126).

Compounding her inability to gain information that would allow her a clear understanding of the past, Harriet and her friend Hely, based on information from the Dufresnes's housekeeper, Ida, believe that a local parolee and meth addict, Danny Ratliff, was her brother's murderer. They pursue him and in the process precipitate a car accident that severely injures Danny's grandmother, and Harriet herself is nearly killed by Danny during one of his meth-fueled rampages. Sadly, Harriet has perpetrated these events only to find, in the end, that Ida's story is incorrect and Danny was actually a friend of Robin's. While in the hospital recovering from Danny's attack, Harriet overhears her father saying to her mother that Danny was "Robin's little friend, don't you remember? He used to come up in the yard and play sometimes. . . . Knocked on the door [after Robin's burial] and said he was sorry he wasn't at the funeral, he didn't have a ride" (Tartt 2002, 543). With a sinking feeling, Harriet realizes how greatly she has misinterpreted the circumstances surrounding Robin's death: "Never had it occurred to her that she might be wrong in her suspicions about Danny Ratliff—simply wrong" (Tartt 2002, 544). In this way, Harriet's attempt to gain control of the slippery, shifting reality of the past nearly leads to disaster for both her and Danny.

The use of the speculative mode, as illustrated through the unreliable perspectives of Libby, Allison, Ida, and others, allows Tartt to depict the past in such a way that shows the reader how unstable memory is and how our understanding of history is created largely from everyone's unreliable recollections and from their own imaginations. In so doing, Tartt rejects society's belief that the accumulation of information can lead to a more complete comprehension of the past. In her novel, Tartt demonstrates that greater amounts of information, some of which may be untrustworthy, will never lead to a clear picture of the past; history will always remain, to some extent, out of reach and inscrutable. Tartt underscores this point by refusing to end the novel with any answers as to who killed Robin or why; Harriet and the reader are as in the dark with regard to these questions as they were at the beginning of the novel.

Critics were divided regarding whether or not Tartt was successful in communicating these themes. Greg Changnon wrote that the novel shows "how difficult it is to get to an objective truth when memory, interpretation and perspective are involved" (Changnon 2003, 4K). Laura Miller found that Tartt's use of popular genre modes "all too often devolve[s] to cliché or cartoon," but Miller also "praise[s] the book's vital characters, its supple conjuring of mood and place, and its dry, dark humor" (Miller 2002). On the other hand, Tom Murray rejected completely the novel's ending, which leaves the reader and Harriet with no enlightened knowledge of the past: "Wasn't that daring, to set the reader up for a revelation that way and then withhold it at the last moment? Wouldn't it have been dishonest to sew things up in a nice, neat bow, when we all know life doesn't really work that way?" (Murray 2002, 1). Gail Caldwell agreed that such ambiguity was tiresome, and that the reader "wind[s] up with lots of exotic, sometimes lovely memories that don't always connect—and nearly as weary as you are enlightened" (Caldwell 2002, D6).

Like Tartt, Elizabeth Kostova questions the ability of our information age to accurately assess the past. Kostova's *The Historian* (2005) is part horror story and part meditation on the task of historians (and other academics) to accumulate information that allows people to understand the past. In Kostova's novel, feelings of horror and dread arise from the realization that information can often be no protection from forestalling the evils of the world. Further, like *The Little Friend*, *The Historian* suggests that the pursuit of the past can potentially lead to self-destruction when the intangible and unknowable past becomes more real than the present. In the novel, a father, and later his daughter (who is never named), find themselves on the trail of the historical Vlad Tepes, the bloodthirsty fifteenth-century Romanian prince who gave rise to the vampire legend made famous by Bram Stoker's 1897 novel, *Dracula*.

The pursuit leads father and daughter to discover that Tepes is a vampire, but a peculiar one in that he is also the novel's titular historian. Tepes turns academics into vampires who then work to maintain his library, which is a collection of information about himself and other evil or nefarious figures throughout history. The novel hints that Tepes uses this "information center" as a means of initiating tragic historical events: "The implication is that Dracula not only takes his place at the head of a procession of eastern European predators ruling by terror which runs through Ivan the Terrible to Stalin, but has actively influenced his successors' career development" (Stevenson 2005). In this way, Dracula becomes a metaphor of what can happen through the study of history. The vampire as academic symbolizes a kind of living death in which one is sustained more through the dead past rather than the present. Dracula states that "As I knew I could not attain a heavenly paradise . . . I became a historian in order to preserve my own history forever" (Kostova 2005, 206). More disturbingly, this fascination with the past leads to destructive consequences in the present, whether it be Dracula's orchestration of contemporary tragedies or the damage to the narrator's family, particularly her mother, who almost becomes a vampire herself. And though Tepes is seemingly defeated at the close of the novel, nevertheless the book ends with the suggestion that Dracula's work continues to be carried out by his vampire minions/historians. In this way, the narrator must continue her involvement with the past, and she will never be free of it.

There is a tension in the novel that arises between the need for information as a means of keeping evil from destroying society and the fear that this information itself can ruin the person who accumulates and tries to make sense of it. This tension is never resolved in the novel. By using the vampire, a fantastic creature, as a metaphor of a life consumed by information, Kostova illuminates for the reader this debate over the efficacy of information gathering in our current culture that might otherwise be difficult to comprehend. Kostova uses a well-known horror figure, Dracula, to help the reader recognize an evolving fear in our twenty-first century society about the positive and negative aspects of information, so often portrayed in our culture as empowering but overwhelming and confusing as well.

Many reviewers found Kostova's speculative novel to be enjoyable as popular fiction but lacking in true literary merit. For instance, Jane Stevenson noted that Kostova's creation of a conceit in which many of the horrific events of the twentieth century are the result of a mythic creature is absurdly facile: "Thus the spectre which is haunting Europe turns out to be not communism, but Count Dracula, a distasteful simplification of the problems of European history" (Stevenson 2005). Peter Bebergal took exception to Kostova's use of the *epistolary,* or letter, format: "The novel's weakest aspect is its format . . . The various letter sequences read more like diary entries than correspondence, and this makes the main characters sound mostly alike" (Bebergal 2005). Janet Maslin found it to be a "ponderous, many-layered book that is exquisitely versed in the art of stalling" (Maslin 2005), and Susanna J. Sturgis concurred that "none of the plot points add up to very much" (Sturgis 2006, 12).

The Historian represents a trend in twenty-first century speculative fiction of refashioning older genre narratives to reflect new concerns, a trend that is also reflected in Cormac McCarthy's *The Road* (2006). McCarthy borrows the well-worn science fiction scenario of the postnuclear "last survivors on earth" and refashions the narrative into a parable about the consequences of where our information and technological know-how are leading us, the inability of information to help us survive, and the importance of basic human emotions and relationships.

In *The Road,* an unnamed father and his young son travel across a post-apocalyptic, nuclear winter landscape toward the southeast coast of America in search of warmer climate. It is not clear what has laid waste to America, but it is the result of some terrible, nameless event that has decimated nearly all human, animal, and plant life. The event has made cannibals and marauders of those humans left alive, and survival requires all the willpower, love, and connection between father and son to maintain hope and the ability to remain "civilized" human beings. The irony is that it is ostensibly this civilization, with its information technology, science, and weaponry, that has led to the very destruction that has forced humans to become savages. Though this motif is similar to previous speculative stories that critique scientific advancement, McCarthy's novel takes a different approach in that it specifically points out that it is information itself, not only science or nuclear weapons, that is not necessarily empowering.

In using the speculative mode to imagine an utterly desolate wasteland that strips its characters to nothing, McCarthy shows that a pursuit of information cannot help father and son with basic survival. This desolation begins to rob the father in particular of his memories and knowledge of the world that existed before: "The names of things slowly following those things into oblivion. Colors. The names of birds. Things to eat. Finally, the names of things one believed to be true. . . . The sacred idiom shorn of its referents and so of reality" (McCarthy 2006, 75). Although the novel laments this absence of knowledge and information, at the same time, it emphasizes that what drives the father and son to stay alive and human is their love for one another rather than information about their surroundings. McCarthy illustrates that if the twenty-first century "road" is an information superhighway, it is a highway that underneath must be sustained by human contact and feeling. The novel's titular road is one that reveals this point. As a result, the reader fears the possibility of cultural collapse yet also hopes that should our technological society fail, there may yet be a spark of humanity that survives in our bonds with one another.

The Road's haunting tribute to human, rather than technological, connection was universally praised by critics. Michael Chabon wrote that McCarthy's novel is a "lyrical epic of horror" that sustains a "great power to move . . . the reader" (Chabon 2007). Mark Holcomb noted the science fiction elements of the novel and concluded that "the freshness he [McCarthy] brings to this end-of-the-world narrative is quite stunning" (Holcomb 2006). Janet Maslin commented on how McCarthy's poetical style made the novel at once appalling and exquisite: "This parable is also trenchant and terrifying, written with stripped-down urgency and fueled by the force of a universal nightmare. *The Road* would be pure misery if not for its stunning, savage beauty" (Maslin 2006). Ron Charles agreed and argued that "*The Road* is a frightening, profound take that drags us into places we don't want to go, forces us to think about questions we don't want to ask" (Charles 2006, BW06).

Although *The Road* and other contemporary speculative texts are cautionary tales about the power of information acquisition, this is not to say that twenty-first century speculative fiction completely condemns the search for knowledge and truth. Rather, such fiction questions the belief that information can be the panacea for all social ills. However, much speculative writing still asserts that knowledge is power and that having access to information remains a means of combating social problems, even if, in the end, this search for truth cannot completely solve those issues. Michael Chabon, in his Pulitzer Prize-winning novel *The Amazing Adventures of Kavalier and Clay* (2000), explores the need to disseminate information and truth about traumatic social events, even if it is through the medium of speculative writing. Chabon's novel focuses on the early world of American comics during the 1930s and 1940s when graphic art matured and characters such as Superman were created by Jewish artists and writers such as such as Jerry Siegel and Joel Schuster as symbolic crusaders against injustice, particularly the threat of Nazi Germany. As noted earlier, these comics became speculative vehicles for highlighting racial prejudice, such as anti-Semitism, in ways that could be palatable for its white, male readership. Further, comic characters such as Superman have been read as imaginative desires on the part of the writers to create a superhero who would fight for the underrepresented and the voiceless, especially racial and ethnic minorities.

In Chabon's novel, the real and imaginary intermix. The titular characters Joe Kavalier and Sam Clay are cousins who represent the real Jewish comic book writers and designers of the early twentieth century. At the same time, the characters' lives are punctuated by extraordinary events, such as Joe's miraculous escape from Nazi-occupied Prague in a box containing the city's famous *Golem,* a fantastical automaton from Jewish folklore. Joe's amazing escape inspires the cousins to create a superhero called "The Escapist," whose superpower is to rescue innocent people from bondage both actual and metaphorical. Specifically, the Escapist helps those who are oppressed by Nazi Germany (though in the comic, Joe and Sam are forced by their publishers to thinly disguise the Nazis as "Razis").

The novel serves as a *metanarrative,* or a text that comments on the writing of fiction as part of the story's action. In this case, Chabon's metanarrative discusses the power and limitations of the speculative mode. Part of the reason that Kavalier and Clay write "The Escapist" is to envision a hero who can destroy and defeat Hitler and the forces of Nazi Germany, which were storming through Europe, incarcerating and murdering millions of Jews. The Escapist is a magician in a Houdini sense—a hero who can get out of any trap—but he also represents what speculative fiction is: a fantasy, an escape from the realities of the world into an alternate one in which one's wishes or dreams come true. For Kavalier and Clay, that wish is for someone to be able to stop the atrocities of the Nazi regime, a regime that would seem to be a phantasm but is not. The Holocaust was not horror fiction but reality.

In one sense, writing "The Escapist" gives Joe and Sam the power to alert Americans to what is happening in Europe. Further, the character allows Joe to articulate his anger and frustration that his family remains in Nazi-occupied Prague. For instance, Joe's first cover art for "The Escapist" illustrates the hero delivering a devastating right hook to Adolf Hitler. Within the pages of the comic, "The war was over; a universal era of peace was declared, the imprisoned and persecuted peoples of Europe—among them, implicitly and passionately, the Kavalier family of Prague—were free" (Chabon 2000, 166). However, this event does not take place in reality. In this way, the novel asks what is the use of speculative fiction if it cannot do anything about such horrors in the real world. Joe ponders this point himself, and he becomes so disillusioned about the efficacy of his work that he eventually enlists in the military to fight the Nazis overseas. He becomes aware that "the true magic of this broken world lay in the ability of the things it contained to vanish, to become so thoroughly lost, that they might never have existed in the first place" (Chabon 2000, 339). This loss includes, heartbreakingly, those Joe knew in Prague who were eventually killed by the Nazis. Nevertheless, Chabon's answer to the question regarding the value of speculative fiction is yes, it is still a valuable and necessary mode of writing. Even if speculative fiction cannot solve problems, it remains an important outlet for authors and readers to discuss and address "those questions we don't want to ask" (Charles 2006, BW06).

Critics found *The Amazing Adventures of Kavalier and Clay* to be at once insightful, moving, and entertaining. Rex Roberts wrote that "Mr. Chabon weaves a complicated skein of images evoking entrapment and escape . . . In this sense, the book is a tour de force, a piece of literary showmanship that brilliantly employs popular culture in the service of high ideals" (Roberts 2001, B6). Amy Benfer agreed that "Many contemporary issues—homosexuality, the role of women in the arts, censorship, anti-Semitism—are addressed, though never with the cloying revisionism that can bog down books that try to use history as a Parable for Our Time" (Benfer 2000). Ken Kalfus added that "The cousins' adventures are leavened by buoyant good humor, wisecracks and shtick, but the story never loses its awareness of the tragedy that roils beneath the surface of our everyday lives and the lives of men in tights" (Kalfus 2000). Finally, Gail Caldwell summarized the novel's importance by noting it "represents the finest in a whole new breed of contemporary fiction. It's full of pizzazz and testosterone and street smarts, with a moral center that tethers its intelligence" (Caldwell 2000, E1).

Bibliography

Balée, Susan. "Spine-Soothing Tales." *The Hudson Review* Autumn 2006: 480–490.

Bebergal, Peter. "Literary Take on Vampires Gives 'Historian' Bite." *The Boston Globe* 15 June 2005. http://www.boston.com/ae/books/articles/2005/06/15/literary_take_on_vampires_gives_historian_bite/

Benfer, Amy. "'The Amazing Adventures of Kavalier and Clay' by Michael Chabon." Sept. 28 2000. Salon.com.

Butler, Octavia. *Fledgling*. New York: Warner Books, 2005.

Caldwell, Gail. "An Ode to the Golden Age of Comic Book Heroes." *The Boston Globe* 19 Nov. 2000: E1.

———. "Other Voices, Other Rooms in Donna Tartt's 'A Little Friend.'" *The Boston Globe* 27 Oct. 2002: D6.

Chabon, Michael. *The Amazing Adventures of Kavalier and Clay*. New York: Picador, 2000.

———. "After the Apocalypse." *The New York Review of Books* 54 (2) (2007). http://www.nybooks.com/articles/19856

Changnon, Greg. "An Odd Coming-of-Age, with a Murderous Twist." *The Atlanta Journal-Constitution* 28 Dec. 2003: 4K.

Charles, Ron. "Apocalypse Now." *The Washington Post* 1 October 2006: BW06.

Cranny-Francis, Anne. *Feminist Fiction: Feminist Uses of Genre Fiction*. Cambridge: Polity, 1990.

Davis, Kathryn. *The Thin Place*. New York: Little, Brown, and Co., 2006.

Donawerth, Jane, and Carol A. Kolmerten, eds. *Utopian and Science Fiction by Women: Worlds of Difference*. Syracuse: Syracuse University Press, 1994.

Due, Tananarive. *The Living Blood*. New York: Washington Square Press, 2001.

Fiske, John. *Understanding Popular Culture*. London: Unwin Hyman, 1989.

Holcomb, Mark. "End of the Line." *Village Voice* 31 Aug. 2006. http://www.villagevoice.com/books/0636,holcomb,74342,10.html

Hopkins, Pauline. *Of One Blood. The Magazine Novels of Pauline Hopkins*. Schomberg Library of Nineteenth-Century Black Women Writers. New York: Oxford University Press, [1903] 1988: 439–621.

Jones, Vanessa E. "'The Living Blood' Gives Supernatural Thrills." *The Boston Globe* 9 Aug. 2001: C15.

Kalfus, Ken. "The Golem Knows." *The New York Times* 24 Sept. 2000. http://www.nytimes.com/books/00/09/24/reviews/000924.24kalfust.html

Kostova, Elizabeth. *The Historian*. New York: Little, Brown, and Co., 2005.

Maslin, Janet. "The Road through Hell, Paved with Desperation." *The New York Times* 25 Sept. 2006. http://www.nytimes.com/2006/09/25/books/25masl.html

———. "Scholarship Trumps the Stake in Pursuit of Dracula." *The New York Times* 13 June 2005. http://www.nytimes.com/2005/06/13/books/13masl.html

McCarthy, Cormac. *The Road*. New York: Knopf, 2006.

———. *All the Pretty Horses*. New York: Vintage, [1992] 1993.

————. *Blood Meridian, Or the Evening Redness in the West.* New York: Vintage, 1985.

Miller, Laura. "'The Historian' by Elizabeth Kostova." June 6 2005. Salon.com.

————. "'The Little Friend' by Donna Tartt." Nov. 11 2002. Salon.com.

Morrison, Toni. "The Site of Memory." *The Norton Anthology of African American Literature,* 2nd ed. New York: Norton, [1987] 2004: 2290–2299.

Murray, Tom. "Who Killed My Brother?" *The San Francisco Chronicle* 27 Oct. 2002.

Nowell-Smith, Geoffrey. "Popular culture." *New Formations* 2 (1987): 80.

Roberts, Rex. "Two Cousins, World War II, and the 'Toons." *The Washington Times* 7 Jan. 2001: B6.

Rosinsky, Natalie M. *Feminist Futures: Contemporary Women's Speculative Fiction.* Ann Arbor: University of Michigan Research Press, 1984.

Smith, Scott. *The Ruins.* New York: Knopf, 2006.

Stevenson, Jane. "Neckrophilia." *The Observer* 24 July 2005. http://books.guardian.co.uk/reviews/generalfiction/0,,1534428,00.html

Sturgis, Susanna J. "Living the Undead Life." *Women's Review of Books* 23 (1) (2006): 11–12.

Suvin, Darko. *Metamorphoses of Science Fiction: On the Poetics and History of a Literary Genre.* New Haven: Yale University Press, 1979.

Tartt, Donna. *The Little Friend.* New York: Knopf, 2002.

Thomas, Sheree R., ed. *Dark Matter: Reading the Bones.* New York: Aspect, 2005.

————. *Dark Matter: A Century of Speculative Fiction from the African Diaspora.* New York: Warner Books, 2000.

Todorov, Tzvetan. *The Fantastic: A Structural Approach to a Literary Genre.* Trans. Richard Howard. Cleveland: Case Western Reserve University Press, 1973.

Williams, Raymond. *Keywords.* London: Fontana, 1983.

Further Reading

Barr, Marleen S. *Lost in Space: Probing Feminist Science Fiction and Beyond.* Chapel Hill: University of North Carolina Press, 1993; Bleiler, Everett, F., and Richard K. Bleiler. *Science Fiction: The Early Years.* Kent: Kent State University Press, 1990; Cranny-Francis, Anne. *Feminist Fiction: Feminist Uses of Genre Fiction.* Cambridge: Polity, 1990; Donawerth, Jane, and Carol A. Kolmerten, eds. *Utopian and Science Fiction by Women: Worlds of Difference.* Syracuse: Syracuse University Press, 1994; Ellis, Kate Ferguson. *The Contested Castle: Gothic Novels and the Subversion of Domestic Ideology.* Urbana: University of Illinois Press, 1989; Goddu, Teresa A. *Gothic America: Narrative, History, and Nation.* New York: Columbia University Press, 1997; Punter, David. *Literature of Terror: A History of Gothic Fictions from 1765 to the Present Day.* New York: Longman, 1980; Rosinsky, Natalie M. *Feminist Futures: Contemporary Women's Speculative Fiction.* Ann Arbor: University of Michigan Research Press, 1984; Suvin, Darko. *Metamorphoses of Science Fiction: On the Poetics and History of a Literary Genre.* New Haven: Yale University Press, 1979; Thomas, Sheree R., ed. *Dark Matter: A Century of Speculative Fiction from the African Diaspora.* New York: Warner Books, 2000; Todorov, Tzvetan. *The Fantastic: A Structural Approach to a Literary Genre.* Trans. Richard Howard. Cleveland: Case Western Reserve University Press, 1973.

DARCIE D. RIVES

SPORTS LITERATURE

Definition. For at least 150 years, sports have been an integral part of our national literature. Although some scholars may define the genre broadly, including mere references to athletic activity in nontraditional texts such as advertisements and television shows, for purposes of this chapter, sports literature is defined as those novels, short stories, poems, and essays that depict the experiences of athletes and spectators in the world of mainstream sports and remind us of how the arena or

---

WHAT IS A SPORTS NOVEL?

Michael Oriard, the field's most prominent critic, states that a sports novel is one "in which sport plays a dominant role or in which the sport milieu is the dominant setting," one that "finds its vision of the individual and his condition in the basic meaning of the sport he [or she] plays" (1982, 6). What Oriard claims for the novel holds true for short fiction, drama, poetry, and literary essays about sports. In broad outline, much sports literature has relied on stock character types—such as the dumb jock, the "stud athlete" (Oriard 1982, 192), and the monomaniacal coach—as well as on hackneyed themes such as the facile correlation between teamwork and victory in the big game.

---

field of play is just as often a stage upon which passionate human dramas about almost every aspect of American culture are performed.

In the hands of especially talented writers, conventions and stock characters are vigorously challenged or bypassed altogether, as sports become a microcosm in which such issues as race, class, gender, and age matter just as much (if not more than) the final outcome of a given contest.

History. The origins of sports literature can be traced to the publication of juvenile books in the late nineteenth century, when in reaction to the increasing violence of dime novels, writers began producing work for young audiences that focused on positive messages conveyed through sports. Gilbert Patten (1866–1945), who in the late nineteenth and early twentieth centuries became "America's most prolific author of juvenile sports novels" (Crowe 2003, 12) with the publication of his Frank Merriwell series, claimed that his works would allow him "an opportunity to preach—by example—the doctrine of a clean mind in a clean and healthy body" (qtd. in Crowe 2003, 13). Patten's immensely popular works helped promote Muscular Christianity, an ideology that equates physical fitness with moral health. In addition to their didactic tone, these novels established a number of conventions regarding character (the hero is "industrious, persistent, honest . . . modest . . . and democratic," among other things) and plot (victory for the hero in a climactic big game) that would be used again and again by writers of both juvenile and adult literature (Oriard 1982, 29–35).

The early twentieth century also saw the emergence of women authors such as Edith Bancroft, whose Jane Allen novels (1917–1922) "explored the subject of girls' athletics more fully" than the work of other female writers of the time. Ultimately, however, these novels "refuse to take sport seriously" (Oriard 1987, 11), as the female protagonists become typical Victorian women, reveling not in athletic competition but in "the joys of mothering" (Oriard 1987, 13).

Conveying positive messages while portraying the excitement of sport has always been the raison d'être of juvenile sports literature, though over time the type and treatment of issues have become ever more complex. In a career spanning from the late 1930s to the 1960s, John Tunis (1889–1975) used sports to spread messages ranging from teamwork to ethnic tolerance. Tunis's "characters possess many heroic and athletic qualities, but their encounters with life are much more realistic, and the outcomes of many of those encounters are distinctly un-Merriwellian" (Crowe 2003, 18). Works such as *Keystone Kids* (1943) and *Rookie of the Year* (1944) depict the trials and tribulations of manager Spike Russell and his scrappy Brooklyn Dodgers. Not only is there plenty of baseball action to satiate the desire of the young sports fan, but there are also clear lessons about the importance of working together to achieve success.

Contemporary novelist and short story writer Chris Crutcher (1946–) has produced juvenile fiction that is worlds apart from the formulaic, moralistic stories of Gilbert Patten or even the more challenging work of John Tunis. In the Foreword to his collection *Athletic Shorts* (1991), Crutcher explains how, despite being criticized for "depicting . . . characters' hardships too graphically, and for using language and ideas that kids don't need to be exposed to" (1991, 2), he remains committed to his vision. Such thematic boldness is epitomized by "In the Time I Get," which deals with a young football player named Louie who must overcome his fear of and prejudice against an acquaintance who has AIDS.

Because our post-Title IX world continues to witness more and more young girls participating in mainstream sports, it is not surprising that there has been a corresponding increase in literature about female athletes, a literature that is also more sophisticated in nature than the work written at the beginning of last century. One especially noteworthy example is Nina Revoyr's *The Necessary Hunger* (1997), a coming-of-age story in which Nancy Takahiro sees basketball as "more a calling than a sport" (1997, 12). As a highly recruited athlete, as a lesbian suffering from the unrequited love of a fellow basketball player, Nancy is about as far as can be from the world of Jane Allen.

Sports literature for young readers has a long, impressive tradition deserving of study, but adult sports literature has attracted a larger readership and more intense scholarly interest. Although one can find depictions of the sporting life in some of the earliest works of our national literature—such as James Fenimore Cooper's Leather Stocking novels (1823, 1826, 1827, 1840, and 1841) or tales from the Old Southwest such as Thomas Bangs Thorpe's "The Big Bear of Arkansas" (1845)— and although late nineteenth-century works such as Mark Twain's *A Connecticut Yankee in King Arthur's Court* (1889) and Frank Norris's "Travis Hallet's Half Back" (1894) use sports and sporting language as an integral part of their narratives, the genre as we know it might be traced back to Ernest Lawrence Thayer's well-known poem "Casey at the Bat" (1888). Though not the first baseball poem to appear in America, "Casey at the Bat" is arguably the most influential in that it addresses "three important themes: the fall of the folk hero, its effect on his community, and the meaning of both to the universe of humans" (Candelaria 1989, 23), thus anticipating a good deal of sports literature that will be written in the next 120 years.

At the beginning of the twentieth century, two writers in particular constructed the foundations of a sports literature meant for adult readers. Two Jack London novels, *The Game* (1905) and *The Abysmal Brute* (1913), used boxing (still considered a disreputable sport and especially so as a subject for serious literature at the time) to explore issues of gender. *The Game* is important for the development of the genre because it serves as a "paradigm" for a "basic theme of sports fiction," namely the "irreconcilable incompatibility between the Woman and the Game" (Oriard 1982, 175). A much more important figure was Ring Lardner, who after getting his start as a sportswriter, turned to writing novels and short stories about baseball and boxing, the most enduring of which is *You Know Me Al* (1914). A novel in letters, the work satirizes Jack Keefe, a provincial, comically obtuse rookie pitcher whose inflated view of his abilities keeps him "a small-time busher even after leaving the bush league" (Candelaria 1989, 28).

In the so-called golden age of sports in the 1920s, when the economic boom following World War I led to an expansion in leisure time that saw spectators flocking to sporting events featuring such nationally celebrated athletes as Babe Ruth (baseball), Jack Dempsey (boxing), and Bobby Jones (golf), literary artists in greater numbers began to examine the effect of sports on American culture. In F. Scott Fitzgerald's *The Great Gatsby* (1925) unflattering portraits of Tom Buchanan, an ex-football player; Jordan Baker, a professional golfer; and Meyer Wolfsheim, a disreputable businessman responsible for fixing the World Series, serve as a clear moral judgment on the general corruption of the times. In the fiction of Ernest Hemingway—particularly *In Our Time* (1925) and *The Sun Also Rises* (1926)—the athlete/bullfighter becomes not a symbol of corruption but a quasi-religious figure, a model of moral conduct in a godless modern world.

It is not football or golf or bullfighting but baseball that has most often drawn the attention of our nation's most gifted writers. Literary interest in baseball is tied to the history of the sport itself. The first written mention of the game in North America appears in 1791; by the 1870s, only a few years after Charles Peverelly's *The National Game* (1866) gave the sport its resilient epithet (Oriard 1982, 69), competitive professional leagues were firmly established. Because the sport came of age as the country did, baseball quickly came to be seen as synonymous with America. Philip Roth, in "My Baseball Years," writes about how baseball was a means of socialization into American culture: "For someone whose roots in America were strong but only inches deep . . . baseball was a kind of secular church that reached into every class and region of the nation and bound millions upon millions of us together" (1975, 180). Former Commissioner of Major League Baseball A. Bartlett Giamatti goes so far as to say that "[b]aseball is part of America's plot . . . the plot of the story of our national life" (1989, 83).

Baseball's prominence in American literature is indebted to the nonfiction writing on sport in the early twentieth century. Richard Orodenker traces this sport's writing tradition and identifies two major categories of writers. The Matties, "graceful, polished writers, baseball's elegant phrasemakers," are epitomized by Grantland Rice, the early twentieth-century sportswriter famous for his overblown style, and much later, by the well-chiseled prose of writers such as John Updike, Gay Talese, and Roger Angell (1996, 10). In contrast, the Rubes, both the optimistic "gee whiz" and the cynical "aw nuts" types, are more interested in "colorful stories" (1996, 10) and the baseball "talk" (1996, 11) used to pass them on. In addition to Ring Lardner, the list of Rubes includes Damon Runyon, Jimmy Cannon, Jimmy Breslin (1996, 11–12), and most recently, Hunter S. Thompson, whose ESPN Page 2 essays, collected in *Hey Rube: Blood Sport, the Bush Doctrine, and the Downward Spiral of Dumbness—Modern History from the Sports Desk* (2004), meditate on the parallels between politics and professional sports (mostly football and basketball) in his own inimitable style.

Since Ring Lardner, "who nearly single-handedly transformed . . . [baseball] from a casual motif in juvenile stories to a formal nuanced metaphor serviceable to serious literature" (Candelaria 1989, 25), writers have been fascinated with the literary possibilities of this sport. A partial list of serious baseball fiction, covering literary modes ranging from the satiric to the mythic to the postmodern, includes Thomas Wolfe's *The Web and the Rock* (1939) and *You Can't Go Home Again* (1940); Bernard Malamud's *The Natural* (1952); Mark Harris's Henry Wiggen novels: *The Southpaw* (1953), *Bang the Drum Slowly* (1956), *A Ticket for a Seamstich*

(1957), and *It Looked Like for Ever* (1979); Robert Coover's *The Universal Baseball Association, Inc., J. Henry Waugh, Prop.* (1968); Philip Roth's *The Great American Novel* (1973); Jay Neugeboren's *Sam's Legacy* (1973); William Brashler's *The Bingo Long Traveling All-Stars and Motor Kings* (1975); W.P. Kinsella's *Shoeless Joe* (1982); and Eric Rolfe Greenberg's *The Celebrant* (1983). More recently, Mark Winegardner's *The Veracruz Blues* (1996), depicting the heyday of the Mexican Leagues, and Don DeLillo's *Underworld* (1997), which connects Bobby Thomson's "shot heard round the world" in 1951 to the Cold War politics of the time, have proven that baseball continues to capture the imagination of some of our nation's most highly regarded writers.

Dramatists have also made compelling use of baseball (and, less often, of other sports) in their work. In the popular imagination, the Broadway musical *Damn Yankees* (adapted from the 1954 Douglass Wallop novel *The Year the Yankees Lost the Pennant*) (Candelaria 1989, 33) continues to entertain audiences to this day. *Old Timers Game* (1988), about an exhibition contest featuring past players from a minor league baseball team, and *Cobb* (1991), which depicts the irascible Ty Cobb at three significant moments in his life, are works by Lee Blessing, a critically acclaimed contemporary playwright. August Wilson's *Fences* (1987) chronicles the last days of Troy Maxon, a prodigious home run hitter resentful of the racially segregated past that prohibited him from showcasing his talents in the major leagues. Significant dramatic works tackling other sports include Arthur Miller's *Death of a Salesman* (1949) and Tennessee Williams's *Cat on a Hot Tin Roof* (1954), both of which feature ex-football players who have trouble adjusting to the real world; Howard Sackler's *The Great White Hope* (1967), loosely based on the life of African American boxer Jack Johnson; and Jason Miller's *That Championship Season* (1972), exploring the tensions that arise during the twenty-fifth reunion of a high school basketball team. Significantly, the plays by Wilson, Arthur Miller, Williams, Sackler, and Jason Miller each won Pulitzer prizes, a testament to the inspiration of sports for many of our nation's most recognized writers.

Poets, too, have made much use of sports in their work, and here again the subject of baseball dominates. Recent anthologies of baseball poetry include *Where Memory Gathers* (1998), edited by Edward R. Ward and *Baseball and the Lyrical Life* (1999), edited by Tom Tolnay. Some collections, such as Don Johnson's *Hummers, Knucklers, and Slow Curves* (1991), are completely devoted to the sport. Two works notable for extended treatment of the subject are Kenneth Koch's book-length *Ko, or Season on Earth* (1959), one of whose multiple narrative lines involves a sensitive, Japanese fastballer who pitches for the Dodgers, and Donald Hall's nine-sectioned meditation on the game simply entitled "Baseball" (1993).

With so much high quality evidence in our literature, it seems almost obvious to conclude, along with Roger Angell, that "[b]aseball is the writer's game" (1991); however, throughout American literary history, there has also been sustained interest in other sports. Boxing, for example, continues to fascinate some of our nation's most popular writers. Although a number of "formulaic boxing novels" (Oriard 1982, 99) were published in the last century, so were original works of fiction such as *The Harder They Fall* (1947) by Budd Schulberg, *The Professional* (1958) by W.C. Heinz, and *Fat City* (1969) by Leonard Gardner. In addition, literary essayists have had much to say about the sport. Norman Mailer's "Ego" (1971), which identifies Muhammad Ali as "the very spirit of the twentieth century" (Halberstam 1999, 713), explores not only the psychology of the then-often-reviled boxer but also America's need for outsized celebrities. In her collection *On Boxing* (1994), Joyce Carol Oates makes an eloquent argument for how "[e]ach boxing match is a story—a unique and highly condensed drama without words" (1994, 8), a tragedy because "it consumes the very excellence it [the punished body] displays" (16). For Oates, the writer's role is to watch the drama unfold and provide what the athletes cannot—a translation of the bodies and their actions into words.

Football has also inspired its fair share of writers. From the early decades of the twentieth century, when the college football novel held sway by addressing "the disparity between the ideals of the university and the glorification of the athlete at the university's expense" (Oriard 1982, 63), to more recent works such as Frederick Exley's *A Fan's Notes* (1968), an autobiographical novel about one man's obsession with football hero Frank Gifford; Dan Jenkins's "outlandishly raunchy" (Oriard 1982, 190) comedy *Semi-Tough* (1972); and Peter Gent's *North Dallas Forty* (1974), a fictional exposé of the brutality of the game, football has served as incredibly fertile ground for the literary imagination. Don DeLillo's *End Zone* (1972), another novel of the gridiron, deserves special note, as it goes far beyond fan adulation, bawdy sexual humor, and graphic depiction of violence to lay bare the limitations of the language we use to represent such things.

The tradition of basketball literature is not as long as that of other major sports; nevertheless, it boasts a body of work notable for quality and thematic diversity. Jay Neugeboren's *Big Man* (1970) and Lawrence Shainberg's *One on One* (1975) are two early examples of the subgenre that explore, among other things, the theme of "creativity within urban limitation" (Oriard 1982, 115). More recently, Charley Rosen has published two novels: *The House of Moses All Stars* (1996), about the adventures of a group of barnstorming Jewish cagers, and *Barney Polan's Game: A Novel of the 1951 College Basketball Scandals* (1997). Paul Beatty's *The White Boy Shuffle* (1996) emphasizes the urban nature of the game and provides an unflinching satirical examination of sports and race in America. Tom LeClair's *Passing Off* (1996), in contrast, is a postmodern suspense novel about an American basketball player in Greece. A fine anthology of basketball literature is offered by editor Dennis Trudell in *Full Court: A Literary Anthology of Basketball* (1996).

Of the recent novels showcasing other major sports, three are distinguished for their postmodern preoccupation with identity. Harry Crews's *Body* (1990) is of note for its incisive critique of gender stereotypes in the world of professional body building. Carol Anshaw's *Aquamarine* (1992) explores the swimmer-protagonist's three possible lives based on important decisions she makes in the wake of a personally disappointing Olympic performance. David Foster Wallace's *Infinite Jest* (1997), which stands out in the field of contemporary American literature for both its scope and erudition, "intertwines sport [tennis] with questions of learning and memory that ultimately shade into a larger meditation on contemporary identity" (Burn 2004, 41). In the last decade of the twentieth century, writers turned to sports to address the complex dynamics of selfhood and, in the process, demonstrated that sports literature is an ever-evolving genre.

Trends and Themes. Whether meant for adult or juvenile readers, sports literature since 2000 builds upon established interests while following new trends in popular culture and global economics. Baseball literature continues to be popular, and works addressing gender, race, and class in sport continue to be published. In addition, relatively new trends are also apparent in this recent literature, including an increasing interest in a wide variety of sports; an increasing number of book-length works on American sports history and present-day sports culture; and literary explorations of the globalization of sports as a money-making entertainment.

Not surprisingly, literature about baseball continues to find an audience. Recent fiction includes Kevin Baker's *Sometimes You See It Coming* (1993; 2003 reissued in paperback) and Patrick Creevy's *Tyrus* (2002), two novels based on the life of Ty Cobb. Baseball, race relations, and the history of Chicago intersect in Peter M. Rutkoff's *Shadow Ball* (2001), which imagines the near-miss integration of baseball long before Jackie Robinson. More personal in its use of baseball history is Mick Cochrane's *Sport* (2001), a coming-of-age story set in the 1960s and featuring a 13-year-old Minnesota Twins fan. An aging scout is the focus of William Littlefield's *Prospect* (1989, reissued in 2001) and Brian Shawver's *The Cuban Prospect* (2003), the latter of which is more of an international thriller than a depiction of baseball between the chalk lines.

Contemporary writers continue to find new ways to present baseball to the reading public. Three recent notable works succeed in this search by treating the intersection of baseball and place. *Crooked River Burning* (2001), by Mark Winegardner explores sports and civic identity, using the misfortunes of the Cleveland Indians baseball team to parallel a city's economic decline. Eugena Pilek's *Cooperstown* (2005) centers on the lives of citizens of a small town who live in the shadow of the Baseball Hall of Fame and must come to terms with the reality behind the baseball myth that gives their small town relevance. Richard Greenberg's drama *Take Me Out* (2003), set in the media crucible of New York City, explores the problems that arise when a talented and popular baseball player announces he is gay. This theme of sexual orientation is especially significant because, up to this point, "[t]he literature of baseball . . . [has been] continuously about male hetero-sexuality; its characters . . . straight men in the process of reinforcing their straight-ness" (Morris 1997, 4).

In addition to full-length works, collections of baseball stories continue to appear on the market in significant numbers, including *Baseball's Best Short Stories* (1997), edited by Paul D. Staudohar; *Bottom of the Ninth: Great Contemporary Baseball Stories* (2003), edited by John McNally; *Dead Balls and Double Curves: An Anthology of Early Baseball Fiction* (2004), edited by Trey Strecker; and *Fenway Fiction: Short Stories from Red Sox Nation* (2005), edited by Adam Emerson Pachter.

As the recent publication of several baseball poetry collections indicates, baseball verse continues to be popular. Notable here is Gene Fehler's *Dancing on the Basepaths* (2001), a single-authored collection devoted entirely to the sport. Other collections include the anthology *Line Drives: 100 Contemporary Baseball Poems* (2002), edited by Brooke Horvath and Tom Wiles. Unlike many such anthologies, this one offers an impressive variety of "previously unanthologized work" (2002, xxiii) loosely arranged to parallel the trajectory of a baseball season. The book includes the work of well-known poets, such as Charles Bukowski's "Betting on the Muse," which compares the abbreviated career of a ball player with the longer and ultimately more satisfying career of a writer; Quincy Troupe's "Poem for My Father," a paean to the negro leagues; and Richard Brautigan's "A Baseball Game," a surrealistic piece depicting what happens when nineteenth-century French poet Charles Baudelaire goes to a professional baseball game. Ranging over more sports is *Way to Go!* (2001), a collection for young audiences edited by Lillian Morrison. Noah Blaustein's *Motion: American Sports Poems* (2001) is an anthology especially noteworthy for its breadth, containing poems ranging from baseball to surfing. Both the "classics" (William Carlos Williams's "At the Ball Game," Marianne Moore's "Baseball and Writing," James Dickey's "For the Death of Vince Lombardi") and more recent works (B.H. Fairchild's "Old Men Playing Basketball" and Gary Soto's "Black Hair") treat such time-honored themes as race and gender, as well as the quest for bodily transcendence.

Because "[s]portswomen simply are not, and haven't really ever been, among sport's more acceptable stories" (Sandoz and Winans 1999, 4), the tradition of sports literature by and about women is not as long. However, with more and more young women participating in high school and collegiate athletics and with the visibility of women's professional leagues such as the WNBA, it is not surprising that these experiences are beginning to be chronicled in the literature. Joli Sandoz's two anthologies of women's writing published in the late 1990s have gone a long way toward solidifying the status of the female athlete in America. The first collection, *A Whole New Ball Game* (1997), features stories and poems from the last one hundred years, whereas the second, *Whatever It Takes* (1999), presents primarily works of nonfiction that serve as an eloquent argument for the long tradition of women's athletics.

The voices of female athletes rise up loud and clear in recent juvenile literature as well. The anthology *Girls Got Game* (2001) features stories and poems about young female protagonists and speakers who look and act much differently from the girls of the Jane Allen novels. Lucy Jane Bledsoe's story "Rough Touch" depicts Ruthie's conflict with her body as both dramatic tension and thematic suggestion. At the end of the story, she plays a game with the boys, taking them all by surprise by going out for a pass and catching it, at which point the narrator announces: "It was hers, the football was hers" (2001, 115).

Refreshingly, not all work by today's female writers defines the sporting experience of girls as a struggle against a patriarchal world. In Grace Butcher's "Basketball," for example, the focus is on the pride the speaker feels in making a layup. The made basket, rather than a significant victory in the gender wars, is what truly matters here. Another noteworthy example is Karol Ann Hoeffner's *All You've Got* (2006), a young adult novel that features a young female volleyball player who "didn't spend a lot of time stressing over how her body looked" but "cared more for how it performed" (2006, 3).

Even juvenile novels by male writers reflect the growing presence of young women in sports. Mike Lupica's *Travel Team* (2006) features a young male protagonist who, according to one of sports literature's many clichés, has a competitive desire on the basketball court that belies his small stature. However, it is important to note that one of the key players on his team is a tough, sharp-shooting girl. Although the two main characters of John Feinstein's *Last Shot* (2006) are not athletes, they are intensely dedicated to and knowledgeable about the game of basketball. Both excellent writers, they win an essay contest and are awarded an all-expenses-paid trip to New Orleans to cover the NCAA Final Four. Significantly, the female is not a clueless interloper in some male preserve; she is a girl who just so happens to be crazy (and well-informed) about basketball.

Other juvenile sports literature offers perspective on different contemporary issues. In a twist on the typical big game narrative, John H. Ritter's *The Boy Who Saved Baseball* (2003) concerns a group of small-town kids who arranged to play a winner-take-all game against unwanted real estate developers. The stakes are raised considerably in Michael Chabon's *Lord of the Rings*-like baseball adventure called

Summerland (2002), in which the very fate of the world hinges on the outcome of a ball game between a team of kids and a team of demons. In a more realistic vein, Chris Crutcher's *Whale Talk* (2001) tells the tale of how several high school misfits come together as a team and achieve not grand victory but the kind of incremental improvement they need to earn their varsity letters, much to the chagrin of the school's bullying football establishment. Significantly, each of these works features a strong, young female athlete.

Whether found in a library, mall bookstore, or online, sports literature continues to proliferate in vigorous variety. The latest in the annual collection of *The Best American Sports Writing* (2006) features essays on underexamined sports such as competitive cheerleading, recreational softball, and professional poker. In addition to literary sports reportage, current magazines have shown a renewed interest in sports fiction. *Golf World* magazine, for example, first published a fiction issue in September of 2005, continuing the practice in 2006, and a short story from *Esquire* (November 2006), "The Death of Derek Jeter" by Michael Martone, has enjoyed an extended life thanks to Internet blogs and message boards that supply a link to the story on the magazine's Web site. In other recent fiction, Darin Strauss's novel *Real McCoy* (2002) narrates the life of a boxer and con artist in the first decade of the twentieth century who is presumably the original "Real McCoy." On a deeper level, the novel explores the issue of artificiality and authenticity in American culture—then and now—and especially in our yearning for genuine sports heroes. Thom Jones also turns to boxing as a subject in more than one story collected in *The Pugilist at Rest* (1994) and *Sonny Liston Was a Friend of Mine* (2000). F.X. Toole's *Rope Burns: Stories from the Corner* (2000) depicts the gritty, violent world of boxing both inside and outside the ring. Another Toole work, his posthumous *Pound for Pound* (2006), is a novel about an ex-boxer who loses his grandson in a traffic accident. Golf is another sport that continues to draw much attention from writers of fiction. The spirituality that can be achieved through golf is a theme in Steven Pressfield's *The Legend of Bagger Vance* (1995), Robert Cullen's *A Mulligan for Bobby Jobe* (2001), and Roland Merullo's humorously pietistic *Golfing with God* (2005). Golf is played primarily for laughs in Dan Jenkins's irreverent *Slim and None* (2005) and Rick Reilly's *Shanks for Nothing* (2006). In each, there is a scattershot approach to satire on topics ranging from feminism to social class distinction to life in a post-9/11 world. Besides boxing and golf, mainstay subjects in the genre, other sports also appear in recent fiction including horse racing in Jane Smiley's sprawling *Horse Heaven* (2000) and surfing in Kem Nunn's thriller *Tijuana Straits* (2004).

In general, writers of mainstream sports fiction take two approaches to attracting readers. First, much recent adult popular fiction on sports features the antics of professional athletes. In *Wild Pitch* (2003), for example, Mike Lupica places a redemption story amid the crude behavior of professional baseball players. Similarly, the lives of professional athletes are blatantly satirized in *Foul Lines: A Pro Basketball Novel* (2006) by Jack McCallum and L. Jon Wertheim, two writers for *Sports Illustrated*. Comic and full of pop cultural allusions, the novel provides genuine insight into how reporters cover professional sports and how professional athletes and those who support them act in private life.

The second strategy many writers employ to attract readers involves combining sports with other popular genres. Golf in a hard-boiled vein is mined by Peter Dexter in *Train* (2003), for example. David Ferrell writes a baseball-serial killer thriller in *Screwball* (2003), and John DeCure has authored two mysteries about a California lawyer and surfer: *Reef Dance* (2001) and *Bluebird Rising* (2003). Although the above writers try for an original approach to sports within the context of something familiar, readers continue to be drawn to literature that merely traffics in sports stereotypes, as exemplified by John Grisham's bestselling *Bleachers* (2003), a novel about Neeley Crenshaw, an ex-high school football player who returns after a considerable absence to his hometown in order to come to terms with his hard-nosed ex-coach, who is now on his deathbed. Nevertheless, for the most part, current writers of sports fiction seek original audience appeal, as can be seen in the case of two recent works focusing on basketball, arguably America's most ascendant sport. Stanley Gordon West offers a heartwarming portrait of small-town high school cagers in *Blind Your Ponies* (2001). In thematic contrast, Sherman Alexie continues to turn to basketball to probe the continuities and dislocations in Native American culture, most recently in the short story "Whatever Happened to Frank Snake Church?" from *Ten Little Indians* (2003). The popular and the serious meet in *Murder at the Foul Line* (2006), a collection of short stories that features the work of such award-winning mystery writers as Lawrence Block, Jeffery Deaver, and S.J. Rosen. This latter work evinces that the "sports-mystery novel," which can be traced back to the 1930s (Oriard 1982, 18), is alive and well.

Nonfiction writing about sports remains strong, with writers turning increasingly to contemporary issues and historical events as subject matter, no doubt appealing to today's readers' appetite for reality-based stories. These writers often produce book-length journalism that seeks the excitement of fiction. For example, in the past few years, a spate of books has appeared focusing on the coach or manager of sports teams to detail the day-to-day practices of winners. Two Pulitzer Prize-winning journalists have authored books that examine the increasingly complex role of coaches in professional sports. H.G. (Buzz) Bissinger's *Three Days in August* (2005) explores the mind and career of St. Louis Cardinals manager Tony LaRussa through a pivotal three-game series in 2003, demonstrating how the successful manager "possesses the combination of skills essential to the trade: part tactician, part psychologist, and part riverboat gambler" (17). In *The Education of a Coach* (2005), David Halberstam reveals New England Patriots coach Bill Belichick to be equally obsessive, a man who "was about one thing only—coaching—and wary of anything that detracted from it," such as the media or egotistical players (21). Don Haskins's (with Daniel Wetzel) *Glory Road* (2005), and Michael Lewis's *Coach* (2005) profile coaches at the amateur level. Haskins, the longtime coach at Texas Western (now University of Texas at El Paso), started an all-black team against Kentucky and won the 1966 NCAA basketball championship. Characterized as a tough and (again) obsessive coach, Haskins rejects the notion that he is some kind of civil rights leader. He started the five best players he had, regardless of their color, because "I was just a coach who hated to get his ass beat and would do anything to avoid it" (120). Billy Fitzgerald, Michael Lewis's high school baseball coach, is more than the stereotypical "Intense Coach" (55). Fitzgerald is described as both an intellectual and a passionate teacher, just the kind of person to make a difference in a younger person's life, something each of the coaches profiled manages to accomplish.

Real-life sporting experiences have been the subject of three very different basketball memoirs. In *Hoop Roots* (2001), John Edgar Wideman compares the act of reading to basketball, which is to him a kind of wonderful jazz played by the body. In his distinctive style, Wideman is part memoirist, part basketball historian, part theorist of race, and part musician, who on the table of contents page issues the following invitation: "Different pieces coming from different places—read them in sequence or improvise." Different in style and tone is Melissa King's *She's Got Next* (2005), which chronicles a young woman's journey toward self-discovery through the unlikely path of pickup basketball. In *My Losing Season* (2002) Pat Conroy also discovers much about himself by reflecting upon his basketball career at The Citadel. Despite a less than successful senior season, one spent under a despotic coach and an unloving father, Conroy, from the perspective of later years, comes to value his experience, arguing that there are more important lessons to be learned from losing than from winning.

In the last several years the presence of women in boxing, our most brutal sport, has been well documented in memoirs such as *Kill the Body, the Head Will Fall* (1997) by Rene Denfeld, *Looking for a Fight* (2000) by Lynn Snowden Picket, *The Boxer's Heart* (2000) by Kate Sekules, and *Without Apology: Girls, Women, and the Desire to Fight* (2005) by Leah Hager Cohen. Not surprisingly, these books examine the pressures of gender as women compete in this most male-dominated of sports; more surprising is the particular perspective each writer derives from her experience. For instance, while Picket ultimately rejects the sport for its brutality, Sekules and Cohen embrace boxing's potential for liberation and self-fulfillment.

Also in the vein of true-to-life sports literature are historical accounts of a great moment in sports and books that follow a high school team's season. It is no surprise that Bissinger's *Friday Night Lights* (1990)—which in meticulous and oftentimes unflattering detail describes the football crazed world of Odessa, Texas—has inspired similar works such as Madeleine Blais's *In These Girls, Hope is a Muscle* (1995), the uplifting story of a girls' basketball team and its successful quest for the Massachusetts state championship; Larry Colton's *Counting Coup: A True Story of Basketball and Honor on the Little Big Horn* (2001); and Michael D'Orso's *Blue Eagle: A Team, a Tribe, and a High School Basketball Season in Arctic Alaska* (2006). The success-story archetype can be found as well in recent historical accounts such as Laura Hillenbrand's *Seabiscuit: An American Legend* (2001) and Mark Frost's *The Greatest Game Ever Played: Harry Vardon, Francis Ouimet, and the Birth of Modern Golf* (2002), two books popular enough to have been made into Hollywood movies. In addition, examining the same pre-World War II time frame, David Margolick has written *Joe Louis vs. Max Schmeling and a World on the Brink* (2005), and Dorothy Ours has published *Man o' War: A Legend Like Lightning* (2006).

Context and Issues. Other writers have chosen to focus not just on a given sport but on the culture that surrounds it. Two prime examples of this are Warren St. John's look at the fans who follow the University of Alabama football team, *Rammer Jammer Yellow Hammer: A Journey into the Heart of Fan Mania* (2004), and Josh Peter's examination of professional bull riders, *Fried Twinkies, Buckle Bunnies, and Bull Riders: A Year Inside the Professional Bull Riders Tour* (2005). Combining a focus on a particular sport and a famous athlete are books about cycling and Lance Armstrong: *It's Not About the Bike: My Journey Back to Life* (2000) and *Every Second Counts* (2003), both by Armstrong and Sally Jenkins, and *Lance Armstrong's War: One Man's Battle Against Fate, Fame, Love, Death, Scandal, and a Few Other Rivals on the Road to the Tour de France* (2005), by Daniel Coyle.

Although there is still much literary focus on baseball, its status as national pastime continues to be challenged by high quality literature focusing on our nation's other sports. This, in part, has to do with the meteoric rise in popularity of basketball in this country in the last 25 years and, more importantly, its stunning success as a global commodity. Walter LaFaber, in his study *Michael Jordan and the New Global Capitalism* (2002), explains the symbiotic relationship between Jordan, the NBA, and the basketball legend's endorsers (particularly Nike), arguing how the sport of basketball grew in popularity both in the United States and in the rest of the world as a result of forward-looking capitalists' entering the global economy. Although imaginative literature has been slow to explore this theme, Paul Beatty's *White Boy Shuffle* (1996)—a novel about an African American basketball star coming of age in Los Angeles at the end of the twentieth century—depicts a world in which the athlete, even in high school, is seen as a commodity to be exploited by advertisers. At this point in our nation's history, with the continuing global popularity of Michael Jordan along with a wave of exciting younger stars (and extremely lucrative marketing tools) such as LeBron James, it seems that basketball may well be, as Bart Giamatti said of baseball not even twenty years ago, "the plot of the story of our national life" (83).

Reception. The body of scholarship in the field of sports literature is small but significant and, not surprisingly, weighted like the literature itself toward the sport of baseball. Wiley Lee Umphlett's *The Sporting Myth and the American Experience* (1975) is a seminal book-length study of the genre. Using as a starting point the idea that "the microcosm of the sporting experience can tell us a great deal about what it means to be an individual in today's world" (18), Umphlett focuses on "the search for identity" (19) theme as it occurs in major sports novels to examine their exploration of "psychological and moral truths about American experience" (28). Also focusing on the quest is Robert Higgs in *The Athlete in American Literature* (1981). Higgs identifies three types of athletes—the Apollonian, the Dionysian, and the Adonic—and meditates on their role in some of the best literature our country has to offer to suggest three different approaches athletes take when pressured to conform to society's codes.

Arguably the most significant scholar in this field is Michael Oriard. An ex-football player whose days with the Fighting Irish of Notre Dame and the Kansas City Chiefs are chronicled in *End of Autumn: Reflections on My Life in Football* (1982), Oriard has written four book-length studies that focus on the genre broadly defined. *Dreaming of Heroes: American Sports Fiction, 1868–1980* (1982) provides a history of sports fiction as well as an overview of prevailing tropes and themes. Like Higgs and Umphlett before him, Oriard focuses on the figure of the sports hero; however, he brings this figure fully into the mainstream by identifying him as not just an athletic type but a national type—"the most widely popular self-made man in America today" (51). As such, he is crucial (not peripheral, as sports figures tend to be viewed) to our understanding of the American mind. Oriard devotes chapters to recurrent themes such as the country versus the city, youth versus age, men versus women, and history versus myth in a variety of novels about baseball, football, basketball, and boxing. *Sporting with the Gods: The Rhetoric of Play and Game in American Culture* (1991) examines how sports language—expressions and metaphors—has worked itself into our culture at large (ix). In *Reading Football: How the Popular Press Created an American Spectacle* (1993) and *King Football: Sport and Spectacle in the Golden Age of Radio, Newsreels, Movies and Magazines,*

The Weekly and The Daily Press (2000), Oriard analyzes a wide variety of texts in order to discover what they reveal about the meaning of football for American spectators.

Christian Messenger has focused exclusively on imaginative literature, authoring two excellent studies on sports fiction: *Sport and the Spirit of Play in American Fiction: Hawthorne to Faulkner* (1981) and its companion work, *Sport and the Spirit of Play in Contemporary Fiction* (1990). Messenger's first study begins with a premise that follows the focus of Umphlett and Higgs: "[t]he sports hero in American fiction," Messenger argues, "has been a special figure, a man apart from mass man" (1981, 1). Like Higgs, Messenger identifies three different "heroic models." The first, The Ritual Sports Hero, is "[a]n Adamic figure who seeks self-knowledge" (1981, 8). The second, The Popular Sports Hero, is "deeply democratic, raw, humorous. . . . he expressed the strength and vitality of westward expansion and growth" (1981, 8). Over time, this type becomes domesticated by the sports arena. The third model, The School Sports Hero, is "more genteel than the Popular Hero and nurtured through American education, privilege, and the assimilation of war through symbolic sports conflict" (1981, 9). Messenger goes on to explain how The Ritual Hero "plays for the self," The School Hero "competes for society's praise," and The Popular Hero "competes for immediate extrinsic rewards: money, fame, records" (1981, 9). In his second book, Messenger explores the sports hero as he or she appears in contemporary American literature, arguing that "[t]he individual sports hero's tensions and achievements within the sports collective is the obsessive subject of American sports fiction" (1990, 24).

Three other scholarly works examine the enduring myths of baseball. Cordelia Candelaria's *Seeking the Perfect Game: Baseball in American Literature* (1989) examines canonical baseball texts and the myths they have created or reinterpreted. In the same vein, Deeanne Westbrook's *Ground Rules: Baseball and Myth* (1996), building upon the work of Claude Levi Strauss, Eric Gould, and Jacques Lacan, argues that baseball literature "has the status of a functional modern mythology" (1996, 9). Broader in scope, David McGimpsey's *Imagining Baseball: America's Pastime and Popular Culture* (2000) studies enduring myths not only in baseball literature, but also in films and television. McGimspey identifies a number of "tropes" in "baseball's cultural products": "baseball is perfect and God-given; baseball is the best sport; baseball is 'naturally' amenable to artistic representation; baseball is America at its best; baseball shows us a nonviolent America where all are judged on merit that can be quantified; baseball is about children; baseball returns sons to fathers" (2000, 2). Some works, such as W.P. Kinsella's *Shoeless Joe* (and its wildly popular movie version *Field of Dreams*), ardently support one or more of these tropes (2000, 35–41), whereas others, such as Jim Bouton's tell-all diary *Ball Four* (1970), deconstruct such nostalgic notions (2000, 45).

Don Johnson focuses exclusively on sports poetry in *The Sporting Muse: A Critical Study of Poetry about Athletes and Athletics* (2004). Johnson organizes his discussion according to sport, allotting chapters for baseball, football, basketball, and golf, as well as chapters exclusively devoted to the work of women poets and the role of the spectator. Regardless of sport or perspective, Johnson observes that

> Most sports poetry falls into one of four types: the memory poem, often about a childhood or adolescent experience on the court or playing field; the action poem, one which attempts to capture the mood and movement in a game or particular play; the

journalistic poem, which records the achievement of an individual or a team as an event; and the celebratory poem, an effort to preserve for posterity the exploits of an heroic player or team. (2004, 135)

Despite the genre's origins and despite the vast body of work, juvenile sports literature has inspired far less scholarship; however, Chris Crowe's *More Than a Game: Sports Literature for Young Adults* (2004) provides a useful taxonomy for understanding the full variety of works published since the days of Frank Merriwell. The works most deserving of critical attention fall under two main categories—the "more-than-a-game novel," "whose main concern is an athlete and his involvement in athletics, but it also has much more character development and some subplots that may be only tangential to sport" (2003, 36); and "[t]he most sophisticated young adult sports novels" called '*sportlerroman*' (2003, 38), a form of the traditional *bildungsroman* apprenticeship novel, where the protagonist is an athlete struggling for maturity" (2003, 21).

Selected Authors. Over the past century, many American writers have used sports in their novels, poems, dramas, and essays to comment on enduring issues in American society. Although many of these works—written by best-selling authors such as Frank Deford, Rick Reilly, Dan Jenkins, and Mike Lupica—enjoy immense popularity and make occasionally incisive comments about our contemporary society, a number of our country's most critically acclaimed writers have challenged conventions of the genre and, in the process, produced original and enduring literature.

Bernard Malamud's first novel, *The Natural* (1952), is without question *the* starting point in the field of contemporary sports literature. Though less than enthusiastically received by critics when it first appeared, *The Natural* is now seen as a seminal attempt to join sports and myth, reality, and fantasy. It is the story of Roy Hobbs, a confident, cocky pitcher who is shot by a strange woman as he is on the verge of making it to the big leagues. When several years later he gets another opportunity to play in the pros, he continues to put his own dreams and goals before the collective by deciding to throw an important game in the pennant race so that he might have the money necessary to satisfy Memo Paris, the woman of his dreams.

WATCHING SPORTS IN A MOVIE

Because we are a nation that loves to watch sports, it is not surprising that sports films outstrip sports literature in terms of popularity. Viewers are drawn to such movies as *Breaking Away* (1979), *Hoosiers* (1986), *Remember the Titans* (2000), and *Glory Road* (2006) because of their "feel good" resolutions, in which teams overcome great odds to achieve success on the field of play. Other films such as *Raging Bull* (1980) and *The Hurricane* (2000) compel attention for the unflinching brutality faced by characters based on real life people and events. Still others generate interest in part because they have been adapted from popular literary works. Among the most significant of these adaptations are *North Dallas Forty* (book 1973; film 1979), *Semi-Tough* (book 1972; film 1977), *The Natural* (book 1952; film 1984) and, more recently, *Friday Night Lights* (book 1990; film 2004; television drama 2006–2007) and *Million Dollar Baby* (short story 2001; film 2004). These films have proven to be just as popular (if not more so) than the original works that inspired them. Sports films have a history that stretches back almost as far as the film industry itself; interest in such works will most likely continue unabated.

As Malamud recounts the Knights' pennant chase, he applies a number of mythic layers to the narrative, depicting Hobbs's exploits on the field through the tropes of Arthurian romance and the fable of the Fisher King. Like King Arthur himself, Hobbs wields a modern-day Excalibur; his sword, however, is a baseball bat named Wonderboy. His seeming heroic quest is leading a team of Knights to the holy grail of a pennant, in the process redeeming the Waste Land of the woeful baseball team and its dispirited fans. Yet the problem with Hobbs is that he, according to Edward Abramson, "lives within baseball and cannot see beyond it. He desires to be a baseball hero rather than a mythic, Grail hero" (1993, 14). He seeks only personal glory and physical satisfaction; he cannot live for anyone other than himself. Unable to see or move beyond his own desires, Hobbs fails again. At the end of the novel, after striking out despite his attempt to get a hit and thereby go against his crooked bargain, he thinks: "I never did learn anything out of my past life, now I have to suffer again" (218).

Published early in the decade after World War II, *The Natural* ultimately asks searing questions about America's values now that the United States is a global superpower. By conflating the classic myths of Arthurian legend with the American myths of success and self-creation, Malamud equates the health of the King (baseball) with the health of the land (America). But America, like the baseball depicted here, is the site of a fallen dream. Hobbs's dishonest dealings clearly allude to the so-called Black Sox scandal in 1919, when it was revealed that players on the Chicago White Sox team had taken payoffs from gamblers to lose World Series games. When a kid says to Hobbs, "Say it ain't true, Roy," (218) Malamud echoes what a boy, as legend would have it, said to "Shoeless" Joe Jackson of 1919 White Sox infamy: "Say it ain't so, Joe." The myth of baseball-America is thus belied by actuality as ideals are warped by personal ambition.

A year after *The Natural* appeared, Mark Harris published the first book in his tetralogy of baseball novels, *The Southpaw* (1953). Narrated and supposedly written by pitcher Henry "Author" Wiggen, these novels ultimately trace the career of their protagonist from fabulous rookie season to reluctant retirement. More than one contemporary review of *The Southpaw* praised Harris for creating a comic novel that was nonetheless "serious." *Bang the Drum Slowly*, which was made into a television movie in 1956 and into a feature film in 1973, received even more acclaim. The third novel in the series, *A Ticket for a Seamstitch* (1957) is widely considered to be the least successful work, in part because the narrative focuses less on Wiggen and more on catcher Piney Woods and his most devoted fan, the "seamstitch" or seamstress of the title. The final novel in the tetralogy, *It Looked Like for Ever* (1979), also received tepid reviews. One notable exception to this reception was the admiration offered by poet and baseball fan Donald Hall in *The New York Times Book Review*.

As a number of critics have noted, Harris's Henry Wiggen tetralogy borrows heavily from Ring Lardner's vernacular presentation of the common baseball player. That common player, however, also often seems to be very much a common man in these novels, confronting the commonplace problem of aging and dying with wit and insight. Fittingly, in *The Southpaw* Wiggen helps the New York Mammoths win a World Series, understandably concluding—with the arrogance of both youth and talent—that he belongs among the elite of professional sports. After giving the crowd an obscene gesture "the old sign—1 finger up," Wiggen defends himself: "I guess all I was saying was they could go their way and I would go mine, and some folks is born to play ball and the rest is born to watch, some folks born to clap and shriek and holler and some folks born to do the doing" (346).

From the élan and vigor of youth Harris turns to the subject of death in *Bang the Drum Slowly*. William J. Schafer identifies the central appeal of the book by noting that the novel "turns, like Housman's 'To an Athlete Dying Young,' around the pity and mystery of the unconscious young struck down untimely" (32). The dying athlete here is Bruce Pearson, a reliable but marginally talented catcher who has Hodgkin's disease. Although he cannot finish the season, Pearson inspires his team to a World Series win, but once dead he is quickly forgotten by his teammates who do not attend his funeral. One player's death does not stop baseball anymore than one person's death stops life. Yet Harris memorializes Pearson by tenderly describing his last moment on a baseball field, the place where he was most alive: "I started off towards the dugout, maybe as far as the baseline, thinking [Pearson] was following, and then I seen that he was not. I seen him standing looking for somebody to throw to, the last pitch he ever caught, and I went back for him, and Mike and Red were there when I got there, and Mike said, 'It is over son,' and he said 'Sure' and trotted on in" (237–238).

The end of baseball for Henry Wiggen comes in *It Looked Like for Ever*, a comic examination of an underrepresented figure in sports literature: the aging athlete. In this novel, Wiggen finds himself suddenly released from the New York Mammoths, and his almost desperate attempts to catch on with another team as a 39-year-old relief pitcher take him from Japan to California to the broadcast booth. Appropriately enough, Wiggen does play again, though his onerously revived career ends suddenly when he is struck by a batted ball. Accepting the inevitable, Wiggen announces "to 1 and all that I was now finally retired from baseball for ever, Nature was Nature, I talked back to Nature once too often and Nature slammed the door" (274). From first appearance as a confident rookie with nothing but seeming glory ahead of him, Wiggen exits baseball as a man made wiser by stark lessons both on and off the field.

In one sense, aging is also the subject of John Updike's Rabbit tetralogy, which chronicles the life, but not necessarily the maturation, of Harry "Rabbit" Angstrom, an ex-high school basketball star. Published roughly a decade apart, these novels— *Rabbit, Run* (1960), *Rabbit Redux* (1971), *Rabbit is Rich* (1981), and *Rabbit at Rest* (1990)—are set mostly in the fictional Pennsylvania town of Brewer, where Angstrom's life unfolds in abundant, realistic detail. Although certain critics have found Updike's realism tiresome, accusing him of writing bloated books, the Rabbit novels have also received significant critical praise, with *Rabbit is Rich* and *Rabbit at Rest* both winning numerous awards, including the Pulitzer Prize for each. Indeed, considered everything from a documentary realist to a social satirist to a theological, existential, and Christian writer, Updike tends to evoke intense, often contradictory reactions in readers and critics who rarely receive him lukewarmly, offering either strong condemnation or unqualified admiration. Although Updike published the four novels under single cover in a book titled *Rabbit Angstrom* (1995), at that time calling the work a "mega-novel" (viii), the Rabbit saga does not end with *Rabbit at Rest*. In 2000 Updike published a novella titled "Rabbit Remembered" in *Licks of Love: Short Stories and a Sequel* in which Rabbit's illegitimate daughter again appears.

In all of the Rabbit portrayals, Updike is careful to depict Harry Angstrom's judgments and actions without authorial criticism, and he staunchly refuses to resolve the tensions in the character's psyche (Boswell *passim*). These novels also attempt to capture the zeitgeist of post–World War II America, principally the four distinctive decades from 1950–1990. Ultimately the tetralogy presents an America in moral and spiritual disarray as the attractions of money, drugs, and sex become ever more alluring; yet the country's energetic and hopeful nature remains constant. In these novels, Updike's view of sports is often more melancholic than celebratory, because sports, as sex and drugs, offer only the briefest kind of transcendence. If, as Daniel Morrissey writes, "Updike's description of Harry Angstrom's soaring golf drive in *Rabbit, Run* was an ecstatic explanation of human union with God" (187), then in these novels much of life is remembering such moments rather than living in them, though Rabbit's frequent sexual encounters represent his attempt to experience both the physical and spiritual fulfillment he used to find regularly in sports. Essentially a seeker, Rabbit is frequently dissatisfied and restless. In *Rabbit, Run,* for example, Angstrom runs away from his wife and an unsatisfactory suburban life. Twenty-six years old and a gadget salesman, he has a difficult time coming to terms with the fact that he is no longer the great sports star. When he is not physically running away from adult responsibilities, he is doing so mentally, by returning to those moments when he performed heroic feats on the basketball court—those times when he was blissfully in sync with himself. The death of his daughter only fuels his desire to run, to stay in flight as it were, like that tremendous golf shot.

By the time of *Rabbit Redux*, however, Angstrom initially seems more resigned to his life. Set in the summer of 1969 with the Apollo moon landing in the background, this novel sees 36-year-old Rabbit working in a print shop at a linotype machine that is soon to be obsolete. At first basketball is used to express Henry Angstrom's sense of pointless change, as he recognizes how different the current game is from the one he played in the late 1940s. Moreover, when his son, Nelson, tells him, "sports are square now. Nobody does it" (18), Angstrom replies, "Well, what isn't square now? Besides pill-popping and draft-dodging. And letting your hair grow down into your eyes" (18–19). Still, Angstrom believes in the power of sports. He wonders: "How can he get the kid [Nelson] interested in sports? If he's too short for basketball, then baseball. Anything, just to put something there, some bliss, to live on later for a while. If he goes empty now he won't last at all, because we get emptier" (25).

Slowly, however, moral certainty seeps away from Rabbit. When his wife leaves him for another man, he begins an affair with an 18-year-old girl who has run away from her rich Connecticut family, and later he harbors a black fugitive and drug dealer. The novel presents drug use, infidelity, and racism graphically and without denunciation. Although Rabbit often perceives himself to be in competition with others in his real life, as he was on the basketball court, his basketball training appears more subtly in the novel. As Rabbit accedes to drug use and increasing sexual promiscuity, it becomes clear that his life mirrors that of the ex-basketball player in that he fits himself—morally, intellectually, and spiritually—with those around him, playing with others in society the way he would play with teammates on the court, not resisting but conforming to the action in a fluid, almost unthinking manner.

This pattern of attempted conformity continues in the final two novels. *Rabbit is Rich* is set in 1979, with gas shortages and the Iranian hostage crisis as backdrop. Now wealthy and operating his dead father-in-law's Toyota dealership, Rabbit tries to conform to middle age. As critic Marshall Boswell notes, Angstrom is at first "content and satisfied," convinced that "his past" is "now solidly behind him" even to the extent that no one calls him Rabbit, using Harry instead (132). The economic malaise in which the country is mired, however, and the fact that Nelson is clearly repeating his father's actions with infidelity and drug use suggest contemporary issues and moral positions that cannot be neatly resolved. Rabbit is still restless, a seeker after ultimate meaning, which he will never find. Boswell furthermore identifies a thematic link with *Rabbit, Run* in the way *Rabbit is Rich* "links sexual redemption with athletic prowess" (183). After a particularly vivid sexual encounter, Rabbit finds his golf game much improved, and Boswell concludes: "[A] good game of golf in Updike is a sure sign of grace" (184).

In the final novel of the tetralogy, *Rabbit at Rest*, Harry Angstrom dies, a fate that is suggested not only by the novel's title but also in its first sentence. Set in 1989, the novel finds Harry Angstrom retired in Florida, where overweight and out of shape, he suffers heart attacks and eventually expires. Here, Updike provides both a detailed description of America in the 1980s and a continuation of the searching that has characterized Rabbit's life. That life features an affair between Rabbit and his daughter-in-law and Nelson's plight as a cocaine addict and embezzler. Fittingly enough, Rabbit's demise is preceded by a pick-up basketball game between him and a teenaged African American boy that momentarily has him feeling "loose and deeply free" (504). Though he wins the game, on old-fashioned shots that the youth derides and grudgingly admires, Rabbit ends up "unconscious [on] the dirt" court (506). Scared, the youth runs away; someone eventually dials 911, and Rabbit is soon dead, the word "Enough" appearing as his final thought (512). Encapsulating Rabbit's life, this last game supplies nothing more lasting than a mere moment of triumph. As Jack B. Moore has argued, however, Harry Rabbit Angstrom's early success as a basketball player defines his subsequent life, principally in the way he measures the success of that life but also in the ways he lives it: as he might in a basketball game, Rabbit "improvises his life, often badly, but with many thrills and great activity" (188).

The Universal Baseball Association, Inc., J. Henry Waugh, Prop. (1968) is Robert Coover's "metacommentary on both myth and history through baseball" (Messenger 1990, 359). The novel concerns a lonely middle-aged man who creates a fantasy baseball game and, with his accountant's penchant for record keeping, a corresponding meticulous history of the league. Waugh rolls dice and the results correspond with events on a series of complicated charts. When Damon Rutherford, the star pitcher in the league—and Waugh's favorite player—falls victim to an unfortunate roll of the dice, Waugh ignores the rules he so carefully created in order to ensure that Jock Casey, Rutherford's killer, is destroyed. The events of The Universal Baseball Association become so much more compelling—and far more real—for Waugh than his actual life that, in the concluding chapter, this alternative world takes over. Waugh himself disappears from the narrative, and the reader is left only with the perspective of his players (his fictional characters), who partake in a quasi-religious commemoration of the two great Association players who were killed a hundred seasons earlier. With the creator out of the picture and his creations assuming a full and seemingly autonomous life of their own, it is easy to agree with Roy Caldwell's contention that the subject of the novel "is not the playing of baseball but the making of fiction" (1987, 162).

Equally challenging is Don DeLillo's postmodern masterpiece *End Zone* (1972). The ostensible subject is collegiate football, but the real subject is language itself—the way it creates reality and gives us a comforting order to our lives. Unlike many of the players who enjoy the order and simplicity of playing for the Logos College Screaming Eagles, Gary Harkness (the protagonist) can see the game—and other games, for that matter—for what it is worth. At the beginning of a chapter that recounts the funeral of an assistant coach, Harkness states: "Most lives are guided by clichés. They have a soothing effect on the mind and they express the kind of widely expressed sentiment that, when peeled back, is seen to be a denial of silence" (69). There is much in the novel to engage the typical sports fan: the autocratic coach; the mercurial star running back; the disaffected troublemaker; the big game against the rival team. However, DeLillo is less interested in presenting these conventions than he is in exploiting them for the purpose of exploring how language often makes pleasant the world we live in and denies the silent, terrifying end zone that is our true reality. Gary Storoff argues that Harkness "searches for a game that will provide his life with significance" (1985, 235). College does not provide the answer, nor do football or the Air Force. They are all games, and "games are at best evasions, unconscious methods of escaping the void" (1985, 244)—the real end zone beyond the boundaries of language itself.

Under the pseudonym of Cleo Birdwell, DeLillo cowrote (with Sue Buck) *Amazons* (1980), a satirical novel, narrated by the first female hockey player, that has intriguing things to say about gender relations. The novel has garnered little scholarly attention, but Philip Nel views the work as important in its status as a starting point for DeLillo's exploration of the theme of gender (2001, 416). Although Birdwell "does little to challenge the structures that maintain an imbalance of power between men and women" (419), she does resist the attempts of reporters and advertisers to objectify her (422). In the end, however, despite the fact that Birdwell is telling her own story, "the point of view feels masculine; only in isolated moments does the book veer toward feminist critique" (419).

DeLillo's magnum opus, *Underworld* (1997), is not a sports novel per se. However, an iconic sporting event—Bobby Thomson's famous home run against the Dodgers claiming the pennant for the 1951 Giants—is absolutely central to the book. The Prologue, separately published as "Pafko at the Wall" (1992), links this moment in baseball history with the testing of a Russian nuclear bomb, which occurred on the very same day. The story becomes "a tale of two blasts." The bomb test signals the beginning of the Cold War, but for the frenzied crowd in the stadium, that news is "overwhelmed by baseball legend" (Duvall 2002, 33) and thus "illustrates the dangerous tendency of baseball to aestheticize and erase international politics" (2002, 35), or at least bury it, metaphorically speaking, underground.

Although the balance of the novel explores other plot lines, the baseball playoff game continues to resonate. In one of the narrative threads, Nick Shay, a waste management specialist, and some of his colleagues attend a very different Dodgers-Giants game, a contest between old rivals that has a striking parallel in international politics. As John Duvall argues, "[b]oth the United States-Russia and the Dodgers-Giants oppositions mean something very different in 1992 than in 1951. Old loyalties and beliefs are rendered archaic. Just as the Dodgers and the Giants left New York to tap into the lucrative West Coast market, so too have market forces rewritten the relationship between America and Russia" (2002, 30). As the colleagues converse, we learn that Nick is supposedly in possession of Thomson's home run ball, the one a young African American boy scrambles to retrieve in the Prologue. Nick has successfully traced ownership of the ball almost all the way back to the end of that game. Despite his best efforts, however, there is a hole in the narrative which he is left to fill with his own belief that this is an authentic object of the past—that, in turn, the past he remembers is itself authentic. Nick's willingness to pay a lot of money for a ball that may or may not be the genuine article suggests the desperate nature of his "quest of what he takes to be a lost authenticity—a sense of himself as someone who was at one time whole and complete and a part of a community" (Duvall 2002, 26). On both the national and personal level, then, the novel is about—at least in part—the way we attempt to connect to our always unknowable past.

Philip Roth's fiction uses sports as a way of critiquing many of our most precious national myths. Unlike Malamud, who employed age-old myths to lend gravitas to the story of a baseball player, Roth in *The Great American Novel* (1973) ruthlessly and humorously debunks the whole myth-making process, creating not just an "anti-baseball novel" (Klinkowitz 1993, 39), but an antimythological one. The novel details the personalities and outrageous events of the 1943 season of the Rupert Mundys, a hapless baseball team from the long forgotten Patriot League. This skewed history is framed by the prolix octogenarian Word Smith, a half senile sportswriter confined to a nursing home who thinks that his story of the league, which has been unceremoniously expunged from the annals of sports history, may well be the great American novel. The league is filled with colorful characters, including Frank Mazuma, a Bill Veeck-like owner who introduces all kinds of entertaining gimmicks into the game; Bob Yamm and O.K. Ockatur, a midget pitcher and batter who face off against each other; Gil Gemesh, the tremendously talented but hotheaded pitcher who is banned from baseball for throwing at an umpire; and Bud Parusha, a one-armed player who plucks the ball from his glove with his mouth. There are outrageous events as well, including a Mundys contest against the inmates of an insane asylum; a Black Sox-like scandal, this one, however, involving a disgruntled Mundy who helps his team to an unlikely win streak with the aid of Jewish Wheaties; and a McCarthyesque inquisition on the presence of Communists in the Patriot League. These outrageous players and situations undercut the sanctimonious traditionalism of characters such as General Oakhart, the president of the league; Glorious Mundy, the original owner of the Mundys and a man for whom baseball was nothing less than a "national religion" (82); and Mister Fairsmith, who "attempted to instruct them [his players] in the Larger Meaning" of the game (136).

Although some critics praise the audacity and comic ingeniousness of *The Great American Novel*, many also view the book as having serious structural flaws as well as a lack of thematic coherence. If the book does not always succeed, it does manage to get across "Roth's purpose," which is "to demythologize mythology" (Siegel 1976, 181). At the end of the novel, when the octogenarian Word Smith, out of publishing options in the United States, sends his book off to Chairman Mao for consideration, he compares himself to the Russian writer Alexander Solzhenitsyn. On the surface, the comparison is ludicrous; however, when Word Smith makes the point that, like the Russian writer, he "refuses to accept lies for truth and myth for reality" (380), he is more or less getting at Roth's "Larger Meaning" behind all the humor and the games.

More recently, Roth's Pulitzer Prize-winning *American Pastoral* (1997) chronicles the life of Seymour Levov (nicknamed The Swede because of his blond hair and blue eyes), who, during World War II, was a high school football, basketball, and baseball star. Some years younger, Nathan Zuckerman (a recurring narrator in

Roth's novels) is in awe of this paragon of athletic ability. "[T]hrough the Swede, the neighborhood entered into a fantasy about itself and about the world, the fantasy of sports fans everywhere: almost like Gentiles (as they imagined Gentiles), our families could forget the way things actually work and make an athletic performance the repository of all their hopes" (3–4). Often over at the Levov's house to play with Seymour's younger brother, the narrator comes to discover a number of John Tunis novels on the athlete's bookshelf. Of particular interest is Tunis's *The Kid from Tompkinsville* (1940), a novel about a baseball player in which "each triumph" of the main character "is rewarded with a punishing disappointment or a crushing incident" (8) in what the narrator calls "the boys' Book of Job" (9). In the balance of the novel, Zuckerman goes on to imagine Levov's life and, in the process, dismantles the myth of the American dream in heart-rending fashion.

Compared to *The Great American Novel*, sports in *American Pastoral* seem to play a relatively minor role; however, Levov's past athletic life is essential for our understanding of his character. As an ex-athlete, as a man who enters smoothly into the WASP world by marrying an Irish girl, a former Miss New Jersey, and as a first-generation American who goes into his father's glove manufacturing business (which, significantly, takes a successful turn when Levov's renown as an athlete helps secure an important client), Levov appears to be living the American dream in all of its glory, having "accumulated the visible signs of an American identity: success in business, sports, and home life" (Stanley 2005, 8). Derek Parker Royal goes so far as to say that "the Swede, as a model of athletic prowess . . . is a stand-in for America itself" (2005, 201).

Because Levov had flown (in the words of the narrator) "the flight of the immigrant rocket, the upward, unbroken immigrant trajectory," he expected that his daughter Merry would be "the highest flier of them all, the fourth-generation child for whom America was to be heaven itself" (122). Instead, Merry, who comes of age during the Vietnam War, grows disgusted by her parents' cozy and isolated upper-class existence and turns into a political radical who blows up the small town's post office, killing several people in the process. In a later phone conversation, his brother Jerry brings up Levov's sporting past in order to criticize him for the kind of banal, unreflective life he has led. He suggests at first that Levov views his situation as a game, but then immediately discards that notion. "For the typical male activity you're the man of action, but this isn't the typical male activity" (280). Following out the metaphor, Merry's behavior is out of bounds for Levov—so far out of the field of play he has no idea how to respond. Jerry continues with his criticism, saying that Levov "[c]an only see [him]self playing ball and making gloves and marrying Miss America. . . . And you thought all that façade was going to come without a cost" (280). If *The Kid from Tompkinsville* was a Book of Job for young boys, then Levov's life, seemingly the epitome of the American dream, is that Bible story in all its disturbing maturity. According to Zuckerman's imaginings, Levov cannot solve his problem; he can only suffer and endure. Unlike *The Great American Novel*, which displays an absurdly comic vision, *American Pastoral* is the tragedy of a man who believes that one can live a dream. Despite differences in tone, each novel is similar in its use of sports to help debunk potent American myths.

Although seriously understudied, Jenifer Levin is, without question, the most significant female voice in sports literature. Her *Water Dancer* (1982) tells the story of Dorey Thomas, a young marathon swimmer who, seeking to overcome a failure in her past, wants to swim the brutal San Antonio Strait off the coast of Washington State. To help her achieve this goal, she approaches Sarge Olssen, a coach whose own son Matt died making the attempt to cross this body of water. The quest to accomplish the goal becomes, in the process, a quest for identity.

Michael Oriard hails this novel as "a major breakthrough in the genre of sports fiction" because "it offers a feminist alternative to the masculine sports myth" that relegates women to second-class status, making them "adjuncts to the [sports] hero's achievements" or even "major obstacles" (1987, 9–10). Unlike her traditional, domesticated mother Carol, who defines herself almost exclusively in terms of her relationship to men, Dorey is quietly but fiercely independent. Her swim across the San Antonio Strait is not a competition in the traditional sense. Even in earlier races, her philosophy has been to focus not on the people who are swimming a given race with her but on the water itself. By novel's end, the mysterious Dorey achieves her goal and, in the process, discovers—or more accurately—develops into her own, natural self. What is more, the act of swimming becomes a kind of self-disclosure. At last, Ilana (Sarge's wife and Dorey's mother-lover) is able to know this water dancer. "Ilana," she calls out near the end of the swim. "Do you know me now?" to which Ilana responds: "Yes . . . I am proud" (1982, 363). As Sharon Carson and Brooke Horvath argue, the novel

> tells us that the skills of endurance, flexibility, strength, and style—all of which Dorey possesses in spades—form the magic pattern of the dancer in water and in life. They are the same skills employed by individuals who are fortunate enough to celebrate themselves for who they are and who flourish in spite of cultural definitions of who they should be. (1991, 46–47)

In two later novels, *Snow* (1983) and *Sea of Light* (1993), Levin continues her exploration of sports, gender, and the quest for identity. *Snow,* through the character of bold, adventurous outdoorswoman named Raina Scott, examines the themes of *Water Dancer:* "woman's endurance, woman's power, woman's desire" (Messenger 1990, 183). *Sea of Light* is told from a variety of perspectives but centers around Babe Delgado, a collegiate swimmer, named by her mother after Babe Didrikson, the phenomenal female athlete of the 1930s and 1940s. After recovering from a plane crash that kills nearly her entire team, Babe enrolls at a smaller school to begin her comeback as an athlete and as a human being. Coached by Bren Allen, who experiences her own emotional struggles due to the untimely death of a lover, and encouraged by the love of a much less talented teammate named Ellie, Babe not only wins a swim meet at novel's end but, much more importantly, recovers from the trauma of the plane crash and begins to reestablish significant relationships with others. Babe's success in the pool, like Dorey's in the San Antonio Strait, is the product of much physical and emotional suffering and sacrifice. Babe's victory does not give her college a championship or help get her back to a Division 1 school; instead, the win symbolizes her successful attempt at self-recovery.

At its best, sports literature has *always* been about much more than the games, athletes, and spectators themselves. Whether assuming the form of a novel, short story, poem, drama, or essay, such literature continues to compel our attention for the simple reason that sports have always revealed deep and enduring truths about the American psyche.

Bibliography

Abramson, Edward. *Bernard Malamud Revisited*. New York: Twayne, 1993.

Angell, Roger. *Once More Around the Park: A Baseball Reader*. New York: Ballantine, 1991.

Bissinger, Buzz. *Three Days in August: Strategy, Heartbreak, and Joy Inside the Mind of a Manager*. New York: Houghton Mifflin, 2005.

Bledsoe, Lucy Jane. "Rough Touch." In *Girls Got Game: Sports Stories and Poems*. Sue Macy, ed. New York: Henry Holt, 2001, 109–116.

Boswell, Marshall. *John Updike's Rabbit Tetralogy: Mastered Irony in Motion*. Columbia, MO: University of Missouri Press, 2001.

Burn, Stephen. "'The Machine Language of the Muscles': Reading, Sport, and the Self in *Infinite Jest*." In *Upon Further Review: Sports in American Literature*. Michael Cocchiarale and Scott D. Emmert, eds. Westport, CT: Praeger, 2004, 41–50.

Caldwell, Roy. "Of Hobby-Horses, Baseball, and Narrative: Coover's *Universal Baseball Association*." *Modern Fiction Studies* 33.1 (1987): 161–171.

Candelaria, Cordelia. *Seeking the Perfect Game: Baseball in American Literature*. Westport, CT: Greenwood, 1989.

Carson, Sharon, and Brooke Horvath. "Sea Changes: Jenifer Levin's *Water Dancer* and the Sociobiology of Gender." *Aethlon* 9.1 (1991): 37–48.

Crowe, Chris. *More Than a Game: Sports Literature for Young Adults*. Lanham, MD: Scarecrow Press, 2003.

Crutcher, Chris. Foreword to *Athletic Shorts*. New York: Greenwillow, 1991.

DeLillo, Don. *End Zone*. New York: Penguin, 1972.

Duvall, John N. *Don DeLillo's Underworld*. New York: Continuum, 2002.

Giamatti, A. Bartlett. *Take Time for Paradise: Americans and Their Games*. New York: Summit Books, 1989.

Halberstam, David. *The Education of a Coach*. New York: Hyperion, 2005.

Harris, Mark. 1956. *Bang the Drum Slowly*. Reprint, Lincoln, NE: University of Nebraska Press, 1984.

———. *It Looked Like for Ever*. New York: McGraw-Hill, 1979.

———. 1953. *The Southpaw*. Reprint, Lincoln, NE: University of Nebraska Press, 1984.

Haskins, Don, and Dan Wetzel. *Glory Road: My Story of the 1966 NCAA Basketball Championship and How One Team Triumphed Against the Odds*. New York: Hyperion, 2005.

Higgs, Robert J. *Laurel and Thorn: The Athlete in American Literature*. Lexington, KY: University of Kentucky Press, 1981.

Hoeffner, Karol Ann. *All You've Got*. New York: Simon Pulse, 2006.

Horvath, Brooke, and Tom Wiles, eds. *Line Drives: 100 Contemporary Baseball Poems*. Carbondale, IL: Southern Illinois University Press, 2002.

Johnson, Don. *The Sporting Muse: A Critical Study of Poetry about Athletes and Athletics*. Jefferson, NC: McFarland, 2004.

Klinkowitz, Jerry. "Philip Roth's Anti-Baseball Novel." *Western Humanities Review* 47.1 (1993): 30–40.

Levin, Jenifer. *Water Dancer*. New York: Plume, 1982.

McGimpsey, David. *Imagining Baseball: America's Pastime and Popular Culture*. Bloomington, IN: Indiana University Press, 2000.

Mailer, Norman. "Ego." In *The Best American Sports Writing of the Century*. David Halberstam, ed. Boston, MA: Houghton Mifflin, 1999, 713–737.

Malamud, Bernard. 1952. *The Natural*. Reprint, New York: Avon Books, 1980.

Messenger, Christian K. *Sport and the Spirit of Play in American Fiction: Hawthorne to Faulkner*. New York: Columbia University Press, 1981.

———. *Sport and the Spirit of Play in Contemporary Fiction*. New York: Columbia University Press, 1990.

Moore, Jack B. "Sports, Basketball, and Fortunate Failure in the Rabbit Tetralogy." In *Rabbit Tales: Poetry and Politics in John Updike's Rabbit Novels*. Lawrence R. Broer, ed. Tuscaloosa, AL: University of Alabama Press, 1998, 170–188.

Morris, Timothy. *Making the Team: The Cultural Work of Baseball Fiction*. Urbana, IL: University of Illinois Press, 1997.

Morrissey, Daniel. "Reveiw of *A Month of Sundays* by John Updike." *Commonweal*, 6 June 1975: 187–188.

Nel, Philip. "*Amazons* in the *Underworld*: Gender, the Body, and Power in the Novels of Don DeLillo." *Studies in Contemporary Fiction* 42.4 (2001): 416–436.

Oates, Joyce Carol. 1987. *On Boxing*. Reprint, Hopewell, NJ: Ecco, 1994.

Oriard, Michael. *Dreaming of Heroes: American Sports Fiction, 1868–1980*. Chicago, IL: Nelson Hall, 1982.

———. *Sporting with the Gods: The Rhetoric of Play and Game in American Culture*. Cambridge: Cambridge University Press, 1991.

———. "From Jane Allen to *Water Dancer*: A Brief History of the Feminist(?) Sports Novel." *Modern Fiction Studies*. 33.1 (1987): 9–20.

Orodenker, Richard. *The Writers' Game: Baseball Writing in America*. New York: Twayne, 1996.

Revoyr, Nina. *The Necessary Hunger*. New York: Simon and Schuster, 1997.

Roth, Philip. *American Pastoral*. Boston, MA: Houghton Mifflin, 1997.

———. *The Great American Novel*. New York: Holt, Rinehart and Winston, 1973.

———. "My Baseball Years." In *Reading Myself and Others*. New York: Farrar, 1975.

Royal, Derek Parker. "Pastoral Dreams and National Identity in *American Pastoral* and *I Married a Communist*." In *Philip Roth: New Perspectives on an American Author*. Derek Parker Royal, ed. Westport, CT: Praeger, 2005, 185–207.

Sandoz, Joli, and Joby Winans, eds. *Whatever It Takes: Women on Women's Sport*. New York: Farrar, 1999.

Schafer, William J. "Mark Harris: Versions of (American) Pastoral." *Critique: Studies in Modern Fiction* 19.1 (1977): 28–48.

Siegel, Ben. "The Myths of Summer: Philip Roth's *The Great American Novel*." *Contemporary Literature* 17.2 (1976): 171–190.

Storoff, Gary. "The Failure of Games in Don DeLillo's *End Zone*." In *American Sport Culture: The Humanistic Dimensions*. Wiley Lee Umphlett, ed. Lewisburg, PA: Bucknell University Press, 1985, 235–245.

Umphlett, Wiley Lee. *The Achievement of American Sport Literature: A Critical Appraisal*. Rutherford, NJ: Fairleigh Dickinson University Press, 1991.

Updike, John. Introduction to *Rabbit Angstrom: A Tetralogy*. New York: Alfred A. Knopf, 1995.

———. *Rabbit at Rest*. New York: Alfred A. Knopf, 1990.

———. *Rabbit Redux*. New York: Alfred A. Knopf, 1971.

Westbrook, Deeanne. *Ground Rules: Baseball and Myth*. Champaign, IL: University of Illinois Press, 1996.

Wideman, John Edgar. 2001. *Hoop Roots*. Reprint, New York: Mariner, 2003.

Further Reading

Bandy, Susan J., and Anne S. Darden. *Crossing Boundaries: An International Anthology of Women's Experiences in Sport*. Champaign, IL: Human Kinetics, 1999; Cocchiarale, Michael, and Scott D. Emmert, eds. *Upon Further Review: Sports in American Literature*. Westport, CT: Praeger, 2004; Darden, Ann. "Outsiders: Women in Sports and Literature." *Aethlon* 15.1 (1997): 1–10; Guttmann, Allen. *A Whole New Ball Game: An Interpretation of American Sports*. Chapel Hill, NC: University of North Carolina Press, 1988; Hye, Allen E. *The Great God Baseball*. Macon, GA: Mercer University Press, 2004; Nelson, Mariah Burton. *The Stronger Women Get, the More Men Love Football: Sexism and the American Culture of Sports*. New York: Harcourt Brace, 1994; Oriard, Michael. *King Football: Sport and Spectacle in the Golden Age of Radio, Newsreels, Movies and Magazines, The Weekly and The Daily Press.* Chapel Hill, NC: University of North Carolina Press, 2000; Rivers, Jacob F. *Cultural Values in the Southern Sporting Narrative.* Columbia, SC: University of South Carolina Press, 2002; Womack, Mari. *Sport as Symbol: Images of the Athlete in Art, Literature and Song.* Jefferson, NC: McFarland, 2003.

MICHAEL COCCHIARALE AND SCOTT D. EMMERT

SPY FICTION

Definition. Most simply defined, spy literature features protagonists who are connected to espionage in some primary way. The protagonists can be either amateur spies or professional operatives and commonly use covert methods to thwart a nation, group, or individual's enemies. Spy stories are most often set against the backdrop of an international political conflict, revolve around secret conspiracies with the potential to change the fate of nations, and occur in environments where nothing is what it seems and everything is potentially dangerous.

The genre shares many characteristics with the British schoolboy adventure story, detective fiction, war prophecy fiction, and the thriller in general. For instance, schoolboy adventure stories flourished in their classic form from the 1850s to the 1920s and celebrated English public schools (which Americans call private schools) as noble institutions that built the character of young men for the good of the nation. Spy authors Erskine Childers, Sapper, John Buchan, Francis Beeding, Graham Greene, John le Carré, and Ian Fleming all draw from this genre's conventions, including its emphasis on the protagonist's maturation, the use of upper-class sportsmen as heroes, the call to action being depicted as thrilling, as well as the importance of playing any game with honor and learning valuable lessons from it, such as hard work, duty, sportsmanship, and masculinity.

Early spy works—including those by William LeQueux, E. Phillips Oppenheim, and Erskine Childers—overlap with war prophecy books, which use fiction in order to warn a country of an impending attack and change its military policies. Childers's *The Riddle of the Sands* (1903) is a classic example of this type of work; it warns of the dangers of a German invasion of Britain across the North Sea and eventually encouraged the British government to develop defensive naval stations on strategic parts of the kingdom's coastline.

Plots of spy novels also differ from crime fiction in that they revolve more heavily around torture, capture, invisibility, secret communications, elaborate disguises, complicated alibis, narrow escapes, and dead drops, and the genre's archetypes include the secret exercise of power, often without traditional ethical constraints, and a profound sense of belonging to an organization that may or may not lead the hero to question the price of loyalty.

HIGH CLASS SPIES

Spy fiction also shares many characteristics with crime fiction; both genres often follow a narrative structure where, at the start of the story, a law is violated and the state finds out about it. The story's hero then attempts to discover who is responsible through the use of informants and struggles with the enemy before defeating him or her and restoring order. However, spy protagonists are usually depicted as more cerebral and of a higher class than police detectives, and they are more likely to be motivated by ethical or political ideals rather than money.

In general, two strains of spy stories exist: one relies on heroic fantasy whereas the other relies on realism and moral relativism. Ian Fleming, the creator of James Bond, is probably best associated with the first strain because his stories revolve around exotic locales, sexual escapades, conspicuous consumerism, and foreign and eccentric criminals whose crimes have massive political consequences. His hero, 007, enjoys being called to a mission, and Fleming depicts spying as an exciting endeavor vital to national security. Popular authors operating in the genre's more realistic vein include John le Carré, Eric Ambler, Graham Greene, and Frederick Forsyth. In these author's novels, spying is more likely to be depicted as an unglamorous activity involving few elements of the action thriller, and the works tend to be more cynical regarding the role of intelligence agencies in the modern world.

History. Although the spy genre is most closely aligned with British storytelling, James Fennimore Cooper's *The Spy* is considered to be the genre's first novel written in English. Published in 1821, the novel is set during the American Revolution and focuses on Harvey Birch, a man suspected of spying for the British but who is actually working for George Washington. The novel spawned a host of dime novel imitations soon after its release, but most scholars do not consider the genre to have truly developed until the turn of the twentieth century.

Traditionally, Erkine Childers's *Riddle of the Sands* (1903) and John Buchan's *The 39 Steps* (1915) are considered two of the first great spy novels. Both works feature amateur spies who are gentleman patriots accidentally swept up in an espionage adventure, and both romanticize the adventure of espionage, depicting it as a thrilling game that breaks the boring routine of life. Perhaps due to the success of these two novels, early spy novelists continued to romanticize espionage as experienced by amateurs until the debut of W. Somerset Maugham's *Ashenden: Or the British Agent (1927)*. This novel is important to the development of the genre because it rejected the heroic trappings of prewar spy fiction and replaced the redemptive nature of spying for the man tired of life with an emphasis on espionage's dull routine, hypocrisy, and ruthlessness. Maugham's *Ashenden* was also one of the first works to feature the spy bureaucracy, although it was not until the later part of WWII that the intelligence agency began to figure regularly and prominently in espionage narratives (Hitz 2004, 38–39).

Although early spy novelist William Le Queux blended romance and espionage in his stories in order to appeal to a female readership, the majority of early spy authors catered to a male readership and few female authors made their mark in the genre before the later part of the twentieth century. One notable exception is Helen MacInnes, a Glasgow-born author, whose first espionage novel, *Above Suspicion*, was published in 1941. MacInnes enjoyed a forty-five-year, highly successful career in which critics praised her for literate, fast-paced, and intricately plotted suspense novels. Her more famous titles include *Assignment in Brittany* (1942), *Decision at Delphi* (1961), and *Ride a Pale Horse* (1984), and her work mostly focuses on the Western struggle against either Nazism or Communism. Like Buchan and Childers, MacInnes favored amateur spies accidentally swept into danger who nevertheless accepted their fate and performed their patriotic duty in warding off political and social threats. Like Le Queux, most of the author's novels also focus on a love story in addition to an espionage plot, but they feature more competent and independent female characters. This last element makes McInnes somewhat unique among early spy writers, who primarily featured women as secondary characters who must be saved by the hero or as characters who wish to participate in male adventures but ultimately discover they are not up to the challenge.

The arrival of Graham Greene marked another important stage in the spy genre's history, as the author was one of the first to explore the psychology of the spy and the ways that spying challenges one's ethics and humanity. Even more so than Maugham, Greene insisted upon showing the anti-heroic side to spying and redirected the genre toward satire and criticism of intelligence organizations—a trend that would be furthered by popular spy novelists such as Len Deighton, Eric Ambler, and John le Carré. The heroes of these authors, for example, are often burned-out agents disillusioned with their own intelligence agency or are ordinary, undistinguished people who do not volunteer to fight an enemy but are rather swept, involuntarily, into a scheme of espionage. These "heroes" often fail to bring down an enemy operation but feel successful merely because they survived the episode in which both enemies and allies worked against them.

Frederick Hitz attributes historical factors to the genre's shift away from romanticized accounts of spying toward more cynical ones in the postwar era. As he explains in *The Great Game*, in the WWII era Stalin and Hitler possessed staunch control over their citizens via police states; thus, in order to stop the spread of totalitarianism and communism, the United States and Britain employed similar spy tactics, causing a spy war to ensue between the East and West. During this battle, Western governments often left their informants in the lurch and plotted assassination attempts. Whereas later, the U.S. government specifically infiltrated and monitored domestic anti-Vietnam War groups and some civil rights protestors. They also developed and tested mind-altering drugs on unsuspecting citizens in hopes of finding weapons to employ on their enemies. For Hitz, this climate explains the creation of novels that emphasize the morally suspect aspects of spying and question the price of loyalty to intelligence organizations. A good example of one such novel is le Carré's *The Spy Who Came in from the Cold* (1963), which explores the ways in which MI-6 deceives its own agent, Alex Leamas, in order to save a ruthless East German spy working for the United Kingdom—a move that eventually leads to the death of Leamas and his lover.

The move toward realism in spy fiction might also be explained by the fact that many of the genre's emerging novelists at the time had served in intelligence capacities during the First or Second World War and thus were able to incorporate their experiences and knowledge of the field into their stories. W. Somerset Maugham, for instance, worked as an intelligence operative during WWI; Graham Greene was stationed in Sierra Leone during World War II, where he worked for the British Foreign Office under Kim Philby (a spy who later defected to the Soviet Union); and John le Carré served in the British Foreign Service from 1959 to 1964, working first as Second Secretary in the British Embassy in Bonn and later as Political Consul in Hamburg.

Ian Fleming, who served in Naval Intelligence throughout World War II, also drew from his experiences as an intelligence officer in his 007 series, but as Fleming demonstrates, not all postwar spy novelists took an anti-heroic approach to the genre, his James Bond novels draw from Buchan's emphasis on the adventure and thrill of spying. Fleming's approach to the spy novel proved just as, if not more, popular among American and European readers in the early Cold War as more realistic novels, especially after John F. Kennedy announced in an interview with *Life* magazine that *From Russia with Love* ranked as one of his top ten favorite books.

In fact, at the time of Fleming's death in August 1964, over 30 million copies of his Bond books had been sold; two years later, at the height of Bond mania, that number had doubled to 60 million; and all of Fleming's novels have since been turned into motion picture films. Attracted to Fleming's success, other writers followed in the author's footsteps by creating fanciful epics of professional spies and arch-villains. Among these were Donald Hamilton, who created a hard-boiled James Bond in his Matt Helm series; Alistair Maclean; Philip McCutchan; John Gardner; Gavin Lyall; Trevanian; and Howard Hunt, an ex-CIA agent and Watergate conspirator, who wrote a series of spy stories even more fantastical than Fleming's in regards to his heroes, sexy women, villains and international conspiracies (Cawelti and Rosenberg 1987, 52).

By the 1970s and 1980s, the spy genre in general turned toward its realistic roots once again in order to explore the moral complexity of espionage due to the aftermath of the Vietnam War, the ongoing Cold War, and political scandals such as Watergate. Characters in these later spy novels often do not know with which side to align themselves, nor do readers, and the story's agents come to realize the ineptness of their agency and its unwillingness to carry out what the spy thinks is just. As a result, these novels' main characters often rebel against their agency and become vigilantes setting out to settle personal scores. These novels also continue to reflect a cynicism regarding patriotism and agency loyalty and focus on the mole, the defector, the double agent, and the traitor within. Most notably, the main villains in these novels are not the Soviets, the Germans, or the Chinese but, rather, conspiracy-plotting members of the protagonist's own intelligence agency. Examples of such stories include Len Deighton's *The Ipcress File* (1968), in which the hero's own section chief proves to be a double agent, and Robert Duncan's *Dragons at the Gate* (1976), which features a CIA agent stationed in Japan betrayed and interrogated by his own agency. Likewise, James Grady's *Six Days of the Condor* (1974) centers around a CIA analyst who leaves one day for lunch only to return and find everyone in his office murdered. Although the analyst manages to escape the initial raid, he must remain on the run for the next six days while a renegade group affiliated with the CIA hunts him down for one of his discoveries.

Trends and Themes. Spy novels have often focused on the possibility of one's own colleague being the enemy, but for most of its history, the spy genre has chosen Germans, Soviets, and Communists for its villains and has rooted itself in the Cold War conflict. However, the end of WWII and the collapse of the Soviet Union in 1991 left subsequent spy authors without a viable, contemporary villain. Many critics writing between the end of the Cold War and the events of September 11, 2001, questioned whether the spy genre could survive as a literary form without an archenemy, especially given the U.S. government's serious consideration of abandoning the Central Intelligence Agency after the USSR's dissolution.

Commenting on the waning popularity of the spy genre, which during the Cold War ranked as an international top-reading choice, with tens of millions of copies sold annually, *The New York Times* critic, Walter Goodman, announced in November 1989 that "The future looks dismal for the trenchcoat set" (Lynds n.d.). Goodman's assessment, which came the same month that the Berlin Wall crumbled, proved accurate for the short term, as sales of bestselling thriller authors plummeted and new authors struggled to find publishing homes. By 1998, two spy fiction icons, Frederick Forsyth and John le Carré had even declared that it was time to accept the fact that the genre was no longer interesting to readers and both began publishing in other fields.

But despite the genre's waning popularity, publishers continued to release the works of those authors who had been highly popular during the Cold War, including Nelson DeMille, W.E.B. Griffin, and David Morrell. A handful of new authors were also able to find success in the genre between 1991 and 2000, including Gayle Lynds, Daniel Silva, Joseph Finder, and Henry Porter, but many of these authors' works continue to revisit the terrain of WWII, the Cold War, and the Soviets, rather than focusing on new threats. To cite just two examples, Porter's *The Brandenburg Gate* (2006) is set in East Germany during the waning days of 1989 and tells the story of a scholar, Dr. Rudi Rosenharte, whose family is being held hostage by the Stasi until he agrees to take part in a dangerous mission, whereas Finder's *Moscow Club* (1995) explores the connections between the Kremlin and U.S. big business after the fall of the Iron Curtain and focuses on a CIA Kremlinologist, Charlie Stone, targeted by both the KGB and the CIA after analyzing a tape provided by a Russian mole.

As recently as 2004, the genre's sustainability was again in question, as reviewers such as Charles McGrath worried that the genre was not keeping up with the current political tides. Writing in *The New York Times,* McGrath specifically remarked: "What's odd is that most of our thriller writers—the people who in the past have taught us most of what we know about intelligence gathering and intelligence failure—don't seem to be interested in the post-9/11 landscape. . . . [T]hey're writing instead about corporate espionage and theological cover-ups in the Middle Ages. To understand what's going on in the world, . . . we readers now have to turn to nonfiction" (Lynds n.d.). Despite McGrath's assertions, however, the spy genre has tackled the post-9/11 landscape and shows signs of flourishing once more. According to PW Newsline, the "espionage/thriller" category experienced a 34 percent increase in sales in 2003—a trend recognized in 2004 by Tom Nolan who remarked in *The Wall Street Journal* that the form appeared to be thriving once again (Lynds n.d.).

Part of the spy fiction revival can be attributed to the events of 9/11, which once again brought issues of intelligence to the forefront of international discussion. As spy fiction writer Gayle Lynds writes, "After those horrifying attacks, Americans abruptly shook off their post–Cold War exhaustion and resumed a vigorous interest in the world at large, searching for information and, ultimately, understanding of what had happened, why it had happened, and what to do about it." (Lynds n.d.) Given that spy fiction is rooted in international politics, conspiracies, secret worlds, and the possibility of large-scale atrocities, the genre was ripe to tackle the post-9/11 landscape, and in March 2005, Edward Wyatt of *The New York Times* acknowledged that it was among one of the first fictional forms to do so (Lynds n.d.). But although spy authors writing since 2000 have begun exploring the fallout of 9/11, including the broader issues of international terrorism and the wars in Iraq and Afghanistan, the genre's writers have also tackled other contemporary issues—most notably the political, economic, and social crises occurring in Africa and industrial espionage conducted by multinational companies.

Reception. Since the late 1990s, the spy genre has not only enjoyed a revival in print but also a resurgence in film and television. Television shows such as *La Femme Nikita* (1997–2001), *Alias* (2001-2006), *24* (2001–2006), *The Agency* (2001), and *Spooks* (MI-5) (2002–) have tackled issues of international terrorism, defectors, doppelgangers, torture, and the moral complexity of espionage whereas films have worked to revive older franchises and novels. Two of the most popular spy films, for instance, are *The Bourne Identity* and *The Bourne Supremacy,* which are loosely based on two 1980s novels by Robert Ludlum bearing the same title. Likewise, Tom Cruise has continued to star in the *Mission: Impossible* franchise, and the most recent James Bond installment, *Casino Royale,* debuted in 2006 to popular acclaim.

The genre has also enjoyed acclaim from the film industry. Steven Spielberg's *Munich* (2005), which focuses on the Mossad's attempt to avenge the 1972 assassination of eleven Israeli Olympians, was nominated for five Academy Awards and two Golden Globes in 2005. Like many recent spy novels, the film calls into question the moral complexities of espionage, in this case as it relates to government-sponsored revenge. George Clooney's *Syriana* won the actor an Academy Award for best supporting actor, and the film was also nominated for best original screenplay. Drawing from recent concerns regarding the role of the United States in the Middle East and its dependence on oil, *Syriana* tells the story of corruption and power related to the oil industry, warns of the peril of backing foreign political leaders for economic gain, and explores the ways a severe lack of economic opportunities fosters the spread of terrorism and religious fundamentalism. Also of note is the 2005 release of *The Constant Gardner*, an adaptation of John le Carré's 2001 novel of the same title, starring Ralph Fiennes and Rachel Weisz. The film and cast both won and were nominated for several industry awards, including The Academy Award's category for Best Supporting Actress and Best Adapted Screenplay, The BAFTA's [British Academy of Film and Television Arts] category for Best Film, and The Golden Globe's for Best Motion Picture—Drama and Best Director—Motion Picture.

Interest in espionage has also filtered into other areas of popular culture. In 2002 the International Spy Museum opened its doors in Washington, D.C. It is the first and only public museum in the United States solely dedicated to espionage and features the largest collection of international spy-related artifacts ever placed on public display. The stories of individual spies are told through film, interactives, and state-of-the-art exhibits, and visitors also learn about basic spy tradecraft and espionage technological gadgetry. Similar museums exist domestically and internationally, including Moscow's KGB Museum, an exhibit within London's Imperial War Museum, and the National Security Agency's National Cryptologic Museum, but unlike the International Spy Museum, they focus on a specific time period or event.

In 2007 an espionage theme park, entitled Spyland, was set to open near Valence, France, and a sister project is under way in Dubai. These theme parks will include roller coaster and water park rides in an environment that illustrates the historical actions of secret agents, the role played by different international spy agencies, and the role spying has played in popular culture. Visitors will be able to access workshops that demonstrate ancient and recent spying techniques, including coding, hidden microphones and cameras, and satellite imagery, and games will be organized for visitors to play the role of a secret agent, with a mission to fulfill, while visiting the amusement park.

Selected Authors. Due to the resurgence in the spy genre, several new authors have entered into print in the last decade, including Daniel Silva, Alex Berenson, Jenny Siler, Joseph Kanon, Francine Mathews, Robert Cullen, Vince Flynn, Brad Thor, Brian Haig, and Raelynn Hillhouse. Spy masters Frederick Forsyth and John le Carré have also returned to the genre, and writers associated with more "literary" endeavors have tried their hand at spy and thriller fiction in recent years.

This last category of authors most notably includes Australian/American author Janet Turner Hospital and John Updike, best known for his works exploring middle American suburbia. In 2006 Updike released *The Terrorist*, a thriller that revolves around Ahmad, the 18-year-old son of a hippieish American mother and an Egyptian exchange student, who embraces Islam and is eventually recruited to blow up the Lincoln Tunnel. Turner Hospital's *Due Preparation for the Plague* was published in 2003 and focuses on the intertwined fates of the survivors and relatives of those who perished in the 1987 hijacking of Flight 64. In addition to addressing the effects of terrorism on its victims' family, the work also addresses contemporary fears and concerns regarding chemical weapons and the government's ability to stop terrorist attacks.

John le Carré's new contributions to the spy genre exemplify contemporary authors' interest in exploring the African terrain, and two of his last three novels have been set in the continent—*The Constant Gardner* (2000) and *Mission Song* (2006). The first focuses on British diplomat Justin Quayle, who is serving in Nairobi when his wife Tessa is raped and murdered during a recent and mysterious visit to Kenya. In his efforts to solve Tessa's murder, Quayle learns that his wife had been compiling data to implicate a multinational drug company using Africans as guinea pigs to test a tuberculosis remedy with fatal side effects. Her report, however, also implicates the British government in the drug scandal, and as Quayle gets closer to the truth, he realizes he is treading in his own government's murky waters. Le Carré's more recent novel, *Mission Song,* is more lighthearted than *The Constant Gardner* but nonetheless explores the terrain of Africa, although none of the action is actually set there. More specifically, the novel's protagonist, Bruno Salvador, is a young Congo native whose fluency in English, French, and several African languages, lands him work with the British Secret Service, which employs him to act as a translator at a secret meeting between Congolese warlords and a shadowy syndicate of Western financiers attempting to bring democracy and economic opportunity to the area. Much like in *The Constant Gardener*, the villain in *Mission Song* is a multinational corporation that adheres to no moral or geographic boundaries in its attempt to turn a profit, and le Carré reminds readers in both works that Africa, much like in colonial times, remains a temptation for outsiders who wish to both save and plunder the continent.

Like le Carré, spy master Frederick Forsyth has returned to the genre in recent years. One of his most recent works, *Avenger* (2003), focuses on vigilante Cal Dexter's pursuit of a Serbian warlord named Zoran Zilic, who escaped Europe with a fortune but not before killing an American aid worker, whose billionaire grandfather now wishes to have Zilic brought to justice. However, this task is complicated by the fact that Zilic is protected in a South American jungle compound by an FBI agent who wishes to use the warlord in order to kill Osama bin Laden, and, in part, the novel, which takes place within weeks of 9/11 and ends on September 10, 2001, explores the moral quagmire of dealing with criminals in order to capture larger ones. Forsyth also tackles issues surrounding the attacks of 9/11 in his latest book *The Afghan* (2006), which begins when a plan to carry out a catastrophic attack on the West is discovered on the computer of a senior al-Qaeda member. In order to combat the further threat of terrorism, the American and British intelligence community attempt to substitute a British operative for an Afghan Taliban leader being held prisoner at Guantánamo Bay and then arrange his release into Afghan custody. The hero must maintain his cover under the closest scrutiny, even as the details of the planned attack are kept beyond his reach.

Like Forsyth, younger spy novelists have also addressed issues surrounding 9/11. For instance, Alex Berenson's *The Faithful Spy* (2006) draws upon *The New York Times* reporter's experience covering the Iraq occupation to tell the fictional story of John Wells, the only American CIA agent ever to penetrate al-Qaeda. Before the attacks on 9/11, Wells had been building his cover in the mountains of Pakistan, but is now ordered home by an al-Qaeda leader planning more attacks on the United States. However, the CIA doesn't know if they can trust Wells any longer, given that he has become a Muslim since living in Pakistan and now finds the United States decadent and shallow, and thus the story grapples with Muslim-American relations in the post 9/11 world, in addition to the likelihood of another al-Qaeda attack on U.S. soil.

Of course, not all spy novelists have abandoned the historical conflicts of the Cold War and the Second World War. Daniel Silva is perhaps one of the most celebrated new authors to enter the spy scene, and his works include *The Secret Servant* (2007), *The Messenger* (2006), *The Confessor* (2003), *The English Assassin* (2002), *The Kill Artist* (2000), and *The Unlikely Spy* (1996) among others. In general, Silva's novels explore past conflicts, but especially WWII, and often trace their effects to the present day. For instance, Silva's *Unlikely Spy* mines the territory of WWII in an historical thriller that centers around the Allies' plans to invade Normandy, whereas *The Confessor* examines Pope Pius XII's silence and lack of action during the Holocaust.

Four-time spy novelist Joseph Kanon has also been successful publishing historical novels that revisit WWII and the Cold War. His works include *Los Alamos* (1997), *The Prodigal Spy* (1998), *The Good German* (2001), and *Alibi: A Novel* (2005) and adopt a postmodern lens through which to view the ethical dilemmas proposed by each conflict. For instance, *The Good German* (which was made into a film in 2006 starring George Clooney and Cate Blanchett) is set in Berlin just several months after the end of the Second World War, and Jake Geismar, a journalist covering the Potsdam Conference, becomes intrigued by the murder of an American soldier whose body washes ashore near the conference grounds. When the military is slow to investigate or provide any details of the murder, Geismar is convinced that a big story looms in the air, but the investigation really serves as Kanon's tool to explore the ethical quandaries of German Nazism, the nation's collective guilt, and the hard ethical dilemmas of the times. Likewise, *Los Alamos,* which won the 1998 Edgar Award for Best First Novel, and *The Prodigal Spy* explore the ethical dilemmas experienced by the scientists developing the atomic bomb and the personal effects felt by a family targeted by McCarthyism, respectively.

Finally, it is important to note that numerous women have begun to experience success in what was once a heavily male-dominated genre. Most notably, these authors include Francine Mathews (a former CIA analyst), Raelynn Hillhouse, and Gayle Lynds (who cowrote several books with Robert Ludlum in addition to her own novels). These women often create stories that revolve around female protagonists, long absent within the genre, while simultaneously addressing some of the most pressing contemporary issues. For instance, Hillhouse's *Outsourced* (2007) revolves around a manager of a private military corporation named Camille Black, who is approached by the CIA to track down and eliminate a man accused of selling arms to terrorist cells throughout the Middle East. That man also happens to be her ex-fiancé, and so the novel explores not only Black's private, personal thoughts but also the role intelligence outsourcing is playing in the War on Terror. Mathews's *Blown* (2005) likewise centers on a female protagonist, Caroline Carmichael, who is about to resign from the CIA when the first reports of a terrorist attack pour in, and she instantly recognizes the hand of an enemy she's battled for years: the 30 April Organization, a neo-Nazi group operating in the United States. Complicating the story is the fact that Caroline's husband, Eric, has infiltrated the terrorist group but has had his cover blown. Arrested in Germany as a 30 April operative, Eric cannot help Caroline, who must work to save both her husband and her country.

Bibliography

Berenson, Alex. *The Faithful Spy*. New York: Random House, 2006.

Finder, Joseph. *Moscow Club*. New York: Viking, 1991.

Forsyth, Frederick. *Avenger*. New York: Thomas Dunne, 2003.

———. *The Afghan*. New York: G.P. Putnam's, 2006.

Hillhouse, Raelynn. *Outsourced*. New York: Forge, 2007.

Hitz, Frederick. *The Great Game: The Myth and Reality of Espionage*. New York: Alfred A. Knopf, 2004.

Hospital, Janette Turner. *Due Preparations for the Plague*. New York: W.W. Norton, 2003.

Kanon, Joseph. *The Good German*. New York: Henry Holt, 2001.

———. *The Prodigal Spy*. New York: Broadway, 1998.

———. *Los Alamos*. New York: Broadway, 1997.

Le Carré, John. *Mission Song*. Boston: Little, Brown, 2006.

———. *The Constant Gardener*. New York: Scribner, 2001.

Lynds, Gayle. "Spy Thrillers Thrive & Surprise." www.thrillwriters.org. Viewed March 2, 2007. http://www.thrillerwriters.org/index.php?option=com_content&task=view&id=23& Itemid=61.

Mathews, Francine. *Blown*. New York: Bantam, 2005.

Porter, Henry. *The Brandenburg Gate*. New York: Atlantic Monthly, 2006.

Silva, Daniel. *The Confessor*. New York: G.P. Putnam's, 2003.

———. *The Unlikely Spy*. New York: Villard, 1996.

Updike, John. *The Terrorist*. New York: Alfred A. Knopf, 2006.

Further Reading

Atkins, John. *The British Spy Novel: Styles in Treachery*. New York: Riverrun Press, 1984; Bloom, Clive, ed. *Spy Thrillers: From Buchan to le Carré*. New York: St. Martin's Press, 1990; Britton, Wesley. *Beyond Bond: Spies in Fiction and Film*. Westport, Connecticut: Praeger, 2005; Cawelti, John, and Bruce Rosenberg. *The Spy Story*. Chicago: University of Chicago Press, 1987; Panek, Leroy. *The Special Branch: The British Spy Novel, 1890–1980*. Bowling Green, Ohio: Bowling Green University Popular Press, 1981.

TRICIA JENKINS

SUSPENSE FICTION

Definition. To label a novel as being a work of suspense is to consign it to a vague place that is hard to define. Readers know suspense when they encounter it, but are hard pressed to explain what elements define the genre. Comprising such varied titles as Thomas Harris's novels about serial killer Hannibal Lecter, Dan Brown's *Da Vinci Code*, and Patricia Highsmith's Tom Ripley series, the genre encompasses romantic suspense, medical and legal thrillers, psychological suspense, political

> ### ELEMENTS OF SUSPENSE FICTION
>
> By and large, certain elements of suspense can be identified and appear in the various subcategories of the genre. Brian Garfield's advice to aspiring authors in the magazine *Writer's Digest* offers several devices that are common to suspense fiction: danger exists, whether of the readily identifiable sort or a more vague uneasiness; the time period over which events unfold is brief; the protagonist is often drawn into the adventure through no volition of his own; and there is a villain of monumental proportions (Moore n.d.). The romantic suspense novel adds its own twists with romantic entanglements that prove dangerous to the heroine, the conspiracy thriller wraps the protagonist up in matters that are historically or politically significant, and medical thrillers throw in a community ravished by, or in danger of being ravished by, a terrible disease.

thrillers, and conspiracy thrillers. Suspense fiction focusing on technology and military exploits can fall into this genre as well.

Each category has its own elements that add to the basic suspense devices to create distinct genres; however, cross pollination is rife and, as a result, new categories are born.

The following categories are the most frequently marketed: romantic suspense, medical thrillers, legal thrillers, psychological suspense, political thrillers, techno thrillers, and conspiracy thrillers. The **spy** novel is another genre that uses elements of suspense.

History. Writers such as Wilkie Collins and Charles Dickens could be considered the grandfathers of the genre, but Erskine Childers's *The Riddle of the Sands* (1903) is often cited as the first modern thriller. In true suspense fashion, two young men accidentally become involved in a German plot to invade England. More aligned with suspense crime fiction, John Buchan's *The Thirty-Nine Steps* (1915) is about an innocent man who becomes entangled in a homicide and is pursued by the good and the bad guys. Robert Ludlum defined the modern thriller with *The Bourne Identity*, published in 1980. A man wakes with amnesia and is startled to find that he has arms and fighting knowledge. His quest is to find his identity while eluding those who don't want him to remember.

There are three major elements of suspense fiction: 1) the idea that time is ticking for the hero and that a resolution must be found quickly, 2) the hero must face grave danger, even though he often doesn't know what he has done to put himself into danger or from whom or what the danger arises, and 3) the hero must rely on his own instinct and courage to both solve the mystery and to keep himself alive. To these basic elements are added the subgenre twists of romance, technology, science, and so on.

Trends and Themes

Romantic Suspense. In 1960 America's Phyllis Whitney's *Thunder Heights* and Britain's Victoria Holt's *Mistress of Mellyn* ushered in the age of the Gothic romance. Working with the conventions established by eighteenth-century authors such as Horace Walpole (*The Castle of Otranto*, 1764), Ann Radcliffe (*The Mysteries of Udolpho,* 1794), and Matthew G. Lewis (*The Monk*, 1796), these novelists, along with such luminaries as Barbara Michaels and Mary Stewart, dominated paperback sales of the modern Gothic from 1969 to 1974.

The conventions of the gothic genre have been incorporated into romantic suspense. A young heroine is removed to an isolated landscape, generally an old family mansion haunted with ghosts and shadowy crimes. In her isolation she must rely on one of two men to help her. One is the villain and one is the hero, and it is usually not clear until the book's end which is which. There are answers to be found about old crimes or the heroine's past, the answers to which place her in danger. Modern romantic suspense novelists have created heroines with more pluck and they often solve their own problems. Romance, however, is still important to the plots.

Phyllis A. Whitney is considered the reigning queen of romantic suspense in a writing career that began in the 1940s with the publication of mysteries for teenagers. She has published over 70 novels. She exerts enormous effort to get the scenic details of her far-flung locations just right, and that exertion has paid off in over five decades of favorable reviews and millions of fans of her romance novels.

By the 1980s the gothic genre was losing popularity, but the category of romantic suspense was just coming into its own. Whitney's novels began being marketed under the new category. The genre under which she is marketed may have changed names, but the formula of Whitney's novels didn't. She adheres to the elements of gothic/suspense fiction, following in the footsteps of Charlotte Bronte and Daphne DuMaurier. Although Phyllis A. Whitney has not published a novel since 1997's *Amethyst Dreams,* she is still at her writing desk, working on an autobiography at the age of 103. Her contributions to the romantic suspense genre have been widespread and almost unfathomably influential.

Barbara Michaels (who also writes as Elizabeth Peters) has produced dozens of romantic suspense novels, some featuring paranormal or supernatural plot elements. Until 1999, Michaels penned a Michaels and Peters novel almost every year. Usually set in the present, the past has a large claim on the plots and the subsequent solution to the story's mysteries. Michaels told Diane Rehm in a 2001 interview that she loves to read and write gothic romances, although she doesn't care to have that label attached to her novels. "'Romantic Suspense' is another term which has been applied to my books and those of other women writers. It is marginally more acceptable than gothic" (Rehm 2001). Michaels is quick to point out, though, that the romance in a story is important. Using the formula of the gothic novel, Michaels twists that genre's elements to suit her own style. Her heroines rely less on the hero to rescue them from their situations and more on their own resolve and pluck. *Other Worlds* (1999) was the last title published under the Michaels name, although Elizabeth Peters novels are still released on a yearly basis.

Sandra Brown began her writing career producing Harlequin romances but quickly moved on to writing longer, less formulaic contemporary romance novels. She is now best known for her romantic suspense, most of which involve the heroines uncovering family secrets for which others will kill. Brown is praised for her fast-paced and twisting plots that usually leave the best secrets until the final pages. Her latest, *Play Dirty* (2007), depicts the framing of a disgraced Dallas Cowboys football player who must find his nemesis before he is killed.

Although reviewers fault Mary Higgins Clark's writing style, they find nothing negative to say about her plots. Clark's two dozen novels all tap into the gothic formula of heroine in trouble with nothing to rely on but her own inner fortitude. Her debut suspense novel was *Where Are the Children* (1975), a terrifying story of the disappearance of a woman's children. Her second attempt at suspense fiction was *A Stranger Is Watching* (1978), which proved her formula's success. Clark has followed her initial success with 20 more novels. Her villains are evil and her heroes are good; her writing is simple, and her plots breathlessly fast. Most of Clark's novels are set in high society New York and all involve dangers.

Many of her earlier novels involved young children in danger, but in recent years Clark has expanded her stories with plots such as financial conspiracies on Wall Street (*Second Time Around*, 2003) and serial stalkers (*Nighttime Is My Time*, 2004). She has also coauthored novels with her daughter, Carol Higgins Clark. The formula has paid off with her books seeing time on the best-sellers' lists and also air time: many have been made into movies.

Catherine Coulter is another author who began writing romances in the Regency category and then moved on to suspense. *Riptide* (2000) received excellent reviews as Coulter adapted to a novel form that was more suspense than romance. The fifth of her FBI adventures featuring agents Savich and Sherlock, *Riptide* features classic suspense traits: disbelieving and unsympathetic police, the heroine's move to an isolated spot, and threatening phone calls. In an interview with *Publishers Weekly*, Coulter addressed some of the concerns of moving from romance to suspense. She said that suspense plots have to be more tightly written than those of the historical romances she penned formerly. The logic of the situation has to be observed as well (Yamashita 2003, 55). This attention to plot and detail has made her FBI suspense series very successful. The most recent title in the series is *Tailspin* (2008).

Tami Hoag made the shift from romance to suspense in the 1990s. Her strength is the amount of detail that goes into her novels. They are well researched and supply the background to the often gruesome crimes in which her characters are involved. Some of her issues are sensitive topics. For example, *Ashes to Ashes* (1999) and its sequel *Dust to Dust* (2000) explore attitudes toward crime victims, prostitutes in the first novel and a gay officer in the second. Hoag's well-developed characters have won her a legion of fans for her 30 books. *The Alibi Man* (2007), was well received by critics.

Moving into romantic suspense after a strong career in historical romances, Iris Johansen creates a taut thriller involving a Greek archaeological dig, a Scottish castle, and terrorists intent on blowing up a nuclear power plant in *Countdown* (2005). More suspense novels followed the commercial success of the *Ugly Duckling* (1991). *Long after Midnight* (1997), *No One to Trust* (2002), and *Final Target* (2001) feature such various plots as corporate corruption, Colombian drug lords, and attempted kidnapping of the president's daughter. In *Fatal Tide* (2003), a woman who had been sold into white slavery teams up with an ex-navy SEAL to find a secret weapon, with the help of dolphins, before the weapon's Middle Eastern developers do. Such wild plots are anchored with well-developed characters, and Johansen's appeal to readers is great. A prolific author, she released four titles in 2006 alone.

Bestselling romance writer Nora Roberts writes romantic suspense in the line of Mary Stewart under the name J.D. Robb, a combination of her sons' initials. The futuristic *In Death* series features police officer Eve Dallas and her husband Roarke. The twenty-seventh installment is *Salvation in Death* (2008).

Medical Thrillers. Although Michael Crichton is perhaps best known for his adventure fiction *Jurassic Park,* his earlier novels, many written under the pseudonym John Lange, were thrillers written while he was medical school in the 1960s. Some of these titles involved medicine-inspired plots. His 1968 *A Case of Need,* filled with details from his work at the Harvard Medical School, won him an Edgar Award. It was *The Andromeda Strain,* published in 1969, that pushed him into a full-time writing career. In the novel, biophysicists race to track down the source of a deadly virus. The book was praised for its technical detail and its pacing and set the stage for the medical thriller genre, in particular the plague novels of such authors as Robin Cook.

Robin Cook is a practicing doctor who debuted with *Coma* (1977), which was made into a successful film written by Michael Crichton in 1978. All of Cook's titles feature medical crises in hospital environments or in the devastated public sector as mysterious viruses spread. The 1987 *Outbreak* and the 1995 *Contagion* are two titles in the epidemic subgenre. Several other titles have had plots revolving around fertility technology that has been abused in frightening ways (*Mutation,* 1989; *Vital Signs,* 1990). In 1999, Cook introduced medical examiner Jack Stapleton, who, along with partner Laurie Montgomery, feature in several more titles. *Foreign Bodies* (2008) is Cook's twenty-eighth medical thriller.

Michael Palmer spent 20 years working as a physician and has used his medical background in his more than a dozen medical thrillers. His 2008 *First Patient* follows the adventures of the President of the United States's best friend who takes on the job of being the President's personal physician after his successor disappears. It appears his friend is going insane and that someone, or something, is behind the President's failing mental health.

Tess Gerritsen's heroines serve in various medical capacities: surgeons, emergency room doctors, and medical examiners. A long time author of romantic suspense, Gerritsen moved into the genre of medical thrillers with *Harvest* (1996). Set in a Boston hospital, the plot involves the unraveling of a secret by a surgical resident. She introduces Detective Jane Rizolli in *The Surgeon* (2002), and Rizzoli teams up with medical examiner Maura Isles in *The Sinner* (2003). The partnership continues in several more titles. Gerritsen's novels are praised for their ability to offer far-fetched plots that seem believable. Meticulously researched, Gerritsen's highly detailed medical scenes add credibility to the suspense and horror readers feel.

Patricia Cornwell and Kathy Reichs are two more authors who critics consistently praise for their extensive details. Cornwell's Kay Scarpetta is a medical examiner for the Commonwealth of Virginia, and Reichs's Tempe Brennan works in both Charlotte, North Carolina, and Quebec, Canada, as a forensic anthropologist. Details of crime scenes and the work that goes on in the morgues are vital to understanding the plots of these authors' books, and both are authorities in their fields.

Cornwell's work in the medical examiner's office lends credibility to her characters' knowledge of forensic science, police work, and the political machinations of state agency employees. Her 1990 *Postmortem* introduced mystery readers to the world of forensic mysteries. *Postmortem* is followed by over a dozen more Scarpetta novels, following the medical examiner as she moves to various states, working in various capacities to solve crimes. The suspense in Cornwell's novels focuses on Scarpetta as she finds herself in dangerous situations due to her inability to leave an investigation alone. In true gothic fashion, she often needs help to extricate herself from a bad situation, but in some installments, she has drawn on her own resourcefulness.

Reichs's experience in the field has helped her books about Temperance "Tempe" Brennan rival those of Cornwell. Brennan debuted in *Deja Dead* (1997), where readers were also introduced to Brennan's archenemy, Montreal Police Inspector Luc Claudel. Grisly forensic details are based on Reichs's own examination of bodies far too decomposed to be identified by pathologists. It is Reichs's ability to combine explanations of forensic procedures with strong storylincs that have captured an ever-increasing fan base for her novels. The television series, *Bones,* is based on Reichs and her character. The tenth Brennan installment is *Devil Bones* (2008).

Karin Slaughter has created Sara Linton, another medical examiner, who is also a pediatrician in a small Georgia town. Six novels have featured Linton, the most recent *Beyond Reach* (2007).

Legal Thrillers. Legal thrillers are popular with mystery readers because the pursuit of justice is usually local and based on a particular crime. John Grisham, a former Mississippi attorney and author of almost 20 best-selling novels, most of which are legal thrillers, has said, "Though Americans distrust the profession as a whole, we have an insatiable appetite for stories about crimes, criminals, trials and all sorts of juicy lawyer stuff" (Grisham 1992, 33). As early as Charles Dickens and Wilkie Collins, the legal thriller was appearing in the marketplace to great popular success. For example, Collins's *The Moonstone* (1868) and *The Woman in White* (1859) contain elements of a legal thriller: an innocent person, the criminal justice system (legal proceedings and courtroom drama) playing an intrinsic part of the storyline (also in Dickens's *Bleak House* [1853]), witness testimony, legal documents (wills, etc.), and lawyers assisting in solving the crime. In the 1930s Erle Stanley Gardner, a practicing attorney, became one of the most prolific and popular authors of courtroom dramas with his creation of Perry Mason.

Many authors of legal thrillers are former attorneys themselves. Grisham, Scott Turow, Richard North Patterson, and Steve Martini are five of the most recognized attorney/authors in the genre. It was Turow's 1987 *Presumed Innocent* that opened the floodgates to courtroom dramas.

Turow's first novel, *One-L* (1977) was written while Turow was a law student at Harvard and documented the difficulties of law school. *Presumed Innocent* was published while Turow was working as an assistant U.S. district attorney in Chicago. The novel was well-received and its publisher, Farrar, Strauss, paid more money for the title than they ever had for a book by a first-time author. Their risk paid off as *Presumed Innocent* hit the bestseller lists. The novel was praised for its insight into the legal system and its refusal to divide the world into simplistic fields of black and white, good and evil. The film, starring Harrison Ford, was released in 1990. Turow's most recent title is *Ordinary Heroes* (2005).

John Grisham's first novel, *A Time to Kill* (1989), was inspired by a courtroom case. His 1994 *The Chamber* garnered more critical acclaim than some of the earlier titles. Grisham's novels, although sometimes criticized for their unrealistic plots, are almost always noted for their characterization and their intense pace. These two elements have led to several of Grisham's titles, among them *A Time to Kill, The Firm* (1991), and *The Pelican Brief* (1992), being made into blockbuster films. His latest is *The Appeal* (2008).

Before turning to fiction writing, Richard North Patterson was a successful lawyer who worked for the prosecution on the Watergate case of the 1970s. His literary career took off after the publication of his second novel, *Degree of Guilt* (1992). The common thread in Patterson's mysteries is the attention paid to the legal system. In the *Conviction* (2005), an eleven-year-old conviction is re-investigated; *Balance of Power* (2003) combines politics and law in issues about gun control; and in *Exile* (2007) the Middle East of today's headlines is at the center of attorney David Wolfe's most difficult case.

Steve Martini is a former journalist and attorney. His skills combine to make him one of the foremost authors of courtroom drama. Most of Martini's titles feature attorney Paul Madriani, whose cases are always part of a larger, more corrupt, political scene. He has been praised for his "torn from the headlines" plots and exceptionally well-drawn and exciting courtroom pyrotechnics. *Shadow of Power* (2008) is the ninth Madriani installment.

As in forensic mysteries, the authors of legal thrillers must clearly explain the points of law upon which a case rests. Legal mysteries often focus on glitches in the legal system or the manipulation of the law by shady attorneys. The protagonists themselves are usually of two types, the idealistic young attorney who is up against a corrupt system, or a jaded lawyer who is closer to the wrong side of the law than to the right. Michael Connelly has created Michael Haller, who is an example of the latter type in *The Lincoln Lawyer* (2005).

Female authors have cornered a large sector of the legal thriller market as well. Lia Matera began publishing fiction after law school, creating the characters Willa Jansson and Laura Di Palma, who have starred in over a dozen titles. Lisa Scottoline is another former lawyer who sets her novels in Philadelphia. Her novels about the all female law firm Rosato and Associates have won her many awards.

Psychological Suspense. Psychological suspense is a fairly vague term. Most novels that fall into this category have characters, usually two, who are testing themselves against their intellectual counterparts. Frequently a criminal will pit his wits against his pursuer. The most famous example is Thomas Harris's serial killer Hannibal Lector in *The Silence of the Lambs* (1988). Imprisoned Lector offers to help FBI Agent Clarice Starling to catch another serial killer known as Buffalo Bill. He plays many mind games with the vulnerable Starling, and the tension mounts as she confronts the killer and Lector escapes. Almost every author creating a serial killer since Harris has had to compete with Lector's presence. Jonathan Kellerman, Jeffrey Deaver, and James Patterson are three writers who have been able to compete successfully with Harris.

Jonathan Kellerman has banked on his expertise as a child psychologist to create 22 novels featuring child psychologist Alex Delaware. Delaware debuts in *When the Bough Breaks* (1985). Like Mary Higgins Clark, Kellerman writes about topical issues. His first Delaware novel, though written before the infamous McMartin Preschool scandal in California, reflected that case's focus on sexually abused children being the only witnesses to crimes. Abused children are often the only leads to crimes in Kellerman's novels, and it is Delaware's job to find out what they know. Suspicion of parents heightens the suspense in a Kellerman novel and the struggle over the validity of a child's testimony that may ruin an innocent adult's life is the focus of *Bad Love* (1993). Most of Kellerman's victims are children, but a death bed confession troubles a young woman in Kellerman's twenty-first Delaware novel *Obsession* (2007).

Although he has written over 20 suspense novels, Jeffery Deaver is best known for his novels about Lincoln Rhyme and Amelia Sachs. The pair debuted in *The Bone Collector* (1997), made into a film starring Denzel Washington and Angelina Jolie. The fast pace and the intricacy of Deaver's plots plant him firmly in the suspense tradition but also give a nod to the police procedural with his close focus on forensic investigation. Deaver's plots lead in many twisting directions and the final one is always kept until the end. Critics found him to be too heavy-handed and overly complex in *The Twelfth Card* (2005), but entertaining nonetheless.

The author is also noted for his character development and ability to create convincing dialogue. The characters of Sachs and Rhyme grow over the course of the series as they face Rhyme's medical problems. Quadriplegic as a result of an accident while investigating a crime scene, Rhyme has a crime lab set up in his New York apartment geared to his needs. Sachs, a police officer, walks the crime scenes for him, reporting back what she sees. The two become lovers and face the obstacles that his health issues and her personal issues bring to the relationship. In many of his interviews, Deaver has said that he creates books based on his reader's wishes. They wish for more Rhyme and Sachs novels and number eight was released in 2008, *The Broken Window*.

The author of dozens of novels and two ongoing series, James Patterson's Alex Cross novels have gained him his largest number of fans. *Along Came a Spider* introduced Cross in 1992. The first 11 Cross novels are called the "Nursery Rhyme" novels for their titles. After *Mary, Mary* (2005), the novel titles began to feature Cross's name. The latest is *Cross Country* (2008). Alex Cross is an African American forensic psychologist who is raising his two children alone in Washington, D.C. A very sensitive man, Cross becomes deeply involved both physically and emotionally in his cases, and he frequently becomes a target for violence himself. Noted for his short quick scenes, Patterson has developed a tense style that appeals to readers and translates well for moviegoers. *Kiss the Girls* (1997) and *Along Came a Spider* (2001) were both made into films starring Morgan Freeman as Cross.

Political Thrillers. Power struggles involving national or international politics make for tautly suspenseful novels as terrorists, power hungry dictators, and drug and weapon cartels clash. Times of war create another dimension to power struggles with spies added to the mix. A final element often present in political thrillers is technology and its use and misuse by those trying to gain or maintain power.

Vince Flynn published his debut novel about Minneapolis, *Term Limits*, in 1997. Since then he has written eight novels featuring such topics as the sale of arms to Iraq (*The Third Option,* 2000) and the race to prevent Saddam Hussein from using nuclear weapons in *Separation of Power* (2001). The 2004 *Memorial Day* moves from the Middle East to the United States as the hero tries to stop terrorists who have brought bombs into the country.

In Stephen Frey's *The Fourth Order* (2007), 150 years after the establishment of The Order, a government agency put in place after the assassination of Abraham Lincoln, the group excels in global surveillance and information gathering. Frey's novels such as *The Power Broker* (2006) and *The Successor* (2007) combine corporate greed with the lust for political power.

Techno and Military Thrillers. Michael Crichton may well be the undisputed master of the modern adventure thriller. His wide-ranging plots, from the 1855 London train robbery of *The Great Train Robbery* (1975), to the H. Rider Haggard-inspired lost world of King Solomon's mines (*Congo,* 1980), to a theme park gone awry featuring cloned dinosaurs (*Jurassic Park,* 1990), are suspenseful and loved by his millions of fans worldwide. Along with Tom Clancy, however, he is considered the master of the techno thriller. Techno thrillers are those whose plots rest on elements of technology: computer, military, biological, and so on. The technology is usually futuristic, but just barely so.

Although DNA technology was behind the creation of modern day dinosaurs, the dinosaurs, not the technology for creating them, predominated. The 1992 *Rising Sun* moved technological cover-ups and political machinations on the parts of both the Japanese and the Americans to the fore. The technological accuracy of *Airframe* (1996) was a result of the in-depth research Crichton does for all his novels. *State of Fear* (2004) provides a look at information manipulation and *Next* (2006) follows the creation of a human/chimp hybrid.

Tom Clancy broke onto the bestseller lists with his 1984 publication of *The Hunt for Red October,* later made into a film starring Sean Connery. He is best known for his post-Cold War thrillers featuring former Marine Jack Ryan, although he has written other action thrillers with Martin H. Greenberg.

Dale Brown is a former Air Force captain who now writes military thrillers featuring Patrick McLanahan. *Strike Force* (2007) is Brown's latest. A geopolitical novel with a plot set in Iran and involving cutting edge military technology, *Strike Force* is the twelfth McLanahan installment. Stephen Coonts's hero is Admiral Jack Grafton. *Liberty* (2007), the latest installment, leads readers on a whirlwind trail of devastation as Grafton makes enemies in the CIA, FBI, and every other law enforcement agency he can alienate as he attempts to locate terrorists before they detonate their bombs on American soil.

Conspiracy Thriller. The conspiracy thriller is a category of suspense fiction in which the hero finds himself embroiled in a secret society or organization that threatens the fate of the nation, and sometimes the world. In this category, only the hero realizes the extent to which the world is in danger and cannot prove his allegations. He must work alone or with a sidekick, romantic or otherwise, to stop the danger. Early examples of the genre include *The Manchurian Candidate* (1952) by Richard Condon and *The Illuminatus! Trilogy* (1976–1977) by Robert Shea and Robert Anton Wilson.

The biggest conspiracy thriller to date is Dan Brown's *The Da Vinci Code* (2003). This phenomenal best seller features symbologist Robert Langdon's race to solve a centuries old mystery involving the Holy Grail and the Knights Templar among other elements. Time is short as Langdon and the granddaughter of a murdered Louvre curator race around France and Rome trying to find the Grail before their enemies do. The thriller was made into a 2006 film starring Tom Hanks.

Bibliography

Grisham, John. "The Rise of the Legal Thriller: Why Lawyers are Throwing the Books at Us." *New York Times*, Book Review Section. 18 Oct. 1992: 33.

Moore, Joe. "Ten Rules for Suspense Fiction by Brian Garfield." http://www.thrillerwriters. org/2008/03/ten-rules-for-suspense-fiction-by-brian.html

Rehm, Diane. Interview with Barbara Michaels. *Diane Rehm Show.* American University Radio. May 29, 2001.

Yamashita, Brianna. "From History to Mystery: A Genre-jumper Explains." *Publishers Weekly* (June 30, 2003): 55.

Further Reading

Anderson, Patrick. *The Triumph of the Thriller: How Cops, Crooks, and Cannibals Captured Popular Fiction.* New York: Random House, 2007; Gannon, Michael B. *Blood, Bedlam, Bullets, and Badguys: A Reader's Guide to Adventure/Suspense Fiction.* Genreflecting Advisory Series. Westport, CT: Libraries Unlimited; Mann, Jessica. "The Suspense Novel."

Classic Crime Fiction. http://www.classiccrimefiction.com/suspense-novel.htm; Regis, Pamela. *A Natural History of the Romance Novel*. Philadelphia: University of Pennsylvania Press, 2003.

PATRICIA BOSTIAN

SWORD AND SORCERY FICTION

Let me live deep while I live; let me know the rich juices of red meat and stinging wine on my palate, the hot embrace of white arms, the mad exultation of battle when the blue blades flame and crimson, and I am content.
—Robert E. Howard "Queen of the Black Coast"

Definition. Casual readers of fantasy fiction are apt to use the terms *fantasy* and *sword and sorcery* interchangeably. Although sword and sorcery is certainly a type of fantasy fiction, as a sports car is a type of automobile, the term was first proposed by Fritz Leiber (1910–1992), the Hugo and Nebula Award-winning speculative fiction author, to distinguish the genre in which he wrote from other medieval fiction, particularly the mythic and epic fantasy, or high fantasy, crafted by J.R.R. Tolkien (1892–1973).

High fantasy, largely invented by William Morris (1834–1896) as an echo of Sir Thomas Malory's tales (e.g., *Le Morte D'Arthur*) and later popularized by Tolkien, tends to proceed at a stately pace, meandering from plot point to plot point, or location to location. Film critic Roger Ebert has written that Tolkien's *Lord of the* Rings trilogy, the most famous of all high fantasy works, "is mostly about leaving places, going places, being places, and going on to other places, all amid fearful portents and speculations. There are a great many mountains, valleys, streams, villages, caves, residences, grottos, bowers, fields, high roads, low roads, and along them the Hobbits and their larger companions travel while paying great attention to mealtimes. Landscapes are described with the faithful detail of a Victorian travel writer. . . . mostly the trilogy is an unfolding, a quest, a journey, told in an elevated, archaic, romantic prose style that tests our capacity for the declarative voice" (Ebert 2001).

Though exotic landscapes are present—even common—in sword and sorcery, they are described differently and for a different purpose. Sword and sorcery arose from a tradition entirely different from Tolkien's ornate, Anglo-Saxon medievalism; by contrast, for American pulp writers like Robert E. Howard (1906–1936), sword and sorcery fiction had to be retooled for specific consumer and marketplace desires during the 1920s and 1930s. The pulps, the television of the time, supplied and demanded quick-moving action. The stories needed to seize readers during the first few sentences so that newsstand browsers would feel compelled to purchase it to discover how the stories ended. Consequently, Howard's stories tended to emphasize dramatic action and tension over, though not necessarily at the expense of, description and setting.

Karl Edward Wagner (1945–1994), the creator of the sword and sorcery hero Kane and a renowned speculative fiction editor, preferred the term *epic fantasy* to *sword and sorcery*, describing it as "a fascinating synthesis of horror, adventure, and imagination . . . the common motif [being] a universe in which magic works and an individual may kill according to his personal code. When the universe is effectively envisioned and the characters are convincingly realized, epic fantasy can command the reader's attention on multiple levels of enjoyment. When the universe is a cardboard stage set and the characters comic book stereotypes, the result is cliché ridden melodrama" (Wagner 1977).

Lin Carter (1930–1988), likewise a renowned fantasy editor and a speculative fiction author, wrote in his introduction to the anthology *Flashing Swords #1* (1973):

> We call a story sword and sorcery when it is an action tale, derived from the traditions of the pulp magazine adventure story, set in a land, age, or world of the author's invention—a milieu in which magic actually works and the gods are real—a story, moreover, which pits a stalwart warrior in direct conflict with the forces of supernatural evil.

Carter simplifies here. He understood that gods did not manifest themselves in all sword and sorcery tales—certainly Howard's Crom never descended from upon high to aid Conan, who frequently swore by him. Dark gods and evil entities are common, however, and sorcerers conjure many a foul creature to confront sword and sorcery heroes. This is true to one of the genre's underlying themes: protagonists must overcome challenges with their own strength and cunning, not through the intercession of benevolent gods or governments. In the strange and hostile lands and situations in which they find themselves, they and their close allies must survive and impose order, meaning, and justice through their own actions. They are almost exclusively existential heroes: armed and able, but alone.

Trends and Themes. Scholar John Flynn has additional, clarifying observations about the genre.

In sword and sorcery, the supernatural is usually depicted as dark and malignant. Users of magic seldom work in the interest of the heroes. Magic is not the delightful, easily manipulated force that brightens fairy tales; rather, it is often associated with demonic forces and is invoked with great effort by lengthy, sinister rituals.

The protagonists of sword and sorcery are most often thieves, mercenaries, or barbarians struggling not for worlds or kingdoms, but for their own gain or mere survival. They are blue-collar rebels fighting against authority, skeptical of civilization and its rulers and adherents. While the strengths and skills of sword and sorcery heroes are romanticized, their exploits take place on a very different stage from one where lovely princesses, dashing nobles, and prophesied saviors are cast as the leads. Sword and sorcery heroes face more immediate problems than those of questing kings. They are cousins of the lone gunslingers of American westerns and the

"Sword-and-Sorcery focuses on the darker, more sinister, and often brutal nature of that struggle [with supernatural forces]. The emphasis is almost always on the might of the sword as contrasted with the power of magic. The protagonist is frequently strong, clever and resourceful, but he (or she) can also be savage, barbaric and brutally ambitious to the point where he often negates his 'goodness.' His heroic challenges repeatedly find him in lost worlds (nearly always tribal or feudal) where the laws of science and reason have been replaced by mysticism and the occult. While he doesn't necessarily deserve to triumph over these forces, the hero's physical courage and tenacity nonetheless make the victory possible"(Jones 2008).

wandering samurai of Japanese folklore, traveling through the wilderness to right wrongs or simply to earn food, shelter, and coin.

Unknown or hazardous lands are an essential ingredient of the genre, and if its protagonists should chance upon inhabited lands, they are often strangers to either the culture or civilization itself.

L. Sprague de Camp (1907–2000) wrote extensively about sword and sorcery. He preferred *heroic fantasy* to Leiber's label (although, aptly enough, the following quote originates from an anthology titled *Swords and Sorcery*). His description captures much of the genre's flavor by noting that

> sword and sorcery is the name of a class of stories laid, not in the world as it is or was or will be, but as it ought to have been to make a good story. The tales collected under this name are adventure-fantasies, laid in imaginary prehistoric or medieval worlds, when (it's fun to imagine) all men were mighty, all women were beautiful, all problems were simple, and all life was adventurous. In such a world, gleaming cities raise their shining spires against the stars; sorcerers cast sinister spells from subterranean lairs; baleful spirits stalk thickets; and the fate of kingdoms is balanced on the bloody blades of broadswords brandished by heroes of preternatural might and valor. (de Camp 1963)

De Camp almost always emphasized sword and sorcery as entertainment. At the time he was writing, fantasy was seldom regarded as worthy of serious study. It was, after all, allegedly written only to amuse. Then too, at the time he was writing, most sword and sorcery fiction was imitative, reflective of the trappings of the genre without understanding the possibilities of its depth.

Context and Issues

THE ELEMENTS OF SWORD AND SORCERY

In the past, sword and sorcery has been either narrowly defined as fiction featuring a barbarian with a loincloth and sword or broadly defined to mean any sort of fantasy where there is action and danger. More careful study can identify four elements that make sword and sorcery different from other fantasy: the environment, the protagonists, the obstacles, and story structure.

- The Environment: Sword and sorcery fiction is set in lands different from our own, where technology is relatively primitive, requiring the protagonists to overcome obstacles face-to-face. Magic works, but seldom at the behest of the heroes, being more often another obstacle used against them by villains or monsters. The landscape is exotic, either a different world or the backwaters of our own.
- The Protagonists: The heroes must survive by their cunning or brawn, frequently both. They are usually strangers or outcasts, rebels imposing their own form of justice on the wild, strange, decadent civilizations which they encounter. They are usually commoners or barbarians; should they hail from the higher ranks of society, they are either discredited or disinherited, or else descended from the lower ranks of nobility (the lowest of the high).
- Obstacles: Sword and sorcery's protagonists must best fantastic dangers, monstrous horrors, and dark sorcery to earn riches, the goodwill of attractive members of the opposite sex, and/or the right to live another day. Horror is a frequent component, but it is a tangible horror that can be confronted and bested, or at the least deflected and avoided.
- Structure: Sword and sorcery is usually crafted with a traditional narrative structure: it has a beginning, middle, and ending; a problem and solution; a climax and resolution. Most important, it moves at a headlong pace and overflows with thrilling action and adventure.

History

The Beginnings. Scholars consider the first fantasy novel to be *The Well at the World's End* (1896) by William Morris, a prominent nineteenth-century socialist who declined the position of poet laureate of England, translated Norse epics, spearheaded the Arts and Crafts movement, and incidentally wrote the first novels set neither on Earth nor in a dream world. From him high fantasy was born, and the line continued through the magnificent Lord Dunsany (1878–1957), the poetic E.R. Eddison (1882–1945), and the brilliantly whimsical James Branch Cabell (1879–1958) to Tolkien, who cast a mold that few authors or publishers have been willing or able to break.

Morris helped birth written fantasy, and thus sword and sorcery, but the subgenre's roots are far older, originating in the epic struggles of mythologies—in the wanderings of Odysseus and the quest of Jason, in the Persian *Shah-Namah* and the Saxon *Beowulf*, in the stories of Sinbad and other heroes from the *Arabian Nights,* and particularly in the Viking sagas, which tremendously influenced Morris, Eddison, and Tolkien. Elements of sword and sorcery also appear in the famous romances *Amadis of Gaul* and *Orlando Furioso,* among others. Volumes have been written about these works, but we will leave them, deserving as they are, to a broader discussion of the history of fantasy fiction.

Room must be made for Lord Dunsany, however, without whom no discussion of modern fantasy can be complete. Born Edward John Moreton Drax Plunkett, Dunsany was an Irish peer. Among other accomplishments, he was a chess champion of Wales, England, and Ireland, soldier, big-game hunter, popular playwright (six of his plays once appeared on Broadway at the same time) and successful novelist.

Most fantasy scholars name Dunsany as Morris's direct successor. Dunsany did craft a handful of fantasy novels, but he is best remembered for eight slim collections of fantastic tales. Many famous fantasy and horror writers name him the greatest fantasy writer of all time, speaking always of his imagination, beautiful prose, and clear conception of man's desperate longings and darkest fears. Though his fantasy work began in 1903, it remains timeless and accessible. It is not the work of a cloistered nobleman, but of a genius gifted with soaring imagination and compassion.

A number of Dunsany's short stories contain heroes and magic blades. His language is courtly and elegant, but unlike much of the prose of the time, there is nothing dense or turgid about it:

> They passed by night over the Oolnar Mountains, each dwarf with his good axe, the old flint war-axe of his fathers, a night when no moon shone, and they went unshod, and swiftly, to come on the demi-gods in the darkness beyond the dells of Ulk, lying faint and idle and contemptible.
>
> And before it was light they found the heathery lands, and the demi-gods lying lazy all over the side of a hill. The dwarfs stole towards them warily in the darkness.
> —"How the Dwarfs Rose Up in War" (1919)

By contrast, E.R. Eddison's masterpiece, *The Worm Ouroboros* (1922), is a more challenging read, because Eddison affected an older style. Many today find the reading labored, but the labor is well rewarded. Eddison painted his scenes with lavish skill:

At the clash the two champions advanced and clasped one another with their strong arms, each with his right arm below and left arm above the other's shoulder, until the flesh shrank beneath the might of their arms that were as brazen bands. They swayed a little this way and that, as great trees swaying in a storm, their legs planted firmly so that they seemed to grow out of the ground like the trunks of oak trees. Nor did either yield ground to other, nor might either win a master hold upon his enemy. So swayed they back and forth for long time, breathing heavily.

Eddison labored over *The Worm Ouroboros* for many years, finally publishing it in 1922. He followed it first with the translation of a Norse epic and then with the translation of a novel that many consider one of the finest Viking novels of all time: *Styrbiorn the Strong.* He later wrote a trilogy set in the heaven of the world of the *Worm,* a unique fantasy but not sword and sorcery.

Just like the most exciting Viking sagas, sword and sorcery features compelling individual duels and the clash of armies, elements first used to great effect in historical fiction. Today, publishers advertise historical horror, historical romance, and historical mystery—even alternate histories and historical political thrillers. In the nineteenth century there was only one flavor: a historical fiction writer was someone who wrote action-packed tales set in distant, exotic places. Readers back then turned to their favorite authors—Alexandre Dumas, Sir Walter Scott, William Morris, Robert Louis Stevenson, and others less known today—for the same thrills modern readers turn to sword and sorcery.

It is in the historical fiction of pulp magazines, however, where the genre's similarities to sword and sorcery become even more striking.

Historical Fiction of the Pulps. The pulp era began around the turn of the twentieth century, before radio and television. Magazines featuring a variety of diverting topics were found on the newsstands, printed on cheap, pulpy paper—hence the term *pulps.* Publishers attempted to print something for almost every reader, in the same way that TV channels attempt to broadcast something for almost every viewer. And like television, most of the product was bad, giving pulp fiction its modern connotations—cheap, sensationalist, and over-the-top writing. As with most popular art forms, though, some gold glittered within the dross, and many famous writers were first published by (or at least appeared later) in the pulps.

Most pulp historical fiction writers crafted tales of action and adventure, and many created serial characters. As in comic books (whose rise in popularity coincides with that of the pulps) and television series, serial characters served two purposes. First, they spared writers the chore of creating a new hero for each story; and second, once serial characters found an accepting editor or readership, they increased the chances of selling the story.

This pulp historical fiction of the early twentieth century (circa 1915–1940) has almost all of the same elements as sword and sorcery. In place of the imaginary land is a distant era that, in the hands of the better writers, appears with greater vividness than many an invented setting. There are heroes who must live by their wits and weapons in deadly borderlands, beset by schemers and intriguers. There are hidden treasures, ancient secrets, and lovely women—some, keen-eyed adventurers of whom heroes should be wary, and others, damsels in need of rescue. There are loyal comrades, implacable foes, powerful but foolish kings, secret societies, fabulous kingdoms, and fraudulent wizards and miracle-workers. In short, the connection between sword and sorcery and pulp historical fiction is obvious, both being fashioned with the same spirit, from love of the same elements.

Historical fiction wasn't the mainstay of the pulps—for the most part westerns and detective fiction were—but many an author wrote "costume pieces." There was H. Bedford Jones, that most prolific of pulp authors (said to write a million words a year), who could be relied upon for tales of the high seas and cavaliers and Dumas-like action. There were Farnham Bishop and Arthur Gilchrist Brodeur, writing together or separately of swordsmen of fortune, and F.R. Buckley, who wrote about battlefield exploits in Renaissance Italy. The pulps saw the engaging, though repetitious, exploits of Zorro, and printed the adventures of Sabatini's Captain Blood. Arthur D. Howden Smith crafted many a bold tale, among them the saga of the Viking Swain and the story of Gray Maiden.

Gray Maiden was a sword first forged for a Pharaoh. In each story the blade is wielded by a different warrior down through history. The sword is sometimes lost or entombed with its wielder, but it is always unearthed to wreak more mischief. It has a supremely sharp blade with supernatural powers—no man who bares her meets his death by sword, though they often perish in other ways.

The Gray Maiden story cycle veers widely in quality—some portions are full of monotonous talking heads, whereas some are fine entertainment. "Thord's Wooing" (1927), one of the Gray Maiden stories, is an excellent Viking tale. Late in the story, in a duel scene provides some sense of its flavor. Bjarni, mortally wounded, seeks to take the life of Thord's mother, Elin.

> "Your doing, witch," He gasped. "Come with me!"
>
> And he hurled his sword straight at her breast. It turned once in the air, hilt over point, a flash of light in the dimness, sped by the last strength of his body even as he collapsed in death. But Gray Maiden flew faster. Thord cast the long blade like an axe, and once more it parried Bjarni's blow. The two swords clattered at Elin's feet.

Gilchrist Brodeur and Farnham Bishop, writing together or separately, could be counted on for exciting tales of clashing arms and mayhem set in the distant past. Their style is sometimes slow, weighted with the pacing of the nineteenth century; yet they should not be too easily disregarded, as their work sometimes springs with amazing vigor. One of the best by either man is a neglected gem of Viking adventure, *He Rules Who Can*, originally serialized in *Argosy*, beginning in November of 1928. Sadly, this Brodeur novel about Harald Hardrada, has never seen reprint.

Selected Authors. While there are other fine authors and other fine tales, two giants stride out of this field, authors famed for both quality and quantity: Talbot Mundy and Harold Lamb. Both of them influenced Robert E. Howard, the true father of sword and sorcery.

Mundy's real name was William Lancaster Gribbon, and before he took up writing he had knocked about India, East Africa, and Germany; married a few women and loved some more; and nearly gotten himself killed several times over. It was while recovering in the hospital after getting blackjacked that he took up writing.

Mundy is best known for two series characters: James Grim, or Jim Grim, an American adventurer working for the British Secret Service, and Tros of Samothrace, the epic Druid warrior. It is Mundy's Tros series that concerns us here. This long cycle of stories was published for the most part as a series of novellas in the pages of *Adventure* magazine (a novel near the end of the cycle appeared in book form). And if any fiction decries its pulp reputation, it is Mundy's Tros of Samothrace. Mundy was a skilled student of human nature who had philosophical leanings. His characters are rich, complex, and well drawn. His plots hinge upon the actions taken by his heroes and villains. Sometimes the stories unfold slowly because they depend upon intrigue, politics, and dialogue, but at the appropriate times they explode with action.

Above all, Mundy was a careful craftsman. Consider the somber tone of the following scene, hardly expected of a typically garish pulp writer:

> He went below, into the cabin where his father's body lay, with Caesar's scarlet cloak spread over it. And for a while he stood steadying himself with one hand on an overhead beam, watching the old man's face, that was as calm as if Caesar's tortures had never racked the seventy-year-old limbs, the firm, proud lip showing plainly through the white beard, the eyes closed as in sleep, the aristocratic hands folded on the breast.
>
> It was dark in there and easy to imagine things. The body moved a trifle in time to the ship's swaying.
>
> —*Tros of Samothrace* (1967 Pyramid reprint)

Tros is a skilled sailor and minor initiate into an ancient and widespread mystical society, a world that Mundy renders entirely believable. His greatest desire is to build the ship of his dreams to sail around the world, but before he can do it he runs afoul of Caesar's ambitions. Caesar is one of Mundy's triumphs, a rascal genius who only fails because his ego eventually grows too large. Tros eventually builds his ship, ends up allied with Cleopatra, and even, near the end, aids his old enemy Caesar. He never manages to sail around the world, though Mundy fully planned to write that story, because his creator died of diabetes before pen went to paper. Fortunately the series ends on a complete note, with all of the hero's Mediterranean adventures resolved.

Harold Lamb was a quiet man fascinated with chronicles of Eastern history from an early age. He wrote the epic Durandal trilogy, amongst other thrilling crusader novels. Later he would become a renowned historian and wealthy screenwriter, penning more than thirty movies for Cecil B. DeMille. First, though, he created a cycle of remarkable historical fiction stories set in locations as fabulous and unfamiliar to most readers as Edgar Rice Burroughs's Mars.

Where many adventure tales are predictable from the first word, Lamb's plots were full of unexpected twists. He wrote convincingly of faraway lands and dealt fairly with their inhabitants, relating without bias the viewpoints of Mongols, Moslems, and Hindus. His stories are rarely profound psychological drama, but Lamb nonetheless breathes humanity into his characters, endowing them with realistic hopes and fears. Unlike the pacing of almost all of his predecessors and most of his contemporaries, his still feels modern—he never stops for slow exposition. His plots thunder forward as though he has envisioned each one for cinema the moment he slid paper into the typewriter.

The most enduring and complex of all Lamb's heroes is his first, Khlit the Cossack. Before Stormbringer keened in Elric's hand, before the Gray Mouser prowled Lankhmar's foggy streets, before Conan trod jeweled thrones under his sandaled feet, Khlit the Cossack rode the steppe. He is the grandfather of all characters in sword and sorcery series.

The Cossack is already old when his saga begins late in the sixteenth century in the grasslands of central Asia. He is an expert horseman and swordsman, unlettered and only a step removed from barbarism, but wise in the ways of war and men. Gruff and taciturn, Khlit is a firm believer in justice and devout in his faith, though not given to prayer or religious musings. He is the friend and protector of many women, but he leaves romance to his sidekicks and allies.

The Khlit stories swim in action, treachery, and places best unseen by mortal men. Consider the following scene, from the novella "The Mighty Manslayer" (1918):

> Mir Turek caught his arm and pointed to the further side.
> "The Bearers of Wealth!" he screamed. "See, the Bearers of Wealth, and their burden. The Tomb of Genghis Khan. We have found the tomb of Genghis Khan!"
> The shout echoed wildly up the cavern, and Khlit thought that he heard a rumbling in the depths of the cavern in answer. He looked where Mir Turek pointed. At first he saw only the veil of smoke. Then he made out a plateau of rock jutting out from the further side. On this plateau, abreast of them, and at the other end of the rock bridge gigantic shapes loomed through the vapor. Twin forms of mammoth size reared themselves, and Khlit thought that they moved, with the movement of the vapor. These forms were not men but beasts that stood side by side. Between them they supported a square object which hung as if suspended in the air.

Throughout the seventeen-part series Khlit yearns for far horizons and strange new sights. He rides alone for a time before rising to lead a Tatar tribe for five tales, later joining forces with the heroic Afghan swordsman and Moslem, Abdul Dost. Khlit always bears his famed curved saber, gilt with the writing of an unknown tongue. It is a deadly blade with its own secret history, disclosed as the series progresses.

The Khlit saga is a remarkable tour de force, and any reader familiar with the works of Robert E. Howard and Fritz Leiber or with the works of those who followed them will recognize familiar elements in this predecessor.

Sword and Planet. Before the mighty Texan Robert E. Howard took up his pen, Edgar Rice Burroughs created—or at least had the first big success—with a genre that some call *sword and planet* and that others describe as *planetary romance*. The concept is simple: an adventurer is dropped in skivvies onto an unknown planet, usually being forced to make do with primitive weapons (but he may have a ray gun slung on a hip with just three shots left). Instead of elves and wizards, there are alien races and the descendants of ancient world masterminds. Rather than magic, there is advanced technology, often poorly understood by the surviving populace and treated like sorcery. In the early pulp days this was science fiction; in retrospect it has a lot more in common with fantasy, especially sword and sorcery.

Before Burroughs came up with Tarzan, he created John Carter, Warlord of Mars. Beginning in 1912, Carter adventured on a world little like the real Mars, with a breathable atmosphere, scheming aliens of varied colors, and lots of lovely, haughty, semi-naked queens and princesses. Carter and his cohorts spend most of the time running around with swords. All of the stories are action-packed cliffhangers. Their biggest flaw is that most have the same plot. Someone's wife/girlfriend/niece is lost/endangered/kidnapped, and the hero must travel across Mars to save them. Not that the female characters lack pluck or courage (they're not wallflowers), but they are, naturally, dated by their time.

Burroughs's work was an outgrowth of the lost race adventures of H. Rider Haggard (of *She* and Alan Quartermain fame), in which the hero journeys to some lost corner of the world to discover ancient civilizations rife with treachery and sinister secrets. Haggard did not quite invent the form, but under his skilled hands it gained popular fame, and he had an enormous influence. His work is still enjoyable today, though most of it speaks matter-of-factly of outmoded conceptions and prejudices, and his plotting is not entirely modern. This does not describe all his work, however; some of his stories, most notably his Viking novel *Eric Brighteyes,* remain fabulous adventures, shot through with swordplay and the supernatural, and they should not be overlooked by sword and sorcery readers.

Haggard's influence can be felt on many writers who thrust their heroes into lost lands (A.E. Merrit became justly famed for doing much the same thing in the early pulp years; his settings dripping with even more magical conceptions). Burroughs merely took things one step further and dropped his heroes into a land that had never existed. He became famous doing it.

Recognizing that sword and planet and sword and sorcery were related fields, early anthologists often packaged authors from both genres under the same covers. Today, science fiction readers look on sword and planet with disdain for the most part, especially those stories set on versions of Mars or Venus that have human-supportable conditions. Fantasy readers seem to have forgotten that such stories even exist.

Many authors crafted sword and planet stories—much of it forgettable. But there were also remarkably enjoyable adventures, written by the likes of Edmund Hamilton, space opera master and science fiction pioneer, and Otis Kline, one-time agent for Robert E. Howard, best remembered today for his somewhat wooden Venusian sword and planet trilogy The Planet of Peril and the novel *The Swordsman of Mars.*

Leigh Brackett, the woman who is probably the very best sword and planet writer, plied her trade in the dying days of the genre. Just as Bach crafted baroque masterpieces in a time that this style was considered old-fashioned and quaint, Brackett penned most of her Martian stories after there was definite evidence that the planet could not possibly exist as she described. Eventually she had to stop writing them altogether, and anyone who laments the end of Ray Bradbury's Martian stories should lament his friend Leigh Brackett's abandoning of Mars as well.

> Carse walked beside the still black waters in their ancient channel, cut in the dead sea-bottom. He watched the dry wind shake the torches that never went out and listened to the broken music of the harps that were never stilled. Lean lithe men and women passed him in the shadowy streets, silent as cats except for the chime and the whisper of the tiny bells the women wear, a sound as delicate as rain, distillate of all the sweet wickedness of the world.
>
> —*The Sword of Rhiannon* (1953)

The sample above only hints at Brackett's mastery with setting. She always evokes a powerful sense of place, and her Mars is a haunting, dimmed, mysterious, and often fatal ruby. Her action scenes are crisp and clean and her plots never flag.

Brackett wrote numerous tales of planets near and far, but she is probably most famous for her Skaith series. She is a well-known contributor to the sci-fi world, having turned in the first draft of *The Empire Strikes Back* to George Lucas shortly before her death in 1978. Brackett's long career also featured other Hollywood triumphs: she wrote the screenplay for *The Big Sleep* with William Faulkner as well as numerous western vehicles for John Wayne.

Although some of Brackett's fiction seems a little dated (her spacemen often smoke and her women sometimes need protecting), she remains surprisingly fresh because of her skill with character and setting, and because her plots are usually unpredictable. So long as they are willing to forgive her planets that cannot be, sword and sorcery readers lucky enough to find her works will be in good hands.

Sword and planet, after many years in the wilderness, has enjoyed a rebirth. In the late 1980s Harry Turtledove launched his Videssos series, about a Roman legion mystically transported to another planet where magic works, and in 1990 William Forstchen created his Lost Regiment series, about a Union regiment flung through a portal to a hostile alien world. Other authors have found additional ways to put fresh spins on this old genre.

Robert E. Howard. Long before Brackett broke into the pulps, a young man named Robert E. Howard set out to become a writer. He had his first success at the age of 17, a success which was followed by many agonizing years of rejection letters. Howard did not give up, though, and he eventually started publishing regularly in *Weird Tales*.

Though never an outstanding success, *Weird Tales* became one of the most influential of all pulp magazines, printing the work of many who later rose to fame as fantasy, horror, and science fiction writers, sometimes in the pages of *Weird Tales* itself. Few pulp magazines today are as widely known or as revered.

Howard himself would rather have been writing historical fiction, a field he loved. But for many years he could not crack the magazines that published his favorite writers, such as Mundy and Lamb. So he started to write for this audience.

Howard told historic tales infused with supernatural horrors, creating characters such as the dour Elizabethan wanderer Solomon Kane, who spent most of his time fighting dreadful things in Africa, and Bran Mak Morn, king of the Picts, who waged a battle against Roman legions knowing that his people would lose it. But Howard also experimented with a prehistory of his own invention in which a king named Kull enjoyed his epic adventures when Atlantis was but a barbarian nation. Only a few of the Kull stories sold, though they possess a dreamy poetic power found otherwise only in Howard's nonfantasy historical fiction.

And then a new character, the inimitable Conan, thrust his way into Howard's consciousness. Howard later wrote that so easily did the stories flow, it was almost as though his creation stood at his shoulder, dictating stories from his life.

> Know, O Prince, that between the years when the oceans drank Atlantis and the gleaming cities, and the years of the rise of the sons of Aryas, there was an age undreamed of, when shining kingdoms lay spread across the world like blue mantles beneath the stars. . . . . Hither came Conan the Cimmerian, black-haired, sullen-eyed, sword in hand, a thief, a reaver, a slayer, with gigantic melancholies and gigantic mirth, to tread the jeweled thrones of the Earth under his sandaled feet.
> —"The Phoenix on the Sword" (1932)

Thus sword and sorcery was born with Kull and Conan. The connection between the real world and the world of these characters is hazy at best. They adventure in a never-neverland of prehistory where supernatural horrors stalk a planet Earth so different that it might as well be one of the other worlds of sword and planet. The map and peoples of their world become familiar through the course of their stories, particularly the longer Conan saga (21 stories in all). Modern readers take for granted many fantastic elements pioneered by Howard: a fantasy world with a map, countries, gods, and a consistent magic system. The complete package originated with Howard.

Howard has his detractors. Some of this has to do with the often low quality of Conan stories written after his death. Tale after tale was authored by others until bookstore shelves groaned under the weight of collected pastiche—more non-Howard Conan stories were written than were those composed by Howard himself, and until just recently the pastiche Conan was the only kind in print.

Then too, the charge of sexism is leveled at Howard. He does not seem to have been sexist himself, even if Conan was. Howard wrote a series centered on the swashbuckling Dark Agnes of France. She was no heroine in a chainmail bikini, but rather, a real woman. Unfortunately, her tales never sold, so Howard stopped writing them. Howard wrote for his market, and so *most* of the women in the Conan series serve the same function as those in a James Bond film. His readers loved him for it.

Those familiar with Conan only from the pastiche, or the movies, or the comic books, do not know the real article, which has far greater range of emotion and zest for life, being is at the same time more primal. Howard is an able plotter with a splendid imagination, but it is in his narrative that Howard truly excels, and this cannot translate into any medium beyond the pages of his work. His scenes are drawn swiftly and skillfully, with a few sharp brush strokes. A movie version of his works is not necessary because his prose is so cinematic to begin with:

> Rising above the black denseness of the trees and above the waving fronds, the moon silvered the river, and their wake became a rippling scintillation of phosphorescent bubbles that widened like a shining road of bursting jewels. The oars dipped into the shining water and came up sheathed in frosty silver. The plumes on the warriors' headpieces nodded in the wind, and the gems on sword hilts and harnesses sparkled frostily.
> —"Queen of the Black Coast" (1934)

Blending historical swashbucklers, horror, tales of lost civilizations, strands from mythology, Jack London's brutal Darwinism, and even a little flavoring from sword and planet works, Howard created something vibrant and new—sword and sorcery.

Howard shot himself in 1936, when he was only 30 years old and at the height of his creative power. He left a large volume of work behind that refused to die with him, though it has only recently begun to be studied by scholars.

Howard's Trail. Catherine L. Moore was the first to follow Howard's path, writing her fantasies while Howard still lived and earning a letter of praise from him. (Howard even sent her copies of his Dark Agnes stories for her perusal.) Moore provided the first innovation in sword and sorcery, introducing a female protagonist. Jirel of Joiry is more than just a "gal Conan," because Moore's prose is a different thing from Robert E. Howard. It is dreamy and surreal and a little reminiscent of the early horror-fantasy writer William Hope Hodgson:

> Presently she began to near one of those luminous patches that resembled fields, and saw now that they were indeed a sort of garden. The luminosity rose from myriads of tiny, darting lights planted in even rows, and when she came near enough she saw that the lights were small insects, larger than fireflies, and with luminous wings which they

beat vainly upon the air, darting from side to side in a futile effort to be free. For each was attached to its little stem, as if they had sprung living from the soil. Row upon row of them stretched into the dark.

—*Jirel Meets Magic* (1935)

Oddly, some of Jirel's tales feel more dated than some of the stories that precede them. In the first for instance, Jirel secretly loves the man trying to conquer her—the old pulp trope of a strong female character who secretly longs to be controlled, presented here by a woman writer. Moore also wrote the very popular Northwest Smith stories, featuring an outer space adventurer. Most of Moore's later work was written in tandem with Henry Kuttner, whom she married. From that point forth the two usually wrote together even if they did not share a byline.

Prior to writing with Moore, Henry Kuttner had produced prolifically on his own. He labored under dozens of pen names and could write commandingly in many different genres. After Robert E. Howard died, Kuttner wrote four sword and sorcery tales for *Weird Tales,* featuring Elak of Atlantis, a slender, civilized prince of Atlantis armed with a rapier. The Elak stories are not nearly as innovative as what had come before, but they overflow with grand scenes of great color and majesty, so that even the shortest reads like an epic.

Kuttner also wrote a short sword and sorcery series for , a rival of *Weird Tales,* that is far more grim than Elak's saga. The two tales feature the brooding Prince Raynor, and in some ways presage the work of Michael Moorcock.

Kuttner died unexpectedly of a heart attack in his early 40s. His colleagues seem to have thought well of him both as a writer and as a human being. Lin Carter related that decades after Kuttner's death, famed science fiction writer Robert Heinlein would get teary-eyed—having to change the subject—after reminiscing about Kuttner for even a little while.

Another *Weird Tales* contributor, Clark Ashton Smith, artist and poet, wrote several series of strange horrific tales set in twilight lands. His prose is bejeweled with descriptions and bizarre imagery, a lush tapestry of words emphasizing tone and style and wit, where character is mostly incidental. Smith was far less interested in swords and barbarians than he was in mages and their spells and the resulting horrors. Today Smith is revered as one of the three greatest *Weird Tales* authors (alongside H.P. Lovecraft and Robert E. Howard), and there is no denying his lasting influence. It was he who wrote first of a decadent Earth of the far future, inspiring Vance's *Dying Earth* and Moorcock's *Hawkmoon* and countless others, but it is his imaginative scope and lush prose that has continued to inspire later writers. Lin Carter wrote that Smith's stories were "darkling and mordant, lit with flashes of jeweled description, studded with exotic names and rare words, pervaded by the lilied languor and dreamlike splendor of a hashish vision"(Carter 1969). There is only room for a brief quote:

> With no other light than that of the four diminutive moons of Xiccarph, each in a different phase but all decrescent, Tiglari had crossed the bottomless swamp of Soorm, wherein no reptile dwelt and no dragon descended—but where the pitch-black ooze was alive with continual heavings and writhings. He had carefully avoided the high causey of white corundum that spanned the fen, and had threaded his way with infinite peril from isle to sedgy isle that shuddered gelatinously beneath him. When he reached the solid shore and the shelter of the palm-tall rushes, he was equally careful to avoid the pale porphyry stairs that would heavenward through dizzy, nadir-cleaving

chasms and along glassy scarps to the ever-mysterious and terrible house of Maal Dweb.

—"The Maze of Maal Dweb" (1933)

Weird Tales was not interested in Fritz Leiber's Lankhmar tales. Fortunately for us all, *Unknown* gave them a home in the early 1940s. In that magazine's pages Leiber launched into a long cycle of sword and sorcery adventures about two wandering rogues, the northern barbarian Fafhrd and the sneaky, city-born thief Gray Mouser. Many other fantasy, science fiction, and horror stories flowed from Leiber's pen, garnering praise and awards, including several Hugos and Nebulas. What differentiates the Fafhrd and the Gray Mouser stories even today is the quality of the writing. We come to care for the two rogues despite their foibles, in part because, while larger than life, they feel human. Leiber's style is clever and sparkles with humor, though the stories are never just comic send-ups.

Most fantasy authors hail Leiber as one of the truly great innovators. Just as no one else has ever equaled the skill with which Howard told of his barbarian hero, no one has yet equaled Leiber's Lankhmar writing at its height. The Lankhmar stories are carefully threaded with action, humor, horror, lust, and humanity. This short passage from "When the Sea King's Away" (1977) provides a small window to his work. The two heroes are exploring a strange passage recently carved out through the sea:

> Soon they were treading along a veritable tunnel in the water, a leaden arch-roofed passageway no wider than the phosphorescently yellow-green path that floored it. The tunnel curved just enough now to left, now to right, so that there was no seeing any long distance ahead. From time to time the Mouser thought he heard faint whistlings and moanings echoing along it. He stepped over a large crab that was backing feebly and saw beside it a dead man's hand emerging from the glowing muck, one shred-fleshed finger pointing the way they were taking.
>
> Fafhrd half turned his head and muttered gravely, "Mark me, Mouser, there's magic in this somewhere!"
>
> The Mouser thought he had never in his life heard a less necessary remark.

Among the many influenced by Leiber are the creators of *Dungeons & Dragons*, who liberated many of Leiber's concepts and overlaid them across the central Tolkienesque game design. (To this day the game also uses a variation on Moorcock's theme of law and chaos to help define its characters.) Leiber continued to write of the two heroes over the course of his lifetime, but naturally his style changed. The later stories take on a meandering prose style that is far less engaging, and the adventures become less interesting.

Norvell Page, famed bard of the pulp vigilante "The Spider," also wrote for *Unknown,* crafting two short Prester John novels. Prester was a character with Conan-like strength, guile, and a genuine sense of humor. He journeys East, encountering action, mysterious sorcerers, and lovely damsels.

These are only the most famous of the pulp sword and sorcery writers. Others appeared in *Weird Tales,* such as Nictin Dyalhis, who crafted a series of stand-alone fantasy adventures; and the mysterious Clifford Ball, a fan stirred by Howard's death to write in his style. There were other writers besides, some who wrote either historicals tinged with sorcery or horror verging on adventure.

After the Pulps. As the pulps died slowly, hit by the triple whammy of paper shortage caused by World War II, a postwar change in mood, and stronger entertainment rivals, sword and sorcery lived on in the new paperback book market—though just barely. For the most part the subgenre lay comatose.

Jack Vance is not, strictly speaking, a sword and sorcery writer. He is one of those gifted authors whose work transcends genres. Readers of both fantasy and science fiction can read his work with delight, and sword and sorcery readers have not neglected his *Dying Earth*, a collection of interlinked short stories shot through with swashbuckling, sorcery, and wondrous imagery. These stories were originally rejected by the magazines, but a small publisher in the 1950s saw their worth and they remain in print today. Other adventure work followed, equally strong and always tinged with space opera or sword and planet filtered through Vance's unique lens.

By the 1970s it was possible to make a living by writing fantasy. Along came award-winning Roger Zelazny, first with a series of short stories centered on Dilvish the Damned, an adventuring swordsman with a postmodern flair, and then with other delightful fiction, including his first Amber series, a high watermark for fantasy and sword and sorcery alike. Set at first on Earth, the series expands through ever more complex and fascinating intrigues and mysteries in parallel worlds, until finally the nature of existence itself is threatened. Magic and action lurk upon nearly every page.

Michael Moorcock experimented with Burroughs-like fiction, then launched into a long, loosely related stories about the eternal champion, a hero who appears in many guises through many parallel worlds, fighting the forces of chaos. Moorcock may have found at least some of his inspiration in the fantasy work of Poul Anderson, whose masterpiece of northern, doom-filled romance, *The Broken Sword* (1954)—as well as the later novel *Three Hearts and Three Lions*—featured many elements now associated with Moorcock: law and chaos, cursed rune swords, and evil, manipulative gods. Elric, the albino swordsman is probably the most famous of Moorcock's characters, but there are others besides: the haunted, elf-like Corum and the obsessed Hawkmoon to name but a few. Moorcock's prose is frequently brilliant, shot through with moments of sad, lyric beauty. It has some of the same sorrow over the human condition that Lord Dunsany conveyed so well, but it is less joyful. Elric knows almost from the start that he is doomed. His soul-sucking sword, Stormbringer, robs strength from others to power him, and it has a dark mind of its own, sometimes striking when Elric would hold his hand.

> It's taking me—the thrice-damned thing is taking me!" Nikorn gurgled horribly, clutching at the black steel with hands turned to claws. "Stop it, Elric—I beg of you, stop it! Please!"
>
> Elric tried again to tug the blade from Nikorn's heart. He could not. It was rooted in flesh, sinew and vitals. It moaned greedily, drinking into it all that was the being of Kiron of Ilmar. It sucked the life-force from the dying man and all the while its voice was soft and disgustingly sensuous. Still Elric struggled to pull the sword free.
>
> —*The Bane of the Black Sword* (1977)

Moorcock still writes in the field today, even generating an occasional Elric prequel (he has already written about Elric's end), but his heart does not really seem to be in it anymore.

A contemporary of Moorcock who is much celebrated by him, M. John Harrison, created a short sword and sorcery novel titled *The Pastel City* (1971). It is the first in a sequence of works about Viroconium, a city that may be a dream of a dream of our own reality, although the first tale in the sequence does not trouble itself with such extratextual concerns. It delivers the familiar sword and sorcery tropes decorated with a veneer of space opera and such fine characterization and description that to a sword and sorcery connoisseur it goes down like fine wine. Having delivered a small masterpiece, Harrison walked away from the field and has not returned.

Moorcock's career was launched during a publishing boom in the 1960s that brought Howard and Burroughs back into print, kept Leiber in paperback, and saw Tolkien rise to worldwide fame. Fantasy could suddenly be found on bookstore shelves in increasing quantities. Imitation rather than innovation began to take over. Rather than a few writers crafting sword and sorcery work with their individual stamp, the 1970s and early 1980s brought us mostly imitation of what had come before. Some writers, such as John Jakes and Gardner Fox, created barbarians of their own and sent them adventuring. Lin Carter drafted multiple series heavily influenced by Burroughs, Howard, Dunsany, and A.E. Merritt, and many others followed suit. Some of the work was polished and entertaining if familiar, but most of it was dreck. The profusion of the material probably contributed to the virtual disappearance of sword and sorcery in the 1980s. Writers were hired to craft more tales of Conan or other Robert E. Howard heroes. As expected, some of this work was much better than others. Accomplished authors—among them David C. Smith, Andrew Offutt, Karl Edward Wagner, and later John Maddox Roberts and John C. Hocking—delivered stories reminiscent of something Howard might have composed. Most of the pastiche, though, was hollow and empty.

The 1970s and 1980s saw the rise of sword and sorcery anthologies, many of which were popular enough to spawn multiple volumes. Lin Carter selected manuscripts for the *Year's Best Fantasy Stories* from 1975 to 1980, in volumes 1 through 6. Though he often published a story of his own (and sometimes two, the second under a pen name), he can perhaps be excused because the stories he chose were among his best. Famed fantasy authors L. Sprague de Camp, Jack Vance, C.J. Cherryh, and Karl Edward Wagner contributed many short stories, and Carter often featured reprints by Robert E. Howard and other luminaries. Lesser known but talented authors also made appearances, including Charles Saunders and Pat McIntosh. Though quality varied, each of these six volumes contained a healthy dose of sword and sorcery. After Carter left, the later books in the series rarely included this genre.

Fantasy author and editor Andrew J. Offutt helmed five volumes of *Swords Against Darkness* from 1977 to 1979. Offutt's selections were similar to Carter's in that they mixed reprints and modern works, including pieces by Poul Anderson, Tanith Lee, Manly Wade Wellman, and Ramsey Campbell. Offutt, however, was able to offer content that was almost exclusively sword and sorcery. Some of it was not especially good, but much of it was. Darrell Schweitzer's haunted Julian the Knight first found a wider audience after being published in this anthology.

There were other series—such as Lin Carter's five-volume Flashing Swords series (each made up of four or five novellas rather than the more typical dozen short stories) as well as the more high-fantasy-oriented Thieves' World books and many fine stand-alones—but two deserve special mention. Jessica Amanda Salmonson edited two volumes of *Amazons* (I and II) in 1979 and 1982. She selected stories of women protagonists slashing and riding into adventure, and most of her choices were more balanced and less shrill than those featured in other sword and sorcery anthologies centered on female adventurers. The most famous of these series was Marion Zimmer Bradley's Sword and Sorceress series.

From 1987 through 1991 Karl Edward Wagner edited *Echoes of Valor*. This three-volume anthology featured few new stories, because what Wagner decided to reprint overlooked or revered but rare works and package them in an affordable format. It was a gold mine for the sword and sorcery or sword and planet aficionado. Volume II, for instance, features a Jirel of Joiry story left out of Moore's collected works, as well as a collaboration between Leigh Brackett and Ray Bradbury that had not been reprinted. Volume III presents three of Nictzin Dyalhis's *Weird Tales* fantasy pieces as well as both of Henry Kuttner's Prince Raynor stories. Wagner would almost surely have followed with more, but this talented editor and author died too young.

Underground in the 1980s. By the mid-1980s sword and sorcery had been all but completely swept from the marketplace. Fantasy as a whole grew in popularity, but the hordes of Tolkien imitators won out against the legions of Conan imitators. Novel markets evaporated, and only a handful of small press magazines welcomed tales of sword and sorcery.

Some have pointed the rise of female editors in the fantasy field, and the resulting backlash against male tropes commonly found in sword and sorcery, as the cause of the genre's decline, but that is too simple an explanation, although it is true that women make up a much larger demographic of fantasy readers today than men do. Some believe sword and sorcery was brought low by the appalling quality of various sword and sorcery movies and a plethora of imitative books. Then video games arrived on the scene, providing for many young men the same kind of thrills that they once experienced vicariously through reading. It might have been the demise of short fiction markets, for the speculative fiction magazines became more and more interested in legitimizing fantasy and science fiction by making it more literary and obscure and by distancing themselves from lowly tales of adventure. Whatever the storm's cause, it left only a few giants standing: Leiber and Moorcock, who were only writing in the field sporadically and had enough clout to have their talent recognized no matter what they wrote, and David Gemmell, who will be discussed in a moment. Nearly everyone else was down for the count, even some less well-known writers who were pushing the genre's envelopes.

The most recognized of these other authors is Michael Shea. Nifft the Lean, Michael Shea's gentleman thief, attracted praise from many circles, including World Fantasy Award winner Tim Powers. Shea himself won the World Fantasy Award for the 1982 collection titled *Nifft the Lean*. His tales have been collected by Baen in recent years and are still in print. Inventive, clever, and exciting, their style is reminiscent of a Vancian-Clark Ashton Smith-Leiber combination at its most indulgent. Shea shares with Vance and Smith a gift for world building, and with Leiber the gift of artful dialogue.

Richard Tierney, sometime cowriter with David C. Smith, created Simon Magus, a magician and ex-gladiator wandering New Testament times and combating Cthulhu-inspired horrors. Most of the tales were collected in *The Scroll of Thoth* in 1997.

Darrel Schweitzer wrote in the late 1970s in elegant prose of a damned, wandering knight. Sir Julian's tales were collected in 1981 and more fantasy has flowed from Schweitzer's pen, including the superlative *Mask of the Sorcerer*, which is decidedly more about sorcery than swords. Schweitzer remains active in the field today, associated with the new *Weird Tales* and writing other fantasy work, although his tone has far more in common with Dunsany than Howard.

Of all these authors, there were three who most closely hewed to the tenets of swords and sorcery as established by Howard, while at the same time forging new paths. A young David C. Smith created Oron in 1979, the first of the new generation of barbarians who actually *felt* barbaric, and the character proved so popular that Smith's publisher had him write prequels, for Oron came to a Wagnerian end at the conclusion of his first adventure.

Then there was Imaro, the creation of Charles Saunders, who sent his character wandering a fantastic Africa. Imaro was the first important black hero of sword and sorcery. The three Imaro novels and a set of related short stories breathe with atmosphere, so much so that the setting is a character unto itself. The customs, people, and places feel real. While the supernatural and fantastic stalk this world, Saunders's storytelling skills present even the ordinary features of this setting, from savanna to jungle, as vivid and new. Saunders's skilful world-building as well as his taut action and suspense scenes create an explosive mix, one that Lin Carter was quick to recognize, printing Imaro tales in several volumes of *The Year's Best Fantasy and Horror* anthology series.

Born the son of mixed parentage in a warrior society, Imaro longs for acceptance, but when he finally earns it, his own pride sets him on another path. A mighty warrior, at heart Imaro is a decent, loving man who hides behind a wall of stoicism he has built both to protect himself during his troubled upbringing and to endure the horrors he has faced. Most other sword and sorcery heroes are rogues born with wanderlust. They are fascinating to see in action, but they are not necessarily people we would care to meet. Imaro, however, is honestly likable.

Finally, and most famously, was Karl Edward Wagner's Kane, marked by God for murder with cold blue eyes, an immortal hero-villain who lusts for knowledge and power. An accomplished manipulator, Kane wanders his world commissioning deeds both good and ill and often carrying them out himself. Wagner was a genius with atmosphere, and the best of the Kane stories are riveting; the worst are maudlin. Like Kane, Wagner dared greatness, sometimes reaching spectacular heights and sometimes failing. Wagner's work is a little like Moorcock's in theme: both writers play with our conceptions of good and evil; and both men created works that when turned this way, show ready flaws, and when turned that way, show gleaming brilliance.

There were other authors writing of heroes adventuring in other times or cultures, such as Keith Taylor's Celtic Bard in his Bard books, and Jessica Amanda Salmonson and Ted Rypel, who drafted tales of adventurous samurai.

With the exception of Shea, these and other authors have either vanished or remained in print only through the auspices of the small press. Smith's work is completely out of print, and Saunders's and Wagner's have been until just recently. For the last twenty years or more sword and sorcery has been relegated to the sidelines, existing for the most part only in limited distribution. Popular authors such as Tanith Lee occasionally dabble with it, but Tolkien-flavored quest fantasy has been continually dominant, save for one important exception.

Born in London, David Gemmell (1948–2006) was expelled from school at age sixteen for organizing a gambling syndicate. Owning a six-feet-four-inch, 230-pound frame, he worked as a laborer and nightclub bouncer before becoming a freelance journalist. In retrospect, these occupations prepared him well to become one of the genre's most skilled and popular writers since Howard.

In 1984, Gemmell published his first novel, *Legend,* a tale of heroes striving to defend a fortress against a vastly larger army. Foremost among the defenders is Druss the Legend, a titanic, indomitable warrior of over 60 years of age, who travels to the fortress to face death not by old age, but in battle. Druss, whose earlier deeds fill later novels, epitomizes the iron-willed soldier who appears frequently in Gemmell's tales, whereas another hero, Rek, is the first of several sword-wielding rogues: an agile man who lacks no skill in battle but who must accept its risk and righteousness in place of women, drink, coin, and self-preservation. Perhaps the most worldly of these reluctant heroes is Jarek Mace, a Robin Hood-William Wallace figure, featured in the excellent stand-alone novel *Morningstar* (1992), by David Gemmell.

Before dying in 2006 from heart disease, Gemmell was prolific, publishing over thirty novels between 1984 and the year of his death. (He smoked heavily as part of his writing process.) These include the eleven-book Drenai Saga, which features *Legend,* and the four-book Rigante Saga. His final novels, *Lord of the Silver Bow* (2005) and *Shield of Thunder* (2006), were the first two parts of a trilogy reimagining Homer's *Iliad.* Gemmell penned 70,000 words of the final part, *The Fall of Kings,* which was being completed by his wife, Stella, and scheduled for publication in 2007. While Gemmell's prose, even in *Legend,* is consistently clear and undemanding, it is especially vivid and polished in these last works, in which memorable characters such as Odysseus sail the Great Green in advance of war.

Because Gemmell's novels often involve climatic battles that determine the fates of nations or races, they can easily be classified as heroic fantasies. However, several elements also mark them as sword and sorcery: warriors and thieves with morals painted in shades of gray; foes who are monstrous, undead, or aided by dark magic; earthy details (e.g., cooking soup in bark bowls); swiftly unfolding action; and courage against almost insurmountable odds, for the sake of liberty—to name the most prevalent. In Gemmell's hands, these elements converge in highly engaging tales (often free of profanity and graphic sex). As succinctly observed by fantasy author Greg Keyes (*The Briar King*), "Gemmell not only knows how to tell a story, he knows how to tell a story you want to hear" (2006). With his passing, the genre has lost arguably its most consistent and productive modern craftsman.

Reception

The New Millennium. Today sword and sorcery remains marginalized, although there are some signs that the pendulum may be swinging in the other direction. Gemmell was a tremendous success in Europe but unwelcome on American shores for many years. Though the foremost of the new sword and sorcery writers, he was not completely alone. Some readers grew tired of high fantasy tropes and found solace in the gritty violence of Glen Cook's Black Company books, which read as a combination of fantasy crossed with military fiction peopled with earthy sword and sorcery heroes. In the late 1990s Matthew Stover delivered two series, the first featuring a Pictish warrior woman (*Iron Dawn,* 1997), the second a warrior transported from his futuristic society to battle with primitive weapons for the amusement of those watching back home (*Heroes Die,* 1999; Tompkins 2008).

Stover's work seems clearly in the sword and sorcery camp, but when the boundary is inexact, it is hard to split hairs with a battle-axe and make certain determinations. Cook's work, for example, seems more like military fiction, albeit with sword and sorcery seasoning. Canadian-born Steven Ericson's Malazan books may be the sign of an even larger swing away from high fantasy by traditional publishers. Phonebook-sized, like the plethora of high fantasy series that dominated the market through the 1990s, the Malazan books are a huge, multipart series replete with action and stuffed with gritty blue-collar heroes. Sword and sorcery scholar Steve Tompkins places Erikson's work clearly in the fold, but others perceive it to be more like epic fantasy with sword and sorcery sensibility, or even the more nebulously defined dark fantasy. Whatever they are, exactly, Malazan books are clearly rooted in sword and sorcery precepts and may indeed be the start of something entirely new.

A handful of writers have found an outlet working for publishing houses that print books based in worlds generated for role-playing games and war games. The most sword-and-sorcery friendly of these publishing firms has been the Warhammer (Electronic Arts) franchise, set in a European Renaissance style world populated by elves, dwarves, humans, and various disturbing things man was not meant to know. Writers such as William King, C.L. Werner, Bryan Craig, and others have fashioned iconic sword and sorcery characters who wander the shared world. King created Gotrek, a skilled and deadly warrior dwarf, and Felix the bard sworn to follow the former and record his exploits until he meets a glorious end. The novels and short stories proved so popular that King left Warhammer in 2003 to craft his own sword and sorcery Terrarch novels for European publishers, leaving his creations Gotrek and Felix to another writer, which is one of the most unfortunate aspects of fashioning characters under contract. Werner has been equally well received by Warhammer fans and outside readers with two very different characters, the first a remorseless and mostly amoral bounty hunter called Brunner; the other a kind of righteous, relentless monster hunter, named Matthias Thulman, fashioned from equal parts Robert E. Howard's Solomon Kane, the Hammer horror movies, and Werner's own imagination.

Aside from the Warhammer books and David Gemmell's tales of soldiers and outlaws, almost no modern sword and sorcery works have achieved widespread, or even marked, popularity, especially when compared with best-selling, epic fantasies such as George R.R. Martin's *A Song of Ice and Fire* or Robert Jordan's *The Wheel of Time*. Although possible reasons for this disparity may include a bias by major publishers against real and perceived flaws in traditional sword and sorcery, such as shallow or stereotypical characters, it seems more likely that the difference is due to a practical consideration (as few epic fantasies lack stereotypes).

Publishers wish to sell as many books as possible, and sweeping, multicharacter, epic fantasies naturally lend themselves to longer tales. In contrast to their epic fantasy counterparts, sword and sorcery heroes tend to resemble sprinters more than marathoners. For example, *The Wheel of Time,* published from 1990 to 2005, consisted of eleven lengthy novels and a prequel, with the story remaining unfinished; by contrast, in Howard's sole novel, *The Hour of the Dragon,* Conan loses and regains a kingdom in 75,000 tumultuous words.

Despite the dominance of epic fantasy in novel-length works, writers of speculative fiction have continued to explore the sword and sorcery genre, selling both traditional and innovative tales to prominent short fiction magazines such as *Black Gate* and *The Magazine of Fantasy and Science Fiction* (F&SF), as well as to Internet publications in recent years (e.g., swordandsorcery.org). Some works are worthy of particular mention.

In 1987, Ellen Kushner (b. 1955) published *Swordspoint,* a critically acclaimed "melodrama of manners" that introduced the duelist Richard St Vier and the erratic scholar Alec. The novel is notable for its nuanced characterization and setting—an intricate juxtaposition of a nameless city akin to eighteenth-century London or Paris and its seedy Riverside district—as well as the protagonists' homosexual relationship. *Swordspoint* was followed by *The Fall of the Kings* (2002) and *The Privilege of the Sword* (2006), and its characters also appeared in a handful of short stories, including "The Swordsman Whose Name Was Not Death" (F&SF, September 1991).

The Magazine of Fantasy and Science Fiction has also showcased, in the tradition of Fafhrd and the Gray Mouser, two of the more fascinating sword-against-sorcery duos to debut in recent years. The first duo, composed of the soldier Vertir and the scribe Kuikan, has appeared in three tales ("For Want of a Nail," March 2003; "After the Gaud Chrysalis," June 2004; and "Of Silence and the Man at Arms," June 2005) by Charles Coleman Finlay, a finalist for the Hugo, Nebula, and John W. Campbell awards. Finlay's stories place the protagonists in exotic, unfriendly surroundings and in situations where survival depends on quick-thinking under duress.

The second consists of two especially odd yet appealing adventurers, the poet Persimmon Gaunt and the long-lived thief Imago Bone, created by Chris Willrich. Editor Gordon van Gelder described their debut, "The Thief with Two Deaths" (June 2000), as "a gorgeous fantasy that owes some of its inspiration to Lord Dunsany's 'The Idle City'"; and Willrich's lush prose is similarly traditional yet fresh:

> Fanned by moonlit palm trees, chaperoned by star-aimed white obelisks slicing the surf's roar into baffled echoes, Persimmon Gaunt stroked the thief's dark hair and smiled.

Gaunt and Bone's journey continues in "King Rainjoy's Tears" (July 2002) and "Penultima Thule" (August 2006).

Most fantasy periodicals print varieties of sword and sorcery occasionally, but among the modern magazines only *Black Gate* actively welcomes it. As a result, in its first ten issues *Black Gate* has showcased a number of writers who may well grow into the genre's new torchbearers. It is too early to know, but some of the writers seem to be creating enduring work. Most certainly, James Enge's three Morlock Ambrosius published tales are alive with splendid world-building, compelling characterization, clever dialogue, and perhaps most daring of all in today's short fiction climate, adventure. Enge's prose is crafted with Leiber's wit and Smith's imagination, and somehow remains supremely approachable while being polished to a high gloss.

These modern heroes bear little outward resemblance to Conan and Jirel, yet they face a similar challenge: in a world that can be strange, wonderful, and terrible, they must survive as well and meaningfully as their prowess and courage allow.

All well-realized fictional characters, and all readers in their daily lives, face this challenge; and it is this commonality of experience that gives the art of storytelling its power. Sword and sorcery tales, woven from the same fabric as ancient myths, can accordingly enlighten and entertain as powerfully as any literary genre—when they are woven well. It is this heritage, and the experience of numerous authors and readers, that qualifies sword and sorcery not as an inferior form of fantasy, but as a distinct and vivid genre.

Bibliography

Anderson, Poul. *The Broken Sword*. New York: Ballantine, 1971.

Bishop, Farnham, and Arthur Gilchrist Brodeur. "The Hand of the Mahdi." *Adventure* 18 Feb. 1920: 8–38.

Bishop, Farnham. "Libertatia." *Adventure* 30 April 1925: 1–73

Bleiler, Richard. *The Index to Adventure Magazine*. San Francisco: Borgo Press, 1990.

Brackett, Leigh. *Martian Quest: The Early Brackett*. Royal Oak, MI: Haffner Press. 2002.

Brackett, Leigh. *Sea-Kings of Mars and Otherworldly Stories*. London: Millenium, 2005.

———. "The Best of Leigh Brackett." In *Story-teller of Many Worlds*. Edmond Hamilton, ed. New York: Nelson/Doubleday, 1977, vii–xiii.

———. *The Book of Skaith: The Adventures of Eric John Stark*. New York: Nelson/Doubleday, 1976.

Brodeur, Arthur Gilchrist. "For the Crown." *Adventure* 20 May 1922: 153–175.

———. "The Doom of the Gods." *Adventure* 18 Nov. 1919: 3–88.

Carter, Lin. *Imaginary Worlds*. New York: Ballantine, 1973.

———, ed. *Dragons, Elves, and Heroes*. New York: Ballantine, 1969.

———, ed. *Flashing Swords #1*. New York: Dell, 1973.

———, ed. *Golden Citites, Far*. New York: Ballantine, 1970.

———, ed. *New Worlds for Old*. New York: Ballantine, 1971.

———. "Of Swordsmen and Sorcerors." Flashing Swords #1. New York: Dell, 1973.

———. "The Maze of Maal Dweb." *The Young Magicians*. Lin Carter, ed. New York: Ballantine Books. 1969.

———, ed. *The Young Magicians*. New York: Ballantine, 1969.

de Camp, L. Sprague, and Lin Carter. *Conan of the Isles*. New York: Ace, 1968.

de Camp, L. Sprague . "Harold Lamb." In *Marching Sands,* by Harold Lamb. New York: Hyperion, 1974, i–ii.

———. "Heroic Fantasy." *Swords and Sorcery*. L. Sprague de Camp, ed. New York: Pyramid Books, 1963, 7–8.

———. *Literary Swordsmen and Sorcerers: The Makers of Heroic Fantasy*. Sauk City, WI: Arkham House, 1976.

Ebert, Roger. "Lord of the Rings: The Fellowship of the Ring." http://rogerebert.suntimes. com/apps/pbcs.dll/article?AID=/20011219/REVIEWS/112190301/102(accesed December 19, 2001).

Eddison, E.R. *The Worm Ouroboros*. New York: Ballantine, 1967 (reprint).

Fox, Gardner. Kothar, Barbarian Swordsman. New York: Leisure Books, 1970.

Gaiman, Neil. "Introduction." In *Return to Lankhmar*. Fritz Leiber, ed. Clarkston, GA: White Wolf Publishing, 1997, 13–15.

Haggard, H. Rider. *Eric Brighteyes*. New York: Zebra, 1978.

———. *The Wanderer's Necklace*. New York: Zebra, 1978.

Hanning, Peter, ed. *Weird Tales*. New York: Carroll & Graf Publishers, Inc., 1990.

Harrison, M. John. *Viroconium*. London: Millenium, 2000.

Hoppenstand, Gary. "Introduction." In *Captain Blood,* by Rafael Sabatini. New York: Penguin, 2003, vi–xix.

Howard, Robert E. *Almuric*. New York: Berkley, 1977.

———. *Bran Mak Morn*. New York: Baen, 1996.

———. *Cormac Mac Art*. New York: Baen, 1995.

———. *Cthulhu: The Mythos and Kindred Horrors*. New York: Baen, 1987.

———. *Kull*. New York: Baen, 1995.

———. *Marchers of Valhalla*. New York: Berkley, 1978.

———. *Pigeons from Hell*. New York: Ace, 1979.

———. *Red Nails*. New York: Berkley, 1977.

———. *Solomon Kane*. New York: Baen, 1995.

———. *Swords of Sharhrazar*. New York: Berkley, 1978.

———. *The Bloody Crown of Conan*. New York: Del Rey, 2003.

———. "The Book of Robert E Howard." Glenn Lord, ed. New York: Zebra, 1976.

———. *The Coming of Conan*. New York: Del Rey, 2002.

———. *The Conquering Sword of Conan*. New York: Del Rey, 2005.

———. *The Last Ride*. New York: Berkley, 1978.

———. *The Lost Valley of Iskander*. New York: Ace, 1974.

———. "The Second Book of Robert E. Howard." Glenn Lord, ed. New York: Zebra, 1976.

Jakes, John. *The Fortunes of Brak*. New York: Dell, 1980.

Jones, Howard. "Defining Sword and Sorcery." *Sword and Sorcery* 2008. http://www.swordandsorcery.org/defining-sword-and-sorcery.htm.

Jones, Robert Kenneth. *The Lure of Adventure*. Mercer Island, WA: Starmont Pulp and Dime Novel Studies, 1989.

Keyes, Greg. Back cover blurb from *Lord of the Silver Bow* by Gemmell, David. New York: Ballantine Books, 2006.

Kuttner, Henry. *The Best of Henry Kuttner*. New York: Nelson/Doubleday, 1975.

Lamb, Harold. *Warriors of the Steppes*. Lincoln: University of Nebraska Press, 2006.

———. *Kirdy: The Road out of the World*. New York: Doubleday, 1933.

———. *Riders of the Steppes*. Lincoln: University of Nebraska Press, 2007.

———. *Swords of the Steppes*. Lincoln: University of Nebraska Press, 2007.

———. *The Mighty Manslayer*. New York: Doubleday, 1969.

———. *Wolf of the Steppes*. Lincoln: University of Nebraska Press, 2006.

Lee, Tanith. *Cyrion*. New York: DAW, 1982.

Leiber, Fritz. *Farewell Lankhmar*. Clarkston, GA: White Wolf Publishing, 1998.

———. *Ill Met in Lankhmar*. Clarkston, GA: White Wolf Publishing, 1995.

———. *Lean Times in Lankhmar*. Clarkston, GA: White Wolf Publishing, 1996.

———. *Return to Lankhmar*. Clarkston, GA: White Wolf Publishing, 1997.

Lord Dunsany. *Time and The Gods*. London: Millenium, 2000.

Louinet, Patrice. "Introduction." In *The Coming of Conan*. Robert E. Howard, ed. New York: Del Rey, 2002.

Moorcock, Michael. *Hawkmoon*. : White Wolf Publishing, 1995.

———. *The Elric Saga: Part I*. New York: Nelson/Doubleday, 1984.

———. *The Elric Saga: Part II*. New York: Nelson/Doubleday. 1984.

———. *Wizardry and Wild Romance: A Study of Epic Fantasy*. Austin: Monkeybrain, Inc., 2004.

Moore, C.L. *Jirel of Joiry*. New York: Ace, 1977.

Mundy, Talbot. *Tros of Samothrace: Helene*. New York: Avon Books, 1967.

———. *Tros of Samothrace: Helma*. New York: Avon Books, 1967.

———. *Tros of Samothrace: Liafail*. New York: Avon Books, 1967.

———. *Tros of Samothrace: Tros*. New York: Avon Books, 1967.

Sabatini, Rafael. *Captain Blood*. New York: Penguin, 2003.

Salmonson, Jessica Amanda, ed. *Heroic Visions*. New York: Ace, 1983.

Sampson, Robert. *Yesterday's Faces: Violent Lives*. Bowling Green, OH: Bowling Green State University Popular Press, 1993.

Saunders, Charles. *Imaro*. San Francisco: Nightshade Books, 2006.

Schweitzer, Darrell, ed. *Discovering Classic Fantasy Fiction*. Rockville, MD: Wildside Press, 1996.

———. *Mask of the Sorcerer*., Rockville, MD: Wildside Press, 1995.

———. *We Are All Legends*. Virginia Beach, VA: Starblaze Editions, 1981.

Smith, Arthur D. Howden. *Gray Maiden*. New York: Longmans/Macmillan, 1929.

———. *Swain's Saga*. New York: Macmillan, 1931.

Smith, Clark Ashton. *Hyperborea*. New York: Ballantine, 1971.

———. *Xiccarph*. New York: Ballantine, 1972.

Smith, David C. *Oron*. New York: Zebra Books, 1978.

Taliaferro, John. *Tarzan Forever: The Life of Edgar Rice Burroughs, Creator of Tarzan*. New York: Scribner, 1999.

Tierney, Richard. *Scroll of Thoth*. Oakland, CA: Chaosium, 1997.

Tompkins, Steven. "After Aquilonia and Having Left Lankhmar: Sword-and-Sorcery since the 1980s." In *The Robert E. Howard Reader*. Darrell Schweitzer, ed. Rockville, MD: Wildside Press, 2008.

Vance, Jack. *Planet of Adventure*. New York: Orb, 1993.

———. *Tales of the Dying Earth*. New York: Orb, 1998.

Wagner, Karl. "Foreword." Red Nails. Robert E. Howard. New York: Berkley. 1977.

———. *Gods in Darkness*. San Francisco: Night Shade Books, 2002.

———. *Midnight Sun*. San Francisco: Night Shade Books, 2003.

Zelazny, Roger. *Dilvish, The Damned*. New York: Del Rey, 1982.

———. *The Chronicles of Amber, Volume I*. New York: Nelson/Doubleday, 1978.

———. *The Chronicles of Amber, Volume II*. New York: Nelson/Doubleday, 1978.

Further Reading

Brackett, Leigh. *Lorelei of the Red Mist*. Royal Oak, MI: Haffner Press, 2007; Harrison, M. John. "The Pastel City." In *Viroconium*. London: Millenium, 2000, 23–152; Howard, Robert E. *The Coming of Conan*. New York: Del Rey, 2005; Jones, Howard. "Defining Sword-and-sorcery." *Sword-and-Sorcery*. 2008. http://www.swordandsorcery.org/defining-sword-and-sorcery.htm; Leiber, Fritz. *Ill Met in Lankhmar*. Clarkston, GA: White Wolf Publishing, 1995; Moorcock, Michael. *The Elric Saga, Part I*. Garden City, New York: Berkley, 1984; Moorcock, Michael. *Wizardry and Wild Romance: A Study of Epic Fantasy*. Austin: Monkeybrain, Inc., 2004; Salmonson, Jessica Amanda, ed. *Heroic Visions*. New York: Ace, 1983; Schweitzer, Darrell, ed. *Discovering Classic Fantasy Fiction*. Rockville, MD: Wildside Press, 1996; Vance, Jack. "The Dying Earth." *Tales of the Dying Earth*. New York: Orb, 1998, 1–131.

HOWARD ANDREW JONES AND ROBERT RHODES